Mastering JavaScript and JScript

Mastering™ JavaScript® and JScript™

James Jaworski

SYBEX®

San Francisco • Paris • Düsseldorf • Soest • London

Associate Publisher: Richard Mills
Contracts and Licensing Manager: Kristine O'Callaghan
Acquisitions & Developmental Editor: Denise Santoro
Editor: Valerie Perry
Project Editor: Rebecca Rider
Technical Editor: David Wall
Book Designer: Kris Warrenburg
Graphic Illustrator: Tony Jonick
Electronic Publishing Specialists: Cyndy Johnsen, Nila Nichols, Grey Magauran, Franz Baumhackl, and Kate Kaminski
Production Coordinator: Shannon Murphy
Indexer: Ted Laux
Cover Designer: Design Site
Cover Illustrator/Photographer: Sergie Loobkoff

Library of Congress Card Number: 99-60013
ISBN: 0-7821-2492-5

Manufactured in the United States of America

10 9 8 7 6 5 4 3 2 1

To Emily, my pumpkin.

ACKNOWLEDGMENTS

I'd like to thank everyone who helped to see this book to completion. In particular, I'd like to thank Margot Maley of Waterside Productions for making it possible and all the great folks at Sybex for their terrific support—especially Denise Santoro, Rebecca Rider, Valerie Perry, David Wall, Shannon Murphy, Cyndy Johnsen, and Richard Mills. Thanks to George Stones for his excellent technical support. I'd also like to thank my wife Lisa, for her patience, love, and understanding; my son Jason, for making great coffee; and my daughter Emily, for her endless entertainment.

CONTENTS AT A GLANCE

Introduction   *xxiii*

PART I: **Getting Started with JavaScript and JScript**   **1**

    Chapter 1: Learning the Fundamentals   3

    Chapter 2: Introducing JavaScript and JScript   27

    Chapter 3: Using Operators, Statements, and Functions   79

    Chapter 4: Handling Events   129

    Chapter 5: Working with Objects   193

PART II: **Using Predefined Objects and Methods**   **245**

    Chapter 6: Creating Frames and Windows   247

    Chapter 7: Processing Forms   289

    Chapter 8: Using Hidden Fields and Cookies   319

    Chapter 9: Working with Links   355

    Chapter 10: Using Images   389

    Chapter 11: Doing Math   413

PART III   **Building Sample Applications**   **431**

    Chapter 12: Accessorizing Your Pages   433

    Chapter 13: Online Catalogs   461

    Chapter 14: Developing Search Tools   497

PART IV: Communicating with Java, ActiveX, and Plug-Ins   529

Chapter 15: Communicating with Java Applets   531

Chapter 16: Scripting ActiveX Components   575

Chapter 17: How Plug-Ins Work   591

PART V: Programming Servers   627

Chapter 18: Using Style Sheets and DHTML   629

Chapter 19: Creating Multimedia Applications   679

PART VI: Programming Servers   713

Chapter 20: Interfacing JavaScript with CGI Programs   715

Chapter 21: Scripting Netscape Servers   739

Chapter 22: Scripting Microsoft Servers   813

Chapter 23: Securing Your Scripts   841

Index   *858*

TABLE OF CONTENTS

Introduction   *xxiii*

PART I   **Getting Started with JavaScript and JScript**   **1**

1   **Learning the Fundamentals**   **3**

The Web   4
The HyperText Markup Language   8
    The Development of HTML   10
    Cascading Style Sheets   11
Helper Applications   11
    External Viewers and Plug-Ins   12
    Using MIME Types to Identify Helpers for File Formats   12
Uniform Resource Locators (URLs)   14
The HyperText Transfer Protocol (HTTP)   15
Common Gateway Interface Programs   16
Java Applets   18
ActiveX—Microsoft Objects   18
A Brief History of JavaScript   19
LiveWire and LiveWire Database Service   22
Active Server Pages, Windows Scripting Host, and Remote Scripting   22
Intranets, Extranets, and Distributed Applications   24
Summary   25

2   **Introducing JavaScript and JScript**   **27**

JavaScript and Browsers, JavaScript and Servers   28
Embedding JavaScript in HTML   34
    Other Language Attributes   35
    Telling Non-JavaScript Browsers to Ignore Your Code   37
    The noscript Tag   39
    The Script Tag's SRC Attribute   41
    JavaScript Entities   43

JavaScript Comments 44
Use of the Document Head 45
Generating HTML 48
Variables—Value Storehouses 50
Types and Variables 51
Types and Literal Values 51
Conversion between Types 62
The Object Type and Arrays 70
Objects and the length Property 76
Summary 77

3 Using Operators, Statements, and Functions 79

Operators and Expressions 80
Arithmetic Operators 81
Logical Operators 82
Comparison Operators 83
String Operators 84
Bit Manipulation Operators 84
Assignment Operators 84
The Conditional Expression Ternary Operator 85
Special Operators 86
Operator Summary Table 87
Operator Precedence 93
JavaScript Programming Statements 94
Assignment Statements 97
Data Declarations 97
The if Statement 98
Loop Statements 100
The switch Statement 108
Function Call Statements 110
Local Variable Declarations 114
The return Statement 117
Object-Access Statements 118
The with Statement 119
The for in Statement 120
The throw, try, and catch Statements 121
Summary 127

4   Handling Events   **129**

What Are Events?   130
How JavaScript Handles Events   131
Handling JavaScript Events   139
  Handling Link Events   142
  Handling Window Events   146
  Handling Image Events   152
  Handling Image Map Events   155
  Handling Form Events   159
Setting Event Handlers from within JavaScript   168
Event Simulation Methods   171
The event Object   173
Event Capturing   178
  The onMouseMove Event   181
Event Bubbling   182
Error Handling   185
  The onError Event Handler   185
  The error Object   187
Summary   190

5   Working with Objects   **193**

What Are Objects?   194
What Is Object-Oriented Programming?   196
  Object Types and Instances   196
  Creating Object Types   197
JavaScript's Object-Based Programming Features   200
The JavaScript Object Model   202
  Using Properties   203
  Using Methods   204
  Creating Instances of Objects   205
Browser Objects   206
  The Browser Object Hierarchy   208
  Hierarchical Object Identifiers   209
Other Predefined Object Types   215
  The Array Object   215
  The Boolean Object   218
  The Date Object   218
  The Function Object   221

The Global Object   223
The Math Object   224
The Number Object   227
The Object Object   227
The String Object   228
Regular Expressions and the RegExp Object   231
Color Constants   231
Defining Object Types   231
Identifying and Assigning Properties   232
Defining Methods   233
Definition of the table Object   234
Using the table Object   236
Adding Properties and Methods to an Object Type   237
Deleting Properties and Methods   240
The event, Event, and Error Objects   241
Summary   242

PART II   Using Predefined Objects and Methods   245

6   Creating Frames and Windows   247

The window Object   248
Opening and Closing Windows   251
Communicating with the User   255
Displaying Status Information   257
Using the Window Synonyms   258
Working with Timeouts   258
Working with Intervals   260
The frame Object   262
Tic-Tac-Toe   263
The document Object   273
Generating Document Contents   275
Accessing Document Contents   276
Working with Colors   279
The navigator Object   280
The screen Object   285
Summary   287

7   Processing Forms   289

The form Object   290
Accessing Forms within JavaScript   292
Accessing Form Elements   292
Using Form Event Handlers   301
   Responding to User Actions   301
Client-Side Form Processing   312
Working with CGI Scripts   312
   Sending Form Data to a CGI Program   312
   Performing Local Form Processing   313
Summary   317

8   Using Hidden Fields and Cookies   319

Maintaining State Information   321
Using Hidden Form Fields   322
JavaScript and Hidden Form Fields   322
   The usesProducts() Function   333
   The askAboutProducts() Function   333
   The processForm3() Function   333
Using Cookies   334
How Is Information Stored in a Cookie?   335
   The NAME=VALUE Field   336
   The expires=DATE Field   336
   The domain=DOMAIN_NAME Field   337
   The path=PATH Field   337
   The secure Field   337
Using JavaScript with Cookies   338
Comparison—Cookies vs. Hidden Form Fields   352
Summary   353

9   Working with Links   355

Uniform Resource Locators (URLs)   356
   The javascript: and about: Protocols   358
The location Object   363
   Example Application Using the location Object   365
The link Object   368
   Example Application Using link—A Pair-Matching Game   369

The link() Method   382
The anchor Object   384
    Internet Explorer's Links and Anchors   385
The history Object   385
Summary   387

10   Using Images   389

The image Object   390
    Image Display Properties   392
    Other Image Properties   393
Dynamic Image Display   393
    The initialize() Function   398
    The displayTable() Function   398
Images and Animation   399
    The initialize() Function   402
    The startAnimation() Function   402
    The setStart() Function   402
    The animate() Function   403
    The goFaster() Function   403
    The goSlower() Function   403
Image Maps and the area Object   403
Working with Image Maps   404
Summary   411

11   Doing Math   413

The Math Object   414
Mathematical Constants   414
Mathematical Functions   415
    Rounding Functions   416
    Comparison Functions   416
    Algebraic Functions   416
    Logarithmic and Exponential Functions   416
    Trigonometric Functions   417
    Random Number Generation   417
Using Math Functions in Scripts   417
Example Project—A JavaScript Calculator   418
    The r Array   426
    The setStartState() Function   426
    The addDigit() Function   426
Summary   429

PART III   **Building Sample Applications**   **431**

12   **Accessorizing Your Pages**   **433**

The Calendar Accessory   434
   The Calendar() Constructor   437
   The displayCalendar() Function   437
   The displayCalendarHeader() Function   437
   The displayDates() Function   438
   The numberOfDays() Function   438
   The writeDate() Function   438
The Calculator Accessory   443
The To-Do List Accessory   448
   The loadNotes() Function   453
   The saveNotes() Function   453
   The encode() Function   453
   The decode() Function   453
The World Clock Accessory   454
Assembling the Desktop   456
Summary   458

13   **Online Catalogs**   **461**

Developing a Catalog without a CGI Program   462
   The displayCatalogForm() Function   465
   The readCookie() Function   465
   The displayRooms() Function   465
   The displayCategories() Function   466
   The displayProducts() Function   466
   The selectRoom() Function   466
   The selectProductType() Function   466
   The selectProduct() Function   466
   The writeDocument() Function   466
   The setCookie() Function   466
   The rooms Array   474
   The roomName() Function   474
   The productCategories Array   474
   The categoryName() Function   474
   The Product() Function   474
   The roomProductCategory() Function   475
   The roomCategories Array   475
   The prod Array   475

Tailoring a Catalog Based on User Preferences	475
The displayCategoryForm() Function	477
The readCookie() Function	477
The displayByRoom() Function	477
The displayByCat() Function	477
The displayByProduct() Function	478
The displayAltView() Function	478
The displayRooms() Function	478
The displayCategories() Function	478
The displayProducts() Function	478
The displayCatList() Function	478
The displayProductsList() Function	478
The altView() Function	478
The selectRoom() Function	479
The selectProductType() Function	479
The selectProduct() Function	479
The selectProductCat() Function	479
The selectFromBigList() Function	479
The writeDocument() Function	479
The setCookie() Function	479
Adding Multimedia Features	485
Summary	495
14 Developing Search Tools	**497**
Search Forms	498
The Topic() Function	501
The topics Array	502
The processArea() Function	502
The displayTopics() Function	502
Search Engines	505
The First Search Engine	505
Connecting Search Forms to Search Engines	507
The Second Search Engine	509
Local Search Engines	515
The Third Search Engine	519
Summary	527

PART IV   **Communicating with Java, ActiveX, and Plug-Ins   529**

15   Communicating with Java Applets   531

What Is Java?   532
   Java Is Platform Independent   532
   Java Is Object Oriented   533
   Java Is Familiar   533
   Java Is Simple and Reliable   534
   The Java API Supports Window and Network Programming   534
   Java Supports Executable Web Content   534
   Java Is Secure   535
   Java Is Free   535
Java vs. JavaScript   535
   Compiled vs. Interpreted   536
   Object-Oriented vs. Object-Based   536
   Strongly Typed vs. Loosely Typed   537
   Browser Window vs. Full Browser Interaction   538
The Java Development Kit   539
Learning Java   540
The Java API   540
Programs vs. Applets   540
   Building Programs from Classes   541
   Organizing Classes into Packages   541
   The main() Method   541
   Java Reserves Certain Keywords   541
   An Example Console Program   541
   An Example Windows Program   543
   An Example Applet   545
LiveConnect and the Internet Explorer Object Model   548
Accessing Java Methods from within JavaScript   548
Accessing Applets from within JavaScript   550
   Declaring Public Classes, Methods, and Variables   551
   Loading an Applet   551
   Using the applet Object   552
   My FancyText Example   553
Using JavaScript in an Applet   555
   Using the MAYSCRIPT Attribute   556
   Importing netscape.javascript   556

Creating a Handle to a JavaScript Window   558
Using getMember()   558
Using eval()   559
Reading Values Entered in a Form   559
Other JSObject Methods   561
GraphIt!   562
The v Variable   568
The xUL and yUL Variables   568
The width and height Variables   568
The xOrig and yOrig Variables   568
The numPoints Variable   568
The xMin, xMax, yMin, and yMax Variables   568
The xDelta and yDelta Variables   569
The add() Method   569
The delete() Method   569
The displayGraph() Method   569
The sortPoints() Method   569
Summary   573

16   Scripting ActiveX Components   575
What Is ActiveX?   576
Using ActiveX Components   577
Accessing ActiveX Components from within JScript   581
Using the ActiveX Control Pad   583
Summary   589

17   How Plug-Ins Work   591
Popular Plug-Ins   592
Plug-Ins in Action   593
Embedded Plug-In Documents   594
How the SRC Attribute Is Processed   595
Plug-In Documents Referenced as URLs   596
Plug-Ins as Embedded Applications   596
Working with MIME Types   597
Determining Installed Plug-Ins   599
How About Plug-Ins Works   602
Detecting Plug-Ins   605
Accessing Plug-Ins from within JavaScript   607

Netscape's Plug-In Documentation   611
  Plugging into LiveVideo   611
  Listening to LiveAudio   612
  The netscape.plugin.Plugin Class   614
Listing Plug-In Methods   615
Synchronizing Multiple Plug-Ins   618
  The play() Function   620
  The stop() Function   620
  The start() Function   620
  The end() Function   620
Assisting Users with Installing Plug-Ins   620
Developing Your Own Plug-Ins   623
Summary   625

PART V   **Programming Servers**   **627**

18   Using Style Sheets and DHTML   **629**
What Are Style Sheets?   630
JavaScript Style Sheets vs. Cascading Style Sheets   631
An Introductory Example   632
Defining Style Sheets   635
  The <STYLE> Tag   636
  The <SPAN> Tag   655
Using the <LINK> Tag to Include Styles   657
Using Multiple Style Sheets   660
Using Internet Explorer's DHTML Capabilities   660
  Accessing HTML Elements as Objects   661
  The Style Property   663
  A Style Sampler   666
  How the Style Sampler Works   672
Summary   676

19   Creating Multimedia Applications   **679**
Using Layers   680
  The Layer Tags   680
  Windowed Elements   682
  The layers Array and layer Object   683
  A Slide Show Example   684

Using Divisions 690
Working with Audio 694
Doing It with Divisions and ActiveX 698
Performing Animation 703
Flying Divisions 706
Using Video 709
Summary 711

PART VI   Programming Servers   713

20   Interfacing JavaScript with CGI Programs   715

When to Use CGI Programs 716
How CGI Programs Work 717
Getting Data from the Web Server 718
Sending Data Back to the Web Server 723
The General Design of a CGI Program 725
ISINDEX Queries 725
Form Processing 725
Server-Side Image-Map Queries 726
Using Custom Hyperlinks to Invoke CGI Programs 726
A Shell Script Example 726
Interfacing JavaScript Scripts with CGI Scripts 730
Returning JavaScript from CGI Programs 734
Summary 737

21   Scripting Netscape Servers   739

Server-Side Scripting with LiveWire 740
A Simple LiveWire Example 741
Building the Example Application 742
Running the Application 745
How the Simple Application Works 746
The LiveWire Compiler 747
Application Manager 748
Server-Side JavaScript Programming 750
Server-Side Objects 751
The request Object 753
The client Object 761
The project Object 761
The server Object 762

File Input and Output   763
  Opening Files   763
  Closing Files   764
  Accessing Files   764
  Locking File Access   766
A Fuller Example—Diskette   766
  The Files of the Diskette Application   767
  Building and Running the Diskette Application   773
State Maintenance   776
  The Client-Cookie Approach   777
  The Client-URL Approach   777
  The Server-IP Approach   778
  The Server-Cookie Approach   778
  The Server-URL Approach   779
  Which Approach Should You Use?   779
Server Functions   780
  The addClient(URL) Function   780
  The debug(expression) Function   780
  The flush() Function   780
  The getOptionValue(name,n) Function   781
  The getOptionValueCount(name) Function   781
  The redirect(URL) Function   781
  The write(expression) Function   781
File-Oriented Systems vs. Database Management Systems   781
  File-Oriented Systems   782
  Database Management Systems   783
LiveWire Database Services to the Rescue   786
Setting Up a Microsoft Access Database for Use with LiveWire   787
Using LiveWire Database Services   791
The database Object   792
  Locks and Connections   793
  Executing SQL   794
  Using the Cursor   795
  Transaction Processing   797
  Error Handling   798
Structured Query Language   798
  Adding, Deleting, and Updating Rows   800
  Querying Tables   801

Updating the Diskette Application 802
    Adding Database Support to Diskette 802
    Viewing the Database 806
    Providing SQL Access to orders 808
Summary 810

22 Scripting Microsoft Servers 813

Active Server Pages 814
    ASP Scripting 815
    Server-Side Objects 818
    Connecting to Databases 835
Windows Scripting Host 835
Remote Scripting 837
Summary 838

23 Securing Your Scripts 841

Internet Security Threats 842
    Threats to the Web Site Manager 842
    Threats to the Web User 843
Web Security Issues 844
    The Webmaster's Perspective 844
    The Web User's Perspective 850
Spying Scripts and JavaScript Security Policy 853
Summary 856

Index *858*

INTRODUCTION

With all of the available Web development technologies, such as HTML, XML, Java, and ActiveX, you are probably wondering why you should invest the time to learn JavaScript. The answer to this question is apparent when you compare the capabilities provided by the current set of Web programming languages:

- HTML is great for creating static Web pages. However, it provides no capabilities to design pages that dynamically respond to user inputs. *JavaScript provides these capabilities.*

- Java and ActiveX are excellent languages for creating components that can be embedded in a Web page. However, their output display is confined, for security reasons, to a limited area of the browser window. In addition, if you want to develop Java and ActiveX components, you'll be undertaking a significant programming investment. *JavaScript provides the capability to develop scripts that can access all aspects of the browser display, and in a secure and easy-to-develop manner.*

- XML is a language for defining other markup languages and will be a significant technology for future Web applications. *Though JavaScript support of XML in current browsers is still very limited, it is certain that there will be a relationship between the two languages.*

JavaScript enables you to integrate HTML documents, Web components (which may have been written in Java and ActiveX), and multimedia plug-ins so that you can develop Web applications that are dynamic, respond to a variety of user inputs, and access advanced browser capabilities such as multimedia, VRML, layers, and style sheets. Further, the LiveConnect feature of Netscape browsers allows JavaScript to directly access the variables and methods of Java applets and to exercise a fine level of control over the operation of plug-ins. The Internet Explorer Object Model provides a similar capability for Microsoft browsers. If these are not compelling enough reasons to learn JavaScript, read on.

JavaScript can also be used to develop server-side Web applications. Both Netscape and Microsoft Web servers support server-side JavaScript. You can use JavaScript to replace all of your CGI scripts that are written in Perl, C, and shell programming languages. Netscape's LiveWire add-on lets you develop integrated client- and server-side applications using JavaScript, greatly simplifying browser-server communication and automatically making the output of server-side scripts available as HTML to browser clients. Microsoft's Active Server Pages (ASP) can be scripted with server-side JScript to develop similar applications on Microsoft's Internet Information Server (IIS).

Finally, JavaScript is the language used by Netscape's LiveWire Database Services to provide connectivity between Web servers and server-external databases. You can use this capability to integrate your Web applications with full-scale databases containing information about your products, customer orders, shipping, or whatever you want. Microsoft's Internet Information Server (IIS) provides the capability to use JScript with the industry-standard Open Database Connectivity (ODBC) database interface. It also integrates JScript with its Windows Scripting Host (WSH) and remote scripting host technologies.

In this book you'll cover all aspects of JavaScript and JScript programming. You'll learn to program Web browsers using client-side scripts, LiveConnect, and the Internet Explorer Object Model. You'll learn how to program Web servers using server-side scripts, LiveWire, Active Server Pages, and Windows Scripting Host. You'll also learn how to program database-enabled applications using server-side JavaScript, LiveWire Database Services, and Structured Query Language (SQL). More important, you'll learn how to combine all of these facets of JavaScript programming to develop integrated Web applications that are attractive, informative, and easy to use.

Conventions Used in This Book

Certain conventions are used in this book to make it easier for you to work with:

Upper- or lowercase? Even though the case does not matter for HTML and JavaScript elements, to help keep them distinct I use all uppercase letters for HTML elements and all lowercase letters for JavaScript elements. (Case *does* matter for Java elements; in my discussions of Java items I use whichever case is appropriate.)

Fonts I use a `monospaced font` to display JavaScript objects, methods, functions, variables, and URLs. (The names of files and directories are also displayed in that font.) Words identifying program parameters or arguments within a syntax explanation (some books refer to these words as "descriptive placeholders") are displayed in *italic*.

➡ Within a script or code listing, you'll see this continuation arrow to indicate a line that is a continuation of the line above it, and which has been broken only to fit it into the book's margins. If you need to type that line of code into a text editor, you should neither break the line nor type a special arrow character. Simply enter both lines of code on a single long line.

Some Experience Required—HTML

This book is aimed at those who want to learn and master JavaScript. You do not need any previous programming experience or knowledge of JavaScript. However, you should have a basic familiarity with HTML, the HyperText Markup Language. Online Appendix A, "Comparing JavaScript and JScript," provides an HTML reference manual. If you are new to HTML, I recommend that you use one of the many online tutorials that are available on the Web to get up to speed. To find one of these tutorials, use your browser's search capabilities to search for the text "HTML tutorial." You can also check the URLs `http://www.sybex.com` and `http://www.jaworski.com/javascript/` for links to online tutorials and other information.

Hardware and Software Requirements

This book is oriented toward Windows 95 and 98 users. However, the JavaScript that you will learn will run on any platform that supports Netscape Communicator, Microsoft Internet Explorer, or the Opera Software Opera browser (`http://www.operasoftware.com`). These include Windows NT, Macintosh, Linux, and UNIX variations. To use this book with Windows 95 and Netscape Communicator or Internet Explorer, I recommend that you have a Pentium or better processor with at least 32 megabytes of RAM. You can get away with a 486 processor and 16 megabytes of RAM, but your browser will start and run very slowly.

To develop server-side JavaScript applications you will need a Netscape or Microsoft Web server. These servers only run on Windows NT (Workstation or Server) and UNIX—there is no Mac version available. I recommend getting Windows NT 4 because it supports both Netscape and Microsoft Web servers. You will need to boost your RAM to a minimum of 32 megabytes. However, 64 megabytes is recommended.

What Browser Should You Use?

To make the best use of this book, I recommend that you use both Netscape Communicator 4.5 or later *and* Microsoft Internet Explorer 4 or later. This book covers JavaScript 1.3, which is fully supported only by the Navigator 4.5 browser provided with Communicator. However, this book also covers JScript 3.1, which is supported by Internet Explorer 4, and JScript 5, which requires Internet Explorer 5. There are incompatibilities between Communicator 4.5, Internet Explorer 4, and Internet Explorer 5. Knowledge of these incompatibilities is important to JavaScript programming, and this book points them out whenever possible. However, the best way to learn JavaScript programming is to use both Netscape and Microsoft browsers to execute your scripts.

How This Book Is Organized

The chapters in this book have three basic elements: background information on a particular aspect of JavaScript, a discussion of how to apply that aspect of JavaScript to the development of Web applications, and programming examples that show JavaScript in action.

This is a large book because there is a lot that you can do with JavaScript and plenty to learn if you want to master all aspects of JavaScript programming. The book is organized into six parts, consisting of 23 chapters. There are also three online bonus chapters, and four online appendices.

Part I—Getting Started with JavaScript and JScript

In Part I (Chapters 1 through 5), you'll cover the elements of the JavaScript language and learn how to write simple scripts. Part I introduces you to JavaScript's syntax and gives you a feel for its use in browser programming. You'll learn about

JavaScript's support of object-based programming and will be introduced to Java-Script's predefined objects. These predefined objects enable your scripts to control the way information is displayed by your browser and also how your browser responds to user events. Mastery of these objects is critical to becoming a proficient JavaScript programmer.

Part II—Using Predefined Objects and Methods

In Part II (Chapters 6 through 11), you'll learn the details of JavaScript's predefined objects, and learn how to use the properties and methods of these objects in sample scripts. When you finish Part II, you will have been thoroughly introduced to JavaScript browser programming and you'll be prepared to go on in Part III to learning how to use JavaScript to create a number of very useful and entertaining scripts.

Part III—Building Sample Applications

In Part III (Chapters 12 through 14) you'll learn how to use JavaScript to create some useful enhancements to your Web pages. In Chapter 12, you'll learn how to implement common desktop accessories in JavaScript and how to integrate them with your Web pages. In Chapter 13, you'll learn how to develop Web-based catalogs, using JavaScript instead of CGI programs. Finally, in Chapter 14, you'll learn how to use JavaScript to interface with existing search engines and to implement browser-side search capabilities.

Part IV—Communicating with Java, ActiveX, and Plug-Ins

In Part IV (Chapters 15 through 17), you'll be introduced to Java applets, ActiveX components, and browser plug-ins and learn how to combine them with JavaScript. Chapter 15 explains how to use JavaScript to load, control, and communicate with Java applets. It also explains how a Java applet can invoke JavaScript functions. Chapter 16 provides an introduction to ActiveX and shows how JScript can be used to script ActiveX objects. Finally, Chapter 17 describes how browser plug-ins work and shows how to use JavaScript to load and communicate with plug-ins.

Part V—Developing Advanced Applications

Part V (Chapters 18 and 19) covers the development of advanced Web applications using new features of JavaScript and JScript. Chapter 18 provides an overview of style sheets and shows how JavaScript style sheets can be used to easily control the ways in which Web documents are presented. It also covers Internet Explorer's extensive support for scripting DHTML. Chapter 19 explains how Navigator layers and features of the Internet Explorer Object Model can be used to develop advanced multimedia applications.

Part VI—Programming Servers

Part VI (Chapters 20 through 23) shows you how to use JavaScript to develop server-side applications. Chapter 20 covers the Common Gateway Interface (CGI) and shows how server-side CGI scripts interact with client-side JavaScript scripts. Chapter 21 introduces LiveWire and LiveWire Database Services and shows how to use JavaScript to create server-side JavaScript applications on Netscape servers. Chapter 22 shows how to script Microsoft servers and covers Active Server Pages (ASP), Windows Scripting Host (WSH), and remote scripting. Finally, Chapter 23 identifies security issues you must consider when developing JavaScript-based Web applications. It also covers the use of signed scripts.

The Web Component

In addition to containing all the listings (scripts, code, and supporting files and graphics) presented and discussed in this book, this book's Web page (`http://www.sybex.com`) contains three bonus chapters and four online appendices that provide additional information about the material covered in the book. The bonus chapters include information on creating Web page widgets, programming games using JavaScript, and working with VRML. The online appendices contain additional information on JavaScript and JScript and provide links to reference manuals for the HTML, JavaScript, Java, ECMAScript, and JScript languages, as well as the World Wide Web Consortium (W3C) Document Object Model (DOM) standard. So that readers may continue to have access to the latest scripting developments, the appendix containing these links will be kept up-to-date.

This Web site will provide a link to the author's home page. His home page will provide you with the most up-to-date information about JavaScript and JScript, and it will answer any questions that you may have about the lessons and examples in this book.

NOTE   The author will be posting updates to this book with the latest news about scripting technologies and information concerning future releases of Netscape Communicator and Microsoft Internet Explorer. Use your Web browser to access the Sybex home page at `http://www.sybex.com`, then follow the links to this book's own Web page for the most current information.

PART I

Getting Started with JavaScript and JScript

■ CHAPTER 1: Learning the Fundamentals

■ CHAPTER 2: Introducing JavaScript and JScript

■ CHAPTER 3: Using Operators, Statements, and Functions

■ CHAPTER 4: Handling Events

■ CHAPTER 5: Working with Objects

CHAPTER

ONE

Learning the Fundamentals

- ■ The Web

- ■ Cascading Style Sheets

- ■ Common Gateway Interface Programs

- ■ JavaScript, JScript, ECMAScript, and the Document Object Model

- ■ Intranets, Extranets, and Distributed Applications

Imagine being able to create interactive multimedia adventure games that anyone can play over the World Wide Web. Imagine being able to create animated product catalogs that not only help your customers find the products they want but enable them to purchase them using secure online payment systems. Imagine being able to create database applications for use by your company's sales force from one end of the country to another via the company's intranet. With Java-Script, you no longer have to imagine, you can do it all.

JavaScript is a new and powerful programming language for the World Wide Web. It not only enables the development of truly interactive Web pages, it is also the essential glue that integrates *Java applets*, *ActiveX Controls*, *browser plug-ins*, *server scripts*, and other Web *objects*, permitting developers to create *distributed applications* for use over the Internet and over corporate *intranets* as well.

If all the terms in the preceding paragraphs are a bit confusing to you, you've come to the right place to begin your involvement with JavaScript and the world of interactive Web page development. In this chapter, I will provide all the background information you need to begin mastering the JavaScript language. I'll start with the concepts that are essential to understanding the operation of the World Wide Web.

NEW! **NOTE**   JavaScript is supported by Netscape Navigator, Microsoft Internet Explorer, and Opera Software's Opera Browser. As such, it is an important tool for both current and future Web development. Throughout this book I will be emphasizing the scripting capabilities provided by Navigator 4.5 (JavaScript 1.3) and Internet Explorer 5 (JScript 5). The Opera 3.5 browser only supports JavaScript 1.1, which is a small subset of the scripting capabilities supported by Navigator and Internet Explorer.

The Web

The World Wide Web, or simply *the Web* for short, is one of the most popular services provided via the Internet. At its best, it combines the appeal of exploring exotic destinations with the excitement of playing a video game, listening to a music CD, or even directing a movie, and you can do it all by means of an intuitive, easy to use, graphical user interface. Probably the most appealing aspect of the Web, however, is the fact that it isn't just for spectators. Once you have some experience with Web *authoring tools*, you can publish yourself—and offer over the Web anything you want to make available, from your company's latest research results to your own documentary on the lives of the rich and famous.

A little history: What exactly *is* the Web? The Web is the collection of all browsers, servers, files, and browser-accessible services available through the Internet. It was created in 1989 by a computer scientist named Tim Berners-Lee; its original purpose was to facilitate communication between research scientists. Berners-Lee, working at the *Conseil Européen pour la Recherche Nucléaire* (CERN), the European Laboratory for Particle Physics, located in Geneva, Switzerland, designed the Web in such a way that documents located on one computer on the Internet could provide links to documents located on other computers on the Internet.

To many, the most familiar element of the Web is the *browser*. A browser is the user's window to the Web, providing the capability to view Web documents and access Web-based services and applications. The most popular browsers are Netscape's Navigator and Microsoft's Internet Explorer, the latest versions of which both support JavaScript. Both browsers are descendants of the *Mosaic* browser, which was developed by Marc Andreessen at the National Center for Supercomputing Applications (NCSA), located at the University of Illinois, Urbana-Champaign. Mosaic's slick graphical user interface (GUI, pronounced "gooey") transformed the Web from a research tool to the global publishing medium that it has become today.

Today's Web browsers extend Mosaic's GUI features with multimedia capabilities and with *browser programming languages* such as Java and JavaScript. These programming languages make it possible to develop Web documents that are highly interactive, meaning they do more than simply connect you to another Web page elsewhere on the Internet. *Web documents created with JavaScript contain programs*—which you, as the user of a browser, run entirely within the context of the Web pages that are currently displayed. This is a major advance in Web publishing technology. It means, for one thing, that you can run Web-based applications without having to install any additional software on your machine.

In order to publish a document on the Web, it must be made available to a Web *server*. Web servers retrieve Web documents in response to browser requests and forward the documents to the requesting browsers via the Internet. Web servers also provide gateways that enable browsers to access Web-related applications, such as database searches and electronic payment systems, as well as other Internet services, such as Gopher and Wide Area Information Search (WAIS).

The earliest Web servers were developed by CERN and NCSA. These servers were the mainstay of the Web throughout its early years. Lately, commercial Web servers, developed by Netscape, Microsoft, and other companies, have become increasingly popular on the Web. These servers are designed for higher performance and to facilitate the development of complex Web applications. They also support the development of server-based applications using JavaScript and Java. Code written in these languages can be integrated very tightly with the server, with the result that server-side programs are executed very efficiently.

Because the Web uses the Internet as its communication medium, it must follow Internet communication *protocols*. A protocol is a set of rules governing the procedures for exchanging information. The Internet's Transmission Control Protocol (TCP) and Internet Protocol (IP) enable worldwide connectivity between browsers and servers. In addition to using the TCP/IP protocols for communication across the Internet, the Web also uses its own protocol, called the HyperText Transfer Protocol (HTTP), for exchanges between browsers and servers. HTTP is used by browsers to request documents from servers and by servers to return requested documents to browsers. Figure 1.1 shows an analogy between the English language and telephony protocols over the phone system on the one hand, and HTTP and TCP/IP over the Internet, on the other hand. Browsers and servers communicate via HTTP over the Internet in the same way that an American and an Englishman would communicate via English over a phone system.

FIGURE 1.1:

An analogy. Browsers and servers communicate via HTTP over the Internet in the same way that an American writer and a British editor would communicate via English over a phone system.

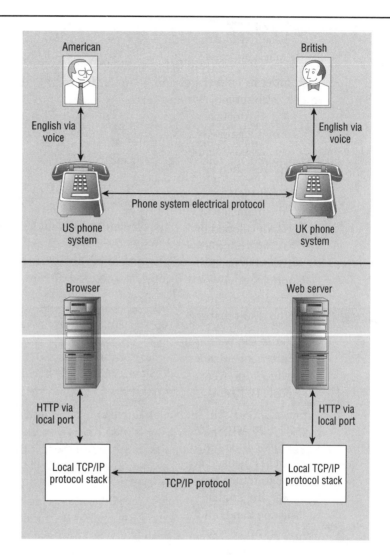

The HyperText Markup Language

The HyperText Markup Language, or HTML, is the *lingua franca* of the Web. It is used to create Web pages and is similar to the codes used by some word processing programs, notably WordPerfect.

HTML uses ordinary ASCII text files to represent Web pages. The files consist of the text to be displayed and the *tags* that specify *how* the text is to be displayed. For example, the following line from an HTML file shows the text of a title between the appropriate title tags.

```
<TITLE>Mastering JavaScript and JScript</TITLE>
```

The use of tags to define the elements of a Web document is referred to as *markup*. Some tags are used to specify the title of a document, others are used to identify headings, paragraphs, and hyperlinks. Still others are used to insert forms, images, multimedia objects, and other features in Web documents.

NOTE   This book assumes that you already have a working knowledge of HTML. This section briefly reviews the important aspects of the language. If you have not used HTML, you should also check out the links to HTML tutorials and reference information located on this book's Web page at http://www.sybex.com.

Tags always begin with a left angle bracket, <, and end with a right angle bracket, >. The name of the tag is placed between these two symbols. Usually, but not always, tags come in pairs, to surround the text that is marked up. Such tags are referred to as *surrounding* tags. For example, HTML documents begin with the <HTML> tag and end with the </HTML> tag. The first tag of a pair of tags is referred to as the *beginning* or *opening* tag and the second tag of the pair is referred to as the *ending* or *closing* tag. The ending tag has the same name as the beginning tag except that a / (a forward slash character) immediately follows the <.

Other tags, known as *separating* tags, do not come in pairs, and have no closing tags. These tags are used to insert such things as line breaks, images, and horizontal rules within marked up text. An example of a separating tag is the <HR> tag, which is used to insert a horizontal rule (a line) across a Web page.

Both surrounding and separating tags make use of *attributes* to specify properties of marked up text. These attributes and their *attribute values*, if any, are included in the tag. For example, a horizontal rule 10 pixels wide may be specified using the following tag:

```
<HR SIZE="10">
```

The above HR tag contains a SIZE attribute that is assigned an attribute value of 10.

NOTE   Attributes and attribute values are placed in the opening tag of a pair of surrounding tags.

Listing 1.1 contains a sample HTML document that illustrates the use of tags in marking up a Web page. Figure 1.2 shows how Netscape Navigator displays this HTML document. The <HTML> and </HTML> tags are used to identify the beginning and end of the HTML document. The document contains a head, identified by the <HEAD> and </HEAD> tags, and a body, identified by the <BODY> and </BODY> tags. The document's head contains a title which is marked by the <TITLE> and </TITLE> tags. (The title appears at the top of the Navigator window.)

Listing 1.1   Example HTML Document

```
<HTML>
<HEAD>
<TITLE>This text is the document's title.</TITLE>
</HEAD>
<BODY>
<H1 ALIGN="CENTER">This is a centered heading.</H1>
<P>This is the first paragraph.</P>
<P>This is the second paragraph.</P>
<HR SIZE="10">
<P ALIGN="CENTER">This paragraph is centered and below the horizontal
rule.</P>
</BODY>
</HTML>
```

FIGURE 1.2:

A browser display of the
HTML document shown in
Listing 1.1

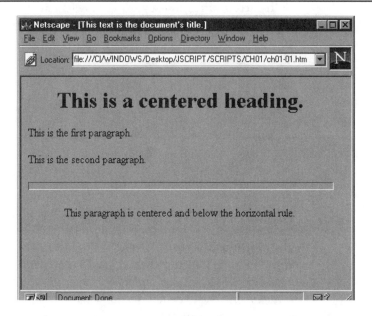

Here are a few items to notice within this listing:

- The document's body contains a Heading 1 that is marked by the <H1> and </H1> tags. The opening <H1> tag uses the ALIGN attribute to center the heading.

- Two paragraphs immediately follow the heading. These paragraphs are marked by the paragraph tags <P> and </P>.

- Following these two paragraphs is a horizontal rule with its SIZE attribute set to 10.

- The last element of the document's body is a paragraph that uses the ALIGN attribute to center the paragraph.

The Development of HTML

HTML was originally developed by Tim Berners-Lee at CERN. Since then, it has evolved through several major revisions. Each revision adds new tags that increase the expressive power of the language. For example, HTML 2 added the capability to include forms within Web documents, and HTML 3.2 added tags for tables and tags that support the use of JavaScript and Java.

As of this writing (winter 1998), HTML 4 is the latest official version of HTML. HTML 4 adds support for international text, greater accessibility, more flexible tables, generic objects, printing, and advanced style sheets.

Although HTML is periodically standardized, the language continues to grow as the result of new tags, attributes, and attribute values that browser developers introduce. Because Netscape and Microsoft hold the largest share of the browser market, they have taken the lead in defining new additions to HTML. These additions are not part of the official HTML language, so they are referred to as *extensions*. Most extensions are eventually integrated into the official version of HTML.

Cascading Style Sheets

Style sheets provide the capability to control the way in which HTML elements are laid out and displayed. For example, you can use style sheets to control the color, font, and spacing used with different HTML elements. Support for Cascading Style Sheets, or CSS, was developed by the World Wide Web consortium and introduced with HTML 3.2, and additional CSS support was added in HTML 4. *Cascading* refers to the capability to use multiple levels of style sheets for a document where one level of style may be used to define another.

Two levels of Cascading Style Sheets have been defined. CSS1 is a simple style sheet mechanism that allows basic styles (for example, fonts, colors and spacing) to be associated with HTML elements. CSS1 is an outgrowth of HTML 3.2 and is supported by Internet Explorer 3 (and later), Navigator 4 (and later), as well as other browsers. CSS2 builds on CSS1 and adds support for media-specific style sheets, content positioning, downloadable fonts, table layout, internationalization, automatic counters and numbering, and other capabilities.

In addition to CSS1 and CSS2, Navigator 4 introduced JavaScript style sheets, or JSS. JSS is similar to CSS1 and makes styles available as JavaScript properties. Chapter 18, "Using Style Sheets and DHTML," introduces style sheets in more detail and shows how styles may be dynamically updated using JavaScript.

Helper Applications

Most graphical Web browsers provide support for viewing images in common graphics formats, such as Graphics Interchange Format (GIF) and Joint Photographic Experts Group (JPEG). Some can even play audio files. However, most browsers do not provide much more than that in terms of multimedia features. Instead of building larger, more complicated browsers to handle many different file formats, browser developers use *helper applications*. When a browser encounters a file type that it does not know how to handle, it searches its list of helper applications to see if it has one that is capable of dealing with the file. If a suitable helper is found, then the browser executes the helper and passes it the name of the file to be run. If an appropriate helper cannot be found, then the browser prompts the user to identify which helper to use, or to save the file for later display.

External Viewers and Plug-Ins

Early helper programs operated independently of the Web browser. These programs, referred to as *external viewers*, were executed separate from the browser and created their own windows to display various types of files. Netscape and Microsoft developed the capability for their second-generation browsers to use *plug-in* or *add-in modules*, which not only execute automatically when needed but display their output in the browser window. Since then, numerous companies have developed plug-in modules to support everything from the three-dimensional worlds created by the Virtual Reality Modeling Language (VRML) to CD-quality audio.

Plug-in modules are generally quicker to load and more efficient than external viewers. Because they execute with the browser, they can be accessed from within the browser environment. Netscape provides the capability to control plug-in modules from Java and JavaScript code via its LiveConnect toolkit. Microsoft provides a similar capability through its Internet Explorer Object Model. You'll learn how to use JavaScript to control plug-ins in Part IV, "Communicating with Java, ActiveX, and Plug-Ins."

Using MIME Types to Identify Helpers for File Formats

So far, I've described how browsers use helper applications to display different types of files, but how does a browser know which helpers to use for a given file? The answer lies in MIME types.

MIME stands for Multipurpose Internet Mail Extensions. MIME was originally developed as a standard for including different types of files in electronic mail. It was subsequently adopted by Web servers and browsers to identify the types of files referenced in a Web page.

MIME identifies file types using a *type/subtype* naming scheme. Examples of common MIME types are text/plain, text/html, image/gif, and video/quicktime. The first component of a MIME type identifies the general type of a file, while the second part identifies the specific type within the general category. For example, the text/plain and text/html types both belong to the text category, but they differ in their subtypes. Table 1.1 lists some common MIME types.

TABLE 1.1: Example MIME Types

MIME Type	Description
text/plain	Generic ASCII text file
text/html	Text file containing HTML
image/gif	Image in Graphics Interchange Format
image/jpeg	Image in Joint Photographic Experts Group format
audio/x-wav	File containing sounds stored in the Windows audio file format
video/mpeg	Video in the Moving Pictures Experts Group format
video/quicktime	Video in the Apple QuickTime format
application/octet-stream	Raw (unformatted) stream of bytes
application/x-javascript	File containing JavaScript source code

Web servers contain configuration files that match file extensions with their MIME types. For example, files that end with the extensions .htm or .html are associated with the text/html MIME type and files that end with .jpg, .jpe, or .jpeg are associated with the image/jpeg MIME type.

Browsers also contain configuration information about MIME types. This information is used to map MIME types to the helper application that displays files of that type.

When a browser requests a file from a Web server, the server uses the file's extension to look up the file's MIME type. The server then identifies the file's MIME type to the browser. The browser uses the file's MIME type to determine which helper application, if any, is to be used to display the file. If the file is to be displayed by an external viewer, the browser waits until the file has been completely received before launching the viewer. If the file is to be displayed by a plug-in, the browser launches the plug-in and passes the file to the plug-in as the file is received. This enables the plug-in to begin displaying the file before it is fully loaded, which is an important capability of audio and video streaming applications.

Uniform Resource Locators (URLs)

A *Uniform Resource Locator*, or URL, is the notation used to specify the addresses of an Internet file or service. You have probably seen numerous examples of URLs. They are included in TV commercials, they're shown on billboards, and they appear in magazine ads. I've even heard people announce them, slash by slash and dot by dot, on the radio. Examples of URLs include `http://home.netscape.com`, `http://www.microsoft.com`, and `ftp://ftp.cdrom.com`.

A URL always contains a *protocol identifier,* such as `http` or `ftp`, and a host name, such as `home.netscape.com`, `www.microsoft.com`, or `ftp.cdrom.com`, which appear in the examples above. Commonly used protocol identifiers are `http`, `ftp`, and `gopher`. The protocol identifier is also referred to as a *scheme.* When writing a URL, the protocol identifier is followed by `://` and then the host name of the computer to which the protocol applies. (In URLs, path names are written using forward slash (/) characters, rather than back slash (\) characters.) For example, to access the main home page of Microsoft on the host named `www.microsoft.com`, you would use the URL `http://www.microsoft.com`. To access the root directory of the File Transfer Protocol (FTP) server hosted at `ftp.cdrom.com`, you would use the URL `ftp://ftp.cdrom.com`.

In addition to the host name, the URL can specify the path and filename of a file to be accessed by adding a single / character followed by the name. For example, from the Sybex Web site, follow the link to my home page for this book, which is located in the `javascript` subdirectory of my Web server's root directory, in the file `index.htm`. The URL for this file is therefore

`http://www.jaworski.com/javascript/index.htm`

(Actually, because my Web server is set up to use the filename `index.htm` by default, it can be omitted from the URL. The URL `http://www.jaworski.com/javascript` would be sufficient to locate the file.)

NOTE   URLs may also contain additional addressing components, such as a port name before the path and filename, and a file offset after the filename.

The File Protocol in URLs

Your browser can use the `file` protocol to access files located on your local machine. Suppose the file `test.htm` was located on your Window 95 Desktop. The path to this file would be `c:\windows\desktop\test.htm`. To open the file with your browser, you would use the following URL:

```
file://localhost/C|/WINDOWS/Desktop/test.htm
```

The host name `localhost` in the URL above is used to refer to the local file system and may be omitted safely. The slash following `localhost`, however, should be retained. The above URL could thus be written as follows:

```
file:///C|/WINDOWS/Desktop/test.htm
```

Note that in both examples above the `C:` drive designation that you are probably most familiar with from DOS conventions is written as `C|` instead.

The HyperText Transfer Protocol (HTTP)

HTTP is the protocol used for communication between browsers and Web servers. HTTP uses a request/response model of communication. A browser establishes a connection with a server and sends URL requests to the server. The server processes the browser's request and sends a response back to the browser.

A browser connects with a Web server by establishing a TCP connection at port 80 of the server. This port is the address at which Web servers "listen" for browser requests. Once a connection has been established, a browser sends a request to the server. This request specifies a request method, the URL of the document, program, or other resource being requested, the HTTP version being used by the browser, and other information related to the request.

Several request methods are available. GET, HEAD, and POST are the most commonly used ones.

The GET method is used to retrieve the information contained at the specified URL. This method may also be used to *submit* data collected in an HTML *form* (the topic of Chapter 7) or to invoke a Common Gateway Interface program (a topic I discuss in the next section, below). When the server processes a GET request, it delivers the requested information (if it can be found). The server inserts at the front of the information an HTTP header that provides data about the server, identifies any errors that occurred in processing the request, and describes the type of information being returned as a result.

The HEAD method is similar to the GET method except that when a Web server processes a HEAD request it only returns the HTTP header data and not the information that was the object of the request. The HEAD method is used to retrieve information about a URL without actually obtaining the information addressed by the URL.

The POST method is used to inform the server that the information appended to the request is to be sent to the specified URL. The POST method is typically used to send form data and other information to Common Gateway Interface (CGI) programs. The Web server responds to a POST request by sending back header data followed by any information generated by the CGI program as the result of processing the request.

The current version of HTTP is HTTP 1.1. It incorporates performance, security, and other improvements to the original HTTP 1. A new version of HTTP, referred to as HTTP-NG, is currently being defined. (The *NG* stands for "next generation.") The goal of HTTP-NG is to simplify the HTTP protocol and make it more extensible.

Common Gateway Interface Programs

The *Common Gateway Interface* is a standard that specifies how external programs may be used by Web servers. Programs that adhere to the Common Gateway Interface standard are referred to as CGI programs. CGI programs may be used to process data submitted with forms, to perform database searches, and to support other types of Web applications such as clickable image maps.

A browser request for the URL of a CGI program comes about as the result of a user clicking a link or submitting a form. The browser uses HTTP to make the request. When a Web server receives the request, the Web server executes the CGI program and also passes it any data that was submitted by the browser. When the CGI program performs its processing it usually generates data in the form of a Web page, which it returns via the Web server to the requesting browser.

The CGI standard specifies how data may be passed from Web servers to CGI programs and how data should be returned from CGI programs to the Web server. Table 1.2 summarizes these interfaces. In Chapter 7, "Processing Forms," and Chapter 20, "Interfacing JavaScript with CGI Programs," you'll study CGI and learn how to create CGI programs.

TABLE 1.2: CGI Summary

Method of Communicating	Interface	Description
Command-line arguments	Web server to CGI program	Data is passed to the CGI program via the command line used to execute the program. Command-line arguments are passed to CGI programs as the result of ISINDEX queries.
Environment variables	Web server to CGI program	A Web server passes data to the CGI program by setting special variables, referred to as environment variables, that are available to the CGI program via its environment.
Standard input stream	Web server to CGI program	A Web server passes data to a CGI program by sending the data to the standard character input stream associated with the CGI program. The CGI program reads the data as if it were manually entered by a user at a character terminal.
Standard output stream	CGI program to Web server	The CGI program passes data back to the Web server by writing it to its standard output stream (for example, to a terminal). The Web server intercepts this data and sends it back to the browser that made the CGI request.

Java Applets

The Java language, developed by Sun Microsystems, Inc., has realized tremendous popularity in the last few years. Although it was originally developed as a language for programming consumer electronic devices, Java has increasingly been adopted as a hardware- and software-independent platform for developing advanced Web applications. Java may be used to write stand-alone applications, but a major reason for its popularity is its ability to develop programs that can be executed by a Web browser.

The Java programs that can be executed by the Web browser are called *applets* rather than applications, because they cannot be run outside of the browser's own window. (*Application* usually implies a complete, stand-alone program.) Programmers create Java applets using built-in programming features of the Java Developer's Kit (JDK). Web pages, written in HTML, reference Java applets using the <APPLET> tag, in much the same way that images are referenced using the <IMAGE> tag. When a Web page that references a Java applet is loaded by a browser, the browser requests the applet code from the Web server. When the browser receives the applet code, it executes the code and allocates a fixed area of the browser window. This area is identified by attributes specified with the <APPLET> tag. The applet is not allowed to update the browser display or handle events outside of its allocated window area.

By way of comparison, JavaScript provides access to the entire Web page, but does not support many of the more advanced object-oriented programming features of Java.

Netscape Navigator and Microsoft Internet Explorer provide the capability for JavaScript scripts to load Java applets, access Java objects, and invoke their methods. Part IV, "Communicating with Java, ActiveX, and Plug-Ins," shows how JavaScript and Java can be combined to produce advanced Web applications.

ActiveX—Microsoft Objects

ActiveX is Microsoft's approach to executing objects other than Java applets in Internet Explorer. The name *ActiveX* was used to make it seem like a new and innovative technology. However, ActiveX is nothing more than Component Object Model (COM) objects that can be downloaded and executed by Internet Explorer. COM traces its origin back to the Object Linking and Embedding (OLE) technology of Microsoft Windows 3.1.

COM objects are instances of *classes* (object types) that are also organized into *interfaces*. Each interface consists of a collection of *methods* (functions). COM objects are implemented inside a *server* (dynamic-link libraries, operating system services, or independent processes) and are accessed via their methods. The *COM library* provides a directory of available COM objects. Over the many years since Windows 3.1, many software components have been developed as COM objects.

ActiveX components are simply COM objects that implement a specific type of interface. They are important in that they provide a means for the large base of COM objects to be reused within Internet Explorer. They also allow older languages, such as C++ and C, to be used to build components for Web applications.

While ActiveX components allow the use of legacy software in Internet Explorer, they also present some drawbacks. The most significant drawback is that ActiveX is only supported by Internet Explore 4 and 5. No other browser (including earlier versions of Internet Explorer) is able to use ActiveX. ActiveX has also been criticized for its poor security. An ActiveX component is not required to behave in a secure manner like a Java applet or JavaScript script. In fact, it has been demonstrated that ActiveX components can be used to steal or modify sensitive information or completely wipe out a user's system. Microsoft has countered this vulnerability by allowing ActiveX components to be digitally signed. This does not prevent ActiveX components from violating security, but, in some cases, it can be used to determine whether a particular Web site is responsible for causing damage.

ActiveX components are useful in intranet applications where all users of a particular company are required to use Internet Explorer and the components are signed by the company or a trusted developer. Because the Internet Explorer Object Model allows ActiveX components to be accessed from JavaScript, JavaScript scripts can be used to integrate the ActiveX components into the intranet applications. Chapter 16, "Scripting ActiveX Components," shows how to script ActiveX components using JavaScript.

A Brief History of JavaScript

Often, one programming language will evolve from another. For example, Java evolved from C++, which evolved from C, which evolved from other languages. This is also the case for JavaScript. Netscape originally developed a language called *LiveScript* to add a basic scripting capability to both Navigator and its

Web-server line of products; when it added support for Java applets in its release of Navigator 2, Netscape replaced LiveScript with JavaScript. Although the initial version of JavaScript was little more than LiveScript renamed, JavaScript has been subsequently updated with each new release of Navigator.

NOTE   Although JavaScript bears the name of Java, JavaScript is a very different language that is used for a very different purpose.

JavaScript supports both Web browser and server scripting. Browser scripts are used to create dynamic Web pages that are more interactive, more responsive, and more tightly integrated with plug-ins, ActiveX components, and Java applets. JavaScript supports these features by providing special programming capabilities, such as the ability to dynamically generate HTML and to define custom event-handling functions.

JavaScript scripts are included in HTML documents via the HTML <SCRIPT> tag. When a JavaScript-capable browser loads an HTML document containing scripts, it evaluates the scripts as they are encountered. The scripts may be used to create HTML elements that are added to the displayed document or to define functions, called *event handlers,* that respond to user actions, such as mouse clicks and keyboard entries. Scripts may also be used to control plug-ins, ActiveX components, and Java applets.

Microsoft implemented JScript in its Internet Explorer 3. The scripting capability of Internet Explorer 3 is roughly equivalent to Navigator 2. Netscape introduced JavaScript 1.1 with Navigator 3 and JavaScript 1.2 with Navigator 4. JavaScript 1.1 added a number of new features, including support for more browser objects and user-defined functions. JavaScript 1.2 added new objects, methods, and properties, and support for style sheets, layers, regular expressions, and signed scripts.

Netscape also supported server-side scripting with its LiveWire and LiveWire Pro (renamed to LiveWire Database Service) features of its Enterprise and Fast-Track Web servers. On the server side, JavaScript is used to more easily develop scripts that process form data, perform database searches, and implement custom Web applications. Server-side scripts are more tightly integrated with the Web server than CGI programs.

Microsoft introduced its version of JavaScript, referred to as JScript, in Internet Explorer 3. JScript is tightly coupled to Internet Explorer and allows almost all HTML elements to be scripted. JScript is compatible with JavaScript 1.2.

Microsoft also included server-side JavaScript support with its Internet Information Server (IIS). It later developed a more general approach to server-side scripting with its Windows Scripting Host and remote scripting technologies. Remote scripting allows Internet Explorer to remotely execute scripts on a server and receive the server script outputs within the context of a single Web page. You'll learn server-side programming in Part VI, "Programming Servers."

Netscape and Microsoft submitted their scripting languages to the European Computer Manufacturers Association (ECMA) for standardization. ECMA released the Standard ECMA-262 in June of 1997. This standard describes the ECMAScript language, which is a compilation of the best features of JavaScript and JScript. An updated version of this standard was released in June of 1998.

Microsoft worked closely with ECMA and updated Internet Explorer 4 and JScript (JScript 3.1) to achieve ECMAScript compliance. Navigator achieved ECMAScript compliance with JavaScript 1.3, which is supported in Navigator 4.06 and 4.5.

Internet Explorer 5 introduced JScript 5, which provides additional scripting capabilities, such as the `try - catch` statement. This statement provides advanced error handling support and will be included in the future ECMAScript 2.

While Netscape and Microsoft were busy introducing new versions of their browsers and scripting languages, another JavaScript-compatible browser was launched by Opera Software (`http://www.operasoftware.com`). Opera browsers 3.2 and 3.5 both support JavaScript 1.1.

Another JavaScript-related standardization effort was initiated by the World Wide Web Consortium to standardize the basic objects that are made available by browsers when processing HTML and XML documents. This effort resulted in a specification known as the Document Object Model (DOM) Level 1. It provides a standard set of objects for representing HTML and XML documents, a standard model of how these objects can be combined, and a standard interface for accessing and manipulating them. The DOM is like an application programming interface (API) for HTML and XML documents. However, the DOM is not a complete API in that it does not specify the events that occur when a user interacts with an HTML or XML document (and methods for handling them). At this time, neither Navigator nor Internet Explorer satisfy the requirements of the DOM.

LiveWire and LiveWire Database Service

LiveWire is a graphical environment for developing and managing Web sites. Netscape created it for use with their servers. One of LiveWire's features is that it supports the development of server-side programs using the JavaScript language. These programs are used in the same way as CGI programs, but they are more closely integrated with Web servers and the HTML pages that reference them. The LiveWire Database Service provides the capability to connect server scripts to databases. Server scripts access databases using the industry-standard Structured Query Language (SQL).

Server-based JavaScript programs are compiled with HTML documents into a platform-independent bytecode format. When a Web browser requests a compiled document, it is translated back into HTML format and sent out to the browser. The server-based scripts remain with the server and are loaded to perform any server-side processing. The HTML document loaded by the browser communicates with the server-side scripts to implement advanced Web applications that are distributed between the browser, server, and other server-side programs, such as database and electronic commerce applications.

LiveWire provides a number of programming objects that JavaScript scripts can use to implement CGI-style programs. These objects simplify the communication between browsers, Web servers, and server-side scripts. Chapter 21, "Scripting Netscape Servers," introduces LiveWire and shows how it is used to develop server-side scripts.

Active Server Pages, Windows Scripting Host, and Remote Scripting

Microsoft's Active Server Pages (ASP) is a server-side scripting environment that is similar to LiveWire. You can use it to include server-side scripts and ActiveX components with HTML pages. The combined HTML and script file is stored as an ASP file. When a browser requests the ASP file from your Web server, the server invokes the ASP processor. The ASP processor reads through the requested file, executes any script commands, and sends the processing results as a Web page to the browser. ASP pages can also invoke ActiveX components to perform tasks, such as accessing a database or performing an electronic commerce transaction. Because ASP scripts run on the Web server and send standard HTML to the browser, ASP is browser independent.

Microsoft introduced ASP with Internet Information Server (IIS) version 3. It also works with IIS 4, Personal Web Server for Windows 95, and Peer Web Server for Windows NT Workstation.

NOTE   Chapter 22, "Scripting Microsoft Servers," covers ASP, WSH, and remote scripting.

As a result of the success of ASP, Microsoft developed Windows Scripting Host (WSH), a technology that allows scripts to be run on Windows 95, 98, and NT 4. WSH is language independent and supports JScript, VBScript, and other languages. It allows scripts to be executed from the Windows Desktop or a console (MS-DOS) window. WSH scripts are complete in themselves and do need to be embedded in an HTML document. WSH is an exciting technology in that it extends the capabilities of JScript beyond the Web to the Windows Desktop and operating system. WSH scripts can be used to replace MS-DOS scripts and provide the capability to take full advantage of the Windows GUI, ActiveX, and operating system functions in JScript scripts.

NOTE   WSH can be freely downloaded from Microsoft's Web site at `http://msdn.microsoft.com/scripting/`.

Microsoft's latest addition to scripting technology is referred to as *remote scripting*. Remote scripting enables client-side scripts, running on Internet Explorer, to execute server-side scripts, running on IIS. This lets Internet Explorer and IIS perform simultaneous processing and communicate with each other within the context of a Web page, allowing the page to be dynamically updated with server information without having to be reloaded. This frees the user from having to reload a Web page during the execution of a Web application and provides for a higher degree of interaction between the browser and Web server. For example, with remote scripting, a Web server can validate form data and provide the user with feedback while the user is still filling out the form.

Remote scripting allows browser/server communication to be accomplished in either a synchronous or asynchronous manner. When synchronous communication is used, a client-side script executes a server-side script and waits for the server-side script to return its result. When asynchronous communication is used, the client-side script executes the server-side script and then continues with its processing without waiting for the server-side script to finish.

NOTE   Remote scripting can be freely downloaded from Microsoft's Web site at `http://msdn.microsoft.com/scripting/`.

Intranets, Extranets, and Distributed Applications

In the last couple of years, corporations have begun to look at ways of deploying TCP/IP networks inside of their companies to take advantage of the full range of standards-based services provided by the Internet. These "company-internal internets" have become known as *intranets*. Intranets may be private networks that are physically separate from the Internet, internal networks that are separated from the Internet by a firewall, or simply a company's internal extension of the Internet.

Companies deploy intranets so that they can make Internet services available to their workers. E-mail, Web browsing, and Web publishing are the most popular of these services. Many companies make Web servers available for their employees' intranet publishing needs. These intranet Web servers allow departments, groups, and individuals within a company to conveniently share information while usually limiting access to the information published on the intranet to company employees.

The popularity of intranets as a way of communicating and of sharing information within a company has brought about a demand for more powerful and sophisticated intranet applications. The eventual goal is for the intranet to provide a common application framework from which a company's core information processing functions can be implemented and accessed. Netscape, Sun, Microsoft, and other Web software providers are focusing on the intranet as the primary application framework for the development of business software.

Because of its client/server architecture and user-friendly browser software, the Web is the perfect model for implementing these common intranet application frameworks. The approach taken by Netscape, Microsoft, and other Web software developers is to use the Web browser as the primary interface by which users connect to the intranet and run intranet and extranet applications. These applications are referred to as *distributed applications* because their execution is distributed in part on the browser (via JavaScript, Java, ActiveX, XML, and other languages); in part on the server (via CGI programs and JavaScript and Java server-side programs); and in part on database and other enterprise servers.

Distributed internet and extranet applications use HTML, JavaScript, Java, XML, and other languages for programming the browser-based user interface portion of the distributed application. They also use JavaScript and Java to perform server-side programming. Other server-side components may be written in Java, C++, or other languages and made available as Common Object Request Broker Architecture (CORBA) or Distributed Component Object Model (DCOM) objects. These objects may also be accessed from JavaScript. Chapter 21, "Scripting Netscape Servers," and Chapter 22, "Scripting Microsoft Servers," cover the use of CORBA and DCOM objects in developing distributed applications.

In many distributed application development approaches, Java is seen as a key technology for developing the components of distributed applications and JavaScript is seen as the essential glue that combines these components into fully distributed Web-based intranet and extranet applications.

Summary

This chapter covered the concepts that are essential to understanding the operation of the Web. You learned about Web development languages, such as HTML, Java, and JavaScript. You also covered related Web technologies, such as HTTP, CGI, LiveWire, ASP, and remote scripting. You should have a basic understanding of how these elements work together to develop Web applications. In the next chapter, you'll begin the exciting process of learning to use JavaScript to write some sample scripts.

CHAPTER

TWO

Introducing JavaScript and JScript

- JavaScript and Browsers, JavaScript and Servers

- Embedding JavaScript in HTML

- Telling Non-JavaScript Browsers to Ignore Your Code

- JavaScript Comments

- Generating HTML

- Types and Variables

This chapter introduces you to the JavaScript language. I'll show you how JavaScript works with both the Netscape and Microsoft browsers and Web servers, and how to embed JavaScript statements in HTML documents. I'll then cover JavaScript's use of *types* and *variables*, and show you how to use *arrays*. By the time you have finished this chapter, you'll be able to write simple scripts and include them in your Web pages.

JavaScript and Browsers, JavaScript and Servers

JavaScript is a script-based programming language that supports the development of both client and server components of Web-based applications. On the client side, it can be used to write programs that are executed by a Web browser within the context of a Web page. On the server side, it can be used to write Web server programs that can process information submitted by a Web browser and then update the browser's display accordingly. Figure 2.1 provides an overview of how JavaScript supports both client and server Web programming.

NOTE   Microsoft's version of JavaScript is named JScript. I use *JavaScript* to refer to both JavaScript and JScript unless I'm referring to one but not the other. In these cases, I'll refer to *Netscape's JavaScript* and *Microsoft's JScript*.

On the left side of the figure, a Web browser displays a Web page. As I mentioned in Chapter 1, "Learning the Fundamentals," this is a result of the browser acting on the instructions contained in an HTML file. The browser reads the HTML file and displays elements of the file as they are encountered. In this case, the HTML file (which the browser has retrieved from a Web server, seen on the right) contains embedded JavaScript code. The process of reading the HTML file and identifying the elements contained in the file is referred to as *parsing*. When a script is encountered during parsing, the browser executes the script before continuing with further parsing.

FIGURE 2.1:

JavaScript supports both client and server Web applications.

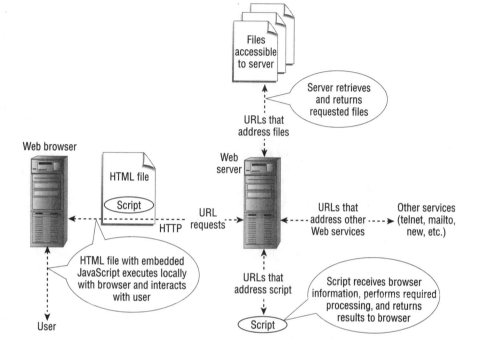

The script can perform actions, such as generating HTML code that affects the display of the browser window. It can perform actions that affect the operation of plug-ins, Java applets, or ActiveX components. The script can also define JavaScript language elements that are used by other scripts. Figure 2.2 summarizes the parsing of HTML files that contain JavaScript scripts.

Some scripts may define functions for handling *events* that are generated by user actions. For example, you might write a script to define a function for handling the event "submitting a form" or "clicking a link." The event handlers can then perform actions such as validating the form's data, generating a custom URL for the link, or loading a new Web page.

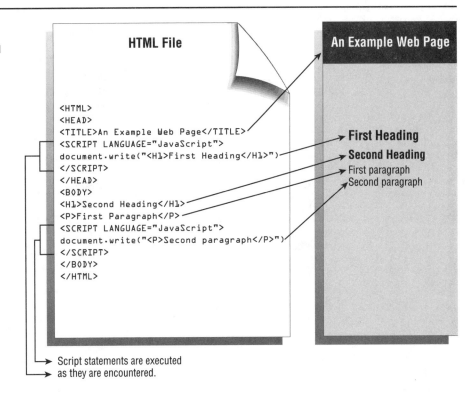

FIGURE 2.2:

HTML files are parsed and displayed one element at a time.

```
HTML File
```
```
<HTML>
<HEAD>
<TITLE>An Example Web Page</TITLE>
<SCRIPT LANGUAGE="JavaScript">
document.write("<H1>First Heading</H1>")
</SCRIPT>
</HEAD>
<BODY>
<H1>Second Heading</H1>
<P>First Paragraph</P>
<SCRIPT LANGUAGE="JavaScript">
document.write("<P>Second paragraph</P>")
</SCRIPT>
</BODY>
</HTML>
```

An Example Web Page

First Heading

Second Heading

First paragraph
Second paragraph

Script statements are executed as they are encountered.

JavaScript's event-handling capabilities provide greater control over the user interface than HTML alone. For example, when a user submits an HTML form, a browser that isn't implementing JavaScript handles the "submit form" event by sending the form data to a CGI program for further processing. The CGI program processes the form data and returns the results to the Web browser, which displays the results to the user. By comparison, when a user submits an HTML form using a browser that *does* implement JavaScript, a JavaScript event-handling function may be called to process the form data. This processing may vary from validating the data (that is, checking to see that the data entered by the user is appropriate for the fields contained in the form) to performing all of the required form processing, eliminating the need for a CGI program. In other words, JavaScript's event-handling capabilities allow the *browser* to perform some, if not all, of the form processing. Figure 2.3 compares JavaScript's event-handling capabilities to those provided by HTML. Besides providing greater control over the user interface, these event-handling capabilities help to reduce network traffic, the need for CGI programs, and the load on the Web server.

FIGURE 2.3:

Event-handling functions enable scripts to respond to user actions.

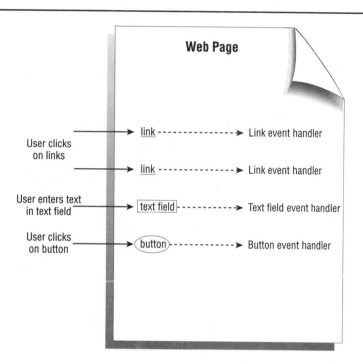

TIP   I'll cover JavaScript's event-handling capabilities more fully in Chapter 4, "Handling Events."

While JavaScript's browser programming capabilities can eliminate the need for *some* server-side programs, others are still required to support more advanced Web applications, such as those that access database information, support electronic commerce, or perform specialized processing. Server-side JavaScript scripts are used to replace traditional CGI programs. Instead of a Web server calling a CGI program to process form data, perform searches, or implement customized Web applications, a JavaScript-enabled Web server can invoke a precompiled JavaScript script to perform this processing. The Web server automatically creates JavaScript objects that tell the script how it was invoked and the type of browser requesting its services; it also automatically communicates any data supplied by the browser.

The script processes the data provided by the browser and returns information to the browser, via the server. The browser then uses this information to update the user's display. Figure 2.4 illustrates how server-side scripts are used.

FIGURE 2.4:

Server-side scripts are used to replace CGI programs.

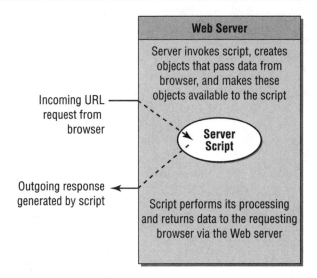

There are several advantages to using server-side JavaScript scripts on Netscape and Microsoft Web servers:

- Because these Web servers have been specially designed for executing JavaScript scripts, they are able to minimize the processing overhead that is usually associated with invoking the script, passing data, and returning the results of script processing.

- You can use JavaScript to replace CGI scripts written in other languages. This eliminates the problems that are usually associated with managing multiple CGI programs, which may have been written in an OS shell language, Perl, tcl, C and other languages. It also provides tighter control over the security of these server-side applications.

- The database extensions integrated within these servers provide a powerful capability for accessing information contained in compatible external databases. These database extensions may be used by server-side scripts.

The database connectivity supported by these servers enables even beginning programmers to create server-side JavaScript programs to update databases with information provided by browsers (usually through forms) and to provide Web users with Web pages that are dynamically generated from database queries. You can imagine how exciting this is for researchers gathering and reporting information over the Web and for entrepreneurs who have catalogs full of products and services to sell over the Web. Figure 2.5 illustrates the use of JavaScript to provide database connectivity to Web applications.

FIGURE 2.5:

Netscape and Microsoft Web servers provide database connectivity to server-side scripts.

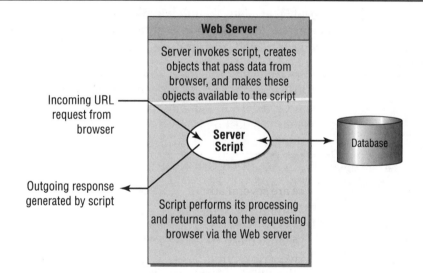

NOTE   In this section, I've provided an overview of the different ways in which JavaScript can be used for browser and server-side Web applications. JavaScript's syntax is the same for both client (browser) *and* server programming; however, the examples I will be using in this chapter mainly reflect how JavaScript relates to browser programming. For examples of JavaScript *server* programming, see the four chapters that make up Part IV, "Programming Servers."

Embedding JavaScript in HTML

JavaScript statements can be included in HTML documents by enclosing the statements between an opening `<script>` tag and a closing `</script>` tag. Within the opening tag, the LANGUAGE attribute is set to `"JavaScript"` to identify the script as being JavaScript as opposed to some other scripting language, such as Visual Basic Script (VBScript). The script tag is typically used as follows:

```
<script language="JavaScript">
 JavaScript statements
</script>
```

The script tag may be placed in either the *head* or the *body* of an HTML document. In many cases, it is better to place the script tag in the head of a document to ensure that all JavaScript definitions have been made before the body of the document is displayed. You'll learn more about this in the subsection, "Use of the Document Head," later in this section.

The traditional first exercise with any programming language is to write a program to display the text *Hello World!* This teaches the programmer to display output, a necessary feature of most programs. A JavaScript script that displays this text is shown in Listing 2.1.

Listing 2.1   **Hello World!**

```
<html>
<head>
<title>Hello World!</title>
</head>
<body>
<script language="JavaScript">
document.write("Hello World!")
</script>
</body>
</html>
```

The body of our example document (the lines between the `<body>` and the `</body>` tags) contains a single element: a script, identified by the `<script>` and `</script>` tags. The opening script tag has the attribute `language="JavaScript"` to identify the script as JavaScript. The script has a single statement, `document.write("Hello World!")`, that writes the text *Hello World!* to the body of the current `document` object. Figure 2.6 shows how the HTML document is displayed by a JavaScript-enabled browser—Netscape Navigator 4.5. The text written by the script becomes part of the HTML document displayed by the browser.

FIGURE 2.6:

The very simple result of Listing 2.1, Hello World!, displayed by Netscape Navigator

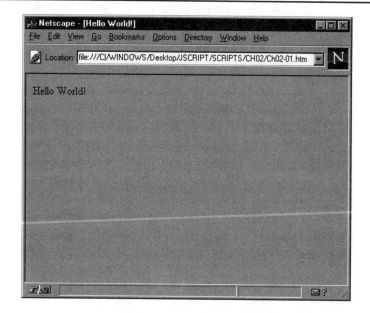

Other Language Attributes

All JavaScript-capable browsers will process JavaScript code if the LANGUAGE attribute is set to *"JavaScript"*. However, the LANGUAGE attribute can also be set to the following other values in order to limit the browsers that are able to process JavaScript code:

JavaScript1.1   Used to limit execution of a script to browsers that support JavaScript 1.1. These browsers are Navigator 3 and later, Internet Explorer 4 and later, and Opera 3.5 and later.

JavaScript1.2   Used to limit execution of a script to browsers that support JavaScript 1.2. These browsers are Navigator 4 and later and Internet Explorer 4 and later.

JavaScript1.3   Used to limit execution of a script to browsers that support JavaScript 1.3. These browsers are limited to Navigator 4.06 and later.

JScript   Used to limit execution of a script to browsers that support JScript. These browsers are limited to Internet Explorer 3 and later.

Table 2.1 identifies which of the above attributes are supported by popular browsers. If a browser does not support an attribute, it will simply ignore the <SCRIPT> tags.

TABLE 2.1: Browser Support of the LANGUAGE Attribute

Browser	JavaScript	JavaScript1.1	JavaScript1.2	JavaScript1.3	JScript
Navigator 2	X				
Navigator 3	X	X			
Navigator 4	X	X	X		
Navigator 4.06	X	X	X	X	
Navigator 4.5	X	X	X	X	
Internet Explorer 3	X				X
Internet Explorer 4	X	X	X		X
Internet Explorer 5	X	X	X		X
Opera 3.21	X	X	X	X	
Opera 3.5	X	X	X	X	

NOTE   The Opera browser reports that it supports the LANGUAGE attribute values `JavaScript`, `JavaScript1.1`, `JavaScript1.2`, and `JavaScript1.3`, but it only supports up to JavaScript version 1.1 as of Opera 3.5.

TIP   To ensure that more browsers are able to execute your scripts, set the LANGUAGE attribute to *"JavaScript"*. Your JavaScript code can then perform checks to detect which type and version of browser is currently executing a script. Chapter 5, "Working with Objects," covers browser detection techniques.

In addition to the LANGUAGE attribute, Internet Explorer 4 and later support the use of conditional compilation directives. These directives are used to limit script execution to selected portions of scripts. Conditional directives are covered in online Appendix A, "Comparing JavaScript and JScript."

Telling Non-JavaScript Browsers to Ignore Your Code

Not all browsers support JavaScript. Older browsers, such as the Netscape Navigator 1 , Internet Explorer 2 and the character-based Lynx browser, do not recognize the script tag and, as a consequence, display as text all the JavaScript statements that are enclosed between <script> and </script>. Figures 2.7 and 2.8 show how the preceding JavaScript script is displayed by Internet Explorer 2 and by DosLynx.

FIGURE 2.7:

Internet Explorer 2 displays the Hello World! script of Listing 2.1 instead of executing it.

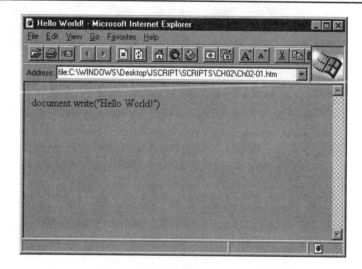

Fortunately, HTML provides a method to conceal JavaScript statements from such JavaScript-challenged browsers. The trick is to use HTML *comment* tags to *surround* the JavaScript statements. Because HTML comments are displayed only within the code used to create a Web page, they do not show up as part of the browser's display. The use of HTML comment tags is as follows:

```
<!- Begin hiding JavaScript
JavaScript statements
// End hiding JavaScript ->
```

The <!-- tag begins the HTML comment and the --> tag ends the comment. The // string identifies a JavaScript comment, as you'll learn later in this chapter in the section, "JavaScript Comments."

FIGURE 2.8:

DosLynx displays the Hello World! script of Listing 2.1 instead of executing it.

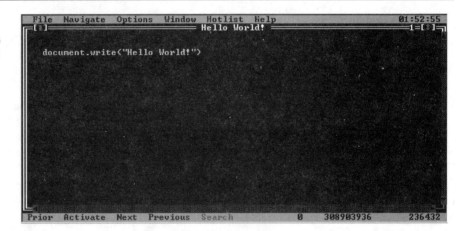

The comment tags cause the JavaScript statements to be treated as comments by JavaScript-challenged browsers. JavaScript-enabled browsers, on the other hand, know to ignore the comment tags and process the enclosed statements as JavaScript. Listing 2.2 shows how HTML comments are used to hide JavaScript statements. Figure 2.9 shows how Internet Explorer 2 displays the HTML document shown in Listing 2.2.

Listing 2.2   **Using HTML Comments to Hide JavaScript Code**

```
<html>
<head>
<title>Using HTML comments to hide JavaScript code</title>
</head>
<body>
<script language="JavaScript">
<!- Begin hiding JavaScript
document.write("Hello World!")
// End hiding JavaScript ->
</script>
</body>
</html>
```

Result of using HTML
comments (Listing 2.2)
with Internet Explorer 2.
Compare to Figures 2.7
and 2.8.

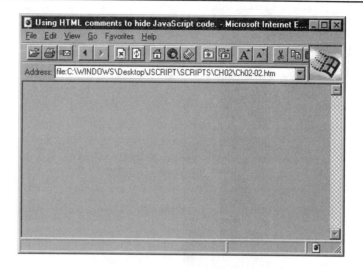

The noscript Tag

Versions 2 and later of Netscape Navigator and versions 3 and later of Microsoft
Internet Explorer support JavaScript. These browsers account for nearly 90 percent
of browser use on the Web and their percentage of use is increasing. This means
that most browser requests come from JavaScript-capable browsers. However,
there are still popular browsers, such as Lynx, that do not support JavaScript. In
addition, both Navigator and Internet Explorer provide users with the option of
disabling JavaScript. The noscript tag was created for those browsers that can't or
won't process JavaScript. It is used to display markup that is an alternative to executing a script. The HTML instructions contained inside the tag are displayed by
JavaScript-challenged browsers (as well as by JavaScript-capable browsers that
have JavaScript disabled). The script shown in Listing 2.3 illustrates the use of
the noscript tag. Figure 2.10 shows the Web page of Listing 2.3 as displayed by a
JavaScript-capable browser. Compare that display to Figure 2.11, which shows
how it is displayed by Internet Explorer 2, a non-JavaScript browser.

Listing 2.3	**Using the noscript Tag**

```
<html>
<head>
<title>Using the noscript Tag.</title>
</head>
<body>
<script language="JavaScript">
<!- Begin hiding JavaScript
document.write("Hello World!")
// End hiding Javascript ->
</script>
<NOSCRIPT>
[JavaScript]
</NOSCRIPT>
</body>
</html>
```

FIGURE 2.10:

Using the noscript
tag with Navigator, a
JavaScript-capable
browser (Listing 2.3).

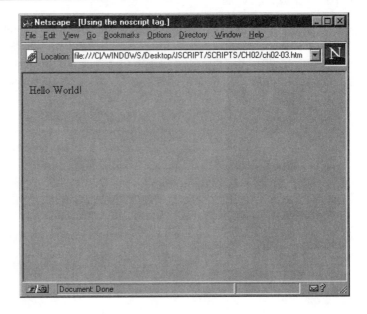

FIGURE 2.11:

Using the noscript tag with Internet Explorer 2, a non-JavaScript browser (Listing 2.3).

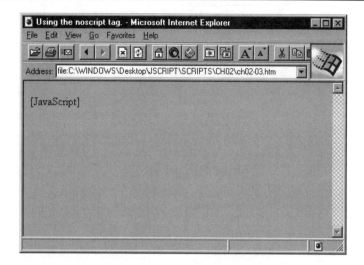

The Script Tag's *SRC* Attribute

The script tag itself provides an alternative way to include JavaScript code in an HTML document, via the tag's SRC attribute, which may be used to specify a *file* containing JavaScript statements. Here's an example of the use of the SRC attribute:

```
<script language="JavaScript" SRC="src.js">
</script>
```

In the above example, the file `src.js` is a file containing JavaScript statements. (The file could have been named anything, but it should end with the `.js` extension; I just chose `src.js` to help you remember the SRC attribute.) Note that the closing `</script>` tag is still required.

If the file `src.js` contains the following code

```
<!- Begin hiding JavaScript
document.write("This text was generated by code in the src.js file.")
// End hiding JavaScript ->
```

then the HTML document shown in Listing 2.4 would produce the browser display shown in Figure 2.12.

Listing 2.4   **Inserting Source JavaScript Files**

```
<html>
<head>
<title>Using the SRC attribute of the script tag.</title>
</head>
<body>
<script language="JavaScript" SRC="src.js">
</script>
</body>
</html>
```

FIGURE 2.12:

Using the SRC attribute of the script tag to include JavaScript code (Listing 2.4)

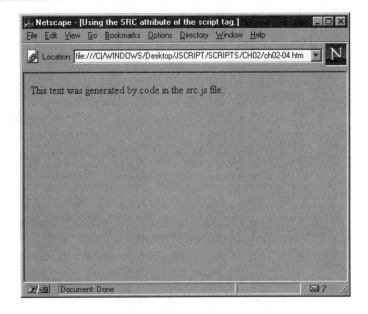

NOTE   The **SRC** attribute may have a URL as its attribute value. Web servers that provide the source file, however, *must* report the file's MIME type as **application/x-javascript**; otherwise, browsers will not load the source file.

JavaScript Entities

JavaScript entities allow the value of an HTML attribute to be provided by a Java-Script *expression*. This allows attribute values to be dynamically calculated during the loading of a Web page.

A JavaScript entity begins with &{ and ends with };. The following example shows how the HREF attribute of a link may be specified by the JavaScript linkTo variable:

```
<A HREF="&{linkTo};">Click here.</A>
```

The value of linkTo, which must be calculated earlier in the script, must be a valid URL.

NOTE   You'll learn about variables in the section, "Variables—Value Storehouses," later in this chapter.

Listing 2.5 shows how the above tag can be used to create a link to this book's Web page.

Listing 2.5   **Using JavaScript Entities**

```html
<html>
<head>
<title>Using the JavaScript entities.</title>
<script language="JavaScript"><!-
linkTo="http://www.jaworski.com/javascript"
// ->
</script>
</head>
<body>
<A HREF="&{linkTo};">Click here.</A>
</body>
</html>
```

WARNING   Microsoft Internet Explorer does not support JavaScript entities. Use of entities with Internet Explorer may lead to scripting errors.

JavaScript Comments

The JavaScript language provides comments of its own. These comments are used to insert notes and processing descriptions into scripts. The comments are ignored (as intended) when the statements of a script are parsed by JavaScript-enabled browsers.

JavaScript comments use the syntax of C++ and Java. The // string identifies a comment that continues to the end of a line. An example of a single line comment follows:

```
// This JavaScript comment continues to the end of the line.
```

The /* and */ strings are used to identify comments that may span multiple lines. The comment begins with /* and continues up to */. An example of a multiple line comment follows:

```
/* This is
an example
of a multiple
line comment */
```

The script shown in Listing 2.6 illustrates the use of JavaScript comments. The script contains four statements that, if they weren't ignored, would write various capitalizations of the text *Hello World!* to the current document. However, since the first three of these statements are contained in comments, and since browsers ignore comments, these statements have no effect on the Web page generated by the script. Figure 2.13 shows how the JavaScript comments in Listing 2.6 are handled by a JavaScript-capable browser.

Listing 2.6 **Using JavaScript Comments**

```
<html>
<head>
<title>Using JavaScript comments</title>
</head>
<body>
<script language="JavaScript">
<!- Begin hiding JavaScript
// document.write("hello world!")
/* document.write("Hello world!")
document.write("Hello World!") */
document.write("HELLO WORLD!")
```

```
// End hiding Javascript ->
</script>
</body>
</html>
```

How JavaScript comments
are handled by a JavaScript-
capable browser
(Listing 2.6)

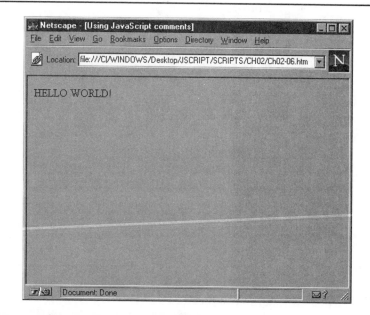

NOTE   Throughout the rest of the book, all browser references will be to JavaScript-capable browsers, unless otherwise specified.

Use of the Document Head

The head of an HTML document provides a great place to include JavaScript definitions. Since the head of a document is processed before its body, placing definitions in the head will cause them to be defined before they are used. This is important because any attempt to use a variable before it is defined results in an error. Listing 2.7 shows how JavaScript definitions can be placed in the head of an HTML document. The script contained in the document head defines a variable named *greeting* and sets its value to the string *Hi Web surfers!* (You'll learn all about variables in the section, "Variables—Value Storehouses," later in this chapter.) The script contained in the document's body then writes the value of the `greeting` variable to the current document. Figure 2.14 shows how this document is displayed.

Listing 2.7   **Using the Head for Definitions**

```
<HTML>
<HEAD>
<TITLE>Using the HEAD for definitions</TITLE>
<SCRIPT language="JavaScript">
<!-
greeting = "Hi Web surfers!"
// ->
</SCRIPT>
</HEAD>
<BODY>
<SCRIPT language="JavaScript">
<!-
document.write(greeting)
// ->
</SCRIPT>
</BODY>
</HTML>
```

FIGURE 2.14:

How the greeting
variable is displayed
(Listing 2.7)

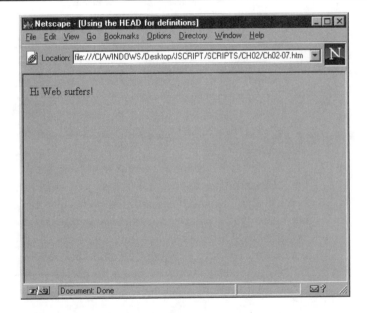

It is important to make sure that all definitions occur before they are used; otherwise an error will be displayed when your HTML document is loaded by a browser. Listing 2.8 contains an HTML document that will generate a "use before definition" error. In this listing, the head contains a JavaScript statement that writes the value of the greeting variable to the current document; however, the greeting variable is not defined until the body of the document. Figure 2.15 shows how this error is displayed by a browser.

Listing 2.8   **Example of Use before Definition**

```
<HTML>
<HEAD>
<TITLE>Use before definition</TITLE>
<SCRIPT language="JavaScript">
<!-
document.write(greeting)
// ->
</SCRIPT>
</HEAD>
<BODY>
<SCRIPT language="JavaScript">
<!-
greeting = "Hi Web surfers!"
// ->
</SCRIPT>
</BODY>
</HTML>
```

FIGURE 2.15:

JavaScript generates an error when a variable is used before it is defined (Listing 2.8).

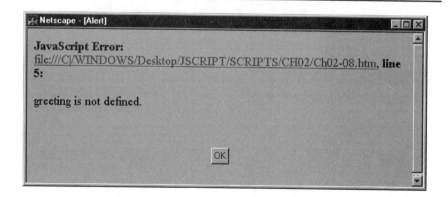

Generating HTML

The examples presented so far have shown how you can use JavaScript to write simple text to the document object. By including HTML tags in your JavaScript script, you can also use JavaScript to generate HTML elements that will be displayed in the current document. The example shown in Listing 2.9 illustrates this concept. Figure 2.16 shows how the Web page generated by this script is displayed.

Listing 2.9	Using JavaScript to Create HTML Tags

```
<HTML>
<HEAD>
<TITLE>Using JavaScript to create HTML tags</TITLE>
<SCRIPT LANGUAGE="JavaScript">
<!-
greeting = "<H1>Hi Web surfers!</H1>"
welcome = "<P>Welcome to <CITE>Mastering JavaScript and
JScript</CITE>.</P>"
// ->
</SCRIPT>
</HEAD>
<BODY>
<SCRIPT LANGUAGE="JavaScript">
<!-
document.write(greeting)
document.write(welcome)
// ->
</SCRIPT>
</BODY>
</HTML>
```

FIGURE 2.16:

Generating HTML from
JavaScript (Listing 2.9)

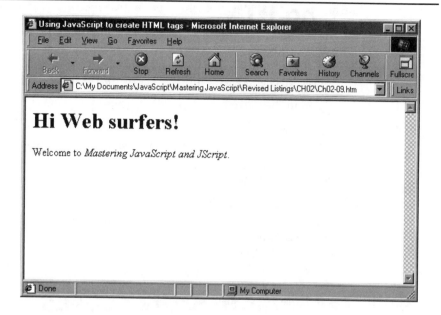

In the script contained in the head of the HTML document, the variables `greeting` and `welcome` are assigned text strings containing embedded HTML tags. These text strings are displayed by the script contained in the body of the HTML document:

- The `greeting` variable contains the heading *Hi Web surfers!*, which is surrounded by the HTML heading tags <H1> and </H1>.

- The `welcome` variable is assigned the string *Welcome to Mastering JavaScript and JScript*.

    - The citation tags, <CITE> and </CITE>, cause the `welcome` variable's string to be cited as a literary reference (which means it shows up in italic).

    - The paragraph tags, <P> and </P>, which surround the `welcome` text are used to mark it as a separate paragraph.

The resulting HTML document generated by the script is equivalent to the following:

```
<HTML>
<HEAD>
<TITLE>Using JavaScript to create HTML tags</TITLE>
</HEAD>
<BODY>
<H1>Hi Web surfers!</H1>
<P>Welcome to <CITE>Mastering JavaScript and JScript</CITE>.</P>
</BODY>
</HTML>
```

So far, I've been making use of variables, such as `greeting` and `welcome`, without having explicitly defined what they are. In the next section, I formally introduce variables.

Variables—Value Storehouses

JavaScript, like other programming languages, uses variables to store values so they can be used in other parts of a program. Variables are names that are associated with these stored values. For example, the variable `imageName` may be used to refer to the name of an image file to be displayed and the variable `totalAmount` may be used to display the total amount of a user's purchase.

Variable names can begin with an uppercase letter (A through Z), lowercase letter (a through z), an underscore character (_), or dollar sign character ($). The remaining characters can consist of letters, the underscore character, the dollar sign character, or digits (0 through 9). Examples of variable names are as follows:

```
orderNumber2
_123
SUM
Image7
Previous_Document
```

Variable names are case sensitive. This means that a variable named `sum` refers to a different value than one named Sum, sUm, or SUM.

Since variable names are case sensitive, it is important to make sure that you use the same capitalization each time you use a variable.

The dollar sign ($) character is reserved for machine-generated code and should not be used in your scripts. In particular, it should not be used for scripts that will be run by earlier browsers that are not fully ECMAScript-compatible.

Types and Variables

Unlike Java and some other programming languages, JavaScript does not require you to specify the *type* of data contained in a variable. (It doesn't even allow it.) In fact, the same variable may be used to contain a variety of different values, such as the text string *Hello World!*, the integer *13*, the floating-point value *3.14*, or the logical value *true*. The JavaScript interpreter keeps track of and converts the type of data contained in a variable.

JavaScript's automatic handling of different types of values is a double-edged sword. On one side, it frees you from having to explicitly specify the type of data contained in a variable and from having to convert from one data type to another. On the other side, since JavaScript automatically converts values of one type to another, it is important to keep track of what types of values should be contained in a variable and how they are converted in expressions involving variables of other types. The next section, "Types and Literal Values," identifies the types of values that JavaScript supports. The later section, "Conversion between Types," discusses important issues related to type conversion.

Types and Literal Values

JavaScript supports four primitive types of values and supports complex types, such as arrays and objects. *Primitive types* are types that can be assigned a single literal value, such as a number, string, or Boolean value. Here are the primitive types that JavaScript supports:

Number Consists of integer and floating-point numbers and the special NaN (not a number) value. Numbers use a 64-bit IEEE 754 format.

Boolean   Consists of the logical values *true* and *false*.

String   Consists of string values that are enclosed in single or double quotes.

Null   Consists of a single value, `null`, which identifies a null, empty, or nonexistent reference.

 Undefined   Consists of a single value, `undefined`, which is used to indicate that a variable has not been assigned a value.

WARNING   The *undefined* value was introduced with the ECMAScript specification and is not supported by browsers that are not fully ECMAScript compatible. This includes Navigator 4.05 and earlier and Internet Explorer 3.

NOTE   You'll learn about the Object type later in this chapter under the section, "The Object Type and Arrays."

In JavaScript, you do not declare the type of a variable as you do in other languages, such as Java and C++. Instead, the type of a variable is implicitly defined based on the literal values that you assign to it. For example, if you assign the integer *123* to the variable `total`, then `total` will support number operations. If you assign the string value *The sum of all accounts* to `total`, then `total` will support string operations. Similarly, if you assign the logical value *true* to `total`, then it will support Boolean operations.

It is also possible for a variable to be assigned a value of one type and then later in the script's execution be assigned a value of another type. For example, the variable `total` could be assigned *123*, then *The sum of all accounts*, and then *true*. The type of the variable would change with the type of value assigned to it. The different types of literal values that can be assigned to a variable are covered in the following subsections.

Number Types—Integers and Floating-Point Numbers

When working with numbers, JavaScript supports both integer and floating-point values. It transparently converts from one type to another as values of one type are combined with values of other types in numerical expressions. For example, integer values are converted to floating-point values when they are used in floating point expressions.

Integer Literals Integers can be represented in JavaScript in decimal, hexadecimal, or octal form:

- A decimal (base 10) integer is what nonprogrammers are used to seeing—the digits 0 through 9, with each new column representing a higher power of 10.

- A hexadecimal (base 16) integer in JavaScript must always begin with the characters 0x or 0X in the two leftmost columns. Hexadecimal uses the letters 0 through 9 to represent the values zero through nine and the letters A through F to represent the values normal people know as 10 through 15.

- An octal (base 8) integer in JavaScript must always begin with the character 0 in the leftmost column. Octal uses only the digits 0 through 7.

Examples of decimal, hexadecimal, and octal integers are provided in Table 2.2.

TABLE 2.2: Examples of Decimal, Hexadecimal, and Octal Integers for the Same Values

Decimal Number	Hexadecimal Equivalent	Octal Equivalent
19	0x13	023
255	0xff	0377
513	0x201	01001
1024	0x400	02000
12345	0x3039	030071

The program shown in Listing 2.10 illustrates the use of JavaScript hexadecimal and octal integers. Figure 2.17 shows how the Web page generated by this program is displayed. Note that the hexadecimal and octal integers are converted to decimal before they are displayed.

Listing 2.10 **Using JavaScript Integers**

```
<HTML>
<HEAD>
<TITLE>Using JavaScript integers</TITLE>
</HEAD>
<BODY>
<SCRIPT LANGUAGE="JavaScript">
<!-
document.write("0xab00 + 0xcd = ")
document.write(0xab00 + 0xcd)
document.write("<BR>")
document.write("0xff - 0123 = ")
document.write(0xff - 0123)
document.write("<BR>")
document.write("-0x12 = ")
document.write(-0x12)
// ->
</SCRIPT>
</BODY>
</HTML>
```

FIGURE 2.17:

Using hexadecimal and octal integers (Listing 2.10)

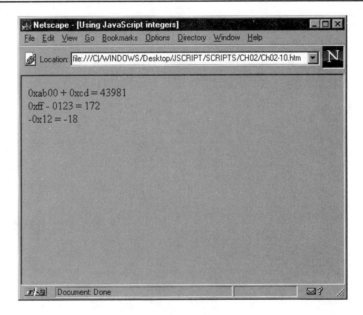

Floating-Point Literals Floating-point literals are used to represent numbers that require the use of a decimal point, or very large or small numbers that must be written using exponential notation.

A floating-point number must consist of either a number containing a decimal point or an integer followed by an exponent. The following are valid floating-point numbers:

```
-4.321
55.
12e2
1e-2
7e1
-4e-4
.5
```

As you can see in the examples above, floating-point literals may contain an initial integer, followed by an optional decimal point and fraction, followed by an optional exponent ("e" or "E") and its integer exponent value. For example, 4e6 equals 4×10 to the sixth power, which equals 4,000,000. Also, the initial integer and integer exponent value may be signed as positive or negative (+ or –). Up to 20 significant digits may be used to represent floating-point values.

The script shown in Listing 2.11 and Figure 2.18 illustrates how JavaScript displays these values. Notice that JavaScript simplifies the display of these numbers whenever possible.

Listing 2.11   **Using Floating-Point Numbers**

```
<HTML>
<HEAD>
<TITLE>Using floating-point numbers</TITLE>
</HEAD>
<BODY>
<SCRIPT LANGUAGE="JavaScript">
<!-
document.write(-4.321)
document.write("<BR>")
document.write(55.)
document.write("<BR>")
document.write(12e2)
document.write("<BR>")
```

```
document.write(1e-2)
document.write("<BR>")
document.write(7e1)
document.write("<BR>")
document.write(-4e-4)
document.write("<BR>")
document.write(.5)
// ->
</SCRIPT>
</BODY>
</HTML>
```

FIGURE 2.18:

How JavaScript displays
floating-point numbers
(Listing 2.11)

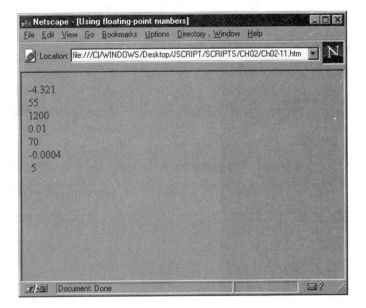

Boolean Values

JavaScript, like Java and unlike C, supports a pure Boolean type that consists
of the two values *true* and *false*. Several logical operators may be used in
Boolean expressions, as you'll learn in Chapter 3 (in the section, "Logical Operators"). JavaScript automatically converts the Boolean values *true* and *false* into
1 and 0 when they are used in numerical expressions. The script shown in Listing 2.12 illustrates this automatic conversion. Figure 2.19 shows the results of
this conversion as displayed by Navigator.

A *Boolean value* is a value that is either true or false. The word *Boolean* is taken from the name of the mathematician George Boole, who developed much of the fundamental theory of mathematical logic.

Listing 2.12   **Conversion of Logical Values to Numeric Values**

```
<HTML>
<HEAD>
<TITLE>Conversion of logical values to numeric values</TITLE>
</HEAD>
<BODY>
<SCRIPT LANGUAGE="JavaScript">
<!-
document.write("true*5 + false*7 = ")
document.write(true*5 +false*7)
// ->
</SCRIPT>
</BODY>
</HTML>
```

FIGURE 2.19:

How logical values are converted to other types (Listing 2.12)

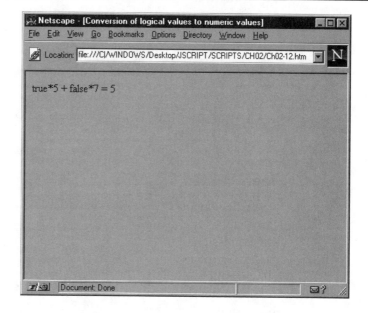

String Values

JavaScript provides built-in support for strings of characters. A string is a sequence of zero or more characters that are enclosed by double (") or single (') quotes. If a string begins with a double quote then it must end with a double quote. Likewise, if a string begins with a single quote then it must end in a single quote.

To insert a quote character in a string, you must precede it by the backslash (\) escape character. The following are examples of the use of the escape character to insert quotes into strings:

```
"He asked, \"Who owns this book?\""
'It\'s Bill\'s book.'
```

The script shown in Listing 2.13 illustrates the use of quotes within strings. Figure 2.20 shows how the strings are displayed. Note that single quotes do not need to be coded with escape characters when they are used within double-quoted strings. Similarly, double quotes do not need to be coded when they are used within single-quoted strings.

Listing 2.13   Using Quotes within Strings

```
<HTML>
<HEAD>
<TITLE>Using quotes within strings</TITLE>
</HEAD>
<BODY>
<SCRIPT LANGUAGE="JavaScript">
<!-
document.write("He said, \"That's mine!\"<BR>")
document.write('She said, "No it\'s not."<BR>')
document.write('That\'s all folks!')
// ->
</SCRIPT>
</BODY>
</HTML>
```

How quotes are inserted
into strings (Listing 2.13)

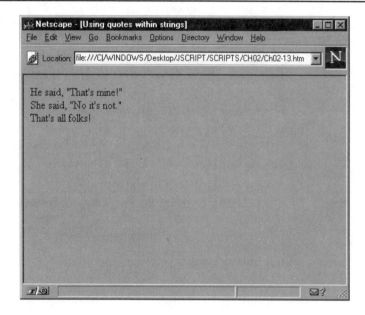

JavaScript defines special formatting characters for use in strings. These characters are identified in Table 2.3.

TABLE 2.3: Special Formatting Characters

Character	Meaning
\'	single quote
\"	double quote
\\	backslash
\n	new line
\r	carriage return
\f	form feed
\t	horizontal tab
\b	backspace

The script shown in Listing 2.14 shows how these formatting characters are used. Figure 2.21 displays the Web page generated by this script. The Web page uses the HTML *preformatted text* tags to prevent the formatting characters from being treated as HTML whitespace characters. (If you are unfamiliar with the pre-formatted text tag, consult online Appendix B, "Accessing Online References.") Notice that the backspace character is incorrectly displayed, the form feed character is ignored, and that the carriage return character is displayed in the same manner as the new line character. Even though these characters are not fully supported in the display of Web pages, they may still be used to insert formatting codes within data and files that JavaScript produces.

Listing 2.14   **Using Special Formatting Characters**

```
<HTML>
<HEAD>
<TITLE>Using special formatting characters</TITLE>
</HEAD>
<BODY>
<PRE>
<SCRIPT LANGUAGE="JavaScript">
<!-
document.write("This shows how the \bbackspace character works.\n")
document.write("This shows how the \ttab character works.\n")
document.write("This shows how the \rcarriage return character
works.\n")
document.write("This shows how the \fform feed character works.\n")
document.write("This shows how the \nnew line character works.\n")
// ->
</SCRIPT>
</PRE>
</BODY>
</HTML>
```

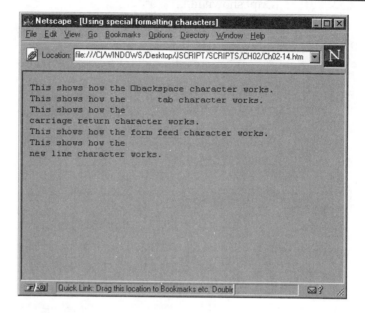

FIGURE 2.21:

This is how formatting characters are handled (Listing 2.14). Note that your Web browser does not process all characters.

The *null* Value

The null value is common to all JavaScript types. It is used to set a variable to an initial value that is different from other valid values. Use of the null value prevents the sort of errors that result from using uninitialized variables. The null value is automatically converted to default values of other types when used in an expression, as you'll see in the section, "Conversion between Types," later in this chapter.

The *undefined* Value

The undefined value indicates that a variable has been created but not assigned a value. Like the null value, the undefined value is common to all JavaScript types and is automatically converted to default values of these types. The undefined value is converted to NaN for numeric types, *false* for Boolean, and "undefined" for strings.

Conversion between Types

JavaScript automatically converts values from one type to another when they are used in an expression. This means that you can combine different types in an expression and JavaScript will try to perform the type conversions that are necessary for the expression to make sense. For example, the expression `"test"` + 5 will convert the numeric 5 to a string *"5"* and append it to the string *"test"*, producing *"test5"*. JavaScript's automatic type conversion also allows you to assign a value of one type to a variable and then later assign a value of a different type to the same variable.

How does JavaScript convert from one type to another? The process of determining when a conversion should occur and what type of conversion should be made is fairly complex. JavaScript converts values when it evaluates an expression or assigns a value to a variable. When JavaScript assigns a value to a variable it changes the type associated with the variable to the type of the value that is assigns.

When JavaScript evaluates an expression, it parses the expression into its component unary and binary expressions based upon the order of precedence of the operators it contains. It then evaluates the component unary and binary expressions of the parse tree. Figure 2.22 illustrates this process. Each expression is evaluated according to the operators involved. If an operator takes a value of a type that is different than the type of an operand, then the operand is converted to a type that is valid for the operator.

Some operators, such as the + operator, may be used for more than one type. For example, `"a"+"b"` results in the string *"ab"* when the + operator is used with string values, but it assumes its typical arithmetic meaning when used with numeric operands. What happens when JavaScript attempts to evaluate `"a"`+3? JavaScript converts the integer 3 into the string *"3"* and yields *"a3"* for the expression. In general, JavaScript will favor string operators over all others, followed by floating-point, integer, and logical operators.

FIGURE 2.22:

Expressions are evaluated based on the types of operators involved.

Expression

Parse Tree

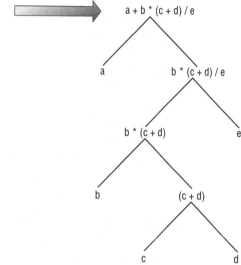

a + b * (c + d) / e

> **NOTE**   Expressions are covered in the section, "Operators and Expressions," in Chapter 3.

The script shown in Listing 2.15 illustrates JavaScript conversion between types when the + operator is used. Figure 2.23 shows how the Web page resulting from this script is displayed.

Listing 2.15   Automatic Conversion between Types

```
<HTML>
<HEAD>
<TITLE>Implicit conversion between types</TITLE>
<SCRIPT LANGUAGE="JavaScript">
<!-
s1="test"
s2="12.34"
i=123
r=.123
```

```
lt=true
lf=false
n=null
// ->
</SCRIPT>
</HEAD>
<BODY>
<H1>Implicit conversion between types</H1>
<TABLE BORDER=2>
<SCRIPT LANGUAGE="JavaScript">
<!-
// Column headings for table
document.write("<TR>")
document.write("<TH>row + column</TH>")
document.write("<TH>string \"12.34\"</TH>")
document.write("<TH>integer 123</TH>")
document.write("<TH>float .123</TH>")
document.write("<TH>logical true</TH>")
document.write("<TH>logical false</TH>")
document.write("<TH>null</TH>")
document.write("</TR>")
// First operand is a string
document.write("<TR>")
document.write("<TH>string \"test\"</TH>")
document.write("<TD>")
document.write(s1+s2)
document.write("</TD><TD>")
document.write(s1+i)
document.write("</TD><TD>")
document.write(s1+r)
document.write("</TD><TD>")
document.write(s1+lt)
document.write("</TD><TD>")
document.write(s1+lf)
document.write("</TD><TD>")
document.write(s1+n)
document.write("</TD>")
document.write("</TR>")
// First operand is an integer
document.write("<TR>")
document.write("<TH>integer 123</TH>")
document.write("<TD>")
document.write(i+s2)
```

```
document.write("</TD><TD>")
document.write(i+i)
document.write("</TD><TD>")
document.write(i+r)
document.write("</TD><TD>")
document.write(i+lt)
document.write("</TD><TD>")
document.write(i+lf)
document.write("</TD><TD>")
document.write(i+n)
document.write("</TD>")
document.write("</TR>")
// First operand is a float
document.write("<TR>")
document.write("<TH>float .123</TH>")
document.write("<TD>")
document.write(r+s2)
document.write("</TD><TD>")
document.write(r+i)
document.write("</TD><TD>")
document.write(r+r)
document.write("</TD><TD>")
document.write(r+lt)
document.write("</TD><TD>")
document.write(r+lf)
document.write("</TD><TD>")
document.write(r+n)
document.write("</TD>")
document.write("</TR>")
// First operand is a logical true
document.write("<TR>")
document.write("<TH>logical true</TH>")
document.write("<TD>")
document.write(lt+s2)
document.write("</TD><TD>")
document.write(lt+i)
document.write("</TD><TD>")
document.write(lt+r)
document.write("</TD><TD>")
document.write(lt+lt)
document.write("</TD><TD>")
document.write(lt+lf)
document.write("</TD><TD>")
document.write(lt+n)
```

```
document.write("</TD>")
document.write("</TR>")
// First operand is a logical false
document.write("<TR>")
document.write("<TH>logical false</TH>")
document.write("<TD>")
document.write(lf+s2)
document.write("</TD><TD>")
document.write(lf+i)
document.write("</TD><TD>")
document.write(lf+r)
document.write("</TD><TD>")
document.write(lf+lt)
document.write("</TD><TD>")
document.write(lf+lf)
document.write("</TD><TD>")
document.write(lf+n)
document.write("</TD>")
document.write("</TR>")
// First operand is null
document.write("<TR>")
document.write("<TH>null</TH>")
document.write("<TD>")
document.write(n+s2)
document.write("</TD><TD>")
document.write(n+i)
document.write("</TD><TD>")
document.write(n+r)
document.write("</TD><TD>")
document.write(n+lt)
document.write("</TD><TD>")
document.write(n+lf)
document.write("</TD><TD>")
document.write(n+n)
document.write("</TD>")
document.write("</TR>")
// ->
</SCRIPT>
</TABLE>
</BODY>
</HTML>
```

FIGURE 2.23:

Conversion table for the + operator (Listing 2.15)

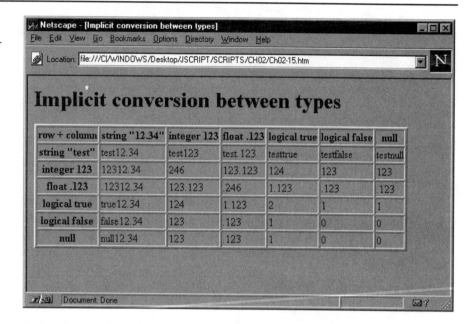

Note that in all cases where string operands are used with a non-string operator, JavaScript converts the other operator into a string:

- Numeric values are converted to their appropriate string value.

- Boolean values are converted to *1* and *0* to support numerical operations.

- The null value is converted to *"null"* for string operations, *false* for logical operations, and 0 for numerical operations.

Let's take a look at Listing 2.15. The script in the document head defines the variables to be used in the table's operations. The s1 and s2 variables are assigned string values. The i and r variables are assigned integer and floating-point values. The lt and lf variables are assigned logical values. The n variable is assigned the null value.

The script in the document body is fairly long. However, most of the script is used to generate the HTML tags for the cells of the conversion table. The script is surrounded by the tags <TABLE BORDER=2> and </TABLE>. The script then generates the cells of the table one row at a time. The <TR> and </TR> tags mark a row of the table. The <TH> and </TH> tags mark header cells. The <TD> and </TD> tags identify normal non-header table cells.

First, the column header row is displayed. Then each row of the table shown in Figure 2.23 is generated by combining the operand at the row heading with the operand at the table heading using the + operator.

NOTE Internet Explorer displays Figure 2.23 slightly differently. If a decimal number has a magnitude less than 1, then Internet Explorer prepends a 0 when displaying the number or converting it to a string value. For example, .123 is displayed as 0.123.

Conversion Functions

Functions are collections of JavaScript code that perform a particular task, and often return a value. A function may take zero or more parameters. These parameters are used to specify the data to be processed by the function. You'll learn more about functions in the "Function Call Statements" section of Chapter 3.

JavaScript provides three functions which are used to perform explicit type conversion. These are `eval()`, `parseInt()`, and `parseFloat()`.

NOTE Functions are referenced by their name with the empty parameter list "()" appended. This makes it easier to differentiate between functions and variables in the discussion of scripts.

The `eval()` function can be used to convert a string expression to a numeric value. For example, the statement `total = eval("432.1*10")`, results in the value *4321* being assigned to the `total` variable. The `eval()` function takes the string value *"432.1*10"* as a parameter and returns the numeric value *4321* as the result of the function call. If the string value passed as a parameter to the `eval()` function does not represent a numeric value, then use of `eval()` results in an error being generated.

The `parseInt()` function is used to convert a string value into an integer. Unlike `eval()`, `parseInt()` returns the first integer contained in the string or *0* if the string does not begin with an integer. For example, `parseInt("123xyz")` returns *123* and `parseInt("xyz")` returns *0*. The `parseInt()` function also parses hexadecimal and decimal integers.

The `parseFloat()` function is similar to the `parseInt()` function. It returns the first floating-point number contained in a string or *0* if the string does not begin with a valid floating-point number. For example, `parseFloat("2.1e4xyz")` returns *21000* and `parseFloat("xyz")` returns *0*.

The script shown in Listing 2.16 illustrates the use of JavaScript's explicit conversion functions. Figure 2.24 shows how the Web page that this script generates is displayed.

| Listing 2.16 | Explicit Conversion Functions |

```
<HTML>
<HEAD>
<TITLE>Using Explicit Conversion Functions</TITLE>
</HEAD>
<BODY>
<H1 ALIGN="CENTER">Using Explicit Conversion Functions</H1>
<SCRIPT LANGUAGE="JavaScript"><!-
document.write('eval("12.34*10") = ')
document.write(eval("12.34*10"))
document.write("<BR>")
document.write('parseInt("0x10") = ')
document.write(parseInt("0x10"))
document.write("<BR>")
document.write('parseFloat("5.4321e6") = ')
document.write(parseFloat("5.4321e6"))
// -></SCRIPT>
</BODY>
</HTML>
```

FIGURE 2.24:

Using the JavaScript conversion functions (Listing 2.16)

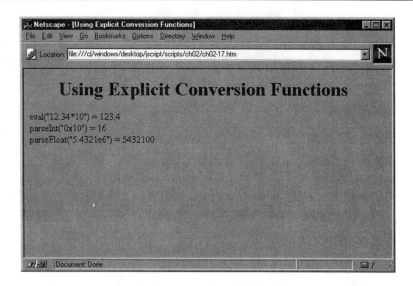

The Object Type and Arrays

In addition to the primitive types discussed in the previous sections, JavaScript supports the Object type. This type is referred to as a complex data type because it is built from the primitive types. I'll address objects in general and the Object type in Chapter 5, "Working with Objects." In this chapter, I'll cover a special JavaScript object—the array.

NOTE   Arrays are a special type of JavaScript object.

Arrays—Accessing Indexed Values

Arrays are objects that are capable of storing a sequence of values. These values are stored in indexed locations within the array. For example, suppose you have a company with five employees and you want to display the names of your employees on a Web page. You could keep track of their names in an array variable named `employee`. You would declare the array using the statement

```
employee = new Array(5)
```

and store the names of your employees in the array using the following statements:

```
employee[0] = "Bill"
employee[1] = "Bob"
employee[2] = "Ted"
employee[3] = "Alice"
employee[4] = "Sue"
```

You could then access the names of the individual employees by referring to the individual elements of the array. For example, you could display the names of your employees using statements such as the following.

```
document.write(employee[0])
document.write(employee[1])
document.write(employee[2])
document.write(employee[3])
document.write(employee[4])
```

The script shown in Listing 2.17 illustrates the use of arrays. Figure 2.25 shows how the Web page this script generates is displayed.

Listing 2.17   Using JavaScript Arrays

```
<HTML>
<HEAD>
<TITLE>Using Arrays</TITLE>
</HEAD>
<BODY>
<H1 ALIGN="CENTER">Using Arrays</H1>
<SCRIPT LANGUAGE="JavaScript"><!-
employee = new Array(5)
employee[0] = "Bill"
employee[1] = "Bob"
employee[2] = "Ted"
employee[3] = "Alice"
employee[4] = "Sue"
document.write(employee[0]+"<BR>")
document.write(employee[1]+"<BR>")
document.write(employee[2]+"<BR>")
document.write(employee[3]+"<BR>")
document.write(employee[4])
// -></SCRIPT>
</BODY>
</HTML>
```

FIGURE 2.25:

Arrays allow multiple values to be stored with a single variable (Listing 2.17).

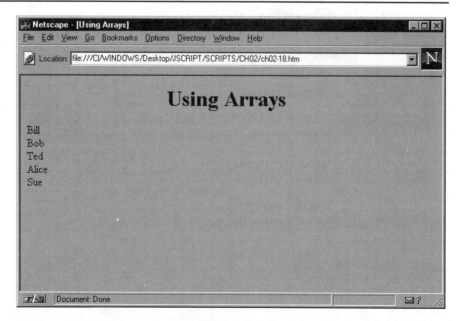

The *length* of an array is the number of elements that it contains. In the example script of Listing 2.17, the length of the employee array is 5. The individual elements of an array are referenced using the name of the array followed by the index of the array element enclosed in brackets. Because the first index is 0, the last index is one less than the length of the array. For example, suppose that you have an array named day of length 7 that contains the names of the days of the week. The individual elements of this array would be accessed as day[0], day[1], ..., day[6].

Declaring Arrays An array must be declared before it is used. An array may be declared using either of the following two statement forms:

- `arrayName = new Array(arrayLength)`

- `arrayName = new Array()`

NOTE A third form of array declaration is discussed in the following subsection, "Constructing Dense Arrays."

In the first form, the length of the array is explicitly specified. An example of this form is

```
days = new Array(7)
```

In the above example, days corresponds to the array name and 7 corresponds to the array length.

In the second array declaration form, the length of the array is not specified and results in the declaration of an array of length 0. An example of using this type of array declaration follows:

```
order = new Array()
```

This declares an array of length 0 that is used to keep track of customer orders. JavaScript automatically extends the length of an array when new array elements are initialized. For example, the following statements create an order array of length 0 and then subsequently extend the length of the array to 100 and then 1000.

```
order = new Array()
order[99] = "Widget #457"
order[999] = "Delux Widget Set #10"
```

When JavaScript encounters the reference to order[99], in the above example, it extends the length of the array to 100 and initializes order[99] to *"Widget #457"*. When JavaScript encounters the reference to order[999] in the third statement, it extends the length of order to 1000 and initializes order[999] to *"Delux Widget Set #10"*.

Even if an array is initially declared to be of fixed initial length, it still may be extended by referencing elements that are outside the current size of the array. This is accomplished in the same manner as with zero-length arrays. Listing 2.18 shows how fixed-length arrays are expanded as new array elements are referenced. Figure 2.26 shows the how the Web page that this script generates is displayed.

Listing 2.18   Extending the Length of an Array

```
<HTML>
<HEAD>
<TITLE>Extending Arrays</TITLE>
</HEAD>
<BODY>
<H1 ALIGN="CENTER">Extending Arrays</H1>
<SCRIPT LANGUAGE="JavaScript"><!-
order = new Array()
document.write("order.length = "+order.length+"<BR>")
order[99] = "Widget #457"
document.write("order.length = "+order.length+"<BR>")
order[999] = "Delux Widget Set #10"
document.write("order.length = "+order.length+"<BR>")
// -></SCRIPT>
</BODY>
</HTML>
```

FIGURE 2.26:

An array's length dynami-
cally expands as new ele-
ments are referenced
(Listing 2.18).

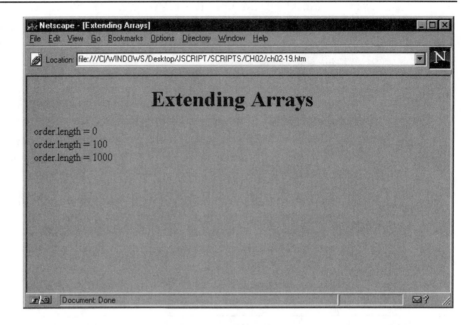

Constructing Dense Arrays A *dense array* is an array that is initially declared
with each element being assigned a specified value. Dense arrays are used in the
same manner as other arrays. They are just declared and initialized in a more efficient manner. Dense arrays are declared by *listing* the values of the array elements
in the array declaration, in place of the array length. Dense array declarations
take the following form:

```
arrayName = new Array(value0, value1, ... , valuen)
```

In the above declaration, because we start counting at zero, the length of the array
is n+1.

When creating short length arrays, the dense array declaration is very efficient.
For example, an array containing the three-letter abbreviations for the days of the
week may be declared using the following statement:

```
day = new Array('Sun','Mon','Tue','Wed','Thu','Fri','Sat')
```

The Elements of an Array JavaScript does not place any restrictions on the
values of the elements of an array. These values could be of different types, or
could refer to other arrays or objects. For example, you could declare an array as
follows:

```
junk = new Array("s1",'s2',4,3.5,true,false,null,new Array(5,6,7))
```

The junk array has length 8 and its elements are as follows:

```
junk[0]="s1"
junk[1]='s2'
junk[2]=4
junk[3]=3.5
junk[4]=true
junk[5]=false
junk[6]=null
junk[7]=a new dense array consisting of the values 5, 6, & 7
```

The last element of the array, junk[7], contains an array as its value. The three elements of junk[7] can be accessed using *a second set of subscripts*, as follows:

```
junk[7][0]=5
junk[7][1]=6
junk[7][2]=7
```

The script shown in Listing 2.19 illustrates the use of arrays within arrays. Figure 2.27 shows the Web page that results from execution of this script.

Listing 2.19   An Array within an Array

```
<HTML>
<HEAD>
<TITLE>Arrays within Arrays</TITLE>
</HEAD>
<BODY>
<H1 ALIGN="CENTER">Arrays within Arrays</H1>
<SCRIPT LANGUAGE="JavaScript"><!-
junk = new Array("s1",'s2',4,3.5,true,false,null,new Array(5,6,7))
document.write("junk[0] = "+junk[0]+"<BR>")
document.write("junk[1] = "+junk[1]+"<BR>")
document.write("junk[2] = "+junk[2]+"<BR>")
document.write("junk[3] = "+junk[3]+"<BR>")
document.write("junk[4] = "+junk[4]+"<BR>")
document.write("junk[5] = "+junk[5]+"<BR>")
document.write("junk[6] = "+junk[6]+"<BR>")
document.write("junk[7][0] = "+junk[7][0]+"<BR>")
document.write("junk[7][1] = "+junk[7][1]+"<BR>")
document.write("junk[7][2] = "+junk[7][2])
// -></SCRIPT>
</BODY>
</HTML>
```

FIGURE 2.27:

An array may contain
another array as the value
of one of its elements
(Listing 2.19).

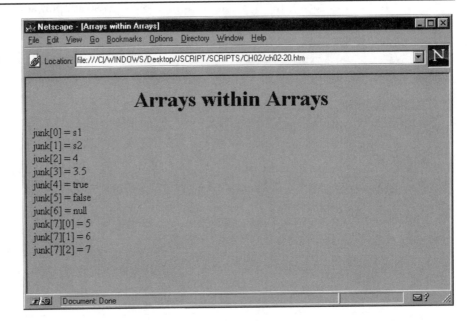

Objects and the *length* Property

JavaScript arrays are implemented as objects. *Objects* are named collections of data that have properties and may be accessed via methods. A *property* returns a value that identifies some aspect of the state of an object. *Methods* are used to read or modify the data contained in an object.

The length of an array is a property of an array. You can access the property of any object in JavaScript by appending a period (.) plus the name of the property to the name of the object, as shown here:

```
objectName.propertyName
```

For example, the length of an array is determined as follows:

```
arrayName.length
```

Now, consider the following array:

```
a = new Array(2,4,6,8,10)
```

The value returned by a.length is *5*.

In addition to the `length` property, arrays also support several methods. These methods and the process of declaring and using JavaScript objects are covered in Chapter 5, "Working with Objects."

Summary

This chapter introduced you to the JavaScript language. You learned how JavaScript works and how JavaScript statements are embedded in HTML documents. You learned about JavaScript's use of types and variables, and how JavaScript automatically converts values of one type to another. In the next chapter, you'll be introduced to JavaScript's operators and programming statements, and learn how functions are created and invoked.

Using Operators, Statements, and Functions

- Operators and Expressions

- Operator Precedence

- Statements and Declarations

- Functions and Function Calls

- Local and Global Variables

- Accessing Objects in Statements

This chapter continues your introduction to the JavaScript language. You'll cover all of the operators provided by JavaScript and learn how expressions are evaluated. You'll learn to use JavaScript's programming statements and develop sample scripts that demonstrate the use of each statement. You'll also learn how to create and invoke *functions*. When you have finished this chapter, you'll be able to write JavaScript scripts that use JavaScript's operators and statements to perform a variety of computations.

Operators and Expressions

In the previous chapter, you used some of the basic operators provided by JavaScript. These include the + operators used with string and numeric types and the = assignment operator. In this section, you'll be introduced to all of the operators provided by Java-Script. These operators are organized into the following categories:

- Arithmetic
- Logical
- Comparison
- String
- Bit manipulation
- Assignment
- Conditional

Let's start with a little terminology. An *operator* is used to transform one or more values into a single resultant value. The values to which the operator applies are referred to as *operands*. The combination of an operator and its operands is referred to as an *expression*.

Expressions are *evaluated* in order to determine the value of the expression. This value is the value that results when the operator is applied to the operands. Some operators, like the = (assignment) operator, result in a value being assigned to a *variable*. Others produce a value that may be used in other expressions.

NOTE   For some operators, such as the * multiplication operator, the *order* of the operands does not matter—for example, x * y = y * x is true for all integers and floating-point numbers. Other operators, such as the + (string concatenation) operator, yield different results for different orderings of their operands. For example, "ab"+"cd" does not equal "cd"+"ab".

Unary operators are operators that are used with only one operand. For example, the unary operator ! is applied to a logical value and returns the *logical not* of that value. Most JavaScript operators are *binary* operators, operators that have two operands. An example of a binary operator is the * (multiplication) operator, which is used to calculate the product of two numbers. For example, the expression 7 * 6 is evaluated as 42 by applying the * operator to the operands 7 and 6.

So far we've only been dealing with simple expressions. More complex expressions can be constructed by combining simple unary and binary expressions. In order to evaluate complex expressions we must *parse* them into their component unary and binary expressions, applying the rules of order or *precedence* (for example, evaluating groups before adding or multiplying them). You'll learn more about parsing expressions later in this chapter, under "Operator Precedence."

NOTE   JavaScript also supports *regular expressions* through the **RegExp** object. You'll learn how to use this object in online Appendix C, "Regular Expressions."

Arithmetic Operators

Arithmetic operators are the most familiar operators because we use them every day to perform common mathematical calculations. The mathematical operators supported by JavaScript are listed in Table 3.1.

TABLE 3.1: Arithmetic Operators

Operator	Description
+	Addition
-	Subtraction or unary negation
*	Multiplication
/	Division
%	Modulus
++	Increment and then return value (or return value and then increment)
—	Decrement and then return value (or return value and then decrement)

NOTE   The % (modulus) operator calculates the *remainder* of dividing two integers. For example, 17 % 3 = 2 because 17/3 = 5 with a remainder of 2.

Logical Operators

Logical operators are used to perform Boolean operations on Boolean operands, such as *logical and, logical or,* and *logical not.* The logical operators supported by JavaScript are listed in Table 3.2.

TABLE 3.2: Logical Operators

Operator	Description
&&	logical and
||	logical or
!	logical not

Comparison Operators

Comparison operators are used to determine whether two values are equal, or to compare numerical values to determine which value is greater than the other. The comparison operators supported by JavaScript are listed in Table 3.3.

TABLE 3.3: Comparison Operators

Operator	Description
==	Equal
===	Strictly equal
!=	Not equal
!==	Strictly not equal
<	Less than
<=	Less than or equal
>	Greater than
>=	Greater than or equal

The equal (==) and not equal (!=) operators perform type conversions before testing for equality. For example, "5" == 5 evaluates to *true*. The strictly equal (===) and strictly not equal (!==) operators do not perform type conversions before testing for equality. For example, "5" === 5 evaluates to *false* and "5" !== 5 returns *true*. The strictly equal (===) and strictly not equal (!==) operators are part of the ECMAScript 1 standard. They were only introduced to Navigator in JavaScript 1.3 and are only supported by Navigator 4.06 and later. They are also supported by Internet Explorer 4 and later.

WARNING   If the <SCRIPT> tag's LANGUAGE attribute is set to "JavaScript1.2", Navigator 4 (and later) treats the equality operator (==) as the strict equality operator. For example, "5" == 5 evaluates to *false*. This is a Navigator flaw.

String Operators

String operators are used to perform operations on strings. JavaScript currently supports only the + *string concatenation* operator. It is used to join two strings together. For example, "ab" + "cd" produces "abcd."

Bit Manipulation Operators

Bit manipulation operators perform operations on the bit representation of a value, such as shifting the bits to the right or the left. The bit manipulation operators supported by JavaScript are listed in Table 3.4.

TABLE 3.4: Bit Manipulation Operators

Operator	Description
&	And
|	Or
^	Exclusive or
<<	Left shift
>>	Sign-propagating right shift
>>>	Zero-fill right shift

Assignment Operators

Assignment operators are used to update the value of a variable. Some assignment operators are combined with other operators to perform a computation on the value contained in a variable and then update the variable with the new value. The assignment operators supported by JavaScript are listed in Table 3.5.

TABLE 3.5: Assignment Operators

Operator	Description
=	Sets the variable on the left of the = operator to the value of the expression on its right
+=	Increments the variable on the left of the += operator by the value of the expression on its right. When used with strings, the value to the right of the += operator is appended to the value of the variable on the left of the += operator.
-=	Decrements the variable on the left of the -= operator by the value of the expression on its right
*=	Multiplies the variable on the left of the *= operator by the value of the expression on its right
/=	Divides the variable on the left of the /= operator by the value of the expression on its right
%=	Takes the modulus of the variable on the left of the %= operator using the value of the expression on its right
<<=	Left shifts the variable on the left of the <<= operator using the value of the expression on its right
>>=	Takes the sign-propagating right shift of the variable on the left of the >>= operator using the value of the expression on its right
>>>=	Takes the zero-filled right shift of the variable on the left of the >>>= operator using the value of the expression on its right
&=	Takes the bitwise *and* of the variable on the left of the &= operator using the value of the expression on its right
l=	Taks the bitwise *or* of the variable on the left of the l= operator using the value of the expression on its right
^=	Takes the bitwise *exclusive or* of the variable on the left of the ^= operator using the value of the expression on its right

The Conditional Expression Ternary Operator

JavaScript supports the conditional expression operator ? : found in Java, C, and C++. This operator is a *ternary* operator since it takes three operands—a condition to be evaluated and two alternative values to be returned based on the truth or falsity of the condition. The format for a conditional expression is as follows:

```
condition ? value1 : value2
```

NOTE A condition is an expression that results in a logical value—for example, *true* or *false*.

If the condition is *true*, *value1* is the result of the expression. Otherwise, *value2* is the result. An example of using this expression follows:

```
(x > y) ? 5 : 7
```

If the value stored in variable x is greater than the value contained in variable y, then *5* is the result of the expression. If the value stored in x is less than or equal to the value of y then *7* is the result of the expression.

Special Operators

JavaScript supports a number of special operators that don't fit into the operator categories covered in the preceding sections:

The comma (,) operator   This operator evaluates two expressions and returns the value of the second expression. Consider the statement a = (5+6) , (2*20). Both expressions, (5+6) and (2*20), are evaluated and the value of the second expression, (40), is assigned to a.

The delete operator   The delete operator is used to delete a property of an object or an element at an array index. For example, delete myArray[5] deletes the sixth element of myArray. You'll learn how to use delete with object properties in Chapter 5, "Working with Objects." The delete operator always returns the *undefined* value as of JavaScript 1.2.

The new operator   The new operator is used to create an instance of an object type. You'll learn how it is used in Chapter 5.

The typeof operator   The typeof operator returns a string value that identifies the type of an operand. Consider the statement, a = typeof 17. The value assigned to a is *number*. Try using typeof with different expressions to see the values that it returns. You can also use it with objects and functions.

The void **operator**   The void operator does not return a value. It is typically used with the *javascript:* protocol to return a URL with no value. Chapter 9, "Working with Links," provides examples of its use.

Operator Summary Table

The script shown in Listing 3.1 illustrates the use of many of the JavaScript operators introduced in the preceding subsections. It generates the HTML table shown in Figure 3.1.

Listing 3.1   JavaScript Operators (ch03-01.htm)

```
<html>
<head>
<title>JavaScript Operators</title>
</head>
<body>
<h1>JavaScript Operators</h1>
<table BORDER="2" CELLPADDING="4" ALIGN="CENTER">
<tr><td>Category</td>
<td>Operator</td>
<td>Description</td>
<td>Usage Example</td>
<td>Value/Result</td></tr>
<tr><td>String</td>
<td>+</td>
<td>concatenation</td>
<td>&quot;Java&quot; + &quot;Script&quot;</td>
<td><script><!-
document.write("Java"+"Script")
// -></script>
</td></tr>
<tr><td ROWSPAN="10">Arithmetic</td>
<td>+</td>
<td>addition</td>
<td>2 + 3</td>
<td><script><!-
document.write(2+3)
// -></script>
</td></tr>
<tr><td ROWSPAN="2">-</td>
```

```
<td>subtraction</td>
<td>6 - 4</td>
<td><script><!-
document.write(6-4)
// -></script>
</td></tr>
<tr><td>unary negation</td>
<td>-9</td>
<td><script><!-
document.write(-9)
// -></script>
</td></tr>
<tr><td>*</td>
<td>multiplication</td>
<td>3 * 4</td>
<td><script><!-
document.write(3*4)
// -></script>
</td></tr>
<tr><td>/</td>
<td>division</td>
<td>15/3</td>
<td><script><!-
document.write(15/3)
// -></script>
</td></tr>
<tr><td>%</td>
<td>modulus</td>
<td>15%7</td>
<td><script><!-
document.write(15%7)
// -></script>
</td></tr>
<tr><td ROWSPAN="2">++</td>
<td>increment and then return value</td>
<td>x=3; ++x</td>
<td><script><!-
x=3
document.write(++x)
// -></script>
</td></tr>
<tr><td>return value and then increment</td>
```

```
<td>x=3; x++</td>
<td><script><!-
x=3
document.write(x++)
// -></script>
</td></tr>
<tr><td ROWSPAN="2">-</td>
<td>decrement and then return value</td>
<td>x=3; -x</td>
<td><script><!-
x=3
document.write(-x)
// -></script>
</td></tr>
<tr><td>return value and then decrement</td>
<td>x=3; x-</td>
<td><script><!-
x=3
document.write(x-)
// -></script>
</td></tr>
<tr><td ROWSPAN="6">Bit Manipulation</td>
<td>&amp;</td>
<td>and</td>
<td>10 &amp; 7</td>
<td><script><!-
document.write(10&7)
// -></script>
</td></tr>
<tr><td>|</td>
<td>or</td>
<td>10 | 7</td>
<td><script><!-
document.write(10|7)
// -></script>
</td></tr>
<tr><td>^</td>
<td>exclusive or</td>
<td>10 ^ 7</td>
<td><script><!-
document.write(10^7)
// -></script>
```

```
</td></tr>
<tr><td>&lt;&lt;</td>
<td>left shift</td>
<td>7 &lt;&lt; 3</td>
<td><script><!-
document.write(7<<3)
// -></script>
</td></tr>
<tr><td>&gt;&gt;</td>
<td>sign-propagating right shift</td>
<td>-7 &gt;&gt; 2</td>
<td><script><!-
document.write(-7>>2)
// -></script>
</td></tr>
<tr><td>&gt;&gt;&gt;</td>
<td>zero-fill right shift</td>
<td>-7 &gt;&gt;&gt; 2</td>
<td><script><!-
document.write(-7>>>2)
// -></script>
</td></tr>
<tr><td ROWSPAN="3">Logical</td>
<td>&amp;&amp;</td>
<td>logical and</td>
<td>true &amp;&amp; false</td>
<td><script><!-
document.write(true&&false)
// -></script>
</td></tr>
<tr><td>||</td>
<td>logical or</td>
<td>true || false</td>
<td><script><!-
document.write(true||false)
// -></script>
</td></tr>
<tr><td>!</td>
<td>not</td>
<td>!true</td>
<td><script><!-
document.write(!true)
```

```
// -></script>
</td></tr>
<tr><td ROWSPAN="6">Comparison</td>
<td>==</td>
<td>equal</td>
<td>3 == 7</td>
<td><script><!-
document.write(3==7)
// -></script>
</td></tr>
<tr><td>!=</td>
<td>not equal</td>
<td>3 != 7</td>
<td><script><!-
document.write(3!=7)
// -></script>
</td></tr>
<tr><td>&lt;</td>
<td>less than</td>
<td>3 &lt; 7</td>
<td><script><!-
document.write(3<7)
// -></script>
</td></tr>
<tr><td>&lt;=</td>
<td>less than or equal</td>
<td>3 &lt;= 7</td>
<td><script><!-
document.write(3<=7)
// -></script>
</td></tr>
<tr><td>&gt;</td>
<td>greater than</td>
<td>3 &gt; 7</td>
<td><script><!-
document.write(3>7)
// -></script>
</td></tr>
<tr><td>&gt;=</td>
<td>greater than or equal</td>
<td>3 &gt;= 7</td>
<td><script><!-
```

```
document.write(3>7)
// -></script>
</td></tr>
<tr><td>Conditional Expression</td>
<td>(condition) ? value1 : value2</td>
<td>if condition is true then value1 else value2</td>
<td>true ? 3 : 7</td>
<td><script><!-
document.write(true?3:7)
// -></script>
</td></tr>
</table>
</body>
</html>
```

FIGURE 3.1:

JavaScript operator
reference (Listing 3.1)

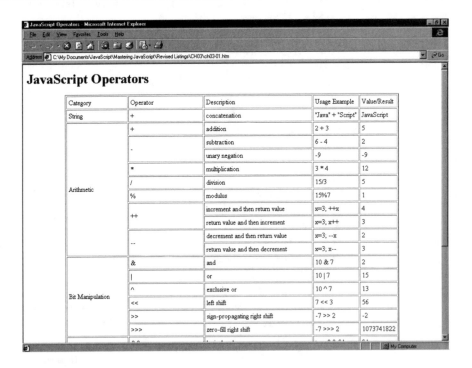

Operator Precedence

The *precedence* of the operator determines which operations are evaluated before others during the parsing and execution of complex expressions. For example, when you evaluate the expression 3 + 4 * 5, you should come up with 23 as your answer and not 35. This is because the multiplication operator, *, has a higher precedence than the addition operator, +. JavaScript defines the precedence and therefore the order of evaluation of all its operators. Table 3.6 summarizes the precedence of the JavaScript operators.

TABLE 3.6: Operator Precedence

Precedence	Operator
1	Parentheses, function call, or array subscript
2	!, ~, -, ++, –, typeof, new, void, delete (see note)
3	*, /, % (see note)
4	+, – (see note)
5	<<, >>, >>> (see note)
6	<, <=, >, >= (see note)
7	==, != , ===. !== (see note)
8	&
9	^
10		
11	&&
12			
13	?:
14	=, +=, -=, *=, /=, %=, <<=, >>=, >>>=, &=, ^=, |= (see note)
15	The comma (,) operator

NOTE: Where more than one operator is listed at a given level, those operators are all of equal priority. I don't mean to imply that =, for example, has a slightly higher priority than += or -= in level 14 above. Rather, it means that as JavaScript reads an expression from left to right at that level of precedence, it will evaluate any of those operators as it comes across them.

To see how you would use Table 3.6 to determine the order of evaluation, consider the following complex expression:

```
a = 3 * (9 % 2) - !true >>> 2 - 1
```

Because parentheses surround 9 % 2 ("nine modulo two"), we evaluate that term first, resulting in the following:

```
a = 3 * 1 - !true >>> 2 - 1
```

NOTE   As mentioned previously, the % (modulus) operator calculates the remainder of dividing two integers. For example, 9 % 2 = 1, because 9/2 = 4 with a remainder of 1.

The highest precedence operator is now the ! negation operator. After an evaluation of !true, we get

```
a = 3 * 1 - false >>> 2 - 1
```

The * operator is the next to be evaluated, resulting in

```
a = 3 - false >>> 2 - 1
```

The two - operators now have the highest precedence. The logical value *false* is converted to *0* and the simple expression 2 - 1 is evaluated to *1*, yielding the following:

```
a = 3 >>> 1
```

Then, because >>> has a higher precedence than =, the expression is evaluated to

```
a = 3
```

Finally, the = assignment operator assigns the integer value *3* to variable a.

JavaScript Programming Statements

The *statements* of any programming language are the instructions from which programs are written. Most programming languages support a common core set of statements, such as assignment statements, if statements, loop statements, and others. These languages differ only in the syntax used for their statements and the degree to which the languages support software development paradigms and programming features such as object-oriented programming, abstract data definition, inference rules, and list processing.

JavaScript provides a complete range of basic programming statements. While it is not an object-oriented programming language, it *is* an object-*based* language, and supports objects, object properties, and methods. You'll learn more about these object-based programming features in Chapter 5, "Working with Objects."

The statements provided by JavaScript are summarized in Table 3.7 and covered in the following subsections.

TABLE 3.7: JavaScript Statement Summary

Statement	Purpose	Example
assignment	Assigns the value of an expression to a variable	`x = y + z`
data declaration	Declares a variable (and optionally assigns a value to it)	`card = new Array(52)`

if	Alters program execution based on the value of a condition	`if (x>y) {`
		`  z = x`
		`}`

switch	Selects from a number of alternatives	`switch (val) {`
		`  case 1:`
		`  // First alternative`
		`  break;`
		`  case 2:`
		`  // Second alternative`
		`  break;`
		`  default:`
		`  // Default action`
		`}`

while	Repeatedly executes a set of statements until a condition becomes false	`while (x!=7) {`
		`  x %= n`
		`  −n`
		`}`

for	Repeatedly executes a set of statements until a condition becomes false	`for(i=0;i<7;++i){`
		`  document.write(x[i])`
		`}`

do while	Repeatedly executes a set of statements while a condition is true	`do {`
		`  // Statements`
		`} while (i>0)`

Continued on next page

TABLE 3.7 CONTINUED: JavaScript Statement Summary

Statement	Purpose	Example
label	Associates a label with a statement	`labelName :` `  statement`
break	Immediately terminates a do, while, or for statement	`if(x>y) break`
continue	Immediately terminates the current iteration of a do, while, or for statement	`if(x>y) continue`
function call	Invokes a function	`x=abs(y)`
return	Returns a value from a function call	`return x*y`

with	Identifies the default object	`with (Math) {`
		`  d = PI * 2 * r;`
		`}`

for in	Iterates over an object's properties	`for (prop in employee) {`
		`  document.write(prop+" ")`
		`}`

throw	Throws an exception	`throw "My Error"`

try	Checks for exceptions	`try {`
		`  // Tricky code`
		`}`
		`catch (exception) {`
		`  // Handle exception`
		`}`

catch	Catches an exception	See above.
delete	Deletes an object property or an array element	`delete a[5]`
method invocation	Invokes a method of an object	`document.write("Hello!")`

NOTE   The throw, try, and catch statements are only supported by Internet Explorer 5 and later. The import and export statements are used with signed scripts and are only supported by Navigator 4 and later. Chapter 23, "Securing Your Scripts," covers the use of the import and export statements.

Here are a few things to keep in mind when writing a series of statements:

- More than one statement may occur on a single line of text, provided that each statement is separated by a semicolon (;). The semicolon is the Java-Script "line separator" indicator.

- No semicolon is needed between statements that occur on separate lines.

- A long JavaScript statement may be written using multiple lines of text. No line-continuation identifier is required for such multiline statements. (In this book, however, I *will* show a continuation arrow, at least in the early chapters when I feel it's helpful for clarifying the extent of long statements that might be unfamiliar to you.)

Assignment Statements

The most basic statement found in almost any programming language is the *assignment* statement. The assignment statement updates the value of a variable based upon an assignment operator and an expression (and, optionally, the current value of the variable being updated). You have seen numerous examples of assignment statements in the earlier sections of this chapter and in Chapter 2, "Starting with JavaScript and JScript." For example, the statement

```
y = x + 10
```

assigns the value of x plus 10 to the y variable.

Data Declarations

Data declarations identify a variable to the JavaScript interpreter. So far you have been declaring simple variables through assignment statements. For example, the statement

```
a = 25
```

causes a to be implicitly declared as an integer variable and initialized to 25. The variable a is referred to as a *global* variable. This means that it can be accessed by all scripts defined in an HTML document. Later in this chapter, in the section titled "Local Variable Declarations," you'll learn how to declare variables that are *local* to a function definition.

Array declarations are another example of data declaration statements. For example, the following array declarations declare array variables:

```
// Declares an array of zero elements
customerNum = new Array()

// Declares an array of 100 null valued elements
productCode = new Array(100)
```

Dense array declarations provide the capability to declare an array and assign initial values to all of the elements of the array. Here are two examples of these declaration statements:

```
// Declares and initializes a seven-element array
day = new Array("Sun","Mon","Tue","Wed","Thu","Fri","Sat")

// Declares and initializes a four-element array
name = new Array("Bob","Sybil","Ricky","Mad Dog")
```

Another type of variable declaration involves the creation of an instance of an object. You'll learn about objects and their creation in Chapter 5, "Working with Objects." For now, instances of objects are created using statements of the following form:

```
variableName = new objectConstructor(p1,p2,...,pn)
```

where *variableName* is the name of a variable that is assigned the newly created object, new is the new object creator, *objectConstructor()* is a function that is used to create the object, and *p1* through *pn* are an optional list of parameters that are used in the object's creation.

The *if* Statement

The if statement provides the capability to alter the course of a program's execution based on an expression that yields a logical value. If the logical value is *true*, a specified set of statements is executed. If the logical value is *false*, the set of statements is skipped (and, optionally, a second set of statements is executed). The if statement comes in two forms. The syntax of the first form is as follows:

```
if ( condition ) {
 statements
 }
```

If the specified condition is *true*, then the statements identified within the braces { and } are executed. Execution then continues with the statement following the if statement. If the specified condition is *false*, then the statements enclosed by braces are skipped and execution continues with the statement following the if statement. For example, the following statement writes the text *Good morning* to the current Web document when the value of the hour variable is less than 12.

```
if(hour<12){
  document.write("Good morning")
}
```

The syntax of the second form of the if statement is similar to the first form except that an else clause is added. The syntax of the second form is as follows:

```
if ( condition ) {
  first set of statements
} else {
  second set of statements
}
```

If the specified condition is *true*, then the first set of statements is executed. If the specified condition is *false*, then the second set of statements is executed. In both cases, execution continues with the statement following the if statement.

An example of the second form of the if statement follows:

```
if(hour<12){
  document.write("Good morning")
}else{
  document.write("Hello")
}
```

The if statement results in the current document being updated with the text *Good morning* if the value of the hour variable is less than 12 or with the text *Hello* if hour is greater than or equal to 12.

NOTE   The braces enclosing the statements in the if and else clauses can be omitted if only one statement is enclosed.

Loop Statements

Loop statements are used to repeat the execution of a set of statements while a particular condition is *true*. JavaScript supports three types of loop statements: the while statement, the do while statement, and the for statement. JavaScript also provides the label, break, and continue statements. The break statement is used to terminate all loop iteration. The continue statement is used to cause a single loop iteration to end immediately and proceed to the next loop iteration. The label statement labels a statement for use with the break and continue statements. These statements are covered in the following subsections.

The *while* Statement

The while statement is a basic loop statement, used to repeat the execution of a set of statements while a specified condition is *true*. The syntax of the while statement is as follows:

```
while ( condition ) {
  statements
  }
```

The while statement evaluates the condition, and if the condition evaluates to *true*, executes the statements enclosed within braces. When the condition evaluates to *false*, it transfers control to the statement following the while statement.

Listing 3.2 provides an example of how the while statement can be used to generate the content of an HTML document. Figure 3.2 shows how the document generated by this script is displayed by a Web browser. The script iterates from 1 to 6, generating six levels of HTML headings. The index variable is incremented each time it passes through the loop.

Listing 3.2   **The *while* Statement (ch03-02.htm)**

```
<HTML>
<HEAD>
<TITLE>Using the While Statement</TITLE>
</HEAD>
<BODY>
<SCRIPT><!-
i=1
while(i<7){
```

```
document.write("<H"+i+">This is a level "+i+" heading."
+"</H"+i+">")
++i
}
// -></SCRIPT>
</BODY>
</HTML>
```

FIGURE 3.2:

Using the while statement to generate an HTML document (Listing 3.2)

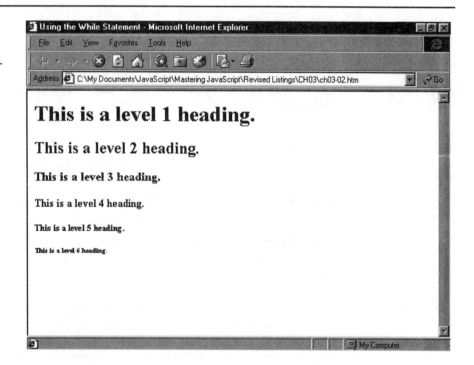

The *do while* Statement

The do while statement, introduced in JavaScript 1.2, is similar to the while statement. The only difference is that the looping condition is checked at the end of the loop, instead of at the beginning. This ensures that the enclosed statements are executed at least once. The syntax of the do while statement is as follows:

```
do {
 statements
while (condition);
```

For example, the following statements display the integers 1 through 10:

```
i = 0
do {
 ++i
 document.writeln(i+"<BR>")
} while (i < 10);
```

The *for* Statement

The for statement is similar to the while statement in that it repeatedly executes a set of statements while a condition is true. It is different from the while statement in that it is designed to update a variable after each loop iteration. The syntax of the for statement is

```
for ( initializationStatement; condition; updateStatement ) {
 statements
}
```

The initialization statement is executed only at the beginning of the for statement's execution. The condition is then tested, and if it is *true*, the statements enclosed within braces are executed. If the condition is *false*, the loop is terminated and the statement following the for statement is executed.

If the statements enclosed within the braces of the for statement are executed, the update statement is executed, and then the condition is retested. The enclosed statements and update statement are repeatedly executed until the condition becomes *false*.

> **NOTE**   The initialization statement, condition, and update statement are optional and may be omitted.

An example for statement follows:

```
a = new Array(2,4,6,8,10)
sum = 0
for (i = 0;i < a.length;++i) {
 sum += a[i]
}
```

The first statement of the above example creates a five-element array with the values 2, 4, 6, 8, and 10. The second statement initializes the variable sum to 0. The for statement begins by initializing the variable i to 0 and tests the length of a to see if it is greater than i. Because i is 0 and a.length is 5, the statement enclosed within the braces is executed and the value of sum is incremented by a[i], which is 2.

The update statement, ++i, is then executed. This causes i to be incremented to 1. The condition is retested and because i is less than 5 the statement enclosed within braces is then re-executed. This time sum is incremented by 4 and its value becomes 6.

The update statement, ++i, is executed a second time and the condition is retested. At this point, you should be able to follow the remainder of the for statement's execution. The for loop continues to iterate until i < a.length is no longer true. This happens when i becomes 5. At this point, sum has become the sum of all the elements of a and its value is 30.

Listing 3.3 shows how the script shown in Listing 3.2 can be updated to use a for statement instead of a while statement. The Web page resulting from the execution of this script is the same as that displayed in Figure 3.2.

Listing 3.3   **Use of the *for* Statement (ch03-03.htm)**

```
<HTML>
<HEAD>
<TITLE>Using the For Statement</TITLE>
</HEAD>
<BODY>
<SCRIPT><!-
for(i=1;i<7;++i)
  document.write("<H"+i+">This is a level "+i+" heading."
  +"</H"+i+">")
// -></SCRIPT>
</BODY>
</HTML>
```

NOTE   The braces enclosing the statements in the for and while statements can be omitted if only one statement is enclosed.

The *label* Statement

Any statement may be labeled, by placing *labelName :* before the statement. For example,

```
MyLabel :
 a = 2 * b
```

causes the above statement to be labeled with the label MyLabel. Labels are used to identify statements. They are typically used to label loop, switch, or if statements. You can reference labeled statements via the break and continue statements, as discussed in the following sections.

The *break* Statement

The break statement is used to terminate execution of a loop and transfer control to the statement following the loop. The break statement consists of the word break, followed by an optional label. When the break statement is encountered, the loop is immediately terminated. An example of its use follows:

```
a = new Array(5,4,3,2,1)
sum = 0
for (i = 0;i < a.length;++i) {
 if (i == 3) break;
 sum += a[i]
}
```

The above for statement executes for i equal to 0, 1, 2, and 3. When i equals 3, the condition of the if statement is true and the break statement is executed. This causes the for statement to immediately terminate. The value of sum is 12 upon termination of the for statement.

Listing 3.4 provides a script that illustrates the use of the break statement. Figure 3.3 shows the Web page generated by this script. The script loops to test the integers from 100 to 1 until it finds one which is evenly divisible by 17. When it finds such a number, it terminates the loop.

Listing 3.4	The *break* Statement (ch03-04.htm)

```
<HTML>
<HEAD>
<TITLE>Using the Break Statement</TITLE>
</HEAD>
<BODY>
```

```
<SCRIPT><!–
for(i=100;i>0;–i){
 document.write(i+"<BR>")
 if(i%17==0) break
}
// –></SCRIPT>
</BODY>
</HTML>
```

FIGURE 3.3:

Using the break state-
ment (Listing 3.4)

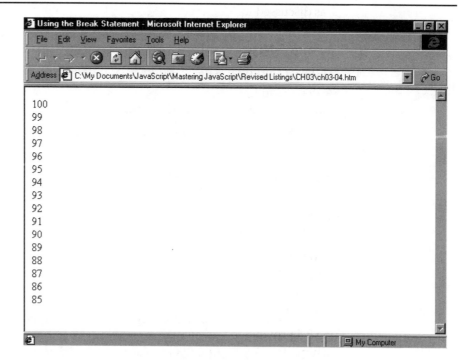

If the break statement is used with a label, then control is transferred to the first
statement following the labeled statement. The labeled statement does not need
to be a loop statement. Consider the following example:

```
test1 :
   if (val > 0) {
      document.write("Greater than zero: ")
      test2 :
         if (val == 2) {
```

```
        document.write(val)
        break test1
    }
    // Other code
}
```

The break statement causes control to transfer to the first statement following the outer if statement (test1).

The *continue* Statement

The continue statement is similar to the break statement in that it affects the execution of the for, do while, or while statement in which it is contained. It differs from the break statement in that it does not completely terminate the loop's execution but only terminates the execution of the statements in the loop's current iteration.

When a continue statement is encountered in a while, do while, or for loop, the rest of the statements being iterated are skipped and control of execution returns to the condition of the loop.

Consider the following while loop as an example:

```
i = 1
sum = 0
while(i<10) {
  i *= 2;
  if (i == 4) continue
  sum += i + 1
}
```

The while loop iterates for i equal to 1, 2, 4, and 8 at the beginning of each loop. However, sum is only updated when i equals 1, 4, and 8. When i equals 2 at the beginning of the loop, it is doubled to 4 as the result of the first statement of the loop's execution. This causes the condition of the if statement to be true and the continue statement to be executed. Execution of the continue statement causes the last statement in the loop to be skipped and control to return to the evaluation of the condition of the while statement. The final value of sum is 29.

NOTE   The continue statement may also be used with a label. The label specifies the loop statement to which the continue statement applies.

Listing 3.5 provides a script that illustrates the use of the continue statement. Figure 3.4 shows the Web page generated by this script. The script prints out the integers between 1 and 10 (exclusive), but uses the continue statement to skip all odd integers.

Listing 3.5 **The *continue* Statement (ch03-05.htm)**

```
<HTML>
<HEAD>
<TITLE>Using the Continue Statement</TITLE>
</HEAD>
<BODY>
<SCRIPT><!-
for(i=1;i<10;++i){
 if(i%2!=0) continue
 document.write(i+"<BR>")
}
// -></SCRIPT>
</BODY>
</HTML>
```

FIGURE 3.4:

Using the continue statement (Listing 3.5)

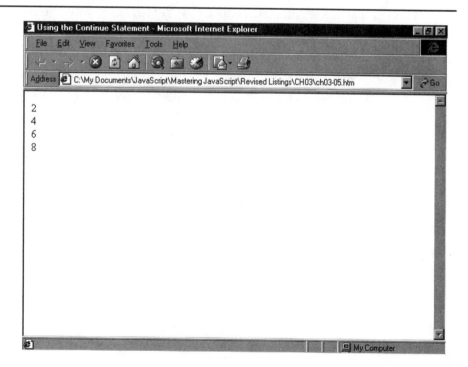

The *switch* Statement

JavaScript 1.2 added the `switch` statement. Its syntax is the same as in Java and C++:

```
switch (expression) {
  case value1:
    statements
    break
      .
      .
      .
  case valuen:
    statements
    break
  default:
    statements
}
```

The `switch` statement evaluates the expression and determines if any of the values (*value1* through *valuen*) match the expression's value. If one of them matches, then the statements for that particular case are executed, and statement execution then continues after the `switch` statement. If there is no matching value, then the statements for the `default` case are executed.

The `break` statements may be omitted. However, if they are omitted, execution continues with the next case (if any).

The following `switch` statement prints the string value of the number corresponding to 1, 2, or 3, or prints *I don't know* otherwise.

```
switch (i) {
  case 1:
    document.writeln("one")
    break
  case 2:
    document.writeln("two")
    break
  case 3:
    document.writeln("three")
    break
  default 1:
    document.writeln("I don't know")
}
```

Listing 3.6 provides a script that illustrates the use of the switch statement. Figure 3.5 shows the Web page generated by this script. The script displays the names of the numbers 1 through 10.

Listing 3.6   The *switch* Statement (ch03-06.htm)

```
<HTML>
<HEAD>
<TITLE>Using the switch Statement</TITLE>
</HEAD>
<BODY>
<SCRIPT LANGUAGE="JavaScript"><!-
for(i=1; i<=10; ++i) {
 switch (i) {
  case 1:
   val = "one"
   break;
  case 2:
   val = "two"
   break;
  case 3:
   val = "three"
   break;
  case 4:
   val = "four"
   break;
  case 5:
   val = "five"
   break;
  case 6:
   val = "six"
   break;
  case 7:
   val = "seven"
   break;
  case 8:
   val = "eight"
   break;
  case 9:
   val = "nine"
   break;
```

```
    case 10:
     val = "ten"
     break;
    default:
     val = "unknown"
   }
   document.writeln(val+"<BR>");
 }
 // ->
 </SCRIPT>
 </BODY>
 </HTML>
```

FIGURE 3.5:

Using the switch state-
ment (Listing 3.6)

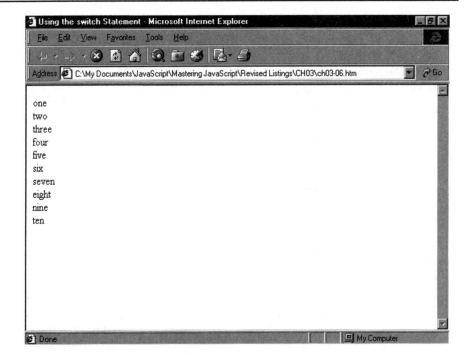

Function Call Statements

Most programming languages support function calls. *Functions* are named blocks
of statements that are referenced and executed as a unit. Data that is required for
the execution of a function may be passed as *parameters* to the function. Functions

may return a value, but are not required to do so. When a function returns a value, the invocation of the function is usually part of an expression. For example, the following statement invokes the `factorial()` function, passing it the integer value 5 as a parameter:

```
n = factorial(5)
```

In the above example, the function call, `factorial(5)`, returns a value which is assigned to the variable n. The `factorial()` function is a hypothetical function and is not defined by JavaScript.

When a function does not return a value, it is usually used to perform an operation that updates a variable or an object that is external to JavaScript. The invocation of a non-value returning function is a complete statement, not merely part of a larger expression. For example, consider the function invocation in the following statement:

```
notifyUser("Product code is invalid")
```

In the above statement, the function `notifyUser()` takes the string *"Product code is invalid"* as a parameter. It then displays this string to the user. The function does not return a value, and therefore, is not on the right side of an assignment statement.

Defining Functions

A function must be defined before it can be used. Function definitions are usually placed in the head of an HTML document, although it is not mandatory to do so. Placing function definitions in the head, however, ensures that the definition occurs before the function is used. The syntax of a function definition is as follows:

```
function functionName(p1, p2, ..., pn) {
 statements
}
```

The function name is the name used to refer to the function in function calls. The parameters are the names of variables that receive the values passed to the function when the function is invoked. The parameters that are passed to a function are referred to as the function's *arguments*. The statements enclosed in braces are executed as the result of a function call.

For example, consider the following function definition:

```
function display(text) {
 document.write(text)
}
```

If the above function is invoked with the statement display("xyz"), the text *xyz* is written to the current Web document. The display("xyz") function call is thus equivalent to the statement document.write("xyz").

Listing 3.7 provides an example of a function definition. Figure 3.6 shows the Web page that this script generates.

Listing 3.7   A Function Definition (ch03-07.htm)

```
<HTML>
<HEAD>
<TITLE>A function definition</TITLE>
<SCRIPT LANGUAGE="JavaScript"><!-
function displayTaggedText(tag, text) {
 document.write("<"+tag+">")
 document.write(text)
 document.write("</"+tag+">")
}
// ->
</SCRIPT>
</HEAD>
<BODY>
<SCRIPT LANGUAGE="JavaScript"><!-
displayTaggedText("H1","This is a level 1 heading")
displayTaggedText("P","This text is the first paragraph of the
document.")
// ->
</SCRIPT>
</BODY>
</HTML>
```

The script in the document head defines the function, displayTaggedText(), that takes two parameters, tag and text. Actual values for tag and text are passed to the function via these parameters when the function is invoked. The function consists of three statements. The first statement writes the left angle bracket, followed by the value of the tag parameter plus a right angle bracket to the current document. The second write statement writes the value of the text variable to the current document. The third statement writes the string </, followed by the value of the tag variable followed by the right angle bracket, to the current document. The displayTaggedText() function does not return a value.

FIGURE 3.6:

Defining and using a
function (Listing 3.7)

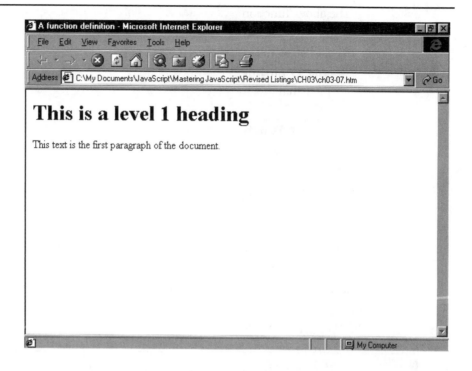

The script in the body of the document executes two function call statements
that invoke the displayTaggedText() function to write a level 1 HTML heading
and a paragraph of text to the current document. The parameters passed in the
first invocation are "H1" and "This is a level 1 heading". The "H1" string is
passed to the displayTaggedText() function via the tag variable. The "This is
a level 1 heading" string is passed via the text variable. The second invocation of displayTaggedText() is handled in the same manner. The string "P" is
passed via tag and "This is a level 1 heading" is passed via text.

Defining Functions with a Variable Number of Parameters

JavaScript provides the capability to define functions that take a variable number
of parameters, using the arguments array. The arguments array is automatically
created by JavaScript for each function invocation. Suppose function f is invoked
with the parameters "test", true, and 77 as in the following statement:

```
f("test",true,77)
```

The array `f.arguments` contains the values of these parameters. In this case, the variables are as follows:

```
f.arguments.length = 3
f.arguments[0] = "test"
f.arguments[1] = true
f.arguments[2] = 77
```

The following function definition illustrates the use of the `arguments` array:

```
function sum() {
 n = sum.arguments.length
 total = 0
 for(i=0;i<n;++i) {
  total += sum.arguments[i]
 }
 return total
}
```

The `sum()` function is designed to add an arbitrary list of parameters. The variable n is assigned the length of the `sum.arguments` array. The `total` variable is used to add the elements of `sum.arguments`.

NOTE   The `this` keyword is used in functions to refer to the current object. Refer to Chapter 5, "Working with Objects," for a description of its use.

Local Variable Declarations

When defining a function, it is often necessary to define variables that will be used to store values calculated by the function. You could declare variables using the declaration statements that you studied in the section, "Data Declarations," earlier in the chapter. However, this causes the function definition to be dependent on these global variables and, as a result, less modular and more difficult to debug. Instead, it is better to declare variables that are used only within the function. These variables, referred to as *local variables*, are accessible only within the function in which they are declared. Figure 3.7 illustrates the difficulties inherent with using global variables within functions.

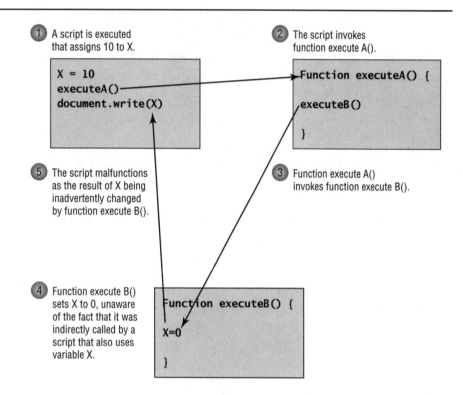

① A script is executed that assigns 10 to X.

② The script invokes function execute A().

```
X = 10
executeA()
document.write(X)
```

```
Function executeA() {

    executeB()

}
```

⑤ The script malfunctions as the result of X being inadvertently changed by function execute B().

③ Function execute A() invokes function execute B().

④ Function execute B() sets X to 0, unaware of the fact that it was indirectly called by a script that also uses variable X.

```
Function executeB() {

    X=0

}
```

Local variables are declared in the same manner as global variables, except that local variable declarations are preceded by the keyword var. The following are examples of local variable declarations:

```
// Declares temp as a local variable
var temp

// Declares index as a local variable and initializes it to 1
var index = 1
```

```
/* Declares the product array with an initial
   capacity of 100 elements */
var product = new Array(100)
```

Local variables may have the same name as global variables. In the case that a local variable and global variable have the same name, all references to the variable name within the function that defines the local variable refer to the local variable of that function and not to the global variable. All references to the variable name outside of the function that defines the local variable are to the global variable. Listing 3.8 provides a script that illustrates the use of global and local variables with the same names. Figure 3.8 displays the Web page that this script generates. The variable x is a local variable in the displaySquared() function and a global variable in the script contained in the document body. Note that the local and global x variables may be updated independently.

Listing 3.8   Use of Global and Local Variables (ch03-08.htm)

```
<HTML>
<HEAD>
<TITLE>Global and Local Variables</TITLE>
<SCRIPT LANGUAGE="JavaScript"><!-
function displaySquared(y) {
var x = y * y
document.write(x+"<BR>")
}
// ->
</SCRIPT>
</HEAD>
<BODY>
<SCRIPT LANGUAGE="JavaScript"><!-
for(x=0;x<10;++x)
 displaySquared(x)
// ->
</SCRIPT>
</BODY>
</HTML>
```

FIGURE 3.8:

An example of using
global and local variables
(Listing 3.8)

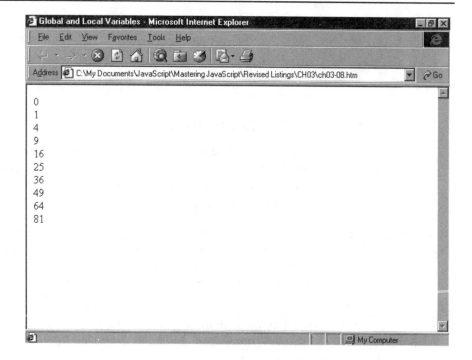

The *return* Statement

The return statement is used to return a value as the result of the processing performed by a function. This value is returned to the statement that invoked the
function. The syntax of the return statement is

```
return expression
```

The expression evaluates to the value to be returned by the function. When the
return statement is encountered, the expression is evaluated and the value to
which the expression evaluates is immediately returned by the function. No subsequent statements of the function are processed.

An example of the use of the return statement is shown in the following function definition:

```
function factorial(n) {
 var sum = 1
 for(i=1;i<=n;++i)
```

```
  sum *= i
 return sum
 }
```

In the above example, sum is calculated as the product of all integers from 1 through n. This value is then returned via the return statement.

Object-Access Statements

Objects are JavaScript data structures that both contain data and provide functions, referred to as *methods*, which are used to perform operations on this data. The individual variables comprising an object are referred to as *properties*. Properties provide access to the data contained in an object.

NOTE   JavaScript objects are covered in Chapter 5. This section focuses on programming statements that use object properties and methods.

Because properties provide access to the values contained in the variables comprising an object, they are usually used in expressions that appear in the right or left side of an assignment statement. For example, suppose the employee variable refers to an object of type employeeRecord that has the employeeID property. The following assignment statement retrieves the value of the employeeID property and assigns it to the id variable.

```
id = employee.employeeID
```

The general syntax used to access the property of an object is

```
variableName.propertyName
```

where the variable name is the name of a variable that refers to an object and the property name is the name of the property to be retrieved.

When a property reference appears in the left side of an assignment statement, the property of the referenced object is updated. In the following example, the employeeID property of the object referred to by the employee variable is updated with the value stored in the id variable.

```
employee.employeeID = id
```

The methods of an object are functions that are used to perform operations on the object. These methods are invoked in a similar manner as properties. However, since methods are functions, they must include the method's parameter list.

An empty parameter list is specified in the same manner as for function calls. The general syntax of a method invocation is shown here:

```
variableName.methodName(p1,p2,...,pn)
```

where the variable name is the name of a variable that refers to an object and the method name is the name of the method to be invoked. The parameters p1 through pn are an optional list of method parameters.

Some methods do not return a value. Their invocation is a complete statement in itself. A common example that you've been using so far is the write() method of the document object:

```
document.write("text to be displayed")
```

Some methods return a value. In this case, the method invocation may appear as part of a larger expression, as in the following example:

```
payroll=0
for(i=0;i<employee.length;++i)
  payroll += employee[i].netPay()
```

In the above example, employee is an array of employeeRecord objects. The net-Pay() method calculates the net pay of each employee based on data contained in the properties of the employeeRecord objects.

The *with* Statement

The with statement is provided as a convenience to eliminate retyping the name of an object that is to be referenced in a series of property references and method invocations. The syntax of the with statement is as follows:

```
with(variableName){
  statements
}
```

The variable name identifies the default object to be used with the statements enclosed in braces. An example of the with statement follows:

```
with(document) {
  write("<H1>With It</H1>")
  write("<P>")
  write("Eliminate object name references with with")
  write("</P>")
}
```

In the above example, the need to prefix each `write()` method invocation with the document object is eliminated because `document` is identified in the `with` statement. Without the `with` statement, the above code would need to be written as

```
document.write("<H1>With It</H1>")
document.write("<P>")
document.write("Eliminate object name references with with")
document.write("</P>")
```

The *for in* Statement

You learned how the `for` statement is used to iterate a set of statements based on a loop condition and an update statement. The `for in` statement is similar to a `for` statement in that it repeatedly executes a set of statements. However, instead of iterating the statements based on the loop condition, it executes the statements for all properties that are defined for an object.

The syntax of the `for in` statement is as follows:

```
for (variableName in objectName) {
 statements
 }
```

The `for in` loop executes the statements enclosed in braces one time for each property defined for `objectName`. Each time the statements are executed, the variable specified by `variableName` is assigned a string identifying the current property name. For example, consider the execution of the following `for in` statement in the case of the `employee` object having the properties `employeeID`, `employeeName`, and `employeeLocation`.

```
for(prop in employee)
    document.write(prop+"<BR>")
```

The above `for in` statement would cause the following text to be written to the current document:

```
employeeID
employeeName
employeeLocation
```

These are the three properties that are defined for the `employee` object.

The *throw*, *try*, and *catch* Statements

Internet Explorer 5 introduced JScript 5, which is the most comprehensive scripting environment supported by any browser (to date). One of the nicest features of JScript 5 is its support for the throw, try, and catch statements. These statements work together to give you advanced control over any errors and exceptions that may arise in your code. If you are a Java programmer, these statements will be familiar to you. JScript uses the same syntax for these statements as Java.

JScript 5 also introduces the error object, which provides a way to handle errors, such as syntax errors and runtime errors, that occur in your documents. You'll study the error object in more detail in Chapter 4, "Handling Events," and Chapter 5, "Working with Objects." For now, just know that it exists and is used with the throw, try, and catch statements.

> **NOTE**
>
> The throw, try, and catch statements only work with Internet Explorer 5. Because these statements will be part of ECMAScript Version 2, it is reasonable to expect them to be supported in Navigator 5.

An *exception* is an error that is generated by your script to call attention to a problem that is discovered during the script's execution. Your script generates an exception so that the error may be handled and resolved. In the parlance of exceptions, you generate an exception by *throwing* it. The code that handles exceptions thrown by your scripts (or the JavaScript interpreter) is referred to as an exception handler. Exception handlers are said to *catch* exceptions. Figure 3.9 provides an overview of the exception handling process.

FIGURE 3.9:

How exception handling works

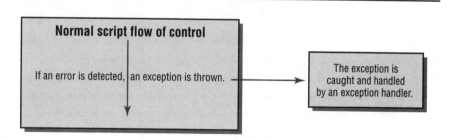

The throw statement is used to throw an exception. Its syntax follows:

```
throw expression
```

The value of *expression* is used to identify the type of error that occurred. For example, the following statement throws an exception named *BadInputFromUser*.

```
throw "BadInputFromUser"
```

TIP   While it isn't mandatory, it's a good idea to throw string values. This will make your code easier to understand and debug.

The try statement and the catch statement work together to support exception handling. Their syntax follows:

```
try {
  statement(s) where an exception may be thrown
}
catch(errorVariable) {
  statement(s) that handle the exception
}
```

The try statement surrounds the statements for which exception handling is to be performed. It is immediately followed by a catch statement that performs the exception handling. The *errorVariable* is used to reference any exception that occurs. It is assigned an instance of the error object. If an exception is thrown during the processing of the statements contained within the try statement, then the *errorVariable* is assigned an error object that identifies the exception, and control immediately transfers to the statements contained within the catch statement. If no exception is thrown during the processing of the statements contained within the try statement, then the catch statement is skipped and control transfers to the statement following the catch statement.

Let's work an example to get a feel for how this all works. Listing 3.9 shows a simple HTML file that contains two scripts, one in the document's head and the other in its body. The script in the document's body iterates i between 0 and 21, passing it as a parameter to the primeTest() function. The script in the document's head defines the primeTest() function. This function checks the parameter n to determine if it is prime. It contains a try statement in which the prime testing is performed. The first if statement checks to see if n is between 1 and 20.

If it is not, then the *It's out of range* exception is thrown and control passes to the catch statement. If n is between 1 and 20 the control passes to the for statement.

Listing 3.9   **An Exception Handling Example (ch03-09.htm)**

```
<HTML>
<HEAD><TITLE>Exception Test</TITLE></HEAD>
<SCRIPT LANGUAGE="JavaScript"><!-
function primeTest(n) {
 document.write("Testing "+n+": ")
 try {
  if(n < 1 || n > 20) throw "It's out of range"
  for(var i = 2; i < n; ++i)
   if(n % i == 0) throw "It's divisible by " + i
  document.writeln("It's prime.<BR>")
 }
 catch (exception) {
  document.writeln(exception+".<BR>")
 }
}
-></SCRIPT>
<BODY>
<P>This script only works with Internet Explorer 5.0, or later.</P>
<SCRIPT LANGUAGE="JavaScript"><!-
for(i = 0; i <= 21; ++i) {
 primeTest(i)
}
-></SCRIPT>
</BODY>
</HTML>
```

The for statement iterates i between 2 and n. If n modulus i is zero, then n is not prime, the *It's divisible by* exception is thrown, and control passes to the catch statement. Otherwise, *It's prime* is written to the document window and the function returns.

The catch statement simply writes the exception to the document window.

Figure 3.10 shows the output that is displayed by primeTest() as the result of the script's processing.

FIGURE 3.10:

The results of the exception processing (Listing 3.9)

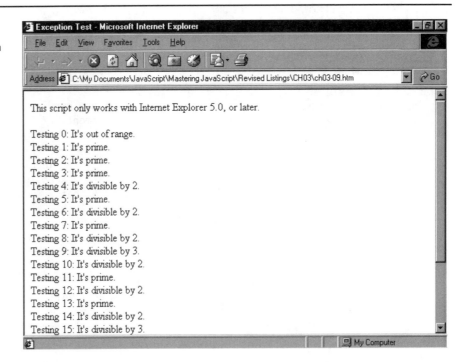

Nesting *try* Statements and Rethrowing Exceptions

JScript 5 allows you to nest `try` statements within each other. By doing so, you can implement multiple levels of exception handling. Figure 3.11 provides an overview of this approach. The `try` and `catch` statements of a lower-level exception handler are enclosed in a higher-level `try` statement. If an exception occurs in the lower-level `try` statement, it is caught by the lower-level `catch` statement. If the lower-level `catch` statement encounters an error in handling the exception, it can throw a new exception that is handled by the higher-level `catch` statement. The lower-level `catch` statement can also rethrow any exception that requires higher-level processing.

Listing 3.10 provides an example of nested exception handling and the rethrowing of exceptions. It consists of two scripts, one in the document head and the other in the document body. The script in the document body iterates i from 1 to 100 and invokes the `selected()` function to determine if the value of i should be displayed. If the `selected()` function returns *true*, then i is displayed.

FIGURE 3.11:

Nested exception handling allows exceptions to be rethrown.

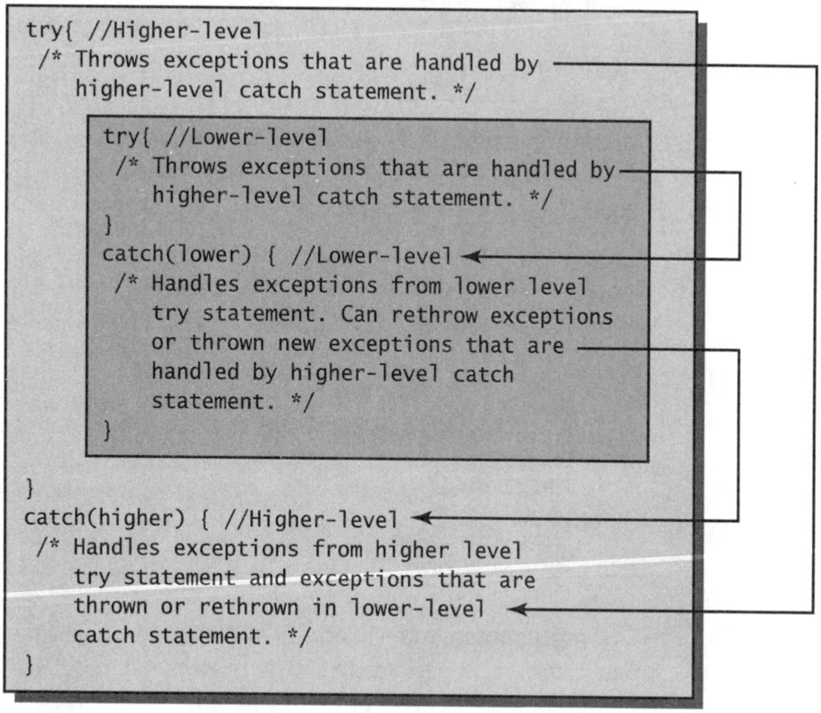

```
try{ //Higher-level
  /* Throws exceptions that are handled by
     higher-level catch statement. */

      try{ //Lower-level
        /* Throws exceptions that are handled by
           higher-level catch statement. */
      }
      catch(lower) { //Lower-level
        /* Handles exceptions from lower level
           try statement. Can rethrow exceptions
           or thrown new exceptions that are
           handled by higher-level catch
           statement. */
      }

}
catch(higher) { //Higher-level
  /* Handles exceptions from higher level
     try statement and exceptions that are
     thrown or rethrown in lower-level
     catch statement. */
}
```

Listing 3.10   Nested Exception Handling (ch03-10.htm)

```
<HTML>
<HEAD><TITLE>Exception Test</TITLE></HEAD>
<SCRIPT LANGUAGE="JavaScript"><!-
function selected(n) {
 try {
  try {
   if (n % 3 == 2) throw "No way"
   if (n % 3 == 1) throw "Try again"
  }
  catch (ex1) {
   if(ex1 == "Try again")
    if (n % 5 == 0) throw "Try again"
   return false
  }
```

```
   if (n % 7 == 3) throw "Try again"
   if (n % 7 != 0) throw "No way"
  }
 catch (ex2) {
  if(ex2 != "Try again") return false
  if(n % 11 != 0) return false
 }
 return true
}
-></SCRIPT>
<BODY>
<P>This script only works with Internet Explorer 5.0, or later.</P>
<SCRIPT LANGUAGE="JavaScript"><!-
for(i = 1; i <= 100; ++i) {
 if (selected(i)) document.writeln(i+"<BR>")
}
-></SCRIPT>
</BODY>
</HTML>
```

The processing of interest occurs in the `selected()` function. This function takes a parameter n and performs a series of tests on it to determine whether it should return *true* or *false*. The `selected()` function contains two sets of `try`/`catch` statements with one set nested within the other. The inner `try` statement checks the value of n % 3. If this value is 2, then the *No way* exception is thrown. If it is 1, then the *Try again* exception is thrown. The `catch` statement processes the *Try again* exception by checking to see if n is divisible by 5. In this case the *Try again* exception is rethrown. Otherwise, the `catch` statement returns a value of *false*.

Two `if` statements appear after the inner `try` statement but before the end of the outer `try` statement. If n % 7 is 3, then the *Try again* exception is thrown. Otherwise, if n % 7 is not 0, then the *No way* exception is thrown.

The outer `catch` statement returns a value of *false* for the *No way* exception and for the *Try again* exception when n is not divisible by 11. If the value of n manages to get through the gauntlet of exceptions, then `selected()` returns a value of *true*.

Figure 3.11 shows the output generated by Listing 3.10. The reason that I put together such a complicated set of exceptions is so that you can trace through the script's code to see how the output of Figure 3.12 is generated. By doing so, you'll have a firm understanding of how nested exception handling and exception rethrowing work.

FIGURE 3.12:

The output generated by
nested exception handlers
(Listing 3.10)

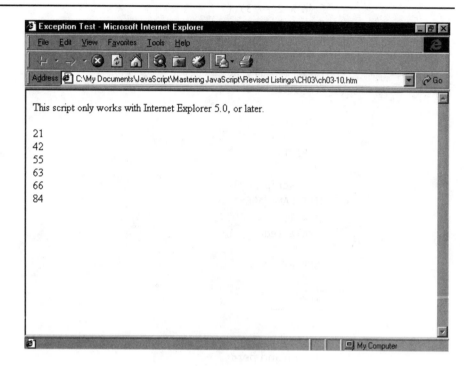

Summary

This chapter introduced you to more elements of the JavaScript language. You covered all of the operators provided by JavaScript and learned how expressions are evaluated using operator precedence. You learned to use JavaScript's programming statements and developed sample scripts that demonstrated the use of these statements. You also learned how to create and invoke functions. In the next chapter, you'll extend your JavaScript programming expertise by learning how JavaScript supports the handling of user-generated events.

CHAPTER

FOUR

4

Handling Events

- How JavaScript Handles Events

- Types of Events

- Setting Event Handlers from within JavaScript

- The *event* Object

- Event Capturing

- Error Handling

Events are the mechanism by which browsers respond to user actions. JavaScript's event-handling features give you the ability to alter the standard way in which a browser reacts to these actions. This enables you to develop Web pages that are more interactive, more responsive, and easier to use.

This chapter illustrates the use of JavaScript's event-handling features. It describes JavaScript's approach to event handling and identifies the event handlers that are predefined by JavaScript. It shows you how to write your own event-handling functions and how to associate them with user interface actions. By the time you finish this chapter, you'll be able to use event-handling functions to develop highly interactive Web pages.

What Are Events?

Events describe actions that occur as the result of user interaction with a Web page or other browser-related activities. For example, when a user clicks a hyperlink or a button, or enters data in a form, an event is generated informing the browser that an action has occurred and that further processing is required. The browser waits for events to occur, and when they do, it performs whatever processing is assigned to those events. The processing that is performed in response to the occurrence of an event is known as *event handling*. The code that performs this processing is called an *event handler*. Figure 4.1 illustrates the notion of an event and the process of event handling.

FIGURE 4.1:

Events and event handling

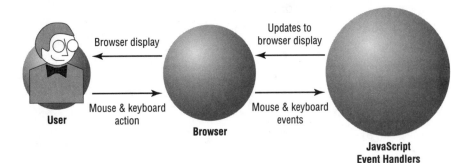

For a simple example of event processing, consider what normally happens when a user clicks a hyperlink that is displayed on a Web page. The default HTML action arising from such an event is that the browser loads and displays the page associated with that URL. With JavaScript, however, you can change that default action by writing a different event handler. Here are just a few things you can do with events using JavaScript event handlers:

- Display a dialog box when a user moves the mouse over a link

- Validate the data a user has just entered into a form

- Load and display an animation sequence when a user clicks a button

- Interact with Java applets and browser plug-ins

JavaScript's event-handling features are what enables JavaScript to create Web pages that come alive and interact with Web users

How JavaScript Handles Events

JavaScript's approach to event handling is a two-step process:

1. Defining the events that can be handled by scripts

2. Providing a standard method of connecting these events to user-supplied JavaScript code

JavaScript defines events for most of the major objects found in Web pages including links, images, image maps, form elements, and windows. The JavaScript language defines special attributes for the tags corresponding to these HTML elements that permit the script to identify event-handling JavaScript code instead of the default HTML event handlers. The values of these attributes are text strings that identify the event-handling code.

Table 4.1 summarizes the events defined by JavaScript that are common to Navigator and Internet Explorer. The first two columns identify the name and tags associated with the HTML element. The third and fourth columns identify and describe the events that JavaScript defines for the HTML element. I'll provide examples of these events throughout this chapter. For now, just try to get a feel for the kinds of events that can be handled through JavaScript.

TABLE 4.1: Events Defined by JavaScript

HTML Element	HTML Tags	JavaScript Event	Description
all elements	Various	***mouseMove	The mouse is moved.
link	<A> ... </A>	click	The mouse is clicked on a link.
		dblClick	The mouse is double-clicked on a link.
		mouseDown	The mouse button is pressed.
		mouseUp	The mouse button is released.
		mouseOver	The mouse is moved over a link.
		mouseOut	The mouse is moved from within a link to outside of that link.
		keyDown	The user presses a key.
		keyUp	The user releases a key.
		keyPress	The user presses and releases a key.
image	<IMG>	abort	The loading of an image is aborted as the result of a user action.
		error	An error occurs during the loading of an image.
		load	An image is loaded and displayed.
		keyDown	The user presses a key.
		keyUp	The user releases a key.
		keyPress	The user presses and releases a key.
area	<AREA>	mouseOver	The mouse is moved over an area of a client-side image map.
		mouseOut	The mouse is moved from within an image map area to outside of that area.
		dblClick	The user double-clicks an area of an image map.

Continued on next page

TABLE 4.1 CONTINUED: Events Defined by JavaScript

HTML Element	HTML Tags	JavaScript Event	Description
document body	`<BODY>` ... `</BODY>`	`click`	The user clicks in the body of a document.
		`dblClick`	The user double-clicks in the body of a document.
		`keyDown`	The user presses a key.
		`keyUp`	The user releases a key.
		`keyPress`	The user presses and releases a key.
		`mouseDown`	The user presses the mouse button.
		`mouseUp`	The user releases the mouse button.
window, frame set, frame	`<BODY>` ... `</BODY>` `<FRAMESET>` ... `</FRAMESET>` `<FRAME>` ... `</FRAME>`	`blur`	A window loses the current input focus.
		`error`	An error occurs when a window is loaded.
		`focus`	A window receives the current input focus.
		`load`	The loading of a window is completed.
		`unload`	The user exits a window.
		`move`	A window is moved.
		`resize`	A window is resized.
		`dragDrop`	The user drops an object onto the window.
form	`<FORM>` ... `</FORM>`	`submit`	A form is submitted by the user.
		`reset`	A form is reset by the user.

Continued on next page

TABLE 4.1 CONTINUED: Events Defined by JavaScript

HTML Element	HTML Tags	JavaScript Event	Description
text field	`<INPUT TYPE = "text">`	blur	A text field loses the current input focus.
		focus	A text field receives the current input focus.
		change	A text field is modified and loses the current input focus.
		select	Text is selected within a text field.
password field	`<INPUT TYPE = "password">`	blur	A password field loses the input focus.
		focus	A password field gains the input focus.
text area	`<TEXTAREA> ... </TEXTAREA>`	blur	A text area loses the current input focus.
		focus	A text area receives the current input focus.
		change	A text area is modified and loses the current input focus.
		select	Text is selected within a text area.
		keyDown	The user presses a key.
		keyUp	The user releases a key.
		keyPress	The user presses and releases a key.
button	`<INPUT TYPE = "button">`	click	A button is clicked.
		blur	A button loses the input
		focus	A button gains the input focus.
		mouseDown	A user presses the left mouse button over a button.
		mouseUp	A user releases the left mouse button over a button.

Continued on next page

TABLE 4.1 CONTINUED: Events Defined by JavaScript

HTML Element	HTML Tags	JavaScript Event	Description
submit	`<INPUT TYPE = "submit">`	click	A submit button is clicked.
		blur	A submit button loses the input focus.
		focus	A submit button gains the input focus.
reset	`<INPUT TYPE = "reset">`	click	A reset button is clicked.
		blur	A reset button loses the input focus.
		focus	A reset button gains the input focus.
radio button	`<INPUT TYPE = "radio">`	click	A radio button is clicked.
		blur	A radio button loses the input focus.
		focus	A radio button gains the input focus.
checkbox	`<INPUT TYPE = "checkbox">`	click	A checkbox is clicked.
		blur	A checkbox loses the input focus.
		focus	A checkbox gains the input focus.
file upload	`<INPUT TYPE = "file">`	blur	A file upload form element loses the input focus.
		change	A user selects a file to be uploaded.
		focus	A file upload form element gains the input focus.
selection	`<SELECT> ... </SELECT>`	blur	A selection element loses the current input focus.
		focus	A selection element receives the current input focus.
		change	A selection element is modified and loses the current input focus.

NOTE   Internet Explorer 4 and later define many events besides those identified in Table 4.1. However, if you use those events, your scripts will not work correctly under Navigator. Throughout this book, I focus on showing you how to write scripts that work with both browsers. Appendix A, "Comparing JavaScript and JScript," provides information about Internet Explorer-only events.

NOTE   Some events can be a combination of other events. For example, the `click` event involves `mouseDown` and `mouseUp` events.

JavaScript recognizes special event-handling attributes for each of the HTML elements identified in Table 4.1. These attributes are used to specify the JavaScript code to be executed in response to a particular event. For example, suppose you wanted to handle the event associated with a user moving the mouse over a particular link. You would connect the link to the event-handling code as follows:

```
<A HREF="http://www.jaworski.com" onMouseOver="event-handling code">
text associated with link</A>
```

The onMouseOver attribute identifies the event handler to be associated with the mouseOver event. The actual code is placed between the quotes. Listing 4.1 provides an example of using the onMouseOver attribute.

Listing 4.1   Example Event Handler (ch04-01.htm)

```
<HTML>
<HEAD>
<TITLE>Example Event Handler</TITLE>
</HEAD>
<BODY>
<H1>Example Event Handler</H1>
<P><A HREF="http://www.jaworski.com/javascript"
onMouseOver=
 "alert('Link to the Mastering JavaScript and JScript Home
 Page.')">Move your mouse over this link and a popup window is
 displayed.</A></P>
</BODY>
</HTML>
```

In Listing 4.1, the JavaScript event-handling code is the following:

```
alert('Link to the Mastering JavaScript and JScript Home Page.')
```

This code consists of a call to the `alert()` method of the `window` object with the string `'Link to the Mastering JavaScript and JScript Home Page.'` passed as a parameter. The `alert()` method displays a popup window with the specified text. Figure 4.2 shows the Web page that is displayed before the mouse is moved over the link. Figure 4.3 shows the popup window that is displayed as the result of handling the `mouseOver` event. Note that if you click the link, the popup window is not displayed. The `click` event is handled by a different event handler. This event handler is specified by the `onClick` attribute.

FIGURE 4.2:

Initial display of the event-handling example from Listing 4.1

FIGURE 4.3:

Popup window resulting from `mouseOver` event of Listing 4.1

The attribute for the `mouseOver` event is `onMouseOver`. The JavaScript code that is executed as the result of the event is provided as the attribute value of the onMouseOver attribute. In general, the name of the event-handling attribute is the name of the event prefixed by *on*. The attributes are case insensitive, which means that you can use **onMouseOver**, **onmouseover**, **ONMOUSEOVER**, or any other upper- and lowercase character combinations.

WARNING   In some rare cases, Internet Explorer only handles an event if the event attribute is uppercase. This is an Internet Explorer bug.

Table 4.2 lists and describes the event-handling attributes of the HTML elements that were presented in Table 4.1. In the following section, you'll learn how to write event handlers for each of these attributes.

TABLE 4.2: Event-Handling Attributes

Event-Handling Attribute	Identifies Code to Execute under These Circumstances
onAbort	The loading of an image is aborted as the result of a user action.
onBlur	A document, window, frame set, or form element loses the current input focus.
onChange	A text field, text area, file upload field, or selection is modified and loses the current input focus.
onClick	A link, client-side image map area, or form element is clicked.
onDblClick	A link, client-side image map area, or document is clicked.
onDragDrop	A dragged object is dropped in a window or frame.
onError	An error occurs during the loading of an image, window, or frame.
onFocus	A document, window, frame set, or form element receives the current input focus.
onKeyDown	The user presses a key.
onKeyPress	The user presses and releases a key.
onKeyUp	The user releases a key.
onLoad	An image, document, or frame set is loaded.
onMouseDown	The user presses a mouse button.
onMouseMove	The user moves the mouse.

Continued on next page

TABLE 4.2 CONTINUED: Event-Handling Attributes

Event-Handling Attribute	Identifies Code to Execute under These Circumstances
onMouseOut	The mouse is moved out of a link or an area of a client-side image map.
onMouseOver	The mouse is moved over a link or an area of a client-side image map.
onMouseUp	The user releases a mouse button.
onMove	The user moves a window or frame.
onReset	A user resets a form by clicking on the form's reset button.
onResize	The user resizes a window or frame.
onSelect	Text is selected in a text field or text area.
onSubmit	A form is submitted.
onUnload	The user exits a document or frame set.

NOTE From now on, I'll follow Netscape's approach and refer to events by the names of their event-handling attributes.

Handling JavaScript Events

To handle any of the JavaScript events identified in Table 4.1, all you have to do is include the event-handling attribute for that event in an appropriate HTML tag and then specify the event-handling JavaScript code as the attribute's value. This usually takes the form of a call to an event-handling function. You've seen an example of this in Listing 4.1. In the following subsections, you'll encounter many more examples of JavaScript event-handling. Before I go off to develop these examples, I'll spend a short time discussing the best way to insert code for the value of an event-handling attribute.

In general, you can insert any JavaScript code for the value of an event-handling attribute. However, if you surround the attribute value with double quotes ("), you must use single quotes (') within your event-handling code. Likewise, if you use single quotes to surround the attribute value, you must use double quotes within your event-handling code. Multiple JavaScript statements must be separated by semi-colons (;). Listing 4.2 provides an example of an event handler that inserts multiple statements within the event-handling attribute.

Listing 4.2   **Event Handler with Multiple Statements in Attribute Value (ch04-01.htm)**

```
<HTML>
<HEAD>
<TITLE>Event Handler With Multiple Statements</TITLE>
<SCRIPT LANGUAGE="JavaScript">
<!-
count=0
//->
</SCRIPT>
</HEAD>
<BODY>
<H1>Event Handler With Multiple Statements</H1>
<P><A HREF="http://www.jaworski.com" ONMOUSEOVER='++count;
alert("You moved your mouse here "+count+" times!")'>Displays
the number of times you move your mouse over this link.</A></P>
</BODY>
</HTML>
```

In the above example, the variable count is initialized to 0 in the document's head. The onMouseOver event handler consists of the following statements:

```
++count; alert("You moved your mouse here "+count+" times!")
```

The semicolon is needed to separate the two statements. The first statement, ++count, increments the count each time the mouse passes over the link. The second statement creates a popup window that displays this information to the user. Figure 4.4 shows how this information is displayed.

FIGURE 4.4:

Popup window that displays the number of times a link was passed over (Listing 4.2)

As a matter of good style, it is best to have a single function call as the value of an event-handling attribute. This makes the event-handling code easier to debug, more modular, and more capable of being reused in other Web pages. Listing 4.3 shows a more complex event handler that is accessed via a single function call.

Listing 4.3   Using Functions as Event Handlers (ch04-03.htm)

```
<HTML>
<HEAD>
<TITLE>Using functions as event handlers</TITLE>
<SCRIPT LANGUAGE="JavaScript">
<!-
function confirmLink() {
 alert("The contents of this link may be objectionable to anyone over
the age of ten.")
 if(confirm("Are you ten years old or younger?")) {
  window.location="http://www.jaworski.com"
 }
}
//->
</SCRIPT>
</HEAD>
<BODY>
<H1>Using functions as event handlers</H1>
<P><A HREF="somewhere" onClick="return false" onMouseOver="confirm-
Link()">Confirms
whether you want to connect via this link.</A></P>
</BODY>
</HTML>
```

The confirmLink() function is defined in the head of the document. This function is the event handler for the onMouseOver event of the link defined in the body of the document. The confirmLink() function invokes the alert() method of the current window to display a warning to the user. This message is shown in Figure 4.5. It then uses the current window's confirm() method to determine the user's age (see Figure 4.6). If the user presses Cancel in the confirm dialog box, then the confirm() method returns *false* and no further action is performed. If the user presses OK in the confirm dialog box then the confirm() method returns *true* and the location property of the current window is set to a new URL. This causes the new document to be loaded without the user ever clicking on a link to that document. In fact, the destination of the link in the body of the Web document is just the dummy URL "somewhere".

However, the clicking of this link is disabled by setting the onClick event handler to return *false*. Whenever a *false* value is returned, the action associated with a click event is canceled. You'll learn more about this feature in later examples.

FIGURE 4.5:

Age warning popup window (Listing 4.3)

FIGURE 4.6:

Confirming the user's age (Listing 4.3)

The important point about Listing 4.3 is that the onMouseOver event handling is performed via a single function call to confirmLink(). This allows confirmLink() to be developed without having to worry about quoting or trying to fit all of its statements in a single attribute value. The result is a much cleaner implementation of the event handler.

NOTE   The event-handling examples I present in this chapter are geared to providing a simple explanation of the mechanics of event handling. I'll develop more sophisticated examples throughout the course of the book after I've covered JavaScript objects beginning in the next chapter.

Handling Link Events

So far, you've seen several examples of handling events associated with links. Let's explore link event handling further before moving on to handling events associated with other HTML elements.

There are nine events that are associated with links, as shown in Table 4.1. In Listings 4.1 through 4.3, I already covered the handling of the onMouseOver event. These examples showed how the onMouseOver event can be used to provide the user with warnings or other information about a link before the user clicks on it. Besides onMouseOver, two other link-related attributes, onMouseOut and onClick, are frequently used with link events.

The onMouseOut event is similar to the onMouseOver event, except that it is triggered when the user *leaves* a link, not when the mouse approaches the link. As such, onMouseOut event handlers generally try to provide information to a user after they have left a link. Listing 4.4 provides an example of an onMouseOut event handler.

Listing 4.4   **Handling *onMouseOut* for Links (ch04-04.htm)**

```
<HTML>
<HEAD>
<TITLE>Handling onMouseOut for links</TITLE>
<SCRIPT LANGUAGE="JavaScript">
<!-
function advertiseLink() {
 alert("The ACME Widget Company is having a 50% off sale on their best
widgets.")
 if(confirm("Would you like to visit them and save 50% on an ACME wid-
get?")) {
  window.location="http://www.jaworski.com/javascript/acme.htm"
 }
}
//->
</SCRIPT>
</HEAD>
<BODY>
<H1>Handling onMouseOut for links</H1>
<P><A HREF="somewhere" ONMOUSEOUT="advertiseLink()">Tells you why you
should connect to this link.</A></P>
</BODY>
</HTML>
```

In the above listing, an advertiseLink() function is defined in the document head. This function is set up to be the event handler for onMouseOut events and is set in the link defined in the body of the HTML document. When a user moves the mouse away from the link, the advertiseLink() function is invoked. The advertiseLink() function first notifies the user via the alert() method that the ACME Widget Company is having a 50-percent-off sale (Figure 4.7). It then uses a confirm() method to ask the user if they want to visit the ACME Widget Company (Figure 4.8). If the user responds by clicking OK, then `advertiseLink()` sets the `location` property of the window to cause the ACME Web page to be loaded (Figure 4.9). If the user clicks Cancel, then the event handling is terminated.

FIGURE 4.7:

Alerting the user to ACME Widget Company's sale (Listing 4.4)

FIGURE 4.8:

Asking the user to link to ACME Widget Company (Listing 4.4)

FIGURE 4.9:

The ACME Widget Company home page is loaded (Listing 4.4)

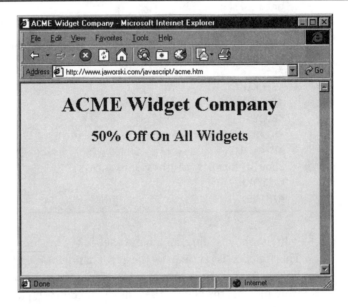

The advertiseLink() function presented above is just one example of how the onMouseOut event can be handled. Of course, it may be an annoying nuisance to your Web users if you badger them with an advertisement every time they refrain from following a link, so exercise a little creativity when you use anything similar to this example.

Another link event handling attribute, onClick, allows the clicking of a hyperlink to be handled in a custom manner. If the onClick event handler returns the value *false*, then the action associated with the click—in this case, the linking to a new document—is canceled. This capability lets the onClick event handler query the user to confirm or deny whether they want to proceed with a link. Listing 4.5 provides an example of this type of onClick event handling.

Listing 4.5   **Handling *onClick* for Links (ch04-05.htm)**

```
<HTML>
<HEAD>
<TITLE>Handling onClick for links</TITLE>
<SCRIPT LANGUAGE="JavaScript">
<!-
function confirmLink() {

  alert("This is the Mastering JavaScript and JScript Home Page.")
  return confirm("Are you sure you want to load this document?")
}
//->
</SCRIPT>
</HEAD>
<BODY>
<H1>Handling onClick for links</H1>
<P><A HREF="http://www.jaworski.com/javascript"
ONCLICK="return confirmLink()">Asks you to confirm
your selection of this link.</A></P>
</BODY>
</HTML>
```

The confirmLink() function is defined in the document head. It alerts the user to the fact that they have selected the Mastering JavaScript and JScript home page and then asks the user to confirm whether they want to link to this page (Figure 4.10).

FIGURE 4.10:

Confirming a user selection
(Listing 4.5)

The results of the confirm() method are then returned. Notice that in the
onClick event handler, the confirmLink() method is not invoked directly, but
rather is invoked as part of a return statement:

```
return confirmLink()
```

This is because the value returned by confirm() and confirmLink() must be
propagated to the point where the event handler was invoked in order for a false
value to cancel the action associated with the clicking of the link. Try removing
the return statement and calling confirmLink() directly. You will find that can-
celing the link is no longer an option.

Handling Window Events

Window events apply to normal HTML documents that contain a body and produce a
display; they also apply to layout documents that replace the document body with a
frame set. (*Layout documents* are used to organize the display of other documents via
frames. If you're unfamiliar with these objects, turn to online Appendix B, " Accessing
Online References" and Chapter 6, "Creating Frames and Windows," for more information.) In this section, I'll look at the event handling associated with both types of
documents. Table 4.1 lists the events that are associated with these window objects.
Listing 4.6 illustrates the handling of the onLoad and onUnload events for a normal
displayable HTML document. When the document is first loaded, the alert message
shown in Figure 4.11 is displayed. As you exit the document, the alert message shown
in Figure 4.12 is displayed.

Listing 4.6   **Handling Load Events in a Content Document (ch04-06.htm)**

```
<HTML>
<HEAD>
<TITLE>Handling load events in a content document</TITLE>
</HEAD>
<BODY onLoad="alert('Hello!')" onUnload="alert('Bye Bye!')">
```

```
<H1>Handling load events in a content document</H1>
<P>This document has a body and is displayed in typical fashion.</P>
</BODY>
</HTML>
```

FIGURE 4.11:

The onLoad message
(Listing 4.6)

FIGURE 4.12:

The onUnload message
(Listing 4.6)

The onLoad event handler is typically used to perform any necessary initialization for Web pages that use Java or plug-ins, or to make a grand entrance by playing an audio file or an animation sequence. You can use it to determine whether all required resources, such as image files, are present before beginning a script's execution. The onUnload event handler performs a similar function—terminating Java applets and plug-ins or enabling a dramatic exit. You'll see examples of using onLoad and onUnload for these purposes in later chapters. Listing 4.7 shows how onLoad and onUnload can be used with layout documents.

Listing 4.7   Handling Load Events in a Layout Document (ch04-07.htm)

```
<HTML>
<HEAD>
<TITLE>Handling load events in a layout document</TITLE>
<SCRIPT LANGUAGE="JavaScript"><!-
function selectFrames(){
 base="frames/"
```

```
newFrames=new
Array("red.htm","yellow.htm","blue.htm","green.htm","white.htm")
 window.firstFrame.location=base+newFrames[Math.round(5*Math.ran-
dom())%5]
 window.secondFrame.location=base+newFrames[Math.round(5*Math.ran-
dom())%5]
}
//->
</SCRIPT>
</HEAD>
<FRAMESET
COLS="*,*" ONLOAD="selectFrames()" ONUNLOAD="alert('Thanks for stopping
by!')">
<FRAME SRC="frames/grey.htm" NAME="firstFrame">
<FRAME SRC="frames/grey.htm" NAME="secondFrame">
</FRAMESET>
</HTML>
```

> **NOTE**
>
> If you are not familiar with Netscape frames, refer to online Appendix B, "Accessing Online References," and Chapter 6, "Creating Frames and Windows."

The HTML document shown in Listing 4.7 defines the `selectFrames()` function to handle the `onLoad` event. Before I describe the processing performed by the `setFrames()` function, I'll discuss what's going on in the frame set part of the document. The frame set tags specify that two frames are to be contained in the document. The frames are to be organized into columns with the first frame named *firstFrame* and the second named *secondFrame*. Initially, both frames display the document at the relative URL `frames/grey.htm`. The `onLoad` attribute of the frame set tag specifies that the `selectFrames()` function should handle the event associated with the frame's loading. The `onUnload` event just displays the popup window with the text *Thanks for stopping by!* when the frame set is exited.

The `selectFrames()` function randomly loads two new documents into `firstFrame` and `secondFrame`. The `newFrames` array contains the names of five documents. A document is randomly selected from the list using the `random()` and `round()` methods of the `Math` object to calculate an index into the `newFrames` array. The `location` property of `firstFrame` and `secondFrame` are set to the randomly selected documents. (You'll learn all about the `Math` and `window` objects in the next chapter.)

When you load Listing 4.7, it opens a two-frame document with both the left and right frames initially set to gray. As soon as the document is loaded, the onLoad event is generated and selectFrames() is invoked to load new frame documents as shown in Figure 4.13. When you exit the document, the message shown in Figure 4.14 is displayed.

FIGURE 4.13:

The onLoad event causes new frames to be loaded (Listing 4.7).

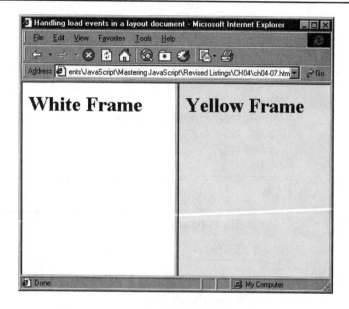

FIGURE 4.14:

The onUnload message displayed when the frame set is exited (Listing 4.7)

While the onLoad and onUnload events are generated at the beginning and end of a document's existence, the onFocus and onBlur events can be triggered several times while a document is loaded. The onFocus event is generally used to restore a document to a default starting state or to continue previously interrupted processing. The onBlur event is used to interrupt the processing being performed on a page, such as the playing of an audio file or an animation, before a new page or area within the current page is activated. Listings 4.8 through 4.10 present an example of the use of onLoad and onUnload event handlers. The frames are organized in column order.

Listing 4.8　　**Defining the Frame Set (ch04-08.htm)**

```
<!- ch04-08.htm ->
<HTML>
<HEAD>
<TITLE>Handling onFocus and onBlur events in a frame</TITLE>
</HEAD>
<FRAMESET COLS="*,*">
<FRAME SRC="frames/doc1.htm">
<FRAME SRC="frames/doc2.htm">
</FRAMESET>
</HTML>
```

Listing 4.9　　**Handling *onBlur* and *onFocus* in Frames (doc1.htm)**

```
<!- doc1.htm ->
<HTML>
<HEAD>
<TITLE>Document 1</TITLE>
<SCRIPT LANGUAGE="JavaScript">
function gotFocus() {
 document.bgColor="#FFFFFF"
}
function lostFocus() {
 document.bgColor="#FF0000";
}
</SCRIPT>
</HEAD>
<BODY onFocus="gotFocus()" onBlur="lostFocus()" BGCOLOR="#FF0000">
<H1>Document 1</H1>
</BODY>
</HTML>
```

Listing 4.10 **Displaying an Alternative Background Color (doc2.htm)**

```
<!- doc2.htm ->
<HTML>
<HEAD>
<TITLE>Document 2</TITLE>
</HEAD>
<BODY BGCOLOR="#FF0080">
<H1>Document 2</H1>
</BODY>
</HTML>
```

The file doc1.htm is the heart of this example. When it is loaded, it displays a reddish-orange color and lists a simple heading. The body tag specifies that the event handlers, gotFocus() and lostFocus(), are used for the onFocus and onBlur events. The document head defines these functions. The gotFocus() function sets the background color of the frame occupied by the document to white. The lostFocus() function resets the color of the frame back to its original color.

Figure 4.15 shows the original state of the frame set. Figure 4.16 shows how the background of the first frame changes to white when it receives the input focus.

FIGURE 4.15:

The frame set in its initial state (Listings 4.8 through 4.10)

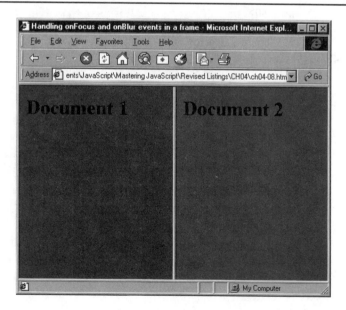

FIGURE 4.16:

The frame set after the first frame receives the input focus (Listings 4.8 through 4.10)

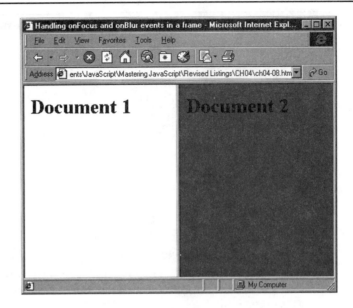

The file doc2.htm is a simple document that merely displays a heading and dark pink background color. It is used to provide contrast for doc1.htm.

Handling Image Events

Image events are used to monitor the progress of image loading. Usually, images are the elements in a Web document that take the longest to load. In many applications, it is important to know whether they have been loaded, are in the process of loading, or have had their loading interrupted. The image events provide this capability. They are summarized in Table 4.1. The onLoad event occurs when an image's loading and display has been completed. In many cases, such as in an image map application, it may be important to wait for the onLoad event to occur before further processing is allowed. The onAbort and onError events are used to respond to any exceptions that may occur in the loading process. Listing 4.11 illustrates the use of these event-handling capabilities.

Listing 4.11	**Image Event Handling (ch04-11.htm)**

```
<HTML>
<HEAD>
<TITLE>Image Event Handling</TITLE>
<SCRIPT LANGUAGE="JavaScript"><!-
function imageLoaded() {
 document.bgColor="#FFFFFF"
 alert(document.images[0].src+" has been loaded.")
}
function imageAborted() {
 alert("Hey! You just aborted the loading of the last image!")
}
function imageError() {
 alert("Error loading image!")
}
//->
</SCRIPT>
</HEAD>
<BODY>
<H1>Image Event Handling</H1>
<P>An image is loaded after this paragraph.</P>
<IMG SRC="image1.gif"
 onLoad="imageLoaded()"
 onAbort="imageAborted()"
 onError="imageError()">
</BODY>
</HTML>
```

The document shown in Listing 4.11 displays a heading, a one-line paragraph, and an image. The image has event handlers that respond to the onLoad, onAbort, and onError events. The onLoad event is handled by the imageLoaded() function. When an image has been loaded, the imageLoaded() function changes the document background color to green and displays an alert dialog box that identifies the name of the image and the fact that it has been loaded. Figure 4.17 shows the document window after the onLoad event has been handled.

The onAbort event occurs as the result of a user action that causes image loading to be aborted, such as clicking the Stop button or changing to a new document. It is handled by the imageAborted() function, which simply notifies the user that they have caused the image's loading to be aborted. Figure 4.18 shows the result of processing the onAbort event.

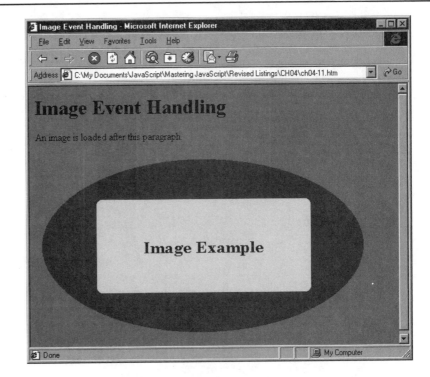

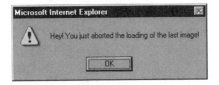

The onError event occurs as the result of an error that prevents an image from loading. A common example of this type of an error is the failure of a Web browser to locate the image. The imageError() function handles the onError event by displaying a notification to the user. Figure 4.19 shows how the onError event is handled as the result of the image file being moved from its specified location.

FIGURE 4.19:

Handling the onError event
for images (Listing 4.11)

Handling Image Map Events

Image maps are a popular feature found on many Web pages. An image map consists of an image that is divided into different areas or regions. When the user clicks on a particular location within the image, a connection is made to the URL associated with that location. This allows the image map to exhibit different responses based on the area clicked by the user. Figure 4.20 summarizes the basic mechanics of image maps.

FIGURE 4.20:

How image maps work

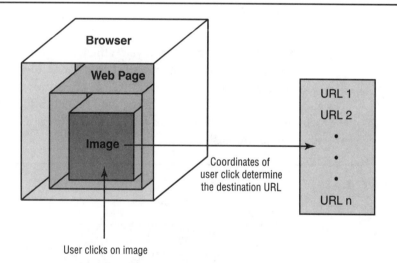

JavaScript supports two types of image maps: *server-side image maps* and *client-side image maps*. Server-side image maps were developed first. As their name implies, most of the processing is performed on the server. The server contains a map file that defines the various regions of the image and associates these regions with specific URLs. When a user clicks on a location in the image, the coordinates of the location are passed to the Web server. The server determines which region was selected and returns the URL associated with that region. The user's browser then connects to this URL. Figure 4.21 summarizes server-side image map processing.

FIGURE 4.21:

How server-side image maps work

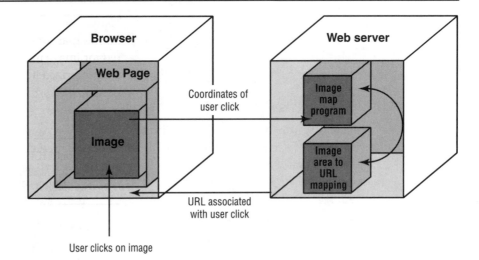

Client-side image maps are a very efficient improvement over server-side image maps. Instead of the map file being maintained on the server, it is embedded in the map element of the HTML file being browsed. This allows the browser to perform all of the processing required to determine which map area the user selected and to choose the destination URL. Figure 4.22 summarizes client-side image map processing.

FIGURE 4.22:

How client-side image maps work

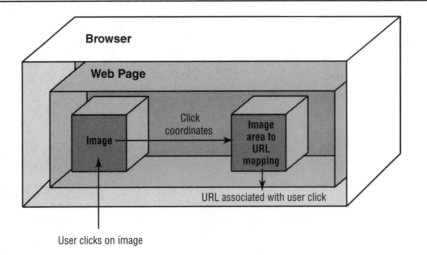

NOTE   Online Appendix B, "Accessing Online References," provides information on the HTML tags used to implement client-side image maps.

JavaScript provides event-handling capabilities that support the processing of client-side image maps. The events supported for image maps are a subset of those that were covered for links, which are summarized in Table 4.1. These events enable custom handling of user image-map clicks and mouse movements around a particular map area.

TIP   In order to use the onMouseOver, onMouseOut, and onDblClick events with the AREA tag, you may have to set the HREF attribute. If the NOHREF attribute is present, these events may not function properly.

Listing 4.12 presents an example of the handling of onMouseOver and onMouseOut events. The document displays a heading and an image that is used as a client-side image map. Note that the image sets the USEMAP attribute to #blockman, which is the name of the image map described by the map tags. The image used in the image map is blockman.gif. It is shown in Figure 4.23 along with the coordinates of various points within the image. These coordinates are used to create the parameters for the area tags that are enclosed by the map tags.

Listing 4.12   Image Map Event Handling (ch04-12.htm)

```
<HTML>
<HEAD>
<TITLE>Image Map Event Handling</TITLE>
<SCRIPT LANGUAGE="JavaScript"><!-
firstTimeOnHead=true
function onHead() {
 if(firstTimeOnHead) {
  alert("You're on my head!")
  firstTimeOnHead=false
 }
}
function myEye() {
 alert("Be careful or you'll poke out my eye!")
}
function myNose() {
 alert("Aaacchhooo!")
}
```

```
function myMouth() {
 alert("Get out of my mouth!")
}
//->
</SCRIPT>
</HEAD>
<BODY>
<H1>Image Map Event Handling</H1>
<IMG SRC="blockman.gif" USEMAP="#blockman">
<MAP NAME="blockman">
<AREA COORDS="80,88,120,125" HREF="ch04-10.htm"
onMouseOver="myEye()">
<AREA COORDS="169,88,208,125" HREF="ch04-10.htm"
onMouseOver="myEye()">
<AREA COORDS="124,147,165,181" HREF="ch04-10.htm"
onMouseOut="myNose()">
<AREA COORDS="92,210,192,228" HREF="ch04-10.htm"
onMouseOut="myMouth()">
<AREA COORDS="6,4,292,266" HREF="ch04-10.htm"
onMouseOver="onHead()">
</MAP>
</BODY>
</HTML>
```

FIGURE 4.23:

Coordinates within
blockman.gif
(Listing 4.12)

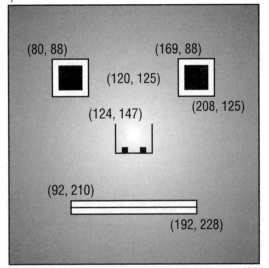

The first and second <AREA> tags (and corresponding area objects) describe rectangles that enclose block man's eyes. Both tags specify that the myEye() function should be called to handle the onMouseOver event. The third area tag describes the rectangle formed by block man's nose. It specifies that the myNose() function should handle the onMouseOut event. The fourth area tag describes the rectangle formed by block man's mouth. It specifies that the onMouseOut event should be handled by the myMouth() function. Finally, the fifth area tag describes the larger rectangle that handles block man's head. This tag handles the onMouseOver event via the onHead() function.

The area tags are processed in a first-come, first-handled order. The browser checks the location of a mouse action with each area tag in the order that the tags appear in the map tag. If the browser gets to the last tag, it is processing a mouse action that occurred outside the other area tags but within the outline of block man's head.

The event-handling functions in this listing are quite simple. The myEye(), myNose(), and myMouth() functions display cute messages using the alert() method. The onHead() function is just a tad more sophisticated. The firstTime-OnHead variable is initialized to *true* when the HTML document is first loaded. The onHead() function displays a message when firstTimeOnHead is *true* and then sets firstTimeOnHead to *false*. This causes the alert message to be displayed only once. Figure 4.24 shows the Web page displayed by a browser as the result of handling the initial onMouseOver event for block man's head.

FIGURE 4.24:

Handling onMouseOver
for AREA tags (Listing 4.12)

Handling Form Events

So far, you have learned to handle events associated with links, windows, images and image maps. However, in most practical JavaScript applications the event handling will be associated with forms. Forms provide a number of sophisticated graphical user interface (GUI) controls such as buttons, checkboxes, and text fields. These controls are associated with a number of events that reflect user actions, such as clicking a button or checkbox or selecting text in a text field. These events are summarized in Table 4.3.

TABLE 4.3: Form Events

Event	Form Element	Event-Handling Attribute
The form is submitted by the user.	Overall form	onSubmit
The form is reset by the user.	Overall form	onReset
A form element loses the input focus.	All form elements	onBlur
A form element receives the input focus.	All form elements	onFocus
A form element is modified and loses the current input focus.	File upload field, select field, text field, or text area	onChange
Text is selected within the text field or text area.	Text field or text area	onSelect
A button or checkbox is clicked.	Button, submit button, reset button, radio button, or checkbox	onClick
A mouse button is pressed or released.	Button	onMouseDown, onMouseUp
A key is pressed, released, or pressed and released.	Text area	onKeyDown, onKeyUp, onKeyPress

I'll present three examples that cover many of the events in Table 4.3. Other examples will be presented in subsequent chapters. The first example, shown in Listing 4.13, illustrates events associated with text field and text area buttons and the onSubmit form event. The second example is presented in Listing 4.14. It illustrates the onClick event used with different types of buttons and checkboxes. The third example is shown in Listing 4.15 and shows how the onChange selection element event is handled.

Listing 4.13   **Text Field and Text Area Event Handling (ch04-13.htm)**

```
<HTML>
<HEAD>
<TITLE>Text Field and Text Area Events</TITLE>
<SCRIPT LANGUAGE="JavaScript"><!-
function nameSelect() {
 if(isBlank(""+document.contest.last.value)) {
  document.contest.last.value="Surname"
  document.contest.last.focus()
  document.contest.last.select()
 }
}
function isBlank(s) {
 var len=s.length
 var i
 for(i=0;i<len;++i) {
  if(s.charAt(i)!=" ") return false
 }
 return true
}
function validate(fieldName,fieldValue) {
 if(isBlank(fieldValue)) {
  alert(fieldName+" cannot be left blank.")
  return false
 }
 return true
}
function validateEmail() {

 validate("The e-mail field",document.contest.email.value)
}
function validateEssay() {
 validate("The essay field",document.contest.essay.value)
}
function validateForm() {
 if(!validate("The last name field",document.contest.last.value))
  return false
```

```
  if(!validate("The e-mail field",document.contest.email.value))
   return false
  if(!validate("The essay field",document.contest.essay.value))
   return false
}
//-></SCRIPT>
</HEAD>
<BODY>
<FORM NAME="contest" ONSUBMIT="return validateForm()">
<H2 ALIGN="CENTER">Contest Application</H2>
<P>Last name:
<INPUT TYPE="TEXT" NAME="last" SIZE="16"
 ONCHANGE="nameSelect()">
First name:
<INPUT TYPE="TEXT" NAME="first" SIZE="12">
Middle Initial:
<INPUT TYPE="TEXT" NAME="initial" SIZE="2"></P>
<P>E-mail address:
<INPUT TYPE="TEXT" NAME="email" SIZE="32"
 ONCHANGE="validateEmail()"></P>
<P>In 50 words or less, state why you should win the contest:</P>
<TEXTAREA NAME="essay" ROWS="5" COLS="40"
 ONCHANGE="validateEssay()"></TEXTAREA>
<P>Submit your winning entry:
<INPUT TYPE="SUBMIT" NAME="go" VALUE="Make me a winner!"></P>
</FORM>
</BODY>
</HTML>
```

The previous listing presents the contest application form shown in Figure 4.25. Event handlers are associated with the last, email, and essay fields of the form as well as with the form as a whole. The last and email fields are text fields and the essay field is a text area field. The onChange event of the last field uses the nameSelect() function to handle the event associated with the changes to the field's contents. The nameSelect() function uses the isBlank() function to determine if the user made changes to the field that resulted in it becoming blank. If the field is left blank, then the field's value is set to Surname, the current focus is set to the field, and the text is selected. Figure 4.26 shows the result of the nameSelect() processing.

FIGURE 4.25:

Contest application form
(Listing 4.13)

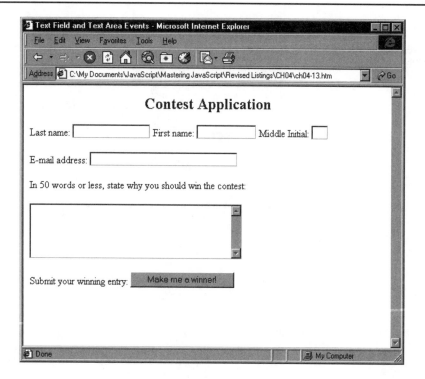

The `email` field uses the `validateEmail()` function to handle the `onChange` event. This function invokes the `validate()` function to check whether the field had been left blank and uses the `alert()` function to send a notification to the user that the field cannot be blank. The `validateEssay()` function is used in the same manner by the `essay` field. The `form` tag specifies that the `onSubmit` event should be handled by the statement `return validateForm()`. When the user clicks the button labeled *Make me a winner!*, the `validateForm()` function is invoked to check whether the `last`, `email`, or `essay` fields are blank and to notify the user if any field is blank. It returns *false* to prevent the form from being submitted with these fields being blank.

The script shown in Listing 4.14 presents the survey form shown in Figure 4.27. This form illustrates the handling of the `onClick` event for buttons and checkboxes. When any of the radio buttons or checkboxes are checked, the `results` text field displays the checked fields. When the button labeled *To Upper Case* is clicked, the `results` field is converted to uppercase. When the Submit or Reset button is clicked, a confirmation window is displayed. Note that the effect of the Submit button may be canceled—with the result that the form is not submitted.

FIGURE 4.26:

Result of nameSelect()
processing (Listing 4.13)

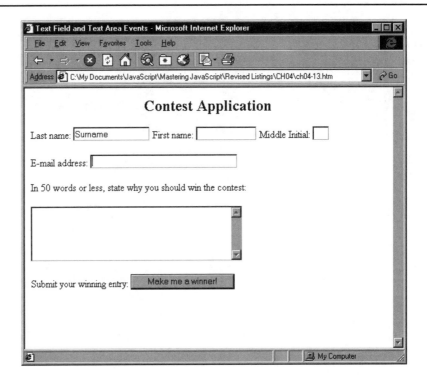

Listing 4.14   Button and Checkbox Event Handling (ch04-14.htm)

```
<HTML>
<HEAD>
<TITLE>Button and Check Box Events</TITLE>
<SCRIPT LANGUAGE="JavaScript"><!-
function showResults() {
 var resultMsg=""
 if(document.survey.age[0].checked) resultMsg+="under 30, "
 if(document.survey.age[1].checked) resultMsg+="between 30 and 60, "
 if(document.survey.age[2].checked) resultMsg+="over 60, "
 if(document.survey.sex[0].checked) resultMsg+="male, "
 if(document.survey.sex[1].checked) resultMsg+="female, "
 if(document.survey.reading.checked) resultMsg+="reading, "
 if(document.survey.eating.checked) resultMsg+="eating, "
 if(document.survey.sleeping.checked) resultMsg+="sleeping, "
 document.survey.results.value=resultMsg
}
```

```
function upperCaseResults() {
 var newResults=document.survey.results.value
 document.survey.results.value=newResults.toUpperCase()
}
//-></SCRIPT>
</HEAD>
<BODY>
<FORM NAME="survey">
<H2 ALIGN="CENTER">Survey Form</H2>
<P><B>Age:</B>
<INPUT TYPE="RADIO" NAME="age" VALUE="under30"
 ONCLICK="showResults()">Under 30
<INPUT TYPE="RADIO" NAME="age" VALUE="30to60"
 ONCLICK="showResults()">30 - 60
<INPUT TYPE="RADIO" NAME="age" VALUE="over60"
 ONCLICK="showResults()">Over 60</P>
<P><B>Sex: </B>
<INPUT TYPE="RADIO" NAME="sex" VALUE="male"
 ONCLICK="showResults()">Male
<INPUT TYPE="RADIO" NAME="sex" VALUE="female"
 ONCLICK="showResults()">Female</P>
<P><B>Interests: </B>
<INPUT TYPE="CHECKBOX" NAME="reading"
 ONCLICK="showResults()"> Reading
<INPUT TYPE="CHECKBOX" NAME="eating"
 ONCLICK="showResults()"> Eating
<INPUT TYPE="CHECKBOX" NAME="sleeping"
 ONCLICK="showResults()"> Sleeping</P>
<P>
<INPUT TYPE="BUTTON" NAME="makeUpper"
 VALUE="To Upper Case" ONCLICK="upperCaseResults()"></P>
<P><B>Results: </B><INPUT TYPE="TEXT" NAME="results" SIZE="50"></P>
<INPUT TYPE="SUBMIT" NAME="submit" VALUE="Submit"
 ONCLICK='return confirm("Sure?")'>
<INPUT TYPE="RESET" NAME="reset"
 ONCLICK='return confirm("Sure?")'>
</FORM>
</BODY>
</HTML>
```

FIGURE 4.27:

Survey form (Listing 4.14)

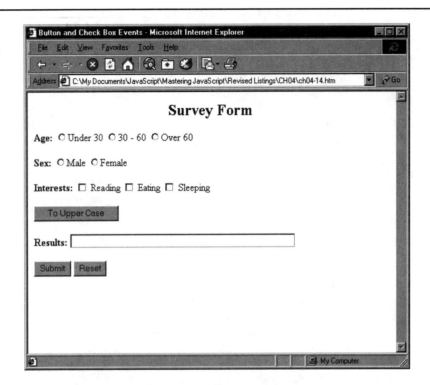

The radio and checkboxes in Listing 4.14 use a single event-handling function—showResults(). This function checks the status of these fields and creates a text message, which it displays in the results field. The upperCaseResults() function handles the onClick event of the makeUpper button by converting the contents of the results field to uppercase. You'll learn more about the mechanics of how this happens in the next chapter on JavaScript objects.

The script in Listing 4.15 presents a menu for the Web Diner page, as shown in Figure 4.28. This form consists of a multiple selection list, from which fast food items are selected, and a text area field, which displays the results of the user's selection. The updateOrder() function handles the onChange event associated with the selection list. It checks through all of the options in the selection list to see which have been selected and displays a formatted text string in the text area field which summarizes the user's selection.

Listing 4.15   Selection List Event Handling (ch04-15.htm)

```
<HTML>
<HEAD>
<TITLE>Handling Selection List Events</TITLE>
<SCRIPT LANGUAGE="JavaScript"><!-
function updateOrder() {
 var orderString=""
 var n=document.diner.entries.length
 for(i=0;i<n;++i) {
  if(document.diner.entries.options[i].selected) {
   orderString+=document.diner.entries.options[i].value+"\n"
  }
 }
 document.diner.summary.value=orderString
}
//-></SCRIPT>
</HEAD>
<BODY>
<FORM NAME="diner">
<H2 ALIGN="CENTER">The Web Diner</H2>
<P><B>Place your order:</B></P>
<SELECT NAME="entries" SIZE="4" MULTIPLE="MULTIPLE"
 ONCHANGE="updateOrder()">
<OPTION VALUE="Hamburger">Hamburger</OPTION>
<OPTION VALUE="Hot Dog">Hot Dog</OPTION>
<OPTION VALUE="Chicken Sandwich">Chicken Sandwich</OPTION>
<OPTION VALUE="French Fries">French Fries</OPTION>
<OPTION VALUE="Onion Rings">Onion Rings</OPTION>
<OPTION VALUE="Soda">Soda</OPTION>
<OPTION VALUE="Milk Shake">Milk Shake</OPTION>
<OPTION VALUE="Coffee">Coffee</OPTION></SELECT>
<P><B>You ordered: </B></P>
<P>
<TEXTAREA NAME="summary" ROWS="4" COLS="20"></TEXTAREA></P>
<P><INPUT TYPE="SUBMIT" NAME="order" VALUE="Let me have it!"></P>
</FORM>
</BODY>
</HTML>
```

FIGURE 4.28:

The Web Diner menu
(Listing 4.15)

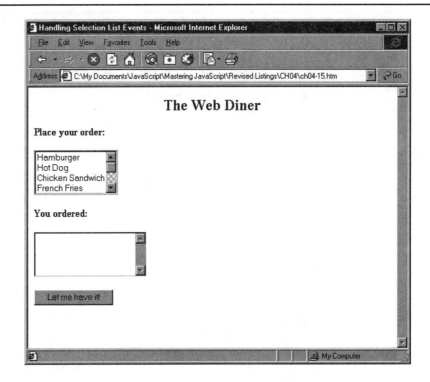

Setting Event Handlers from within JavaScript

Until now, I have been explicitly identifying event handlers using the event attribute of the tag to which the event handlers apply. You can also identify event handlers from within JavaScript. This capability adds greater flexibility in specifying event handlers.

NOTE   The capability to set event handlers from within JavaScript was introduced with JavaScript 1.1.

As you'll learn in Chapter 5, "Working with Objects," most of the individual elements of an HTML document can be accessed as objects that are automatically created by JavaScript. These objects have properties that specify the values of data items associated with the object. For example, in Listing 4.15, the entries selection list is identified by the following object:

```
document.diner.entries
```

The number of options in the selection list is a property of the list and is identified by the following:

```
document.diner.entries.length
```

Objects that are associated with events, such as links and form elements, have properties that identify the functions used to handle these events. For example, in Listing 4.15, the onChange event handler associated with the entries selection list is identified by the following property:

```
document.diner.entries.onchange
```

Instead of specifying updateOrder() as the event handler for entries in its input tag definition, we could have used the following JavaScript statement:

```
document.diner.entries.onchange=updateOrder
```

If we used this approach, the above statement would need to be placed in a script that is executed *after* the entries input tag is defined, or else a JavaScript error would result.

When an event-handling function is explicitly assigned to the event property of an object, the trailing parentheses () are omitted. It is important that both the object and the function be defined prior to the assignment statement.

TIP   Use all lowercase letters for the event property. Some browsers will not recognize the property if it is mixed case.

Listing 4.16 illustrates the process of setting event handlers from within JavaScript, and Figure 4.29 shows the Web page that is generated. It consists of a single Click Me! button that, when clicked, causes the text *Set by handler1* or *Set by handler2* to be alternately displayed in a text field. The input tag of the Click Me! button does not identify a event handler via the onClick attribute. Instead, a script follows the form definition that assigns handler1 to document.test.clickMe.onclick. This script causes the initial event handler for the onClick event of the Click Me! button to be handler1().

Listing 4.16   Setting Event Handlers from within JavaScript (ch04-16.htm)

```
<HTML>
<HEAD>
<TITLE>Setting event handlers from within JavaScript</TITLE>
<SCRIPT LANGUAGE="JavaScript"><!-
function handler1() {
 document.test.result.value="Set by handler1"
 document.test.clickMe.onclick=handler2
}
function handler2() {
 document.test.result.value="Set by handler2"
 document.test.clickMe.onclick=handler1
}
//-></SCRIPT>
</HEAD>
<BODY>
<FORM NAME="test">
<INPUT TYPE="BUTTON" NAME="clickMe" VALUE="Click Me!">
<P><INPUT TYPE="TEXT" NAME="result" SIZE="20"></P>
</FORM>
<SCRIPT LANGUAGE="JavaScript"><!-
 document.test.clickMe.onclick=handler1
//-></SCRIPT>
</BODY>
</HTML>
```

When handler1() is invoked to handle the onClick event, it sets the result text field to *Set by handler1* and then changes the onClick event handler to handler2(). The next time the Click Me! button is clicked, handler2() handles the onClick event. The handler2() function sets the result field to *Set by handler2* and changes the onClick event handler back to handler1().

This simple example illustrates the flexibility and power of explicitly assigning event handlers from within JavaScript. There is an additional benefit to assigning event handlers from within JavaScript. If you set the LANGUAGE attribute of the SCRIPT tag to anything other than "JavaScript", then earlier browsers, such as Navigator 2, will not be able to see your scripts. If you also use an event-handling attribute to set an event handler, then older browsers will look for an event-handling function and not be able to find it (because it is hidden by the LANGUAGE attribute). This results in a scripting error. On the other hand, if you specify event handlers from within your scripts, then you can avoid this type of error.

FIGURE 4.29:

Setting event handlers
from within JavaScript
(Listing 4.16)

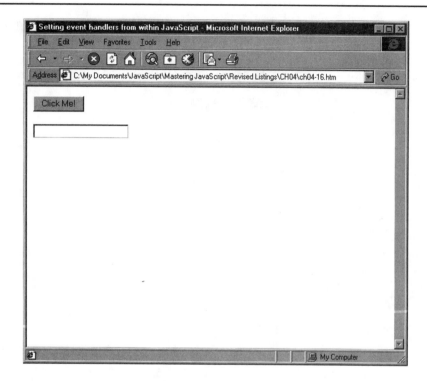

Event Simulation Methods

In the previous section, you learned how HTML elements are represented by
JavaScript objects, and how certain properties of these objects can be used to
assign event handlers. In addition to these properties, some objects have methods
that can be used to *simulate* the occurrence of events. When an event simulation
method is invoked, the object to which it refers acts as if the event is taking place.
For example, button objects have the click() method that, when invoked, causes
the button's event handler to be invoked.

Listing 4.17 provides an example of event simulation. Figure 4.30 shows the
Web page displayed by this document. It consists of two buttons—Button 1 and
Button 2.

FIGURE 4.30:

An event simulation
example (Listing 4.17)

Listing 4.17	**Simulating Events (ch04-17.htm)**

```
<HTML>
<HEAD>
<TITLE>Simulating Events</TITLE>
<SCRIPT><!-
function button1Clicked() {
 document.test.button2.click()
}
function button2Clicked() {
 alert("Button 2 was clicked!")
}
//-></SCRIPT>
</HEAD>
<BODY>
<FORM NAME="test">
<INPUT TYPE="BUTTON" NAME="button1" VALUE="Button 1"
```

```
 ONCLICK="button1Clicked()">
 <INPUT TYPE="BUTTON" NAME="button2" VALUE="Button 2"
 ONCLICK="button2Clicked()">
 </FORM>
 </BODY>
 </HTML>
```

When you click on Button 1, the function button1Clicked() is invoked; it executes the following statement:

```
document.test.button2.click()
```

which causes Button 2 to act as if it is being clicked. This results in Button 2's event handler, button2Clicked(), being invoked. The button2Clicked() function then displays the alert message shown in Figure 4.31.

FIGURE 4.31:

Button 2's event handler is invoked (Listing 4.17).

The *event* Object

The event object was introduced in JavaScript 1.2 as a mechanism to provide additional information about events. This information is provided through the object's properties (refer to Table 4.4). As you can see from Table 4.4, the event object is implemented differently by Navigator and Internet Explorer. The properties that are available to a particular event object instance depend on the type of event that occurs and the type of browser that is executing the script. For example, a mouseDown event will have the pageX and pageY properties under Navigator and the x and y properties under Internet Explorer.

NOTE JavaScript objects, properties, and methods are covered in Chapter 5, "Working with Objects."

TABLE 4.4: Properties of the event Object

Property	Browser	Description
data	Navigator	An array of strings containing the URLs of objects dropped as the result of a **DragDrop** event.
height and width	Navigator	The height and width of a window or frame (in pixels).
pageX and pageY	Navigator	The cursor's horizontal and vertical position in pixels, relative to the page.
screenX and screenY	Navigator Internet Explorer	The cursor's horizontal and vertical position in pixels, relative to the screen.
layerX and layerY	Navigator	The cursor's horizontal and vertical position in pixels, relative to the layer in which the event occurred. When used with the resize event, layerX and layerY specify the width and height of the object to which the event is targeted.
clientX and clientY	Internet Explorer	The cursor's horizontal and vertical position in pixels, relative to the Web page in which the event occurred.
offsetX and offsetY	Internet Explorer	The cursor's horizontal and vertical position in pixels, relative to the container in which the event occurred.
x and y	Internet Explorer	The cursor's horizontal and vertical position in pixels, relative to the document in which the event occurred.
target	Navigator	The object to which the event was originally sent.
srcElement	Internet Explorer	The object to which the event was originally sent.
type	Navigator Internet Explorer	The type of event that occurred.
which	Navigator	Either the mouse button (left = 1, middle = 2, and right = 3) that was pressed or the ASCII value of a pressed key.

Continued on next page

TABLE 4.4 CONTINUED: Properties of the event Object

Property	Browser	Description
keyCode	Internet Explorer	Identifies the Unicode key code associated with a key press.
button	Internet Explorer	Identifies the mouse button that was pressed when the event occurred. Values are 0 No button 1 Left button 2 Right button 4 Middle button
modifiers	Navigator	Identifies the modifier keys (ALT_MASK, CONTROL_MASK, SHIFT_MASK, and META_MASK) associated with a mouse or key event.
altKey, ctrlKey, and shiftKey	Internet Explorer	Set to *true* or *false* to indicate whether the Alt, Control, or Shift keys were pressed when the event occurred.
cancelBubble	Internet Explorer	Set to *true* or *false* to cancel or enable event bubbling (see the section, "Event Bubbling," later in this chapter).
fromElement and toElement	Internet Explorer	Specifies the HTML element being moved from or to.
reason	Internet Explorer	Used to indicate the status of data transfer for data source objects (refer to Chapter 22, "Scripting Microsoft Servers").
returnValue	Internet Explorer	Set to *true* or *false* to indicate the event handler's return value. Same as returning *true* or *false* from the event handler.
srcFilter	Internet Explorer	Specifies the filter object that caused an onfilterchange event (refer to Chapter 18, "Using Style Sheets and DHTML").

Whenever an event occurs, an event object is automatically generated. This object is made available to event handlers in one of two different ways, depending on the browser (Navigator or Internet Explorer) you are using. Internet Explorer defines a global object, named **event**, that can be accessed from your event handling function. For example, the following code accesses the global event object in an event handler:

```
function myEventHandler() {
  // Access the Internet Explorer event object
  // to display the mouse's x and y position when the
  // event occurred.
  alert(event.screenX+","+event.screenY)
}
```

Navigator does not define a global event object. Instead, it implicitly passes an event object to event handling functions. To use this extra parameter, you can simply rewrite the above function to take an eventObject parameter:

```
function myEventHandler(eventObject) {
  // Access the Navigator event object
  // to display the mouse's x and y position when the
  // event occurred.
  alert(eventObject.screenX+","+ eventObject.screenY)
}
```

You can combine both approaches by explicitly passing the event object to the event handling function in your event handling attributes. This will ensure compatibility between Internet Explorer and Navigator. Listing 4.18 provides an example. When you open ch04-18.htm in your browser, it displays the Web page shown in Figure 4.32. (The code for this example is available on the Sybex Web site at http://www.sybex.com.) Click on the link and an alert displays the coordinates of your mouse's position at the time of the click. Refer to Figure 4.33.

Listing 4.18　　**Using the *event* Object with Navigator and Internet Explorer (ch04-18.htm)**

```
<HTML>
<HEAD>
<TITLE>Using the event Object</TITLE>
<SCRIPT><!-
function clickHandler(eventObject) {
  alert(eventObject.screenX+","+ eventObject.screenY)
}
//-></SCRIPT>
</HEAD>
<BODY>
<H1>Using the event Object</H1>
```

```
<A HREF="javascript:void(0)" onClick="clickHandler(event)">Click this
link.</A>
</BODY>
</HTML>
```

FIGURE 4.32:

Click the link to invoke the
event handler (Listing 4.18).

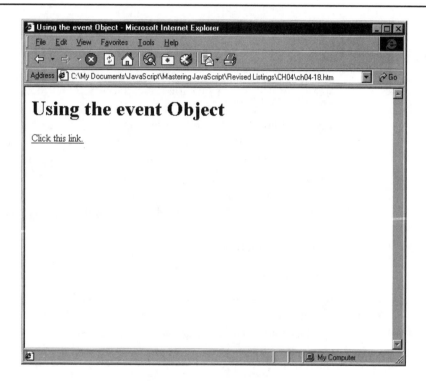

FIGURE 4.33:

The event object allows
you to determine the
coordinates of the mouse
when the event occurred
(Listing 4.18).

NOTE   The event object is only supported by version 4 (Navigator or Internet Explorer) or
later browsers.

The key to supporting compatibility with Navigator and Internet Explorer is to pass the `event` object as a parameter to the event handling function. This is done in the `onClick` attribute of the document's link. The `clickHandler()` function takes the object as a parameter and then processes the event independently of the browser type.

Event Capturing

Navigator 4 and later provide the capability for `window`, `document`, and `layer` objects to capture the events of lower-level objects that are displayed in the window, document, and layer. For example, all the events associated with a form can be captured and processed by a document's event handlers. This is a useful capability if you want to centralize all the event handling that occurs in a document. (I generally avoid this approach because it relies on Navigator-specific code.) In order to set up a window, document, or layer to capture events, you simply invoke the object's `captureEvents()` method and pass it the type of event that you want to capture. For example, to capture all of a document's click events, you simply invoke `captureEvents()` as follows:

```
document.captureEvents(Event.CLICK)
```

> **NOTE**
> The `window` and `document` objects are covered in Chapter 5, "Working with Objects." The `layer` object is a Navigator-specific object that is covered in Chapter 18, "Using Style Sheets and DHTML."

The `Event.CLICK` parameter that you pass to `captureEvents()` is unique to Navigator. The `Event` object specifies constants for event types and special keys. It is defined by Navigator as a distinct object from the `event` object. To identify a particular event type, use `Event.NAME` where NAME is the name of the event in uppercase without the preceding *ON*. Some examples of this convention are as follows:

```
Event.CLICK
Event.DBLCLICK
Event.MOUSEDOWN
Event.MOUSEUP
```

The Event object is also used to specify constants for special keys. These constants are as follows:

```
Event.ALT_MASK
Event.CONTROL_MASK
Event.META_MASK
Event.SHIFT_MASK
```

NOTE   The Meta key corresponds to the Command key on the Macintosh.

In addition to the captureEvents() method, the window, document, and layer objects also support the releaseEvent() and routeEvent() methods. The releaseEvents() method is used to turn off event capturing. The routeEvent() method passes a captured event to its normal destination. Both methods take the same argument as the captureEvents() method. The handleEvent() method may be used to directly invoke an object's event handler. It is used as follows:

```
object.handleEvent(Event.TYPE)
```

TYPE is the type of event to be handled, such as CLICK or MOUSEDOWN.

The example provided in Listing 4.19 shows how to use event capturing and the Event object. Remember, these capabilities are unique to Netscape Navigator 4 or later. When you open ch04-19.htm with Navigator, it displays the Web page shown in Figure 4.34. Click anywhere in the document while holding down a combination of the Alt, Control, and Shift keys. The document captures the mouseDown event and displays an alert dialog that identifies which of the special keys were pressed. Refer to Figure 4.35.

Listing 4.19   Using Event Capturing and the *event* Object (ch04-19.htm)

```
<HTML>
<HEAD>
<TITLE>Event Capturing and the Event Object</TITLE>
<SCRIPT><!-
function mouseDownHandler(eventObject) {
  specialKeys = "Special keys: "
  if(eventObject.modifiers & Event.ALT_MASK) specialKeys += "ALT "

if(eventObject.modifiers & Event.CONTROL_MASK) specialKeys += "CONTROL
"
  if(eventObject.modifiers & Event.META_MASK) specialKeys += "META "
  if(eventObject.modifiers & Event.SHIFT_MASK) specialKeys += "SHIFT "
  alert(specialKeys)
```

```
}
//-></SCRIPT>
</HEAD>
<BODY>
<H1>Event Capturing</H1>
<P>This only works with Navigator 4 or later.</P>
<P>Click anywhere in the document.</P>
<SCRIPT><!-
document.captureEvents(Event.MOUSEDOWN)
document.onmousedown = mouseDownHandler
//-></SCRIPT>
</BODY>
</HTML>
```

FIGURE 4.34:

The document object captures all mouseDown events on the page (Listing 4.19).

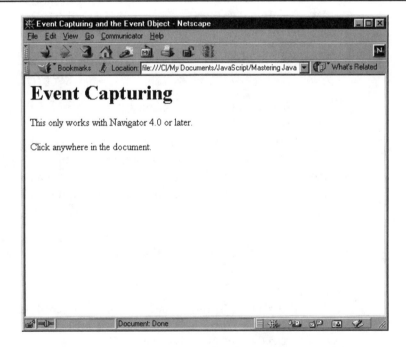

FIGURE 4.35:

The event object provides masks for identifying any special keys pressed by the user (Listing 4.19).

Note that in the mouseDownHandler() function of Listing 4.19, the constants, Event.ALT_MASK, Event.CONTROL_MASK, Event.META_MASK, and Event.SHIFT_MASK are *anded* with the eventObject.modifiers value. The modifiers property contains a string of bits that identify which of the special keys were pressed. By *anding* the special key event constants to modifiers, you can obtain a Boolean value identifying whether a particular key was pressed.

The *onMouseMove* Event

The onMouseMove event must be captured when used with Navigator. This event is not associated with any particular object. Listing 4.20 shows how to use event capturing with the onMouseMove event. Because the example uses event capturing, it will only work with Navigator 4 or later. Figure 4.36 shows the Web page displayed by this script. When you move your mouse around the Web page, the coordinates of the mouse's position are shown in the default status location. Refer to the bottom of Figure 4.36.

Listing 4.20   Using Event Capturing with the *onMouseMove* Event (ch04-20.htm)

```
<HTML>
<HEAD>
<TITLE>Using the onMouseMove Event</TITLE>
<SCRIPT><!-
function mouseMoveHandler(eventObject) {
 window.defaultStatus =
   "(" + eventObject.screenX + "," + eventObject.screenY + ")"
}
//-></SCRIPT>
</HEAD>
<BODY>
<H1>Capturing the onMouseMove Event</H1>
<P>This only works with Navigator 4 or later.</P>
<P>Move your mouse around the document.</P>
<SCRIPT><!-
document.captureEvents(Event.MOUSEMOVE)
document.onmousemove = mouseMoveHandler
//-></SCRIPT>
</BODY>
</HTML>
```

FIGURE 4.36:

The onMouseMove event
can be used to track the
mouse's movement and
location (Listing 4.20).

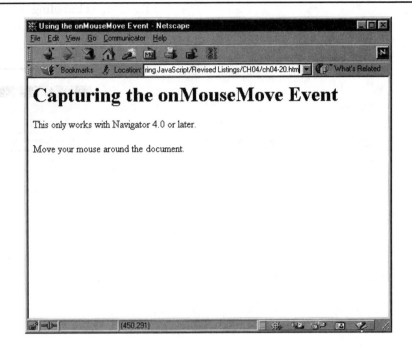

Event Bubbling

Internet Explorer does not support Navigator's event capturing approach.
Instead, it uses an approach called *event bubbling* that can be used to achieve the
same results. In Internet Explorer, when an event occurs, it is directed toward the
lowest-level object to which the event applies. For example, suppose a user clicks
a button contained in a form. The button's onClick event handler is invoked to
handle the event. When the button's event handler is finished processing the
event, the event *bubbles* up to the form's onClick event handler. The form's
onClick event handler handles the event and then the event bubbles up to the
document's onClick handler. The document's onClick handler then handles the
event. If any of the button, form, or document event handlers are omitted, the
event just bubbles up to the next higher event handler. If you keep the document's object hierarchy in mind, you should visualize events bubbling up from
lower-level objects to the higher-level objects in which they are contained.

Listing 4.21 provides an example of event bubbling. Figure 4.37 shows the Web page it displays. Click the button and three alert boxes are displayed, one from each event handler. Figures 4.38 through 4.40 show these dialog boxes.

FIGURE 4.37:

The onClick event is bubbled from the button's onClick event handler to the onClick event handler of the form and document (Listing 4.21).

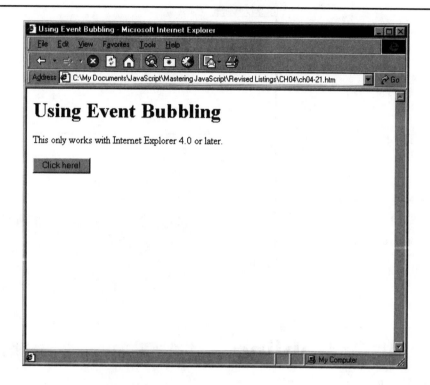

Listing 4.21   **Using Event Bubbling with the *onClick* Event (ch04-21.htm)**

```
<HTML>
<HEAD>
<TITLE>Using Event Bubbling</TITLE>
<SCRIPT><!-
function buttonClickHandler() {
 alert("The onClick event was handled by buttonClickHandler()")
}
function formClickHandler() {
 alert("The onClick event was handled by formClickHandler()")
}
function documentClickHandler() {
 alert("The onClick event was handled by documentClickHandler()")
```

```
}
//--></SCRIPT>
</HEAD>
<BODY ONCLICK="documentClickHandler()">
<H1>Using Event Bubbling</H1>
<P>This only works with Internet Explorer 4 or later.</P>
<FORM ONCLICK="formClickHandler()">
<INPUT TYPE="BUTTON" ONCLICK="buttonClickHandler()"
VALUE="Click here!">
</FORM>
</BODY>
</HTML>
```

FIGURE 4.38:

The onClick event is handled by the button's onClick event handler (Listing 4.21).

FIGURE 4.39:

The onClick event is handled by the form's onClick event handler (Listing 4.21).

FIGURE 4.40:

The onClick event is handled by the document's onClick event handler (Listing 4.21).

In order to cancel event bubbling for a particular event, set

```
event.cancelBubble = true
```

in the event's handler. For example, the following code cancels the bubbling of onClick events in Listing 4.21:

```
function buttonClickHandler() {
 alert("The onClick event was handled by buttonClickHandler()")
 event.cancelBubble = true
}
```

NOTE   Setting the event.cancelBubble property to *true* only affects bubbling for the current event. It has no impact on subsequent events.

Error Handling

There is nothing more frustrating for a user than loading a Web page and receiving an endless sequence of scripting errors. As script writers, our goal should be to create scripts that are error free. Unfortunately, due to the subtle incompatibilities between Navigator and Internet Explorer, it is likely that some errors will eventually find their way into our scripts. On the positive side, JavaScript and JScript both provide the capability to handle errors during a script's execution. JavaScript 1.1 and later provide error handling support through the error event and the onError event handling attribute. JScript 5 (currently only supported by Internet Explorer 5) provides superior exception handling support via the error object and the throw, try, and catch statements. I'll cover both of these approaches in the following sections.

The *onError* Event Handler

The error event was introduced in JavaScript 1.1 to provide the capability to handle errors associated with the loading of images or documents. The onError event handler of the image object (refer to the section, "Handling Image Events," earlier in this chapter) is used to handle image-related loading errors. The onError event handler of the window object is used to handle errors that occur during the loading and processing (syntax and runtime errors) of a document.

The function that you use to handle onError differs from other event handling functions in that it is automatically passed three parameters by the browser (both Internet Explorer and Navigator):

errorMessage   The error message associated with the error

url   The URL of the document in which the error occurred

line   The line number at which the error occurred

You can use these parameters to provide custom error information to your users. In addition, the value returned by your onError event handler determines whether standard error messages are displayed to the user. A *true* return value causes the standard error message to be suppressed. A *false* return value causes the standard error message to be displayed.

To use onError in a way that works with both Navigator and Internet Explorer, set the window.onerror property to your event handling function. Internet Explorer does not handle the onError attribute of the <BODY> tag correctly.

NOTE   Setting the window.onerror property to null prevents runtime errors from being displayed to users of Navigator (but not Internet Explorer).

Listing 4.22 provides an example of using onError that works with both Internet Explorer and Navigator. Figure 4.41 shows the Web page that is displayed. When you click the Click Here to Generate an Error button, the button's onClick event handler tries to invoke the nonexistent createAnError() function. This results in a runtime error. The errorHandler() function handles the error by displaying the error message shown in Figure 4.42.

Listing 4.22   **Using the *onError* Event Handler (ch04-22.htm)**

```
<HTML>
<HEAD>
<TITLE>Handling Errors with onError</TITLE>
<SCRIPT><!-
function errorHandler(errorMessage,url,line) {
  document.write("<P><B>Error message:</B> "+errorMessage+"<BR>")
  document.write("<B>URL:</B> "+url+"<BR>")
  document.write("<B>Line number:</B> "+line+"</P>")
  return true
}
```

```
onerror = errorHandler
// -></SCRIPT>
</HEAD>
<BODY>
<H1>Handling Errors with onError</H1>
<FORM>
<INPUT TYPE="BUTTON" ONCLICK="createAnError()"
VALUE="Click here to generate an error.">
</FORM>
</BODY>
</HTML>
```

FIGURE 4.41:

Click the button to generate a runtime error (Listing 4.22).

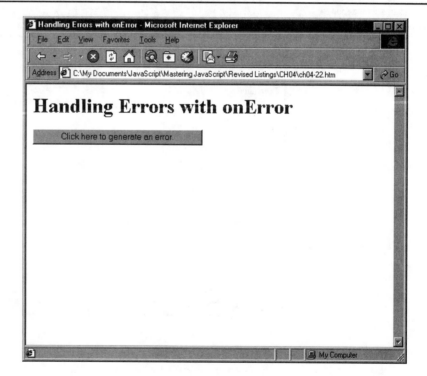

The *error* Object

Internet Explorer 5 (JScript 5) introduced the throw, try, and catch statements. These statements allow you to handle runtime errors with minimal impact on your script's normal flow of execution. Chapter 3, "Using Operators, Statements, and Functions," introduces these statements and provides examples of their use. Internet Explorer 5 also introduced the `error` object. Instances of this object are created and thrown when an error occurs during a script's execution. The `try` and `catch` statements are used to handle these runtime errors.

The `error` object has two properties, `number` and `description`. The `number` property is used to specify an error number. It is a two-byte number and needs to be *anded* with *0xFFFF* in order to produce a 16-bit integer value. The `description` property provides a description of the error.

FIGURE 4.42:

The runtime error is handled and an error message is displayed (Listing 4.22).

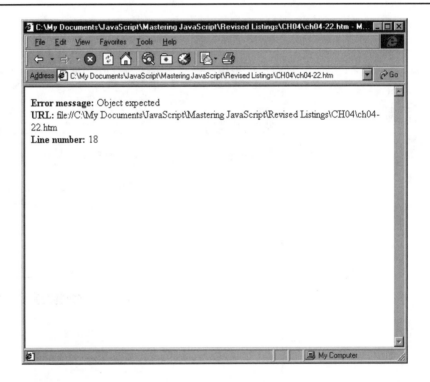

Listing 4.23 shows how the `error` object and the `try` and `catch` statements are used to handle runtime errors. Figure 4.43 shows the Web page it generates. Click the Click Here to Generate an Error button. This results in the `generateError()` function being invoked. This function uses a `try` statement to invoke the nonexistent `createAnError()` function, resulting in a runtime error. The runtime error is caught by the `catch` statement. The `number` and `description` properties of the error object are used to display the error message shown in Figure 4.44.

FIGURE 4.43:

Click the button to generate a runtime error (Listing 4.23).

FIGURE 4.44:

The runtime error is handled and an error message is displayed (Listing 4.23).

Listing 4.23   **Using the *error* Object to Handle Errors (ch04-23.htm)**

```
<HTML>
<HEAD>
<TITLE>Handling Errors with the error Object</TITLE>
<SCRIPT><!-
function generateError() {
 try {
  createAnError()
 }
 catch(errorObject) {
  errorMessage = "Guess what I caught?\n\n"
  errorMessage += "Error number: " + (errorObject.number & 0xFFFF)
  errorMessage += "\n" + errorObject.description
  alert(errorMessage)
 }
}
// -></SCRIPT>
</HEAD>
<BODY>
<H1>Handling Errors with the error Object</H1>
<FORM>
<INPUT TYPE="BUTTON" ONCLICK="generateError()"
VALUE="Click here to generate an error.">
</FORM>
</BODY>
</HTML>
```

Summary

This chapter illustrated the use of JavaScript's event-handling capabilities. It
described JavaScript's approach to event handling and identified the event handlers that are predefined by JavaScript. You learned how to write your own
event-handling functions and how to associate them with user interface actions.
In the next chapter, you'll learn about JavaScript's support of objects and how to
create your own objects and methods in JavaScript.

CHAPTER
FIVE

5

Working with Objects

- What Are Objects?

- What Is Object-Oriented Programming?

- The JavaScript Object Model

- Color Constants

- Defining Object Types

- Deleting Properties and Methods

One of the most important features of JavaScript is that it is an object-based language. This simplifies the design of JavaScript programs and enables them to be developed in a more intuitive, modular, and reusable manner.

This chapter describes JavaScript's support of objects and object-based programming. It introduces the JavaScript Object Model and summarizes the predefined JavaScript objects. It also shows how to create your own object types. When you finish this chapter, you'll be able to define and use objects in your Web pages.

TIP Part II, "Using Predefined Objects and Methods," provides detailed descriptions and examples of JavaScript's predefined objects.

What Are Objects?

Most people know that objects are entities that exist in the real world of people, places, and things. But they also exist in the cyber world of computers and networking. Examples of real-world objects include you, the book you are reading, and the lamp that you use to provide you with light. Examples of cyber-world objects are the Web pages that you create and the individual HTML elements they contain. It is these types of objects that I will be discussing in relation to JavaScript.

An object consists of two things:

- A collection of *properties* that contain data

- *Methods* that enable operations on the data contained in those properties

When you view something as an object, you look at it in terms of its properties and methods. Table 5.1 identifies some of the properties and methods that could apply to the example objects mentioned in the previous paragraph.

TABLE 5.1: Examples of Objects, Properties, and Methods

Object	Properties	Methods

You
(real-world object)
	`height`
	`weight`
	`hairColor`
		`eat()`
		`exercise()`
		`grow()`

This book
(real-world object)
	`pages`
	`currentPage`
		`turnPageForward()`
		`turnPageBackward()`
		`goToPage()`

A lamp (real-world object)	`onOffState`	`turnOn()` `turnOff()`

A Web page
(cyber-world
object)
	`title`
	`bgColor`
	`links`
		`open()`
		`close()`
		`write()`

An HTML button (cyber-world object)	`name` `value`	`setLabel()`

You've already seen several examples of JavaScript objects. You've used the `document` object and its `write()` method in many of the scripts in previous chapters. You've also used the `alert()` method of the `window` object to display messages to the user. The fields of a form are also objects. You've seen how the `value` property of a field can be used to test and set the field's value. By the time you finish this chapter, you will have encountered all of the predefined JavaScript objects and learned how to create objects of your own.

NOTE JavaScript is not a full object-oriented language—there are a few object-oriented programming features that it lacks. However, JavaScript is an object-based language, and provides several important object-oriented programming features. In order to learn why these features are important and how to use these features correctly, I'll begin by reviewing object-oriented programming in general and then identify which object-oriented programming features JavaScript supports.

What Is Object-Oriented Programming?

The field of software engineering has evolved over the 50 or so years of the computer's existence. This evolution has brought about different approaches and strategies to the task of creating high-quality software while minimizing development time and costs. The most successful development approach currently in use is the object-oriented approach. This approach *models* the elements of a software application as objects—by modeling I mean object types are named, their properties are identified, and their methods are described. Once an object type is defined, it can then be used to create specific instances of other objects of that type and to construct other, more complex object types.

> **NOTE**   Object-oriented programming is sometimes referred to by the acronym, OOP.

> **NOTE**   An object type is referred to as a *class* in object-oriented languages such as Java and C++.

Object Types and Instances

An *object type* is a template from which specific objects of that type are created. It defines the properties and methods that are common to all objects of that type. For example, let's consider a person's mailing address as an object type. I'll name it `mailAddress` and give it the properties of `streetAddress`, `city`, `state`, and `postalCode`. In addition to these properties, I'll define `changeAddress()` as a method for changing one person's address and `findAddress()` as a method for finding out another person's address. Don't worry about how I'm doing this—you'll learn that later—for this explanation just focus on what's being done.

When I define the `mailAddress` object type, I haven't specified anyone's address. I've only developed a template for the creation of an address—kind of like a blank Rolodex card. The address type can be *instantiated*, which is the programming term for creating a specific *instance* of that type of object; in this case it would mean creating a specific person's address record. This is similar to producing a Rolodex card, filling it in, and sticking it in the Rolodex.

The capability to define an object type from which specific object instances can then be created is a very basic but important feature of object-oriented software development.

Creating Object Types

While the definition and instantiation of object types is a basic feature of object-oriented languages, it is not the only feature these languages provide. The ability to use object types to define *other* object types is what really gives object-oriented programming its power. There are two major ways in which this is accomplished: through *object composition* and *inheritance*.

Object Composition

One approach to developing object types is to define primitive object types that serve as simple building blocks from which more complex types may be composed. This approach is referred to as *object composition*. Consider the process of building a house. At some point, somebody must construct the boards, nails, and glass panes that are used as the basic building blocks for constructing most homes. These building objects are assembled into more complex objects such as doors, windows, and prefabricated walls. These more complex objects are then, in turn, assembled into larger objects that eventually are integrated into a finished home. In the same way that boards, nails, glass panes, and other simple objects are used to construct a wide variety of different homes, simple object types are used in programming to create more complex object types which are eventually integrated into a final software application. For example, the `mailAddress` object may be used to create an employment application form, which is itself used to create a personnel database system.

Object composition is closely related to and depends on the capability to support *object reuse*. When an object type is defined, it is often very desirable that it be defined in such a way that it can be reused in other software applications. This simplifies the development of other applications, and naturally leads to cost and schedule savings. The reuse of software objects is just as important as the reuse of technology in other engineering disciplines. Imagine the state of the automotive industry if the wheel had to be reinvented for every new type of car that's been developed.

Encapsulation—Packaging Objects　Software objects are reusable when they follow certain design principles. One of the most important of these principles is *encapsulation*. Encapsulation is the packaging of the properties and methods of an object into a container with an appropriately defined interface. The object's interface must provide the methods and properties that enable the object to be used in the manner that is intended, and must do it without providing methods or properties that would allow the object to be misused. If this abstract description is difficult to fathom, consider the interface of an automobile. Auto designers provide standardized steering, braking, and throttling capabilities in all cars, since these capabilities are basic to driving. However, no automobile manufacturer provides drivers with the capability to manually control the firing of spark plugs from the dashboard. Even if drivers were provided with this capability, they more than likely could not use it to any advantage.

Modularity and Information Hiding   Encapsulation depends upon two important concepts for its success. The first concept, *modularity*, refers to an object's being complete in and of itself and not accessing other objects outside their defined interfaces. Modular objects are said to be "loosely coupled," which means that dependencies between objects are minimized, and internal changes to an object do not require changes in other objects that make use of the object. The second concept, *information hiding*, refers to the practice of limiting information about an object to that which is required to use the object's interface. It is accomplished by removing information about the internal operation of an object from the object's interface.

Inheritance—A Hierarchical Approach to Object Design

The second major way of constructing object types from other object types is through *inheritance*. In this approach, higher-level, more abstract object types are defined from which lower-level, more concrete object types are derived. When a lower-level object type is created, it identifies one or more higher-level object types as its *parent* types. The *child* type inherits all of the properties and methods of its parents. This eliminates the need to redefine these properties and methods. The child type is free to redefine any of the methods that it inherits or to add new properties and methods. This enables the child type to tailor its inherited characteristics to new situations.

As an example, consider the various types of objects that may be constructed to implement a scrolling marquee. At the highest level, a `genericMarquee` may be constructed that has the basic properties `scrolledText` and `scrollRate`. It may provide basic methods, such as `startScrolling()` and `stopScrolling()`. From this generic marquee, more complex marquees may be created. For example, `horizontalMarquee` and `verticalMarquee` object types may be constructed that add the property `scrollDirection` to those inherited from `genericMarquee`. These, in turn, may be further refined into marquees which use colored text and backgrounds. The properties `textColor` and `backgroundColor` and the methods `randomTextColor()` and `randomBackgroundColor()` could be added.

Using inheritance, more sophisticated, tailored object types can be created from those that are already defined. This is done by just adding the properties and methods needed to differentiate the new objects from their parents. Once a useful object type is created, it can then be reused many times to create several child objects and numerous generations of offspring.

Classification and Inheritance Object-oriented programming languages, such as Java and C++ (but not JavaScript), refer to an object's type as its *class*, and provide the capability to develop child classes from parent classes using inheritance. The resulting class structure is referred to as a *classification scheme*. The classification schemes that result from object-oriented development mimic those that are fundamental to the way we as human beings acquire and organize knowledge. For example, we develop general class names, such as *animal*, that we use to refer to large groups of real-world objects. We then develop names of subclasses, such as *mammal*, *bird*, and *insect*, which we use to refine our concept of animal. We continue to develop more detailed classes that differentiate between objects of the same class. The same sort of classification process is carried out by developers of object-oriented programs.

Single and Multiple Inheritance Part of the reason that inheritance is a successful approach to object development is that it mimics the way we acquire and organize knowledge—it is therefore *intuitive* to us. In addition to this, inheritance is *efficient*, because it only requires you to define the properties and methods that are unique for an object's type.

Some languages, notably Java, enforce a more restricted form of inheritance, known as *single inheritance*. Single inheritance requires that a child class have only one parent. However, a parent may have multiple children. Since a child class inherits its properties and methods from a single parent, it is an exact duplicate of its parent before it adds its own unique properties and methods.

Other languages, notably C++, support *multiple inheritance*. As you might expect, multiple inheritance allows child classes to inherit their properties and methods from more than one parent class. Multiple inheritance is much more powerful than single inheritance, because it allows independent, but complementary, branches of the class structure to be fused together into a single branch.

Multiple inheritance does, however, introduce some difficulties with respect to name resolution. Suppose that class C is the child of both class A and class B. Suppose also that both class A and B define different save() methods. Which of these two methods is inherited by class C? How does the compiler determine which method to use for objects of class C? Although it is certainly possible to develop naming schemes and compilers that resolve naming difficulties resulting from multiple inheritance, these solutions often require a significant amount of additional compilation and runtime processing.

Polymorphism—Many Methods with the Same Name While at first it may appear to be undesirable to have many methods of the same name, the capability to do so is actually a feature of object-oriented programming. *Polymorphism* is the capability to take on different forms. It allows an object type to define several different implementations of a method. These methods are differentiated by the types and number of parameters they accept. For example, several different print() methods may be defined, each of which is used to print objects of different object types. Other print() methods may be defined which take a different number of parameters. The interpreter, compiler, or runtime system selects the particular print() method that is most appropriate for the object being printed. Polymorphism allows the programmer to use a standard method, such as print(), to perform a particular operation and to define different forms of the method to be used with different parameters. This promotes standardization and reusable software and eliminates the need to come up with many slightly different names to distinguish the same operation being performed with different parameters.

JavaScript's Object-Based Programming Features

In the previous section, you learned about the capabilities that are common to object-oriented programming languages. JavaScript does not support several of the capabilities described, but Java does support them. You won't be studying Java until Part IV, "Communicating with Java, ActiveX, and Plug-Ins," but it is worth your while to become familiar with the object-oriented programming capabilities described in the previous section. That way, when you do get to Part IV, you'll be ready to start learning how Java applets can be integrated with JavaScript scripts.

In this section, you'll learn which object-oriented programming capabilities JavaScript supports and how they are used to develop object-based JavaScript programs.

JavaScript is not a fully object-oriented programming language. It does not support the basic object-oriented programming capabilities of classification, inheritance, encapsulation, and information hiding. However, this is not as bad as it first appears. JavaScript is a scripting language, not a full programming language. The features that it does provide are geared toward providing a capability to quickly and easily generate scripts that execute in the context of a Web page or a server-side application.

JavaScript is referred to as an *object-based* language. It supports the development of object types and the instantiation of these types to create object instances. It provides great support for object composition, but only fair support for modularity and object reuse. Table 5.2 summarizes JavaScript's object-based programming capabilities.

TABLE 5.2: JavaScript's Object-Based Programming Capabilities

Capability	Description
Object types	JavaScript supports both predefined and user-defined object types. However, JavaScript does not provide capabilities for type enforcement. An object of any type may be assigned to any variable.
Object instantiation	Object types are instantiated using the **new** operator to create specific object instances.
Object composition	Object types may be defined in terms of other predefined or user-defined object types.
Modularity	JavaScript code may be defined in a modular fashion, but JavaScript does not provide any features that enforce modular software development.
Object reuse	JavaScript software may be reused via the **SRC** attribute of the **SCRIPT** tag. Software may be made available for reuse via the Internet.
Information hiding	JavaScript does not provide any capabilities to support information hiding.
Encapsulation	Because JavaScript lacks information hiding capabilities, it cannot be used to develop encapsulated object types. Any method or property that is defined for a type is always directly accessible.
Inheritance	JavaScript does not provide any language features that support inheritance between object types.
Classification	Because JavaScript does not support inheritance, it cannot be used to develop a hierarchy of object types.
Polymorphism	JavaScript supports polymorphism using the `arguments` array for function definitions.

Although JavaScript does not provide all of the features of full object-oriented programming languages, such as Java, it does provide a suite of object-based features that are specially tailored to browser and server scripting. These features include a number of predefined browser and server objects and the capability to access related objects through the properties and methods of other objects. If this seems very abstract at this point, don't worry—you'll see several concrete examples of these features throughout this chapter as well as in Part II, "Using Predefined Objects and Methods."

The JavaScript Object Model

JavaScript supports a simple object model that is supported by a number of predefined objects. The *JavaScript Object Model* centers around the specification of object types that are used to create specific object instances. Object types under this model are defined in terms of properties and methods:

- Properties are used to access the data values contained in an object. Properties, by default, can be updated as well as read, although some properties of the predefined JavaScript objects are read-only.

- Methods are functions that are used to perform operations on an object. Methods may use the object's properties to perform these operations.

NOTE   This chapter describes the JavaScript Object Model as implemented by both Navigator and Internet Explorer. Each of these browsers provide additional browser-specific objects, methods, and properties. Online Appendix A, "Comparing JavaScript and JScript," covers these additional browser-specific objects of Navigator and Internet Explorer.

Using Properties

An object's properties are accessed by combining the object's name and its property name as follows:

```
objectName.propertyName
```

For example, the background color of the current Web document is identified by the bgColor property of the predefined document object. If you wanted to change the background color to white, you could use the following JavaScript statement:

```
document.bgColor="white"
```

The above statement assigns the string "white" to the bgColor property of the predefined document object. Listing 5.1 shows how this statement can be used in an example script. Figure 5.1 shows the Web page that it produces. Several buttons are displayed with the names of different colors. When a button is clicked, the button's onClick event handler changes the background of the document by setting the document.bgColor property.

Listing 5.1   **Using JavaScript Properties (ch05-01.htm)**

```html
<HTML>
<HEAD>
<TITLE>Using Properties</TITLE></HEAD>
<BODY>
<H1>Using Properties</H1>
<FORM>
<P><INPUT TYPE="BUTTON" NAME="red" VALUE="Red"
 ONCLICK='document.bgColor="red"'></P>
<P><INPUT TYPE="BUTTON" NAME="white" VALUE="White"
 ONCLICK='document.bgColor="white"'></P>
<P><INPUT TYPE="BUTTON" NAME="blue" VALUE="Blue"
 ONCLICK='document.bgColor="blue"'></P>
</FORM>
</BODY>
</HTML>
```

FIGURE 5.1:

Using properties to
change background colors
(Listing 5.1)

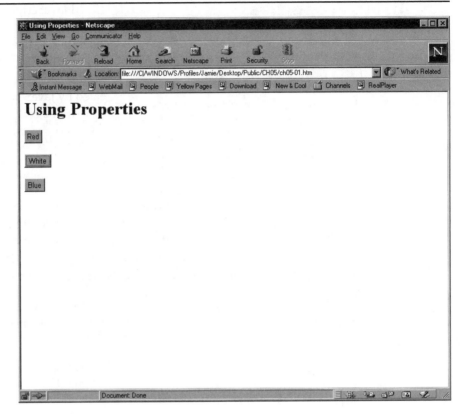

Using Methods

An object's methods are accessed in the same manner as its properties:

objectName.methodName(parameterList)

The parameters, if any, are separated by commas. The parentheses must be used even if no parameters are specified. An example of a method invocation is

    r=Math.random()

The random() method of the predefined Math object is invoked. This method returns a random floating-point number between 0 and 1. The number is then assigned to the r variable.

You have been using the methods of predefined JavaScript objects since your first script in Chapter 2, "Introducing JavaScript and JScript." You've used the `write()` method of the `document` object to generate HTML entities that are written to the current document. You've also used the `alert()` method of the `window` object to display popup dialog boxes. In the next section, you'll be introduced to some of the objects that are automatically created by JavaScript-capable browsers. Later in this chapter, all of the predefined JavaScript objects will be introduced in summary form. Part II of this book will show you how to use each of these predefined objects in your Web pages.

Creating Instances of Objects

Instances of objects of a particular object type are created using the `new` operator. You've previously used the `new` operator to create array objects. The same syntax is used to create objects of other types:

```
variable = new objectType(parameters)
```

The `objectType(parameters)` portion of the above statement is referred to as the *constructor*. Some object types have more than one constructor. Constructors differ in the number of parameters that they allow.

For example, `Date` is a predefined JavaScript object type. To create an instance of `Date` with the current date and time and assign it to the `currentDate` variable, you would use the following statement:

```
currentDate = new Date()
```

In the above statement, the `Date()` constructor does not take any parameters. The `Date` object type also allows object instances to be created for a specified date. For example, the following statement creates an instance of `Date` for January 1, 1999:

```
currentDate = new Date(99,1,1)
```

The constructor used in the above statement, `Date(99,1,1)`, takes three parameters. The `Date` object type provides other constructors in addition to the ones described in this section. (The `Date` object type is formally introduced later in this chapter in the section, "The `Date` Object Type.")

Browser Objects

When a Web page is loaded by a JavaScript-capable browser, the browser creates a number of JavaScript objects that provide access to the Web page and the HTML elements it contains. These objects are used to update and interact with the loaded Web page. Table 5.3 identifies these objects and summarizes their use.

TABLE 5.3: Browser Objects

Object	Use
`window` object	To access a browser window or a frame within a window. The `window` object is assumed to exist and does not require the `"window."` prefix when referring to its properties and methods.
`document` object	To access the document that is currently loaded into a window. A **document** object refers to an HTML document that provides content, that is, one that has **HEAD** and **BODY** tags.
`location` object	To represent a URL. It can be used to create a URL object, access parts of a URL, or modify an existing URL.
`history` object	To maintain a history of the URLs accessed within a window.
`frame` object `frames` array	To access an HTML frame. The `frames` array is used to access all frames within a window.
`link` object `links` array	To access a text- or image-based source anchor of a hypertext link. The `links` array is used to access all `link` objects within a document. Internet Explorer combines the `link` object with the **anchor** object.
`anchor` object `anchors` array	To access the target of a hypertext link. The **anchors** array is used to access all **anchor** objects within a document.
`image` object `images` array	To access an image that is embedded in an HTML document. The `images` array is used to access all `image` objects within a document.
`area` object	To access an area within a client-side image map.
`applet` object `applets` array	To access a Java applet. The `applets` array is used to access all applets in a document.
`event` object `Event` object	To access information about the occurrence of an event. The **event** object provides information about a specific event. The **Event** (capitalized) object provides constants that are used to identify events.
`form` object `forms` array	To access an HTML form. The `forms` array is used to access all forms within a document.

Continued on next page

TABLE 5.3 CONTINUED: Browser Objects

Object	Use
`elements` object	To access all form elements (fields or buttons) contained within a form.
`text` object	To access a text field of a form.
`textarea` object	To access a text area field of a form.
`radio` object	To access a set of radio buttons of a form or to access an individual button within the set.
`checkbox` object	To access a checkbox of a form.
`button` object	To access a form button that is not a submit or reset button.
`submit` object	To access a submit button of a form.
`reset` object	To access a reset button of a form.
`select` object `option` object	To access a select list of a form. The `option` object is used to access the elements of a select list.
`password` object	To access a password field of a form.
`hidden` object	To access a hidden field of a form.
`FileUpload` object	To access a file upload element of a form.
`navigator` object	To access information about the browser that is executing a script.
`screen` object	To access information about the size and color depth of a user's screen.
`embed` object `embeds` array	To access an embedded object. The `embeds` array provides access to all embedded objects in a document.
`mimeType` object `mimeTypes` array	To access information about a particular MIME type supported by a browser. The `mimeTypes` array is an array of all `mimeType` objects supported by a browser. Internet Explorer provides tacit support for `mimeTypes`, returning an empty array.
`plugin` object `plugins` array	To access information about a particular browser plug-in. The `plugins` array is an array of all plug-ins supported by a browser. Internet Explorer provides tacit support for `plugins`, returning an empty array.

Table 5.3 summarizes the predefined objects that are created by a JavaScript-capable browser when a Web page is loaded. JavaScript also supports object

types that are independent of the Web page that is loaded. These objects are described in the section, "Other Predefined Object Types," later in this chapter.

The Browser Object Hierarchy

Your browser creates the objects presented in Table 5.3 as the results of Web pages that you design. For example, if you create a Web page with three forms, then the forms array will contain three form objects corresponding to the forms that you have defined. Similarly, if you define a document with seven links, then the links array will contain seven link objects that correspond to your links.

The browser objects are organized into a hierarchy that corresponds to the structure of loaded Web documents and the current state of the browser. This hierarchy is referred to as an *instance hierarchy*. The window and navigator objects are the highest-level objects in this hierarchy.

The *window* Object

The window object represents a browser window, and it has properties that are used to identify the objects of the HTML elements that comprise that window. For example, the frames array is a property of a window object. If the window uses the frame set tag to define multiple frames, then the frames array contains the frame object associated with each frame. The window's location property refers to the location object that contains the URL associated with the window. The window's screen property may be used to obtain the user's screen dimensions and color depth.

If a window contains displayable content, as opposed to a frame set tag, then the window object's document property refers to the document object associated with the window. The document object contains properties that reference objects that are displayed in the window. These properties include the links, anchors, images, and forms arrays. The links array identifies all link objects contained in a document. The anchors array identifies all named anchors. Link objects refer to the source of a hyperlink, while anchor objects refer to the named destinations of a link. The images, applets, and forms arrays identify all image, applet, and form objects contained in a document. A document's area property refers to an area within a client-side image map that is defined in the document. A document's history property refers to a history object that contains a list of URLs that the user has visited within a particular window.

NOTE
Internet Explorer combines the `link` and `anchor` objects. Both links and anchors can be accessed via the `anchors` array.

A `document` object's `forms` array identifies all `form` objects that are defined in the document. Although a document may define any number of forms, usually only one form is defined. The `form` object provides access to the individual elements defined for a particular form via the `elements` array. The `elements` array refers to `text`, `textarea`, `radio`, `checkbox`, `button`, `submit`, `reset`, `select`, `password`, `hidden`, and `FileUpload` form fields. These fields may also be individually accessed by their names. You'll learn how to use form-related objects in Chapter 7, "Processing Forms," and Chapter 20, "Interfacing JavaScript with CGI Programs."

The *navigator* Object

The `navigator` object, like the `window` object, is a top-level object in the browser hierarchy. The `navigator` object is used to describe the configuration of the browser being used to display a window. Two of its properties, `mimeTypes` and `plugins`, contain the list of all MIME types and plug-ins supported by the browser. Internet Explorer returns empty arrays for the `mimeTypes` and `plugins` properties.

Hierarchical Object Identifiers

Because your browser organizes the various objects of a Web page according to the instance hierarchy described in the previous section, a hierarchical naming scheme is used to identify these objects. For example, suppose an HTML document defines three forms, and the second form has seven elements. Also suppose the fifth element of the second form is a radio button. You can access the name of this radio button using the following identifier:

```
document.forms[1].element[4].name
```

The above identifier refers to the name of the fifth element of the second form of the current document. (Remember that array indices begin at 0.) You could display this name using the following statement:

```
document.write(document.forms[1].element[4].name)
```

NOTE   You do not have to identify the **window** object when you refer to the current window's properties and methods—your browser will assume the current **window** object by default. There is one exception, however: in event-handling code, it is the current **document** object that is assumed by default.

In most cases, you can refer to a property or method of a browser-created object by starting with **document** and using the property names of the objects that contain the object (such as **links**, **anchors**, **images**, and **forms**) to identify the object within the instance hierarchy. When you have named the object in this fashion, you can then use the object's property or method name to access the data and functions defined for that object.

Listing 5.2 provides an example of using hierarchical names to access the elements defined within a Web document. The document defines a number of functions in the document head. It begins by invoking the **open()** method of the **window** object to open a second browser window. This second window is assigned to the **outputWindow** variable and is used to write the description of the objects defined for the HTML document shown in Listing 5.2. The **open()** method takes two parameters—the URL of the document to be loaded in the window and a window name. Because you don't want to load a document at another URL, set the URL parameter to a blank string.

Listing 5.2   **Using Hierarchical Object Identifiers (ch05-02.htm)**

```
<HTML>
<HEAD>
<TITLE>Using Hierarchical Object Identifiers</TITLE>
<SCRIPT LANGUAGE="JavaScript"><!--
outputWindow = open("","output")
function setupWindow() {
 outputWindow.document.write("<HTML><HEAD><TITLE>Output
  Window</TITLE></HEAD><BODY>")
}
function describeBrowser() {
 outputWindow.document.write("<H2>Browser Properties</H2>")
 outputWindow.document.write(navigator.appCodeName+" ")
 outputWindow.document.write(navigator.appName+" ")
 outputWindow.document.write(navigator.appVersion+"<BR>")
 outputWindow.document.write(navigator.mimeTypes.length+" MIME
```

```
  types are defined. ")
 outputWindow.document.write(navigator.plugins.length+"
  plug-ins are installed.")
}
function describeWindow() {
 outputWindow.document.write("<H2>Window Properties</H2>")
 outputWindow.document.write("Frames: "+frames.length+"<BR>")
 outputWindow.document.write("URL: "+location.href+"<BR>")
}
function describeDocument() {
 outputWindow.document.write("<H2>Document Properties</H2>")
 describeLinks()
 describeForms()
}
function describeLinks(){
 outputWindow.document.write("<H3>Links</H3>")
 outputWindow.document.write("This document contains "
  +document.links.length+" links:<BR>")
 for(i=0;i<document.links.length;++i)
  outputWindow.document.write(document.links[i].href+"<BR>")
}
function describeForms() {
 outputWindow.document.write("<H3>Forms</H3>")
 for(i=0;i<document.forms.length;++i) describeForm(i)
}
function describeForm(n) {
 outputWindow.document.write("Form "+n+" has "
  +document.forms[n].elements.length+" elements:")
 for(j=0;j<document.forms[n].elements.length;++j)
  outputWindow.document.write(" "
   + document.forms[n].elements[j].name)
 outputWindow.document.write("<BR>")
}
function finishWindow() {
 outputWindow.document.write("<FORM><INPUT Type='button'
  Value='Close Window' onClick='window.close()'></FORM>")
 outputWindow.document.write("</BODY></HTML>")
}
// -></SCRIPT></HEAD>
<BODY>
<H1>Using Hierarchical Object Identifiers</H1>
<P><A HREF="http://www.jaworski.com/javascript">Link to
```

```
Mastering JavaScript and JScript home page.</A></P>
<P><A HREF="http://home.netscape.com/">Link to Netscape's home
 page.</A></P>
<FORM>
<P><INPUT TYPE="TEXT" NAME="textField1"
 VALUE="Enter text here!"></P>
<P><INPUT TYPE="CHECKBOX" NAME="checkbox1"
 CHECKED="CHECKED">I'm checkbox1.</P>
<P><INPUT TYPE="CHECKBOX" NAME="checkbox2"> I'm checkbox2.</P>
<INPUT TYPE="SUBMIT" NAME="submitButton" VALUE="Click here!">
</FORM>
<SCRIPT LANGUAGE="JavaScript"><!-
setupWindow()
describeBrowser()
describeWindow()
describeDocument()
finishWindow()
// -></SCRIPT>
</BODY>
</HTML>
```

The `setupWindow()` function is used to generate the head of the second document and its opening body tag. It uses the `outputWindow` variable to select the second window as the target for writing. This function and other functions in the script write their output using statements of the following form:

```
outputWindow.document.write()
```

These statements tell JavaScript to write to the `document` object of the `window` object identified by the `outputWindow` variable.

The `describeBrowser()` function displays some of the `navigator` object's properties to the second window. It also uses the `outputWindow` variable to select this window. It displays the `appCodeName`, `appName`, `appVersion`, and uses the `length` property of the `mimeTypes` and `plugins` arrays to determine the number of MIME types and plug-ins supported by the browser.

The `describeWindow()` function displays some properties of the original (first) window. It displays the number of frames defined by the window and the URL of the document loaded into the window. Since the window does not define any frames, the length of the `frames` array is 0. The `href` property of the window's `location` object is used to get the text string corresponding to the URL. The URL displayed when you execute the script will be different depending on the directory from which you run the files of this chapter.

The describeDocument() function displays some of the properties associated with the current document in the second window. It invokes the describeLinks() and describeForms() functions to perform this processing.

The describeLinks() function uses the length property of the links array to identify the number of links contained in the document. It then executes a for loop to display the URL associated with each of these links. The href attribute of the link object is used to get the text string corresponding to the URL.

The describeForms() function uses the length property of the forms array to iterate through the document's links and display each one. The displayForm() function is used to display each form.

The displayForm() function uses the length property of the elements array of each form object to identify the number of elements contained in a form. It takes a single parameter, identified by the n variable. This parameter identifies the index into the forms array of the form object being displayed. The name of each field element is displayed by referencing the name property of each object contained in the elements array of each form object identified in the forms array. This is a good example of using hierarchical object naming to access the lower-level elements of an HTML document.

The finishWindow() function appends the following HTML to the body of the document displayed in the second window:

```
<FORM>
<INPUT Type='button' Value='Close Window'
 onClick='window.close()'>
</FORM>
</BODY>
</HTML>
```

The form is used to create a button, labeled *Close Window*, that is used to close the second window. The onClick attribute of the INPUT tag is assigned the event handling code, window.close(), which is used to close the window upon clicking the button. The window object should be explicitly referenced in event handlers to ensure that the current window is closed and not the current document. The </BODY> and </HTML> tags are used to end the displayed document.

The main body of the HTML document defines two links—one to the *Mastering JavaScript and JScript* home page and one to Netscape's home page. The document then defines a form with four elements—a text field, two check boxes, and a Submit button.

The script contained in the main body of the document invokes the `setup-indow()`, `describeBrowser()`, `describeWindow()`, `describeDocument()`, and `finishWindow()` functions to display the contents of the first window in the second window referenced by the `outputWindow` object. This script is placed at the end of the document so that the various HTML elements of the document are defined when the script is invoked.

A second window is created to display the various properties of the document. The Web browser displays this second window as shown in Figure 5.2. When the user clicks the Close Window button, the original document, shown in Figure 5.3, is displayed. You can also use your browser's Window pull-down menu to switch between the two windows.

FIGURE 5.2:

The output window
(Listing 5.2)

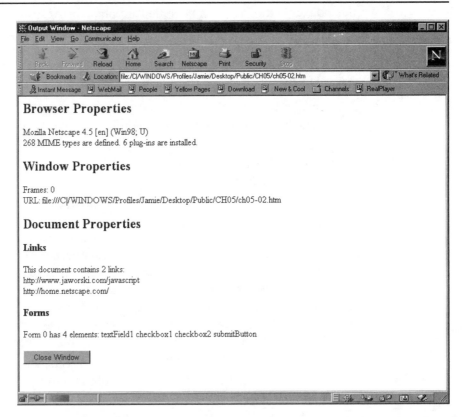

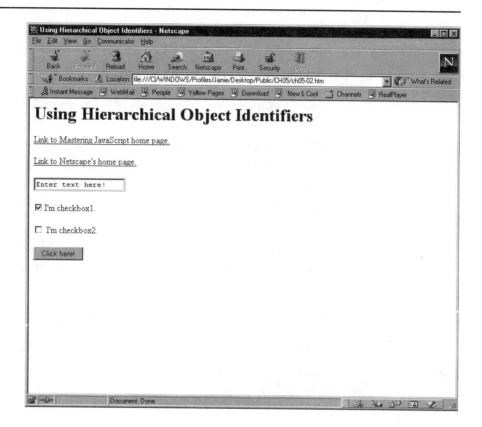

Other Predefined Object Types

In addition to the predefined browser objects discussed in earlier sections, JavaScript also provides general-purpose object types that support common operations. These object types (except the RegExp object type) are defined by the ECMAScript 1 specification and are described in the following sections.

The *Array* Object

The Array object allows arrays to be accessed as objects. The ECMAScript 1 specification defines two properties for the Array object: length and prototype. The length property identifies the length of an array. The prototype property is a property that is supported by all object types. It allows additional properties and methods to be defined for an object type. It is covered in the section, "Adding Properties and Methods to an Object Type," later in this chapter.

ECMAScript 1 defines the following `Array` methods:

`toString()`   Returns a string version of an array. Array elements are separated by commas.

`join(separator)`   Returns a string version of an array. Array elements are separated by the *separator* string. If no separator is specified, a comma is used.

`reverse()`   Reverses the elements of an array, that is, the last element appears first and the first element appears last.

`sort(comparisonFunction)`   Sorts the elements of an array according to a comparison function. If no comparison function is specified, the array elements are sorted in dictionary order. If a comparison function is specified, it should take two parameters, `p1` and `p2`, and return a negative integer if `p1` is less than `p2`, zero if `p1` equals `p2`, and a positive integer if `p1` is greater than `p2`.

Listing 5.3 illustrates the use of the above methods. It creates an array of integers 0 through 10 and applies the `toString()`, `join(':')`, `reverse()`, and `sort()` methods to it. Figure 5.4 shows the results it displays.

Listing 5.3   **Using the Methods of the *Array* Object (ch05-03.htm)**

```
<HTML>
<HEAD>
<TITLE>Using Arrays</TITLE>
<SCRIPT LANGUAGE="JavaScript"><!-
// -></SCRIPT></HEAD>
<BODY>
<H1>Using Arrays</H1>
<SCRIPT LANGUAGE="JavaScript"><!-
myArray = [0, 1, 2, 3, 4, 5, 6, 7, 8, 9, 10]
```

```
document.write("myArray: "+myArray+"<P>")
document.write("myArray.toString(): "+myArray.toString()+"<P>")
document.write("myArray.join(':'): "+myArray.join(':')+"<P>")
document.write("myArray.reverse(): "+myArray.reverse()+"<P>")
document.write("myArray.sort: "+myArray.sort())
// -></SCRIPT>
</BODY>
</HTML>
```

FIGURE 5.4:

The results of applying Array methods (Listing 5.3)

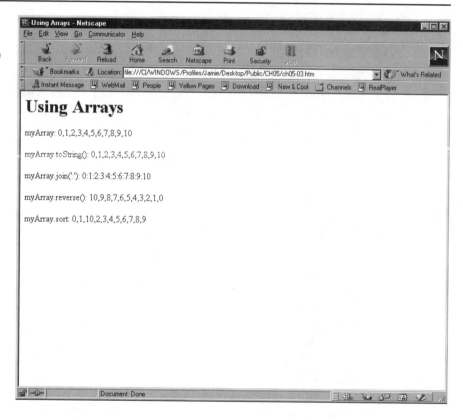

The *Boolean* Object

The Boolean object allows Boolean values to be accessed as objects. It supports the prototype property and the toString() and valueOf() methods. The toString() method returns the string equivalent of a Boolean value. The valueOf() method returns *true* or *false* depending on the value of the underling object.

Boolean objects are created by identifying their value as an argument to the constructor:

```
myBoolean = new Boolean(false)
yourBoolean = new Boolean(true)
```

The *Date* Object

The Date object type provides a common set of methods for working with dates and times. These methods are summarized in Table 5.4. The methods with UTC in their name refer to Universal Coordinated Time, which is the time set by the World Time Standard. The Date object type supports the prototype property. Instances of the Date object type may be created with any of the constructors shown in Table 5.5. Listing 5.4 illustrates the use of the Date object type.

TABLE 5.4: Methods of the *Date* Object

Method	Description
getDate() getUTCDate() setDate() setUTCDate()	Returns or sets the day of the month of the Date object.
getDay() getUTCDay()	Returns the day of the week of the Date object.
getHours() getUTCHours() setHours() setUTCHours()	Returns or sets the hour of the Date object.
getMilliseconds() getUTCMilliseconds() setMilliseconds() setUTCMilliseconds()	Returns or sets the milliseconds value of the Date object.
getMinutes() getUTCMinutes() setMinutes() setUTCMinutes()	Returns or sets the minutes of the Date object.

Continued on next page

TABLE 5.4 CONTINUED: Methods of the *Date* Object

Method	Description
getMonth() getUTCMonth() setMonth() setUTCMonth()	Returns or sets the month of the **Date** object.
getSeconds() getUTCSeconds() setSeconds() setUTCSeconds()	Returns or sets the seconds of the **Date** object.
getTime() setTime()	Returns or sets the time of the **Date** object.
getTimeZoneOffset()	Returns the time zone offset (in minutes) of the **Date** object.
getYear() getFullYear() getUTCFullYear() setYear() setFullYear() setUTCFullYear()	Returns or sets the year of the **Date** object. The full year methods use four-digit year values.
toGMTString()	Converts a date to a string in Internet GMT (Greenwich Mean Time) format.
toLocaleString()	Converts a date to a string in *locale* format, which means the format commonly used in the geographical region in which the user is located.
toString()	Returns a string value of a **Date** object.
valueOf()	Returns the number of milliseconds since midnight January 1, 1970.
toUTCString()	Returns a string that represents the time in UTC.

TABLE 5.5: Date Constructors

Constructor	Description
Date()	Creates a **Date** instance with the current date and time.
Date(*dateString*)	Creates a **Date** instance with the date specified in the *dateString* parameter. The format of the *dateString* is "*month day, year hours:minutes:seconds*".

Continued on next page

TABLE 5.5 CONTINUED: Date Constructors

Constructor	Description
Date(*milliseconds*)	Creates a Date instance with the specified number of milliseconds since midnight January 1, 1970.
Date(*year*, *month*, *day*, *hours*, *minutes*, *seconds*, *milliseconds*)	Creates a Date instance with the date specified by the year, month, day, hours, minutes, seconds, and milliseconds integers. The year and month parameters must be supplied. If other parameters are included, then all preceding parameters must be supplied.

Listing 5.4   **Using the *Date* Object (ch05-04.htm)**

```
<HTML>
<HEAD>
<TITLE>Using the Date Object Type</TITLE>
</HEAD>
<BODY>
<H1>Using the Date Object Type</H1>
<SCRIPT LANGUAGE="JavaScript"><!-
currentDate = new Date()
with (currentDate) {
  document.write("Date: "+getMonth()+"/"+getDate()+"/"+getYear()
   +"<BR>")
  document.write("Time: "+getHours()+":"+getMinutes()+":"
   +getSeconds())
}
// -></SCRIPT>
</BODY>
</HTML>
```

The above document uses the methods of the Date object type to write the current date and time to the current document object. The currentDate variable is assigned a new Date object that is created using the new operator and the Date() constructor. A with statement is used to make the object stored with current-Date the default object for object references. The two write() method invocations use the getMonth(), getDate(), getYear(), getHours(), getMinutes(), and getSeconds() methods to access the various components of a Date object. Figure 5.5 shows the Web page generated by Listing 5.4.

FIGURE 5.5:

Using the Date object type
(Listing 5.4)

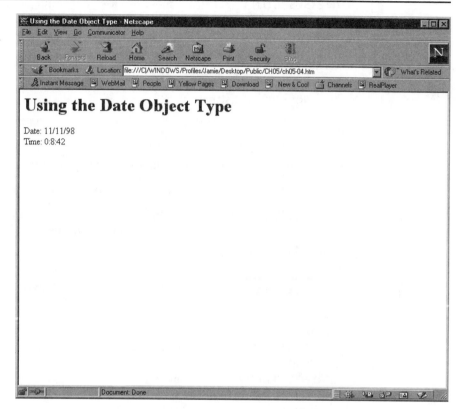

The *Function* Object

The Function object allows functions to be accessed as objects. It can be used to dynamically create and invoke a function during a script's execution. The ECMAScript 1 specification identifies the length and prototype properties. The length property identifies the number of parameters defined for a function. Navigator and Internet Explorer define the arguments property and the caller property. The arguments property is an array that identifies the arguments that are passed to a function when it is invoked. The caller property identifies the function that invoked a particular function. Navigator also defines the arity property, which is identical to the length property.

The ECMAScript 1 specification defines the `toString()` and `valueOf()` methods. The `toString()` method returns a string representation of the function. The `valueOf()` method returns the function itself. Navigator also defines the `call()` and `apply()` methods, which can be used to invoke a `Function` object.

`Function` objects are created by supplying the function's parameters and body to the `Function()` constructor:

```
variable = new Function("p1", "p2", ..., "pn", "body")
```

The opening and closing brackets ({ and }) of the function body are not specified. The following function returns x-squared plus y-squared:

```
myFunction = new Function("x", "y", "return x*x + y*y")
```

Listing 5.5 illustrates the use of the `Function` object. It creates a function that surrounds a string with braces ([and]). Figure 5.6 shows the results that are displayed by Listing 5.5.

Listing 5.5   **Using the *Function* Object (ch05-05.htm)**

```
<HTML>
<HEAD>
<TITLE>Using the Function Object</TITLE>
<BODY><H1>
<SCRIPT LANGUAGE="JavaScript"><!-
addBraces = new Function("s","return '['+s+']'")
document.write(addBraces("This"))
document.write(addBraces("is"))
document.write(addBraces("a"))
document.write(addBraces("test."))
// -></SCRIPT>
</H1></BODY>
</HTML>
```

FIGURE 5.6:

The results of the dynamically-created function (Listing 5.5).

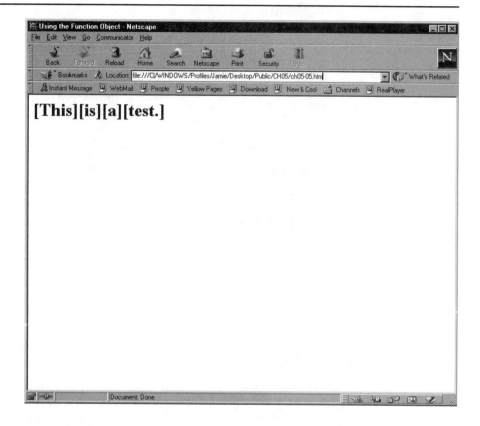

The *Global* Object

The ECMAScript specification defines the Global object to associate an object with the globally-accessible variables and functions defined in earlier versions of JavaScript. Navigator and Internet Explorer implement the Global object, but do not allow it to be explicitly created (via new Global()) or referenced (via "Global."). Instead, its properties and methods are referenced directly as global variables and functions.

The ECMAScript specification defines two constant properties: NaN and Infinity. The NaN constant means *not a number*. The Infinity property represents positive infinity. Methods defined for the Global object are as follows:

escape(*string*)   Converts the *string* into a new string where certain characters are converted into escape sequences in accordance with RFC 1738.

eval(*x*)   Evaluates and returns the value of the expression *x*.

isFinite(*number*)   Returns *true* if *number* is finite and *false* otherwise.

isNaN(*number*)   Returns *true* if *number* is not a number and *false*, otherwise.

parseFloat(*string*)   Parses the *string* as a floating-point value.

parseInt(*string*, *radix*)   Parses the *string* as an integer of base *radix*.

unescape(*string*)   Converts strings encoded by escape() back to their original value.

The above methods can be used to support numerical tests and URL encoding/decoding in accordance with RFC 1738.

The *Math* Object

The Math object provides a standard library of mathematical constants and functions. The constants are defined as properties of Math, and are listed in Table 5.6. The functions are defined as methods of Math, and are summarized in Table 5.7. Specific instances of Math are not created because Math is a built-in object and not an object type. Listing 5.6 illustrates the use of the Math object; Figure 5.7 shows the Web page it generates.

TABLE 5.6: Math Properties

Property	Description
E	Euler's constant
LN2	The natural logarithm of 2
LN10	The natural logarithm of 10
LOG2E	The base 2 logarithm of e

Continued on next page

TABLE 5.6 CONTINUED: Math Properties

Property	Description
LOG10E	The base 10 logarithm of e
PI	The constant p
SQRT1_2	The square root of _
SQRT2	The square root of 2

TABLE 5.7: Math Methods

Method	Description
abs(x)	Returns the absolute value of x
acos(x)	Returns the arc cosine of x in radians
asin(x)	Returns the arc sine of x in radians
atan(x)	Returns the arc tangent of x in radians
atan2(x,y)	Returns the angle of the polar coordinate corresponding to (x,y)
ceil(x)	Returns the least integer that is greater than or equal to x
cos(x)	Returns the cosine of x
exp(x)	Returns e^x
floor(x)	Returns the greatest integer that is less than or equal to x
log(x)	Returns the natural logarithm of x
max(x,y)	Returns the greater of x and y
min(x,y)	Returns the lesser of x and y
pow(x,y)	Returns x^y
random()	Returns a random number between 0 and 1
round(x)	Returns x rounded to the closest integer
sin(x)	Returns the sine of x
sqrt(x)	Returns the square root of x
tan(x)	Returns the tangent of x

Listing 5.6	Using the *Math* Object (ch05-06.htm)

```
<HTML>
<HEAD>
<TITLE>Using the Math Object</TITLE>
</HEAD>
<BODY>
<H1>Using the Math Object</H1>
<SCRIPT LANGUAGE="JavaScript"><!-
document.write(Math.PI+"<BR>")
document.write(Math.E+"<BR>")
document.write(Math.ceil(1.234)+"<BR>")
document.write(Math.random()+"<BR>")
document.write(Math.sin(Math.PI/2)+"<BR>")
document.write(Math.min(100,1000)+"<BR>")
// -></SCRIPT>
</BODY>
</HTML>
```

FIGURE 5.7:

Example of using the Math object (Listing 5.6)

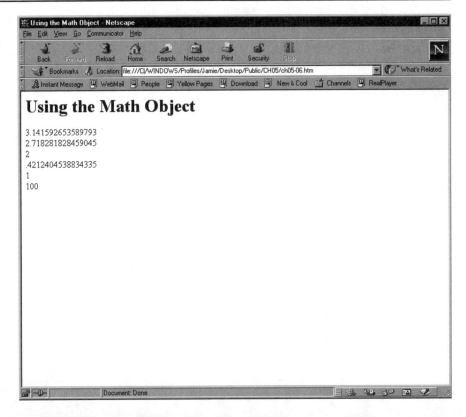

The *Number* Object

The Number object type allows numbers to be treated as objects. The ECMA-Script 1 specification defines the following Number properties:

MAX_VALUE   The number is the maximum possible numeric value.

MIN_VALUE   The number is the minimum possible numeric value.

NaN   The number is not a number.

NEGATIVE_INFINITY   The number is negative infinity.

POSITIVE_INFINITY   The number is positive infinity.

prototype   The prototype property that is supported by all object types.

The above properties are used to identify numbers as having special characteristics. They are not normally used in scripts. Instead, use the properties and methods of the Global object.

The ECMAScript 1 specification defines the following Number methods:

toString(*radix*)   Returns a string that represents the number in base *radix*.

valueOf()   Returns the numeric value of the Number object.

Instances of the Number object are created by supplying a numeric value to the Number() constructor:

```
myNumber = new Number(123.456)
```

The *Object* Object

The Object object is the base object from which all other objects are derived. Its properties and methods are available to other object types.

The Object object supports the prototype and constructor properties. The constructor property identifies the name of the object's constructor.

The Object object supports the toString() and valueOf() methods. The toString() method converts an object to a string representation. The valueOf() method returns the primitive value (number, string, or Boolean) of an object if one is associated with the object. Otherwise, it returns the object itself.

Object objects can be created by supplying a number, string, Boolean value, or function in the Object() constructor. However, this is rarely done. Instead, it is better to use the constructor of the specific object type (that is, Number(), String(), Boolean(), or Function()).

The *String* Object

The String object type allows strings to be accessed as objects. It supports the length and prototype properties. The length property identifies the string's length in characters.

The String object type provides a set of methods for manipulating strings. The methods defined in the ECMAScript 1 specification are summarized in Table 5.8. Any JavaScript string value or variable containing a string value is able to use these methods. Both Netscape and Internet Explorer define String methods in addition to those contained in Table 5.8. These additional methods are covered in online Appendix A, "Comparing JavaScript and JScript."

TABLE 5.8: String Methods

Method	Description
charAt(index)	Returns a string that consists of the character at the specified index of the string to which the method is applied.
charCodeAt(index)	Returns the Unicode encoding of the character at the specified index.
fromCharCode(codes)	Creates a string from a comma-separated sequence of character codes.
indexOf(pattern)	Returns the index of the first string specified by the *pattern* parameter that is contained in a string. Returns *-1* if the pattern is not contained in the string.
indexOf(pattern, startIndex)	Same as the previous method except that searching starts at the position specified by *startIndex*.
lastIndexOf(pattern)	Returns the index of the last string specified by the *pattern* parameter that is contained in a string. Returns *-1* if the pattern is not contained in the string.
lastIndexOf(pattern, startIndex)	Same as the previous method except that searching starts at the position specified by *startIndex*.
split(separator)	Separates a string into an array of substrings based upon the *separator*.

Continued on next page

TABLE 5.8 CONTINUED: String Methods

Method	Description
substring(startIndex)	Returns the substring of a string beginning at *startIndex*.
substring(startIndex, endIndex)	Returns the substring of a string beginning at *startIndex* and ending at *endIndex*.
toLowerCase()	Returns a copy of the string converted to lowercase.
toString()	Returns the string value of the object.
toUpperCase()	Returns a copy of the string converted to uppercase.
valueOf()	Returns the string value of the object.

Listing 5.7 illustrates the use of the String object type. The script in the document body begins by defining the function displayLine(), which displays text followed by the <BR> tag. The displayLine() function is used to display several text strings which are modified using sample string methods. Figure 5.8 shows the Web page generated by Listing 5.7.

Listing 5.7   Using the *String* Object (ch05-07.htm)

```
<HTML>
<HEAD>
<TITLE>Using the String Object Type</TITLE>
</HEAD>
<BODY>
<SCRIPT LANGUAGE="JavaScript"><!-
function displayLine(text) {
 document.write(text+"<BR>")
}
s = new String("This is a test of the JavaScript String methods.")
displayLine('s = '+s)
displayLine('s.charAt(1) = '+s.charAt(1))
displayLine('s.charCodeAt(1) = '+s.charCodeAt(1))
displayLine('s.indexOf("is") = '+s.indexOf("is"))
displayLine('s.lastIndexOf("is") = '+s.lastIndexOf("is"))
displayLine('s.substring(22,32) = '+s.substring(22,32))
displayLine('s.toLowerCase() = '+s.toLowerCase())
displayLine('s.toUpperCase() = '+s.toUpperCase())
```

```
split = s.split(" ")
for(i=0; i<split.length; ++i)
 displayLine('split['+i+'] = '+split[i])
// –></SCRIPT>
</BODY>
</HTML>
```

FIGURE 5.8:

Using the String object
(Listing 5.7)

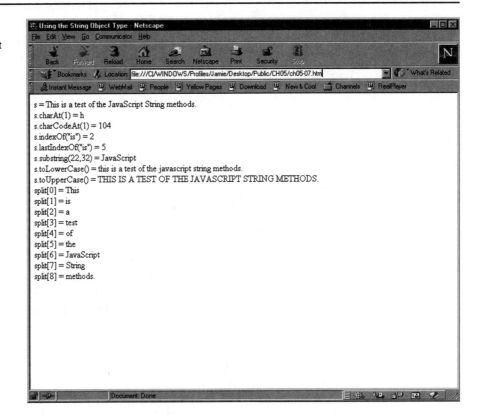

Creating *String* Objects

String objects may be created in the same manner as other JavaScript objects using the new operator. For example, the variable text may be assigned the string "I am a string" using the following statement:

```
text = new String("I am a string")
```

The above statement is equivalent to:

```
text = "I am a string"
```

Regular Expressions and the *RegExp* Object

Support for *regular expressions* was introduced in JavaScript 1.2. Regular expressions are string expressions that describe a pattern of characters. They provide a powerful capability for finding patterns in text strings and performing search and replace operations on text. Regular expressions make use of a very compact, powerful, but somewhat arcane syntax that is covered in detail in online Appendix C, "Regular Expressions." In JavaScript, regular expressions are implemented using the RegExp object. The RegExp object is also covered in Appendix C.

NOTE   Although regular expressions were not included in the ECMAScript 1 specification, they will be included in ECMAScript 2.

Color Constants

JavaScript defines a number of color constants that can be used with methods and functions that take color parameters. Some of these color constants are `"red"`, `"orange"`, `"yellow"`, `"green"`, `"blue"`, `"white"`, `"black"`, and `"brown"`. A complete list of the color constants can be found in online Appendix B, "Accessing Online References."

Defining Object Types

JavaScript provides the capability for you to define your own object types and create specific object instances. To create a new object type, you simply define a function that is used to construct specific instances of the object type. Essentially, this constructor function does two things:

- It assigns values to the object type's properties.
- It identifies other functions to be used as the object type's methods.

As an example of defining a new object type, we'll create the `table` object type. This object type will be used to create simple tables using JavaScript and write them to the current document.

The function used as a constructor of an object type must have the same name as the object type.

Identifying and Assigning Properties

The first thing that we'll do is identify the properties of the `table` object type. The number of rows and columns of the table are obvious properties with which to start. Let's name these properties `table.rows` and `table.columns`. We'll also need to define a property to store the elements of the table. Let's call this property `table.data` and let it be an array of the following length:

```
table.rows * table.columns
```

Because HTML allows some table cells to be designated as header cells, let's also define the property `table.header` as an array of the same length as above, `table.rows * table.columns`, where each element is a Boolean value indicating whether a table cell is a header cell. Finally, let's define a property, `table.border`, that identifies the border width of the table. The following code shows how the table constructor would be defined using the items we just identified:

```
function table(rows,columns) {
  this.rows = rows
  this.columns = columns
  this.border = 0
  this.data = new Array(rows*columns)
  this.header = new Array(rows*columns)
}
```

As you can see, the `table()` constructor takes the parameters `rows` and `columns`, and assigns them to `this.rows` and `this.columns`. The `this` prefix is a special keyword that is used to refer to the current object. For example, the statement `this.rows = rows` assigns the value stored in the `rows` parameter to the `rows` property of the current object. Similarly, `this.columns = columns` assigns the `columns` parameter to the `columns` property of the current object. The parameters to the `table()` constructor do not have to be named rows and columns—they could have been named x and y. However, it is common to see parameters named after the object type properties to which they are assigned.

The `border` property of the current object is set to the default value of 0. This results in the creation of a borderless table. As mentioned earlier, the `data` and `header` properties are each assigned an array of size `rows * columns`.

In order to create an object that is an instance of the `table` object type, you use the new operator in conjunction with the `table` constructor. For example, the following statement creates a table of three rows by four columns and assigns it to the t variable:

```
t = new table(3,4)
```

Defining Methods

So far, we've defined the properties of the `table` object type. However, we'll need to define some methods to update the values of the `data`, `header`, and `border` properties and to write the `table` object to a `document` object.

Methods are defined by assigning the name of an already defined function to a method name in an object type constructor. For example, suppose the `table_setValue()` function is defined as follows. This function sets the value of the table cell at the specified `row` and `column` parameters to the `value` parameter.

```
function table_setValue(row,col,value) {
  this.data[row*this.columns+col]=value
}
```

We can use the above-defined `table_setValue()` function as the `setValue()` method of the `table` object type by including the following statement in the `table` constructor:

```
this.setValue = table_setValue
```

Note that trailing parentheses are not used in the above statement. The new table constructor is as follows:

```
function table(rows,columns) {
  this.rows = rows
  this.columns = columns
  this.border = 0
  this.data = new Array(rows*columns)
  this.header = new Array(rows*columns)
  this.setValue = table_setValue
}
```

An example of invoking the setValue() method for the table object stored in the t variable follows:

```
t.setValue(2,3,"Hello")
```

The above statement sets the table data value at row 2 and column 3 to "Hello".

Definition of the *table* Object

Listing 5.8 provides a complete definition of the table object. Note that functions must be defined before they can be assigned to a method name.

Listing 5.8   **Definition of the *table* Object (table.js)**

```
function table_getValue(row,col) {
 return this.data[row*this.columns+col]
}
function table_setValue(row,col,value) {
 this.data[row*this.columns+col]=value
}
function table_set(contents) {
 var n = contents.length
 for(var j=0;j<n;++j) this.data[j]=contents[j]
}
function table_isHeader(row,col) {
 return this.header[row*this.columns+col]
}
function table_makeHeader(row,col) {
 this.header[row*this.columns+col]=true
}
function table_makeNormal(row,col) {
 this.header[row*this.columns+col]=false
}
function table_makeHeaderRow(row) {
 for(var j=0;j<this.columns;++j)
   this.header[row*this.columns+j]=true
}
function table_makeHeaderColumn(col) {
 for(var i=0;i<this.rows;++i)
   this.header[i*this.columns+col]=true
}
function table_write(doc) {
```

```
doc.write("<TABLE BORDER="+this.border+">")
for(var i=0;i<this.rows;++i) {
 doc.write("<TR>")
 for(var j=0;j<this.columns;++j) {
  if(this.header[i*this.columns+j]) {
   doc.write("<TH>")
   doc.write(this.data[i*this.columns+j])
   doc.write("</TH>")
  }else{
   doc.write("<TD>")
   doc.write(this.data[i*this.columns+j])
   doc.write("</TD>")
  }
 }
 doc.writeln("</TR>")
}
doc.writeln("</TABLE>")
}
function table(rows,columns) {
 this.rows = rows
 this.columns = columns
 this.border = 0
 this.data = new Array(rows*columns)
 this.header = new Array(rows*columns)
 this.getValue = table_getValue
 this.setValue = table_setValue
 this.set = table_set
 this.isHeader = table_isHeader
 this.makeHeader = table_makeHeader
 this.makeNormal = table_makeNormal
 this.makeHeaderRow = table_makeHeaderRow
 this.makeHeaderColumn = table_makeHeaderColumn
 this.write = table_write
}
```

Listing 5.8 adds the getValue(), set(), isHeader(), makeHeader(), make-Normal(), makeHeaderRow(), makeHeaderColumn(), and write() methods to the table definition introduced in the previous section.

The getValue() method returns the data value stored at a specified row and column. The set() method stores an array of values as the contents of a table. The makeHeader() and makeNormal() methods are used to identify whether a cell should or should not be a header cell. The makeHeaderRow() and makeHeader-Column() methods are used to designate an entire row or column as consisting of header cells. The write() method is used to write a table to a document object.

Using the *table* Object

Listing 5.9 provides an example of the use of the table object. The document's body contains a script that creates, initializes, and displays a three-row by four-column table object. Using the SRC attribute of the script tag, it includes the table.js file presented in the previous section. It begins by creating a table object and assigning it to the t variable. It then creates an array, named contents, that contains a list of values. The set() method is invoked to assign the contents array to the cells of the table stored at t. The table's border property is set to 4 pixels, and the cells of column 0 are designated as header cells. Finally, the write() method is used to write the table to the current document object. Figure 5.9 shows the Web page resulting from the script of Listing 5.9.

Listing 5.9   **Using the *table* Object (ch05-09.htm)**

```
<HTML>
<HEAD>
<TITLE>Defining Object Types</TITLE>
<SCRIPT LANGUAGE="JavaScript" SRC="table.js"><!-
// -></SCRIPT>
</HEAD>
<BODY>
<H1>Defining Object Types</H1>
<SCRIPT LANGUAGE="JavaScript"><!-
t = new table(3,4)
contents = new Array("This","is","a","test","of","the","table",
  "object.","Let's","see","it","work.")
t.set(contents)
t.border=4
t.makeHeaderColumn(0)
t.write(document)
// -></SCRIPT>
</BODY>
</HTML>
```

FIGURE 5.9:

An example table
(Listing 5.9)

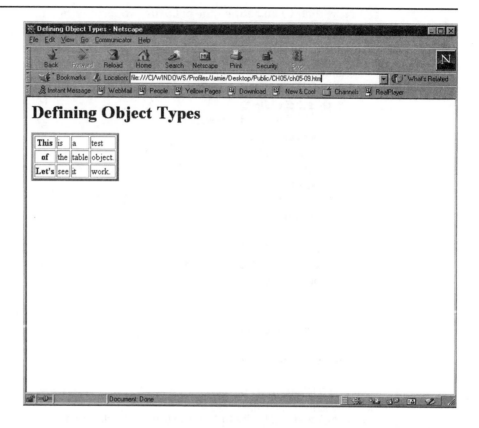

Adding Properties and Methods to an Object Type

Object types that can be instantiated with the new operator are referred to as *instantiable* object types. They include all user-defined object types and most of the predefined object types. Examples of object types that are not instantiable are Math and Global. JavaScript provides the capability to add properties and methods to already defined instantiable object types via the prototype property.

For example, suppose we wanted to add a background color attribute to the table object type defined in previous section. We could add the new attribute with the following statement:

```
table.prototype.bgColor = "cyan"
```

The above statement uses the prototype property of the table object type to create a new property called bgColor to represent the background color of the table.

Now that we've defined the `bgColor` property, we should create an additional method called `colorWrite()` that writes a table using the `bgColor` property. The following function performs this processing:

```
function table_colorWrite(doc) {
  doc.write("<TABLE BORDER="+this.border+"BGCOLOR="
   +this.bgColor+">")
  for(var i=0;i<this.rows;++i) {
   doc.write("<TR>")
   for(var j=0;j<this.columns;++j) {
    if(this.header[i*this.columns+j]) {
     doc.write("<TH>")
     doc.write(this.data[i*this.columns+j])
     doc.write("</TH>")
    }else{
     doc.write("<TD>")
     doc.write(this.data[i*this.columns+j])
     doc.write("</TD>")
    }
   }
   doc.writeln("</TR>")
  }
  doc.writeln("</TABLE>")
}
```

We can use the `table_colorWrite()` function in the listing above as the `color-Write()` method by including the following statement in our script:

```
table.prototype.colorWrite=table_colorWrite
```

Listing 5.10 updates the script shown in Listing 5.9 to make use of the new `bgColor` property and the `colorWrite()` method. Figure 5.10 shows the Web page that results from Listing 5.10. Note that we did not have to modify the original `table.js` file that is included via the SRC attribute.

TIP   Always create an object of the object type being modified before using the object type's **prototype** property. This will ensure that any new properties and methods are correctly added.

Listing 5.10   **Updating an Object Type Definition (ch05-10.htm)**

```
<HTML>
<HEAD>
<TITLE>Updating Object Types</TITLE>
<SCRIPT LANGUAGE="JavaScript" SRC="table.js"><!-
// -></SCRIPT>
</HEAD>
<BODY>
<H1>Updating Object Types</H1>
<SCRIPT LANGUAGE="JavaScript"><!-
function table_colorWrite(doc) {
 doc.write("<TABLE BORDER="+this.border+" BGCOLOR="+this.bgColor+">")
 for(var i=0;i<this.rows;++i) {
  doc.write("<TR>")
  for(var j=0;j<this.columns;++j) {
   if(this.header[i*this.columns+j]) {
    doc.write("<TH>")
    doc.write(this.data[i*this.columns+j])
    doc.write("</TH>")
   }else{
    doc.write("<TD>")
    doc.write(this.data[i*this.columns+j])
    doc.write("</TD>")
   }
  }
  doc.writeln("</TR>")
 }
 doc.writeln("</TABLE>")
}

t = new table(3,4)
table.prototype.bgColor="cyan"
table.prototype.colorWrite=table_colorWrite
contents = new
Array("This","is","a","test","of","the","table","object.",
 "Let's","see","it","work.")
t.set(contents)
t.border=4
t.makeHeaderColumn(0)
```

```
t.colorWrite(document)
// -></SCRIPT>
</BODY>
</HTML>
```

FIGURE 5.10:

Tables with a background
color (Listing 5.10)

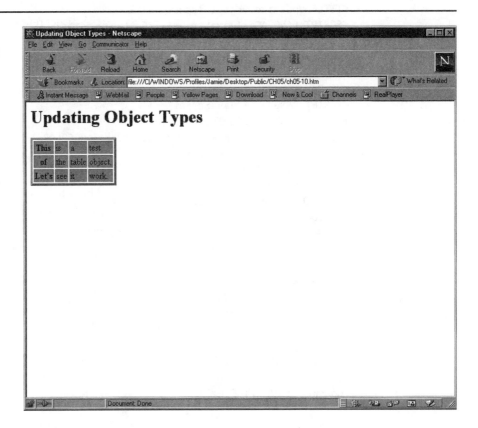

Deleting Properties and Methods

The delete operator was introduced in Chapter 3, "Using Operators, Statements, and Functions," where you learned how it can be used to delete an element of an array. The `delete` operator can also be used to delete a property or method of a user-defined object. Its syntax is as follows:

```
delete objectName.propertyName
delete objectName.methodName
```

For example, suppose the `myTable` variable refers to a `table` object. The following statement deletes the `header` property of the object referenced by `myTable`:

```
delete myTable.header
```

There are few occasions in which it is desirable to delete a property or method of an existing object. As such, the `delete` operator is rarely used.

The *event, Event,* and *Error* Objects

In Chapter 4, "Handling Events," you learned how to handle events and errors. You covered the `event`, `Event`, and `error` objects. Now that you know what objects are, we'll go over the properties and methods of these objects.

An instance of the `event` object is created whenever an event occurs during the execution of a script. Navigator and Internet Explorer each define a different set of properties for the `event` object. Both browsers use the `type` property to identify the type of event that occurred and the `screenX` and `screenY` properties to identify the screen location at which the event occurred. Navigator and Internet Explorer also implement some similar properties with different names as summarized in Table 5.9.

TABLE 5.9: Similar Navigator and Internet Explorer *Event* Properties

Navigator Property	Internet Explorer Property	Description
`pageX, pageY`	`clientX, clientY`	The location of the event relative to the Web page
`target`	`srcElement`	The event source
`which`	`button`	The mouse button associated with the event
`key`	`keyCode`	The Unicode character code of the character corresponding to the key press
`modifiers`	`altKey, ctrlKey, shiftKey`	The state of the Alt, Control, or Shift keys

Summary

This chapter described JavaScript's support of objects and object-based programming. It introduced the JavaScript Object Model and summarized the predefined JavaScript objects. It also showed you how to create your own objects and methods. In the next chapter, you'll learn how to use predefined JavaScript objects that allow you to create and manage multiple frames and windows. The next chapter will expand upon the window and other objects that were introduced in this chapter.

PART II

Using Predefined Objects and Methods

■ CHAPTER 6: Creating Frames and Windows

■ CHAPTER 7: Processing Forms

■ CHAPTER 8: Using Hidden Fields and Cookies

■ CHAPTER 9: Working with Links

■ CHAPTER 10: Using Images

■ CHAPTER 11: Doing Math

CHAPTER

SIX

6

Creating Frames and Windows

- Opening and Closing Windows

- Simple Communication Windows—Messages, Prompts, and Status Bars

- Using the Window *Synonyms*

- Frames and Frame Sets

- Generating Document Contents

- Browser Identification

- Working with Colors

This chapter shows you how to use five important JavaScript objects: the `window`, `frame`, `document`, `navigator`, and `screen` objects. It describes how to use them to create and manage multiple frames and windows in your Web pages. It also shows how to obtain version information about the browsers that execute your scripts. When you have finished this chapter, you'll be able to use frames and windows to effectively organize your Web pages.

The *window* Object

The `window` object is basic to all browser scripts. Like the `navigator` object, the `window` object is a top-level object that is automatically defined by your browser. A separate `window` object is defined for each window that is opened. If you use Navigator, these windows are listed under the Window menu item from the Communicator pull-down menu as shown in Figure 6.1. Internet Explorer does not have a similar capability.

FIGURE 6.1:

Your browser's Window pull-down menu lists all of the windows that are currently opened.

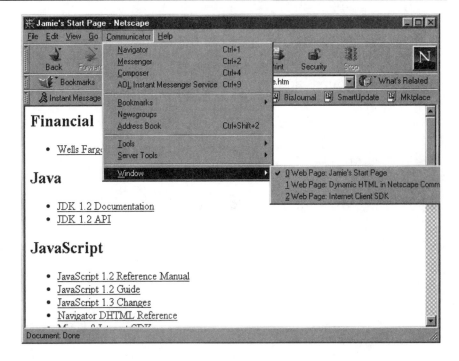

The `window` object is so important to writing browser scripts that the current `window` object is assumed by default in many cases and may be omitted. For example, when you use the statement:

```
document.write("Write this text to the current window.")
```

in a script, JavaScript assumes that you are referring to the current window object and executes the following statement:

```
window.document.write("Write this text to the current window.")
```

In addition, the `window` object has several *synonyms* that let you refer to the current `window` object being displayed by your browser, as well as to other related window objects. These synonyms are implemented as properties of the `window` object. You'll learn about these synonyms in the section "Using the Window Synonyms," later in this chapter.

Tables 6.1 and 6.2 summarize the properties and methods of the `window` object that both Navigator and Internet Explorer support. These properties and methods are described in the following sections. Online Appendix A, "Comparing JavaScript and JScript," identifies properties and methods that are unique to either Navigator or Internet Explorer.

TABLE 6.1: Properties of the `window` Object

Property	Description
`closed`	Identifies whether the window is closed.
`defaultStatus`	Specifies the default status message that appears on the status bar on the bottom of the browser window.
`document`	An object that refers to the current document being displayed in a window.
`frames`	An array that consists of all frame objects contained in a window object.
`history`	Refers to the window's `history` object, which contains a list of URLs last loaded into the window.
`length`	Identifies the number of frames contained in a `window`.
`location`	An object that identifies the URL associated with a `window` object.
`name`	Identifies the name of the window.
`offscreen-Buffering`	Boolean value that specifies whether offscreen buffering of window information should be used. Offscreen buffering is used to load all of a window's elements before displaying the window.

Continued on next page

TABLE 6.1 CONTINUED: Properties of the window Object

Property	Description
opener	Identifies the window object that caused a window to be created and opened.
parent	A synonym that identifies the window containing a particular window.
self	A synonym that identifies the current window being referenced.
status	Specifies a temporary message that appears on the status bar on the bottom of the browser window.
top	A synonym that refers to the topmost browser window in a series of nested windows.
window	A synonym that identifies the current window being referenced.

TABLE 6.2: Methods of the window Object

Method	Description
alert(text)	Displays an alert dialog box.
blur()	Removes focus from a window.
clearInterval(interval)	Clears a previously set interval timer.
clearTimeout(timer)	Clears a previously set timeout.
close()	Closes the specified window.
confirm(text)	Displays a confirm dialog box.
focus()	Gives focus to a window.
open(url,name,[options])	Opens a new window and creates a new window object.
prompt(text,defaultInput)	Displays a prompt dialog box.
scroll(x,y)	Scrolls a window to the specific location.
setInterval(expression, milliseconds)setInterval (function, milliseconds, [arguments])	Repeatedly evaluates an expression or invokes a function after the elapse of a specified time interval. The *arguments* are a possibly empty comma-separated list of arguments to the function to be invoked. Returns an interval reference that can be cleared by clearInterval().
setTimeout(expression, milliseconds)setTimeout (function, milliseconds, [arguments])	Evaluates an expression or invokes a function after a timeout period has elapsed. The *arguments* are possibly an empty comma-separated list of arguments to the function to be invoked. Returns a timer reference that can be cleared by clearTimer().

Opening and Closing Windows

When you launch your browser it creates and opens a window to display your startup page. This is the most common way that a `window` object is created. In most cases, the window that you open during browser startup stays open until you exit your browser. When you open a new Web document or a local file with your browser, you usually *replace* the document contained in the opened window and do not create or open a new window. In Netscape Navigator, new windows are created and opened when you select New ➢ Navigator Window from the File menu. In Microsoft Internet Explorer, you use the New Window menu item to create a new window. When a new window is created, it can be accessed from the browser's Window pull-down menu as shown in Figure 6.1.

The `open()` and `close()` methods may be used from within JavaScript to open and close browser windows. The `open()` method opens a new Web browser window at a specified URL with a given set of options. A newly created object is returned as the result of invoking `open()`. This object is usually assigned to a variable, which is used to keep track of the window. The syntax of the `open()` method is as follows:

```
variable = open(url, name, [options])
```

where *variable* is the name of the variable to which the `window` object is assigned, *url* is the URL of the document to open in the window, *name* is the name to be associated with the window, and *options* can be used to specify different characteristics of the window. The name may be used in the target attribute of a `<form>` tag or an `<a>` tag.

The options, if supplied, consist of a set of comma-separated *option=value* pairs. The options that both Navigator and Internet Explorer support are shown in Table 6.3. Browser-specific options are covered in Online Appendix A, "Comparing JavaScript and JScript."

TABLE 6.3: Options of the open() Method

Option	Values	Description
toolbar	Yes no	The window has a tool bar.
location	Yes no	The window displays the location field.
directories	Yes no	The window provides directory buttons.

Continued on next page

TABLE 6.3 CONTINUED: Options of the open() Method

Option	Values	Description
status	Yes no	The window has a status bar.
menubar	Yes no	The window has a menu bar.
scrollbars	Yes no	The window provides scroll bars.
resizable	Yes no	The window is resizable.
width	Integer	The width of the window in pixels.
height	Integer	The height of the window in pixels.

NOTE: The values 1 and 0 may be used instead of yes and no.

An example of the use of the open() method follows:

```
win = open("http://www.sybex.com","sybex")
```

The above statement opens a new window and loads the Sybex home page, located at http://www.sybex.com, into the window. The window is given the name *sybex* and is assigned to the win variable.

The close() method is used to close a window that has been opened. For example, win.close() can be used to close the window opened above.

Listings 6.1 and 6.2 provide a colorful example of how the open() and close() methods are used in an example Web page. Listing 6.1 creates a Web page that announces a New Year's Eve party. Figure 6.2 shows the party invitation that is generated by Listing 6.1.

Listing 6.1   **Opening a New Window (ch06-01.htm)**

```
<HTML>
<HEAD>
<TITLE>Party</TITLE>
<SCRIPT LANGUAGE="JavaScript"><!-
function directions() {
 open("ch06-02.htm","map")
}
// -></SCRIPT>
</HEAD>
```

```
<BODY>
<H1>New Years Eve Party!</H1>
<P><B>When:</B> December 31, 1999 8pm</P>
<P><B>Where:</B> 613 Beyer Way #504</P>
<P><B>Dress:</B> Casual </P>
<FORM>
<INPUT TYPE="BUTTON" VALUE="Click for directions"
 ONCLICK="directions()">
</FORM>
<P>RSVP by December 28th.
<A HREF="mailto:jamie@jaworski.com">
 <I>jamie@jaworski.com</I></A></P>
</BODY>
</HTML>
```

Listing 6.2	Closing a Window (ch06-02.htm)

```
<HTML>
<HEAD>
<TITLE>Directions</TITLE>
</HEAD>
<BODY ONLOAD="defaultStatus='It's at the big star!'">
<FORM>
<INPUT TYPE="BUTTON" VALUE="Close window"
 ONCLICK="window.close()">
</FORM>
<IMG SRC="map.gif">
</BODY>
</HTML>
```

When a user clicks on the Click for Directions button shown in Figure 6.2, a new window is created and opened using the document of Listing 6.2. This window is shown in Figure 6.3. (If you select the Window menu item from the Communicator pull-down menu, you can verify that a new window has been created—see Figure 6.4.) Clicking on the Close window button closes the second window.

FIGURE 6.2:

A party invitation
(Listing 6.1)

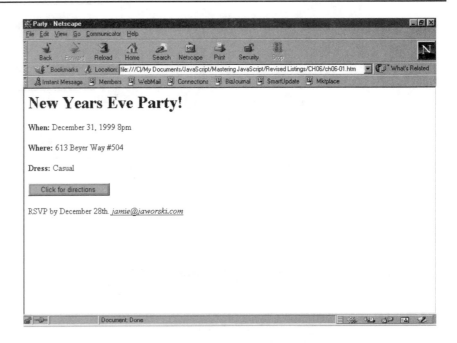

FIGURE 6.3:

Directions to the party (Listing 6.2)

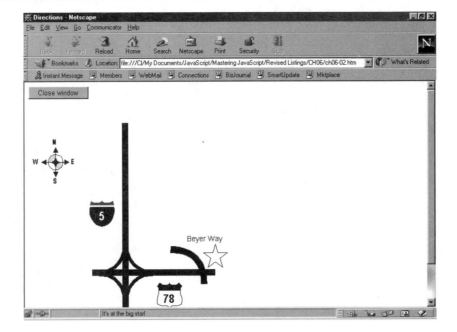

FIGURE 6.4:

A new window is created
(Listings 6.1 and 6.2).

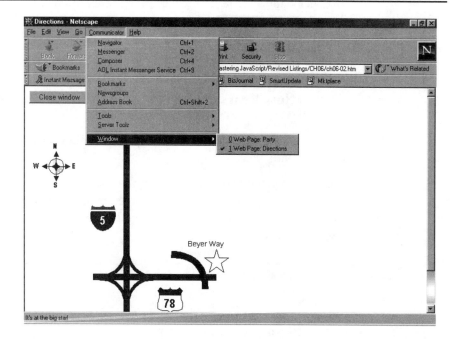

The `directions()` function of Listing 6.1 uses the `open()` method to open the file `ch06-02.htm` (see Listing 6.2). It assigns the name `"map"` to the newly created window.

As shown in Listing 6.2, the `onClick` event handler of the Close window button invokes the `close()` method to close and dispose of the second window.

Communicating with the User

Some of the most useful methods provided by the `window` object are those that support dialog with the user. These methods are as follows:

- The `alert()` method displays a dialog box containing a message and an OK button. You use the `alert()` method to provide the user with critical information that must be acknowledged, by means of an OK button.

- The `confirm()` method is similar to the `alert()` method except that it produces a dialog box with a message, an OK button, and a Cancel button. The `confirm()` method returns *true* if the user clicks OK and *false* if the user clicks Cancel. You use the confirm() method to inform the user and ask him to confirm whether he wants to perform a particular action.

- The prompt() method displays a message to the user and prompts the user to type information into a text field. It provides the capability to display default text in the text field. You use the prompt() method to obtain text input from the user such as a name or a URL. The value entered by the user is the return value of the prompt method.

You've used these methods in Chapter 4, "Handling Events," and Chapter 5, "Working with Objects."

Listing 6.3 provides an example of the use of each of these three methods. Figure 6.5 shows the initial page displayed by this script. When you open this script in your browser, you can click on the buttons provided to see an example of each type of dialog box.

Listing 6.3   Dialog Box Demo (ch06-03.htm)

```
<HTML>
<HEAD>
<TITLE>Dialog box demo</TITLE>
</HEAD>
<BODY>
<FORM>
<INPUT TYPE="BUTTON" VALUE="Alert"
 ONCLICK="alert('An alert dialog box.')">
<INPUT TYPE="BUTTON" VALUE="Confirm"
 ONCLICK="confirm('A confirm dialog box.')">
<INPUT TYPE="BUTTON" VALUE="Prompt"
 ONCLICK="prompt('A prompt dialog box.','Type something!')">
</FORM>
</BODY>
</HTML>
```

FIGURE 6.5:

Dialog box demo opening
display (Listing 6.3)

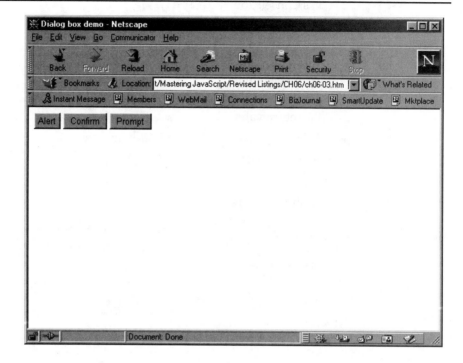

Displaying Status Information

The window object provides two properties that can be used to display status information in the browser's status bar:

- The defaultStatus property specifies a permanent default status message.

- The status property specifies a transient status message that appears as the result of a user action such as moving a mouse to a particular window location.

Use the defaultStatus property to show any messages that you want permanently displayed.

Using the Window Synonyms

As mentioned earlier in the section "The `window` Object," the `window` object provides several properties that are used as synonyms to identify the current `window` object as well as related objects. The `window` and `self` properties both refer to the current window being referenced. The `parent` property is used in multi-frame windows and refers to the window that contains a particular window. The `opener` property refers to the window from which a particular window was opened. The `top` property is used with framed windows. It refers to the topmost window containing a particular window.

Working with Timeouts

The `setTimeout()` and `clearTimeout()` methods provide a clever way to wait a specified amount of time for a user to perform a particular action and, if the action does not occur within the specified time, perform timeout processing. The `setTimeout()` method identifies an expression to be evaluated after a specified number of milliseconds; it is this expression that performs the timeout processing.

The `setTimeout()` method returns a value that is used to identify the timeout. It is usually assigned to a variable as shown in the following example:

```
timVar = setTimeout("timeoutProcessing()",10000)
```

In the above statement, the `setTimeout()` method is invoked to perform the timeout processing specified by the `timeoutProcessing()` function after 10,000 milliseconds (10 seconds) have elapsed. The `setTimeout()` method returns a value that identifies the timeout. This value is assigned to the `timVar` variable.

The `clearTimeout()` method is used to cancel a timeout before it occurs and prevent the timeout processing from being performed. It takes the value of the timeout as an argument. For example, to clear the timeout created above, use the following statement:

```
clearTimeout(timVar)
```

The above statement clears the timeout identified by `timVar`. This prevents the `timeoutProcessing()` from being invoked after the timeout period has occurred.

Listing 6.4 provides a more concrete example of performing timeout processing. It generates the Web page shown in Figure 6.6 and sets a 10-second timeout for the user to click on the provided button. If the user does not click on the button within 10 seconds the alert dialog box shown in Figure 6.7 is displayed. If the user does click on the button within 10 seconds the button's `onClick` event handler clears the timeout and congratulates the user.

Listing 6.4   A Timeout Processing Example (ch06-04.htm)

```
<HTML>
<HEAD>
<TITLE>Timeout Program</TITLE>
<SCRIPT LANGUAGE="JavaScript"><!-
function setTimer() {
 timer=setTimeout("alert('Too slow!')",10000)
}
function clearTimer() {
 clearTimeout(timer)
 alert("Congratulations!")
}
// -></SCRIPT>
</HEAD>
<BODY>
<SCRIPT LANGUAGE="JavaScript"><!-
setTimer()
// -></SCRIPT>
<FORM>
<INPUT TYPE="BUTTON" VALUE="Click here within ten seconds."
 ONCLICK="clearTimer()">
</FORM>
</BODY>
</HTML>
```

FIGURE 6.6:

Opening window for time-out processing example (Listing 6.4)

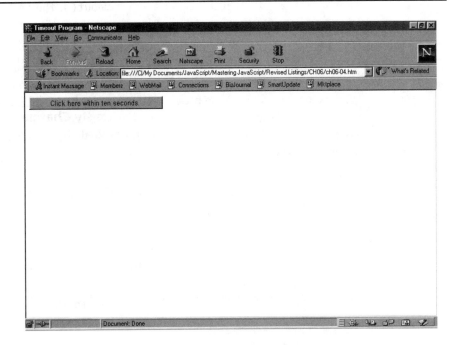

FIGURE 6.7:

This is what happens when a timeout occurs (Listing 6.4).

Working with Intervals

The sbetInterval() and clearInterval() methods were introduced in JavaScript 1.2. These methods are used to repeatedly execute a function or expression every so many milliseconds. This capability is very useful in performing animation, as you'll learn in Chapter 19, "Creating Multimedia Applications." The setInterval() method is similar to setTimeout(). The difference is that set-Timeout() executes a function or expression once, while setInterval() executes it repeatedly. Listing 6.5 provides an example of using setInterval(). It changes the document background color every three seconds. Figure 6.8 provides a snapshot of its output.

Listing 6.5   **Using *setInterval()* to Repeatedly Change the Document Background Color (ch06-05.htm)**

```
<HTML>
<HEAD>
<TITLE>Using setInterval()</TITLE>
<SCRIPT LANGUAGE="JavaScript1.2"><!-
colors = new Array("red","orange","green","blue","brown","purple",
 "gray","white")
colorIndex = 0
function changeColor() {
 document.bgColor = colors[colorIndex]
 colorIndex = (colorIndex + 1) % colors.length
}
function startColorChange() {
 setInterval("changeColor()",3000)
}
window.onload = startColorChange
// -></SCRIPT>
</HEAD>
<BODY BGCOLOR="white">
<H1>Changing Background Colors</H1>
<P>The <CODE>setInterval()</CODE> method is used to repeatedly change
the document background color every three seconds.</P>
</BODY>
</HTML>
```

FIGURE 6.8:

The document background
color changes every three
seconds (Listing 6.5).

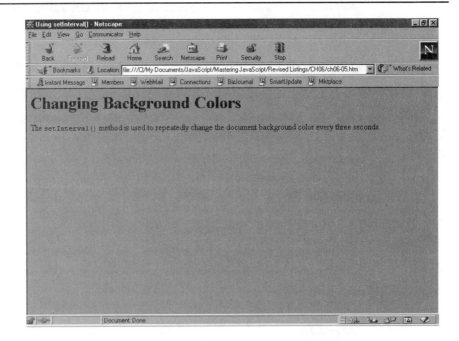

The *frame* Object

Frames are an HTML innovation developed by Netscape. They enable you to partition a window into independent display areas and organize and control the information displayed in these areas in powerful ways. You've already been exposed to frames in Chapter 4, "Handling Events." Their use is summarized in this section in preparation for introducing the frame object.

An HTML file can contain either a document body or a *frame set*. You already know what a document body is, but what is a frame set? Frame sets are used to organize frames. If a file contains a document body, it uses the <body> tags to specify the document's contents. If a file contains a frame set, it uses the <frameset> tags instead of the <body> tags, to enclose one or more <frame> tags which are used to identify the individual frames contained in the frame set. Frame sets can also be nested within each other. The <frame> tags identify other HTML files to be loaded in the frame. These files can contain a document body or another (nested) frame set.

The <frameset> tag supports the ROWS and COLS attributes. These attributes are used to lay out the frames contained in the frame set. By default, they specify the dimensions of the frame set, in pixels.

Frame objects are automatically created by your browser and they enable your scripts to control how frames are used. These frame objects allow you to load, based on user-generated or other events, new documents into frames. For example, a common use of frames is to use one frame as a clickable table of contents and use another frame to display the sections the user has selected.

The properties and methods of the frame object are the same as the window object with one exception—the frame object does not support the close() method. Navigator and Internet Explorer actually implement frame objects as window objects. That's because frame objects are also windows in the sense that a frame can contain a document body or a frame set. This important characteristic of frames allows multiple nested frame sets to be displayed in a single browser window.

Tic-Tac-Toe

In order to learn how to use frames and have some fun at the same time, in this section you're going to use frames to create a tic-tac-toe game. Several HTML and JavaScript files work together to implement this game.

Listing 6.6 shows the contents of the ttt.htm file, which provides the main entry point into the game. When you open the ttt.htm file with your browser it displays the window shown in Figure 6.9. It displays a 3×3 tic-tac-toe grid in the upper-left corner and a Restart button in the lower-right corner.

Listing 6.6   The Main Tic-Tac-Toe File (ttt.htm)

```
<HTML>
<HEAD>
<TITLE>Tic Tac Toe</TITLE></HEAD>
<FRAMESET ROWS="300,*" COLS="300,*" BORDER=0>
<FRAME SRC="board.htm">
<FRAME SRC="values.htm">
<FRAME SRC="blank.htm">
<FRAME SRC="control.htm">
</FRAMESET>
</HTML>
```

FIGURE 6.9:

The initial tic-tac-toe display (Listing 6.6)

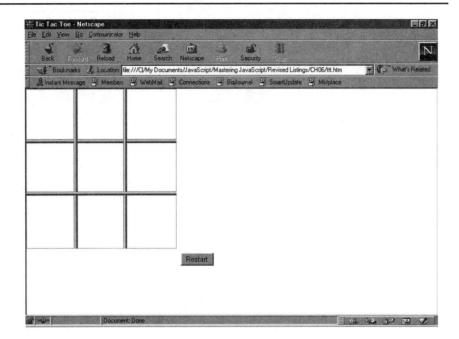

FIGURE 6.9:

The initial tic-tac-toe display (Listing 6.6)

The Top-Level Frame Set

The `ttt.htm` file is the top-level frame set. This file creates a frame set that has two rows and two columns. The first row and first column are 300 pixels wide and the second row and column use the rest of the window. The frame set does not have a border.

The four frames making up the frame set load the HTML files `board.htm`, `values.htm`, `blank.htm`, and `control.htm`. The tic-tac-toe grid is created by the `board.htm` file that is loaded into the first frame. The Restart button is created by the `control.htm` file that is loaded in the fourth frame. The files `values.htm` and `blank.htm` do not display information in their respective frames.

The *board.htm* File   Listing 6.7 shows the contents of `board.htm`. This file creates a second-level nested frame set, which is displayed in the first frame of the top-level frame set; this is itself defined in `ttt.htm`. The frame set defined by `board.htm` is organized into a 3×3 grid of 100-pixel×100-pixel squares. The documents loaded into these squares are contained in the files `square0.htm` through `square8.htm`.

Listing 6.7   **The Frames of the Tic-Tac-Toe Board (board.htm)**

```
<HTML>
<HEAD>
<TITLE>Tic Tac Toe</TITLE></HEAD>
<FRAMESET ROWS="100,100,100" COLS="100,100,100">
<FRAME SRC="square0.htm">
<FRAME SRC="square1.htm">
<FRAME SRC="square2.htm">
<FRAME SRC="square3.htm">
<FRAME SRC="square4.htm">
<FRAME SRC="square5.htm">
<FRAME SRC="square6.htm">
<FRAME SRC="square7.htm">
<FRAME SRC="square8.htm">
</FRAMESET>
</HTML>
```

Before going on to see what's in the square files, let's look at the remaining three frames defined in ttt.htm.

The *values.htm* File   The values.htm file is shown in Listing 6.8. It contains a single form with nine hidden fields, each assigned the value of *no one*. Later on in the discussion I'll show how this hidden form is used.

Listing 6.8   **A Hidden Form (values.htm)**

```
<HTML>
<HEAD>
<TITLE>Values</TITLE>
</HEAD>
<BODY>
<FORM>
<INPUT TYPE="HIDDEN" VALUE="no one">
<INPUT TYPE="HIDDEN" VALUE="no one">
<INPUT TYPE="HIDDEN" VALUE="no one">
<INPUT TYPE="HIDDEN" VALUE="no one">
<INPUT TYPE="HIDDEN" VALUE="no one">
<INPUT TYPE="HIDDEN" VALUE="no one">
<INPUT TYPE="HIDDEN" VALUE="no one">
<INPUT TYPE="HIDDEN" VALUE="no one">
```

```
<INPUT TYPE="HIDDEN" VALUE="no one">
</FORM>
</BODY>
</HTML>
```

The *blank.htm* File   The file blank.htm, shown in Listing 6.9, contains a blank
HTML file that is used as a dummy placeholder to fill up the third frame defined
in ttt.htm. It does not display any information in the browser window.

Listing 6.9   **A Blank Document (blank.htm)**

```
<HTML>
<HEAD>
<TITLE>Blank</TITLE>
</HEAD>
<BODY>
</BODY>
</HTML>
```

The *control.htm* File   Listing 6.10 shows the contents of the control.htm file. It
implements the Restart button by invoking the restart() function. This function
restarts the tic-tac-toe game to its original state using the following statement:

```
parent.location.href="ttt.htm"
```

This statement uses the parent property of the current window to access the window containing the frame set defined by ttt.htm. It then sets the href property
of the window's location, causing the ttt.htm file to be reloaded.

Listing 6.10   **Implementing the Restart Button (control.htm)**

```
<HTML>
<HEAD>
<TITLE>Blank</TITLE>
<SCRIPT LANGUAGE="JavaScript"><!-
function restart() {
 parent.location.href="ttt.htm"
}
// -></SCRIPT>
</HEAD>
```

```
<BODY>
<FORM>
<P ALIGN="CENTER">
<INPUT TYPE="Button" VALUE="Restart" onClick="restart()">
</P>
</FORM>
</BODY>
</HTML>
```

The Second-Level Frame Set

Now that we've covered the top-level frame set defined by ttt.htm, let's look into the second-level frame set defined by board.htm. As shown in Listing 6.7, this frame set defines nine frames containing the files square0.htm through square8.htm. Listing 6.11 shows as an example the contents of the square4.htm file. All nine files are identical except that the fourth line of each file sets the cell variable to a value that indicates which grid cell is occupied by a square. For instance, square0.htm sets cell to 0, square1.htm sets cell to 1, and square8.htm sets cell to 8.

Listing 6.11   A Sample Square (square4.htm)

```
<HTML>
<HEAD>
<TITLE>Blank</TITLE>
<SCRIPT LANGUAGE="JavaScript"><!-
cell=4
// -></SCRIPT>
</HEAD>
<SCRIPT LANGUAGE="JavaScript" SRC="ttt.js"><!-
// -></SCRIPT>
</HEAD>
<BODY onFocus="playerMoves()">
</BODY>
</HTML>
```

The important point to notice about the square files is that the onFocus event of each file invokes the playerMoves() function. You may wonder where this function is defined. It's defined in the ttt.js file, which is included in each square file via the SRC attribute of the `<script>` tag included in each file's head. The `ttt.js` file provides the JavaScript code that is at the heart of the tic-tac-toe game's operation. This file is shown in Listing 6.12.

Listing 6.12   **The JavaScript Code That Implements the Tic-Tac-Toe Game (ttt.js)**

```
function isBlank(n) {
 if(owns("player",n) || owns("computer",n)) return false
 return true
}
function owns(who,i) {
 var fr = parent.parent.frames[1]
 var doc = fr.document
 var field = doc.forms[0].elements[i]
 if(field==null || field.value==who) return true
 else return false
}
function setOwner(who,n) {
 var fr = parent.parent.frames[1]
 var doc = fr.document
 var field = doc.forms[0].elements[n]
 field.value=who
}
function ticTacToe(who,n1,n2,n3) {
 if(owns(who,n1) && owns(who,n2) && owns(who,n3)) {
  parent.parent.frames[3].focus()
  return true
 }
 return false
}
function isTicTacToe(who) {
 if(ticTacToe(who,0,1,2)) return true
 if(ticTacToe(who,3,4,5)) return true
 if(ticTacToe(who,6,7,8)) return true
 if(ticTacToe(who,0,3,6)) return true
 if(ticTacToe(who,1,4,7)) return true
 if(ticTacToe(who,2,5,8)) return true
 if(ticTacToe(who,0,4,8)) return true
 if(ticTacToe(who,2,4,6)) return true
 return false
```

```
}
function gameOver() {
 numMoves = 0
 for(i=0;i<9;++i) {
  if(!isBlank(i)) ++numMoves
 }
 if(numMoves==9) return true
 if(isTicTacToe("player")) return true
 if(isTicTacToe("computer")) return true
 return false
}
function computerMoves() {
 if(gameOver()) return -1
 var newMove = Math.round(9*Math.random())
 while(!isBlank(newMove)) {
  newMove = (newMove + 1) % 9
 }
 setOwner("computer",newMove)
 return newMove
}
function playerMoves() {
 if(!gameOver() && isBlank(cell)) {
  setOwner("player",cell)
  var move = computerMoves()
  location.href="o.htm"
  if(move!=-1) parent.frames[move].location.href="x.htm"
 }
}
function showWinner() {
 if(isTicTacToe("player")) alert("Congratulations! You win.")
}
function showLoser() {
 if(isTicTacToe("computer")) alert("Sorry. You Lose.")
}
```

In order to understand just what ttt.js does, open ttt.htm with your browser, and after the document has been loaded, click on one of the tic-tac-toe squares, as shown in Figure 6.10. An O appears in the square that you click; the computer responds by marking an X in another square.

FIGURE 6.10:

Playing tic-tac-toe

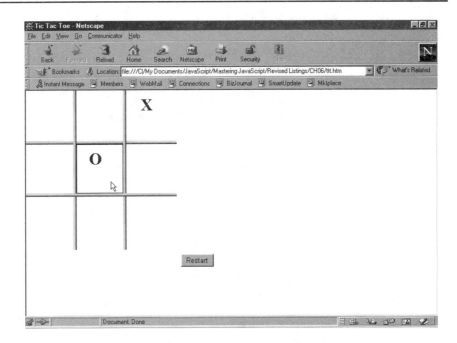

Click once more and the computer responds again; continue clicking on blank squares until the game is over. The computer plays randomly, so you *should* win at least once in a while. If you or the computer wins, then an alert dialog box up to inform you of the result. If neither of you wins, all of the squares are filled in, as in the paper version of the game.

Investigating *ttt.js*

Now that you know how the game works, let's analyze ttt.js. It defines 10 functions: isBlank(), owns(), setOwner(), ticTacToe(), isTicTacToe(), gameOver(), computerMoves(), playerMoves(), showWinner(), and showLoser().

The playerMoves() function is invoked when you click on a square in the tic-tac-toe grid. It uses the isBlank() function to determine whether the square is empty. The cell variable identifies which square has been clicked on. If the game is not over and the cell is blank, the setOwner() function is invoked to set the owner of the cell as the player. The computerMoves() function is invoked to get the program's next move. The `playerMoves()` function then loads the `o.htm` file into the frame by setting the `href` property of the document's location. This marks the frame with an O to indicate that it belongs to the player. The `o.htm` file also notifies the user if and when he or she has won the tic-tac-toe game. If the program is unable to make a move, it returns a value of -1. The `if` statement checks to see if the computer has moved, and if so, loads the `x.htm` file into the frame. This file marks the frame with an X and notifies the user if the computer has won the game.

The `isBlank()` function uses the `owns()` function to determine whether the player or the computer currently owns a cell. If either owns a cell then it returns *false*. Otherwise, it returns *true*.

The `owns()` function performs some fairly intricate processing. It sets the `doc` variable to the document loaded in the second frame of the top-level frame set. This is the document created when the `values.htm` file is loaded. I could have used the `top` property instead of `parent.parent` to access the top-level frame set. The `frames` array contains all of the `frame` objects in the frame set. The element `frames[1]` refers to the second frame. The `document` property of the `frame` object refers to the document that is loaded in the second frame. The `field` variable is assigned the element of the index (`i`) of the first form contained in the `values.htm` document. The value of this field is checked to see if it equals the value passed via the `who` argument. If the values match, then *true* is returned. Otherwise, *false* is returned. The values of the hidden fields of the form contained in the document generated by `values.htm` are used to maintain the state of the tic-tac-toe game. You'll learn more about using hidden fields in Chapter 8, "Using Hidden Fields and Cookies."

The `setOwner()` function updates the ownership of a cell by setting the *n*th cell's owner to the value of the `who` parameter. It uses `parent.parent` to access the top-level frame set, `frames[1].document` to access the frame containing the `values.htm` document, and `elements[n].value` to access the value of the *n*th hidden field in this document. It then assigns the value of `who` to this field.

The `ticTacToe()` function checks to see if the player identified by `who` owns all three of the cells specified by n1, n2, and n3. If tic-tac-toe has occurred, it sets the tic-tac-toe input focus to the frame containing the Restart button and returns a value of *true*. The `isTicTacToe()` function uses the `ticTacToe()` function to check each of the eight possible tic-tac-toe combinations.

The gameOver() function checks to see if all squares have been played or either the player or computer has made tic-tac-toe. If any of these occur, the game if over and *true* is returned. Otherwise, *false* is returned.

The computerMoves() function makes a random move for the computer. If the game is over, it returns -1. Otherwise, it uses the random() and round() methods of the Math object to generate a random integer between 0 and 8. It uses the randomly generated integer and a while statement to look for the next blank cell. When it finds a blank cell, it sets the owner of the cell to the computer and returns the frame number associated with the cell.

The showWinner() and showLoser() functions are used by the o.htm and x.htm files (Listings 6.13 and 6.14) to check to see if either the player won (showWinner()) or the computer won (showLoser()). These functions are invoked when the o.htm and x.htm files are loaded.

Listing 6.13   **Displaying an O (o.htm)**

```
<HTML>
<HEAD>
<TITLE>O</TITLE>
<SCRIPT LANGUAGE="JavaScript" SRC="ttt.js"><!-
// -></SCRIPT>
</HEAD>
<BODY onLoad="showWinner()">
<H1 ALIGN="CENTER">O</H1>
</BODY>
</HTML>
```

Listing 6.14   **Displaying an X (x.htm)**

```
<HTML>
<HEAD>
<TITLE>X</TITLE>
<SCRIPT LANGUAGE="JavaScript" SRC="ttt.js"><!-
// -></SCRIPT>
</HEAD>
<BODY onLoad="showLoser()">
<H1 ALIGN="CENTER">X</H1>
</BODY>
</HTML>
```

The *document* Object

The document object is a very important JavaScript object. It allows you to update a document that is being loaded and to access the HTML elements contained in a loaded document. It provides many properties that help you to access these elements, as shown in Table 6.4. Many of these properties are objects that we'll be studying in subsequent chapters. Table 6.5 identifies the methods of the document object that are supported by Navigator and Internet Explorer.

TABLE 6.4: Properties of the document Object

Property	Description
alinkColor	Identifies the value of the **alink** attribute of the **\<body>** tag.
anchor	An object that refers to an array contained in a document. See Chapter 9, "Working with Links."
anchors	An array of all the anchors contained in a document. See Chapter 9.
applet	An object that refers to an applet that is contained in a document. See Chapter 15, "Communicating with Java Applets."
applets	An array of all the applets contained in a document. See Chapter 15.
area	An object that refers to an image map area contained in a document. See Chapter 10, "Using Images."
bgColor	Identifies the value of the **bgcolor** attribute of the **\<body>** tag.
cookie	Identifies the value of a cookie. See Chapter 8, "Using Hidden Fields and Cookies."
domain	Identifies the domain name of the server from which the document is loaded.
embeds	An array of all the plug-ins contained in a document. See Chapter 17, "How Plug-Ins Work."
fgColor	Identifies the value of the **text** attribute of the **\<body>** tag.
form	An object that refers to a form contained in a document. See Chapter 7, "Processing Forms."
Forms[]	An array of all the forms contained in a document. See Chapter 7.
image	An object that refers to an image contained in a document. See Chapter 10, "Using Images."
Images[]	An array of all the images contained in a document. See Chapter 10.

Continued on next page

TABLE 6.4 CONTINUED: Properties of the document Object

Property	Description
lastModified	The date that a document was last modified.
link	An object that refers to a link contained in a document. See Chapter 9, "Working with Links."
links	An array of all the links contained in a document. See Chapter 9.
linkColor	Identifies the value of the link attribute of the <body> tag.
plugin	An object that refers to a plug-in contained in a document. See Chapter 17, "How Plug-Ins Work."
Plugins[]	An array of objects that describe the plug-ins supported by a browser.
referrer	The URL of the document that provided the link to a document. See Chapter 9, "Working with Links."
title	The document's title.
URL	The URL of a document. See Chapter 9.
vlinkColor	Identifies the value of the vlink attribute of the <body> tag.

TABLE 6.5: Methods of the document Object

Method	Description
close()	Closes a stream (see note following) used to create a document object.
open([mimeType][,"replace"])	Opens a stream used to create a document object with the optional MIME type. The "replace" parameter is used with the text/html MIME type to replace the current document in the history list.
write(expr1[,expr2,...,exprN])	Writes the values of the expressions to a document.
writeln(expr1[,expr2,...,exprN])	Writes the values of the expressions to a document followed by a new-line character.

NOTE   The term, "stream," in Table 6.5 refers to a sequence of input or output characters. In the case of the open() and close() methods, it refers to the sequence of characters that constitute the document being created.

Generating Document Contents

You already know how to use the methods of the document object to generate HTML. For instance, you've used write() and writeln() extensively to write HTML code to a document as it is loaded in a window. The document object also provides two additional methods—open() and close()—that can help you to generate the contents of a document. Both of these additional methods work with the write() and writeln() methods.

The open() method allows you to update a document that is in a window other than the current window. For example, suppose the variable win2 refers to a window that you have created. You can use open() to generate the document loaded into win2 as follows:

```
win2.document.open()
      .
      .
      .
win2.document.write()
win2.document.writeln()
      .
      .
      .
win2.document.close()
```

In the above example, the open() method opens the document for writing, the write() and writeln() methods are used to write to the document, and the close() method is used to close the document after writing has been completed. The vertical dots indicate code lines that were omitted.

The open() method takes two optional string parameters that specify the MIME type of the document being generated and whether the document should replace the current document in the history list. If the MIME type parameter is omitted, the *text/html* MIME type is assumed. If the MIME type parameter is supplied, then the "replace" parameter may also be used.

Your browser will display the document according to its MIME type. For example, if you open a document with the *image/gif* MIME type, then it will display the document as a GIF image. However, in order to create the GIF image you must write the GIF header and pixel data to the document.

If you use open() with a MIME type that is not supported directly by your browser it will look to see if it has a plug-in that supports the MIME type. If a suitable plug-in exists, your browser will load the plug-in and pass the contents of the document to the plug-in as the document is written. You'll learn more about using open() and close() with plug-ins in Chapter 17, "How Plug-Ins Work."

NOTE   If open() is unable to open a document for any reason, then it returns the value null. If open() is able to open a document it will return a value other than null.

Accessing Document Contents

The document object provides several properties that can be used to access the contents of an HTML document. These properties were listed in Table 6.4 earlier in the chapter. In many cases, the document properties refer to objects that are contained within the displayed document. You'll learn how to use these objects in subsequent chapters.

Listing 6.15 provides an example of using the properties of the document object to summarize the objects that are contained in a document. (That is, it lists the objects that are contained in the document and displays a count of how many of each type are contained.) This example also shows how to use the open() method to generate the contents of a document that is contained in another window.

Listing 6.15   **Accessing Document Contents (ch06-15.htm)**

```
<HTML>
<HEAD>
<TITLE>Accessing Document Contents</TITLE>
<SCRIPT LANGUAGE="JavaScript"><!-
function createSummary() {
 win2 = open("","window2")
 win2.document.open("text/plain")
 win2.document.writeln("Title: "+document.title)
 win2.document.writeln("Links: "+document.links.length)
```

```
win2.document.writeln("Anchors: "+document.anchors.length)
win2.document.writeln("Forms: "+document.forms.length)
win2.document.writeln("Images: "+document.images.length)
win2.document.writeln("Applets: "+document.applets.length)
win2.document.writeln("Embeds: "+document.embeds.length)
win2.document.close()
}
// -></SCRIPT>
</HEAD>
<BODY>
<A NAME="#top"></A>
<P><A HREF="http://www.jaworski.com/javascript">
 <IMG SRC="master.gif"></A>
<A HREF="http://www.sybex.com/"><IMG SRC="sybex.gif"></A></P>
<FORM>
<INPUT TYPE="BUTTON" NAME="Help" VALUE="Help"
  ONCLICK="alert('Click one of the above images.')">
</FORM>
<SCRIPT LANGUAGE="JavaScript"><!-
setTimeout("createSummary()",5000)
// -></SCRIPT>
</BODY>
</HTML>
```

When you open the file shown in Listing 6.15, it generates the Web page shown in Figure 6.11. This Web page has two images that are used as the source of links. It also contains a form with one button and an internal anchor (not visible) that names the top of the document. After five seconds, your browser creates a new window and displays the document shown in Figure 6.12. This action is caused by the script contained in the body of Listing 6.15. It contains a single statement that sets a five-second timeout before invoking the createSummary() function.

The createSummary() function is defined in the document's head. It creates a new window using the open() method of the window object. This new window is blank; it is assigned to the win2 variable. The document contained in the new window is opened using the text/plain MIME type. A series of writes to the document are performed and then the document is closed. The write statements access the properties of the document that is displayed in the first window, and summarize these properties in the second window. These properties describe the document title and identify the number of links, anchors, forms, images, applets, and plug-ins contained in the document.

FIGURE 6.11:

The opening window
(Listing 6.15)

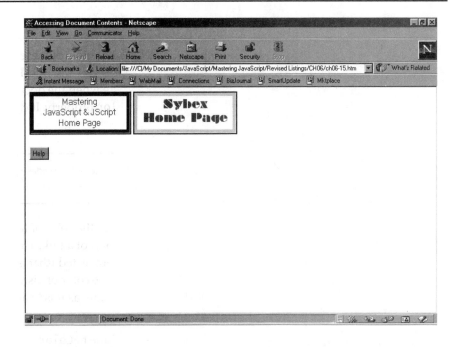

FIGURE 6.12:

The document summary
window (Listing 6.15)

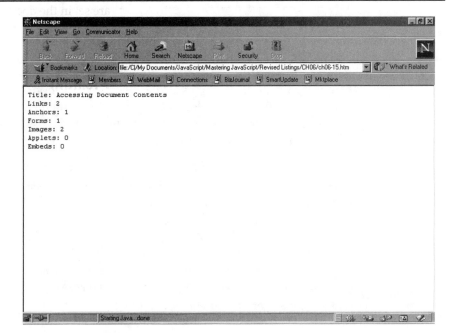

Working with Colors

The document object provides several properties that allow you to change the colors used to display Web pages. Unfortunately, most of these properties must be specified before the body of a document has been laid out. This means that the properties must be set by scripts that execute when the document's header is processed. An exception to this is the bgColor property. It can be used to change a document's background color at any time.

NOTE
     Online Appendix B, "Accessing Online References," provides links to color charts that identify color names and color codes.

The fgColor property allows you to change the color of text that is displayed in a document. It applies to all text that is not part of a link. The linkColor property specifies the color for links that have not been visited (that is, ones not clicked on), and the vlinkColor property specifies the color of visited links. Finally, the alinkColor property specifies the color of a link as it is to appear while it is being clicked.

Listing 6.16 provides an example of using the bgColor, fgColor, and link-Color attributes. It generates the document display shown in Figure 6.13. Note that the fgColor and linkColor attributes are set in the document header so that they can go into effect when the document body is laid out. The bgColor attribute is set in the document body.

Listing 6.16   **Using Color Attributes (ch06-16.htm)**

```
<HTML>
<HEAD>
<TITLE>Changing Colors</TITLE>
<SCRIPT LANGUAGE="JavaScript"><!-
document.fgColor="white"
document.linkColor="yellow"
// -></SCRIPT>
</HEAD>
<BODY>
<H1>Changing Colors</H1>
<P>This Web page shows how document colors can be changed.</P>
<P>Here is a <A HREF="nowhere">sample link</A>.</P>
<SCRIPT LANGUAGE="JavaScript"><!-
```

```
document.bgColor="black"
// -></SCRIPT>
</BODY>
</HTML>
```

FIGURE 6.13:

A grayscale version of the
document generated by
Listing 6.16

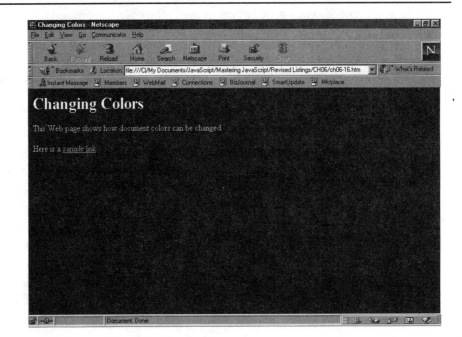

The *navigator* Object

The navigator object provides information about the type and version of the browser that is used to run a script. You can use this object to determine the capabilities of a user's browser and run code that is supported by that browser. Navigator and Internet Explorer both support the navigator object (even though it was named after Netscape's browser). The navigator properties that Navigator and Internet Explorer support differ slightly. These properties are identified in Table 6.6.

TABLE 6.6: Properties of the navigator Object

Property	Browser Support	Description
appCodeName	Navigator 2 Internet Explorer 3	The code name of the browser.
AppMinorVersion	Internet Explorer 4	The minor version number of the browser.
appName	Navigator 2 Internet Explorer 3	The name of the browser.
appVersion	Navigator 2 Internet Explorer 3	The version of the browser.
browserLanguage	Internet Explorer 4	The language in which the browser is configured.
connectionSpeed	Internet Explorer 4	The speed at which the browser is connected to the network.
cookieEnabled	Internet Explorer 4	Whether the browser is configured to accept cookies.
cpuClass	Internet Explorer 4	The type of microprocessor used to execute the browser.
onLine	Internet Explorer 4	Whether the browser currently has an online connection.
Language	Navigator 4 Internet Explorer 4	The language in which the browser is configured.
mimeTypes	Navigator 3 Internet Explorer 4	An array of all MIME types currently supported by the browser.
platform	Navigator 4 Internet Explorer 4	The operating system platform on which the browser executes.
plugins	Navigator 3 Internet Explorer 4	An array of all plug-ins currently installed on the browser.
systemLanguage	Internet Explorer 4	The default language of the operating system.
userAgent	Navigator 2 Internet Explorer 3	The user-agent header sent in the HTTP protocol from the browser to the server.
userLanguage	Internet Explorer 4	The human language used by the user.
userProfile	Internet Explorer 4	An object that provides access to user profile information.

Both Navigator and Internet Explorer support the javaEnabled() and taint-Enabled() methods. The javaEnabled() method returns a Boolean value that indicates whether the user has enabled the use of Java on his browser. The taintEnabled() method returns a Boolean value that indicates whether the user has enabled data tainting. *Data tainting* is a security mechanism implemented in JavaScript 1.1. It is covered in Chapter 23, "Securing Your Scripts." Internet Explorer always returns *false* when taintEnabled() is invoked. In addition to these methods, Navigator also supports the preference() method. The preference() method is used by unsigned scripts to get and set security-related properties. It is covered in Chapter 23.

The navigator object, like the window object, is a top-level object in the browser object model in that it is not a property of some other higher-level object. Listing 6.17 shows how it is used to acquire information about the user's browser. Figure 6.14 shows the output it displays for Navigator 4.5. Figure 6.15 shows the output it displays for the version of Internet Explorer that is distributed with Windows 98.

Listing 6.17   Using Navigator Properties (browser.htm)

```
<HTML>
<HEAD>
<TITLE>Detecting Browser Capabilities</TITLE>
<SCRIPT LANGUAGE="JavaScript">
function displayNavigatorProperties() {
 with(document) {
  write("<B>appName: </B>")
  writeln(navigator.appName+"<BR>")
  write("<B>appVersion: </B>")
  writeln(navigator.appVersion+"<BR>")
  write("<B>appCodeName: </B>")
  writeln(navigator.appCodeName+"<BR>")
  write("<B>platform: </B>")
  writeln(navigator.platform+"<BR>")
  write("<B>userAgent: </B>")
  writeln(navigator.userAgent+"<BR>")
  write("<B>language: </B>")
  writeln(navigator.language+"<BR>")
  write("<B>Number of mimeTypes: </B>")
  writeln(navigator.mimeTypes.length+"<BR>")
  write("<B>Number of plugins: </B>")
```

```
   writeln(navigator.plugins.length)
  }
 }
 function displayExplorerProperties() {
  with(document) {
   write("<B>appName: </B>")
   writeln(navigator.appName+"<BR>")
   write("<B>appVersion: </B>")
   writeln(navigator.appVersion+"<BR>")
   write("<B>appMinorVersion: </B>")
   writeln(navigator.appMinorVersion+"<BR>")
   write("<B>appCodeName: </B>")
   writeln(navigator.appCodeName+"<BR>")
   write("<B>platform: </B>")
   writeln(navigator.platform+"<BR>")
   write("<B>cpuClass: </B>")
   writeln(navigator.cpuClass+"<BR>")
   write("<B>userAgent: </B>")
   writeln(navigator.userAgent+"<BR>")
   write("<B>cookieEnabled: </B>")
   writeln(navigator.cookieEnabled+"<BR>")
   write("<B>browserLanguage: </B>")
   writeln(navigator.browserLanguage+"<BR>")
   write("<B>userLanguage: </B>")
   writeln(navigator.userLanguage+"<BR>")
   write("<B>systemLanguage: </B>")
   writeln(navigator.systemLanguage+"<BR>")
   write("<B>onLine: </B>")
   writeln(navigator.onLine+"<BR>")
   write("<B>Number of mimeTypes: </B>")
   writeln(navigator.mimeTypes.length+"<BR>")
   write("<B>Number of plugins: </B>")
   writeln(navigator.plugins.length+"<BR>")
   write("<B>userProfile: </B>")
   writeln(navigator.userProfile)
  }
 }
 function displayBrowserProperties() {
  if(navigator.appName=="Netscape")
   displayNavigatorProperties()
  else
   if(navigator.appName=="Microsoft Internet Explorer")
```

```
        displayExplorerProperties()
}
displayBrowserProperties()
</SCRIPT>
</HEAD>
<BODY>
</BODY>
</HTML>
```

FIGURE 6.14:

The navigator properties displayed by Navigator 4.5 (Listing 6.17)

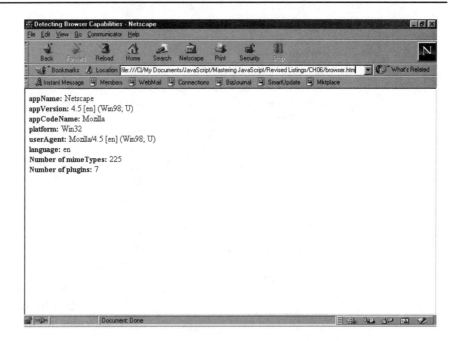

The script contains three functions: displayBrowserProperties(), display-NavigatorProperties(), and displayExplorerProperties(). The display-BrowserProperties() function uses the navigator.appName property to determine the browser type and invokes either displayNavigatorProperties() or displayExplorerProperties() depending on the value of navigator.appName.

FIGURE 6.15:

The navigator properties displayed by Internet Explorer 4 running under Windows 98 (Listing 6.17)

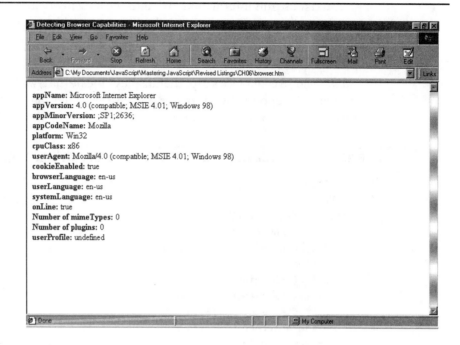

FIGURE 6.15:

The navigator properties displayed by Internet Explorer 4 running under Windows 98 (Listing 6.17)

The *screen* Object

The screen object is an object that is a property of the window object. It provides information about the dimensions and color depth of the user's screen. The screen properties supported by both Navigator and Internet Explorer follow:

- height is the current height of the user's screen (in pixels).

- width is the current width of the user's screen (in pixels).

- colorDepth is the number of bits per color currently supported by the user's screen/video card. For example, 8-bits of color depth corresponds to 256 colors since 2 raised to the 8th power is 256.

You can use this information to determine how to organize the information you display to the user. In addition, both Navigator and Internet Explorer support browser-specific screen properties. These additional properties are covered in online Appendix A, "Comparing JavaScript and JScript."

Listing 6.18 contains a script that displays the `height`, `width`, and `colorDepth` properties supported by a browser. Figure 6.16 shows the results it displays when I run it on my notebook computer.

Listing 6.18   Displaying the Properties of the *screen* Object (screen.htm)

```
<HTML>
<HEAD>
<TITLE>Test</TITLE>
<SCRIPT LANGUAGE="JavaScript">
function displayScreenProperties() {
 with(document) {
  write("<B>height: </B>")
  writeln(screen.height+"<BR>")
  write("<B>width: </B>")
  writeln(screen.width+"<BR>")
  write("<B>colorDepth: </B>")
  writeln(screen.colorDepth+"<BR>")
 }
}
displayScreenProperties()
</SCRIPT>
</HEAD>
<BODY>
</BODY>
</HTML>
```

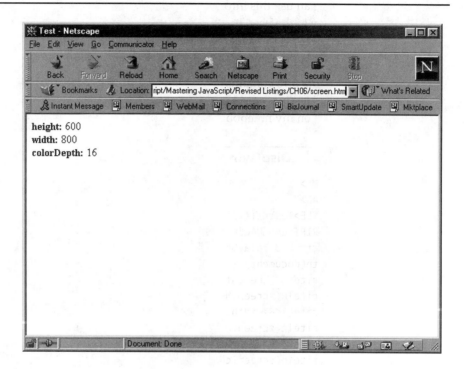

FIGURE 6.16:

The screen properties displayed by my browser (Listing 6.18)

Summary

This chapter showed you how to use the predefined window, frame, document, navigator, and screen objects to create and manage Web pages with multiple windows and frames. It also provided several examples of using windows and frames to organize your Web pages. In the next chapter, you'll learn how to use predefined JavaScript objects to implement local form-processing functions.

CHAPTER
SEVEN

7

Processing Forms

- The form Object

- Accessing Forms within JavaScript

- Accessing Form Elements

- Using Form Event Handlers

- Performing Local Form Processing

- Working with CGI Scripts

Forms provide you with an important capability for Web page development—they allow you to gather information from individuals who browse your Web pages. This is especially important if you use your Web site to advertise or sell your products. Forms make it easy to collect information from your Web page users. They provide a full range of graphical user interface (GUI) controls and they automatically submit the data they collect to your Web server. This data can then be processed by CGI programs, server-side JavaScript scripts built upon Netscape's LiveWire, server-side JScript scripts written as Microsoft's Active Server Pages, or other types of server-side scripts.

JavaScript provides a number of features that can be used to enhance the forms that you develop for your particular Web applications. These features allow you to validate form data before it is submitted to your server and to exercise greater control of the interaction between your forms and Web users.

This chapter introduces the form object and discusses the JavaScript objects that are associated with form fields and GUI controls. It shows how to use the properties and methods of these objects, and how to handle form-related events. When you finish this chapter you will know how to use JavaScript to create forms that perform local processing and will be able to use these forms to communicate with CGI programs.

NOTE   If you are unfamiliar with the HTML tags used to create forms, consult `http://www.sybex.com`. Use the catalog to access this book's Web page. From this page, follow the link to the author's home page, which will provide links to HTML tutorials and reference documents.

The *form* Object

JavaScript provides the form object to enable your scripts to interact with and exercise control over HTML forms. The form object is accessed as a property of the document object. Your browser creates a unique form object for every form that is contained in a document. These objects can be accessed via the document .forms[] array.

The form object is important because it provides you with access to the forms contained in your documents and allows you to respond to form-related events.

Table 7.1 lists the properties of the form object as of JavaScript 1.3. These properties provide access to a form's attributes and allow you to work with a form's fields and GUI controls. In JavaScript 1.3, the form object provides three methods, handleEvent(), submit(), and reset(). The handleEvent() method is used to invoke a form's event handler for a specified event. The submit() and reset() methods are used to submit a form or reset a form's entries to their default values. (The events that forms handle are covered in Chapter 4 and in the section, "Using Form Event Handlers," later in this chapter.)

NOTE   The Internet Explorer object model defines additional properties and methods for the form object and the objects that are contained in a form. These properties and methods support Internet Explorer's implementation of DHTML and are covered in Chapter 18, "Using Style Sheets and DHTML."

TABLE 7.1: Properties of the form Object

Property	Description
action	Provides access to the HTML action attribute of the \<form> tag
button	An object representing a button GUI control
checkbox	An object representing a checkbox field
elements	An array containing all the fields and GUI controls included in a form
encoding	Provides access to the HTML enctype attribute of the \<form> tag
FileUpload	An object representing a file-upload form field
hidden	An object representing a hidden form field
length	Provides access to the length of the elements array
method	Provides access to the HTML method attribute of the \<form> tag
name	Identifies the name of the form
password	An object representing a password field
radio	An object representing a radio button field
reset	An object representing a reset button
select	An object representing a selection list

Continued on next page

TABLE 7.1 CONTINUED: Properties of the form Object

Property	Description
submit	An object representing a submit button
target	Provides access to the HTML target attribute of the <form> tag
text	An object representing a text field
textarea	An object representing a text area field

Accessing Forms within JavaScript

Because form objects are properties of documents, they are accessed by referencing the documents in which they are contained. If you name a form when you create it, then you can access the form by its name. Forms are named using the form's name attribute. For example, if you create a form named employeeData you can access the form's method property using employeeData.method.

You can also use the forms property of the document object to access the forms contained in a particular document. The forms property is an array that contains an entry for each form contained in a document. Suppose that the employeeData form is the third form contained in the document loaded into the current window. You can access the form's method property using document.forms[2].method or document.forms["employeeData"].method.

Accessing Form Elements

A form may contain a wide variety of fields and GUI controls. These form components are referred to as *elements* of the form and are objects in their own right. Table 7.2 lists and summarizes the objects that may be contained in a form.

TABLE 7.2: The Objects That May Be Contained in a Form

Object	Description
button	A general-purpose button for implementing GUI controls
checkbox	A clickable field that allows multiple selections from within a group
FileUpload	A field that allows a user to specify a file to be submitted as part of the form
hidden	A field that may contain a value but is not displayed within a form
password	A text field in which the values that a user enters are hidden via mask characters
radio	A clickable field that allows only a single selection from within a group
reset	A button that is used to reset the contents of a form to its default state
select	A list from which individual list items may be selected
submit	A button that is used to submit the data entered into a field
text	A single-line field for entering text
textarea	A multiline field for entering text

If the elements of a form are named using an HTML name attribute, then the element can be accessed using this name. For example, suppose that you have a form named form1 that contains a text field named ssn. You can access the value of this field using form1.ssn.value.

In most cases, you will access the elements of a form using the elements array property of the form object. This array contains an object for each element of a form. Suppose that the ssn field of the form1 form is the seventh element defined in the form. You can access the value of the ssn field using form1.elements[6] .value.

The objects described in Table 7.2 reference the elements of a form and have properties and methods of their own as summarized in Tables 7.3 and 7.4.

TABLE 7.3: Properties of Form Elements

Object	Property	Description
button	name	Provides access to the button's name attribute
	type	Identifies the object's type
	value	Identifies the object's value
checkbox	checked	Identifies whether the checkbox is currently checked
	defaultChecked	Identifies whether the checkbox is checked by default
	name	Provides access to the checkbox's HTML name attribute
	type	Identifies the object's type
	value	Identifies the object's value
FileUpload	name	Provides access to the object's name attribute
	type	Identifies the object's type attribute
	value	Identifies the object's value
hidden	name	Provides access to the object's name attribute
	type	Identifies the object's type
	value	Identifies the object's value
password	defaultValue	Identifies the object's default value
	name	Provides access to the object's name attribute
	type	Identifies the object's type
	value	Identifies the object's value
radio	checked	Identifies whether the radio button is currently checked
	defaultChecked	Identifies whether the radio button is checked by default

Continued on next page

TABLE 7.3 CONTINUED: Properties of Form Elements

Object	Property	Description
	name	Provides access to the object's **name** attribute
	type	Identifies the object's type
	value	Identifies the object's value
reset	name	Provides access to the object's **name** attribute
	type	Identifies the object's type
	value	Identifies the object's value
select	length	Identifies the length of the select list
	name	Provides access to the object's **name** attribute
	options	An array that identifies the options supported by the select list
	selectedIndex	Identifies the first selected option within the select list
	type	Identifies the object's type
submit	name	Provides access to the object's **name** attribute
	type	Identifies the object's type
	value	Identifies the object's value
text	defaultValue	Identifies the default text to be displayed in the text field
	name	Provides access to the object's **name** attribute
	type	Identifies the object's type
	value	Identifies the object's value

Continued on next page

TABLE 7.3 CONTINUED: Properties of Form Elements

Object	Property	Description
textarea	defaultValue	Identifies the default text to be displayed in the text area field
	name	Provides access to the object's **name** attribute
	type	Identifies the object's type
	value	Identifies the object's value

NOTE All form elements have the **form** property. This property references the form in which the element is contained. All form elements except the **hidden** element provide the **handleEvent()** method for directly invoking the element's event handlers.

TABLE 7.4: Methods of Form Elements

Object	Method	Description
button	click()	Simulates the button being clicked
	blur()	Removes focus from the button
	focus()	Gives focus to the button
checkbox	click()	Simulates the checkbox being clicked
	blur()	Removes focus from the checkbox
	focus()	Gives focus to the checkbox
FileUpload	blur()	Removes focus from the file upload field
	focus()	Gives focus to the file upload field
	select()	Selects the input area of the file upload field
hidden	none	

Continued on next page

TABLE 7.4 CONTINUED: Methods of Form Elements

Object	Method	Description
password	blur()	Removes input focus from the password field
	focus()	Gives input focus to the password field
	select()	Highlights the text displayed in the password field
radio	click()	Simulates the clicking of the radio button
	blur()	Removes focus from the radio button
	focus()	Gives focus to the radio button
reset	click()	Simulates the clicking of the reset button
	blur()	Removes focus from the reset button
	focus()	Gives focus to the reset button
select	blur()	Removes focus from the selection list
	focus()	Gives focus to the selection list
submit	click()	Simulates the clicking of the submit button
	blur()	Removes focus from the submit button
	focus()	Gives focus to the submit button
text	blur()	Removes focus from the text field
	focus()	Gives focus to the text field
	select()	Highlights the text in the text field
textarea	blur()	Removes focus from the text area
	focus()	Gives focus to the text area
	select()	Highlights the text in the text area

Listing 7.1 shows how the individual forms and form elements can be accessed in multiform documents. It creates the three-form document shown in Figure 7.1. When you click the Submit button of the first form, the onSubmit() handler invokes the displayFormData() function. Note that it does this in the context of a return statement. This causes the form submission to be aborted when display-FormData() returns a *false* value. This is always the case because displayForm-Data() always returns *false*.

Listing 7.1   **Accessing the Elements of a Form (formacc.htm)**

```
<HTML>
<HEAD>
<TITLE>Multiform Document Example</TITLE>
<SCRIPT LANGUAGE="JavaScript"><!-
function displayFormData() {
 win2=open("","window2")
 win2.document.open("text/plain")
 win2.document.writeln("This document has "+
  document.forms.length+" forms.")
 for(i=0;i<document.forms.length;++i) {
  win2.document.writeln("Form "+i+" has "+
   document.forms[i].elements.length+" elements.")
  for(j=0;j<document.forms[i].elements.length;++j) {
   win2.document.writeln((j+1)+" A "+
    document.forms[i].elements[j].type+" element.")
  }
 }
 win2.document.close()
 return false
}
// -></SCRIPT>
</HEAD>
<BODY>
<H1>Multiform Document Example</H1>
<FORM ACTION="nothing" onSubmit="return displayFormData()">
<H2>Form 1</H2>
<P>Text field: <INPUT TYPE="TEXT" NAME="f1-1"
 VALUE="Sample text"></P>
<P>Password field: <INPUT TYPE="PASSWORD" NAME="f1-2"></P>
<P>Text area field:
<TEXTAREA ROWS="4" COLS="30"
```

```
              NAME="f1-3">Write your novel here.</TEXTAREA></P>
<P><INPUT TYPE="SUBMIT" NAME="f1-4" VALUE="Submit">
<INPUT TYPE="RESET" NAME="f1-5"></P>
</FORM>
<HR>
<FORM>
<H2>Form 2</H2>
<P><INPUT TYPE="CHECKBOX" NAME="f2-1" VALUE="1"
 CHECKED> Check me!</P>
<P><INPUT TYPE="CHECKBOX" NAME="f2-1" VALUE="2"> No.
 Check me!</P>
<P><INPUT TYPE="CHECKBOX" NAME="f2-1" VALUE="3"> Check all of
 us!</P>
<P><INPUT TYPE="RADIO" NAME="f2-2" VALUE="1"> AM</P>
<P><INPUT TYPE="RADIO" NAME="f2-2" VALUE="2" CHECKED> PM</P>
<P><INPUT TYPE="RADIO" NAME="f2-2" VALUE="3"> FM</P>
<INPUT TYPE="FILE" NAME="f2-3">
</FORM>
<HR>
<FORM>
<H2>Form 3</H2>
<INPUT TYPE="HIDDEN" NAME="f3-1">
<SELECT NAME="f3-2" SIZE="4">
<OPTION VALUE="">Item 1</OPTION>
<OPTION VALUE="">Item 2</OPTION>
<OPTION VALUE="" SELECTED>Item 3</OPTION>
<OPTION VALUE="">Item 4</OPTION>
<OPTION VALUE="">Item 5</OPTION>
</SELECT>
</FORM>
</BODY>
</HTML>
```

The displayFormData() function creates and opens a separate window and assigns the window object to the win2 variable. It then opens the window's document with a text/plain MIME type. It uses the forms array of the document object of the first window to determine how many forms are contained in the document. It then writes this information to the document contained in win2. Next, it identifies the number of elements in each form using the length property of the form's elements array. Finally, it displays the type property of each form element via win2, as shown in Figure 7.2.

FIGURE 7.1:

A multiform document
(Listing 7.1)

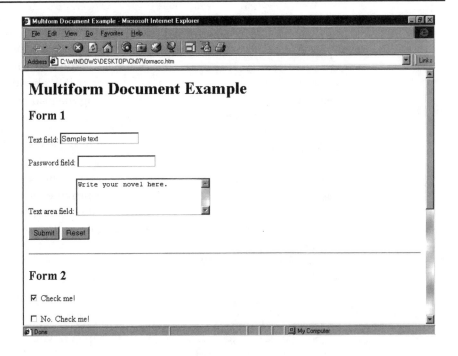

FIGURE 7.2:

A summary of the contents
of the multiform document
(Listing 7.1)

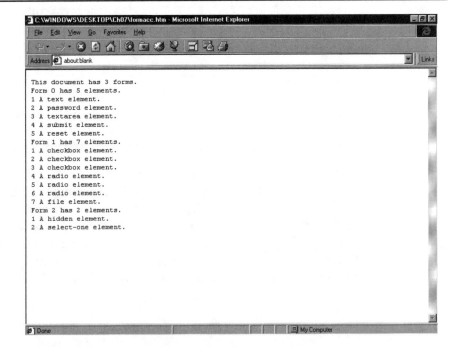

Using Form Event Handlers

JavaScript's ability to handle form-related events is a very powerful tool for customizing form behavior. It allows you to control the user's interaction with your forms and to process form data as the user enters it. It also allows you to process form data locally at the user's browser, reducing the load on your communication bandwidth and on your Web server.

Form event handlers respond to events that indicate the user has performed an input action, such as filling in a text field, clicking a button, or submitting an entire form. These event handlers check the data entered by the user and then either prompt the user to correct any errors or provide the user with other feedback on the data that was entered. Form event handlers may also be used to adaptively present new forms to a user based upon the user's response to prior forms.

Responding to User Actions

Event handling in general, and form event handling in particular, are introduced in Chapter 4. If you have not already read Chapter 4, you should do so before continuing on in this chapter.

Within Chapter 4, Table 4.2 identifies all of the JavaScript event-handling attributes and Table 4.7 identifies which event-handling attributes apply to forms and form elements. From Table 4.7 you can see that most form events fall into the following categories:

Clicks and checks   These are the most common types of form events. A user clicks a button or checks a checkbox to provide information or to perform an action. These events are handled by event-handling functions that provide feedback to the user on the results of the actions taken in response to the click or check.

Text changes   Text changes are another common type of form event. The user enters data into a text field or text area, an event is generated, and the event handler validates the user's entry and performs further processing based on the user's input.

List selection   When a user selects an item from a selection list, event-handling code is used to verify that the selection is consistent with other inputs and to perform any processing indicated by the selection.

Change of focus   Change-of-focus events occur when a form element, such as a text field or selection list, receives or loses the current input focus. These events usually do not require special event handling. However, JavaScript provides the capability to do so, when required.

Form submission and reset   These events are generated when a user clicks a submit or reset button. Form-submission events are typically handled by validating all of the data entered by the user, performing any local processing on that data, and then forwarding the data to a CGI program or other server-side script.

Because you have already covered form event handling in Chapter 4, I'm not going to bore you with any more trivial examples. Instead we'll use JavaScript's event-handling capabilities to create a form-based Hangman game—something that is impossible to do in HTML alone.

If you're not already familiar with Hangman, here's a short description of the game. Hangman is a game where you try to guess a word, one letter at a time. You are initially presented with a word pattern where each letter of the word to be guessed is represented by an underscore (_) character. This tells you how many letters are in the word, but nothing more. When you guess a letter that is in the word, the underscore representing that letter is replaced by the letter you guessed correctly. This tells you that you've guessed the correct letter and shows you where the letter appears in the word. You continue to guess until you run out of guesses or you guess all of the letters of the word.

Your status in terms of guesses is depicted in a gallows—that's why it's called Hangman. Each time you guess incorrectly, a "body part" is added to the victim being hanged. You are only allowed seven incorrect guesses (head, upper and lower torso, two arms, two legs) before the game is over. The purpose of the game is not to be morbid, but to improve your word recognition skills.

Before going on to learn how the game is implemented using form event handling, you should play a few games. Start the game by opening hangman.htm from your browser. The file is located on the Sybex Web site in the ch07 folder. At startup, it presents the display shown in Figure 7.3. Play the game by clicking any of the buttons labeled *A* through *Z*. If you guess correctly, the game will display the position of the letter in the Word to Guess text field as shown in Figure 7.4. If you guess incorrectly, a part of your body will be hung in the gallows as shown in Figure 7.5. If you continue to guess incorrectly, your complete effigy will be hung (see Figure 7.6), an alert dialog box will tell you that you lost, and the game will start again. If you are clever enough to guess the word before you are hung, an alert dialog box will tell you that you won, and the game will start over. Clicking the Start Again button will immediately restart the game with a new word to guess.

NOTE　　If you try to modify any of the form's text fields an alert message will be displayed that tells you not to mess with that field.

FIGURE 7.3:

The Hangman opening display (Listing 7.2)

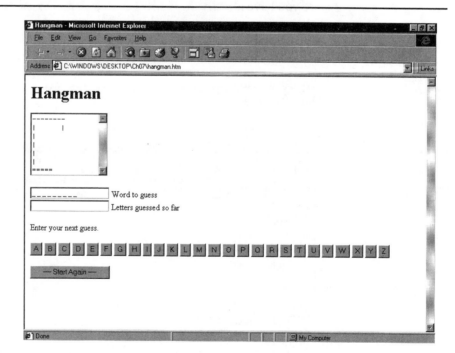

FIGURE 7.4:

You guessed correctly
(Listing 7.2).

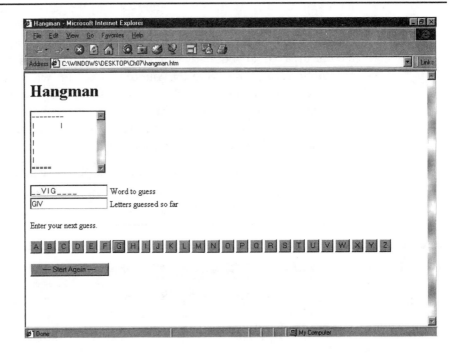

FIGURE 7.5:

You guessed incorrectly
(Listing 7.2).

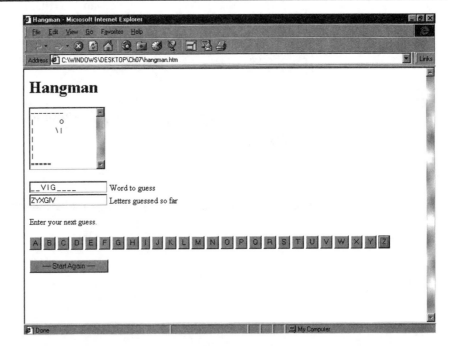

FIGURE 7.6:

You're hung (Listing 7.2).

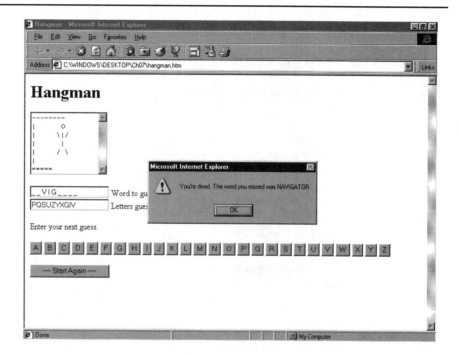

Listing 7.2 shows the contents of the hangman.htm file. This file is fairly long, but don't worry; I'll go over it one small piece at a time. The file contains two scripts: one in the document head and one in the document body. I'll start with the script in the document head because that's the part your browser processes first.

Listing 7.2　　**A JavaScript Hangman Game (hangman.htm)**

```
<HTML>
<HEAD>
<TITLE>Hangman</TITLE>
<SCRIPT LANGUAGE="JavaScript"><!-
gallows = new Array("----\n|        |\n|\n|\n|\n|\n\n=====",
"----\n|        O\n|\n|\n|\n|\n\n=====",
"----\n|        O\n|        |\n|\n|\n|\n\n=====",
"----\n|        O\n|       \\|\n|\n|\n|\n\n=====",
"----\n|        O\n|       \\|/\n|\n|\n|\n\n=====",
"----\n|        O\n|       \\|/\n|        |\n|\n|\n\n=====",
```

```
"----\n|      O\n|      \\|/\n|       |\n|      /\n|\n=====",
"----\n|      O\n|      \\|/\n|       |\n|      / \\\n|\n====
=")
guessChoices = new
Array("JavaScript","Navigator","LiveConnect","LiveWire")
function startAgain() {
 guesses = 0
 max = gallows.length-1
 guessed = " "
 len = guessChoices.length - 1
 toGuess = guessChoices[Math.round(len*Math.random())]
 .toUpperCase()
 displayHangman()
 displayToGuess()
 displayGuessed()
}
function stayAway() {
 document.game.elements[3].focus()
 alert("Don't mess with this form element!")
}
function displayHangman() {
 document.game.status.value=gallows[guesses]
}
function displayToGuess() {
 pattern=""
 for(i=0;i<toGuess.length;++i) {
  if(guessed.indexOf(toGuess.charAt(i)) != -1)
   pattern += (toGuess.charAt(i)+" ")
  else pattern += "_ "
 }
 document.game.toGuess.value=pattern
}
function displayGuessed() {
 document.game.guessed.value=guessed
}
function badGuess(s) {
 if(toGuess.indexOf(s) == -1) return true
 return false
}
function winner() {
 for(i=0;i<toGuess.length;++i) {
  if(guessed.indexOf(toGuess.charAt(i)) == -1) return false
```

```
 }
 return true
}
function guess(s){
 if(guessed.indexOf(s) == -1) guessed = s + guessed
 if(badGuess(s)) ++guesses
 displayHangman()
 displayToGuess()
 displayGuessed()
 if(guesses >= max){
 alert("You're dead. The word you missed was "+toGuess+".")
  startAgain()
 }
 if(winner()) {
  alert("You won!")
  startAgain()
 }
}
// -></SCRIPT>
</HEAD>
<BODY>
<H1>Hangman</H1>
<FORM NAME="game">
<PRE>
<TEXTAREA NAME="status" ROWS="7" COLS="16"
 ONFOCUS="stayAway()"></TEXTAREA>
</PRE><P>
<INPUT TYPE="TEXT" NAME="toGuess"
 ONFOCUS="stayAway()"> Word to guess<BR>
<INPUT TYPE="TEXT" NAME="guessed"
 ONFOCUS="stayAway()"> Letters guessed so far<BR>
<P>Enter your next guess.</P>
<INPUT TYPE="BUTTON" VALUE=" A " ONCLICK="guess('A')">
<INPUT TYPE="BUTTON" VALUE=" B " ONCLICK="guess('B')">
<INPUT TYPE="BUTTON" VALUE=" C " ONCLICK="guess('C')">
<INPUT TYPE="BUTTON" VALUE=" D " ONCLICK="guess('D')">
<INPUT TYPE="BUTTON" VALUE=" E " ONCLICK="guess('E')">
<INPUT TYPE="BUTTON" VALUE=" F " ONCLICK="guess('F')">
<INPUT TYPE="BUTTON" VALUE=" G " ONCLICK="guess('G')">
<INPUT TYPE="BUTTON" VALUE=" H " ONCLICK="guess('H')">
<INPUT TYPE="BUTTON" VALUE=" I " ONCLICK="guess('I')">
<INPUT TYPE="BUTTON" VALUE=" J " ONCLICK="guess('J')">
```

```
<INPUT TYPE="BUTTON" VALUE=" K " ONCLICK="guess('K')">
<INPUT TYPE="BUTTON" VALUE=" L " ONCLICK="guess('L')">
<INPUT TYPE="BUTTON" VALUE=" M " ONCLICK="guess('M')">
<INPUT TYPE="BUTTON" VALUE=" N " ONCLICK="guess('N')">
<INPUT TYPE="BUTTON" VALUE=" O " ONCLICK="guess('O')">
<INPUT TYPE="BUTTON" VALUE=" P " ONCLICK="guess('P')">
<INPUT TYPE="BUTTON" VALUE=" Q " ONCLICK="guess('Q')">
<INPUT TYPE="BUTTON" VALUE=" R " ONCLICK="guess('R')">
<INPUT TYPE="BUTTON" VALUE=" S " ONCLICK="guess('S')">
<INPUT TYPE="BUTTON" VALUE=" T " ONCLICK="guess('T')">
<INPUT TYPE="BUTTON" VALUE=" U " ONCLICK="guess('U')">
<INPUT TYPE="BUTTON" VALUE=" V " ONCLICK="guess('V')">
<INPUT TYPE="BUTTON" VALUE=" W " ONCLICK="guess('W')">
<INPUT TYPE="BUTTON" VALUE=" X " ONCLICK="guess('X')">
<INPUT TYPE="BUTTON" VALUE=" Y " ONCLICK="guess('Y')">
<INPUT TYPE="BUTTON" VALUE=" Z " ONCLICK="guess('Z')"><P>
<INPUT TYPE="BUTTON" NAME="restart" VALUE="—
  Start Again —"
 ONCLICK="startAgain()">
<SCRIPT LANGUAGE="JavaScript"><!-
startAgain()
// -></SCRIPT>
</FORM>
</BODY>
</HTML>
```

The script defines two arrays, gallows and guessChoices, and eight functions—startAgain(), stayAway(), displayHangman(), displayToGuess(), displayGuessed(), badGuess(), winner(), and guess(). Each of these is discussed in the following paragraphs.

The *gallows* Array

This array contains eight string entries that correspond to the eight states that the gallows pole may be in: empty, head hanging, head and upper torso hanging, and so on. The strings may look very cryptic. That's because new lines are represented by the new-line character (\n) and back slashes are represented by a pair of back slashes (\\). These are the standard escape characters used by JavaScript, Java, C, and C++. Try decoding and drawing each of the strings in the gallows array to get a better feel for how these escape characters are used.

The *guessChoices* Array

This array contains four words. These are the words that the user is required to guess. One word from this array is randomly selected for each play of the game. You can add or replace the words contained in this array to tailor Hangman with your own word list.

The *startAgain()* Function

This function starts and restarts the Hangman game. It initializes variables used by the program and then invokes the functions required to display the hangman, show the word to be guessed, and display the letters that the user has already guessed. The guesses variable keeps track of how many incorrect guesses the user has made. It is used to select which element of the gallows array is to be displayed. The max variable determines how many guesses the user can make before he or she is hung. The guessed variable is initialized to " " (one space) to indicate that the user has not yet guessed any letters.

NOTE   The value " " is used instead of "" (no space) because the indexOf() method of the string object does not work correctly for the value "".

The len variable is used to calculate the maximum array subscript of the guessChoices array. The toGuess variable is set to a randomly selected word in the guessChoices array. This word is then converted to uppercase. The display-Hangman() function displays the hangman figure in the status text area. The displayToGuess() function displays the word being guessed in the toGuess text field. The displayGuessed() function displays the letters guessed by the user in the guessed text field. When the game is first started or restarted, the display-Guessed() function is used to blank out the guessed text field.

The *stayAway()* Function

This function is called by the onFocus event handlers of the form's text fields to warn the user not to mess around with these fields. This is to discourage the user from trying to change the content of these fields. Note that it moves the input focus to the "A" button before it displays the alert box.

The *displayHangman()* Function

This function displays the hangman character figure in the status text area. It does this by setting the value property of the status field of the game form of the current document to the gallows array entry corresponding to the number of incorrect guesses.

The *displayToGuess()* Function

This function displays a word pattern based on the word to be guessed and the letters the user has currently guessed. If a user has guessed a letter of the word then that letter is displayed. Otherwise, an underscore character is displayed in place of the letter. It loops through each letter of the word contained in toGuess and uses the indexOf() method of the string object to determine whether that letter is contained in the guessed string. The word pattern is then written to the toGuessed text field.

The *displayGuessed()* Function

This function writes the value of the guessed variable to the guessed text field to inform the user of the letters that he or she has already tried. The guessed variable is updated each time a user makes a new letter guess.

The *badGuess()* Function

This function returns *true* if the letter represented by the s parameter is not in the word contained in the toGuess variable. It returns *false*, otherwise. It is used to determine whether the user has guessed incorrectly.

The *winner()* Function

This function checks each letter in the word contained in the toGuess variable and returns *false* if any letter is not in the string contained in the guessed variable. It returns *true* otherwise. It is used to determine whether the user has correctly guessed all letters of the toGuess word.

The *guess()* Function

This function is invoked whenever the user clicks a button with the letters *A* through *Z*. It is invoked by the button's onClick event handler and passes the letter associated with the button via the s parameter. Here's how it works:

1. The guess() function first checks to see if the letter is currently in the list of letters the user has already guessed, and adds the letter to the list if it is not.

2. It then checks to see if the letter is an incorrect guess, and increments the guesses variable accordingly.

3. Next, it invokes the appropriate functions to redisplay the form's text fields.

4. It then checks to see if the user has run out of guesses, and if so, alerts the user that he or she has been hung.

5. Finally, it invokes the winner() function to determine if the user has correctly guessed all letters of the toGuess word, and, if so, tells the user that he or she has won.

The form displayed by the browser is named game. It contains the text area named status, the text fields named toGuess and guessed, the buttons labeled *A* through *Z*, and the Start Again button. Each of these form elements performs event handling which supports the processing of the Hangman game. This event handling is as follows:

status, toGuess, and guessed   These fields handle the onFocus event by invoking the stayAway() function to tell the user to not mess with the field's contents.

A through Z   These buttons handle the onClick event by invoking the guess() function and passing as a parameter the letter associated with the button.

Start Again   This button invokes the startAgain() function to reinitialize the game's variables and restart the game.

The script contained in the document body contains the single statement, start-Again(), which initializes the variables used in the game and displays the contents of the form's text fields.

Client-Side Form Processing

The Hangman game of the previous section is a great example of the power of local form processing. However, unless your sole purpose in Web programming is to entertain those who browse your Web page, you'll probably want to use forms to return some data to your Web server. This brings up the very important question of which processing should be performed locally via browser-side scripts and which should be performed on the server? For the most part this question is easy to answer: "If it can be performed on the browser then do it." It's a pretty good rule of thumb. However, as with most rules of thumb, there are cases that create exceptions to the rule. For example, if you don't want anyone to know how you process the form data, then don't do it locally on the browser. Anyone can figure out your processing approach by examining your JavaScript code. Another consideration is performance. If your Web application requires a time- or resource-intensive computation, you can avoid upsetting your user by having the data sent back to your high-performance server for processing. However, in most cases forms processing is short and quick and no noticeable impact is made on browser performance.

Working with CGI Scripts

Before the advent of JavaScript, the data the forms collected from users was submitted to Common Gateway Interface (CGI) programs. The CGI programs performed all processing on the form data and sent the results of that processing back to the browser so that it could be displayed to users. The sections, "The Hypertext Transfer Protocol (HTTP)" and "Common Gateway Interface Programs," of Chapter 1 provide a summary of the methods by which browsers communicate with CGI programs. In this section, I'll show how to use JavaScript scripts to communicate with CGI programs. More importantly, I'll show how to use JavaScript to perform local processing of form data before sending the data to CGI programs.

Sending Form Data to a CGI Program

When a form sends data to a CGI program it uses either the GET or POST method. These methods are specified by setting the method attribute of the form to either "get" or "post". If the GET method is used, the form encodes and appends its data to the URL of the CGI program. When a Web server receives the encoded URL, it passes the form data to the CGI program via a program variable known as an *environment* variable. If the POST method is used, the Web server passes the form's data to the CGI program via the program's standard input. The POST method is preferred over the GET method because of data size limitations associated with environment variables. The method property of the form object allows a form's method to be set within JavaScript.

A form's ACTION attribute specifies the URL of the CGI program to which a form's data is to be sent. The action property of the form object allows this URL to be set or changed within JavaScript. This allows a script to send a form's data to one of several CGI programs, depending upon the form's contents as entered by a user. For example, you can have a general-purpose form that collects information on users interested in your product line and then process that data in different ways depending upon the demographic data supplied by the user.

In most cases, form data is encoded using the URL encoding scheme identified by the following MIME type:

```
application/x-www-form-urlencoded
```

However, it is likely that another scheme

```
multipart/form-data encoding
```

will become popular because of its support for file uploads. This encoding scheme is discussed in RFC 1867, which can be found at the URL http://www .jaworski.com/javascript/rfc1867.txt. The encoding property of the form object identifies what encoding scheme was specified by the form's ENCTYPE attribute. The encoding property may also be used to change this attribute.

NOTE   An RFC (literally a Request for Comments) is a document that is used to describe a particular aspect of the Internet, such as a protocol standard or a coding scheme.

Performing Local Form Processing

Having covered the basic form properties that control a form's interaction with a CGI program, let's investigate how JavaScript can be used to locally process a form's data and then send the processed data to the Web server.

When a form is submitted, either as the result of a user clicking a submit button or the invocation of a form's submit() method, all of the data contained in the form's fields are sent to the Web server. This is both inefficient and undesirable because we can use JavaScript to preprocess a form's data.

The secret to using JavaScript to send processed form data to CGI programs is to use a *summary form* to hold the data that is the result of any local form processing. Once a form's data has been initially processed, it is put into a summary form, and then the summary form is sent to the CGI program for any additional processing that is required. Listing 7.3 illustrates this concept. A Web page is designed with two forms. The first form is visible to the user and is the form used to collect raw input data. This form is shown in Figure 7.7. It provides the user with four selection lists with which the user can select a particular type of automobile.

Listing 7.3   **Using a Summary Form to Support Local Processing (orderform.htm)**

```
<HTML>
<HEAD>
<TITLE>Submitting the results of local form processing</TITLE>
<SCRIPT LANGUAGE="JavaScript"><!-
function processOrder() {
 order = ""
 order += document.orderForm.model.selectedIndex
 order += document.orderForm.doors.selectedIndex
 order += document.orderForm.color.selectedIndex
 sel = document.orderForm.accessories
 for(i=0;i<sel.length;++i)
  if(sel.options[i].selected) order += i
 document.submitForm.result.value = order
 document.submitForm.submit()
 return false
}
// -></SCRIPT>
</HEAD>
<BODY>
<H1>Select your next car:</H1>
<PRE>Model          Doors     Color     Accessories</PRE>
<FORM ACTION="" NAME="orderForm"
 ONSUBMIT="return processOrder()">
<SELECT NAME="model" SIZE="3">
<OPTION>Big Blob</OPTION>
<OPTION>Wild Thing</OPTION>
<OPTION>Penny Pincher</OPTION>
<OPTION>Class Act</OPTION>
```

```
</SELECT>
<SELECT NAME="doors" SIZE="3">
<OPTION>2 doors</OPTION>
<OPTION>4 doors</OPTION>
</SELECT>
<SELECT NAME="color" SIZE="3">
<OPTION>red</OPTION>
<OPTION>white</OPTION>
<OPTION>blue</OPTION>
<OPTION>black</OPTION>
<OPTION>brown</OPTION>
<OPTION>silver</OPTION>
<OPTION>pink</OPTION>
</SELECT>
<SELECT NAME="accessories" SIZE="3" MULTIPLE="MULTIPLE">
<OPTION>air conditioning</OPTION>
<OPTION>CD player</OPTION>
<OPTION>bigger engine</OPTION>
<OPTION>fancy dashboard</OPTION>
<OPTION>leather seats</OPTION>
</SELECT>
<P><INPUT TYPE="SUBMIT" NAME="order" VALUE="I'll take it!"></P>
</FORM>
<FORM ACTION="http://www.jaworski.com/cgi-bin/echo.cgi"
       METHOD="POST" NAME="submitForm">
<INPUT TYPE="HIDDEN" NAME="result">
</FORM>
</BODY>
</HTML>
```

When the first form is submitted, the onSubmit event handler invokes the processOrder() function as the argument of a return statement. If the return statement returns *false*, then the form is not submitted. If the return statement returns *true*, then the form *is* submitted. Because processOrder() *always* returns *false*, the form will never be submitted. Instead, processOrder() fills in the invisible field in the second form and submits the second form to a CGI program located on my Web server. This CGI program is located at the URL http://www.jaworski.com/cgi-bin/echo.cgi. It merely echoes back any form fields that it has received from the browser. Figure 7.8 provides an example of the CGI program's output.

FIGURE 7.7:

The form that is presented to the user (Listing 7.3)

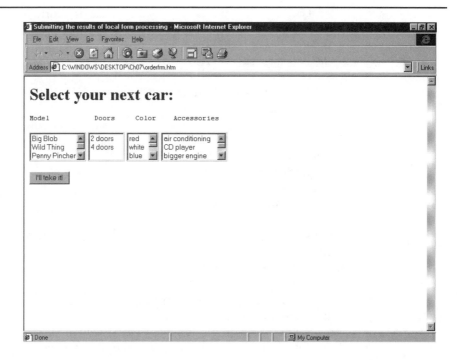

FIGURE 7.8:

The form data that is echoed by the Web server (Listing 7.3)

I'll summarize what I've covered so far. The first form is used to gather automobile selection data from the user. When the first form is submitted, `process-Order()` is invoked to process this data locally on the user's browser. `processOrder()` then inserts the processed data into the second form (named `submitForm`) and submits the second form to my Web server. The Web server then echoes the form fields back to the browser.

The processing performed by `processOrder()` is quite simple, but it illustrates how locally processed form data can be sent to a Web server. Here are the steps:

1. `processOrder()` begins by setting the `order` variable to a string that contains the indices of the list items selected in the `model`, `doors`, and `colors` selection lists. Each of these three lists is a single-selection list.

2. For each item in the multiple-selection `accessories` list, `processOrder()` checks to see if the item has been selected, and appends the index of each selected `accessories` item to the string stored in the `order` variable.

3. The `processOrder()` function then sets the invisible `results` field of `submitForm` to the value stored in `order`. By doing so, it has placed all of the first form's results into a single field in `submitForm`.

4. The `processOrder()` function then invokes the `submit()` method of `submitForm` to send the `result` field to my Web server.

While you may not be impressed by the complexity of the processing performed by `processOrder()`, you should realize the value of the approach that it takes. This approach allows you to design your forms so that they are most appealing to your end users. When the user submits a filled-out form, you can process the form's results and send the results to your Web server in whatever format is most efficient for your CGI or other server-side programs.

Summary

This chapter introduced the `form` object and discussed the JavaScript objects that are associated with form fields and GUI controls. It showed you how to use the properties and methods of these objects and how to handle form-related events. In the next chapter, you will learn how to enhance your forms by using hidden form fields and "cookies."

CHAPTER
EIGHT

8

Using Hidden Fields and Cookies

- Maintaining State Information

- Using Hidden Form Fields

- Using Cookies

- How Is Information Stored in a Cookie?

- Comparison—Cookies vs. Hidden Form Fields

The Web was originally designed to be *stateless*, in the sense that all Web servers would process URL requests in the same manner, independent of any previous requests. This enabled the first Web servers to be fast and efficient by not requiring them to maintain information about the browsers requesting URLs. Browsers also operated in a stateless fashion, processing new URL requests independent of previous requests.

The stateless design of the Web works well in most cases. When a browser requests a particular Web page, the Web server that provides that page will serve it up to the browser in the same way every time. Similarly, all Web browsers requesting a particular Web page always request that page in the same way. However, there are situations in which you *want* the processing of one Web page to be dependent on the processing of previous pages. For example, you may want to enable a user to complete a series of forms where the user's responses to the first form determine which forms are provided next. For instance, you may want to create a form that collects general information about the user, such as name and address, and link it to subsequent forms to collect more information. However, those forms will vary depending on what country the user has entered in the first form.

A number of capabilities have been successively introduced to enable Web applications to be built upon the stateless design of the Web. *Hidden form fields* were introduced first, followed by HTTP "cookies." These capabilities were introduced to allow CGI programs to maintain information about individual Web browsers. With JavaScript's support of browser-side scripting, the use of hidden fields and cookies can be taken to new levels.

In this chapter you'll learn how to use hidden fields and cookies to maintain browser state information and how you can use this information in your scripts to develop more capable and powerful Web applications. When you've finished this chapter you'll be able to read and update hidden fields and cookies using JavaScript and locally implement on the browser side much of the complex state-related processing that would otherwise be performed by server-side CGI programs.

Maintaining State Information

To gain a greater understanding of the problem of maintaining state information, let's explore the example discussed in this chapter's introduction. Suppose that you want to develop a Web page that presents a related series of forms to a user as follows:

Form One   Collects the user's name, address, phone number, and e-mail address.

Form Two   Asks the user which of your products he or she currently uses.

Form Three   Asks the user to evaluate the products that he or she uses.

Say the user receives the first form, fills it out, and submits it. It goes to a CGI program located on your Web server. This CGI program processes the form's data and sends the second form to the user. The user fills out the second form and submits it. It goes to the same or perhaps a different CGI program on your server. When this CGI program receives the second form's data it has no way of knowing that the second form's data is related to the data of the first form. Therefore, it cannot combine the results of the two forms in its database. The same problem occurs with the CGI program that receives the third form's data.

There is a work-around to this problem. You can have the user enter some small piece of common information, like his e-mail address, in all three forms. When the second and third forms are submitted to your Web server, a CGI program can combine their data based upon the common e-mail address. This work-around allows your CGI programs to continue to operate in a stateless manner. However, your users suffer by having to reenter their e-mail address in all three forms. While this may not seem to be much of an inconvenience, it is noticeable, and it detracts from the appeal of your forms.

What would be even better is if somehow your CGI program could remember the e-mail address that was entered into the first form and attach it to the second and third forms that it sends to your browser. *Hidden form fields* (discussed next) were invented to provide CGI programs with this specific capability.

Using Hidden Form Fields

Hidden form fields are text fields that are not displayed and cannot be modified by a user. Forms with hidden fields are dynamically generated by CGI programs as the result of processing data submitted by other forms.

A CGI program sets a hidden field to a particular value when the server sends a form to a browser. When a user fills out and submits a form containing a hidden field, the value originally stored in the field is returned to the server. The server uses the information stored in the hidden field to maintain state information about the user's browser. To see how this works, let's examine how hidden fields can be used in the three-form example discussed in the previous section.

When a user fills out the name and address information and submits form 1, the CGI program on your server processes the form data by creating a record in a database and sending form 2 back to the user. However, instead of sending a static form 2, it dynamically *generates* a form 2 that contains a hidden field, with the field's value set to the e-mail address that was submitted in the first form.

When the user fills out and submits form 2, the hidden field (still with the user's e-mail address) is sent to your CGI program. Your CGI program can now relate the data of the second form to that of the first because they both have the same value in the e-mail address field. (This is true even though the user did not have to retype his or her e-mail address in the second form). The same process is carried out for the third form, after which the CGI program sends back a Web page to the user, thanking him or her for filling out the forms.

JavaScript and Hidden Form Fields

At this point, you are probably wondering what any of this has to do with JavaScript. JavaScript's browser-side programming features take full advantage of and enhance the capabilities provided by hidden fields. With JavaScript, you can eliminate the need to send three forms back and forth between the user's browser and your CGI programs. A JavaScript script can perform the processing of all three forms locally on the user's browser and then consolidate the forms' results before sending them to a CGI program.

To see how JavaScript can use hidden fields to implement our three-form customer survey, open the survey.htm file (Listing 8.1) with your browser. This file uses the hidden form, control.htm, shown in Listing 8.2. Your browser will display the first form of a three-form series, as shown in Figure 8.1. Fill out this form, and click the Next button. Make sure you that you fill in the E-mail Address field; otherwise, you will receive the alert message shown in Figure 8.2.

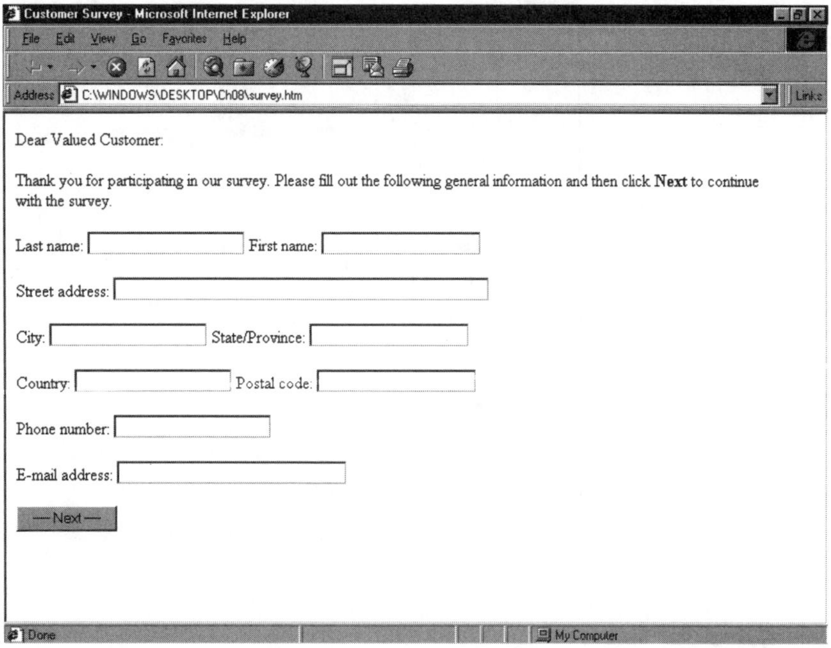

FIGURE 8.1:

The first form of the customer survey asks the user to enter general name and address information. (Listing 8.3)

> **Customer Survey - Microsoft Internet Explorer**
>
> File Edit View Go Favorites Help
>
> Address C:\WINDOWS\DESKTOP\Ch08\survey.htm   Links
>
> Dear Valued Customer:
>
> Thank you for participating in our survey. Please fill out the following general information and then click **Next** to continue with the survey.
>
> Last name: [   ]   First name: [   ]
>
> Street address: [   ]
>
> City: [   ]   State/Province: [   ]
>
> Country: [   ]   Postal code: [   ]
>
> Phone number: [   ]
>
> E-mail address: [   ]
>
> [— Next —]
>
> Done   My Computer

FIGURE 8.2:

If the user skips the E-mail Address field, the form validation alert notifies the user that this information is necessary. (Listing 8.3)

Microsoft Internet Explorer

You must fill in your e-mail address!

[OK]

After you click the Next button, the form shown in Figure 8.3 is displayed. This form asks you to identify which products you use. Click on the check box of at least one of these fictitious products.

FIGURE 8.3:

The second form of the customer survey asks users which products they use. (Listing 8.4)

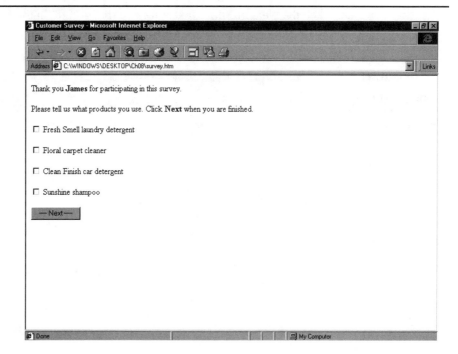

NOTE If you do not select at least one of the four products, the third part of the form will be skipped.

After you click the Next button of the second form, the third form is displayed, as shown in Figure 8.4. The third form asks you to evaluate the products that you selected in the second form. Use the radio buttons to perform your product evaluation.

When you click the Next button on the third form, all of the values of the three forms are collectively sent to the CGI program located at http://www.jaworski .com/cgi-bin/thanks.cgi. This CGI program reads these values and then sends back the thank-you message shown in Figure 8.5.

FIGURE 8.4:

The third form of the customer survey asks customers how they like the products. (Listing 8.5)

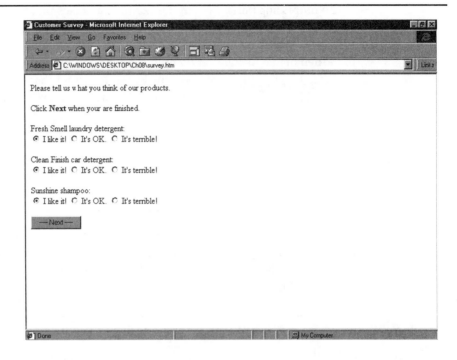

FIGURE 8.5:

The thank-you message is displayed after the user completes the survey.

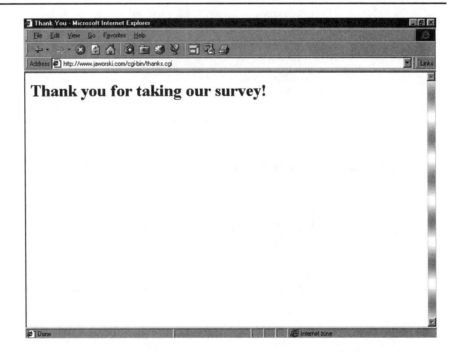

The processing performed in the example all takes place on the user's browser. A CGI program is not required until after all three forms have been filled out. The values of these forms are stored in a separate invisible form that consists entirely of hidden fields. As the user completes each form, the values of the current form are stored in the hidden fields of the invisible form. When the user has completed the third form (or completed the second form without checking any products) the invisible form is submitted to the CGI program. This is much more efficient than having a CGI program process the results of each form separately.

TIP   If you were creating a real survey, you would dress up the form with graphics and a catchier layout.

The `survey.htm` file shown in Listing 8.1 defines a two-frame set. The first frame loads the file `form1.htm` (Listing 8.3) and the second frame loads `control.htm` (Listing 8.2). The BORDER attribute of the frame set is set to 0 to avoid displaying a distracting border between frames.

Listing 8.1   **Defining the Survey's Frame Set (survey.htm)**

```
<HTML>
<HEAD>
<TITLE>Customer Survey</TITLE>
</HEAD>
<FRAMESET COLS="*,10" BORDER=0>
<FRAME SRC="form1.htm">
<FRAME SRC="control.htm">
</FRAMESET>
</HTML>
```

Listing 8.2   **The Survey's Hidden Form (control.htm)**

```
<HTML>
<HEAD>
<SCRIPT LANGUAGE="JavaScript"><!-
// -></SCRIPT>
</HEAD>
<BODY>
<FORM ACTION="http://www.jaworski.com/cgi-bin/thanks.cgi"
```

```
 NAME="controlForm"
 METHOD="post" TARGET="_top">
<INPUT TYPE="HIDDEN" NAME="lastName" VALUE="">
<INPUT TYPE="HIDDEN" NAME="firstName" VALUE="">
<INPUT TYPE="HIDDEN" NAME="street" VALUE="">
<INPUT TYPE="HIDDEN" NAME="city" VALUE="">
<INPUT TYPE="HIDDEN" NAME="state" VALUE="">
<INPUT TYPE="HIDDEN" NAME="country" VALUE="">
<INPUT TYPE="HIDDEN" NAME="zip" VALUE="">
<INPUT TYPE="HIDDEN" NAME="phone" VALUE="">
<INPUT TYPE="HIDDEN" NAME="email" VALUE="">
<INPUT TYPE="HIDDEN" NAME="products" VALUE="">
<INPUT TYPE="HIDDEN" NAME="evaluation" VALUE="">
</FORM>
</BODY>
</HTML>
```

The control.htm file defines a form with 11 hidden fields. Because all of the form's fields are hidden, the form is not displayed. These fields are filled in with the data collected by the three visible forms that are displayed to the user.

The form's NAME attribute is set to "controlForm". This allows the form to be referenced by name by the JavaScript code that executes with the forms contained in the first frame.

The form's ACTION attribute is set to the URL of my CGI program and its METHOD attribute is set to "post". When the form is submitted, this CGI program receives the data that has been stored in the hidden fields and returns a thank-you message to the user. The form's TARGET attribute is "_top". This causes the thank-you message to be displayed in the full window occupied by survey.htm rather than in the frame occupied by control.htm.

The form1.htm file displays the form shown in Figure 8.1 in the first frame of the frame set. It contains a single script that defines the processForm1() function. This function handles the onClick event that is generated when the user clicks on the Next button. It sets the form1 variable to document.forms["form-One"] so that it can be used as a shortcut (to avoid having to retype the document prefix). It then checks to see if the email field is blank. If it is blank then it displays an alert dialog box to the user; otherwise it continues on with its processing. The controlForm variable is used as a shortcut to the hidden form stored in the second frame. All of the fields from form1 are then copied into the hidden fields of controlForm. Finally, the form2.htm (Listing 8.4) file is loaded into the first frame and formTwo replaces formOne.

Listing 8.3   **The First Form of the Survey (form1.htm)**

```
<HTML>
<HEAD>
<TITLE>Customer Survey: General Information</TITLE>
<SCRIPT LANGUAGE="JavaScript"><!-
function processForm1() {
 form1 = document.forms["formOne"]
 if(form1.email.value=="")
  alert("You must fill in your e-mail address!")
 else {
  controlForm = parent.frames[1].document.controlForm
  controlForm.lastName.value=form1.lastName.value
  controlForm.firstName.value=form1.firstName.value
  controlForm.street.value=form1.street.value
  controlForm.city.value=form1.city.value
  controlForm.state.value=form1.state.value
  controlForm.country.value=form1.country.value
  controlForm.zip.value=form1.zip.value
  controlForm.phone.value=form1.phone.value
  controlForm.email.value=form1.email.value
  location.href="form2.htm"
 }
}
// -></SCRIPT>
</HEAD>
<BODY>
<P>Dear Valued Customer:</P>
<P>Thank you for participating in our survey. Please fill out
 the following general information and then click <B>Next</B> to
 continue with the survey.</P>
<FORM ACTION="" NAME="formOne">
<P>Last name: <INPUT TYPE="TEXT" NAME="lastName">
 First name: <INPUT TYPE="TEXT" NAME="firstName"></P>
<P>Street address: <INPUT TYPE="TEXT" SIZE="50" NAME="street">
 </P>
<P>City: <INPUT TYPE="TEXT" NAME="city">
 State/Province: <INPUT TYPE="TEXT" NAME="state"></P>
<P>Country: <INPUT TYPE="TEXT" NAME="country">
```

```
Postal code: <INPUT TYPE="TEXT" NAME="zip"></P>
<P>Phone number: <INPUT TYPE="TEXT" NAME="phone"></P>
<P>E-mail address: <INPUT TYPE="TEXT" SIZE="30" NAME="email">
 </P>
<P></P>
<INPUT TYPE="BUTTON" NAME="next" VALUE="— Next —"
 onClick="processForm1()">
</FORM>
</BODY>
</HTML>
```

The `form2.htm` file displays the form shown in Figure 8.3. It contains two scripts—one in the document head and the other in the document body. The script in the document body is executed when the Web page is generated. This script is used to insert the first name of the user into the text that is displayed above the form.

Listing 8.4   **The Second Form of the Survey (form2.htm)**

```
<HTML>
<HEAD>
<TITLE>Customer Survey: Product Usage</TITLE>
<SCRIPT LANGUAGE="JavaScript"><!-
function processForm2() {
 controlForm = parent.frames[1].document.controlForm
 form2 = document.forms["formTwo"]
 products = ""
 if(form2.laundry.checked) products += "1"
 else products += "0"
 if(form2.carpet.checked) products += "1"
 else products += "0"
 if(form2.car.checked) products += "1"
 else products += "0"
 if(form2.shampoo.checked) products += "1"
 else products += "0"
 controlForm.products.value=products
 location.href="form3.htm"
}
// -></SCRIPT>
</HEAD>
<BODY>
```

```
<SCRIPT LANGUAGE="JavaScript"><!-
document.write("<P>Thank you <B>"+parent.frames[1].document.control-
Form.firstName.value+"</B> ")
document.writeln("for participating in this survey.</P>")
// -></SCRIPT>
<P>Please tell us what products you use. Click <B>Next</B> when you are
finished.</P>
<FORM NAME="formTwo">
<P><INPUT TYPE="CHECKBOX" NAME="laundry"> Fresh Smell laundry deter-
gent</P>
<P><INPUT TYPE="CHECKBOX" NAME="carpet"> Floral carpet cleaner</P>
<P><INPUT TYPE="CHECKBOX" NAME="car"> Clean Finish car detergent</P>
<P><INPUT TYPE="CHECKBOX" NAME="shampoo"> Sunshine shampoo</P>
<P></P>
<P><INPUT TYPE="BUTTON" NAME="next" VALUE="— Next —"
onClick="processForm2()"></P>
</FORM>
</BODY>
</HTML>
```

The script in the document head defines the processForm2() function. This function handles the onClick event that is generated when the user clicks on the Next button. It sets the hidden products field of controlForm based upon the products the user has checked off. It then loads form3.htm (Listing 8.5) as the replacement for form2.htm in the first frame.

Listing 8.5   **The Third Form of the Survey (form3.htm)**

```
<HTML>
<HEAD>
<TITLE>Customer Survey: Product Evaluation</TITLE>
<SCRIPT LANGUAGE="JavaScript"><!-
function usesProducts() {
 productsUsed = parent.frames[1].document.controlForm.products.value
 usage = new Array(productsUsed.length)
 productsInUse=false
 for(i=0;i<usage.length;++i) {
  if(productsUsed.charAt(i)=="0") usage[i]=false
  else{
   usage[i]=true
   productsInUse=true
```

```
   }
  }
  return productsInUse
 }
 function askAboutProducts() {
  document.writeln('<P>Please tell us what you think of our
products.</P>')
  document.writeln('<P>Click <B>Next</B> when your are finished.</P>')
  document.writeln('<FORM NAME="formThree">')
  if(usage[0]){
   document.writeln('<P>Fresh Smell laundry detergent:<BR>')
   document.writeln('<INPUT TYPE="RADIO" NAME="laundry"')
   document.writeln('VALUE="like" CHECKED> I like it!')
   document.writeln('<INPUT TYPE="RADIO" NAME="laundry"')
   document.writeln('VALUE="ok"> It\'s OK.')
   document.writeln('<INPUT TYPE="RADIO" NAME="laundry"')
   document.writeln('VALUE="dislike"> It\'s terrible!')
   document.writeln('</P>')
  }
  if(usage[1]){
   document.writeln('<P>Floral carpet cleaner:<BR>')
   document.writeln('<INPUT TYPE="RADIO" NAME="carpet"')
   document.writeln('VALUE="like" CHECKED> I like it!')
   document.writeln('<INPUT TYPE="RADIO" NAME="carpet"')
   document.writeln('VALUE="ok"> It\'s OK.')
   document.writeln('<INPUT TYPE="RADIO" NAME="carpet"')
   document.writeln('VALUE="dislike"> It\'s terrible!')
   document.writeln('</P>')
  }
  if(usage[2]){
   document.writeln('<P>Clean Finish car detergent:<BR>')
   document.writeln('<INPUT TYPE="RADIO" NAME="car"')
   document.writeln('VALUE="like" CHECKED> I like it!')
   document.writeln('<INPUT TYPE="RADIO" NAME="car"')
   document.writeln('VALUE="ok"> It\'s OK.')
   document.writeln('<INPUT TYPE="RADIO" NAME="car"')
   document.writeln('VALUE="dislike"> It\'s terrible!')
   document.writeln('</P>')
  }
  if(usage[3]){
   document.writeln('<P>Sunshine shampoo:<BR>')
   document.writeln('<INPUT TYPE="RADIO" NAME="shampoo"')
```

```
        document.writeln('VALUE="like" CHECKED> I like it!')
        document.writeln('<INPUT TYPE="RADIO" NAME="shampoo"')
        document.writeln('VALUE="ok"> It\'s OK.')
        document.writeln('<INPUT TYPE="RADIO" NAME="shampoo"')
        document.writeln('VALUE="dislike"> It\'s terrible!')
        document.writeln('</P>')
    }
    document.writeln('<P></P><P>')
    document.writeln('<INPUT TYPE="BUTTON" NAME="next"')
    document.writeln('VALUE="-- Next --" ')
    document.writeln(' onClick="processForm3()"></P>')
    document.writeln('</FORM>')
}
function processForm3() {
    controlForm = parent.frames[1].document.controlForm
    form3 = document.forms["formThree"]
    evaluation = ""
    for(i=0;i<form3.elements.length-1;++i)
        if(form3.elements[i].checked)
            evaluation += form3.elements[i].value + " "
    controlForm.evaluation.value=evaluation
    controlForm.submit()
}
// -></SCRIPT>
</HEAD>
<BODY>
<SCRIPT LANGUAGE="JavaScript"><!-
if(usesProducts()) askAboutProducts()
else parent.frames[1].document.controlForm.submit()
// -></SCRIPT>
</BODY>
</HTML>
```

The form3.htm file, unlike form1.htm and form2.htm, consists almost entirely of JavaScript code. Most of the code is contained in the script located in the document's head. A small script is contained in the document's body. This script invokes the usesProducts() function to determine whether the user had checked any products when he filled out formTwo. If the user had checked at least one product, the askAboutProducts() function is invoked to generate formThree.

Otherwise, the controlForm is submitted as is, without the user having to fill in formThree.

The script in the document head defines three functions:

- usesProducts()
- askAboutProducts()
- processForm3()

These functions are discussed in the following subsections.

The *usesProducts()* Function

This function checks the hidden products field of controlForm to determine what products the user checked off when filling in formTwo. It initializes the usage array based upon this information. It sets productsInUse to *true* if the user has checked off any products in formTwo and to *false* otherwise. It then returns this value as a result.

The *askAboutProducts()* Function

This function generates the HTML content of formThree. It creates a short text introduction to the form, generates the <form> tag, and then generates a set of three radio buttons for each product the user selected in formTwo. It then generates a Next button for the form, setting the form's onClick event handler to processForm3(). Finally, it generates the closing </form> tag.

The *processForm3()* Function

This function handles the onClick event generated when the user clicks on the Next button after filling out form3. It summarizes the radio buttons checked by the user and stores this summary in the hidden evaluation field of control-Form. It then submits the data contained in controlForm.

Using Cookies

Hidden form fields were introduced to enable CGI programs to maintain state information about Web browsers. They work well in situations where the state information is to be maintained for a short period of time, as is the case when a user fills out a series of forms. However, hidden fields do not allow state information to be maintained in a *persistent* manner. That is, hidden fields can only be used within a single browser session. When a user exits the browser, the information contained in a hidden form field is lost forever.

Netscape developed the *cookie* as a means to store state-related and other information in a persistent manner. The information stored in a cookie is maintained between browser sessions; it survives when the user turns off his or her machine. Cookies allow CGI and other programs to store information on Web browsers for significantly longer time periods.

NOTE   Cookies are supported by Netscape Navigator, Internet Explorer, and most other major browsers.

A cookie consists of information sent by a server-side program in response to a URL request by the browser. The browser stores the information in the local cookie file ("the cookie jar") according to the URL of the CGI program sending the cookie. This URL may be generalized, based upon additional information contained in the cookie. Different browsers will store the cookie in different files. For example, Netscape Navigator stores cookies in a file named `cookies .txt`. Internet Explorer stores cookies in multiple files in the `\windows\cookies` directory.

WARNING   Internet Explorer 3 correctly processes cookies only when a document is read from the Web via an HTTP connection. In particular, it does not support cookies when a document is read from the local file system.

When a browser requests a URL from a Web server, the browser first searches the local cookie files to see if the URL of any of its cookies matches the URL that it is requesting. The browser then sends the Web server, as part of the URL request, the information contained in the matching cookie or cookies.

Cookies provide CGI programs with the capability to store information on browsers. Browsers return this information to CGI programs when they request the URL of the CGI program. CGI programs update cookies when they respond to browser URL requests. In this manner, a CGI program can use browsers to maintain state information and have the browsers return this information whenever they invoke the CGI program.

To get a better feel for how cookies work, let's revisit the three-form example introduced in the beginning of this chapter. The goal is to implement a sequence of forms where each form expands upon the information gathered in previous forms. In order to do this, a CGI program must be able to relate the data received in later forms to that received in earlier forms. The solution is for the CGI program to identify related forms using data that is common to these forms. A person's e-mail address is a common example of this identifying data.

Cookies provide a persistent mechanism for storing identifying data. When a browser submits form 1 to a CGI program, the CGI program responds by sending form 2 to the browser. A cookie containing the user's e-mail address accompanies this second form. When the browser submits form 2, it returns any cookies that match the CGI program to which the form is submitted. This causes the user's e-mail address to be returned with the submitted form 2 data. The CGI program then sends form 3 to the browser. When the user submits form 3, the browser again checks the local cookie file and sends any related cookies.

Cookies are obviously more powerful than hidden form fields. Since cookies can persist between browser sessions, they may be used to store permanent user data, such as identification information (e-mail address) and preferences (frames, background colors, and so on), as well as state information (the current page in an online book).

How Is Information Stored in a Cookie?

A cookie is created when a CGI program includes a Set-Cookie header as part of an HTTP response. This response is generated when a browser requests the URL of the CGI program. The syntax of the Set-Cookie header is:

```
Set-Cookie: NAME=VALUE
[; expires=DATE][; path=PATH][; domain=DOMAIN_NAME][; secure]
```

The *NAME=VALUE* field (discussed next) is required. The other fields are optional; however, they should all appear on the same line as the Set-Cookie header.

NOTE   More than one Set-Cookie header may be sent in a single HTTP response.

The *NAME=VALUE* Field

This field contains the essential data being stored in a cookie. For example, when used to store my e-mail address it could appear as `email=jamie@jaworski.com`. A semicolon, comma, or white-space character is not allowed in the `NAME=VALUE` string per the cookie specification. Applications are free to develop their own encoding scheme for these strings.

The expires=*DATE* Field

This field specifies the expiration date of a cookie. If it is omitted, the cookie expires at the end of the current browser session. The date is specified in the following format:

```
Weekday, DD-Mon-YY HH:MM:SS GMT
```

Weekday is the day of the week. *DD* is the day of the month. *Mon* is the first three letters of the month. *YY* is the year (e.g., 97). *HH* is hours. *MM* is minutes. *SS* is seconds. The GMT time zone is always used. An example date is

```
Monday, 20-Sep-10 12:00:00 GMT
```

The above date is noon GMT on September 20th, 2010. Although cookies store the year in a two-digit year format, there is no year 2000 (Y2K) problem associated with them. Browsers accept the year 10 as the year 2010. If cookies are still around in the middle of the 21st century, then browsers of that era will need to be updated to support dates in the later part of that century.

TIP   Cookies that specify long-term user preferences should specify an expiration date of several years to help ensure that the cookies will be available as needed in the future. Cookies that specify short-term state information should expire in days, at which point the expired (stale) cookies are automatically destroyed.

The domain=*DOMAIN_NAME* Field

When a cookie is stored in the local file system, it is organized by the URL of the CGI program that sent the cookie. The `domain` field is used to specify a more general domain name to which the cookie should apply. For example, suppose the URL of the CGI program that sends a cookie has the domain *athome.jaworski.com*. A `domain=jaworski.com` field in a cookie would associate that cookie with all hosts in the *jaworski.com* domain, not just the single host *athome.jaworski.com*. The domain field cannot be used to associate cookies with top-level domains *.com*, *.mil*, *.edu*, *.net*, *.org*, *.gov*, and *.int*. Any domain name that is not part of the top-level domains (for example, *ca.us*) must include an extra subdomain. For example, *sd.ca.us* is allowed, but *ca.us* is not.

The path=*PATH* Field

This field is used to specify a more general path for the URL associated with a cookie. For example, suppose the URL of a CGI program is `http://www.jaworski.com/cgi-bin/js-examples/ch08/test.cgi`. The *path* of that CGI program is `/cgi-bin/js-examples/ch08/`. In order to associate a cookie with all of my CGI programs in this example, I could set `path=/cgi-bin`.

The *secure* Field

If the `secure` field is specified, then a cookie is only sent over a secure communication channel (HTTPS servers).

When a browser sends matching cookies back to a Web server, it sends an HTTP request header in the following format:

```
Cookie: NAME1=VALUE1; NAME2=VALUE2; ... NAMEN=VALUEN
```

NAME1 through NAMEN identify the cookie names and VALUE1 through VALUEN identify their values.

NOTE   You can find Netscape's original documentation on cookies at `http://www.netscape.com/newsref/std/cookie_spec.html`.

Using JavaScript with Cookies

Cookies provide a powerful feature for Web application development, but using them with CGI programs can be somewhat messy. You have to design your programs to send cookies via the HTTP response header and to receive cookies via the HTTP request header. While this is not difficult to implement, it means that more processing is performed on the server and not on the browser.

JavaScript, on the other hand, can take full advantage of cookies by reading and setting them locally on the browser, eliminating the need for the cookies to be processed by CGI programs. A JavaScript script can then forward any information the CGI program requires to perform its processing. By using JavaScript to maintain cookies and perform as much processing as possible on the browser, CGI programs can be greatly simplified, and in most cases, eliminated.

The cookie associated with a document is set using the document's `cookie` property. When you set a cookie you must provide the same cookie fields that would be provide by a CGI program. For example, consider the following statements:

```
email="jamie@jaworski.com"
expirationDate="Thursday, 01-Dec-11 12:00:00 GMT"
document.cookie="email="+email+";expires="+expirationDate
```

These statements set the value of the `cookie` property of the current document to the string `"email=jamie@jaworski.com; expires=Thursday, 01-Dec-11 12:00:00 GMT"`. Note that the `expires` field is required to keep the cookie from expiring after the current browser session. `Domain`, `path`, and `secure` fields can also be used when a `cookie` property is set.

When the value of the cookie is retrieved using the statement

```
cookieString=document.cookie
```

the `cookieString` variable will be assigned the value `"email=jamie@jaworski .com"`. If multiple cookies had been set for the current document, then `cookieString` would contain a list of semicolon-separated `name=value` pairs. For example, consider the following statements:

```
email="jamie@jaworski.com"
firstName="Jamie"
lastName="Jaworski"
expirationDate="Thursday, 01-Dec-11 12:00:00 GMT"
document.cookie="email="+email+";expires="+expirationDate
document.cookie="firstName="+firstName
```

```
+";expires="+expirationDate
document.cookie="lastName="+lastName+";expires="+expirationDate
cookieString=document.cookie
```

The value of `cookieString` includes the `name=value` pairs of the `email`, `firstName`, and `lastName` cookies. This value is `"email=jamie@jaworski.com; firstName=Jamie; lastName=Jaworski"`.

NOTE   Bill Dortch provides a number of resuable cookie-processing functions at `http://www.hidaho.com`.

In order to get a feel for how cookies are accessed via JavaScript, run the file `cooktest.htm` shown in Listing 8.6. It will display the form shown in Figure 8.6. This form allows you to enter the text of a cookie and then set the cookie by clicking the Set Cookie button. The new value of the cookie is displayed at the top of the Web page.

Listing 8.6   **A Cookie Test Program (cooktest.htm)**

```html
<HTML>
<HEAD>
<TITLE>Cookie Test</TITLE>
<SCRIPT LANGUAGE="JavaScript"><!--
function updateCookie() {
 document.cookie=document.form1.cookie.value
 location.reload(true)
}
// --></SCRIPT>
</HEAD>
<BODY>
<SCRIPT LANGUAGE="JavaScript">
 <!--document.write("Your current cookie value is: '"+
   document.cookie+"'")// -->
</SCRIPT>
<FORM ACTION="" NAME="form1">
<P>Enter new cookie: <INPUT TYPE="TEXT" SIZE="60"
 NAME="cookie"></P>
<INPUT TYPE="BUTTON" NAME="setCookie" VALUE="Set Cookie"
 onClick="updateCookie()">
</FORM>
</BODY>
</HTML>
```

The cookie test program's
opening screen tells the
user what the current
cookie value is and
prompts him or her to enter
a new cookie. (Listing 8.6)

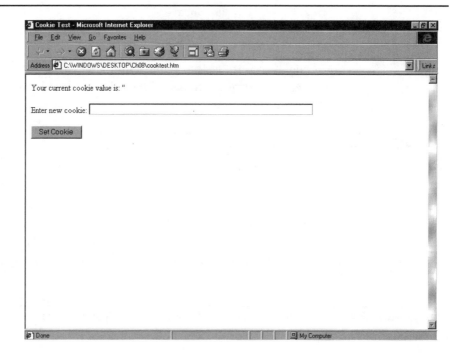

To see how this script works, enter the cookie shown in Figure 8.7 and click on
the Set Cookie button. The new cookie is displayed as shown in Figure 8.8. Experiment with this program by entering cookies with different or no expiration
dates, terminating your browser, and restarting it to see what cookies have per-
sisted between browser sessions.

The cookie test program is very simple. This attests to the power and flexibility
with which JavaScript supports cookies. The program consists of two scripts—
one in the document head and one in the document body. The script in the document body displays the current cookie values that are available to the document.
The script in the document head handles the `onClick` event associated with the
Next Cookie button by setting a cookie with the value entered by the user. It then
reloads the current `cooktest.htm` document so that the updated cookie value is
displayed. Note that the cookie test program runs locally without the need for a
CGI program. For Web applications that do not require you to collect information
from users, the combination of JavaScript and cookies can, in many cases, eliminate the need to develop CGI programs.

FIGURE 8.7:

An example of how to enter the text of a cookie (Listing 8.6)

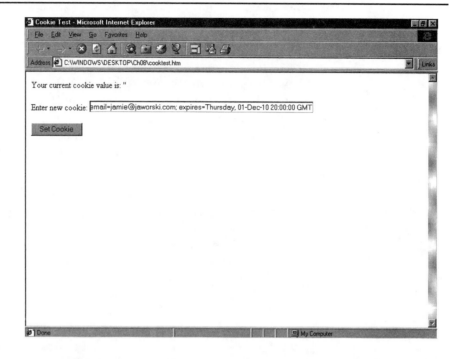

FIGURE 8.8:

When the page reloads, the new cookie is displayed. (Listing 8.6)

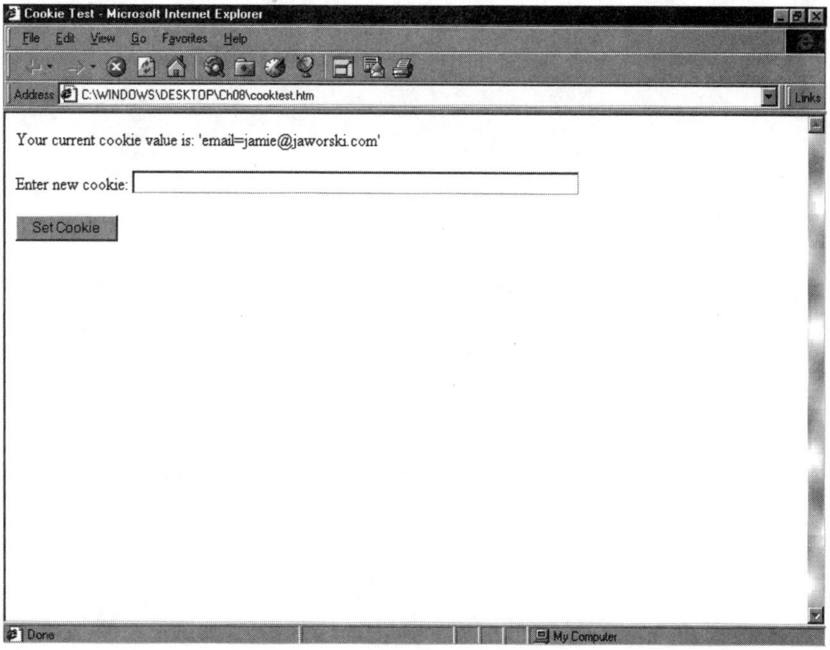

As another example of how JavaScript and cookies can be combined to build Web applications that execute entirely on the browser, we'll develop a JavaScript application that quizzes users about their understanding of historical facts.

Open quiz.htm with your browser, and it displays the Web page shown in Figure 8.9. Click on the radio button corresponding to the correct answer and then click on the Continue button. The Web page is redisplayed with a new question and an updated score. If you select the wrong answer, you are notified with an alert message and the question is redisplayed. When you have successfully answered all of the questions in the quiz, you will be congratulated with the Web page shown in Figure 8.10.

FIGURE 8.9:

The Quiz Program opening display lists a quiz question and a group of possible answers. (Listing 8.7)

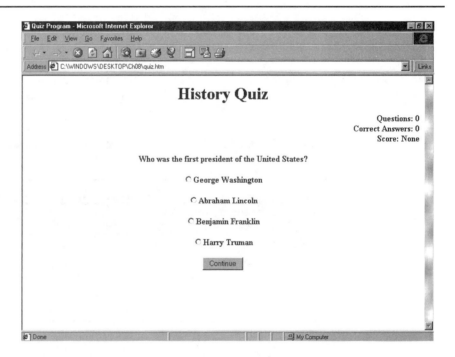

FIGURE 8.10:

The Quiz Program final display tells users how well they scored. (Listing 8.7)

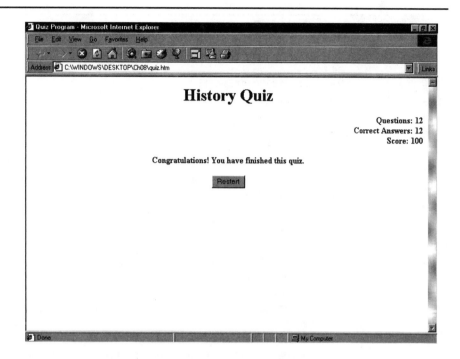

The `quiz.htm` file is shown in Listing 8.7. It consists almost entirely of JavaScript code. This code is organized into three scripts. Two of the scripts are in the document's head and the other, a short script, is located in the document's body. The second script of the document's head loads the JavaScript code contained in the `history.js` file (Listing 8.8), which contains the questions that are used in the quiz. The quiz questions are contained in a separate file so that the quiz can be easily tailored to different sets of questions.

TIP   You can improve the quiz by adding graphics and links to related topics.

Listing 8.7   **Quiz Program (quiz.htm)**

```
<HTML>
<HEAD>
<TITLE>Quiz Program</TITLE>
<SCRIPT LANGUAGE="JavaScript"><!-
//Question object
function Question() {
 this.question=Question.arguments[0]
 var n=Question.arguments.length
 this.answers = new Array(n-2)
 for(var i=1; i<n-1; ++i)
  this.answers[i-1]=Question.arguments[i]
 this.correctAnswer=Question.arguments[n-1]
}
function readCookie() {
 currentQuestion=0
 numberOfQuestions=0
 correctAnswers=0
 score="None"
 cookie=document.cookie
 currentQuestion=getNumberValue(cookie,"currentQuestion")
 numberOfQuestions=getNumberValue(cookie,"numberOfQuestions")
 correctAnswers=getNumberValue(cookie,"correctAnswers")
 if(numberOfQuestions>0)
  score=Math.round(correctAnswers*100/numberOfQuestions)
}
function getNumberValue(s,n) {
 s=removeBlanks(s)
 var pairs=s.split(";")
 for(var i=0;i<pairs.length;++i) {
  var pairSplit=pairs[i].split("=")
  if(pairSplit[0]==n) {
   if(pairSplit.length>1) return parseInt(pairSplit[1])
   else return 0
  }
 }
 return 0
}
function removeBlanks(s) {
 var temp=""
```

```
 for(var i=0;i<s.length;++i) {
  var c=s.charAt(i)
  if(c!=" ") temp += c
 }
 return temp
}
function askNextQuestion() {
 document.writeln("<H4 ALIGN='CENTER'>"
  +qa[currentQuestion].question+"</H4>")
 displayAnswers()
}
function displayAnswers() {
 document.writeln('<FORM NAME="answerForm">')
 for(var ii=0;ii<qa[currentQuestion].answers.length;++ii) {
  document.writeln('<H4 ALIGN="CENTER">')
  document.writeln('<INPUT TYPE="RADIO" NAME="answer"> ')
  document.writeln(qa[currentQuestion].answers[ii])
  if(ii+1==qa[currentQuestion].answers.length) {
   document.writeln('<BR><BR><INPUT TYPE="BUTTON"')
   document.writeln('NAME="continue" VALUE="Continue" ')
   document.writeln(' onClick="checkAnswers()">')
  }
  document.writeln('</H4>')
 }
 document.writeln('</FORM>')
}
function checkAnswers() {
 var numAnswers=qa[currentQuestion].answers.length
 var correctAnswer=qa[currentQuestion].correctAnswer
 for(var jj=0;jj<numAnswers;++jj) {
  if(document.answerForm.elements[jj].checked) {
   if(jj==correctAnswer){
    correct()
    break
   }else{
    incorrect()
    break
   }
  }
 }
 if(jj==numAnswers){
  incorrect()
  break
```

```
  }
 }
}
function correct() {
 ++currentQuestion
 ++numberOfQuestions
 ++correctAnswers
 updateCookie()
 location.reload(true)
}
function incorrect() {
 ++numberOfQuestions
 updateCookie()
 alert("Incorrect!")
 location.reload(true)
}
function updateCookie() {
 document.cookie="currentQuestion="+currentQuestion
 document.cookie="numberOfQuestions="+numberOfQuestions
 document.cookie="correctAnswers="+correctAnswers
}
function endQuiz() {
 document.cookie="currentQuestion=0"
 document.cookie="numberOfQuestions=0"
 document.cookie="correctAnswers=0"
 document.writeln('<FORM NAME="finishedForm">')
 document.write("<H4 ALIGN='CENTER'>")
 document.write("Congratulations! You have finished this quiz.")
 document.writeln('<BR><BR><INPUT TYPE="BUTTON" NAME="restart"
  VALUE="Restart" ')
 document.writeln(' onClick="restartQuiz()">')
 document.writeln("</H4>")
 document.writeln('</FORM>')
}
function restartQuiz() {
 location.reload(true)
}
// -></SCRIPT>
<SCRIPT LANGUAGE="JavaScript" SRC="history.js"><!-
// -></SCRIPT>
```

```
</HEAD>
<BODY>
<SCRIPT LANGUAGE="JavaScript"><!-
readCookie()
document.writeln("<H1 ALIGN='CENTER'>"+pageHeading+"</H1>")
document.writeln("<P ALIGN='RIGHT'><B>Questions: "
 +numberOfQuestions+"<BR>")
document.writeln("Correct Answers: "+correctAnswers+"<BR>")
document.writeln("Score: "+score+"</B></P>")
if(currentQuestion >= qa.length) endQuiz()
else askNextQuestion()
// -></SCRIPT>
</BODY>
</HTML>
```

We'll examine the code contained in the body of quiz.htm and then study the
code in the document's head. After that we'll cover history.js.

The Code in the Document Body

The code in the body of quiz.htm is very short. The readCookie() function is
invoked to read the cookies associated with the document and use the cookie's
name=value pairs to initialize the script's variables to the current state of the quiz.
The cookies contain the number of the current question, the number of questions
asked so far, and the number of correct answers. Next, the script creates a document heading based on the value of the pageHeading variable. (The pageHeading
variable is initialized in history.js.)

The number of questions asked, number of correct answers, and quiz score
are then displayed. The script checks to see if the value of currentQuestion is
equal to or greater than the length of the qa array. (The qa array is also defined
in history.js.) It is used to store all of the quiz's questions and answers. If the
currentQuestion variable is greater than or equal to the length of the qa array,
then all questions have been asked and the endQuiz() function is invoked to
end the quiz. Otherwise, the askNextQuestion() function is invoked to present
the user with another question.

The Code in the Document Head

The first script in the head of `quiz.htm` defines 12 functions. These functions are used as described in the following subsections.

The *Question()* Function This function is used in `history.js` to create `Question` objects. It uses the `arguments` property of the `function` object to determine how many arguments were passed in the `Question()` invocation. The first argument is the text of the question. The last argument is an integer that identifies the correct answer. All arguments between the first and the last are used to define the answers to a question.

The *readCookie()* Function This function reads the cookies of the current document and sets the `currentQuestion`, `numberOfQuestions`, and `correctAnswers` variables. It then uses these values to calculate the value of the `score` variable.

The *getNumberValue()* Function This function is used by `readCookie()` to parse the cookie string `s` and return the value associated with a particular name `n`. It does this by removing all blanks from `s` and then splitting `s` by means of the field separator ";". Having separated the string into `name=value` fields, it then separates these fields by "=". It checks to see if the name component of the split field matches `n` and returns the value associated with the name as an integer. If the name does not have a value it returns 0.

The *removeBlanks()* Functions This function removes all blanks contained in a string and returns this value as a result.

The *askNextQuestion()* Function This function displays the current question in a centered Heading 4. It then invokes `displayAnswers()` to display the possible answers associated with this question.

The *displayAnswers()* Function This function displays the possible answers of the current question as a form. A radio button is displayed with each answer. A Continue button follows the answers. The Continue button's `onClick` event handler is set to the `checkAnswers()` function.

The *checkAnswers()* Function This function is invoked when a user answers a question and clicks on the Continue button. It determines how many answers are associated with a question and then checks the radio button of each answer to see if it is checked. When it finds a checked button it determines whether the checked button is the correct answer. If the answer is correct it invokes the `correct()` function; otherwise it invokes the `incorrect()` function. If no radio buttons have been clicked, the `incorrect()` function is invoked.

The *correct()* Function This function increments the `currentQuestion`, `numberOfQuestions`, and `correctAnswers` variables and invokes `updateCookie()` to write the values of these variables to the document's cookie jar. It then reloads the `quiz.htm` file to process the next question.

The *incorrect()* Function This function increments the `numberOfQuestions` variable and invokes `updateCookie()` to write the value of this variable to the document's cookie jar. It then reloads the `quiz.htm` file to reprocess the same question.

The *updateCookie()* Function This function uses the document's cookie jar to temporarily store the program's state while the `quiz.htm` file is reloaded. It stores the values of the `currentQuestion`, `numberOfQuestions`, and `correctAnswers` variables.

The *endQuiz()* Function This function ends the quiz by setting the document's cookies back to their initial state. It then displays a form that congratulates the user for finishing the quiz and displays a Restart button so that the user can restart the quiz if she or he wishes. The `onClick` event handler for the Restart button is `restartQuiz()`.

The *restartQuiz()* Function This function handles the clicking of the Restart button by reloading the `quiz.htm` file so that the quiz may be restarted.

The Source File

Having gone through the description of `quiz.htm`, the `history.js` file (Listing 8.8) is easy to understand. It defines the `pageHeading` variable that is used to display the heading on each quiz page. It then creates the `qa` array. Each element of `qa` is a `Question` object. Twelve questions are defined. Feel free to add your own questions or delete the ones that I've created—you can change the entire content of the quiz by modifying `history.js`. You can also substitute your own question file for `history.js` by modifying the SRC attribute value of the second script of `quiz.htm`.

Listing 8.8   **Quiz Questions (history.js)**

```
//Heading displayed on the quiz page
pageHeading="History Quiz"
//Questions
qa = new Array()
qa[0] = new Question("Who was the first president
  of the United States?",
 "George Washington",
 "Abraham Lincoln",
 "Benjamin Franklin",
 "Harry Truman",
 0)
qa[1] = new Question("When did Columbus discover America?",
 "1249",
 "1942",
 "1492",
 "1294",
 2)
qa[2] = new Question("Who commanded the Macedonian army?",
 "Napoleon",
 "Alexander the Great",
 "Cleopatra",
 "George Patton",
 1)
qa[3] = new Question("Where did Davy Crockett lose his life?",
 "The Spanish Inquisition",
 "The Alamo",
 "Miami, Florida",
 "On the Oregon Trail",
 1)
qa[4] = new Question("Who was the first man to
  walk on the moon?",
 "Louis Armstrong",
 "Buzz Armstrong",
 "Jack Armstrong",
 "Neil Armstrong",
 3)
qa[5] = new Question("Who wrote the <I>Scarlet Letter</I>?",
 "Michael Crichton",
 "Ernest Hemingway",
```

```
  "Nathaniel Hawthorne",
  "Charles Dickens",
  2)
qa[6] = new Question("Eli Whitney invented:",
  "Mad Cow's Disease",
  "the Cotton Gin",
  "whisky",
  "the automobile",
  1)
qa[7] = new Question("Who was known as the King of the Fauves?",
  "Salvatore Dali",
  "Henri Matisse",
  "Pablo Picasso",
  "Vincent Van Gogh",
  1)
qa[8] = new Question("Who discovered the force of gravity?",
  "Isaac Newton",
  "Galileo",
  "Copernicus",
  "Albert Einstein"
  ,0)
qa[9] = new Question("Who created HTML?",
  "Tim Berners-Lee",
  "Marc Andreessen",
  "Bill Gates",
  "Jim Barksdale",
  0)
qa[10] = new Question("Leonardo da Vinci was born in Greece.",
  "True",
  "False",
  1)
qa[11] = new Question("Louisiana was purchased from France.",
  "True",
  "False",
  0)
```

This example shows how JavaScript can use cookies to create a complex Web application without the use of a CGI program. All of the cookie processing is performed locally on the browser.

Comparison—Cookies vs. Hidden Form Fields

Now that you've learned how both hidden fields and cookies can be used to maintain state information, you may be wondering which one you should use and when. In general, cookies are the preferred option because they allow persistent storage of state information, whereas hidden fields do not. However, cookies may not be the right choice for all applications. Table 8.1 summarizes the trade-offs between cookies and hidden fields.

TABLE 8.1: Cookies vs. Hidden Fields

Trade-Off	Cookies	Hidden Fields
Ease of use	Requires cookie string parsing	Requires form setup and access
Browser support	Navigator, Internet Explorer, other browsers	Almost all browsers
Server support	May not be supported by some servers	Supported by all servers
Performance	Slower—requires disk I/O	Faster—implemented in RAM
Persistent storage	Supported	Not Supported
Availability	Maximum cookie storage may be reached	No practical storage limitation

Both cookies and hidden fields are easy to use; however, both also have some coding overhead associated with them. Cookie strings need to be parsed when they are read. Hidden fields require invisible forms to be set up. As far as ease of use is concerned, I prefer cookies because all of the setup processing is performed in JavaScript.

Even though cookies are supported by Navigator, Internet Explorer, and other browsers, they are not supported by all browsers. On the other hand, hidden fields are supported by all HTML 2–compatible browsers.

Not all Web servers support cookies, though they do support hidden form fields. Cookies are not as performance efficient as hidden fields because cookie operations require disk I/O to the local cookie file. However, in most applications this performance difference is not noticeable.

Cookies provide persistent storage. That is their biggest advantage and why they were developed in the first place. If you require persistent storage, then you have to use cookies.

Cookies may not always be available to your scripts. The cookie specification states that a browser cannot claim that it is cookie capable unless it provides a minimum cookie storage capacity of 300 (currently, this limit is not a problem for most browsers). However, with the increase in cookie popularity, it could be an issue in the future. In addition, most browsers limit the number of cookies that can be stored for a given domain. Netscape Navigator 4 has a 20-cookie-per-domain limit and Internet Explorer 3 has a single-cookie-per-domain limit. Hidden fields do not have any practical limits.

Summary

In this chapter you learned how to use hidden fields and cookies to maintain browser state information. You learned how JavaScript enhances the capabilities that both hidden fields and cookies provide by maximizing local processing and reducing the need for CGI programming. In the next chapter, you'll learn how to work with the link-related objects that are available in JavaScript. You'll learn how to attach scripts to link events and how to use the `location` object to dynamically load Web pages under script control.

CHAPTER
NINE

9

Working with Links

- Uniform Resource Locators (URLs)

- The *javascript:* and *about:* Protocols

- The location Object

- The link Object

- The link() Method

- The anchor Object

- The history Object

The ability to quickly move from one Web page to another in search of information (and entertainment) is at the heart of the Web's popularity. With a click of the mouse, we can travel from a Web page about native cultures to recipes for exotic foods. The single-click simplicity with which we traverse the Web is provided by *links*.

Most links are *static*. Static links always take you to the same destination. This type of link can be written entirely in HTML. Other links are *dynamic*, such as those used to link forms to CGI programs. When you submit a form, especially a search form, the Web page to which you link is often a page that is generated according to data submitted with the form. Until JavaScript, most dynamic links were created using CGI programs. Now, with JavaScript, you can develop browser-side dynamic links, which can eliminate the need for CGI programming and reduce the load on your Web server.

In this chapter, you'll learn how to use JavaScript objects that provide control over the way that links are implemented. You'll learn how use the `location` object to load documents at various URLs, how to attach JavaScript code to a document's links, and how to use the `history` object to keep track of the URLs that have been visited within a window. When you finish this chapter, you'll be able to use link-related objects to implement dynamically programmable links within your own Web pages.

Uniform Resource Locators (URLs)

A Uniform Resource Locator, or URL, is the standard type of Internet address used on the Web. It is used to locate resources and services associated with a variety of protocols. The syntax of a URL varies with the particular protocol used to access a resource or service. For example, most URLs do not contain spaces, but URLs that use the *javascript:* protocol may include spaces, as you'll learn later in this section.

The most common format of a URL is as follows:

```
protocol//hostname[:port] path search hash
```

The `protocol` element of the URL syntax above identifies the protocol to be used to access a resource or service. Examples of protocols include *http:*, *ftp:*, *mailto:*, and *file:*. More-specialized JavaScript protocols are presented later in this section.

The `hostname` element of the URL identifies the fully qualified domain name of the host where the resource is located. Examples are `home.netscape.com`, `www.w3.org`, `www.microsoft.com`, and `java.sun.com`.

The `port` element of the URL identifies the TCP port number to use with the protocol. The port is optional. If it is omitted, the colon preceding the port is also omitted, and the protocol's "well-known" port is assumed. *Well-known ports* are the ports that servers "listen to" when implementing a protocol. For example, the well-known port of HTTP is 80.

The `path` element of the URL is the directory/file path to the resource. It is written in the UNIX forward-slash format. An example path is `/javascript/index.htm`. The path is usually relative to a directory used by the server. For example, my Web server uses the following directory as the base directory from which it services HTTP requests:

```
/usr/local/etc/httpd/htdocs
```

Thus, the URL

```
http://www.jaworski.com/javascript/index.htm
```

addresses the following file:

```
/usr/local/etc/httpd/htdocs/javascript/index.htm.Verify the above
base address.
```

The `search` element of the URL identifies a query string passed in a URL. Query strings are data that is passed to CGI programs via the `QUERY_STRING` environment variable. The query string begins with a question mark (?) followed by the query data. Spaces are encoded using plus (+) signs. For example, the query string *?tall+dark+handsome* passes the words *tall*, *dark*, and *handsome* to a CGI program.

The `hash` element of the URL identifies a named file offset. It consists of a hash character (#) (some of you may know this as a pound sign) followed by the name of the anchor associated with the file offset. For example, if you want to create a link to the part of the file associated with the anchor `section3`, you would append the hash `#section3` to the link's URL.

The *javascript*: and *about*: Protocols

In addition to the standard protocols used with URLs, Netscape Navigator supports the *javascript:* and *about:* protocols. Internet Explorer supports the *javascript:* protocol but not the *about:* protocol.

The *javascript:* Protocol

This protocol is used to evaluate a JavaScript expression and load a Web page that contains the value of the expression. If the expression does not evaluate to a defined value, then no Web page is loaded.

> **NOTE** Spaces may be included in URLs that use the *javascript:* protocol.

In order to see how the *javascript:* protocol works, open your browser and load the following URL:

```
javascript:Date()
```

As shown in Figure 9.1, this URL (which, incidentally, contains a space) opens a document that displays the value of the current date.

Try opening the following URL with Netscape Navigator:

```
javascript:"<H1>"+"What's up?"+"</H1>"
```

This one results in the document shown in Figure 9.2 being displayed. Note that the H1 tags were used to display *What's up?* as a Heading 1. Figure 9.3 shows what happens when you use Internet Explorer to display the same URL.

FIGURE 9.1:

Using the *javascript:* protocol to display the current date

FIGURE 9.2:

Using Netscape Navigator and the *javascript:* protocol to display HTML tags

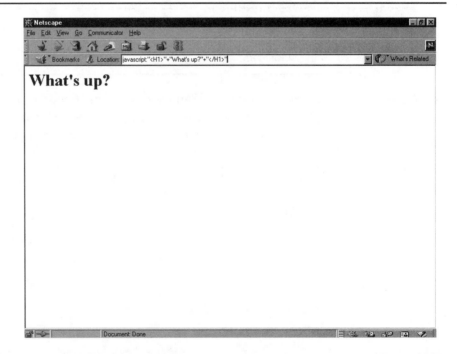

FIGURE 9.3:

Using Internet Explorer and the *javascript:* protocol to display HTML tags

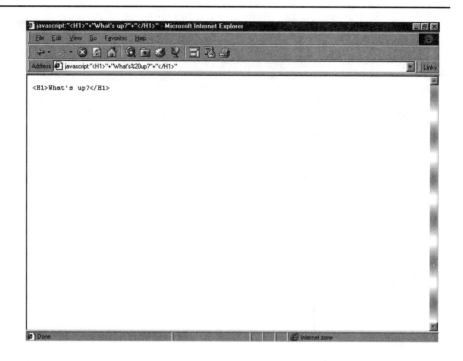

TIP

The URL, *javascript:void(0)*, can be used to create a link that does nothing when the user clicks on it. The **void()** operator is used to evaluate an expression without returning a value.

Netscape Navigator 4.06 and later versions support a JavaScript console window that you can use to debug your scripts. To open this window, simply open the URL *javascript:*, as shown in Figure 9.4. Internet Explorer does not support this feature.

FIGURE 9.4:

FIGURE 9.4:

Using the *javascript:* protocol to open the JavaScript console window

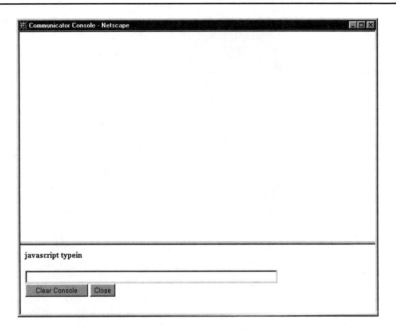

The *about:* Protocol

This protocol provides access to built-in Navigator information. The URL *about:* loads a Web page that identifies the current Navigator version and other related information as shown in Figure 9.5. Loading *about:* has the same result as selecting About Netscape from the Navigator Help pull-down menu.

If the *about:cache* URL is loaded, then Navigator displays statistics on the current state of its cache, as shown in Figure 9.6.

If the *about:plugins* URL is loaded, then Navigator displays information about the plug-ins that are currently configured, as shown in Figure 9.7. The resulting display is the same as that obtained by selecting About Plugins from the Help menu.

FIGURE 9.5:

Loading *about:* displays the same information as selecting About Netscape from Navigator's Help menu.

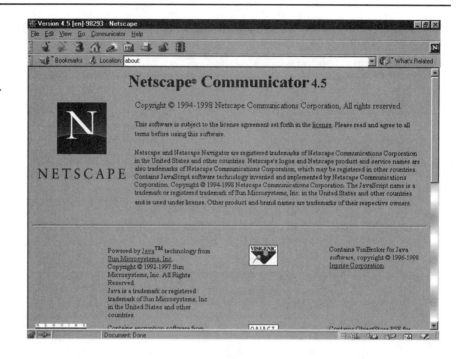

FIGURE 9.6:

Loading *about:cache* displays information about the current state of the disk cache.

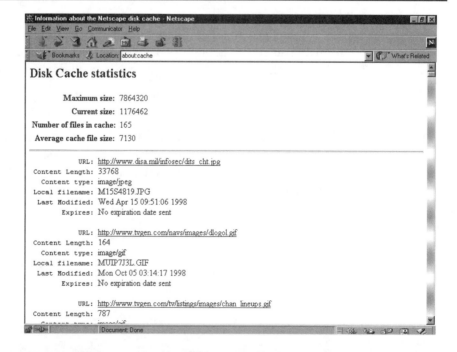

FIGURE 9.7:

Loading *about:plugins* displays information about the plug-ins your browser has installed.

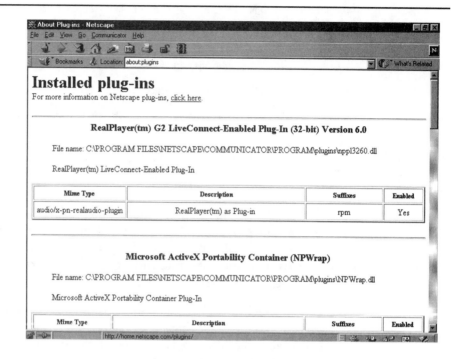

The *location* Object

JavaScript uses the location object to access the URL of the current document that is loaded in a window. The location object contains properties that describe the various parts of the URL. These properties are summarized in Table 9.1.

TABLE 9.1: Properties of the location Object

Property	Description
hash	The anchor part of the URL (if any)
host	The hostname:port part of the URL
hostname	The hostname part of the URL
href	The entire URL

Continued on next page

TABLE 9.1 CONTINUED: Properties of the `location` Object

Property	Description
`pathname`	The pathname part of the URL
`port`	The port part of the URL
`protocol`	The protocol part of the URL, which includes the colon following the protocol name
`search`	The query string part of the URL

The `location` object is a property of the `window` object. If the `location` object of a window is modified, then the browser attempts to load the document specified by the modified URL into the window. For this reason, you should use the `href` property to modify the entire URL at a single time, rather than sequentially modifying each of the parts of the URL.

NOTE The document object also contains a location property. This property is read-only and cannot be modified to load a new document. You should not plan on using this property, because it will be deleted in future versions of JavaScript. Instead, use the `href` property of the `location` property of the `window` object.

The `location` object has two methods—`reload()` and `replace()`. The `reload()` method causes the current document of a window to be reloaded according to the policy used by the browser's Reload button. This policy allows a document to be reloaded from the server in one of the following three ways:

Every time The document is reloaded from the server every time.

Once per session The document is reloaded from the server once per session if the document's date on the server indicates that it is newer than the document stored in cache. If the document is not in the cache, it is loaded from the server.

Never The document is reloaded from cache, if possible. Otherwise, it is loaded from the server.

If true is passed as an argument to the reload() method, then the document is unconditionally loaded from the server.

The replace() method takes a URL as a parameter and loads the document at the specified URL over the current document in the current document history list. This prevents the user from returning to the previous document by clicking the browser's Back button.

The location object does not have any events.

Internet Explorer (but not Navigator) supports the assign() method. It is very similar to replace() in that it takes a URL as an argument and loads the document references by the URL.

Example Application Using the *location* Object

The location object is a simple object with which to work. It is usually used to load a new document or to access individual parts of a document's URL. Listing 9.1 provides an example of the location object's use.

Listing 9.1   Using the *location* Object (load-url.htm)

```
<HTML>
<HEAD>
<TITLE>Load URL</TITLE>
</HEAD>
<FRAMESET ROWS="200,*" BORDER=10>
<FRAME SRC="url-form.htm">
<FRAME SRC="blank.htm">
</FRAMESET>
</HTML>
```

Open the file load-url.htm with your browser, and it will display the form shown in Figure 9.8. This form lets you enter simple URLs that use the *file:*, *http:*, and *ftp:* protocols. You can enter a host name and path to further specify the URLs. When you click on the Load URL button, the document at the specified URL is displayed in the bottom frame of the window, as shown in Figure 9.9.

FIGURE 9.8:

The Load URL form lets you enter a URL part by part (Listing 9.1).

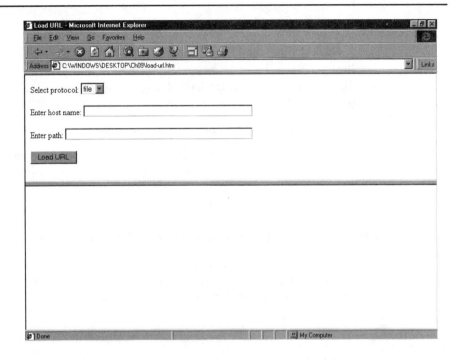

FIGURE 9.9:

The Load URL form lets you load Netscape's home page (Listing 9.1).

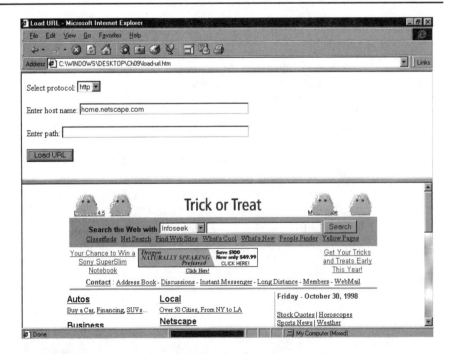

The `load-url.htm` file is shown in Listing 9.1. It sets up a two-row frame set. The file `url-form.htm` is loaded in the top row and `blank.htm` is loaded in the bottom row. The `url-form.htm` file is shown in Listing 9.2 and the `blank.htm` file is shown in Chapter 6, "Creating Frames and Windows."

Listing 9.2   **A Form for Entering a URL (url-form.htm)**

```
<HTML>
<HEAD>
<TITLE>Load URL</TITLE>
<SCRIPT LANGUAGE="JavaScript"><!-
function loadFrames() {
 ix = document.URLform.protocol.options.selectedIndex
 urlString = document.URLform.protocol.options[ix].value+"//"
 urlString += document.URLform.hostname.value
 path =      document.URLform.path.value
 if(path.length > 0) {
  if(path.charAt(0)!="/") path = "/"+path
 }
 urlString += path
 parent.frames[1].location.href=urlString
}
// -></SCRIPT>
</HEAD>
<BODY>
<FORM ACTION="" NAME="URLform">
<P>Select protocol:
<SELECT NAME="protocol" SIZE="1">
<OPTION VALUE="file:" SELECTED="SELECTED">file</OPTION>
<OPTION VALUE="http:">http</OPTION>
<OPTION VALUE="ftp:">ftp</OPTION></SELECT></P>
<P>Enter host name:
<INPUT TYPE="TEXT" NAME="hostname" SIZE="45"></P>
<P>Enter path:
<INPUT TYPE="TEXT" NAME="path" SIZE="50"></P>
<P></P>
<INPUT TYPE="BUTTON" NAME="load" VALUE="Load URL"
 ONCLICK="loadFrames()">
</FORM>
</BODY>
</HTML>
```

There is a single script in the head of `url-form.htm`. This script defines the `loadFrames()` function, which is invoked to handle the `onClick` event of the Load URL button. It determines which of the `protocol` options were selected and uses that option to build `urlString`. It appends the string "//" and the value of the `hostname` field to `urlString` followed by the value of the `path` variable. The `path` variable is set based on the value of the `path` field. If the first character of the `path` field is not "/", then it prepends a slash to the `path` variable before appending its value to `urlString`. Finally, it loads the document specified by `urlString` in the second frame by setting the frame's `location.href` property to `urlString`.

The *link* Object

The `link` object encapsulates a text or image link contained in a document. It is a property of the `document` object. The `links` array is an array of all links contained in a document and is also a property of the `document` object. A `link` object is similar to a `location` object in that it contains a URL. Because of this, `link` objects have many of the same properties as `location` objects; these properties are shown in Table 9.2. The only additional property that the `link` object has in comparison with the `location` object is the `target` property. This property is the HTML `target` attribute of the link and identifies the window where the document referenced by the link's URL is to be loaded.

TABLE 9.2: Properties of the `link` Object

Property	Description
hash	The anchor part of the URL (if any)
host	The hostname:port part of the URL
hostname	The hostname part of the URL
href	The entire URL
pathname	The pathname part of the URL
port	The port part of the URL
protocol	The protocol part of the URL. It includes the colon following the protocol name.
search	The query string part of the URL
target	The link's HTML `target` attribute

The `link` object has one method, `handleEvent()`, which takes an **event** object as an argument and invokes the appropriate event handler for that event. It has nine events—`onClick`, `onDblClick`, `onKeyDown`, `onKeyPress`, `onKeyUp`, `onMouse-Down`, `onMouseUp`, `onMouseOver`, and `onMouseOut,` as described in Chapter 4, "Handling Events."

NOTE   Internet Explorer combines the `link` object with the **anchor** object. You'll learn about the **anchor** object later in this chapter. Internet Explorer's combined implementation has additional properties, methods, and events besides those described in this section.

The following section presents an example of using the `link` object. After this example, the `JavaScript link()` method is introduced.

Example Application Using *link*—A Pair-Matching Game

To see how the `link` object may be used in a Web application, we'll develop a JavaScript version of a familiar pattern-matching game. In this game, you are faced with an array of 16 cards. These 16 cards represent eight pairs of matching images, randomly arranged. Initially, you see only the backs of the cards; the images are hidden facedown. Your goal is to turn over one card and then another to see if the images on the cards match. If they do, the pair remains faceup, and you take another turn—that is, you try to find another pair by choosing two of the remaining cards. Whenever the second card of one of your attempts doesn't match the first card, both of those two cards flip over again, and you must take another turn. You continue taking turns until you have uncovered all the matching pairs.

To get a better feel for how the game is played, open the file `click1.htm` with your browser. You will see a display similar to the one shown in Figure 9.10. In order to play the game, click on any one of the cards, as shown in Figure 9.11. Now click on any other card, as shown in Figure 9.12. Your objective is to click on a card whose image matches the first. Your odds at getting it right are 1 out of 15. However, with repeated tries you will be able to improve those odds. If the card you clicked on is a match, the matching images will remain faceup until the end of the game. If you missed, click on the Continue button to try again. The mismatched pair you clicked is then hidden (that is, turned facedown) again. Continue taking turns until you have finally turned over all of the pairs, two cards at a time. By the time you have won a game, you will be ready to go on to see how the game is implemented.

NOTE In Chapter 10, "Using Images," you will learn how to enhance the pair-match program with JavaScript's dynamic image-display capabilities.

FIGURE 9.10:

The pair match opening screen shows all cards turned over. (Listings 9.3 through 9.6)

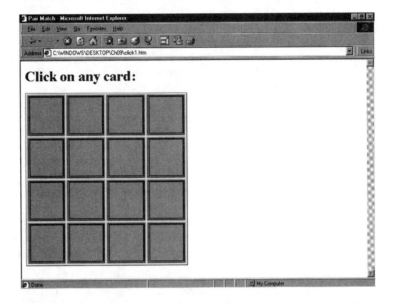

FIGURE 9.11:

A single image has been clicked—try to find a match! (Listings 9.3 through 9.6)

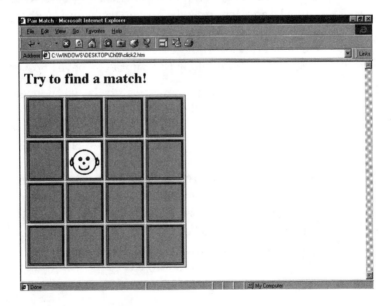

FIGURE 9.12:

Two images have been clicked. They don't match, so you must click the Continue button to take your next turn. (The images will automatically flip facedown again.) (Listings 9.3 through 9.6)

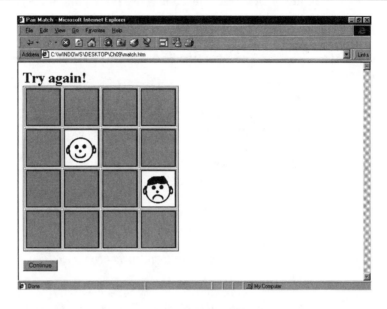

FIGURE 9.13:

The game has been won—all images have been matched (Listings 9.3 through 9.6).

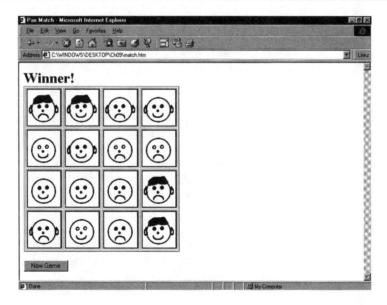

Listing 9.3 contains the code of the `click1.htm` file. This file is rather short, considering the complexity of the pair-matching application, and consists mostly

of JavaScript code. The code is organized into three scripts—two in the header and one in the body.

Listing 9.3   The Startup File for the Pair-Matching Game (click1.htm)

```
<HTML>
<HEAD>
<TITLE>Pair Match</TITLE>
<SCRIPT LANGUAGE="JavaScript" SRC="pairs.js"><!-
// -></SCRIPT>
<SCRIPT LANGUAGE="JavaScript"><!-
function readCookie() {
 var cookie=document.cookie
 if(nameDefined(cookie,"displayedImages")){
  displayedImages=getCookieValue(cookie,"displayedImages")
 }else{
  displayedImages="0000000000000000"
 }
 if(nameDefined(cookie,"imageSequence")){
  imageSequence=getCookieValue(cookie,"imageSequence")
 }else{
  imageSequence=permuteString("0123456701234567")
 }
 initializeImageArray()
 initializeDisplayedArray()
}
function displayCell(n) {
 var f="none.gif"
 if(displayed[n]) f=images[n]
 document.write('<A HREF="click2.htm" ')
 document.write('onClick="userClick('+n+')">')
 document.write('<IMG SRC="'+f+'" WIDTH="80" HEIGHT="83">')
 document.write('')
}
function userClick(n) {
 document.cookie="displayedImages="+displayedImages
 document.cookie="imageSequence="+imageSequence
 document.cookie="click1="+n
}
// -></SCRIPT>
</HEAD>
<BODY BGCOLOR="#FFFFFF">
```

```
<H1>Click on any card:</H1>
<SCRIPT LANGUAGE="JavaScript"><!-
readCookie()
displayTable()
// -></SCRIPT>
</BODY>
</HTML>
```

The script in the document's body invokes the readCookie() function to read the cookies used by click1.htm. (Cookies were covered in Chapter 8, "Using Hidden Fields and Cookies." If you skipped Chapter 8, you should go back and read it before going on.) The displayTable() function is used to display the table of images shown in Figure 9.10.

The first header script imports JavaScript code from the pairs.js file (Listing 9.4). The code in pairs.js is common to click2.htm (Listing 9.5) and match.htm (Listing 9.6), which are also used in the pair-matching program.

The second header script contains the functions readCookie(), displayCell(), and useClick(). These functions are unique to click1.htm. However, modified versions of these functions are used in click2.htm and match.htm. Their use in click1.htm is described in the following subsections.

NOTE   To fully understand readCookie(), displayCell(), and userClick() you'll need to read the description of pairs.js (Listing 9.4 later in this section).

The *readCookie()* Function

This function reads the cookies that are available to click1.htm and looks for cookies that have the names displayedImages and imageSequence. The displayed-Images cookie contains 16 characters which are either 0 or 1. The value 1 at position n indicates that the user has successfully matched the nth image. The value 0 indicates that they have not. The imageSequence is a permuted string that identifies which of the 16 image positions are occupied by image pairs 0 through 7. The initializeImageArray() function is invoked to initialize the images array with the file names of the images that are at each image position. The initialize-DisplayedArray() is invoked to initialize the displayed array with Boolean values based upon the displayedImages cookie.

The *displayCell()* Function

This function creates the image link of each cell of the 4-row-by-4-column image table shown in Figure 9.10. Each cell links to the `click2.htm` file. The image associated with the link is either `none.gif` (corresponding to a hidden image) or one of the images contained in the `images` array. The `onClick` event of the link is handled by the `userClick()` function, which is passed the index (n) of the table cell being displayed. When `userClick()` returns, the `click2.htm` file is loaded, since it is the HREF attribute of the image link.

The *userClick()* Function

This function handles the `onClick` event associated with each of the table's image-link cells. It updates the document's `displayedImages` and `imageSequence` cookies, and creates a third cookie, `click1`, which stores the index of the cell that was clicked.

The `pairs.js` file shown in Listing 9.4 contains the common code used by `click1.htm`, `click2.htm`, and `match.htm`. It defines the `images` and `displayed` arrays, and seven functions: `nameDefined()`, `removeBlanks()`, `getCookie-Value()`, `permuteString()`, `initializeImageArray()`, `initializeDisplayed-Array()`, and `displayTable()`. These arrays and functions are discussed in the following subsections.

Listing 9.4   **Common Code for the Pair-Matching Game (pairs.js)**

```
images = new Array(16)
displayed = new Array(16)
function nameDefined(c,n) {
 var s=removeBlanks(c)
 var pairs=s.split(";")
 for(var i=0;i<pairs.length;++i) {
  var pairSplit=pairs[i].split("=")
  if(pairSplit[0]==n) return true
 }
 return false
}
function removeBlanks(s) {
 var temp=""
 for(var i=0;i<s.length;++i) {
  var c=s.charAt(i)
```

```
  if(c!=" ") temp += c
 }
 return temp
}
function getCookieValue(c,n) {
 var s=removeBlanks(c)
 var pairs=s.split(";")
 for(var i=0;i<pairs.length;++i) {
  var pairSplit=pairs[i].split("=")
  if(pairSplit[0]==n) return pairSplit[1]
 }
 return ""
}
function permuteString(s) {
 var len=s.length
 var sArray = new Array(len)
 for(var i=0;i<len;++i) sArray[i]=s.charAt(i)
 for(var i=0;i<len;++i) {
  var currentValue=sArray[i]
  ix=Math.round(Math.random()*(len-1))
  sArray[i]=sArray[ix]
  sArray[ix]=currentValue
 }
 t=""
 for(var i=0;i<len;++i) t+=sArray[i]
 return t
}
function initializeImageArray() {
 for(var i=0;i<16;++i) {
  var ch=imageSequence.charAt(i)
  var n=parseInt(ch)
  if(n>3) images[i]="frown"+(n-3)+".gif"
  else images[i]="smile"+(n+1)+".gif"
 }
}
function initializeDisplayedArray() {
 for(var i=0;i<16;++i) {
  var ch=displayedImages.charAt(i)
  if(ch=="1") displayed[i]=true
  else displayed[i]=false
 }
}
```

```
function displayTable(){
 document.writeln('<TABLE BORDER="2">')
 for(var i=0;i<4;++i) {
  document.writeln('<TR>')
  for(var j=0;j<4;++j) {
   document.writeln('<TD>')
   document.writeln('<SCRIPT LANGUAGE="JavaScript">')
   document.writeln('displayCell('+(i*4+j)+')')
   document.writeln('</SCRIPT>')
   document.writeln('</TD>')
  }
  document.writeln('</TR>')
 }
 document.writeln('</TABLE>')
}
```

The *images* Array

This array contains the names of the image files that are displayed in each cell of the table.

The *displayed* Array

This array consists of 16 Boolean values, indicating which images have been matched by the user.

The *nameDefined()* Function

This function checks the cookie passed via the c argument to see if it contains a name=value pair with the name passed by the n argument. It returns true if a matching name is found and false otherwise.

The *removeBlanks()* Function

This function returns a string that has all blank spaces removed.

The *getCookieValue()* Function

This function returns the value of the name=value pair of the cookie passed via the c argument and the name passed via the n argument.

The *permuteString()* Function

This function is passed a string s and returns a string t where t is a random permutation of s. It is used to randomly distribute the images contained in the image table.

The *initializeImageArray()* Function

This function is invoked by readCookie() to initialize the images array based upon the imageSequence cookie value. The files smile1.gif through smile4.gif correspond to imageSequence values 0 through 3. The files frown1.gif through frown4.gif correspond to imageSequence values 4 through 7.

The *initializeDisplayedArray()* Function

This function initializes the Boolean displayed array based on the displayed-Images cookie.

The *displayTable()* Function

This function displays the Image Link table. It generates the HTML code for the table as a whole, as well as for each of its rows and for all of its cells. It writes a script that invokes the displayCell() function as the contents of each table cell. The displayCell() function is invoked when the table is being formatted. It generates each cell's image link.

When a user clicks on any image link displayed by click1.htm, the userClick() function is invoked to handle the event. Each image displayed by click1.htm is used as the anchor of a link. The destination of this link is click2.htm; this file processes the second click of a pair of clicks. Its code is shown in Listing 9.5.

The only differences between click2.htm and click1.htm are in click2's implementation of the readCookie(), displayCell(), and userClick() functions. These differences are explained in the following subsections.

The *readCookie()* Function

In click2.htm, readCookie() reads three cookies: displayedImages, image-Sequence, and click1. The additional click1 cookie contains the index of the image that the user selected with his or her first click.

The *displayCell()* Function

In click2.htm, the displayCell() function displays an image if it has already been matched by the user (i.e., if displayed[n] is true) or if it was selected on the user's first click. Also, all links created by click2.htm now point to match.htm. When a user clicks on a link, userClick() is invoked to handle the onClick event, then match.htm is loaded.

The *userClick()* Function

In click2.htm, the userClick() function creates an additional cookie, click2, that records the user's second image selection.

Listing 9.5　　　**The Document Used to Process the Second Click (click2.htm)**

```
<HTML>
<HEAD>
<TITLE>Pair Match</TITLE>
<SCRIPT LANGUAGE="JavaScript" SRC="pairs.js"><!-
// -></SCRIPT>
<SCRIPT LANGUAGE="JavaScript"><!-
function readCookie() {
 var cookie=document.cookie
 displayedImages=getCookieValue(cookie,"displayedImages")
 imageSequence=getCookieValue(cookie,"imageSequence")
 click1=parseInt(getCookieValue(cookie,"click1"))
 initializeImageArray()
 initializeDisplayedArray()
}
function displayCell(n) {
 var f="none.gif"
 if(displayed[n] || click1==n) f=images[n]
 document.write('<A HREF="match.htm" ')
 document.write('onClick="userClick('+n+')">')
 document.write('<IMG SRC="'+f+'" WIDTH="80" HEIGHT="83">')
 document.write('</A>')
}
function userClick(n) {
 document.cookie="displayedImages="+displayedImages
 document.cookie="imageSequence="+imageSequence
 document.cookie="click1="+click1
 document.cookie="click2="+n
```

```
}
// -></SCRIPT>
</HEAD>
<BODY BGCOLOR="#FFFFFF">
<H1>Try to find a match!</H1>
<SCRIPT LANGUAGE="JavaScript"><!-
readCookie()
displayTable()
// -></SCRIPT>
</BODY>
</HTML>
```

The match.htm file is loaded each time the user has clicked on two cards. It checks to see if the images match and whether the game has been won. It is similar to click1.htm and click2.htm but has some changes and additional functions, as follows:

The Script in the Document's Body

The script in the document's body invokes the displayMatchStatus() function before going on to display the image table. The displayMatchStatus() function determines whether the user has matched a pair of images, and it displays an appropriate heading. After the image table is displayed, a form with a single button is generated. The button's label is *New Game* if the user has just matched all image pairs and *Continue* otherwise. Clicking on the button results in click1.htm being reloaded.

The *readCookie()* Function

The readCookie() function reads four cookies: displayedImages, imageSequence, click1, and click2.

The *displayCell()* Function

The displayCell() function displays an image if its index is click1 or click2 or if that image has already been matched. It does not generate image links for the table's cells. Simple images are used instead. By the time a user gets to match.htm he or she will not be clicking on an image. Instead, he or she will click on the New Game or Continue button.

The *displayMatchStatus()* Function

This function checks to see if a user has matched two images. In this case, click1 must be different from click2 (the user can't click on the same image twice) and the value of the images array for both clicks must be the same (the image files must match). If the user has successfully matched two images then the value of the displayed array is updated to reflect the fact that the images match. The displayed-Images cookie value is then updated, based upon the revised displayed array. The winner() function is invoked to determine whether all images have been matched, and an appropriate heading is displayed.

The *winner()* Function

This function checks to see if all images have been matched. If they have, then it returns true. Otherwise, it returns false.

Listing 9.6	The Document Used to Check for Matching Clicks (match.htm)

```
<HTML>
<HEAD>
<TITLE>Pair Match</TITLE>
<SCRIPT LANGUAGE="JavaScript" SRC="pairs.js"><!-
// -></SCRIPT>
<SCRIPT LANGUAGE="JavaScript"><!-
function readCookie() {
 var cookie=document.cookie
 displayedImages=getCookieValue(cookie,"displayedImages")
 imageSequence=getCookieValue(cookie,"imageSequence")
 click1=parseInt(getCookieValue(cookie,"click1"))
 click2=parseInt(getCookieValue(cookie,"click2"))
 initializeImageArray()
 initializeDisplayedArray()
}
function displayCell(n) {
 var f="none.gif"
 if(displayed[n] || click1==n || click2==n) f=images[n]
 document.write('<IMG SRC="'+f+'" WIDTH="80" HEIGHT="83">')
}
function displayMatchStatus() {
 if(click1!=click2 && images[click1]==images[click2]){
  displayed[click1]=true
```

```
     displayed[click2]=true
     displayedImages=""
     for(var i=0;i<16;++i) {
      if(displayed[i]) displayedImages+="1"
      else displayedImages+="0"
     }
     if(winner()){
      document.writeln("<H1>Winner!")
      displayedImages="0000000000000000"
      imageSequence=permuteString("0123456701234567")
      state="winner"
     }else{
      document.writeln("<H1>They matched!")
      state="matched"
     }
    }else{
     document.writeln("<H1>Try again!")
     state="notMatched"
    }
    document.cookie="displayedImages="+displayedImages
    document.cookie="imageSequence="+imageSequence
   }
   function winner() {
    for(var i=0;i<16;++i)
     if(displayed[i]!=true) return false
    return true
   }
   // -></SCRIPT>
   </HEAD>
   <BODY BGCOLOR="#FFFFFF">
   <SCRIPT LANGUAGE="JavaScript"><!-
   readCookie()
   displayMatchStatus()
   displayTable()
   document.write('<FORM><INPUT TYPE="BUTTON" NAME="goToClick1"')
   if(state=="winner") document.writeln(' VALUE="New Game" ')
   else document.writeln(' VALUE="Continue" ')
   document.write('onClick="window.location.href=')
   document.write("'click1.htm'")
   document.writeln('"></FORM>')
   // -></SCRIPT>
   </BODY>
   </HTML>
```

The *link()* Method

The link object is not the only way of creating a link. A link may be created using the link() method of the String object. This method takes the hypertext reference (HREF) attribute of the link as a parameter and creates a link to the specified HREF. For example, the following statements create a link to the author's *Mastering JavaScript and JScript* home page:

```
mjLink="Mastering JavaScript and
JScript".link("http://www.jaworski.com/javascript/")
document.writeln(mjLink)
```

The above statements result in the following HTML being generated for the current document:

```
<A HREF="http://www.jaworski.com/javascript/">Mastering JavaScript and
JScript</A>
```

As another example, consider Listing 9.7. It contains the code of the linkx.htm file and generates the Web page shown in Figure 9.14.

Listing 9.7   Using the *link()* Method (linkx.htm)

```
<HTML>
<HEAD>
<TITLE>Using the link() Method</TITLE>
</HEAD>
<BODY>
<H1>Using the link() Method</H1>
<SCRIPT LANGUAGE="JavaScript"><!-
text=new Array(5)
text[0]="Mastering JavaScript and JScript Home Page"
text[1]="Sybex Home Page"
text[2]="Netscape Home Page"
text[3]="Microsoft Home Page"
text[4]="JavaSoft Home Page"
linkx=new Array(5)
linkx[0]=text[0].link("http://www.jaworski.com/javascript/")
linkx[1]=text[1].link("http://www.sybex.com")
linkx[2]=text[2].link("http://home.netscape.com")
linkx[3]=text[3].link("http://www.microsoft.com")
linkx[4]=text[4].link("http://www.javasoft.com")
```

```
for(var i=0;i<linkx.length;++i)
 document.writeln("<P>"+linkx[i]+"</P>")
// -></SCRIPT>
</BODY>
</HTML>
```

FIGURE 9.14:

The `link()` method
makes it easy to insert URLs
in a Web page (Listing 9.7).

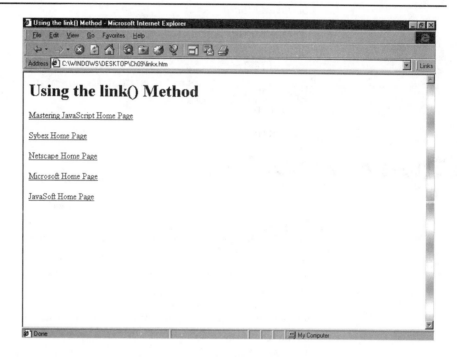

The `linkx.htm` file creates an array of strings, called `text`, with the following anchor text:

Mastering JavaScript and JScript Home Page

Sybex Home Page

Netscape Home Page

Microsoft Home Page

JavaSoft Home Page

It then creates an array of links, called `linkx`, using the `link()` method of the `String` object. These links are to the following URLs:

- `http://www.jaworski.com/javascript/`
- `http://www.sybex.com`
- `http://home.netscape.com`
- `http://www.microsoft.com`
- `http://www.javasoft.com`

Finally, it writes these links to the current document using the `writeln()` method of the `document` object.

The *anchor* Object

The anchor object represents an anchor that is used as a named offset within an HTML document. It is a property of the `document` object. The `anchors` array contains all of the anchors of a document. The `anchor` object has no properties, methods, or events. It is used to keep track of the named offsets that are defined relative to an HTML document. For example, `anchors.length` can be used to step through all of a document's anchors.

An anchor object is also a `link` object if it contains an HREF attribute. In this case, it will have an entry in both the `anchors` and `links` arrays.

The `anchor()` method is a method of the `String` object that can be used to generate the hypertext used to create an `anchor` object. It is similar to the `link()` method. For example, the following code can be used to create an anchor in the current document:

```
anchorString="Section 5".anchor("sect5")
document.write(anchorString)
```

The anchor created by the above code is equivalent to the following HTML:

```
<A NAME="sect5">Section 5</A>
```

Internet Explorer's Links and Anchors

Internet Explorer combines the `link` object with the `anchor` object. In the Internet Explorer object model, the `document.links[]` array refers to a collection of `anchor` and `area` objects. (You'll learn about `area` objects in the next chapter.) A *link* is differentiated from an *anchor* in that the `anchor` object's `href` property is set if the anchor represents a link and its `name` property is set if it represents a named anchor. It is possible for an `anchor` object to be used as both a link and an anchor. In this case, both properties will be set. The important thing to remember is that either `href` or `name` must be set.

NOTE Internet Explorer's implementation of the **anchor** object is quite extensive. It supports additional properties and methods that implement the Internet Explorer object model. In addition to the nine events supported by Navigator's `link` object, Internet Explorer's **anchor** object supports the `onBlur`, `onDragStart`, `onError-Update`, `onFilterChange`, `onFocus`, `onHelp`, `onMouseMove`, and `onSelect-Start` events.

The *history* Object

The `history` object is used by Navigator to keep track of the URLs that have been displayed within a window during the current browser session. It displays this information in the History list that is accessed via Navigator's Go menu. The `history` object is a property of the `window` object. The `history` object has no events, but it has the four following properties:

current   The URL of the current document displayed in the window

length   The length of the History list

next   The next URL in the History list

previous   The previous URL in the History list

NOTE Internet Explorer does not support the **current**, **next**, and **previous** properties of the **history** object.

The `history` object has three methods—`back()`, `forward()`, and `go()`—which can be used to travel to documents contained in the History list:

back() Loads the previous document in the History list. It produces the same effect as clicking on your browser's Back button.

forward() Loads the next document in the History list. It produces the same effect as clicking on your browser's Forward button.

go() Goes to a specific document in the History list. It can take either an integer parameter (positive or negative, indicating whether to go forward or back in the History list) or a string parameter (a keyword—see the next two items).

go(n) When $n>0$, this method loads the document that is n entries ahead (forward) in the History list. When $n=0$, it reloads the current document. When $n<0$, go loads the document that is n entries behind (back) in the History list.

go(string) When used in this manner, `go()` loads the closest document in the History list whose URL contains this string as a substring. For example, `history.go("chargers")` loads the closest History entry that contains the string `"chargers"` in its URL.

The JavaScript `history` object may be used to help users navigate your Web site. For example, it can be used to create simple direction buttons that allow users to revisit previously traversed Web pages. More elaborate navigation aids may be developed using a standard site-navigation form.

JavaScript security places restrictions on the use of the `history` object. In particular, a script that executes as part of a document in one frame can only access the `history` object of a different frame if the `history` object refers to documents that are loaded from the same Web server as the script's document. This restriction is implemented by both Navigator and Internet Explorer. Chapter 23, "Securing Your Scripts," covers this and other aspects of JavaScript security in more detail. It also shows how signed scripts can be used to avoid some security restrictions.

Summary

In this chapter, you learned how to use link-related objects to exercise greater control over your document's links. You learned how to load documents via the `location` object, how to attach JavaScript code to a document's links, and how to use the `history` object to keep track of the URLs that have been visited within a window. In the next chapter, you'll learn how to use JavaScript's `image` and `area` objects to perform animation and to implement advanced client-side image map programs.

CHAPTER
TEN

Using Images

- The image Object and Its Properties

- Dynamic Image Display

- Images and Animation

- Image Maps and the area Object

- Working with Image Maps

10

The old adage that a picture is worth a thousand words has never been more appropriate than it is to the Web. Images transform Web pages from fancy formatted text to professional graphical presentations. They allow drawings, photographs, and other graphics to be used to present the information that words alone cannot describe. Images can also be used as the source anchor for links or as clickable image maps. When images are used with links, they provide a highly intuitive approach to navigating the Web.

Until JavaScript, however, images could not be displayed dynamically because HTML's image-display capabilities have one significant limitation—once you've displayed an image, you cannot change it without loading a new Web page. JavaScript overcomes the static image-display limitations of HTML by allowing you to dynamically update images without having to load a new Web page. This single JavaScript feature can greatly enhance the attractiveness of your Web pages. It allows you to provide timely graphical feedback in response to user actions and can be used to include sophisticated animation sequences in your Web pages.

In this chapter, you'll learn how to use the excellent image-handling features that JavaScript provides. I'll cover the `image` object and show you how to control the way images are displayed with respect to surrounding text. You'll learn how to dynamically display images in your Web pages and how to use dynamic images to create animation effects. You'll also learn how to develop sophisticated client-side image maps using the `area` object. When you've finished this chapter, you'll be able to use images to create Web applications that are highly informative, user-friendly, and entertaining.

The *image* Object

The `image` object provides access to the images that are loaded with a document. It is a property of the `document` object. The `images` array contains an entry for each `<img>` tag that is specified within a document. The `images` array is also a property of the `document` object.

The properties of the `image` object that are supported by both Navigator and Internet Explorer are shown in Table 10.1. These properties reflect the attributes of the `<img>` tag. Internet Explorer supports many more properties than those shown in Table 10.1. These additional properties support Internet Explorer's implementation of Dynamic HTML. (Refer to Chapter 18, " Using Style Sheets and DHTML.")

TABLE 10.1: Image Properties

Property	Description
border	The value of the <img> tag's BORDER attribute
complete	Identifies whether an image has been completely loaded
height	The value of the <img> tag's HEIGHT attribute
hspace	The value of the <img> tag's HSPACE attribute
lowsrc	The value of the <img> tag's LOWSRC attribute
name	The value of the <img> tag's NAME attribute
prototype	Used to add user-specified properties to an image object
src	The value of the <img> tag's SRC attribute
vspace	The value of the <img> tag's VSPACE attribute
width	The value of the <img> tag's WIDTH attribute

The image object has no methods that are common to Internet Explorer and Navigator. Navigator defines the handleEvent() method, which is used to directly invoke an image's event handler. Internet Explorer defines 10 methods that support event handling and DHTML. Online Appendix A, "Comparing JavaScript and JScript," covers the differences between Internet Explorer's and Navigator's implementation of the image object. Both Internet Explorer and Navigator support the events listed in Table 4.1. Internet Explorer supports additional events, as described in Appendix A.

The image object type allows new image objects to be explicitly created with the keyword and a *constructor*. (Constructors were introduced in Chapter 5, "Working with Objects.") The Image() constructor is used to create and preload images that aren't initially displayed as part of a Web page. These image objects are stored in the browser's cache and are used to replace images that have already been displayed.

An example of creating a cached image via the Image() constructor follows:

```
cachedImage = new Image()
cachedImage.src = "myImage.gif"
```

The first statement creates a new image object and assigns it to the cachedImage variable. The second statement sets the image object's src property to the image file myImage.gif. This causes myImage.gif to be loaded into the browser cache. The loaded image can then be referenced using the cachedImage variable.

The image constructor takes optional width and height parameters. For example, myImage = new Image(40,50) creates an image object that is 40 pixels wide and 50 pixels high.

NOTE Images that are created using the Image() constructor are not accessible via the images array.

Image Display Properties

Before I get into dynamic image display, I'll cover the image properties that affect the way an image is displayed with respect to surrounding text. These properties reflect the attributes of the <img> tag used to place an image in a document.

The border property identifies the thickness of an image's border in pixels. Images that are created using the Image() constructor have their border set to 0. The border property is read-only.

The height and width properties of an image specify the height and width of the window area in which the image is to be displayed. If the image is larger than the specified area, the browser will scale the image to fit in the allocated space. The height and width properties can be specified in pixels or as a percentage of the window's dimensions; a percent sign (%) is used to specify a percentage value. Images that are created using the Image() constructor have their height and width properties set to their actual dimensions. The height and width properties are read-only.

The hspace and vspace properties are used to specify a margin between an image and surrounding text. The hspace attribute specifies the size of an image's left and right margins in pixels. The vspace attribute specifies an image's top and bottom margins in pixels. Images that are created using the Image() constructor have their hspace and vspace properties set to 0. These properties are read-only.

Other Image Properties

The `image` object has other properties that can be used to monitor and control image loading and display:

The `name` property is a read-only property that specifies the image's `name` attribute.

The `lowsrc` property can be modified to quickly load and display a low-resolution image while a slower loading high-resolution image is being loaded.

The `src` property is used to load a new image in the place of a currently displayed image. (You'll learn more about this property in the next section on dynamic image display.)

The `complete` property is a read-only property that indicates whether an image has been completely loaded.

The `prototype` property allows other user-defined properties to be created for all objects of the `image` object type. (This property is covered in Chapter 5, "Working with Objects.")

Dynamic Image Display

JavaScript's dynamic image display capabilities are easy to use. Just follow these three steps:

1. Use the `Image()` constructor to create `image` objects for storing the images that you'll display dynamically.

2. Load the image files associated with the newly created images by setting the image's `src` attribute to the image file's name.

3. Display the images by setting the `src` attribute of an image in the document's `images` array to the `src` attribute of a cached image.

For example, suppose you have a document that contains two <img> tags. When the document is loaded by your browser, the image files that are specified in the

`<img>` tags' `src` attributes are displayed. You can load and display two new images using the following JavaScript code:

```
//Step 1: Create image objects
newImage1 = new Image()
newImage2 = new Image()
//Step 2: Load the image files
newImage1.src = "new1.gif"
newImage2.src = "new2.gif"
//Step 3: Display the images
document.images[0].src = newImage1.src
document.images[1].src = newImage2.src
```

In Chapter 9, "Working with Links," you developed an image pair-matching program. This program was designed to illustrate link event handling and to develop your skills in using cookies. The program did not take advantage of JavaScript's dynamic image display capabilities, and as a result, it required a new Web page to be loaded whenever a new image was displayed. Now that you know how to display images dynamically, let's revise the pair-matching program to take advantage of these capabilities.

A revised pair-matching program is contained in Listing 10.1. This single file (`pairs.htm`) takes the place of the `click1.htm`, `click2.htm`, `match.htm`, and `pairs.js` files used in Chapter 9. It also implements the image map program in a much smoother fashion, because it does not load an entire Web page to display a single image. Figure 10.1 shows the program's opening display. Figure 10.2 provides a sample snapshot of a game in mid-progress. You can play the new game by downloading the `pairs.htm` file from this book's page on the Sybex Web site. When you open the file, you should immediately notice the improvement in the way the program displays images.

Listing 10.1   Pair Matching Revisited (pairs.htm)

```
<HTML>
<HEAD>
<TITLE>Pair Match</TITLE>
<SCRIPT LANGUAGE="JavaScript"><!–
function initialize() {
 imageSource=new Array(9)
 for(var i=0;i<9;++i) imageSource[i]=new Image()
 imageSource[0].src="smile1.gif"
 imageSource[1].src="smile2.gif"
```

```
    imageSource[2].src="smile3.gif"
    imageSource[3].src="smile4.gif"
    imageSource[4].src="frown1.gif"
    imageSource[5].src="frown2.gif"
    imageSource[6].src="frown3.gif"
    imageSource[7].src="frown4.gif"
    imageSource[8].src="none.gif"
    imageSequence=new Array(16)
    for(var i=0;i<16;++i) imageSequence[i]=i%8
    for(var i=0;i<16;++i) {
     var currentValue=imageSequence[i]
     var ix=Math.round(Math.random()*(15))
     imageSequence[i]=imageSequence[ix]
     imageSequence[ix]=currentValue
    }
    click0=0
    click1=0
    click2=0
   }
   function displayTable(){
    document.writeln('<TABLE BORDER="2">')
    for(var i=0;i<4;++i) {
     document.writeln('<TR>')
     for(var j=0;j<4;++j) {
      document.writeln('<TD>')
      document.write('<A HREF="javascript:void(0)" ')
      document.write('onClick="userClick('+(i*4+j)+')">')
      document.write('<IMG SRC="none.gif" WIDTH="80" HEIGHT="83">')
      document.write('</A>')
      document.writeln('</TD>')
     }
     document.writeln('</TR>')
    }
    document.writeln('</TABLE>')
   }
   function userClick(n) {
    if(click0==0){
     click0=1
     click1=n
     document.images[n].src=imageSource[imageSequence[n]].src
    }else if(click0==1){
```

```
            click0=0
            click2=n
            document.images[n].src=imageSource[imageSequence[n]].src
            if(click1==click2 ||
             imageSequence[click1]!=imageSequence[click2])
              setTimeout("resetImages()",1500)
          }
        }
        function resetImages() {
          document.images[click1].src=imageSource[8].src
          document.images[click2].src=imageSource[8].src
        }
        // -></SCRIPT>
        </HEAD>
        <BODY BGCOLOR="#FFFFFF">
        <H1>Try to find a matching pair!</H1>
        <SCRIPT LANGUAGE="JavaScript"><!-
        initialize()
        displayTable()
        // -></SCRIPT>
        <FORM>
        <P ALIGN="CENTER">
        <INPUT TYPE="BUTTON" NAME="replay" VALUE="Play again!"
         ONCLICK="window.location='pairs.htm'">
        </P>
        </FORM>
        </BODY>
        </HTML>
```

The pairs.htm file contains a large script in the document's head and a small script in the document's body. The script in the document's body invokes the initialize() function to initialize the arrays and variables used in the program. It invokes the displayTable() function to display the table of image links.

The script in the document's head defines four functions: initialize(), displayTable(), userClick(), and resetImages(). The use of these functions is described in the following subsections.

FIGURE 10.1:

The revised pair-matching program takes advantage of dynamic image display (Listing 10.1).

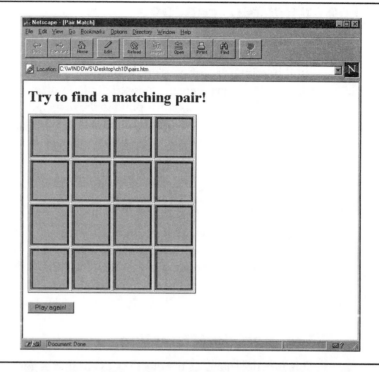

FIGURE 10.2:

A snapshot of the pair-matching program's display—recognize anyone (Listing 10.1)?

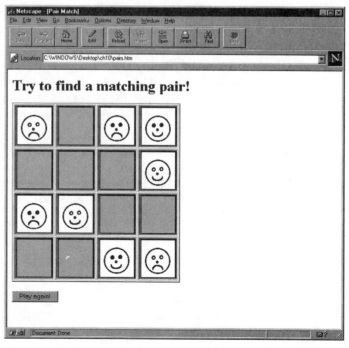

The *initialize()* Function

This function initializes the arrays and variables used throughout the script. The imageSource array is used to load and cache the images to be displayed throughout the script's execution. The imageSequence array is used to identify in which table cells the images are to be stored. It randomizes the location of pairs of the digits 0 through 7. These digits correspond to the first eight images stored in imageSource. The click0 variable is used to keep track of whether the user has clicked on the first or second image of the two-image sequence. The click1 and click2 variables identify the index of the image that the user clicked.

The *displayTable()* Function

This function displays the initial image link table. It is similar to the displayTable() function used in Chapter 9, "Working with Links." However, it displays the table only once—when the document is loaded. Thus, it displays the none.gif image in each table cell. The table images are updated dynamically by the userClick() function.

The *userClick()* Function

This function handles the onClick event that is generated when a user clicks an image link. If the user has clicked the first image of the two-click sequence, then the click variable is set to 1, click1 is set to the index of the clicked cell, and the image associated with the cell is displayed. If the user has clicked the second image of the two-click sequence, then the click variable is reset to 0, click2 is set to the index of the clicked cell, and the image associated with the cell is displayed. If the images do not match, then the resetImages() function is invoked to reset the image display after a 1.5 second timeout period.

The *resetImages()* Function

This function resets the table cells pointed to by the click1 and click2 variables; it resets them to the none.gif image.

Images and Animation

JavaScript's dynamic image display capabilities can be used to create animation effects. *Animation* basically involves displaying one image after another in sequence. The quality of the animation depends on the quality of the images displayed, the delay between successive image displays, and the ability of your browser to reduce any deviations in this delay.

The quality of the images displayed depends on your taste in choosing images or your artistic skills in creating them; we can't provide you with much help in those areas. The delay between images is usually a fraction of a second (assuming that all images are downloaded prior to performing the animation). Higher-performance computers may be able to minimize this delay and reduce deviations in the average delay. These deviations are caused by the performance load on your system that results from other concurrently executing tasks.

Even if you already know the basics of how to perform animation, there are a few tips that will improve your results. These are as follows:

- Make sure that all images are loaded before you start your animation sequence. This will eliminate any additional delays associated with image loading.

- Schedule successive image displays using the onLoad event handler of the <img> tag to which the images are to be written. This will ensure that an image has been loaded and displayed before the next image is processed.

- Use the setTimeout() method of the window object to implement delays between images. This method will help to reduce any deviations in your average delay.

- Experiment with the delay value to see what delay is best for your animation. Although a lower delay value provides a smoother animation, a delay that is too small can result in images being displayed at a comically quick pace.

The file animate.htm provides a simple example of JavaScript animation. It displays a five-frame animation of me working out (see Figure 10.3). The first and last frames are the same; so are the second and fourth frames. Admittedly, this is not a very exciting animation, but it illustrates the principles of animation without getting wrapped up in the images being displayed. You can apply these principles to your own animation needs. If you haven't already done so, open `animate.htm` with your browser. Experiment with the faster and slower buttons to change the delay between successive images. Notice how this delay affects the quality of the animation.

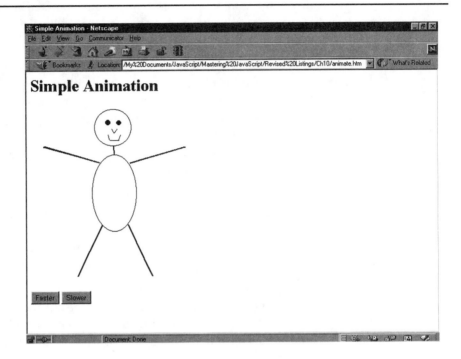

The `animate.htm` (Listing 10.2) file is rather short compared to other scripts. The script in the document's body simply invokes the `initialize()` function to create and load the animation images, set the value of the `delay` variable, and initialize other variables. Note that the `onLoad` event handler of the `<img>` tag invokes the `setStart()` function to start the animation. The `setStart()` function sets the `start` variable to *true*. The `animate()` function waits until `start` is *true* before beginning the animation.

Listing 10.2   **JavaScript Animation (animate.htm)**

```
<HTML>
<HEAD>
<TITLE>Simple Animation</TITLE>
```

```
<SCRIPT LANGUAGE="JavaScript"><!-
function initialize() {
 start=false
 imageSource=new Array(5)
 for(var i=0;i<5;++i){
  imageSource[i]=new Image()
  imageSource[i].src="image"+i+".gif"
 }
 delay=500
 delta=100
 nextImage=1
 startAnimation()
}
function startAnimation() {
 interval=setInterval('animate()',delay)
}
function setStart() {
 start = true
}
function animate() {
 if(start==true){
  i=nextImage
  ++nextImage
  nextImage%=5
  if(imageSource[i].complete)
   document.display.src=imageSource[i].src
 }
}
function goFaster() {
 clearInterval(interval)
 delay-=delta
 if(delay<100) delay=100
 startAnimation()
}
function goSlower() {
 clearInterval(interval)
 delay+=delta
 startAnimation()
}
// -></SCRIPT>
```

```
</HEAD>
<BODY BGCOLOR="#FFFFFF">
<SCRIPT LANGUAGE="JavaScript"><!-
initialize()
// -></SCRIPT>
<H1>Simple Animation</H1>
<IMG NAME="display" SRC="image0.gif" onLoad="setStart()">
<BR>
<FORM>
<INPUT TYPE="BUTTON" NAME="faster" VALUE="Faster" ONCLICK="goFaster()">
<INPUT TYPE="BUTTON" NAME="slower" VALUE="Slower" ONCLICK="goSlower()">
</FORM>
</BODY>
</HTML>
```

The script in the document's head defines four functions: initialize(), start-Animation(), setStart(), animate(), goFaster(), and goSlower(). The use of these functions is described in the following subsections.

The *initialize()* Function

This function creates and loads the images used in the animation and sets the delay variable to 500. Since the delay is specified in milliseconds, this initial delay is a half-second. The delta variable is set to 100. This variably is used to increment or decrement the delay when the user clicks the Slower or Faster buttons. The nextImage variable identifies the next image to be displayed.

The *startAnimation()* Function

This function invokes the animate() function at an interval of delay milliseconds.

The *setStart()* Function

Sets the value of start to *true* to begin the animation.

The *animate()* Function

This function performs the actual animation. It displays the next image, and updates nextImage to point to a new image.

The *goFaster()* Function

This function handles the onClick event associated with the Faster button by decreasing the delay value by the amount indicated by the delta variable.

The *goSlower()* Function

This function handles the onClick event associated with the Slower button by increasing the delay value by the amount indicated by the delta variable.

Image Maps and the *area* Object

Clickable image maps provide a graphical, intuitive, and easy-to-use way to navigate the Web. An image map is an image that is divided into different areas, each of which is associated with its own URL. When a user clicks a particular area of the image map, the document at the URL associated with the area is loaded. Chapter 4, "Handling Events," introduces image maps and shows how to handle image map events.

JavaScript supports client-side image maps and provides the area object as a way of handling user actions related to specific image areas. These areas are defined by the <area> tag. For more information on how to use these tags, consult online Appendix B, "Accessing Online References."

The properties of the area object that are common to Navigator and Internet Explorer are shown in Table 10.2. These properties reflect the HREF and TARGET attributes of the <area> tag and are equivalent to those of the location and link objects that you studied in Chapter 9, "Working with Links." The area object does not have any methods that are common to Navigator and Internet Explorer. It has three common events, onDblClick, onMouseOut, and onMouseOver, as described in Chapter 4.

TABLE 10.2: Area Properties

Property	Description
hash	The file offset part of an **area** object's HREF attribute
host	The host name part of an **area** object's HREF attribute
hostname	The host:port part of an **area** object's HREF attribute
href	An **area** object's complete HREF attribute
pathname	The path name part of an **area** object's HREF attribute
port	The port part of an **area** object's HREF attribute
protocol	The protocol part of an **area** object's HREF attribute
search	The query string part of an **area** object's HREF attribute
target	An **area** object's TARGET attribute

Working with Image Maps

The HTML <map> and <area> tags can be used to implement effective client-side image maps. However, as is usually the case, JavaScript provides some additional features that further enhance the capabilities of HTML. With respect to image maps, these features are the onMouseOver and onMouseOut events associated with the area object. The onMouseOver event is generated when a user moves the mouse pointer over an image area. The onMouseOut event is generated when a user moves the mouse pointer away from an image area. Of the two events, the onMouseOver event is generally more useful. To illustrate its use, I'll create an image map for lazy people. With this image map, users will not have to *click* the image for an action to be performed—they only have to move the mouse over an image area.

The imap.htm file is shown in Listing 10.3. It creates a simple two-frame document with map.htm (Listing 10.4) loaded in the first frame. Open imap.htm with your Web browser; the two-frame document shown in Figure 10.4 is displayed.

Listing 10.3   A Client-Side Image Map (imap.htm)

```
<HTML>
<HEAD>
<TITLE>Client-Side Image Maps</TITLE>
</HEAD>
<FRAMESET COLS="415,*" BORDER="1">
<FRAME SRC="map.htm">
<FRAME SRC="blank.htm">
</FRAMESET>
</HTML>
```

Listing 10.4   Creating the Image Map (map.htm)

```
<HTML>
<HEAD>
<TITLE>Client-Side Image Maps</TITLE>
<SCRIPT LANGUAGE="JavaScript"><!-
function goWhatsNew() {
 parent.frames[1].location.href="whatsnew.htm"
}
function goProducts() {
 parent.frames[1].location.href="products.htm"
}
function goCompany() {
 parent.frames[1].location.href="company.htm"
}
function goField() {
 parent.frames[1].location.href="field.htm"
}
// -></SCRIPT>
</HEAD>
<BODY BGCOLOR="#FFFFFF">
<MAP NAME="bizmap">
  <AREA NAME="whatsNew" COORDS="219,250,50" shape="circle"
   HREF="javascript:void(0)" onMouseOver="goWhatsNew();
      return true">
  <AREA NAME="products" COORDS="205,226,100" shape="circle"
   HREF="javascript:void(0)" onMouseOver="goProducts();
      return true">
```

```
      <AREA NAME="company" COORDS="192,202,155" shape="circle"
        HREF="javascript:void(0)" onMouseOver="goCompany()">
      <AREA NAME="field" COORDS="183,189,188" shape="circle"
        HREF="javascript:void(0)" onMouseOver="goField()">
    </MAP>
    <IMG SRC="map.gif" BORDER="0" USEMAP="#bizmap">
    </HTML>
```

FIGURE 10.4:

The image map opening display provides an interesting company home page (Listing 10.3).

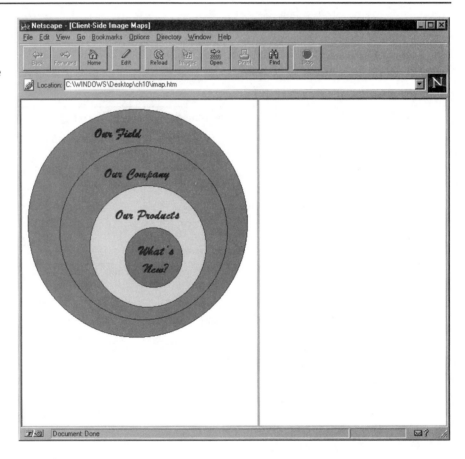

The map.htm file creates a client-side image map and defines four <area> tags. These <area> tags correspond to each of the four circles of the map.gif file. The HREF attribute of each <area> tag is set to the URL javascript:void(0). This URL causes user clicks to be ignored. The onMouseOver events of the four <area> tags are handled by invoking the goWhatsNew(), goProducts(), goCompany(), and goField() functions, as appropriate. These functions display the files shown in Listings 10.5 through 10.8. (In a real company home page, the files shown in Listings 10.5 through 10.8 would contain real links, as opposed to the fake ones shown in the example.)

Listing 10.5   What's New! (whatsnew.htm)

```
<HTML>
<HEAD>
<TITLE>What's New!</TITLE>
</HEAD>
<BODY BGCOLOR="#FFFFFF">
<H1 ALIGN="CENTER">What's New!</H1>
<DL>
<DT><I>October 10, 2000</I></DT>
<DD>Our lastest virtual widget has been released...</DD>
<DT><I>February 29, 2000</I></DT>
<DD>We've developed a special millenium leap year widget...</DD>
<DT><I>January 1, 2000</I></DT>
<DD>Our X Widget has led the way into the 21st century...</DD>
</DL>
</BODY>
</HTML>
```

Listing 10.6   Our Products! (products.htm)

```
<HTML>
<HEAD>
<TITLE>Our Products!</TITLE>
</HEAD>
<BODY BGCOLOR="#FFFFFF">
<H1 ALIGN="CENTER">Our Products!</H1>
<P>Our product line includes the following
  state-of-the-art widgets:</P>
<DL>
<DT><A HREF="javascript:void(0)">X Widget</A></DT>
<DD>The most advanced widget available today.</DD>
<DT><A HREF="javascript:void(0)">Y Widget</A></DT>
<DD>A low power version of the X Widget.</DD>
<DT><A HREF="javascript:void(0)">Z Widget</A></DT>
<DD>Our lowest cost X-compatible widget. </DD>
```

```
</DL>
</BODY>
</HTML>
```

Listing 10.7   **Our Company! (company.htm)**

```
<HTML>
<HEAD>
<TITLE>Our Company!</TITLE>
</HEAD>
<BODY BGCOLOR="#FFFFFF">
<H1 ALIGN="CENTER">Our Company!</H1>
<P>XYZ Corporation has remained at the forefront of advanced
   widget research. We have pioneered the development of the
   new X widget, the low power Y widget, and the low cost Z
   widget....</P>
</BODY>
</HTML>
```

Listing 10.8   **Our Field! (field.htm)**

```
<HTML>
<HEAD>
<TITLE>Our Field!</TITLE>
</HEAD>
<BODY BGCOLOR="#FFFFFF">
<H1 ALIGN="CENTER">Our Field!</H1>
<P>Our field has witnessed a number of breakthroughs in the
   last year. Advanced widget research at the university level
   has led to whole new ways of designing widgets. New widget
   designs have revolutionized the end products built from these
   widgets....</P>
</BODY>
</HTML>
```

When you move your mouse over the What's New? circle, the second frame displays the relevant page, as shown in Figure 10.5. When you move your mouse over the Our Products circle, the second frame shows the document shown in Figure 10.6. Move your mouse over the Our Company and Our Field circles and the frame shows the documents shown in Figures 10.7 and 10.8. Isn't this much more efficient than having to move *and* click individual image areas?

FIGURE 10.5:

The What's New? document display provides up-to-date news about a company (Listing 10.5).

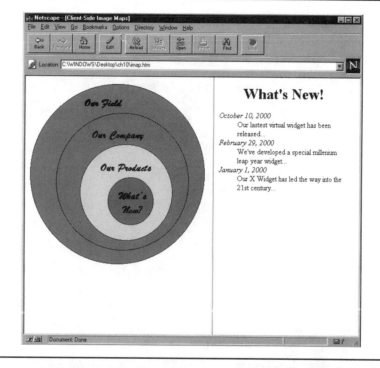

FIGURE 10.6:

The Our Products document display provides access to information about a company's products (Listing 10.6).

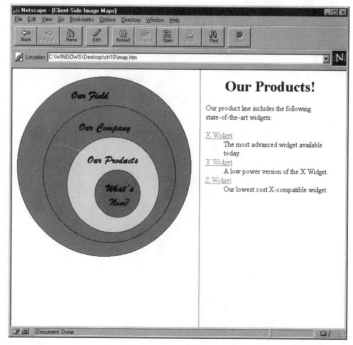

FIGURE 10.7:

The Our Company document display provides high-level information about a company (Listing 10.7).

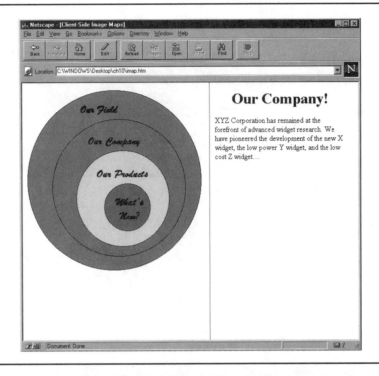

FIGURE 10.8:

The Our Field document display provides new information about the technical fields in which the company is engaged (Listing 10.8).

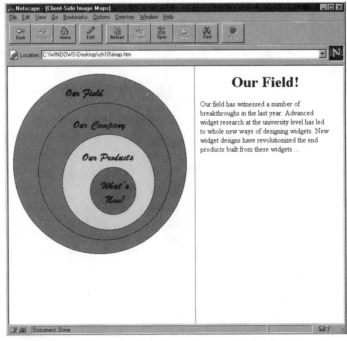

Summary

In this chapter, you learned how to use the image-handling features provided by JavaScript. You were introduced to the `image` object and you learned how to control the way images are formatted with respect to surrounding text. You also learned how to dynamically display images in your Web pages. You covered the basics of animation and learned how to use dynamic images to create animation effects. You also learned how to use the `area` object to enhance the attractiveness of client-side image maps. You've covered quite a bit of material in this chapter. The following chapter will be much lighter. You'll learn how to use the mathematical constants and functions provided by JavaScript's `Math` object.

CHAPTER
ELEVEN

Doing Math

- The Math Object

- Mathematical Constants

- Mathematical Functions

- Using Math Functions in Scripts

Almost every useful or entertaining program performs some sort of mathematical computation. Game programs use random number generators to shuffle cards, roll dice, or add variety to computer actions. Word processing programs use plenty of tedious arithmetic to determine how pages should be displayed or laid out in hardcopy form. Graphics programs use trigonometric functions to display different geometrical shapes. And so on.

Web programs have an equal affinity for math. Some game programs use a random number generator. Web sales forms calculate sales totals based on the prices of the products that a user selects. Search engines rank the search value of Web pages based on a variety of formulae ranging from simple to complex.

In this chapter, you'll learn about the extensive library of mathematical functions and constants that are provided by JavaScript's Math object. You'll learn how to use the Math object to perform simple computations, and you'll create a JavaScript calculator that illustrates the use of the constants and functions provided by the Math object. When you finish this chapter, you'll have a thorough understanding of JavaScript's math capabilities.

The *Math* Object

The Math object is a predefined JavaScript object. It is a built-in object that is defined by the ECMAScript standard and supported by both Navigator and Internet Explorer. The Math object cannot be instantiated like Date and String to create specific object instances. Rather, it is always available, anytime a JavaScript browser is running. Think of the Math object as a library of mathematical constants and functions. The constants are properties of Math and the functions are its methods. Learning to use the Math object involves familiarizing yourself with these properties and methods.

Mathematical Constants

For a scripting language, JavaScript provides a rich collection of mathematical constants—more than you'll need unless you are a mathematician, engineer, or scientist. These constants are described in Table 11.1.

TABLE 11.1:   Math Constants Used in JavaScript

Constant	Description
E	Euler's constant. It is found everywhere in computational math and is the base for natural logarithms.
LN2	The natural logarithm of 2. This is a handy constant for converting between natural logarithms and base 2 logarithms.
LN10	The natural logarithm of 10. Like LN2, it is used in logarithm conversions.
LOG2E	The base 2 logarithm of E. It is used in base 2 to base E logarithm conversions.
LOG10E	The base 10 logarithm of E. It is used in base 10 to base E logarithm conversions.
PI	Another famous mathematical constant, PI is the ratio of the circumference of a circle to its diameter.
SQRT1_2	The square root of 1/2 is used in many trigonometric calculations.
SQRT2	The square root of 2 is commonly used in algebraic formulas.

The mathematical constants are accessed as Math.constant where constant is one of the constants listed above. For example, pi times Euler's constant divided by the square root of two is written as follows:

```
Math.PI*Math.E/Math.SQRT2
```

Mathematical Functions

The Math object provides 18 mathematical functions that run the gamut from rounding to random number generation. These functions have been organized into the following categories:

- Rounding
- Comparison
- Algebraic
- Logarithmic and exponential

- Trigonometric
- Random number generation

To use any of the mathematical functions, invoke them as methods of the Math object. For example, the cosine of pi divided by 2 is written as

```
Math.cos((Math.PI/2))
```

The categories of Math functions are described in the following paragraphs.

Rounding Functions

The round(), floor(), and ceil() functions are used to approximate floating-point numbers with integers. The round() function returns the closest integer to a floating-point number. The floor() function returns the greatest integer that is less than or equal to a floating-point number. Similarly, the ceil() function returns the least integer that is greater than or equal to a floating-point number.

Comparison Functions

The min() and max() functions are used to compare two numbers. The min() function returns the lesser of the two numbers, and the max() function returns the greater. These functions are often used in operations that rely on sorting.

Algebraic Functions

The abs() function calculates the absolute value of a number. It is very useful in calculating the distance between two numbers. It is also commonly found in solutions to algebraic problems. The sqrt() function calculates the square root of a number.

Logarithmic and Exponential Functions

JavaScript provides the natural logarithm function, log(). Base 2 or 10 logarithms can be calculated using the logarithm constants (LN2, LN10, LOG2E, LOG10E) to convert between different bases.

The power function, pow(), calculates a number raised to a power.

The exponential function, exp(), calculates Euler's constant raised to a power. The function exp(x) is the same as pow(Math.E,x).

Trigonometric Functions

JavaScript provides seven trigonometric function: cos(), sin(), tan(), acos(), asin(), atan(), and atan2(). Trig functions are used to calculate the position and relationship of points on circles, ellipses, waves, and other curved objects with respect to Cartesian coordinates. You probably won't use these functions unless you are involved in science or engineering.

Random Number Generation

The random() function generates a pseudorandom number between 0 and 1. You'll continue to use random() with many of the examples of this book—especially with games.

Using Math Functions in Scripts

When you use Math constants or functions in a script you must precede the constant or function reference with the keyword Math. However, this often brings clutter to your scripts. You can use the with statement to help eliminate this clutter in math-intensive scripts. For example, the following two statements are equivalent:

Statement 1

```
with (Math) {
 y=sqrt(pow(cos(x),2)+pow(sin(x),2))
 }
```

Statement 2

```
y=Math.sqrt(Math.pow(Math.cos(x),2)+ Math.pow(Math.sin(x),2))
```

Example Project—A JavaScript Calculator

Math can be a somewhat passionless subject. The same is true for the Math object. We've already covered all of JavaScript's mathematical constants and functions. To liven things up a bit, let's use these constants and functions to build an advanced scientific calculator.

Download math.htm from this book's page on the Sybex Web site. When you open this file, you will notice that it displays the calculator shown in Figure 11.1. This calculator is the same as most calculators that you've used before except that it has some of JavaScript's mathematical constants and functions attached to it. The purpose of the calculator is not to come up with a new calculator design but to illustrate the use of the JavaScript Math object. For example, click on the e button. Your browser display should look like Figure 11.2. Select log(x) from the Functions selection list, as shown in Figure 11.3. Now click on the Apply button to calculate the natural log of e. The answer is 1—just as you'd expect. Figure 11.4 shows the result of this calculation. Play with the calculator to get a good feel for how it operates.

FIGURE 11.1:

This calculator's keys are attached to JavaScript Math methods (Listing 11.1).

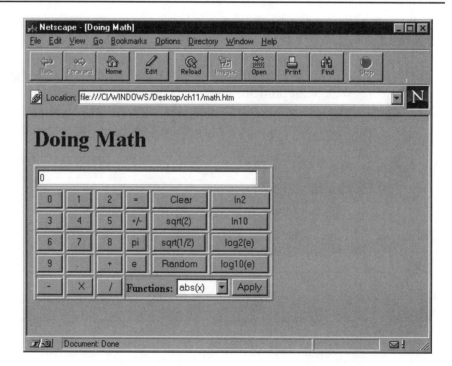

FIGURE 11.2:

Clicking the e button causes Euler's constant to be displayed (Listing 11.1).

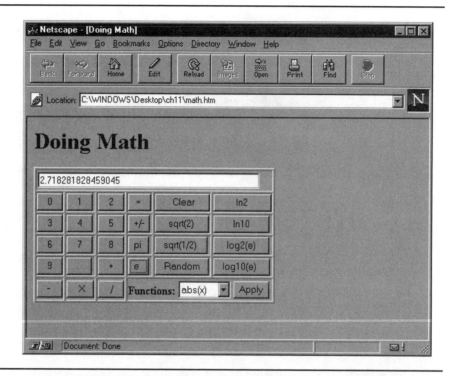

FIGURE 11.3:

Selecting log(x) allows you to apply log(x) to e (Listing 11.1).

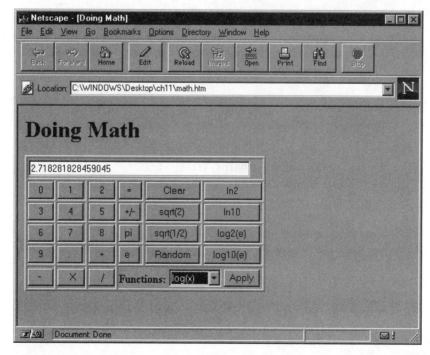

FIGURE 11.4:

Applying log(x) to e
results in an answer of 1
(Listing 11.1).

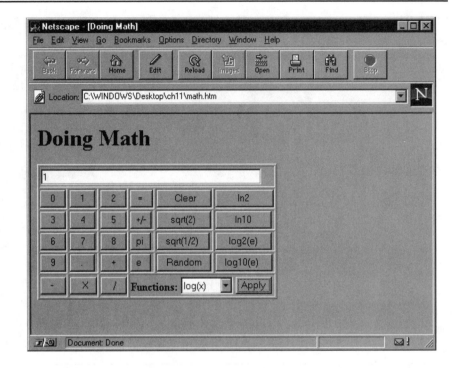

Listing 11.1 shows the math.htm file that implements the calculator. This is a
fairly long file and is about half HTML and half JavaScript. The HTML creates the
nice-looking form used as the calculator. The JavaScript provides the computations behind the buttons.

Listing 11.1	A JavaScript Calculator (math.htm)

```
<HTML>
<HEAD>
<TITLE>Doing Math</TITLE>
<SCRIPT LANGUAGE="JavaScript"><!-
r = new Array(2)
function setStartState(){
 state="start"
 r[0] = "0"
 r[1] = "0"
 operator=""
 ix=0
}
```

```
function addDigit(n){
 if(state=="gettingInteger" || state=="gettingFloat")
  r[ix]=appendDigit(r[ix],n)
 else{
  r[ix]=""+n
  state="gettingInteger"
 }
 display(r[ix])
}
function appendDigit(n1,n2){
 if(n1=="0") return ""+n2
 var s=""
 s+=n1
 s+=n2
 return s
}
function display(s){
 document.calculator.total.value=s
}
function addDecimalPoint(){
 if(state!="gettingFloat"){
  decimal=true
  r[ix]+="."
  if(state=="haveOperand" || state=="getOperand2") r[ix]="0."
  state="gettingFloat"
  display(r[ix])
 }
}
function clearDisplay(){
 setStartState()
 display(r[0])
}
function changeSign(){
 if(r[ix].charAt(0)=="-") r[ix]=r[ix].substring(1,r[ix].length)
 else if(parseFloat(r[ix])!=0) r[ix]="-"+r[ix]
 display(r[ix])
}
function setTo(n){
 r[ix]=""+n
 state="haveOperand"
 decimal=false
 display(r[ix])
}
```

```
function calc(){
 if(state=="gettingInteger" || state=="gettingFloat" ||
  state=="haveOperand"){
  if(ix==1){
   r[0]=calculateOperation(operator,r[0],r[1])
   ix=0
  }
 }else if(state=="getOperand2"){
  r[0]=calculateOperation(operator,r[0],r[0])
  ix=0
 }
 state="haveOperand"
 decimal=false
 display(r[ix])
}
function calculateOperation(op,x,y){
 var result=""
 if(op=="+"){
  result=""+(parseFloat(x)+parseFloat(y))
 }else if(op=="-"){
  result=""+(parseFloat(x)-parseFloat(y))
 }else if(op=="*"){
  result=""+(parseFloat(x)*parseFloat(y))
 }else if(op=="/"){
  if(parseFloat(y)==0){
   alert("Division by 0 not allowed.")
   result=0
  }else result=""+(parseFloat(x)/parseFloat(y))
 }
 return result
}
function performOp(op){
 if(state=="start"){
  ++ix
  operator=op
 }else if(state=="gettingInteger" || state=="gettingFloat" ||
  state=="haveOperand"){
  if(ix==0){
   ++ix
   operator=op
  }else{
   r[0]=calculateOperation(operator,r[0],r[1])
```

```
    display(r[0])
    operator=op
   }
  }
  state="getOperand2"
  decimal=false
}
function applyFunction(){
 var selectionList=document.calculator.functions
 var selIX=selectionList.selectedIndex
 var sel=selectionList.options[selIX].value
 if(sel=="abs") r[ix]=Math.abs(r[ix])
 else if(sel=="acos") r[ix]=Math.acos(r[ix])
 else if(sel=="asin") r[ix]=Math.asin(r[ix])
 else if(sel=="atan") r[ix]=Math.atan(r[ix])
 else if(sel=="ceil") r[ix]=Math.ceil(r[ix])
 else if(sel=="cos") r[ix]=Math.cos(r[ix])
 else if(sel=="exp") r[ix]=Math.exp(r[ix])
 else if(sel=="floor") r[ix]=Math.floor(r[ix])
 else if(sel=="log") r[ix]=Math.log(r[ix])
 else if(sel=="sin") r[ix]=Math.sin(r[ix])
 else if(sel=="sqrt") r[ix]=Math.sqrt(r[ix])
 else r[ix]=Math.tan(r[ix])
 decimal=false
 display(r[ix])
}
// -></SCRIPT>
</HEAD>
<BODY>
<SCRIPT LANGUAGE="JavaScript"><!-
setStartState()
// -></SCRIPT>
<H1>Doing Math</H1>
<FORM NAME="calculator">
<TABLE BORDER="BORDER" ALIGN="CENTER">
<TR>
<TD COLSPAN="6"><INPUT TYPE="TEXT" NAME="total" VALUE="0"
 SIZE="44"></TD></TR>
<TR>
<TD><INPUT TYPE="BUTTON" NAME="n0" VALUE="  0   "
 ONCLICK="addDigit(0)"></TD>
<TD><INPUT TYPE="BUTTON" NAME="n1" VALUE="  1   "
```

```
 ONCLICK="addDigit(1)"></TD>
<TD><INPUT TYPE="BUTTON" NAME="n2" VALUE="   2    "
 ONCLICK="addDigit(2)"></TD>
<TD><INPUT TYPE="BUTTON" NAME="equals" VALUE="  =    "
 ONCLICK="calc()"></TD>
<TD ROWSPAN="1"><INPUT
TYPE="BUTTON" NAME="clearField" VALUE="    Clear    "
 ONCLICK="clearDisplay()"></TD>
<TD COLSPAN="1"><INPUT
TYPE="BUTTON" NAME="ln2" VALUE="       ln2         "
 ONCLICK="setTo(Math.LN2)"></TD></TR>
<TR>
<TD><INPUT TYPE="BUTTON" NAME="n3" VALUE="   3    "
 ONCLICK="addDigit(3)"></TD>
<TD><INPUT TYPE="BUTTON" NAME="n4" VALUE="   4    "
 ONCLICK="addDigit(4)"></TD>
<TD><INPUT TYPE="BUTTON" NAME="n5" VALUE="   5    "
 ONCLICK="addDigit(5)"></TD>
<TD COLSPAN="1" ROWSPAN="1"><INPUT TYPE="BUTTON"
 NAME="sign" VALUE=" +/- " ONCLICK="changeSign()"></TD>
<TD ROWSPAN="1"><INPUT TYPE="BUTTON" NAME="sqrt2"
 VALUE="  sqrt(2)    " ONCLICK="setTo(Math.SQRT2)"></TD>
<TD COLSPAN="1" ROWSPAN="1"><INPUT TYPE="BUTTON" NAME="ln10"
 VALUE="      ln10       " ONCLICK="setTo(Math.LN10)"></TD></TR>
<TR>
<TD><INPUT TYPE="BUTTON" NAME="n6" VALUE="   6    "
 ONCLICK="addDigit(6)"></TD>
<TD><INPUT TYPE="BUTTON" NAME="n7" VALUE="   7    "
 ONCLICK="addDigit(7)"></TD>
<TD><INPUT TYPE="BUTTON" NAME="n8" VALUE="   8    "
 ONCLICK="addDigit(8)"></TD>
<TD COLSPAN="1" ROWSPAN="1"><INPUT
TYPE="BUTTON" NAME="pi" VALUE=" pi   "
 ONCLICK="setTo(Math.PI)"></TD>
<TD COLSPAN="1" ROWSPAN="1"><INPUT
TYPE="BUTTON" NAME="sqrt12" VALUE="sqrt(1/2) "
 ONCLICK="setTo(Math.SQRT1_2)"></TD>
<TD COLSPAN="1" ROWSPAN="1"><INPUT
TYPE="BUTTON" NAME="log2e" VALUE="  log2(e)   "
 ONCLICK="setTo(Math.LOG2E)"></TD></TR>
<TR>
```

```
<TD><INPUT TYPE="BUTTON" NAME="n9" VALUE="   9   "
 ONCLICK="addDigit(9)"></TD>
<TD><INPUT TYPE="BUTTON" NAME="decimal" VALUE="   .   "
 ONCLICK="addDecimalPoint()"></TD>
<TD><INPUT TYPE="BUTTON" NAME="plus" VALUE="   +   "
 ONCLICK="performOp('+')"></TD>
<TD COLSPAN="1" ROWSPAN="1"><INPUT TYPE="BUTTON" NAME="e"
 VALUE="  e  " ONCLICK="setTo(Math.E)"></TD>
<TD COLSPAN="1" ROWSPAN="1"><INPUT TYPE="BUTTON"
 NAME="random" VALUE="Random"
 ONCLICK="setTo(Math.random())"></TD>
<TD COLSPAN="1" ROWSPAN="1"><INPUT TYPE="BUTTON" NAME="log10e"
 VALUE="log10(e)  " ONCLICK="setTo(Math.LOG10E)"></TD></TR>
<TR>
<TD><INPUT TYPE="BUTTON" NAME="minus" VALUE="   -   "
 ONCLICK="performOp('-')"></TD>
<TD><INPUT TYPE="BUTTON" NAME="multiply" VALUE="   X   "
 ONCLICK="performOp('*')"></TD>
<TD><INPUT TYPE="BUTTON" NAME="divide" VALUE="    /   "
 ONCLICK="performOp('/')"></TD>
<TD COLSPAN="3" ROWSPAN="1"><B>Functions: </B>
<SELECT NAME="functions" SIZE="1">
<OPTION VALUE="abs" SELECTED="SELECTED">abs(x)</OPTION>
<OPTION VALUE="acos">acos(x)</OPTION>
<OPTION VALUE="asin">asin(x)</OPTION>
<OPTION VALUE="atan">atan(x)</OPTION>
<OPTION VALUE="ceil">ceil(x)</OPTION>
<OPTION VALUE="cos">cos(x)</OPTION>
<OPTION VALUE="exp">exp(x)</OPTION>
<OPTION VALUE="floor">floor(x)</OPTION>
<OPTION VALUE="log">log(x)</OPTION>
<OPTION VALUE="sin">sin(x)</OPTION>
<OPTION VALUE="sqrt">sqrt(x)</OPTION>
<OPTION VALUE="tan">tan(x)</OPTION>
</SELECT>
<INPUT TYPE="BUTTON" NAME="apply" VALUE="Apply"
 onClick="applyFunction()"></TD></TR>
</TABLE>
</FORM>
</BODY>
</HTML>
```

The document contains two scripts: one in the head and one in the body. The script in the document's body invokes the `setStartState()` function to perform all necessary initializations. The script in the document's head defines the r array and 12 functions. These are described in the following paragraphs.

The *r* Array

This array is used to hold two numbers, entered by the user, that are used as the operands of an arithmetic calculation.

The *setStartState()* Function

This function performs all variable initialization. It sets the `state` variable to *start*, the current operands to *0*, the current operator to *""* (null string), and the index of the current operand (`ix`) to *0*.

The `state` variable may be set to any of the following states:

start   This state indicates the program has just loaded/reloaded or that the Clear button has been pressed.

gettingInteger   This state is entered when the user tries to enter an integer via the calculator's keypad.

gettingFloat   This state is entered when the user tries to enter a floating-point number and when the user clicks the decimal point button.

haveOperand   This state is entered when the user completes the entry of an integer or floating-point number by pressing = or a JavaScript constant, or selecting/applying a JavaScript function.

getOperand2   This state is entered when the user clicks an arithmetic operator (+, -, X, or /).

The *addDigit()* Function

This function handles the clicking of a digit (0 through 9). If the current state is *gettingInteger* or *gettingFloat*, then the digit is appended to the current operand. Otherwise, the current operand is initialized to the digit and the state is set to *gettingInteger*. The calculator's `total` field is then updated.

The *appendDigit()* Function

This function is invoked by addDigit() to append a digit to the current operand. If the value of the current operand is *0*, then the digit becomes the value of the current operand. Otherwise, it is appended to the current operand. Note that operands are maintained as string values.

The *display()* Function

This function displays a string (usually the current operand) in the total field of the calculator form.

The *addDecimalPoint()* Function

This function handles the clicking of the decimal point button. If the current state is *gettingFloat*, then the decimal point is ignored. Otherwise, it appends a decimal point to the current operand or creates a new operand equal to *0.* (zero followed by a decimal point). It then sets the current state to *gettingFloat* and updates the value of the total field.

The *clearDisplay()* Function

This function invokes the setStartState() function to reinitialize the calculator, and invokes display() to update the total field.

The *changeSign()* Function

This function handles the clicking of the change sign (+/-) button. It converts the current operand from negative to positive or vice versa. It then updates the calculator's total field.

The *setTo()* Function

This function handles the clicking of any of the JavaScript constants. It sets the value of the current operand to the constant and the current state to *haveOperand*. The decimal flag is set to *false* to indicate that a decimal point is not longer in effect. The calculator's total field is then updated with the value of the new operand.

The *calc()* Function

This function handles the clicking of the calculate (=) key. If the current state is *gettingInteger*, *gettingFloat*, or *haveOperand*, it checks `ix` to determine if the current operand is *1* or *0*. If `ix` is *1* then the user has entered two operands and an operator. The `calculateOperation()` function is invoked to calculate the result of applying the operator to the two operands. The resultant value is stored in the first operand and the number of operands (`ix`) is set to *0*.

If the current state is *getOperand2*, then `calculateOperation()` is invoked to calculate the result of applying the current operator to the first operand and itself. The resultant value is stored in the first operand and the number of operands (`ix`) is set to *0*.

After performing state-specific processing, the current state is set to *haveOperand*, the `decimal` flag is set to *false*, and the calculator's `total` field is updated.

The *calculateOperation()* Function

This function is invoked by `calc()` and `performOp()` to calculate the value of applying a binary operator to two operands. It handles addition, subtraction, multiplication, and division operations. It also checks for division by 0.

The *performOp()* Function

This function handles the clicking of a binary (two-value) operator, such as +, -, X, or /. If the current state is *start*, it increments the number of operands and sets the `operator` variable to the operator selected by the user.

If the current state is *gettingInteger*, *gettingFloat*, or *haveOperand*, then this function checks the number of operands in use (`ix`). If `ix` is *0*, indicating that the current operand is the first operand, then it increments the number of operands and sets the `operator` variable to the operator selected by the user. If `ix` is *1*, the `calculateOperation()` method is invoked to calculate the current operation entered by the user. The result is assigned to the first operand, and this operand is displayed in the calculator's `total` field. The `operator` variable is assigned the new operator.

The *applyFunction()* Function

This function responds to the clicking of the Apply button by applying the currently selected JavaScript function to the current operand. It then displays the new operand value in the calculator's `total` field.

Summary

In this chapter you learned how to use the mathematical functions and constants provided by JavaScript's Math object. You used these functions and constants to create a JavaScript calculator. This chapter marks the end of Part II, "Using Predefined Objects and Methods." You have now covered the important objects, methods, and properties that are predefined by JavaScript. In Part III, "Building Sample Applications," you'll learn to use them in some practical Web applications. To download the bonus chapter, "Creating Web Page Widgets," please visit the Sybex Web site at http://www.sybex.com. Click the catalog link and search for *Mastering JavaScript and JScript*. Follow the link to the book's page and click the Downloads button. This bonus chapter provides several examples of JavaScript Web page widgets that can enhance the appearance of your Web pages.

PART III

Building Sample Applications

- CHAPTER 12: Accessorizing Your Pages
- CHAPTER 13: Online Catalogs
- CHAPTER 14: Developing Search Tools

CHAPTER
TWELVE

12

Accessorizing Your Pages

- The Calendar Accessory

- The Calculator Accessory

- To-Do List

- World Clock

- Assembling the Desktop

One of the reasons for the success of window-based operating systems is their ability to take the objects of your physical desktop—the clock, calendar, notepad, calculator, files, and so on—and make them available in electronic form. Software such as MacOS and Microsoft Windows was developed around this desktop metaphor. The World Wide Web, on the other hand, was designed using the metaphor of a library—we access electronic documents and view electronic pages. Now the Web and the desktop are beginning to converge. The browser is being integrated into window-based operating systems and desktop programs are being executed on the Web.

In the first bonus online chapter, "Creating Web Page Widgets," you have the opportunity to develop several widgets that enhance the effectiveness of your Web pages. (To download this bonus chapter, please visit the Sybex Web site at http://www.sybex.com. Click on the Catalog link and search for *Mastering JavaScript and JScript*. Follow the link to the book's page and click the Downloads button.) These widgets are generic and can be tailored to a variety of needs. In this chapter, you'll learn how to develop JavaScript components that are not only eye-catching, but also useful. As you have probably guessed by now, you'll be developing desktop accessories—a calendar, a calculator, a to-do list, and a clock—that you'll be able to use with your own Web pages. By themselves, these simple accessories won't likely make you a more productive person, but I will show you how you can incorporate such accessories into your Web applications, which may be very useful for your business or personal needs.

The Calendar Accessory

The first accessory that you'll develop is a calendar. Calendars are required by anyone who works or lives by a schedule. I constantly consult a calendar to schedule meetings, conferences, travel, and parties. In most cases, a simple monthly view is all I need to make these scheduling decisions. Why would I want to put a calendar on a Web page? Well, if I were the leader of a rock band, I would like to tell my fans when and where to go for my next month's gigs. If I were an astronomer, I'd let people know when to look for interesting celestial events. If I were a soccer coach, I'd inform my players when practices and games would be held. Get the idea? In short, when there's a need to publicize a schedule, making it available electronically is a good way to do it.

The calendar that you'll develop in this section is only a calendar—it won't let you publish your schedule, it will just show you the days of the month. However, it can easily be added as an accessory to any schedule-publishing application, as you'll see in Chapter 21, "Scripting Netscape Servers."

NOTE   When you run the calendar scripts of this chapter, they will display a calendar for the current month. The screen captures shown in this chapter were current for the month in which this chapter was written. Thus, your display and the chapter's screens will differ.

Listing 12.1 defines a `Calendar` object that displays the monthly calendar shown in Figure 12.1. The `calendar.js` serves as a building block for a general calendar application. It defines six functions: the `Calendar()` constructor, `displayCalendar()`, `displayCalendarHeader()`, `displayDates()`, `numberOfDays()`, and `writeDate()`. These functions are used as explained in the following subsections.

Listing 12.1   The Calendar Object (calendar.js)

```
function Calendar() {
 var len = Calendar.arguments.length
 if(len == 2){
  this.month = Calendar.arguments[0]
  this.year = Calendar.arguments[1]
 }else{
  today = new Date()
  this.month = today.getMonth()
  this.year = today.getYear()
 }
 this.display = displayCalendar
}
function displayCalendar() {
 document.writeln("<TABLE BORDER='0' BGCOLOR='white'>")
 displayCalendarHeader(this.month,this.year)
 if(displayCalendar.arguments.length>0){
  var day = displayCalendar.arguments[0]-1
  displayDates(day,this.month,this.year,true)
 }else displayDates(0,this.month,this.year,false)
 document.writeln("</TABLE>")
}
function displayCalendarHeader(month,year) {
 var days = new Array("Sun","Mon","Tue","Wed","Thu",
  "Fri","Sat")
 var months = new Array("January","February","March","April",
```

```
  "May","June","July","August","September","October",
  "November","December")
 document.writeln("<TR><TH COLSPAN='7'><H2 ALIGN='CENTER'>")
 document.writeln(months[month])
 document.writeln(" 19"+year+"</H2></TH></TR>")
 document.writeln("<TR>")
 for(var i=0;i<days.length;++i)
  document.writeln("<TH> "+days[i]+" </TH>")
 document.writeln("</TR>")
}
function displayDates(day,month,year,shade) {
 d = new Date(year,month,1)
 var startDay = d.getDay()
 var numDays = numberOfDays(month,year)
 var numRows = Math.floor((numDays+startDay)/7)
 if((numDays+startDay)%7 > 1) ++numRows
 var currentDate=0
 for(var i=0;i<numRows;++i) {
  document.writeln("<TR>")
  for(var j=0;j<7;++j) {
   if(shade && day==currentDate)
    document.write("<TD BGCOLOR='red'>")
   else document.write("<TD>")
   if(currentDate>=numDays) document.write(" ")
   else if(currentDate>0){
    ++currentDate
    writeDate(currentDate)
   }else if(i*7+j>=startDay){
    ++currentDate
     writeDate(currentDate)
   }else document.write(" ")
   document.writeln("</TD>")
  }
  document.writeln("</TR>")
 }
}
function numberOfDays(month,year) {
 var numDays=new Array(31,28,31,30,31,30,31,31,30,31,30,31)
 n = numDays[month]
 if(month == 1 && year % 4 == 0) ++n
 return n
}
function writeDate(n) {
 document.write("<H3 ALIGN='CENTER'>"+n+"</H3>")
}
```

FIGURE 12.1:

Displaying the calendar (Listing 12.1)

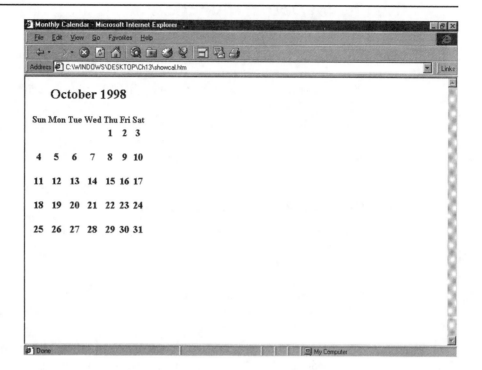

The *Calendar()* Constructor

This is the constructor for the Calendar object. It checks the number of arguments passed to it and creates a calendar using the current date or a specified month and year. It also defines the display() method using the displayCalendar() function.

The *displayCalendar()* Function

This function displays a monthly calendar as an HTML table. It invokes display-CalendarHeader() to display the table header and displayDates() to display the actual calendar dates. If a day of the month is passed as an argument to this function, then that day is highlighted in red when the calendar is displayed.

The *displayCalendarHeader()* Function

This function displays the calendar header—month, year, and days of the week.

The *displayDates()* Function

This function displays the days of the month. It figures out which day the month should begin on by creating a Date object for the first day of the month and by accessing its getDay() method. It invokes the numberOfDays() function to get the number of days in a particular month. It calculates the number of rows in the calendar table and then fills in those rows with the appropriate dates. If the shade argument is set to *true*, then the specified day is highlighted in red. Calendar days outside of the current month are ignored (a non-breaking space, , is used to fill the calendar entry of these days).

The *numberOfDays()* Function

This function calculates the number of days in a month. It takes leap years into account.

The *writeDate()* Function

This function writes the cells of the calendar table as centered Heading 3s.

To see how the Calendar object and functions of the calendar.js file work, open showcal.htm (Listing 12.2) with your browser. It generates the display shown in Figure 12.1. The file showcal.htm is a simple HTML file with two scripts—one to read calendar.js and one to create and display a calendar. You can use calendar.js in your scripts in a similar fashion.

Listing 12.2   **Displaying the Calendar (showcal.htm)**

```
<HTML>
<HEAD>
<TITLE>Monthly Calendar</TITLE>
<SCRIPT LANGUAGE="JavaScript" SRC="calendar.js"><!-
// -></SCRIPT>
</HEAD>
<BODY>
<SCRIPT LANGUAGE="JavaScript"><!-
cal=new Calendar()
cal.display()
// -></SCRIPT>
</BODY>
</HTML>
```

Because `calendar.js` is fairly modular, its functions can be used to build larger calendar applications. Let's do so now as a prelude to using `calendar.js` in your own Web applications.

Open `cal.htm` with your browser, and it displays the Web page shown in Figure 12.2. At the top of your screen are three buttons for displaying different monthly views. If you click on the left arrow, the previous month is displayed, as shown in Figure 12.3. If you click on the right arrow, the next month is displayed. Of course, if you click on the Current Month button, the current month's calendar is displayed.

FIGURE 12.2:

The Calendar program opening display (Listing 12.3)

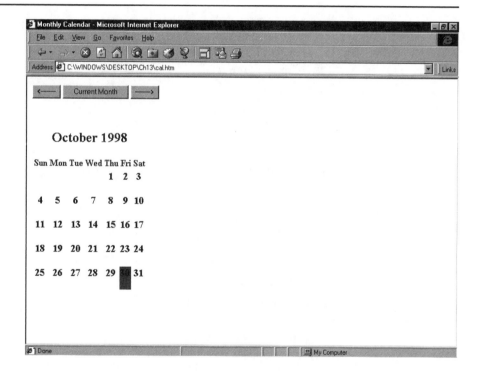

The button controls at the top of the calendar were added by creating a two-frame set. The buttons are placed in the top frame set, and the calendar is displayed in the bottom frame set. Listing 12.3 shows how the frame sets were set up.

FIGURE 12.3:

Displaying the previous
month (Listing 12.3)

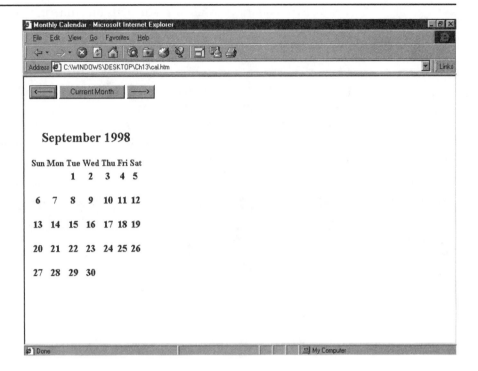

Listing 12.3   Setting Up a Two-Frame Calendar (cal.htm)

```
<HTML>
<HEAD>
<TITLE>Monthly Calendar</TITLE>
<FRAMESET ROWS="77,*" BORDER="0">
<FRAME SRC="control.htm">
<FRAME SRC="calendar.htm">
</FRAMESET>
</HTML>
```

The control.htm file (Listing 12.4) is used to display the buttons in the top frame. Note that two hidden fields are used to hold the values of the current month and year of the calendar being displayed. These values are initially set to 99 and 0. The calendar.htm file recognizes these values as invalid and sets them to the values of the current month to mark them as invalid entries. (You can't have a month 99 and year 0 has long since passed—the calendar doesn't work for all historical dates.)

Listing 12.4   The Calendar Controls (control.htm)

```
<HTML>
<HEAD>
<TITLE>Monthly Calendar</TITLE>
<SCRIPT LANGUAGE="JavaScript"><!-
function updateCalendar(month,year) {
 document.forms[0].monthValue.value=month
 document.forms[0].yearValue.value=year
 parent.frames[1].location.reload(true)
}
function previousMonth() {
 month=document.forms[0].monthValue.value
 year=document.forms[0].yearValue.value
 -month
 if(month<0) {
  if(year==0) month=0
  else{
   -year
   month=11
  }
 }
 updateCalendar(month,year)
}
function currentMonth() {
 var today=new Date()
 updateCalendar(today.getMonth(),today.getYear())
}
function nextMonth() {
 month=document.forms[0].monthValue.value
 year=document.forms[0].yearValue.value
 ++month
 if(month>11) {
  if(year==99) month=11
  else{
   ++year
   month=0
  }
 }
}
```

```
    updateCalendar(month,year)
  }
  // -></SCRIPT>
  </HEAD>
  <BODY>
  <FORM NAME="changeMonth">
  <INPUT TYPE="HIDDEN" NAME="monthValue" VALUE="99">
  <INPUT TYPE="HIDDEN" NAME="yearValue" VALUE="0">
  <INPUT TYPE="BUTTON" NAME="previous" VALUE="<----"
   onClick="previousMonth()">
  <INPUT TYPE="BUTTON" NAME="current" VALUE="Current Month"
   onClick="currentMonth()">
  <INPUT TYPE="BUTTON" NAME="next" VALUE="---->"
   onClick="nextMonth()">
  </FORM>
  </BODY>
  </HTML>
```

The previousMonth(), currentMonth(), and nextMonth() functions are used to handle the events associated with the clicking of the three buttons. They update the month and year as appropriate and invoke updateCalendar() to store the new month and year values in the monthValue and yearValue hidden fields. The updateCalendar() function then reloads the bottom frame so that the calendar displayed reflects the new month and year values.

The calendar.htm file (Listing 12.5) displays the calendar in the bottom frame. It uses the calendar.js file to accomplish this purpose. It contains a small script which reads the monthValue and yearValue fields of the control.htm file and creates a calendar for the specified month and year. If the month is 99 then the script sets the month and year to the current date and updates the monthValue and year-Value fields with these values. If the month and year are current, then the current date is highlighted in red on the calendar.

Listing 12.5   The Calendar Update Frame (calendar.htm)

```
  <HTML>
  <HEAD>
  <TITLE>Monthly Calendar</TITLE>
  <SCRIPT LANGUAGE="JavaScript" SRC="calendar.js"><!-
  // -></SCRIPT>
  </HEAD>
```

```
<BODY>
<SCRIPT LANGUAGE="JavaScript"><!-
formRef = parent.frames[0].document.forms[0]
month = parseInt(formRef.monthValue.value)
year = parseInt(formRef.yearValue.value)
today = new Date()
if(month==99) {
 month = today.getMonth()
 year = today.getYear()
 formRef.monthValue.value=""+month
 formRef.yearValue.value=""+year
}
cal=new Calendar(month,year)
if(month==today.getMonth() && year==today.getYear())
 cal.display(today.getDate())
else cal.display()
// -></SCRIPT>
</BODY>
</HTML>
```

The Calculator Accessory

You've already learned, in Chapter 11, "Doing Math," how to develop the second desktop accessory—a calculator. However, the calculator that you developed in Chapter 11 was meant to help you learn how to use JavaScript's Math object and would be a little bit of an overkill for most users on a Web page. The calc.htm file shown in Figure 12.4 (Listing 12.6) removes all of the extra functions used to show off JavaScript's math library and won't scare off any of your Web users.

Why would you want to include a calculator on a Web page? A calculator is a nice feature if you are involved in any type of Web-based sales. When a customer selects a series of products and sees their total price automatically calculated, he or she may often want to double-check the calculations. Did they add the right sales tax? Did they charge the right shipping rate? Did they add the numbers correctly? Having a calculator available to your customers offers them a convenient way to perform these checks. They may even create a bookmark to your Web page just to have the calculator available from their browser!

FIGURE 12.4:

The simplified calculator
(Listing 12.6)

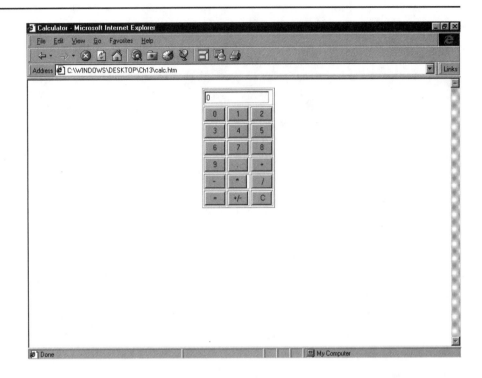

Listing 12.6   **The Revised Calculator Program (calc.htm)**

```
<HTML>
<HEAD>
<TITLE>Calculator</TITLE>
<SCRIPT LANGUAGE="JavaScript"><!-
r = new Array(2)
function setStartState(){
 state="start"
 r[0] = "0"
 r[1] = "0"
 operand=""
 ix=0
}
function addDigit(n){
 if(state=="gettingInteger" || state=="gettingFloat")
  r[ix]=appendDigit(r[ix],n)
```

```
 else{
  r[ix]=""+n
  state="gettingInteger"
 }
 display(r[ix])
}
function appendDigit(n1,n2){
 if(n1=="0") return ""+n2
 var s=""
 s+=n1
 s+=n2
 return s
}
function display(s){
 document.calculator.total.value=s
}
function addDecimalPoint(){
 if(state!="gettingFloat"){
  decimal=true
  r[ix]+="."
  if(state=="haveOperand" || state=="getOperand2") r[ix]="0."
  state="gettingFloat"
  display(r[ix])
 }
}
function clearDisplay(){
 setStartState()
 display(r[0])
}
function changeSign(){
 if(r[ix].charAt(0)=="-") r[ix]=r[ix].substring(1,r[ix].length)
 else if(parseFloat(r[ix])!=0) r[ix]="-"+r[ix]
 display(r[ix])
}
function calc(){
 if(state=="gettingInteger" || state=="gettingFloat" ||
  state=="haveOperand"){
  if(ix==1){
   r[0]=calculateOperation(operand,r[0],r[1])
   ix=0
  }
```

```
        }else if(state=="getOperand2"){
         r[0]=calculateOperation(operand,r[0],r[0])
         ix=0
        }
        state="haveOperand"
        decimal=false
        display(r[ix])
       }
       function calculateOperation(op,x,y){
        var result=""
        if(op=="+"){
         result=""+(parseFloat(x)+parseFloat(y))
        }else if(op=="-"){
         result=""+(parseFloat(x)-parseFloat(y))
        }else if(op=="*"){
         result=""+(parseFloat(x)*parseFloat(y))
        }else if(op=="/"){
         if(parseFloat(y)==0){
          alert("Division by 0 not allowed.")
          result=0
         }else result=""+(parseFloat(x)/parseFloat(y))
        }
        return result
       }
       function performOp(op){
        if(state=="start"){
         ++ix
         operand=op
        }else if(state=="gettingInteger" || state=="gettingFloat" ||
         state=="haveOperand"){
         if(ix==0){
          ++ix
          operand=op
         }else{
          r[0]=calculateOperation(operand,r[0],r[1])
          display(r[0])
          operator=op
         }
        }
        state="getOperand2"
        decimal=false
```

```
}
// -></SCRIPT>
</HEAD>
<BODY>
<SCRIPT LANGUAGE="JavaScript"><!-
setStartState()
// -></SCRIPT>
<FORM NAME="calculator">
<TABLE BORDER="BORDER" ALIGN="CENTER">
<TR>
<TD COLSPAN="3"><INPUT TYPE="TEXT" NAME="total" VALUE="0"
 SIZE="15"></TD></TR>
<TR>
<TD><INPUT TYPE="BUTTON" NAME="n0" VALUE="    0    "
 ONCLICK="addDigit(0)"></TD>
<TD><INPUT TYPE="BUTTON" NAME="n1" VALUE="    1    "
 ONCLICK="addDigit(1)"></TD>
<TD><INPUT TYPE="BUTTON" NAME="n2" VALUE="    2    "
 ONCLICK="addDigit(2)"></TD>
</TR>
<TR>
<TD><INPUT TYPE="BUTTON" NAME="n3" VALUE="    3    "
 ONCLICK="addDigit(3)"></TD>
<TD><INPUT TYPE="BUTTON" NAME="n4" VALUE="    4    "
 ONCLICK="addDigit(4)"></TD>
<TD><INPUT TYPE="BUTTON" NAME="n5" VALUE="    5    "
 ONCLICK="addDigit(5)"></TD>
</TR>
<TR>
<TD><INPUT TYPE="BUTTON" NAME="n6" VALUE="    6    "
 ONCLICK="addDigit(6)"></TD>
<TD><INPUT TYPE="BUTTON" NAME="n7" VALUE="    7    "
 ONCLICK="addDigit(7)"></TD>
<TD><INPUT TYPE="BUTTON" NAME="n8" VALUE="    8    "
 ONCLICK="addDigit(8)"></TD>
</TR>
<TR>
<TD><INPUT TYPE="BUTTON" NAME="n9" VALUE="    9    "
 ONCLICK="addDigit(9)"></TD>
<TD><INPUT TYPE="BUTTON" NAME="decimal" VALUE="    .    "
 ONCLICK="addDecimalPoint()"></TD>
```

```
<TD><INPUT TYPE="BUTTON" NAME="plus" VALUE="   +   "
 ONCLICK="performOp('+')"></TD>
</TR>
<TR>
<TD><INPUT TYPE="BUTTON" NAME="minus" VALUE="   -   "
 ONCLICK="performOp('-')"></TD>
<TD><INPUT TYPE="BUTTON" NAME="multiply" VALUE="   *   "
 ONCLICK="performOp('*')"></TD>
<TD><INPUT TYPE="BUTTON" NAME="divide" VALUE="   /   "
 ONCLICK="performOp('/')"></TD>
</TR>
<TR>
<TD><INPUT TYPE="BUTTON" NAME="equals" VALUE="   =   "
 ONCLICK="calc()"></TD>
<TD COLSPAN="1" ROWSPAN="1"><INPUT TYPE="BUTTON"
 NAME="sign" VALUE=" +/-  " ONCLICK="changeSign()"></TD>
<TD><INPUT TYPE="BUTTON" NAME="clearField" VALUE="   C   "
 ONCLICK="clearDisplay()"></TD>
</TR>
</TABLE>
</FORM>
</BODY>
</HTML>
```

The To-Do List Accessory

When you're browsing the Web, would you like to take notes on a particular Web page and have those notes available to you whenever you revisit the page? I know I would. You could take notes to summarize the important points of a Web-based document, to identify other relevant URLs, or just to keep track of when or why you last visited the page.

This section presents an approach to maintaining private notes on public Web sites. In keeping with the desktop metaphor, it implements this approach in terms of a to-do list—a very handy tool for people who have a lot to do! It can easily be tailored to a general-purpose notepad by just changing its heading.

Download `notes.htm` from this book's page on the Sybex Web site. When you open it, you will notice that it generates the display shown in Figure 12.5. Now type a list of things that you have to do—your to-do list—as shown in Figure 12.6. Exit your browser, wait a few seconds, and then reopen `notes.htm`. Your notes are still there, on that Web page! The best thing about it is that nobody else can read them. This may not seem all that exciting, but it is an important capability. You can add the same type of note area to your Web pages. People can jot down notes to themselves about your Web pages, and when they return to your Web page, their notes will still be there—but only for their own use.

How does `notes.htm` (Listing 12.7) work? You probably guessed it—cookies. Cookies are used to store the notes entered by the user. These notes are stored on the user's system, so you don't have to worry about making disk space available for them. When users revisit your Web page, they are automatically reloaded by their browsers.

FIGURE 12.5:

The to-do list opening display (Listing 12.7)

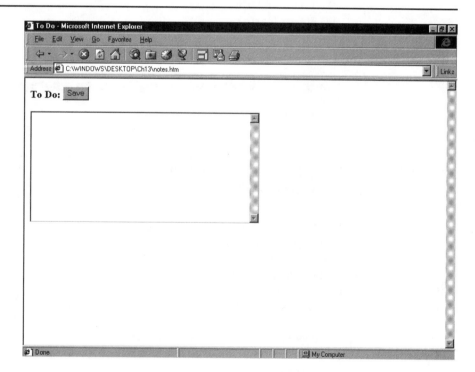

FIGURE 12.6:

The to-do list reads the cookie the next time it starts (Listing 12.7).

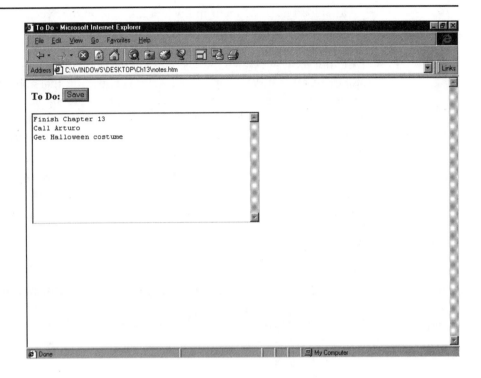

Listing 12.7   **The To-Do List Script (notes.htm)**

```
<HTML>
<HEAD>
<TITLE>To Do</TITLE>
<SCRIPT LANGUAGE="JavaScript" SRC="cookie.js"><!-
// -></SCRIPT>
<SCRIPT LANGUAGE="JavaScript"><!-
function loadNotes() {
 var cookie=document.cookie
 if(nameDefined(cookie,"toDo")) {
  todo=getCookieValue(cookie,"toDo")
  todo=decode(todo)
 }else todo=""
 document.forms[0].notes.value=todo
}
```

```
function saveNotes() {
 todo=window.document.forms[0].notes.value
 todo=encode(todo)
 var newCookie = "toDo="+todo+"; expires="
 newCookie += "Tuesday, 09-Nov-10 23:12:40 GMT"
 document.cookie=newCookie
}
function encode(s) {
 t=""
 for(var i=0;i<s.length;++i) {
  ch=s.charAt(i)
  if(ch=="/") t += "//"
  else if(ch==" ") t += "/b"
  else if(ch==",") t += "/."
  else if(ch==";") t += "/:"
  else if(ch=="\n") t += "/n"
  else if(ch=="\r") t += "/r"
  else if(ch=="\t") t += "/t"
  else if(ch=="\b") t += "/b"
  else t += ch
 }
 return t
}
function decode(s) {
 t=""
 if(s==null) return
 for(var i=0;i<s.length;++i) {
  var ch=s.charAt(i)
  if(ch=="/") {
   ++i
   if(i<s.length){
     ch=s.charAt(i)
     if(ch=="/") t += ch
     else if(ch==".") t += ","
     else if(ch==":") t += ";"
     else if(ch=="n") t += "\n"
     else if(ch=="r") t += "\r"
     else if(ch=="t") t += "\t"
     else if(ch=="b") t += " "
   }
  }else t += ch
}
```

```
 return t
}
// -></SCRIPT>
</HEAD>
<BODY>
<FORM>
<H3>To Do:
<INPUT NAME="save" TYPE="BUTTON" VALUE="Save"
 onClick="saveNotes()"></H3>
<TEXTAREA NAME="notes" ROWS="12" COLS="50"
 VALUE=""></TEXTAREA>
</FORM>
<SCRIPT LANGUAGE="JavaScript"><!-
 loadNotes()
// -></SCRIPT>
</BODY>
</HTML>
```

The notes.htm file uses the cookie-reading functions of cookie.js (Listing 12.8). You've already used these functions in Chapter 9, "Working with Links," and Chapter 10, "Using Images." They are nameDefined(), removeBlanks(), and get-CookieValue().

Listing 12.8   **Common Cookie Functions (cookie.js)**

```
function nameDefined(c,n) {
 var s=removeBlanks(c)
 var pairs=s.split(";")
 for(var i=0;i<pairs.length;++i) {
  var pairSplit=pairs[i].split("=")
  if(pairSplit[0]==n) return true
 }
 return false
}
function removeBlanks(s) {
 var temp=""
 for(var i=0;i<s.length;++i) {
  var c=s.charAt(i)
  if(c!=" ") temp += c
 }
```

```
 return temp
 }
function getCookieValue(c,n) {
 var s=removeBlanks(c)
 var pairs=s.split(";")
 for(var i=0;i<pairs.length;++i) {
  var pairSplit=pairs[i].split("=")
  if(pairSplit[0]==n) return pairSplit[1]
 }
 return ""
 }
```

The file notes.htm defines four other functions—loadNotes(), saveNotes(), encode(), and decode()—to process the text that is entered into its text area field. These functions are used as explained in the following subsections.

The *loadNotes()* Function

This function uses nameDefined() and getCookieValue() to read the value of the toDo cookie. It invokes decode() to decode the cookie value.

The *saveNotes()* Function

This function reads the notes entered into the text area field and invokes encode() to encode them in a form that is suitable for storage in a cookie. It then creates a new toDo cookie with a 2010 expiration date. (I picked 2010 arbitrarily. There is no reason you can't go beyond the year 2010.)

The *encode()* Function

White-space characters, semicolons, and commas cannot be stored as part of a cookie's *name=value* pair. This function encodes such strings into a form that is suitable for cookie storage. The conversions carried out by the encode() function are listed in Table 12.1.

The *decode()* Function

This function decodes a stored cookie string in accordance with Table 12.1.

TABLE 12.1:   String to Cookie Encoding Performed by encode() and decode()

String character	Cookie character
/	//
space	/b
,	/.
;	/:
\n	/n
\r	/r
\t	/t
\b	/b

The World Clock Accessory

The Web never sleeps. Someone could be browsing your Web page at any time of the day. They could be viewing it from Europe, Asia, Africa, Australia, or North or South America. In some cases, you may want to display the current date and time along with your Web page.

When people view your Web page, they are more concerned about the time of day where they are than the time of day where your Web page is located. If you add the time to your Web pages via a CGI program, you will have a hard time converting your time to the local time of your Web users. Fortunately, JavaScript can be easily used to display the user's local time and identify the user's time-zone offset from Greenwich Mean Time (GMT).

After downloading this chapter's code, open clock.htm with your browser, and your browser will display the day of the week, the date, your local time, and your time-zone offset from GMT, as shown in Figure 12.7. Take a closer look at your browser display. Notice the seconds tick by. Your browser updates the time on one-second intervals. This allows you to update the time as your Web page sits on your user's browser. You can even tell your user how long he or she has used your Web page—an important capability if you decide to charge someone based on access time.

FIGURE 12.7:

The world-clock display
(Listing 12.9)

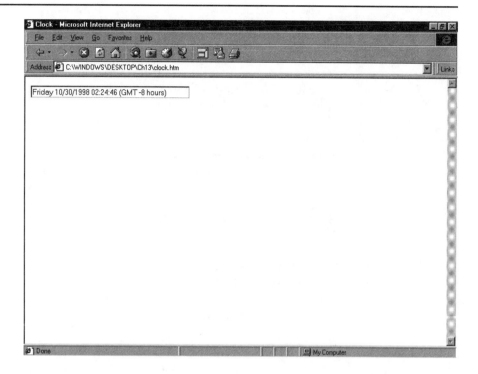

The script used in clock.htm (Listing 12.9) is fairly short, but it illustrates some important points. The clock text field takes its value directly from the dateTime() function. The tick() function is then invoked to start the clock running. This function updates the value of the clock field and then sets a one-second timeout so it can reinvoke itself. The dateTime() function returns a string containing the day, date, time, and time-zone offset.

Listing 12.9	A Clock Script (clock.htm)

```
<HTML>
<HEAD>
<TITLE>Clock</TITLE>
<SCRIPT LANGUAGE="JavaScript"><!-
function dateTime() {
 var days = new Array("Sunday","Monday","Tuesday","Wednesday",
  "Thursday","Friday","Saturday")
```

```
 var now = new Date()
 var result = days[now.getDay()]+" "
 result += now.toLocaleString()
 var tzOffset=-now.getTimezoneOffset()/60
 if(tzOffset<0) result += " (GMT "+tzOffset+" hours)"
 else result += " (GMT +"+tzOffset+" hours)"
 return result
 }
 function tick() {
 document.forms[0].clock.value=dateTime()
 setTimeout("tick()",1000)
 }
 // -></SCRIPT>
 </HEAD>
 <BODY>
 <FORM>
 <INPUT NAME="clock" TYPE="TEXT" SIZE="40"
 VALUE="&{dateTime()};">
 </FORM>
 <SCRIPT LANGUAGE="JavaScript"><!-
 tick()
 // -></SCRIPT>
 </BODY>
 </HTML>
```

Assembling the Desktop

Now that you've developed the clock, calendar, calculator, and to-do list, wouldn't you like to put them all together in one Web page? You'll learn how to do that so you can see them working together and envision how to integrate them with your own Web pages. The hard part has been completed—the accessories have been developed. All you need to do now is to assemble them into a common desktop.

Open desktop.htm, and you'll see the Web page shown in Figure 12.8. You can watch the clock tick, flip through the calendar, make some notes, or calculate how much your next raise should be.

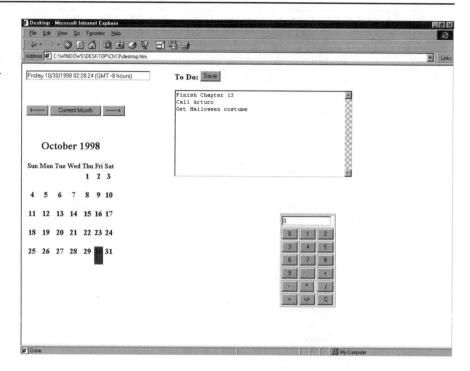

FIGURE 12.8:

The desktop display integrates each of the desktop accessories (Listing 12.10).

The desktop.htm file (Listing 12.10) is the first of two levels of frame sets. It defines two columns that contain the files cal-clock.htm (Listing 12.11) and notes-calc.htm (Listing 12.12). The cal-clock.htm file creates a frame set for displaying the clock and the calendar. The notes-calc.htm file creates a frame set for displaying the to-do list and the calculator. Notice how simple it was to integrate all four accessories into a single Web application.

Listing 12.10   Defining the Top-Level Frame Set (desktop.htm)

```
<HTML>
<HEAD>
<TITLE>Desktop</TITLE>
<FRAMESET COLS="350,*" BORDER="0">
<FRAME SRC="cal-clock.htm">
<FRAME SRC="notes-calc.htm">
</FRAMESET>
</HTML>
```

Listing 12.11   **Defining the Left Frame Set (cal-clock.htm)**

```
<HTML>
<HEAD>
<TITLE>Desktop</TITLE>
<FRAMESET ROWS="80,*" BORDER="0">
<FRAME SRC="clock.htm">
<FRAME SRC="cal.htm">
</FRAMESET>
</HTML>
```

Listing 12.12   **Defining the Right Time Set (notes-calc.htm)**

```
<HTML>
<HEAD>
<TITLE>Desktop</TITLE>
<FRAMESET ROWS="325,*" BORDER="0">
<FRAME SRC="notes.htm">
<FRAME SRC="calc.htm">
</FRAMESET>
</HTML>
```

Summary

In this chapter, you learned how to develop four common desktop accessories—a calendar, a calculator, a clock, and a to-do list—and integrate them into a Web page-based application: a Web desktop. You are finally learning how to develop scripts that are both useful and reusable. In the next chapter, you'll develop some examples of online catalogs and order forms that use JavaScript to simplify the customer ordering process.

CHAPTER
THIRTEEN

13

Online Catalogs

- Developing a Catalog without a CGI Program

- Tailoring a Catalog Based on User Preferences

- Adding Multimedia Features

The Web has become a showcase for almost everything that is new or innovative. New products, services, and technologies are frequently introduced to the world via corporate Web sites and through ads appearing on popular Web pages. Smaller companies with fewer products are able to provide information on their products in a small number of Web pages. Larger companies, like IBM, Microsoft, and Sun Microsystems, have so many products that they only describe their latest and greatest products on their top-level Web pages and provide access to everything else via online catalogs.

Catalogs are important to online merchants, both resellers and manufacturers. Sales catalogs must be highly attractive to stimulate interest in products and must be easy to use in order to help close the sale.

Online catalogs are used for reasons other than product information and sales. Web-based libraries use catalogs to provide information on book availability. Museums catalog their exhibits and collectors catalog their collections. Multimedia catalogs are especially impressive.

The primary purpose of a catalog is to facilitate access to information. HTML-based catalogs present static Web pages that use CGI programs to fetch product information. In these catalogs, a user fills out a catalog search form and submits it to a CGI program. The CGI program returns the Web page of the selected product. With JavaScript, much of the catalog processing can be performed on the browser. Catalogs can be dynamically tailored based on user preferences and can be implemented without the need for CGI programs. JavaScript catalogs can also make optimal use of multimedia features.

In this chapter, you'll learn to use JavaScript to create sophisticated catalogs. You'll learn how to develop catalogs that do not require CGI programs and that can be tailored to user preferences. When you finish this chapter you'll be able to develop catalogs that are attractive, informative, and easy to use.

Developing a Catalog without a CGI Program

Small catalogs are usually implemented entirely in HTML; ordinary links are used to guide users to the information they want. Large catalogs are typically implemented using a series of HTML forms that provide a front-end search interface for a CGI program; the user enters product search criteria into the HTML forms, submits them to the CGI program, and a Web page containing the requested product information is returned.

JavaScript can be used to implement small to medium catalogs without the need for CGI programs. Even if CGI programs are required, JavaScript can help to reduce their complexity.

When implementing a catalog in JavaScript, you should include as much catalog indexing information as possible within the script. This will allow your script to implement the catalog search functions locally without requiring CGI processing.

Figure 13.1 provides an example of a JavaScript-only product catalog. The catalog is organized according to the room of the house in which a product is used. Run this script by opening `catalog.htm` (Listing 13.1) from the code listings on the Sybex Web site. Select Bed Room from the Room selection list and click the Select Room button. You'll see that the values of the Types of Products selection list is updated based on the room that is selected. Select Electronics from this selection list and click the Select Product Type button. The Products selection list is now updated with electronics products for the bedroom. Select Clock Radio from this list and click the Select Product button. As you can see in Figure 13.2, the lower-left frame contains a photo of the product, and the lower-right frame contains a short description of the selected product. I had to create 71 product images and 71 product descriptions for this example. For a real catalog, you would have to supply the images and descriptions appropriate to your products.)

Listing 13.1   The Catalog's Top-Level Frame Set (catalog.htm)

```
<HTML>
<HEAD>
<TITLE>XYZ Company Catalog</TITLE>
</HEAD>
<FRAMESET ROWS="235,*" BORDER="10">
<FRAME SRC="catform.htm">
<FRAME SRC="products.htm">
</FRAMESET>
</HTML>
```

The `catalog.htm` file shown in Listing 13.1 sets up a top-level frame set that organizes the catalog into a two-row form. The `products.htm` file shown in Listing 13.2 sets up a two-column frame set for the bottom half of the window.

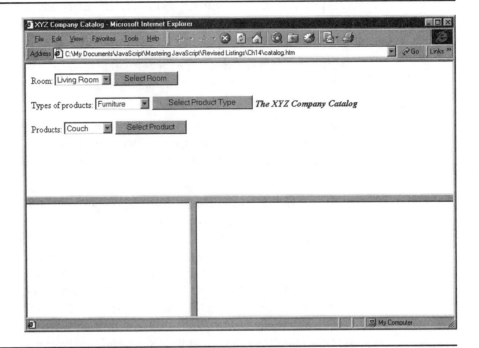

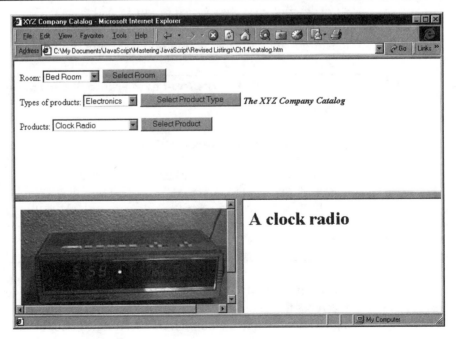

Listing 13.2   **The Frame Set Used to Display the Product Image and Description (products.htm)**

```
<HTML>
<HEAD>
<TITLE>XYZ Company Catalog</TITLE>
</HEAD>
<FRAMESET COLS="300,*" BORDER="10">
<FRAME SRC="blank.htm">
<FRAME SRC="blank.htm">
</FRAMESET>
</HTML>
```

The `catform.htm` file (Listing 13.3) implements the catalog form shown in the top half of the browser's display. It consists of four scripts—three in the document's head and one in the document's body. The script in the document's body invokes the `displayCatalogForm()` function to cause the catalog's form to be displayed. The first two scripts in the document's head insert code from the files `cookie.js` (Listing 13.4) and `products.js` (Listing 13.5). The third script in the document's head defines 10 functions, which are used as described in the following sections.

The *displayCatalogForm()* Function

This is the main function used to create the catalog form. It invokes the `read-Cookie()` function to read the user's current form selections. It then invokes the `displayRooms()`, `displayCategories()`, and `displayProducts()` functions to display the elements of the form.

The *readCookie()* Function

This function reads the `room` and `cat` (product category) cookie values to determine what form elements are currently selected by the user.

The *displayRooms()* Function

This function displays the Room selection list and the Select Room button. The `rooms` array is defined in the `products.js` file.

The *displayCategories()* Function

This function displays the Types of Products selection list and the Select Product Type button. The roomCategories array is defined in the products.js file.

The *displayProducts()* Function

This function displays the Products selection list and the Select Product button. The prod array is defined in the products.js file.

The *selectRoom()* Function

This function handles the onClick event of the Select Room button. It sets cat to the first product category associated with the room and invokes setCookie() to store the room and cat variables as cookies.

The *selectProductType()* Function

This function handles the onClick event of the Select Product Type button. It updates the cat variable based on the user's selection and invokes setCookie() to store the updated cat variable as a cookie.

The *selectProduct()* Function

This function handles the onClick event of the Select Product button. It displays the product image and description files in the lower frames of the window.

The *writeDocument()* Function

This function is used to load the appropriate files in the lower window frames.

The *setCookie()* Function

This function updates the room and cat cookies and reloads the current document to update the catalog form's display.

Listing 13.3   The Code That Implements the Catalog Form (catform.htm)

```
<HTML>
<HEAD>
<TITLE>XYZ Company Catalog</TITLE>
<SCRIPT LANGUAGE="JavaScript" SRC="products.js"><!-
// -></SCRIPT>
<SCRIPT LANGUAGE="JavaScript" SRC="cookie.js"><!-
// -></SCRIPT>
<SCRIPT LANGUAGE="JavaScript"><!-
function displayCatalogForm() {
 readCookie()
 document.writeln('<FORM>')
 displayRooms()
 displayCategories()
 displayProducts()
 document.writeln('</FORM>')
}
function readCookie() {
 var cookie=document.cookie
 room="li"
 cat="fu"
 if(nameDefined(cookie,"room"))
  room=getCookieValue(cookie,"room")
 if(nameDefined(cookie,"cat"))
  cat=getCookieValue(cookie,"cat")
}
function displayRooms() {
 document.write('<P>')
 document.write('Room: ')
 document.writeln('<SELECT name="roomField">')
 for(var i=0;i<rooms.length;++i) {
  if(room==rooms[i]){
   document.write('<OPTION SELECTED')
  }else document.write('<OPTION')
  document.write(' VALUE="'+rooms[i]+'">')
  document.writeln(roomName(rooms[i]))
 }
 document.writeln('</SELECT>')
 document.write(' <INPUT type="BUTTON" value="Select Room" ')
 document.writeln('onClick="selectRoom()">')
```

```
  document.writeln('</P>')
 }
 function displayCategories() {
  document.write('<P>')
  document.write('Types of products: ')
  document.writeln('<SELECT name="catField">')
  for(var i=0;i<roomCategories.length;++i) {
   if(room==roomCategories[i].room) {
    if(cat==roomCategories[i].cat)
     document.write('<OPTION SELECTED')
    else document.write('<OPTION')
    document.write(' VALUE="'+roomCategories[i].cat+'">')
    document.writeln(categoryName(roomCategories[i].cat))
   }
  }
  document.writeln('</SELECT>')
  document.write(' <INPUT type="BUTTON" ')
  document.write('value="Select Product Type" ')
  document.writeln('onClick="selectProductType()">')
  document.writeln(' <B><I>The XYZ Company Catalog</B></I>')
  document.writeln('</P>')
 }
 function displayProducts() {
  document.write('<P>')
  document.write('Products: ')
  document.writeln('<SELECT name="productField">')
  for(var i=0;i<prod.length;++i) {
   if(room==prod[i].room) {
    if(cat==prod[i].category) {
     document.write('<OPTION VALUE="')
      document.write(i+'">')
     document.writeln(prod[i].name)
    }
   }
  }
  document.writeln('</SELECT>')
  document.write(' <INPUT type="BUTTON" ')
  document.write('value="Select Product" ')
  document.writeln('onClick="selectProduct()">')
  document.writeln('</P>')
 }
 function selectRoom() {
```

```
  var field=window.document.forms[0].roomField
  var ix=field.selectedIndex
  room=field.options[ix].value
  for(var i=0;i<roomCategories.length;++i) {
   if(room==roomCategories[i].room){
    cat=roomCategories[i].cat
    break
   }
  }
  setCookie()
}
function selectProductType() {
 var field=window.document.forms[0].catField
 var ix=field.selectedIndex
 cat=field.options[ix].value
 setCookie()
}
function selectProduct() {
 var field=window.document.forms[0].productField
 var ix=field.selectedIndex
 prodIX=field.options[ix].value
 writeDocument(0,"products/"+prod[prodIX].image)
 writeDocument(1,"products/"+prod[prodIX].desc)
}
function writeDocument(n,s) {
 var doc=parent.frames[1].frames[n].location = s
}
function setCookie() {
 var newCookie = "room="+room
 window.document.cookie=newCookie
 newCookie = "cat="+cat
 window.document.cookie=newCookie
 window.location="catform.htm"
}
// -></SCRIPT>
</HEAD>
<BODY bgColor="white">
<SCRIPT LANGUAGE="JavaScript"><!-
displayCatalogForm()
// -></SCRIPT>
</BODY>
</HTML>
```

The cookie.js file includes the cookie-reading functions used in previous examples.

Listing 13.4   **Functions for Reading Cookies (cookie.js)**

```
function nameDefined(c,n) {
 var s=removeBlanks(c)
 var pairs=s.split(";")
 for(var i=0;i<pairs.length;++i) {
  var pairSplit=pairs[i].split("=")
  if(pairSplit[0]==n) return true
 }
 return false
}
function removeBlanks(s) {
 var temp=""
 for(var i=0;i<s.length;++i) {
  var c=s.charAt(i)
  if(c!=" ") temp += c
 }
 return temp
}
function getCookieValue(c,n) {
 var s=removeBlanks(c)
 var pairs=s.split(";")
 for(var i=0;i<pairs.length;++i) {
  var pairSplit=pairs[i].split("=")
  if(pairSplit[0]==n) return pairSplit[1]
 }
 return ""
}
```

The products.js file (Listing 13.5) contains the product database used by the catalog.

Listing 13.5   **The Catalog's Product Database (products.js)**

```
rooms = new Array("li","di","be","ki","ba")
function roomName(room) {
 if(room=="li") return "Living Room"
 if(room=="di") return "Dining Room"
```

```
 if(room=="be") return "Bed Room"
 if(room=="ki") return "Kitchen"
 if(room=="ba") return "Bath Room"
 return "Unknown"
}
productCategories = new Array("fu","ca","li","el","ac",
 "ap","cb","si","to","ba")
function categoryName(cat) {
 if(cat=="fu") return "Furniture"
 if(cat=="ca") return "Carpeting"
 if(cat=="li") return "Lighting"
 if(cat=="el") return "Electronics"
 if(cat=="ac") return "Accessories"
 if(cat=="ap") return "Appliances"
 if(cat=="cb") return "Cabinets"
 if(cat=="si") return "Sinks"
 if(cat=="to") return "Toilets"
 if(cat=="ba") return "Bath and Shower"
 return "Unknown"
}
function Product(id,name,category,room)    {
 this.id=id
 this.name=name
 this.category=category
 this.room=room
 this.image="i"+id+".jpg"
 this.desc="d"+id+".htm"
}
function roomProductCategory(room,cat) {
 this.room=room
 this.cat=cat
}
var i=0
roomCategories = new Array()
roomCategories[i] = new roomProductCategory("li","fu"); ++i
roomCategories[i] = new roomProductCategory("li","ca"); ++i
roomCategories[i] = new roomProductCategory("li","li"); ++i
roomCategories[i] = new roomProductCategory("li","el"); ++i
roomCategories[i] = new roomProductCategory("li","ac"); ++i
roomCategories[i] = new roomProductCategory("di","fu"); ++i
roomCategories[i] = new roomProductCategory("di","ca"); ++i
roomCategories[i] = new roomProductCategory("di","li"); ++i
```

```
roomCategories[i] = new roomProductCategory("di","ac"); ++i
roomCategories[i] = new roomProductCategory("be","fu"); ++i
roomCategories[i] = new roomProductCategory("be","ca"); ++i
roomCategories[i] = new roomProductCategory("be","li"); ++i
roomCategories[i] = new roomProductCategory("be","el"); ++i
roomCategories[i] = new roomProductCategory("be","ac"); ++i
roomCategories[i] = new roomProductCategory("ki","ap"); ++i
roomCategories[i] = new roomProductCategory("ki","cb"); ++i
roomCategories[i] = new roomProductCategory("ki","li"); ++i
roomCategories[i] = new roomProductCategory("ki","ac"); ++i
roomCategories[i] = new roomProductCategory("ba","si"); ++i
roomCategories[i] = new roomProductCategory("ba","to"); ++i
roomCategories[i] = new roomProductCategory("ba","li"); ++i
roomCategories[i] = new roomProductCategory("ba","ba"); ++i
roomCategories[i] = new roomProductCategory("ba","ac"); ++i
var i=0
prod=new Array()
//Living room products
prod[i]=new Product(i,"Couch","fu","li"); ++i
prod[i]=new Product(i,"Sofa","fu","li"); ++i
prod[i]=new Product(i,"Arm chair","fu","li"); ++i
prod[i]=new Product(i,"Long table","fu","li"); ++i
prod[i]=new Product(i,"Side table","fu","li"); ++i
prod[i]=new Product(i,"Persian rug","ca","li"); ++i
prod[i]=new Product(i,"Cheap rug","ca","li"); ++i
prod[i]=new Product(i,"Ceiling light","li","li"); ++i
prod[i]=new Product(i,"Floor light","li","li"); ++i
prod[i]=new Product(i,"Table light","li","li"); ++i
prod[i]=new Product(i,"Big TV","el","li"); ++i
prod[i]=new Product(i,"Small TV","el","li"); ++i
prod[i]=new Product(i,"Entertainment Center","el","li"); ++i
prod[i]=new Product(i,"Stereo","el","li"); ++i
prod[i]=new Product(i,"Large painting","ac","li"); ++i
prod[i]=new Product(i,"Small painting","ac","li"); ++i
prod[i]=new Product(i,"Large fake plant","ac","li"); ++i
prod[i]=new Product(i,"Small fake plant","ac","li"); ++i
prod[i]=new Product(i,"Expensive knick knack","ac","li"); ++i
prod[i]=new Product(i,"Cheap knick knack","ac","li"); ++i
//Dining room products
prod[i]=new Product(i,"Expensive dining set","fu","di"); ++i
prod[i]=new Product(i,"Cheap dining set","fu","di"); ++i
prod[i]=new Product(i,"China cabinet","fu","di"); ++i
```

```
prod[i]=new Product(i,"Serving table","fu","di"); ++i
prod[i]=new Product(i,"Stain-proof rug","ca","di"); ++i
prod[i]=new Product(i,"Plastic floor covering","ca","di"); ++i
prod[i]=new Product(i,"Chandalier","li","di"); ++i
prod[i]=new Product(i,"Ceiling lamp","li","di"); ++i
prod[i]=new Product(i,"China set","ac","di"); ++i
prod[i]=new Product(i,"Silver set","ac","di"); ++i
//Bed room products
prod[i]=new Product(i,"King bed","fu","be"); ++i
prod[i]=new Product(i,"Queen bed","fu","be"); ++i
prod[i]=new Product(i,"Single bed","fu","be"); ++i
prod[i]=new Product(i,"End table","fu","be"); ++i
prod[i]=new Product(i,"Dresser","fu","be"); ++i
prod[i]=new Product(i,"Lamb skin carpet","ca","be"); ++i
prod[i]=new Product(i,"Bear skin carpet","ca","be"); ++i
prod[i]=new Product(i,"Ceiling lamp","li","be"); ++i
prod[i]=new Product(i,"Table lamp","li","be"); ++i
prod[i]=new Product(i,"Clock Radio","el","be"); ++i
prod[i]=new Product(i,"Electronic head board","el","be"); ++i
prod[i]=new Product(i,"Pillow set","ac","be"); ++i
prod[i]=new Product(i,"Linen set","ac","be"); ++i
prod[i]=new Product(i,"Bed spread","ac","be"); ++i
//Kitchen products
prod[i]=new Product(i,"Refrigerator","ap","ki"); ++i
prod[i]=new Product(i,"Stove - oven","ap","ki"); ++i
prod[i]=new Product(i,"Microwave oven","ap","ki"); ++i
prod[i]=new Product(i,"Toaster","ap","ki"); ++i
prod[i]=new Product(i,"Coffee maker","ap","ki"); ++i
prod[i]=new Product(i,"Dish washer","ap","ki"); ++i
prod[i]=new Product(i,"Deluxe cabinets","cb","ki"); ++i
prod[i]=new Product(i,"Standard cabinets","cb","ki"); ++i
prod[i]=new Product(i,"Deluxe counter","cb","ki"); ++i
prod[i]=new Product(i,"Standard counter","cb","ki"); ++i
prod[i]=new Product(i,"Ceiling light","li","ki"); ++i
prod[i]=new Product(i,"Counter light","li","ki"); ++i
prod[i]=new Product(i,"Cookware","ac","ki"); ++i
prod[i]=new Product(i,"Storage containers","ac","ki"); ++i
prod[i]=new Product(i,"Wall clock","ac","ki"); ++i
//Bath room products
prod[i]=new Product(i,"Deluxe sink","si","ba"); ++i
prod[i]=new Product(i,"Standard sink","si","ba"); ++i
prod[i]=new Product(i,"Deluxe toilet","to","ba"); ++i
```

```
prod[i]=new Product(i,"Standard toilet","to","ba"); ++i
prod[i]=new Product(i,"Ceiling light","li","ba"); ++i
prod[i]=new Product(i,"Wall light","li","ba"); ++i
prod[i]=new Product(i,"Deluxe bath tub","ba","ba"); ++i
prod[i]=new Product(i,"Standard bath tub","ba","ba"); ++i
prod[i]=new Product(i,"Shower stall","ba","ba"); ++i
prod[i]=new Product(i,"Wall cabinet","ac","ba"); ++i
prod[i]=new Product(i,"Towel rack","ac","ba"); ++i
prod[i]=new Product(i,"Towels","ac","ba"); ++i
```

The *rooms* Array

This array contains the two-letter room identifiers used as shortcuts to refer to rooms.

The *roomName()* Function

This function returns the full room name associated with a room identifier.

The *productCategories* Array

This array contains the two-letter product category identifiers used as shortcuts to refer to product categories.

The *categoryName()* Function

This function returns the full product category name associated with its two-character identifier.

The *Product()* Function

This function is the constructor for the Product object. It assigns the product's id, name, cat, and room properties. It also identifies the image and description files associated with the product.

The *roomProductCategory()* Function

This function is the constructor for the `roomProductCategory` object. It is used to map rooms to product categories.

The *roomCategories* Array

This array consists of `roomProductCategory` objects, which are used to assign product categories to rooms.

The *prod* Array

This array identifies all of the products in the catalog.

Tailoring a Catalog Based on User Preferences

You now know how to implement catalogs using JavaScript, but JavaScript can do much more! HTML-only catalogs are not very user friendly—it's pretty much take it or leave it when it comes to user preferences. That's because you have to program a CGI program to implement those preferences. With JavaScript, implementing preferences is a snap! For example, you can use cookies to store preferences between browser sessions. More importantly, you won't be wasting your server's CPU time running unneeded CGI programs.

Figure 13.3 shows how the catalog that was developed in the previous section can be enhanced to allow for user preference selection. Note the Catalog View selection list and the Select View Preference button, which are used to select different views of the catalog. Start by selecting By Product Category from the selection list and then clicking the Select View Preference button. The form is updated to allow selection by product category rather than by room. Now select Electronics (Bed Room) from the Types of Products list and click the Select Product Type button. The Products list is then updated with the bedroom electronics products. Finally, select Clock Radio from the Products list and click the Select Product button. The appropriate product image and description files are displayed in the lower frames of the window. (Refer to Figure 13.4.)

FIGURE 13.3:

Adding catalog view preferences (Listing 13.6)

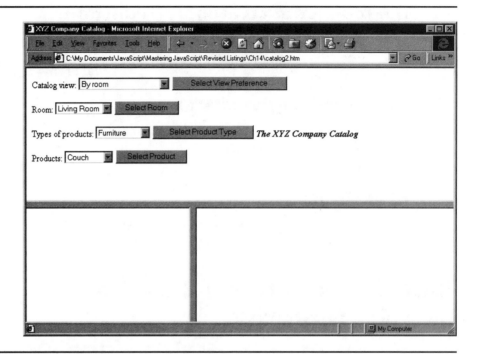

FIGURE 13.4:

Selecting a product via a different view. (Listing 13.6)

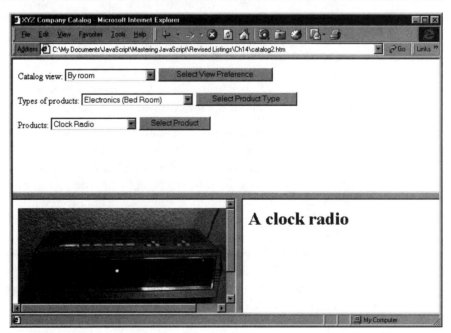

The catalog2.htm file updates the catalog.htm file to use the catform2.htm file instead of catform.htm.

Listing 13.6   **The Updated Catalog's Top-Level Frame Set (catalog2.htm)**

```
<HTML>
<HEAD>
<TITLE>XYZ Company Catalog</TITLE>
</HEAD>
<FRAMESET ROWS="235,*" BORDER="10">
<FRAME SRC="catform2.htm">
<FRAME SRC="products.htm">
</FRAMESET>
</HTML>
```

The catform2.htm file (Listing 13.7) updates the catform.htm file from the previous discussion to provide alternative catalog views. The changes to catform.htm are as described in the following sections.

The *displayCategoryForm()* Function

This function is updated to implement the room, product category, and product views.

The *readCookie()* Function

This function reads an additional cookie—the view cookie—which is used to track the catalog view that the user selects.

The *displayByRoom()* Function

This function displays the room-oriented catalog view.

The *displayByCat()* Function

This function displays the product category–oriented catalog view.

The *displayByProduct()* Function

This function displays the product-oriented catalog view.

The *displayAltView()* Function

This function displays the Catalog View selection list and the Select View Preference button.

The displayRooms() Function

No change from the previous discussion of Listing 13.3.

The *displayCategories()* Function

No change from the previous discussion of Listing 13.3.

The *displayProducts()* Function

No change from the previous discussion of Listing 13.3.

The *displayCatList()* Function

This function displays the Types of Products selection list and Select Product Type button.

The *displayProductsList()* Function

This function displays an alphabetical list of products. It identifies the room associated with each product.

The *altView()* Function

This function handles the onClick event of the Select View Preference button by storing the user-selected view in a cookie.

The *selectRoom()* Function

No change from the previous discussion of Listing 13.3.

The *selectProductType()* Function

No change from the previous discussion of Listing 13.3.

The *selectProduct()* Function

No change from the previous discussion of Listing 13.3.

The *selectProductCat()* Function

This function handles the onClick event of the Select Product Type button. It updates the document's cookies based on the user's selection.

The *selectFromBigList()* Function

This function handles the onClick event of the Select Product button and invokes writeDocument() to display the product's image and description files in the window's lower frames.

The *writeDocument()* Function

No change from the previous discussion of Listing 13.3.

The *setCookie()* Function

This function provides additional support to handle the view cookie.

Listing 13.7   **A Catalog Form That Supports Different Catalog Views (catform2.htm)**

```
<HTML>
<HEAD>
<TITLE>XYZ Company Catalog</TITLE>
<SCRIPT LANGUAGE="JavaScript" SRC="products.js"><!-
// -></SCRIPT>
```

```
<SCRIPT LANGUAGE="JavaScript" SRC="cookie.js"><!-
// -></SCRIPT>
<SCRIPT LANGUAGE="JavaScript"><!-
function displayCatalogForm() {
 readCookie()
 if(view=="byRoom") displayByRoom()
 else if(view=="byCat") displayByCat()
 else displayByProduct()
}
function readCookie() {
 var cookie=document.cookie
 room="li"
 cat="fu"
 view="byRoom"
 if(nameDefined(cookie,"room"))
  room=getCookieValue(cookie,"room")
 if(nameDefined(cookie,"cat"))
  cat=getCookieValue(cookie,"cat")
 if(nameDefined(cookie,"view"))
  view=getCookieValue(cookie,"view")
}
function displayByRoom() {
 document.writeln('<FORM>')
 displayAltView()
 displayRooms()
 displayCategories()
 displayProducts()
 document.writeln('</FORM>')
}
function displayByCat() {
 document.writeln('<FORM>')
 displayAltView()
 displayCatList()
 displayProducts()
 document.writeln('</FORM>')
}
function displayByProduct() {
 document.writeln('<FORM>')
 displayAltView()
 displayProductsList()
 document.writeln('</FORM>')
}
```

```
function displayAltView() {
 document.write('<P>')
 document.write('Catalog view: ')
 document.writeln('<SELECT name="viewField">')
 document.write('<OPTION VALUE="byRoom" SELECTED>By room')
 document.write('<OPTION VALUE="byCat">By product category')
 document.write('<OPTION VALUE="byProd">Alphabetical by product')
 document.writeln('</SELECT>')
 document.write(' <INPUT type="BUTTON" ')
 document.write('value="Select View Preference" ')
 document.writeln('onClick="altView()">')
 document.writeln('</P>')
}
function displayRooms() {
 document.write('<P>')
 document.write('Room: ')
 document.writeln('<SELECT name="roomField">')
 for(var i=0;i<rooms.length;++i) {
  if(room==rooms[i]){
   document.write('<OPTION SELECTED')
  }else document.write('<OPTION')
  document.write(' VALUE="'+rooms[i]+'">')
  document.writeln(roomName(rooms[i]))
 }
 document.writeln('</SELECT>')
 document.write(' <INPUT type="BUTTON" value="Select Room" ')
 document.writeln('onClick="selectRoom()">')
 document.writeln('</P>')
}
function displayCategories() {
 document.write('<P>')
 document.write('Types of products: ')
 document.writeln('<SELECT name="catField">')
 for(var i=0;i<roomCategories.length;++i) {
  if(room==roomCategories[i].room) {
   if(cat==roomCategories[i].cat)
    document.write('<OPTION SELECTED')
   else document.write('<OPTION')
   document.write(' VALUE="'+roomCategories[i].cat+'">')
   document.writeln(categoryName(roomCategories[i].cat))
  }
 }
```

```
           document.writeln('</SELECT>')
           document.write(' <INPUT type="BUTTON" ')
           document.write('value="Select Product Type" ')
           document.writeln('onClick="selectProductType()">')
           document.writeln(' <B><I>The XYZ Company Catalog</B></I>')
           document.writeln('</P>')
         }
         function displayProducts() {
          document.write('<P>')
          document.write('Products: ')
          document.writeln('<SELECT name="productField">')
          for(var i=0;i<prod.length;++i) {
           if(room==prod[i].room) {
            if(cat==prod[i].category) {
             document.write('<OPTION VALUE="')
              document.write(i+'">')
             document.writeln(prod[i].name)
            }
           }
          }
          document.writeln('</SELECT>')
          document.write(' <INPUT type="BUTTON" ')
          document.write('value="Select Product" ')
          document.writeln('onClick="selectProduct()">')
          document.writeln('</P>')
         }
         function displayCatList() {
          document.write('<P>')
          document.write('Types of products: ')
          document.writeln('<SELECT name="catListField">')
          for(var i=0;i<productCategories.length;++i) {
           for(var j=0;j<roomCategories.length;++j) {
            if(productCategories[i]==roomCategories[j].cat) {
             if(cat==productCategories[i])
              document.write('<OPTION SELECTED')
             else document.write('<OPTION')
              var optionValue=roomCategories[j].room
               +productCategories[i]
             document.write(' VALUE="'+optionValue+'">')
             document.write(categoryName(productCategories[i])+" ")
              document.writeln('('+roomName(roomCategories[j].room)+')')
            }
```

```
  }
 }
 document.writeln('</SELECT>')
 document.write(' <INPUT type="BUTTON" ')
 document.write('value="Select Product Type" ')
 document.writeln('onClick="selectProductCat()">')
 document.writeln('</P>')
}
function displayProductsList() {
 document.write('<P>')
 document.write('Products: ')
 document.writeln('<SELECT name="allProductsField">')
 var sortedOptions = new Array(prod.length)
 for(var i=0;i<prod.length;++i) {
  sortedOptions[i]=prod[i].name+" ("
  sortedOptions[i]+=roomName(prod[i].room)+")"
  sortedOptions[i]+="|"+i
 }
 sortedOptions.sort()
 for(var i=0;i<sortedOptions.length;++i){
  document.write('<OPTION VALUE="')
  var parts=sortedOptions[i].split("|")
  document.writeln(parts[1]+'">'+parts[0])
 }
 document.writeln('</SELECT>')
 document.write(' <INPUT type="BUTTON" ')
 document.write('value="Select Product" ')
 document.writeln('onClick="selectFromBigList()">')
 document.writeln('</P>')
}
function altView() {
 var field=window.document.forms[0].viewField
 var ix=field.selectedIndex
 view=field.options[ix].value
 setCookie()
}
function selectRoom() {
 var field=window.document.forms[0].roomField
 var ix=field.selectedIndex
 room=field.options[ix].value
 for(var i=0;i<roomCategories.length;++i) {
  if(room==roomCategories[i].room){
```

```
    cat=roomCategories[i].cat
    break
   }
  }
 setCookie()
}
function selectProductType() {
 var field=window.document.forms[0].catField
 var ix=field.selectedIndex
 cat=field.options[ix].value
 setCookie()
}
function selectProduct() {
 var field=window.document.forms[0].productField
 var ix=field.selectedIndex
 prodIX=field.options[ix].value
 writeDocument(0,"products/"+prod[prodIX].image)
 writeDocument(1,"products/"+prod[prodIX].desc)
}
function selectProductCat() {
 var field=window.document.forms[0].catListField
 var ix=field.selectedIndex
 var fieldValue=field.options[ix].value
 room=fieldValue.substring(0,2)
 cat=fieldValue.substring(2,4)
 setCookie()
}
function selectFromBigList() {
 var field=window.document.forms[0].allProductsField
 var ix=field.selectedIndex
 prodIX=field.options[ix].value
 writeDocument(0,"products/"+prod[prodIX].image)
 writeDocument(1,"products/"+prod[prodIX].desc)
}
function writeDocument(n,s) {
 var doc=parent.frames[1].frames[n].location = s
}
function setCookie() {
 var newCookie = "room="+room
 window.document.cookie=newCookie
 newCookie = "cat="+cat
 window.document.cookie=newCookie
```

```
    newCookie = "view="+view
    window.document.cookie=newCookie
    window.location="catform2.htm"
}
// -></SCRIPT>
</HEAD>
<BODY bgColor="white">
<SCRIPT LANGUAGE="JavaScript"><!-
displayCatalogForm()
// -></SCRIPT>
</BODY>
</HTML>
```

Adding Multimedia Features

When you put your catalog online you want to make it interesting for the user to browse. One way that you can do that is to add multimedia features to your catalogs. High-quality graphics are a must. In addition, you can add audio and video.

TIP   Because audio and video can be time-consuming to access over the Internet, especially for users with low-bandwidth lines, it's a good idea to implement controls that allow users to specify whether or not they want to wait for audio and video files to be loaded.

It is easy to add audio support to the product catalog developed in earlier sections of this chapter. After downloading `catalog3.htm` from this book's page on the Sybex Web site, open it and select any product. The audio confirmation dialog box displayed in Figure 13.5 is displayed. Click OK and an audio file is played using your browser's audio player (see Figure 13.6).

Only a few small changes are needed to support audio product descriptions. The `catalog3.htm` (Listing 13.8) file is used to reference the `catform3.htm` (Listing 13.9) file, which updates `catform2.htm` by including a reference to `playSound()` in the `selectFromBigList()` and `selectProduct()` functions. The `playSound()` function displays the confirmation dialog box, and upon positive user confirmation, loads the appropriate file. This file is then played by your audio player. The audio file is identified in the updated **Product** object constructor shown in Listing 13.10. The **Product** constructor creates a sound property for each product.

FIGURE 13.5:

The audio confirmation dialog box (Listing 13.9)

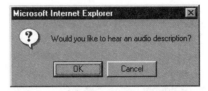

FIGURE 13.6:

The Windows media player

Listing 13.8	The Multimedia Catalog's Top-Level Frame Set (catalog3.htm)

```
<HTML>
<HEAD>
<TITLE>XYZ Company Catalog</TITLE>
</HEAD>
<FRAMESET ROWS="235,*" BORDER="10">
<FRAME SRC="catform3.htm">
<FRAME SRC="products.htm">
</FRAMESET>
</HTML>
```

Listing 13.9	The Catalog Form Updated to Support Audio Files (catform3.htm)

```
<HTML>
<HEAD>
<TITLE>XYZ Company Catalog</TITLE>
<SCRIPT LANGUAGE="JavaScript" SRC="product3.js"><!-
// -></SCRIPT>
```

```
<SCRIPT LANGUAGE="JavaScript" SRC="cookie.js"><!-
// -></SCRIPT>
<SCRIPT LANGUAGE="JavaScript"><!-
function displayCatalogForm() {
 readCookie()
 if(view=="byRoom") displayByRoom()
 else if(view=="byCat") displayByCat()
 else displayByProduct()
}
function readCookie() {
 var cookie=document.cookie
 room="li"
 cat="fu"
 view="byRoom"
 if(nameDefined(cookie,"room"))
  room=getCookieValue(cookie,"room")
 if(nameDefined(cookie,"cat"))
  cat=getCookieValue(cookie,"cat")
 if(nameDefined(cookie,"view"))
  view=getCookieValue(cookie,"view")
}
function displayByRoom() {
 document.writeln('<FORM>')
 displayAltView()
 displayRooms()
 displayCategories()
 displayProducts()
 document.writeln('</FORM>')
}
function displayByCat() {
 document.writeln('<FORM>')
 displayAltView()
 displayCatList()
 displayProducts()
 document.writeln('</FORM>')
}
function displayByProduct() {
 document.writeln('<FORM>')
 displayAltView()
 displayProductsList()
 document.writeln('</FORM>')
}
```

```
function displayAltView() {
 document.write('<P>')
 document.write('Catalog view: ')
 document.writeln('<SELECT name="viewField">')
 document.write('<OPTION VALUE="byRoom" SELECTED>By room')
 document.write('<OPTION VALUE="byCat">By product category')
 document.write('<OPTION VALUE="byProd">Alphabetical by product')
 document.writeln('</SELECT>')
 document.write(' <INPUT type="BUTTON" ')
 document.write('value="Select View Preference" ')
 document.writeln('onClick="altView()">')
 document.writeln('</P>')
}
function displayRooms() {
 document.write('<P>')
 document.write('Room: ')
 document.writeln('<SELECT name="roomField">')
 for(var i=0;i<rooms.length;++i) {
  if(room==rooms[i]){
   document.write('<OPTION SELECTED')
  }else document.write('<OPTION')
  document.write(' VALUE="'+rooms[i]+'">')
  document.writeln(roomName(rooms[i]))
 }
 document.writeln('</SELECT>')
 document.write(' <INPUT type="BUTTON" value="Select Room" ')
 document.writeln('onClick="selectRoom()">')
 document.writeln('</P>')
}
function displayCategories() {
 document.write('<P>')
 document.write('Types of products: ')
 document.writeln('<SELECT name="catField">')
 for(var i=0;i<roomCategories.length;++i) {
  if(room==roomCategories[i].room) {
   if(cat==roomCategories[i].cat)
    document.write('<OPTION SELECTED')
   else document.write('<OPTION')
   document.write(' VALUE="'+roomCategories[i].cat+'">')
   document.writeln(categoryName(roomCategories[i].cat))
  }
 }
 document.writeln('</SELECT>')
```

```
document.write(' <INPUT type="BUTTON" ')
document.write('value="Select Product Type" ')
document.writeln('onClick="selectProductType()">')
document.writeln(' <B><I>The XYZ Company Catalog</B></I>')
document.writeln('</P>')
}
function displayProducts() {
document.write('<P>')
document.write('Products: ')
document.writeln('<SELECT name="productField">')
for(var i=0;i<prod.length;++i) {
 if(room==prod[i].room) {
  if(cat==prod[i].category) {
   document.write('<OPTION VALUE="')
    document.write(i+'">')
   document.writeln(prod[i].name)
  }
 }
}
document.writeln('</SELECT>')
document.write(' <INPUT type="BUTTON" ')
document.write('value="Select Product" ')
document.writeln('onClick="selectProduct()">')
document.writeln('</P>')
}
function displayCatList() {
document.write('<P>')
document.write('Types of products: ')
document.writeln('<SELECT name="catListField">')
for(var i=0;i<productCategories.length;++i) {
 for(var j=0;j<roomCategories.length;++j) {
  if(productCategories[i]==roomCategories[j].cat) {
   if(cat==productCategories[i])
    document.write('<OPTION SELECTED')
   else document.write('<OPTION')
    var optionValue=roomCategories[j].room
     +productCategories[i]
   document.write(' VALUE="'+optionValue+'">')
   document.write(categoryName(productCategories[i])+" ")
    document.writeln('('+roomName(roomCategories[j].room)+')')
  }
 }
}
```

```
document.writeln('</SELECT>')
document.write(' <INPUT type="BUTTON" ')
document.write('value="Select Product Type" ')
document.writeln('onClick="selectProductCat()">')
document.writeln('</P>')
}
function displayProductsList() {
document.write('<P>')
document.write('Products: ')
document.writeln('<SELECT name="allProductsField">')
var sortedOptions = new Array(prod.length)
for(var i=0;i<prod.length;++i) {
 sortedOptions[i]=prod[i].name+" ("
 sortedOptions[i]+=roomName(prod[i].room)+")"
 sortedOptions[i]+="|"+i
}
sortedOptions.sort()
for(var i=0;i<sortedOptions.length;++i){
 document.write('<OPTION VALUE="')
 var parts=sortedOptions[i].split("|")
 document.writeln(parts[1]+'">'+parts[0])
}
document.writeln('</SELECT>')
document.write(' <INPUT type="BUTTON" ')
document.write('value="Select Product" ')
document.writeln('onClick="selectFromBigList()">')
document.writeln('</P>')
}
function altView() {
var field=window.document.forms[0].viewField
var ix=field.selectedIndex
view=field.options[ix].value
setCookie()
}
function selectRoom() {
var field=window.document.forms[0].roomField
var ix=field.selectedIndex
room=field.options[ix].value
for(var i=0;i<roomCategories.length;++i) {
 if(room==roomCategories[i].room){
  cat=roomCategories[i].cat
  break
 }
```

```
 }
 setCookie()
}
function selectProductType() {
 var field=window.document.forms[0].catField
 var ix=field.selectedIndex
 cat=field.options[ix].value
 setCookie()
}
function selectProduct() {
 var field=window.document.forms[0].productField
 var ix=field.selectedIndex
 prodIX=field.options[ix].value
 writeDocument(0,"products/"+prod[prodIX].image)
 writeDocument(1,"products/"+prod[prodIX].desc)
 playSound("products/"+prod[prodIX].sound)
}
function selectProductCat() {
 var field=window.document.forms[0].catListField
 var ix=field.selectedIndex
 var fieldValue=field.options[ix].value
 room=fieldValue.substring(0,2)
 cat=fieldValue.substring(2,4)
 setCookie()
}
function selectFromBigList() {
 var field=window.document.forms[0].allProductsField
 var ix=field.selectedIndex
 prodIX=field.options[ix].value
 writeDocument(0,"products/"+prod[prodIX].image)
 writeDocument(1,"products/"+prod[prodIX].desc)
 playSound("products/"+prod[prodIX].sound)
}
function playSound(s) {
 var q="Would you like to hear an audio description?"
 if(confirm(q)){
  window.location.href=s
 }
}
function writeDocument(n,s) {
 var doc=parent.frames[1].frames[n].location = s
}
function setCookie() {
```

```
var newCookie = "room="+room
window.document.cookie=newCookie
newCookie = "cat="+cat
window.document.cookie=newCookie
newCookie = "view="+view
window.document.cookie=newCookie
window.location="catform3.htm"
}
// -></SCRIPT>
</HEAD>
<BODY bgColor="white">
<SCRIPT LANGUAGE="JavaScript"><!-
displayCatalogForm()
// -></SCRIPT>
</BODY>
</HTML>
```

Listing 13.10   **The Updated *Product* Object (product3.js)**

```
rooms = new Array("li","di","be","ki","ba")
function roomName(room) {
 if(room=="li") return "Living Room"
 if(room=="di") return "Dining Room"
 if(room=="be") return "Bed Room"
 if(room=="ki") return "Kitchen"
 if(room=="ba") return "Bath Room"
 return "Unknown"
}
productCategories = new Array("fu","ca","li","el","ac",
 "ap","cb","si","to","ba")
function categoryName(cat) {
 if(cat=="fu") return "Furniture"
 if(cat=="ca") return "Carpeting"
 if(cat=="li") return "Lighting"
 if(cat=="el") return "Electronics"
 if(cat=="ac") return "Accessories"
 if(cat=="ap") return "Appliances"
 if(cat=="cb") return "Cabinets"
 if(cat=="si") return "Sinks"
 if(cat=="to") return "Toilets"
 if(cat=="ba") return "Bath and Shower"
 return "Unknown"
```

```
}
function Product(id,name,category,room)   {
 this.id=id
 this.name=name
 this.category=category
 this.room=room
 this.image="i"+id+".jpg"
 this.desc="d"+id+".htm"
 this.sound="a"+id+".wav"
}
function roomProductCategory(room,cat) {
 this.room=room
 this.cat=cat
}
var i=0
roomCategories = new Array()
roomCategories[i] = new roomProductCategory("li","fu"); ++i
roomCategories[i] = new roomProductCategory("li","ca"); ++i
roomCategories[i] = new roomProductCategory("li","li"); ++i
roomCategories[i] = new roomProductCategory("li","el"); ++i
roomCategories[i] = new roomProductCategory("li","ac"); ++i
roomCategories[i] = new roomProductCategory("di","fu"); ++i
roomCategories[i] = new roomProductCategory("di","ca"); ++i
roomCategories[i] = new roomProductCategory("di","li"); ++i
roomCategories[i] = new roomProductCategory("di","ac"); ++i
roomCategories[i] = new roomProductCategory("be","fu"); ++i
roomCategories[i] = new roomProductCategory("be","ca"); ++i
roomCategories[i] = new roomProductCategory("be","li"); ++i
roomCategories[i] = new roomProductCategory("be","el"); ++i
roomCategories[i] = new roomProductCategory("be","ac"); ++i
roomCategories[i] = new roomProductCategory("ki","ap"); ++i
roomCategories[i] = new roomProductCategory("ki","cb"); ++i
roomCategories[i] = new roomProductCategory("ki","li"); ++i
roomCategories[i] = new roomProductCategory("ki","ac"); ++i
roomCategories[i] = new roomProductCategory("ba","si"); ++i
roomCategories[i] = new roomProductCategory("ba","to"); ++i
roomCategories[i] = new roomProductCategory("ba","li"); ++i
roomCategories[i] = new roomProductCategory("ba","ba"); ++i
roomCategories[i] = new roomProductCategory("ba","ac"); ++i
var i=0
prod=new Array()
//Living room products
prod[i]=new Product(i,"Couch","fu","li"); ++i
```

```
prod[i]=new Product(i,"Sofa","fu","li"); ++i
prod[i]=new Product(i,"Arm chair","fu","li"); ++i
prod[i]=new Product(i,"Long table","fu","li"); ++i
prod[i]=new Product(i,"Side table","fu","li"); ++i
prod[i]=new Product(i,"Persian rug","ca","li"); ++i
prod[i]=new Product(i,"Cheap rug","ca","li"); ++i
prod[i]=new Product(i,"Ceiling light","li","li"); ++i
prod[i]=new Product(i,"Floor light","li","li"); ++i
prod[i]=new Product(i,"Table light","li","li"); ++i
prod[i]=new Product(i,"Big TV","el","li"); ++i
prod[i]=new Product(i,"Small TV","el","li"); ++i
prod[i]=new Product(i,"Entertainment Center","el","li"); ++i
prod[i]=new Product(i,"Stereo","el","li"); ++i
prod[i]=new Product(i,"Large painting","ac","li"); ++i
prod[i]=new Product(i,"Small painting","ac","li"); ++i
prod[i]=new Product(i,"Large fake plant","ac","li"); ++i
prod[i]=new Product(i,"Small fake plant","ac","li"); ++i
prod[i]=new Product(i,"Expensive knick knack","ac","li"); ++i
prod[i]=new Product(i,"Cheap knick knack","ac","li"); ++i
//Dining room products
prod[i]=new Product(i,"Expensive dining set","fu","di"); ++i
prod[i]=new Product(i,"Cheap dining set","fu","di"); ++i
prod[i]=new Product(i,"China cabinet","fu","di"); ++i
prod[i]=new Product(i,"Serving table","fu","di"); ++i
prod[i]=new Product(i,"Stain-proof rug","ca","di"); ++i
prod[i]=new Product(i,"Plastic floor covering","ca","di"); ++i
prod[i]=new Product(i,"Chandalier","li","di"); ++i
prod[i]=new Product(i,"Ceiling lamp","li","di"); ++i
prod[i]=new Product(i,"China set","ac","di"); ++i
prod[i]=new Product(i,"Silver set","ac","di"); ++i
//Bed room products
prod[i]=new Product(i,"King bed","fu","be"); ++i
prod[i]=new Product(i,"Queen bed","fu","be"); ++i
prod[i]=new Product(i,"Single bed","fu","be"); ++i
prod[i]=new Product(i,"End table","fu","be"); ++i
prod[i]=new Product(i,"Dresser","fu","be"); ++i
prod[i]=new Product(i,"Lamb skin carpet","ca","be"); ++i
prod[i]=new Product(i,"Bear skin carpet","ca","be"); ++i
prod[i]=new Product(i,"Ceiling lamp","li","be"); ++i
prod[i]=new Product(i,"Table lamp","li","be"); ++i
prod[i]=new Product(i,"Clock Radio","el","be"); ++i
prod[i]=new Product(i,"Electronic head board","el","be"); ++i
prod[i]=new Product(i,"Pillow set","ac","be"); ++i
```

```
prod[i]=new Product(i,"Linen set","ac","be"); ++i
prod[i]=new Product(i,"Bed spread","ac","be"); ++i
//Kitchen products
prod[i]=new Product(i,"Refrigerator","ap","ki"); ++i
prod[i]=new Product(i,"Stove - oven","ap","ki"); ++i
prod[i]=new Product(i,"Microwave oven","ap","ki"); ++i
prod[i]=new Product(i,"Toaster","ap","ki"); ++i
prod[i]=new Product(i,"Coffee maker","ap","ki"); ++i
prod[i]=new Product(i,"Dish washer","ap","ki"); ++i
prod[i]=new Product(i,"Deluxe cabinets","cb","ki"); ++i
prod[i]=new Product(i,"Standard cabinets","cb","ki"); ++i
prod[i]=new Product(i,"Deluxe counter","cb","ki"); ++i
prod[i]=new Product(i,"Standard counter","cb","ki"); ++i
prod[i]=new Product(i,"Ceiling light","li","ki"); ++i
prod[i]=new Product(i,"Counter light","li","ki"); ++i
prod[i]=new Product(i,"Cookware","ac","ki"); ++i
prod[i]=new Product(i,"Storage containers","ac","ki"); ++i
prod[i]=new Product(i,"Wall clock","ac","ki"); ++i
//Bath room products
prod[i]=new Product(i,"Deluxe sink","si","ba"); ++i
prod[i]=new Product(i,"Standard sink","si","ba"); ++i
prod[i]=new Product(i,"Deluxe toilet","to","ba"); ++i
prod[i]=new Product(i,"Standard toilet","to","ba"); ++i
prod[i]=new Product(i,"Ceiling light","li","ba"); ++i
prod[i]=new Product(i,"Wall light","li","ba"); ++i
prod[i]=new Product(i,"Deluxe bath tub","ba","ba"); ++i
prod[i]=new Product(i,"Standard bath tub","ba","ba"); ++i
prod[i]=new Product(i,"Shower stall","ba","ba"); ++i
prod[i]=new Product(i,"Wall cabinet","ac","ba"); ++i
prod[i]=new Product(i,"Towel rack","ac","ba"); ++i
prod[i]=new Product(i,"Towels","ac","ba"); ++i
```

Summary

In this chapter, you learned how to use JavaScript to create a variety of catalogs. You learned how to develop catalogs without the need for CGI programs. You also learned to tailor your catalogs based on user preferences and to add multimedia features to your catalogs. In the next chapter, you'll learn how to use JavaScript to implement custom site searches and navigation aids.

CHAPTER

FOURTEEN

14

Developing Search Tools

- Search Forms

- Search Engines

- Connecting Search Forms to Search Engines

- Creating Local Search Engines

Some of the most frequently visited Web sites are those that help you to find other Web pages. AltaVista, Yahoo, Infoseek, and Lycos are some of the many popular search sites. In addition, many large sites, such as Microsoft's and CNN's, provide site-specific search capabilities.

JavaScript makes implementing search capabilities in your Web pages easy. You can use JavaScript to develop a full-featured search interface to connect to existing search engines, or to implement your own browser-based search scripts.

In this chapter, you'll learn to integrate search capabilities into your Web pages. You'll learn to use JavaScript to write interfaces to search engines and to implement local search capabilities. When you finish this chapter, you'll be able to incorporate advanced search features into your Web pages.

Search Forms

Search forms are used to gather search information from a user and forward it to one or more search engines. The search engines then perform the search and forward the search results back to the user. Because the search form is what the user sees when he or she performs the search, it is important to provide an interface that is flexible, efficient, and easy to use.

JavaScript-based search forms have a major advantage over those that are implemented in HTML alone—they allow form-related events to be handled locally. This lets you develop forms that can dynamically adapt to entries the user may have made previously. These dynamic forms help users to specify search criteria more easily and efficiently. Dynamic search forms can also be used to present a more flexible and intuitive interface to the user. They can also be used to validate form data and provide users with suggestions on how to enter data correctly.

NOTE   In this chapter, I've provided three different search engines for different purposes. For each example in the chapter, I'll instruct you to rename `engines1.htm`, `engines2.htm`, or `engines3.htm` to simply `engines.htm` in order to run the appropriate search engine in the particular example being discussed. Go ahead and rename `engines1.htm` to `engines.htm` before running the first example.

To get a better feel for how JavaScript can be used to enhance a search interface, consider the search form shown in Figure 14.1. This form allows you to select a particular Web technology area of interest and then a specific topic within that area. Download this chapter's code from this book's page on the Sybex Web site. Then open the file search.htm (Listing 14.1) with your browser to see how this form works.

FIGURE 14.1:

The search form opening display (Listings 14.1 through 14.3)

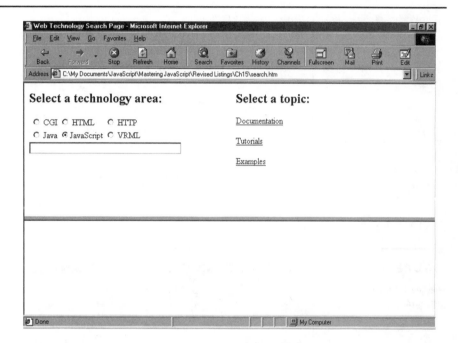

When you click a Select a Technology Area radio button, the list of topic links to the right changes to reflect the area you selected. For this example, click the HTTP technology area and the list of topics is updated with links that are specific to HTTP—Specification, Security, and Versions—as shown in Figure 14.2. Click the Security link; a Web search engine form is displayed, as shown in Figure 14.3. Note that the area and topic the user selected—in this case HTTP security—are automatically inserted into the search text field. Forms such as the ones shown in this example make it much easier for the user to formulate a search query. Later in this chapter, in "Connecting Search Forms to Search Engines," you'll learn how to connect this form to a search engine.

FIGURE 14.2:

Selecting a technology area
(Listings 14.1 through 14.3)

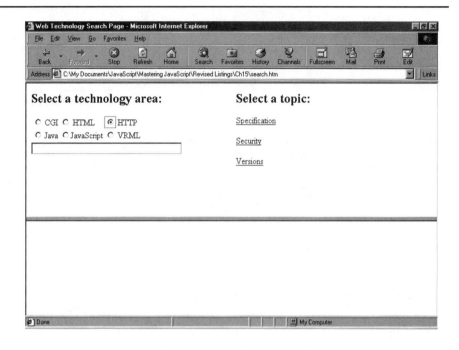

FIGURE 14.3:

Selecting a search engine
(Listing 14.4)

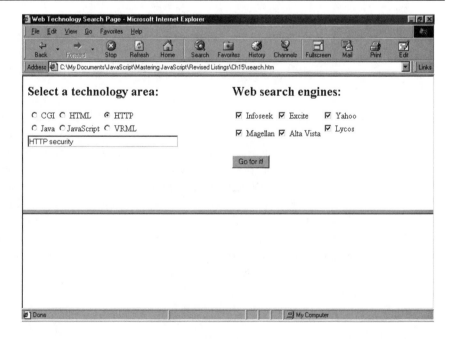

Listing 14.1 contains the search.htm file. This file sets up a two-frame set with sform.htm (Listing 14.2) loaded into the top frame. Listing 14.2 shows that sform.htm breaks the top frame into two columns, with topic.htm loaded into the left frame. The topic.htm file is shown in Listing 5.3.

Listing 14.1   The Search Form's Top-Level Frame Set (search.htm)

```
<HTML>
<HEAD>
<TITLE>Web Technology Search Page</TITLE>
</HEAD>
<FRAMESET ROWS="250,*" BORDER="10">
<FRAME SRC="sform.htm">
<FRAME SRC="blank.htm">
</FRAMESET>
</HTML>
```

Listing 14.2   The Search Form's Second-Level Frame Set (sform.htm)

```
<HTML>
<HEAD>
<TITLE>Web Technology Search Page</TITLE>
</HEAD>
<FRAMESET COLS="*,*" BORDER="0">
<FRAME SRC="topic.htm">
<FRAME SRC="blank.htm">
</FRAMESET>
</HTML>
```

The topic.htm file implements the search form. It creates the radio button form shown in the upper-left frame of Figure 14.1 and implements the following functions and arrays.

The *Topic()* Function

This function is the constructor of the search's Topic object. A Topic object consists of a topic title and a string of keywords to search for that are related to this topic.

The *topics* Array

The topics array is an array of the arrays of all topics supported for each technology area. For example, topics[0] identifies the topics related to the CGI area, topics[1] identifies the topics related to HTML, and so on.

The *processArea()* Function

This function determines which technology area radio button is checked and invokes displayTopics() to display the topics related to the technology area.

The *displayTopics()* Function

This function creates the document shown in the upper-right frame of the window. It creates a link for each topic in the topics array related to the technology area. The engines.htm file is the destination of each link. The setSearch() function is the onClick event handler for each link. The setSearch() function displays the link's search string in the text field of the frame located in the upper left of the window.

Listing 14.3   **Implementing the Search Form (topic.htm)**

```
<HTML>
<HEAD>
<TITLE>Web Technologies Search Form</TITLE>
<SCRIPT LANGUAGE="JavaScript"><!-
function Topic(desc,search) {
 this.desc=desc
 this.search=search
}
topics = new Array()
topics[0] = new Array(
 new Topic("Tutorials","CGI tutorial"),
 new Topic("Documentation","CGI documentation"),
 new Topic("Examples","CGI example"),
 new Topic("Using cookies","CGI cookies")
)
topics[1] = new Array(
 new Topic("HTML 2.0","HTML 2.0"),
 new Topic("HTML 3.0","HTML 3.0"),
```

```
  new Topic("HTML 3.2","HTML 3.2"),
  new Topic("Extensions","HTML extensions"),
  new Topic("Tutorials","HTML tutorial")
)
topics[2] = new Array(
  new Topic("Specification","HTTP specification"),
  new Topic("Security","HTTP security"),
  new Topic("Versions","HTTP version")
)
topics[3] = new Array(
  new Topic("Documentation","Java documentation"),
  new Topic("Tutorials","Java tutorial"),
  new Topic("Examples","Java example"),
  new Topic("Shareware","Java shareware")
)
topics[4] = new Array(
  new Topic("Documentation","JavaScript documentation"),
  new Topic("Tutorials","JavaScript tutorial"),
  new Topic("Examples","JavaScript example")
)
topics[5] = new Array(
  new Topic("Documentation","VRML documentation"),
  new Topic("Tutorials","VRML tutorial"),
  new Topic("Examples","VRML example"),
  new Topic("Web sites","VRML sites")
)
function processArea() {
 var thisForm=window.document.forms[0]
 var elements=thisForm.elements
 for(var i=0;i<topics.length;++i) {
  if(elements[i].checked) displayTopics(i)
 }
}
function displayTopics(n) {
 var doc=parent.frames[1].document
 doc.open()
 doc.writeln('<HTML>')
 doc.writeln('<HEAD>')
 doc.writeln('<SCRIPT LANGUAGE="JavaScript">')
 doc.writeln('function setSearch(s) {')
 doc.writeln('text=parent.frames[0].document.forms[0].srch')
 doc.writeln('text.value=s')
```

```
doc.writeln('}')
doc.writeln('</SCRIPT>')
doc.writeln('</HEAD>')
doc.writeln('<BODY BGCOLOR="white">')
doc.writeln('<H2>Select a topic:</H2>')
for(var i=0;i<topics[n].length;++i) {
 doc.writeln('<P><A HREF="engines.htm" ')
 doc.writeln('onClick="setSearch(\''
  +topics[n][i].search+'\')">')
 doc.writeln(topics[n][i].desc+'</A></P>')
 }
 doc.writeln('</BODY>')
 doc.writeln('</HTML>')
 doc.close()
}
// -></SCRIPT>
</HEAD>
<BODY BGCOLOR="white">
<FORM>
<H2>Select a technology area:</H2>
<TABLE>
<TR><TD><P>
<INPUT TYPE="RADIO" NAME="area" VALUE="cgi"
 onClick="processArea()"> CGI</P></TD>
<TD><P>
<INPUT TYPE="RADIO" NAME="area" VALUE="html"
 onClick="processArea()"> HTML</P></TD>
<TD><P>
<INPUT TYPE="RADIO" NAME="area" VALUE="http"
 onClick="processArea()"> HTTP</P></TD>
</TR>
<TR><TD><P>
<INPUT TYPE="RADIO" NAME="area" VALUE="java"
 onClick="processArea()"> Java</P></TD>
<TD><P>
<INPUT TYPE="RADIO" NAME="area" VALUE="javascript"
 CHECKED="CHECKED" onClick="processArea()">JavaScript</P>
<TD><P>
<INPUT TYPE="RADIO" NAME="area" VALUE="vrml"
 onClick="processArea()"> VRML</P></TD>
</TR>
</TABLE>
```

```
<INPUT TYPE="text" NAME="srch" SIZE="40">
</FORM>
<SCRIPT LANGUAGE="JavaScript"><!-
processArea()
// -></SCRIPT>
</BODY>
</HTML>
```

Search Engines

Search engines are programs (usually CGI scripts) that perform a search and generate search results. They commonly use one or more databases to keep track of a large collection of URLs for Web pages, and the keywords the pages contain. JavaScript scripts can make use of and enhance the capabilities provided by these CGI-based search engines. The following sections show how to design a JavaScript-based search page and how to connect your scripts to available search engines.

The First Search Engine

The `engines1.htm` file (see Listing 14.4) is the first of three search "engines" that you'll be creating in the examples in this chapter. You must rename this file `engines.htm` for it to be used with the current version of our search form. This file is not in itself a search engine—in fact, this version doesn't actually perform any searching at all. Instead, it displays a handful of popular and freely available Web search engines, shown in the upper-right frame of Figure 14.3. It also handles the `onClick` event of the Go for It! button using the `goSearch()` function (which is a function stub that will be implemented in `engines2.htm` and `engines3.htm`, search engines that are introduced in later sections of this chapter). These search engines are introduced in the sections "The Second Search Engine" and "The Third Search Engine."

NOTE The file `engines1.htm` that we're using in this example will be the basis of the other two engines that we develop later in the chapter; `engines2.htm` will make use of the six Web search engines listed in this example to perform actual searching, and `engines3.htm` will be adapted for use as a local search engine.

Listing 14.4   **Selecting a Search Engine (engines1.htm)**

```
<HTML>
<HEAD>
<TITLE>Web Search Engines</TITLE>
<SCRIPT LANGUAGE="JavaScript"><!-
function goSearch() {
 doc = top.frames[1].document
 doc.write("<H2>This function is implemented in ")
 doc.write("<CODE>engines2.htm</CODE> and ")
 doc.writeln("<CODE>engines3.htm</CODE>.</H2>")
}
// -></SCRIPT>
</HEAD>
<BODY BGCOLOR="white">
<H2>Web search engines:</H2>
<FORM>
<TABLE>
<TR>
<TD><INPUT TYPE="CHECKBOX" CHECKED NAME="infoseek"> Infoseek
</TD>
<TD><INPUT TYPE="CHECKBOX" CHECKED NAME="excite"> Excite
</TD>
<TD><INPUT TYPE="CHECKBOX" CHECKED NAME="yahoo"> Yahoo
</TD>
</TR>
<TR>
<TD><INPUT TYPE="CHECKBOX" CHECKED NAME="magellan"> Magellan
</TD>
<TD><INPUT TYPE="CHECKBOX" CHECKED NAME="altaVista"> Alta Vista
</TD>
<TD><INPUT TYPE="CHECKBOX" CHECKED NAME="lycos"> Lycos</P>
</TD>
</TR>
</TABLE>
<P><INPUT TYPE="BUTTON" VALUE="Go for it!"
 onClick="goSearch()"></P>
</FORM>
</BODY>
</HTML>
```

Connecting Search Forms to Search Engines

In order to perform a search, you must pass the search criteria gathered from the user (via the search form) to the CGI program implementing the search engine. This search criteria is generally passed in the form of a *query string*.

A query string passes data to a CGI program via the URL used to access the CGI program. It consists of a question mark (?) followed by the data to be passed. For example, the following URL passes the string *This is a test* to my echo-query.cgi CGI program:

```
http://www.jaworski.com/cgi-bin/echo-query.cgi?This+is+a+test
```

You may have noticed in the above URL that spaces are encoded with plus signs (+) when they are passed via query strings. Other codings are used to pass special characters and binary data as described in RFC 1738, "Uniform Resource Locators (URL)." This RFC is available at http://nic.mil/ftp/rfc/rfc1738.txt. The coding of form data is covered in the HTML 4 specification (http://www.w3.org/TR/REC-html40/html40.txt).

Listing 14.5 shows how search data can be passed to more than one search engine at the same time. It builds upon the first example shown in this chapter by adding the JavaScript necessary to implement the goSearch() function. First, you must rename engines2.htm as engines.htm (in order to install that file as the new search engine for the search form introduced in the previous section). Then open search.htm with your browser. Finally, make sure that you are connected to the Internet, because the engines2.htm file contains links to connect your search form to popular online search engines.

For this example, click the VRML radio button and then on the Examples link. The Web Search Engines form appears in the upper-right frame. Click the Go for It! button to perform a search for the string "VRML example" using all of the six major search engines. The search results produced by these engines are provided in six separate frames at the bottom of the window (refer to Figure 14.4). You can click the links in each of these frames to find more information on VRML examples. Wouldn't it be impressive to provide the same search capabilities in your Web pages?

Figure 14.5 shows the results of a search that uses only four search engines. Figure 14.6 shows the results of a single engine search.

FIGURE 14.4:

Using all six search engines at once (Listing 14.5)

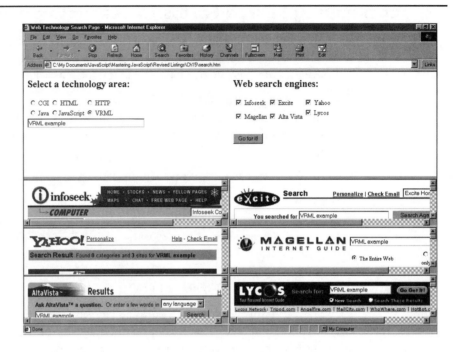

FIGURE 14.5:

Using four search engines (Listing 14.5)

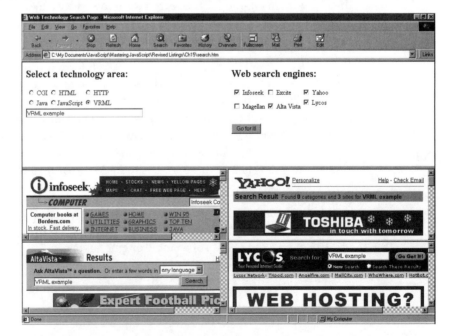

FIGURE 14.6:

Using a single search engine (Listing 14.5)

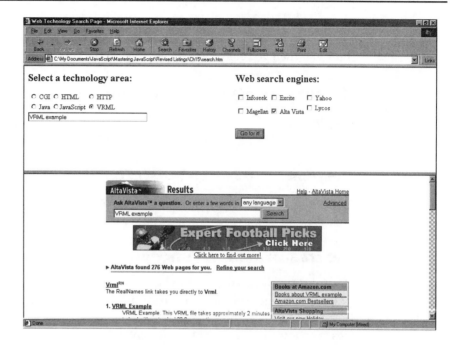

The Second Search Engine

The engines2.htm search engine is more of a transmission than an engine. It takes the search string produced by the search form introduced in the previous section and converts it into a form that can be used with popular Web search engines. It then prompts these engines to perform a search of the search string and displays the results they return in separate frames. The functions implemented by engines2.htm are presented in the following paragraphs.

The *goSearch()* Function

This function handles the onClick event of the Go for It! button and initiates the search. It retrieves the search string contained in the text field of the frame in the upper left corner of the window, and converts it to a URL query string using the convertToQueryString() function. It determines how many search sites the user selected in the Web Search Engines form, creates that many frames to store the query results, and waits two seconds before invoking loadFrames() to load the search results into these frames. The two-second delay is used to make sure that the new frames are created before the search is initiated. I could have also used an onLoad event handler to check for form loading. If you have a low-powered computer then you may wish to increase this delay.

The *convertToQueryString()* Function

This function converts spaces in the search string to plus signs (+) so that the search string can be passed via a query string.

The *numberOfSearchSites()* Function

This function determines how many Web search sites were chosen by the user in the Web search engines form.

The *createFrames()* Function

This function creates the required number of frames to display the search results by loading the appropriate document (from the set of documents named frames2.htm through frames6.htm) into the lower frame of the window. These files are shown in Listings 14.6 through 14.11.

The *loadFrames()* Function

This function uses the loadNextFrame() function to perform the search, and loads the results into the frames created by the createFrames() function. The loadNextFrame() function is passed the frame that the search results should be loaded into; it is also passed the index of the next search site to be considered as a candidate for searching.

The *loadNextFrame()* Function

This function uses a search site to perform a search and stores the results in a designated frame. The frameObj parameter identifies the frame in which the search results should be loaded. The start parameter identifies the index of the next search site to be considered as a candidate for searching. If the check box at the specified index is not checked, then subsequent check boxes are examined for the next search site to be used. This function prepares the URLs necessary to using the Infoseek, Excite, Yahoo, Magellan, AltaVista, and Lycos search engines, and appends the value of the searchString variable to these URLs. The search is initiated by setting the destination frame's location property to the search URL.

NOTE
The URLs of the search engines used in loadNextFrame() were determined by trial and error, playing with the search engines at each search site. The conventions used in these URLs are specific to each site.

Listing 14.5   Connecting to Other Search Engines (engines2.htm)

```html
<HTML>
<HEAD>
<TITLE>Web Search Engines</TITLE>
<SCRIPT LANGUAGE="JavaScript"><!-
function goSearch() {
 searchString=parent.frames[0].document.forms[0].srch.value
 searchString=convertToQueryString(searchString)
 var n=numberOfSearchSites()
 createFrames(n)
 setTimeout("loadFrames("+n+")",2000)
}
function convertToQueryString(s) {
 var result=""
 for(var i=0;i<s.length;++i)
  if(s.charAt(i)==' ') result+="+"
  else result+=s.charAt(i)
 return result
}
function numberOfSearchSites() {
 var result=0
 var elements=window.document.forms[0].elements
 for(var i=0;i<elements.length-1;++i)
  if(elements[i].checked) ++result
 return result
}
function createFrames(n) {
 if(n>1)
  parent.parent.frames[1].location.href="frames"+n+".htm"
}
```

```
function loadFrames(n) {
 var mainFrame=parent.parent.frames[1]
 var newStart
 if(n==1) loadNextFrame(mainFrame,0)
 else if(n==2) {
  newStart=loadNextFrame(mainFrame.frames[0],0)
  loadNextFrame(mainFrame.frames[1],newStart)
 }else if(n==3) {
  newStart=loadNextFrame(mainFrame.frames[0],0)
  newStart=loadNextFrame(mainFrame.frames[1],newStart)
  loadNextFrame(mainFrame.frames[2],newStart)
 }else if(n==4) {
  newStart=loadNextFrame(mainFrame.frames[0].frames[0],0)
  newStart=loadNextFrame(mainFrame.frames[0].frames[1],newStart)
  newStart=loadNextFrame(mainFrame.frames[1].frames[0],newStart)
  loadNextFrame(mainFrame.frames[1].frames[1],newStart)
 }else if(n==5) {
  newStart=loadNextFrame(mainFrame.frames[0].frames[0],0)
  newStart=loadNextFrame(mainFrame.frames[0].frames[1],newStart)
  newStart=loadNextFrame(mainFrame.frames[1].frames[0],newStart)
  newStart=loadNextFrame(mainFrame.frames[1].frames[1],newStart)
  loadNextFrame(mainFrame.frames[2],newStart)
 }else if(n==6) {
  newStart=loadNextFrame(mainFrame.frames[0].frames[0],0)
  newStart=loadNextFrame(mainFrame.frames[0].frames[1],newStart)
  newStart=loadNextFrame(mainFrame.frames[1].frames[0],newStart)
  newStart=loadNextFrame(mainFrame.frames[1].frames[1],newStart)
  newStart=loadNextFrame(mainFrame.frames[2].frames[0],newStart)
  loadNextFrame(mainFrame.frames[2].frames[1],newStart)
 }
}
function loadNextFrame(frameObj,start) {
 var elements=window.document.forms[0].elements
 for(var i=start;i<elements.length-1;++i) {
  if(elements[i].checked){
   var searchURL="http://"
   if(elements[i].name=="infoseek")
    searchURL+="guide-p.infoseek.com/Titles?qt="
   else if(elements[i].name=="excite")
    searchURL+="www.excite.com/search.gw?search="
   else if(elements[i].name=="yahoo")
    searchURL+="search.yahoo.com/bin/search?p="
```

```
      else if(elements[i].name=="magellan")
       searchURL+="searcher.mckinley.com/searcher.cgi?query="
      else if(elements[i].name=="altaVista"){
       searchURL+="www.altavista.digital.com"
       searchURL+="/cgi-bin/query?pg=q&what=web&fmt=.&q="
      }else if(elements[i].name=="lycos")
       searchURL+="www.lycos.com/cgi-bin/pursuit?query="
      searchURL+=searchString
      frameObj.location.href=searchURL
      return (i+1)
    }
   }
   return start
}
// -></SCRIPT>
</HEAD>
<BODY BGCOLOR="white">
<H2>Web search engines:</H2>
<FORM>
<TABLE>
<TR>
<TD><INPUT TYPE="CHECKBOX" CHECKED NAME="infoseek"> Infoseek
</TD>
<TD><INPUT TYPE="CHECKBOX" CHECKED NAME="excite"> Excite
</TD>
<TD><INPUT TYPE="CHECKBOX" CHECKED NAME="yahoo"> Yahoo
</TD>
</TR>
<TR>
<TD><INPUT TYPE="CHECKBOX" CHECKED NAME="magellan"> Magellan
</TD>
<TD><INPUT TYPE="CHECKBOX" CHECKED NAME="altaVista"> Alta Vista
</TD>
<TD><INPUT TYPE="CHECKBOX" CHECKED NAME="lycos"> Lycos</P>
</TD>
</TR>
</TABLE>
<P><INPUT TYPE="BUTTON" VALUE="Go for it!"
 onClick="goSearch()"></P>
</FORM>
</BODY>
</HTML>
```

The following `frames*.htm` files are used by the `engines2.htm` file to create frames to display the results of the Web search engines. The `double.htm` file splits a frame into a two-column frame set.

Listing 14.6   **Displaying the Results of Two Search Engines (frames2.htm)**

```
<HTML>
<FRAMESET ROWS="*,*" BORDER="5">
<FRAME SRC="blank.htm">
<FRAME SRC="blank.htm">
</FRAMESET>
</HTML>
```

Listing 14.7   **Displaying the Results of Three Search Engines (frames3.htm)**

```
<HTML>
<FRAMESET ROWS="*,*,*" BORDER="5">
<FRAME SRC="blank.htm">
<FRAME SRC="blank.htm">
<FRAME SRC="blank.htm">
</FRAMESET>
</HTML>
```

Listing 14.8   **Displaying the Results of Four Search Engines (frames4.htm)**

```
<HTML>
<FRAMESET ROWS="*,*" BORDER="5">
<FRAME SRC="double.htm">
<FRAME SRC="double.htm">
</FRAMESET>
</HTML>
```

Listing 14.9   Displaying the Results of Five Search Engines (frames5.htm)

```
<HTML>
<FRAMESET ROWS="*,*,*" BORDER="5">
<FRAME SRC="double.htm">
<FRAME SRC="double.htm">
<FRAME SRC="blank.htm">
</FRAMESET>
</HTML>
```

Listing 14.10   Displaying the Results of Six Search Engines (frames6.htm)

```
<HTML>
<FRAMESET ROWS="*,*,*" BORDER="5">
<FRAME SRC="double.htm">
<FRAME SRC="double.htm">
<FRAME SRC="double.htm">
</FRAMESET>
</HTML>
```

Listing 14.11   Creating Two Columns (double.htm)

```
<HTML>
<FRAMESET COLS="*,*" BORDER="5">
<FRAME SRC="blank.htm">
<FRAME SRC="blank.htm">
</FRAMESET>
</HTML>
```

Local Search Engines

A local search engine is one that implements search algorithms on the browser instead of using a server-based CGI program. The main advantage of local search engines is that they take the processing load off of your server and put it on the browser. Their main disadvantage is that they are downloaded to the browser and are therefore limited in the amount of search data that they can contain. Local search engines may be impractical for searching large Web sites, such as those of Microsoft, IBM, and Sun, but they may be the perfect solution for searching the Web sites of small to medium-sized companies. Local search engines may also be combined with server-based search engines to take some of the processing load off the server-based search engines.

Keyword Search Scripts

For small to medium-sized Web sites, simple *keyword search scripts* may be used as local search engines. These scripts present a selection list of terms (keywords) that categorize or describe Web pages that you think may be of interest to the user. The keywords you provide should be categories that you think the page's topics might fall into, or words or phrases that you think users might use to describe the page's content. For example, for a document about server-side Web programming, you might list the keywords *CGI*, *LiveWire*, and *Perl* as categories, and/or *programming*, *client/server*, and so on as descriptions.

The advantages of keyword scripts are that they are small, user-friendly, and easy to develop. Their main disadvantage is that they become unwieldy when the number of keywords used becomes large.

Keyword search scripts can be created in such a way that when the user clicks on a keyword, the URLs for relevant Web pages are displayed. Of course, you can also create a script that first offers topic or category keywords (as you first saw in search.htm at the beginning of the chapter), which would link to more-detailed lists of keywords that are linked to specific URLs. This latter approach is the one we've been building up to throughout the chapter, and is the approach I'll be illustrating with the following listing.

Listing 14.12 provides an example of a local search engine that provides lists of keywords to choose from in various categories and at various levels of focus (for documents of interest to the entire company, to a company division, or to a single department). To run this example, rename engines3.htm to engines.htm to use it with the search form developed in the first section of this chapter. After renaming it, open search.htm and, for this example, try the following keyword searches:

1. Click the Java radio button in the Select a Technology Area frame, then click the Documentation link in the Select a Topic frame.

2. Scroll to the right (if necessary) in the upper panel to see the choices offered by the Search Depth form.

3. Choose the Department button to perform a department-level search, then click the Go for It! button. The search results are shown in Figure 14.7.

FIGURE 14.7:

Searching for documents related to Java at the department level (Listing 14.12)

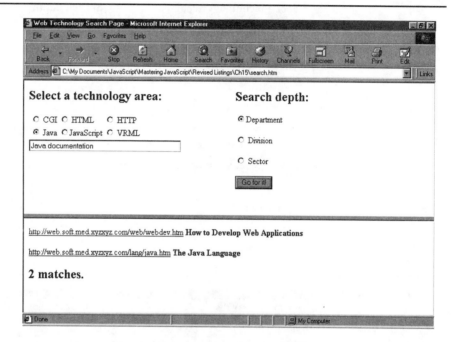

The Search Depth form in this example provides local search capabilities at different levels, in this case at department, division, and sector levels. I chose these levels to reflect the differences in scope you might want to address within a company's organization. In this example, the company is considered to be comprised of sectors, which are made up of divisions, which consist of departments. Documents that are intended for readership at the sector level are for the use of all divisions and departments within the sector. Other documents may be intended for both the division and sector levels, and still others may be of interest only within a department.

When you perform a similar search for JavaScript documentation at the division level, you see the result shown in Figure 14.8. Searching for VRML tutorials at the sector level produces the result shown in Figure 14.9.

FIGURE 14.8:

Searching for documents
relating to JavaScript at the
division level
(Listing 14.12)

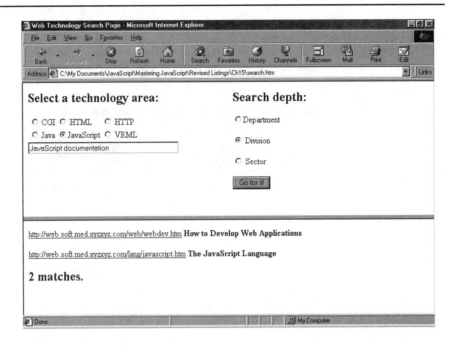

FIGURE 14.9:

Searching for documents
relating to VRML at the sector level (Listing 14.12)

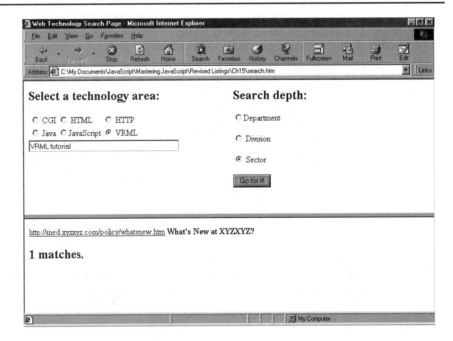

The Third Search Engine

The `engines3.htm` file implements the local search engine using the following functions. Note that the JavaScript code it includes is contained in `db.js`.

The *goSearch()* Function

This function handles the `onClick` event of the Go for It! button and initiates the search. It retrieves the search string contained in the text field of the frame in the upper left corner of the window, and converts it to a URL query string using the `convertToQueryString()` function. It then invokes `performSearch()` to perform the search and `listURLs()` to display the search results.

The *convertToQueryString()* Function

This function converts spaces in the search string to plus signs (+) so that it can be passed via a query string.

The *performSearch()* Function

This function searches the search database for each word in the search string.

The *buildHitList()* Function

This function creates a list of all URLs that are candidates for the search. This `hitList` is implemented as indices into the `deptURLs`, `divURLs`, or `sectURLs` arrays defined in `db.js`. The `scope` variable is set to 0, 1, or 2 by the `onClick` event handlers of the Department, Division, and Sector radio buttons.

The *updateSearch()* Function

This function performs the central search processing. It creates a `mask` array the same size as `hitList`, setting the default search value to `false`. It then finds the search word identified by the `s` variable in the `dictionary` array (defined in `db.js`). It sets the values of the `mask` array to `true` depending on whether the value of `s` is contained in a document in the list of URLs specified by the `scope` variable. Refer to the description of the `db` array (defined in `db.js`) for more information on how this is accomplished. The values of the elements of the `mask` array are then logically *AND*ed with the values of the elements of the `hitList` array to identify which URLs are still search candidates.

The *listURLs()* Function

This function uses the `hitList` array to display the URLs and their descriptions in the lower frame of the window. The `urlSet` variable is assigned the `deptURLs`, `divURLs`, or `sectURLs` array depending upon the value of `scope`. It then uses `urlSet` and the `urlDescs` array to display and describe the URLs that have met the search criteria. The `urlSet` and the `urlDescs` array are defined in `db.js` (Listing 14.13).

Listing 14.12   **A Local Search Engine (engines3.htm)**

```
<HTML>
<HEAD>
<TITLE>Local Search Engine</TITLE>
<SCRIPT LANGUAGE="JavaScript" SRC="db.js"><!-
// -></SCRIPT>
<SCRIPT LANGUAGE="JavaScript"><!-
scope=0
function goSearch() {
 searchString=parent.frames[0].document.forms[0].srch.value
 searchString=convertToQueryString(searchString)
 performSearch()
 listURLs()
}
function convertToQueryString(s) {
 var result=""
 for(var i=0;i<s.length;++i)
  if(s.charAt(i)==' ') result+="+"
  else result+=s.charAt(i)
 return result
}
function performSearch() {
 strings=searchString.split("+")
 buildHitList()
 for(var i=0;i<strings.length;++i)
  updateSearch(strings[i])
}
function buildHitList() {
 if(scope==0) hitList = new Array(deptURLs.length)
 else if(scope==1) hitList = new Array(divURLs.length)
 else if(scope==2) hitList = new Array(sectURLs.length)
 for(var i=0;i<hitList.length;++i) hitList[i]=true
}
```

```
function updateSearch(s) {
 var mask = new Array(hitList.length)
 for(var i=0;i<mask.length;++i) mask[i]=false
 for(var i=0;i<dictionary.length;++i) {
  if(dictionary[i]==s) {
   for(var j=0;j<db[i][scope].length;++j) {
     mask[db[i][scope][j]]=true
   }
  }
 }
 for(var i=0;i<hitList.length;++i)
  hitList[i]=hitList[i] && mask[i]
}
function listURLs() {
 doc=parent.parent.frames[1].document
 doc.open()
 var hitCount=0
 var urlSet = deptURLs
 if(scope==1) urlSet=divURLs
 else if(scope==2) urlSet=sectURLs
 doc.writeln("<HTML><BODY BGCOLOR='white'>")
 for(var i=0;i<hitList.length;++i) {
  if(hitList[i]) {
   ++hitCount
   doc.writeln("<P>"+urlSet[i].link(urlSet[i])+" ")
   doc.writeln("<B>"+urlDescs[scope][i]+"</B></P>")
  }
 }
 doc.writeln("<H2>"+hitCount+" matches.</H2>")
 doc.writeln("</BODY></HTML>")
 doc.close()
}
// -></SCRIPT>
</HEAD>
<BODY BGCOLOR="white">
<H2>Search depth:</H2>
<FORM>
<P><INPUT TYPE="RADIO" CHECKED NAME="depth" VALUE="dept"
 onClick="scope=0">Department
</P><P><INPUT TYPE="RADIO" NAME="depth" VALUE="div"
 onClick="scope=1"> Division
</P><P><INPUT TYPE="RADIO" NAME="depth" VALUE="sect"
```

```
  onClick="scope=2"> Sector
  </P>
  <P><INPUT TYPE="BUTTON" VALUE="Go for it!"
   onClick="goSearch()"></P>
  </FORM>
  </BODY>
  </HTML>
```

The *db.js* file contains the search database used by engines3.htm. It consists of the array described in the following sections.

The *dictionary* Array   This array contains all of the keywords that are supported by the search engine. The list presented here is small. Most search engines would have a list containing between 100 and 1,000 words.

The *deptURLs* Array   This array identifies the department-level URLs that are covered by the search engine. My script lists only a few, for example purposes. A list of hundreds of URLs would be more normal for a real application, and would still be manageable by most local search engines.

The *divURLs* Array   This array identifies the division-level URLs that are covered by the search engine.

The *sectURLs* Array   This array identifies the sector-level URLs that are covered by the search engine.

The *urlDescs* Array   This array provides a description of the department, division, and sector URLs. It is an array of arrays of descriptions that can be indexed by the scope variable (see Listing 14.12, engines3.htm) to provide department, division, or sector URL descriptions.

The *db* Array   This array is the heart of the search database. Each element of db contains information on a specific word in the dictionary array. For example, db[0] contains information pertaining to the keyword *CGI*, db[1] contains information pertaining to the keyword *Tutorial*, and db[18] contains information pertaining to the keyword *Sites*. In addition, every db[n] is itself a three-element array, for it contains the aforementioned information at the department, division, and sector levels, respectively. For example, in the listing below, db[5][0] is an array containing the indices for the HTML keyword for department-level URLs. These URLs are deptURLs[0], deptURLs[1], deptURLs[2], deptURLs[5], deptURLs[6], and deptURLs[8]. Similarly, db[5][1] is an array containing the indices for the HTML keyword for division-level URLs. These URLs are divURLs[0], divURLs[1], divURLs[3], divURLs[4], divURLs[5], and divURLs[6].

> **NOTE**
>
> The elements of the **db** arrays are initialized as strings to avoid ambiguities in the array definitions. For example, `new Array(5)` results in a new array of five elements, and `new Array("5")` results in a new array of one element whose value is `"5"`.

Listing 14.13   The Search Database (db.js)

```
dictionary = new Array(
 "CGI",
 "tutorial",
 "documentation",
 "example",
 "cookies",
 "HTML",
 "2.0",
 "3.0",
 "3.2",
 "extensions",
 "HTTP",
 "specification",
 "security",
 "version",
 "Java",
 "shareware",
 "JavaScript",
 "VRML",
 "sites"
)
deptURLs = new Array(
 "http://web.soft.med.xyzxyz.com/web/webdev.htm",
 "http://web.soft.med.xyzxyz.com/web/webtut.htm",
 "http://web.soft.med.xyzxyz.com/web/examples.htm",
 "http://web.soft.med.xyzxyz.com/spec/http.htm",
 "http://web.soft.med.xyzxyz.com/spec/vrml.htm",
 "http://web.soft.med.xyzxyz.com/lang/java.htm",
 "http://web.soft.med.xyzxyz.com/lang/javascript.htm",
 "http://web.soft.med.xyzxyz.com/lang/vrml.htm",
 "http://web.soft.med.xyzxyz.com/lang/html.htm"
)
```

```
divURLs = new Array(
 "http://soft.med.xyzxyz.com/standards/webpage.htm",
 "http://soft.med.xyzxyz.com/standards/code.htm",
 "http://soft.med.xyzxyz.com/standards/http.htm",
 "http://soft.med.xyzxyz.com/tutorials/html.htm",
 "http://soft.med.xyzxyz.com/tutorials/cgi.htm",
 "http://soft.med.xyzxyz.com/tutorials/java.htm",
 "http://soft.med.xyzxyz.com/tutorials/javascript.htm",
 "http://soft.med.xyzxyz.com/tutorials/vrml.htm"
)
sectURLs = new Array(
 "http://med.xyzxyz.com/policy/web.htm",
 "http://med.xyzxyz.com/policy/whatsnew.htm"
)
urlDescs = new Array(
 new Array(
  "How to Develop Web Applications",
  "A Web Tutorial",
  "Examples of Web Application Development",
  "The HTTP Specification",
  "The VRML Specification",
  "The Java Language",
  "The JavaScript Language",
  "The VRML Language",
  "The HTML Language"
 ),
 new Array(
  "Web Page Design Standards",
  "Coding Standards",
  "The HTTP Specification",
  "An HTML Tutorial",
  "A CGI Tutorial",
  "A Java Tutorial",
  "A JavaScript Tutorial",
  "A VRML Tutorial"
 ),
 new Array(
  "The XYZXYZ Company Web Policy",
  "What's New at XYZXYZ?"
 )
)
```

```
db = new Array(dictionary.length)
db[0]=new Array(
 new Array("0","1","2"),
 new Array("0","1","4"),
 new Array()
)
db[1]=new Array(
 new Array("1"),
 new Array("3","4","5","6","7"),
 new Array("1")
)
db[2]=new Array(
 new Array("0","3","4","5","6","7","8"),
 new Array("0","1","2"),
 new Array("1")
)
db[3]=new Array(
 new Array("2"),
 new Array("3","4","5","6","7"),
 new Array()
)
db[4]=new Array(
 new Array("0","3"),
 new Array("1","2","4"),
 new Array()
)
db[5]=new Array(
 new Array("0","1","2","5","6","8"),
 new Array("0","1","3","4","5","6"),
 new Array("0","1")
)
db[6]=new Array(
 new Array("0","1","2","8"),
 new Array("0","1","3"),
 new Array("0")
)
db[7]=new Array(
 new Array("8"),
 new Array("0"),
 new Array("0")
)
```

```
db[8]=new Array(
 new Array("0","8"),
 new Array("0","3"),
 new Array("0","1")
)
db[9]=new Array(
 new Array("0","1","8"),
 new Array("0","3"),
 new Array("0","1")
)
db[10]=new Array(
 new Array("3"),
 new Array("2"),
 new Array()
)
db[11]=new Array(
 new Array("0","3","4"),
 new Array("0","1","2"),
 new Array()
)
db[12]=new Array(
 new Array(),
 new Array("0","1","2","4"),
 new Array("0","1")
)
db[13]=new Array(
 new Array("3","4"),
 new Array("0","1","2"),
 new Array("0","1")
)
db[14]=new Array(
 new Array("0","1","2","5"),
 new Array("0","1","5"),
 new Array("0","1")
)
db[15]=new Array(
 new Array("2"),
 new Array("4","5"),
 new Array()
)
```

```
db[16]=new Array(
 new Array("0","1","2","6"),
 new Array("0","1","6"),
 new Array("0","1")
)
db[17]=new Array(
 new Array("4","7"),
 new Array("7"),
 new Array("1")
)
db[18]=new Array(
 new Array("7"),
 new Array("7"),
 new Array("1")
)
```

Summary

In this chapter, you learned how to develop and integrate JavaScript-based search capabilities in your Web pages. You learned how to connect your scripts to existing Web search engines and how to implement local search engines using JavaScript. This chapter was the last one in Part III, "Building Sample Applications." In Part IV, "Communicating with Java, ActiveX, and Plug-Ins," you'll learn to interface JavaScript with its namesake—the Java programming language. You'll also learn how to load, interact with, and control Java applets, ActiveX components, and plug-ins using JavaScript scripts.

PART IV

Communicating with Java, ActiveX, and Plug-Ins

■ CHAPTER 15: Communicating with Java Applets

■ CHAPTER 16: Scripting ActiveX Components

■ CHAPTER 17: How Plug-Ins Work

CHAPTER

FIFTEEN

15

Communicating with Java Applets

- What Is Java?

- Java vs. JavaScript

- LiveConnect and the Internet Explorer Object Model

- Accessing Java Methods from Within JavaScript

- Accessing Applets from Within JavaScript

- Using JavaScript in an Applet

Java is a very powerful and popular language that supports the development of browser-neutral Web-based applications. It provides a number of capabilities that complement those that JavaScript provides. In this chapter, you'll learn the similarities and differences between Java and JavaScript and learn how to develop simple Java programs and applets. You'll learn how to use Navigator and Internet Explorer to enable communication between JavaScript scripts and Java applets. You'll also learn how to invoke JavaScript functions from within applets. By the time you finish this chapter, you'll be able to create Web applications that integrate scripts and applets.

What Is Java?

The rapid growth in the popularity of the Java language is nothing short of a phenomenon. In less than a year, Java went from a relatively unknown alpha version to an incredibly successful Version 1 release. Java has since been endorsed by every major computer hardware and software vendor. Its remarkable success is summed up by the fact that Microsoft, its chief rival, not only supports Java with Internet Explorer, but also sells J++, a popular Java development environment. In this section I'll explore the features of Java that set it apart from other programming languages.

Java Is Platform Independent

Java's phenomenal success is due to the fact that it provides the capability to develop compiled software that runs, without modification, on a large variety of operating system platforms—including Microsoft Windows, Apple Macintosh, IBM OS/2, Linux, and several varieties of UNIX. In addition, and perhaps more importantly, specially designed Java programs known as *applets* run in the context of Java-enabled Web browsers, such as Netscape Navigator and Microsoft Internet Explorer.

NOTE   Java is distributed by JavaSoft, a subsidiary of Sun Microsystems, as the Java Development Kit (JDK), a complete set of tools for developing Java applications. The latest version of the JDK can be obtained from JavaSoft via its Web site; browse the URL `http://www.javasoft.com` and follow the appropriate links.

The Java Virtual Machine (JVM) is the key to Java's platform independence. JVM provides a machine-independent and operating system–independent platform for the execution of Java code. The JVM is a program that runs on your host operating system (OS) or is embedded in a browser. The JVM executes Java programs that are compiled into the JVM byte code. This byte code is the native machine language of the JVM and does not vary among JVM implementations.

When Java is ported to a new platform, be it an OS or a browser, the JVM itself is ported, yet its interface to compiled Java programs remains the same. The code required to port the JVM to the host OS or browser varies from system to system. In addition to the JVM, this code is required to port the Java application programming interface (API). The Java API is a common set of software packages that all Java implementations support. Much of the API is itself written in Java and runs on the JVM. However, some parts of the API, such as the windowing and networking software, are written in C++. The JVM, together with the additional software required to support the Java API, is referred to as the *Java Runtime Environment (JRE)*.

Java Is Object Oriented

Java is an object-oriented language and provides all of the benefits of object-oriented programming: classification, inheritance, object composition, encapsulation, and polymorphism. Java supports single inheritance, but not multiple inheritance; however, it provides the interface construct that can be used to obtain the benefits of multiple inheritance without having to deal with any of its drawbacks.

NOTE   Refer to Chapter 5, "Working with Objects," for a complete discussion of object-oriented programming concepts.

Java Is Familiar

One of the most striking characteristics of Java, at least from a programmer's perspective, is its familiarity. Java is based on C++ and retains much of its syntax. This makes the language very easy to learn for C++ programmers. Because JavaScript is also based on both C++ and Java, Java's syntax will be easy for you to learn. However, because Java is a full object-*oriented* language (as opposed to an object-*based* language, like JavaScript), you will have to learn some additional programming constructs.

NOTE   Online Appendix B, "Accessing Online References," provides links to a reference manual and other information about the Java language and API.

Java Is Simple and Reliable

Although Java is based on C++, it is simpler and easier to use. This is because the designers of Java eliminated many of the complex and dangerous features of C++, such as pointers and address manipulation. By doing so, Java's creators also increased its overall reliability, making it an attractive language for mission-critical applications.

The Java API Supports Window and Network Programming

Another attractive feature of Java is the extensive API that comes as a standard part of the JDK. The API provides portable libraries for the development of window- and network-based programs. The same API is used to develop console-based programs, windowed programs, network clients and servers, applets, and fully distributed Web-based applications. It also supports the development of multithreaded programs.

Java Supports Executable Web Content

The capability to develop applets for use in Web applications is one of the most attractive features provided by Java. *Applets* are programs that execute in the context of a browser window; thus, they allow executable content to be embedded in a Web page. This enables Web pages to be more dynamic and interactive and greatly increases the number and types of Web applications that can be supported.

NOTE   Chapter 1, "Learning the Fundamentals," presents applets within the context of a general introduction to client- and server-side Web programming technologies. Chapter 5, "Working with Objects," discusses some of Java's object-oriented programming features.

Java Is Secure

The power and flexibility that applets provide requires ironclad security on the part of the Java runtime system. This high level of security is required to prevent malicious applets from disclosing or damaging the information stored on the user's computer. Java provides several levels of security protection. At the language level, Java has eliminated dangerous programming features such as pointers, memory allocation and deallocation operators, and automatic type conversion.

At the compiler level, the Java compiler performs extensive checks that prevent errors and ensure that the compiled code does not contain any inconsistencies that could allow objects to be accessed in ways other than explicitly allowed.

At the runtime level, the Java runtime system prevents applets from performing actions that could result in damage to or disclosure of information stored on your computer.

Java Is Free

Finally, if none of the above features is compelling enough to go with Java, Sun gives the JDK away for free—it is publicly available at JavaSoft's Web site, `http://www.javasoft.com/products/index.html`.

Java vs. JavaScript

Although Java and JavaScript have similar names, there are a number of significant differences between the two languages. These differences do not make one language superior to the other—the features of both languages are well suited to their respective programming niches. For example, JavaScript is designed to supplement the capabilities of HTML with scripts that are capable of responding to Web page events. As such, it has complete access to all aspects of the browser window. Java is designed to implement executable content that can be embedded in Web pages. For this purpose, it is endowed with much more powerful programming capabilities. However, these capabilities are confined to a limited area of the browser window.

Java and JavaScript complement each other well. Java is the industrial-strength programming language for developing advanced Web objects. JavaScript is the essential glue that combines HTML, Java applets, plug-ins, server-side programs, and other Web components into fully integrated Web applications. While Java's forte is in Web component development, JavaScript excels at component integration. The following subsections identify the differences between these two languages. These discussions also show how their differences enable each language to achieve its respective Web programming goals.

Compiled vs. Interpreted

The most obvious difference between Java and JavaScript is that Java is compiled and JavaScript is interpreted. As you would expect, there is a good reason for this difference.

Java is intended to be used to develop secure, high-performance Web applications. The JVM executes compiled bytecodes rather than interpreting source Java statements. The bytecode instruction set is designed for quick and efficient execution, allowing Java to achieve performance comparable to native code compilers.

JavaScript, on the other hand, is intended to create scripts that can be embedded in HTML documents. These scripts control the way the documents are laid out and define functions to handle user events. JavaScript can be viewed as an extension to HTML that provides additional capabilities for browser and document control. From this perspective, it is important that JavaScript be included in HTML as source code—so the browser can inspect the code. This is the reason why it is an interpreted language instead of a compiled language, like Java.

Although compiled JavaScript scripts would be inappropriate for Web page development because of the need for cross-platform support, there is no reason why server-side scripts should not be compiled. In Chapter 21, "Scripting Netscape Servers," you'll learn how Netscape's LiveWire tools provide a unique approach to integrating server-side scripts with Web pages.

Object-Oriented vs. Object-Based

Java and JavaScript differ in the degree to which they support object-oriented programming. Java is fully committed to object-oriented programming and supports all object-oriented programming features except multiple inheritance. Even so, Java's use of single inheritance combined with its interface construct provides the benefits of multiple inheritance while retaining the simple class structure that is characteristic of single inheritance. Java's commitment to object-oriented programming stems from the fact that it was originally intended to be used to develop software for consumer electronic devices. Full support of object-oriented programming is integral to the development of the simple and reliable software components that characterize these devices.

JavaScript does not share Java's commitment to object-oriented programming. JavaScript's approach is to take what's most useful from object-oriented programming and discard everything else. For example, JavaScript supports object types, instantiation, composition, reuse, and polymorphism, but it does not support classification and inheritance.

The reasons for JavaScript's pick-and-choose attitude toward object-oriented programming are based on the nature of the objects that JavaScript is compelled to support. Objects, such as windows, frames, documents, forms, and so on, are the reason for JavaScript's existence. These objects are accessed more effectively using the document object model, introduced in Chapter 5, "Working with Objects," than using a pure object-oriented approach.

Strongly Typed vs. Loosely Typed

JavaScript is a *loosely-typed* language and Java is *strongly typed*. A *loosely-typed* language is one in which data of one type is automatically converted to another type during the runtime execution of a program or script. On the other hand, a *strongly-typed* language is one that flags inappropriate type conversions as errors instead of converting data types. Strongly-typed languages flag type-conversion errors during program compilation, loading, and execution. The difference between loosely- and strongly-typed languages is suggestive of the ways in which each type is intended to be used.

Java focuses on the development of software that is secure and reliable. Strong typing is absolutely essential to achieving each of these goals. The ability to restrict operations on objects to only those that are explicitly defined is basic to Java's security approach. This control is needed to ensure that objects are not accessed in ways that circumvent the security checks imposed by the JVM.

Strong typing is also important to developing reliable software. Software reliability studies have repeatedly shown that automatic type conversion is a contributing factor in many common programming errors.

JavaScript's decision to go with loose typing can be viewed as a trade-off between expediency and reliability. This is characteristic of most scripting languages. By not enforcing strong typing, a scripting language confers more power and responsibility on the programmer. It says, "I'm going to permit you to perform this operation. It may be dangerous, but I trust your judgment."

JavaScript's support of loose typing is consistent with its role as a Web scripting language. Rather than forcing you to clutter your scripts with the extra code needed to perform explicit type conversion, it automatically performs these conversions for you. This reduces the overall size of your scripts and lets you focus on the pertinent aspects of your Web application.

Browser Window vs. Full Browser Interaction

Perhaps the most important differences between Java and JavaScript lie in their different capabilities for interacting with the user, the browser, and the rest of the Web. These differences determine which applications each language can support.

Java applets are intended to be *embedded* in Web pages, and their capabilities reflect this intent. Applets are assigned a limited area of the browser window in which they are allowed to interact with the user. Applets are not allowed to display information in other areas of the browser window or to respond to events that occur as the result of actions taken with respect to other window areas. This precludes Java from providing the controls for Web page layout and event-handling support that we have seen are possible with JavaScript.

JavaScript scripts are not employed in the same manner as Java applets. JavaScript scripts are not confined to a limited area of the browser window; rather, they are allowed to control the display of an entire Web page, to handle all events that occur with respect to a window, and to interact with other frames and windows. These total Web-page control capabilities enable JavaScript to carry out its role of being the glue that integrates HTML, Java, plug-ins, and server-side scripts into complete Web applications.

Even though JavaScript has considerably more latitude than Java in Web page control, it is faced with similar security restrictions. Navigator and Internet Explorer prevent scripts that are loaded from one server from accessing the properties of documents that are loaded from other servers. This restriction prevents a script from accessing sensitive data entered in another frame or window and sending it to an arbitrary Internet host.

The Java Development Kit

In order to work the examples in this and later chapters, you will need to obtain and install a copy of the Java Development Kit (JDK) on your computer. The latest version of the JDK may be obtained by following the appropriate links from the JavaSoft home page at `http://www.javasoft.com`. Figure 15.1 shows the JavaSoft home page. It contains a number of useful links that you can follow to learn more about Java. The JDK is free to download, but make sure that you read and agree with Sun's license agreement before downloading the JDK. I use version 1.2 of the JDK for the examples in this chapter. This version has been renamed as Java 2.

FIGURE 15.1:

The JavaSoft home page

NOTE   The examples in this book assume that you install the JDK in the directory `c:\jdk1.2` of your hard disk. I recommend that you install the JDK in this directory in order to avoid any problems in completing the examples.

Learning Java

Besides giving away the JDK for free, Sun wanted to make sure that you would be able to use it. They have included an extensive online tutorial at their Web site `http://www.javasoft.com/docs/books/tutorial/index.html`. I highly recommend that you take this tutorial if you intend to program in Java. Although Java is simple and easy to use, a complete introduction to Java is beyond the scope of this book. We get you started in this chapter, by showing you how to develop a Java console program, a window program, and some applets. For those of you who already know Java or are adept at learning new languages, you may find everything you need concerning Java in online Appendix B, "Accessing Online Resources," which provides links to reference information about the Java language.

The Java API

One of the benefits of using Java is that it comes with an extensive application programming interface (API). This API provides access to all of the objects and methods that you need to develop sophisticated window and network programs and Java applets. Sun provides excellent documentation for the Java API at its Web site `http://www.javasoft.com/products/jdk/1.2/docs/api/index.html`. This documentation can be viewed online or downloaded to your computer.

Programs vs. Applets

Java is a general-purpose software development language. You can use it to create Web applets that run in the context of a Web browser. But Java can also be used to develop stand-alone console and window programs that run independently of a browser and the Web. The term *console program* refers to text mode programs, such as DOS and UNIX command-line programs, that do not use a windowing system, such as Microsoft Windows or the X Window System. Java *window programs* are distinguished from Microsoft Windows programs in that they can execute on Microsoft Windows (95, 98, or NT), the X Window System, Motif, and the Macintosh windowing system. In this section, you'll learn how to develop all three types of Java programs. In addition, later chapters will focus more on applets in particular.

Java is an easy programming language to learn—especially if you've already programmed in JavaScript. Start by browsing Sun's online Java tutorial or the Java reference links included in online Appendix B, "Accessing Online Resources," to get a feel for the language and how it compares to JavaScript. You will find that Java's syntax is very similar to JavaScript's, but of course there are some differences between the two languages. In order to get you up and programming in Java, I'll list the most important differences here and then illustrate them in the programming examples covered in the following subsections.

Building Programs from Classes

Java programs are built from *classes*. Classes are analogous to object types in JavaScript. They define *variables* (also called *fields*) and methods that correspond to JavaScript's properties and methods.

Organizing Classes into Packages

Related classes are organized into *packages*. When you write a Java program, you can access previously defined classes by *importing* them into your program.

The *main()* Method

The `main()` method is the first method that is executed when you run a standalone Java program.

Java Reserves Certain Keywords

Java uses keywords, like `public` and `static`, to identify additional properties of variables.

An Example Console Program

The traditional first program in any language displays the text *Hello World!*, with the objective being to create a small program that produces a visible result. In keeping with this tradition, Listing 15.1 shows the simplest possible Java program—a program that you'll soon create. Open an MS-DOS window and compile the program using the Java compiler as follows:

```
javac ConsolePrg.java
```

Then run the program using the following command line:

```
java ConsolePrg
```

It will display the text *Hello World!* to the console window.

Listing 15.1   **A Java Console Program (ConsolePrg.java)**

```
import java.lang.System;
class ConsolePrg {
 public static void main (String args[]) {
  System.out.println("Hello World!");
 }
}
```

Now that you are a Java programmer, let's review the program's source code. It begins with an `import` statement that imports the `System` class from the `java.lang` package into your program. By importing it, you make it available for use in your program.

Following the `import` statement is the declaration of the `ConsolePrg` class. This class declaration ends with the last closing brace (}).

Within the `ConsolePrg` class, we define the `main()` method. This method is declared as `public`, `static`, and `void`. The `public` keyword identifies it as publicly accessible. The `static` keyword specifies that `main()` is used with the `ConsolePrg` class as a whole, rather than with an instance of the class. The `void` keyword identifies `main()` as not returning a value.

The one and only statement within `main()` prints the text, *Hello World!,* on the console window. It invokes the `println()` method for the `out` variable of the System class. The `println()` method is similar to the JavaScript `writeln()` method. The `System.out` variable identifies the console as the object to which the output is to be displayed. It is a standard variable provided by the `System` class.

NOTE   In practice, `java.lang.System` is always imported, by default, regardless of whether it is identified in an import statement. The import statement was included in this example only so that we could cover it in the context of the first program.

An Example Windows Program

Now that you understand a little about Java programs, let's write a window-based version of the *Hello World!* program. It will quickly get you up to speed writing stand-alone Java window programs.

Compile WindowsPrg.java (Listing 15.2) using the statement

```
javac WindowsPrg.java
```

and then run it using

```
java WindowsPrg
```

It displays the window shown in Figure 15.2. Now we're making progress! When you've finished marveling at your creation, you can close it by clicking on the X in the upper-right corner of the program's title bar.

FIGURE 15.2:

A Java window program

The program begins by importing java.awt.*; and java.awt.*;. This tells the Java compiler to import all classes in the java.awt and java.awt.event packages. These packages contain the classes used for window program development and event handling.

The class WindowsPrg is declared as a public class that extends the Frame class. The Frame class is a class of the java.awt package that defines the main window of an application program. Three methods and an inner class are declared for the WindowsPrg class, as discussed next.

The *main()* Method

The main() method is the first method to be executed when the WindowsPrg program is run. It creates an object of the WindowsPrg class and assigns it to the program variable. The program variable is declared as an object of the WindowsPrg class.

The *WindowsPrg()* Constructor

This is the constructor for the WindowsPrg class. Like all constructors, it does not specify a return value. It invokes the super() method to set the window's title bar to the text "A Java Windows Program". The super() method is a way of calling the constructor of WindowsPrg's parent class (Frame). The Frame() constructor takes a string as a parameter and displays it as the document's title. You may want to look up the description of the Frame class in the Java API.

WindowsPrg() then invokes the pack() method to pack the contents of the window. This is a standard method that is called when a window is constructed to place and organize any window components within the window. The window is resized to 500 by 250 pixels using the setSize() method. An event handler for the window-closing event is defined using the addWindowListener() method.

The window is displayed using the show() method. The pack(), setSize (), and show() methods are inherited from the Frame class by WindowsPrg.

The *paint()* Method

The paint() method is called to draw a window when it is initially displayed or needs to be redrawn. It takes a Graphics object as a parameter. The Graphics object is where the screen updates are drawn. The first statement invokes the setFont() method of the Graphics class to set the drawing font to 48-point, bold and italic Times Roman. The Font() constructor is used to create this font. The second statement invokes the setColor() method to set the drawing color to red. The Color class provides a set of color constants. The third statement invokes the drawString() method to draw the text "Hello World!" on the screen at the offset (100,125) within the Graphics object.

The *WindowEventHandler* Class

The WindowEventHandler class is an inner class of WindowsPrg that is used to handle the event associated with the application window. It extends the WindowAdapter class, which provides default event handlers for window-related events. The windowClosing() method handles the closing of the application window by invoking the exit() method of the System class. This results in the program's termination.

Listing 15.2   **A Java Window Program (WindowsPrg.java)**

```java
import java.awt.*;
import java.awt.event.*;
public class WindowsPrg extends Frame {
 public static void main(String args[]){
  WindowsPrg program = new WindowsPrg();
 }
 public WindowsPrg() {
  super("A Java Windows Program");
  pack();
  setSize(500,250);
  addWindowListener(new WindowEventHandler());
  show();
 }
 public void paint(Graphics g) {
  g.setFont(new Font("TimesRoman",Font.BOLD+Font.ITALIC,48));
  g.setColor(Color.red);
  g.drawString("Hello World!",100,125);
 }
 class WindowEventHandler extends WindowAdapter {
  public void windowClosing(WindowEvent e){
   System.exit(0);
  }
 }
}
```

An Example Applet

Now that you can develop Java window programs, you're ready to create an applet. Remember, applets execute in the context of a browser window. This means that you have to develop and compile the applet and then create an HTML document that displays the applet as part of a Web page. Listing 15.3 contains the source code of an applet I've named *WebApp*. Compile it using the following statement:

```
javac WebApp.java
```

This creates the WebApp.class file, which is the compiled applet code.

NOTE

Make sure that your browser has Java enabled before trying to run the remaining examples in this chapter.

Listing 15.3   **A Java Applet (WebApp.java)**

```java
import java.awt.*;
import java.applet.*;
public class WebApp extends Applet {
 public void paint(Graphics g) {
  g.setFont(new Font("TimesRoman",Font.BOLD+Font.ITALIC,48));
  g.setColor(Color.red);
  g.drawString("Hello World!",50,100);
 }
}
```

The `web.htm` file shown in Listing 15.4 contains an HTML document that inserts the applet as part of a Web page. Open `web.htm` with your browser. Figure 15.3 shows the Web page that is displayed. The gray area of the Web page is the applet's display area. I purposely set the document's background to white so that the applet would stand out.

Listing 15.4   **An HTML File That Displays a Java Applet (web.htm)**

```html
<HTML>
<HEAD>
<TITLE>A Java Applet</TITLE>
</HEAD>
<BODY BGCOLOR="white">
<APPLET CODE="WebApp.class" WIDTH=400 HEIGHT=200>
[WebApp applet]
</APPLET>
</BODY>
</HTML>
```

FIGURE 15.3:

A Java applet

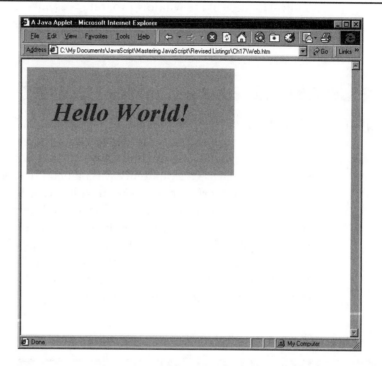

The <applet> tag shown in Listing 15.4 contains three attributes: CODE, WIDTH, and HEIGHT. The CODE attribute identifies the Java bytecode file of the applet to be loaded. The WIDTH and HEIGHT attributes identify the dimensions of the applet's display area. Any text between the <applet> and </applet> tags is displayed by browsers that are not capable of or configured to handle applets. A non-Java-capable browser would display the phrase *[WebApp applet]* in place of the applet.

The applet's code will be easy to follow because you've used the same methods in the window programming example. In fact, applets use many of the standard java.awt window classes. The classes of the java.applet package are imported in addition to the java.awt classes. The WebApp class is declared as a class that extends the Applet class. The Applet class is the common ancestor of all applet classes in the Java class hierarchy.

The WebApp class does not define a main() method. This is because it is not a stand-alone program. It defines the paint() method to draw the Graphics object of the applet display area. The paint() method works in the same way as for window programs. The three statements contained in the paint() method are identical to those of the window program presented in the previous section except that the text is drawn at location (50,100) instead of (100,125).

LiveConnect and the Internet Explorer Object Model

Netscape Navigator 3 was the first browser to support communication between JavaScript and Java. This capability was named LiveConnect by Netscape. Live-Connect also supports communication with Navigator plug-ins. Microsoft implemented most of the features of LiveConnect in Internet Explorer 4. However, Microsoft did much more than simply reimplement LiveConnect. In its Internet Explorer Object Model, Microsoft provided the capability for scripts, applets, and ActiveX components to be seamlessly integrated within the context of a Web page. Chapter 16, "Scripting ActiveX Components," shows how ActiveX components can be used with scripts and applets.

Accessing Java Methods from within JavaScript

One of the easiest ways to use Java in JavaScript is to invoke Java methods directly in your scripts. For example, consider the following Java statement, which displays the text *Hello World!* to the Java console window:

```
java.lang.System.out.println("Hello World!")
```

Using Netscape Navigator, you can execute this statement directly from within a JavaScript script, as shown in Listing 15.5. To see how this script works, download this chapter's code and open `console.htm` with Navigator 4 or later. It will display the Web page shown in Figure 15.4. To view the Java console window, select Tools ➤ Java Console from the Communicator pull-down menu. The window shown in Figure 15.5 will be displayed.

NOTE   Because this approach only works with Navigator, I do not recommend using it in your Web applications.

Listing 15.5   Calling Java Methods (console.htm)

```
<HTML>
<HEAD>
<TITLE>Calling Java Methods</TITLE>
</HEAD>
<BODY>
<P>This script writes the text, <EM>Hello World!</EM>
 to the Java console window.</P>
<SCRIPT LANGUAGE="JavaScript"><!-
java.lang.System.out.println("Hello World!")
// -></SCRIPT>
</BODY>
</HTML>
```

FIGURE 15.4:

The browser window
(Listing 15.5)

FIGURE 15.5:

The Java console window
(Listing 15.5)

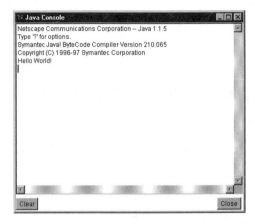

Accessing Applets from within JavaScript

As you learned in the previous section, accessing Java methods from within JavaScript is easy. When it comes to accessing the methods and variables of *applets* from within your Javascript scripts, however, the following steps must be taken:

1. The applet methods and variables to be accessed must be declared as `public`.

2. The applet must be loaded before it can be accessed.

3. The applet must be accessed using JavaScript's `applet` object.

By simply following the above three steps, you'll be able to access the methods and properties of applets in your scripts. In addition to the above three steps, Netscape recommends that the applet be compiled with the Netscape `java40 .jar` file in your CLASSPATH. This file contains packages that provide additional security and allow Java applets to access JavaScript objects. In practice, you do not need to compile your applets with `java40.jar` unless you want to access JavaScript objects from within your applets.

NOTE   Your scripts can also use "faceless" applets, which do not display GUI output, but can be used to perform internal computations.

Declaring Public Classes, Methods, and Variables

In order to access a method or variable used by an applet, the method or variable must be declared as `public` and must be declared as part of a `public` class. In practice, this is easy to accomplish—you use the `public` keyword in the class, method, or variable declaration. Listing 15.6 provides an example of an applet that displays a text string within its applet window. The `setText()` method is declared as `public`, making it accessible to JavaScript code. This method is used to change the text that is displayed by the applet. Note that the `FancyText` subclass of `applet` is also declared as `public`.

Listing 15.6   An Applet That Displays Text (FancyText.java)

```java
import java.applet.*;
import java.awt.*;
public class FancyText extends Applet {
 String text="I like Java!";
 Font font = new Font("TimesRoman",Font.BOLD+Font.ITALIC,36);
 public void paint(Graphics g) {
  g.setFont(font);
  g.drawString(text,30,30);
 }
 public void setText(String s) {
  text=s;
  repaint();
 }
}
```

Loading an Applet

An applet must be completely loaded before you can access its variables and methods. Although there is no `onLoad` event defined for the `applet` object, you can use the `window` object's `onLoad` event handler by specifying it in a document's `<body>` tag.

Consider the example shown in Listing 15.7. This example loads the applet shown in Listing 15.6. The onLoad event handler invokes the accessApplet() function after the document (and therefore the applet) has been loaded. I'll complete the discussion of Listing 15.7 after covering the applet object in the next section.

Listing 15.7   **Loading and Accessing an Applet (use-app1.htm)**

```
<HTML>
<HEAD>
<TITLE>Accessing Applets</TITLE>
<SCRIPT LANGUAGE="JavaScript"><!-
function accessApplet() {
 setTimeout("changeText('I like JavaScript!')",2000)
 setTimeout("changeText('I like JavaScript and Java!')",4000)
 setTimeout("changeText('I like Java!')",6000)
 setTimeout("accessApplet()",8000)
}
function changeText(s) {
 window.document.fancyText.setText(s)
}
// -></SCRIPT>
</HEAD>
<BODY onLoad="accessApplet()">
<APPLET CODE="FancyText.class" NAME="fancyText"
 WIDTH=450 HEIGHT=150>
[The FancyText Applet]
</APPLET>
</BODY>
</HTML>
```

Using the *applet* Object

The applet object is provided by JavaScript to enable JavaScript code to access Java variables and methods. This object has a single property—the name property—and no methods or event handlers. The name property is used to access the name attribute of the <applet> tag.

The `applet` object is a property of the `document` object. Individual applets can be accessed by name. For example, in the `changeText()` function of Listing 15.7, the statement

```
window.document.fancyText.setText(s)
```

is used to invoke the `setText()` method of the applet named *fancyText*.

The `applets` array is also a property of the `document` object. This array provides access to all applets that are defined for a particular document.

My FancyText Example

Listings 15.6 and 15.7 provide a complete example of how JavaScript code is able to access a Java applet. To run this example, compile `FancyText.java` with your Java compiler. This will produce the `FancyText.class` byte-code file.

`FancyText.class` is loaded via the `<applet>` tag shown in Listing 15.7. The applet is named *fancyText*. When the `use-app1.htm` file is loaded, the `accessApplet()` function is invoked to handle the `onLoad` event. This function sets four timeouts. The first timeout invokes `changeText()` after two seconds, passing it the `I like JavaScript!` string. The second timeout invokes `changeText()` after four seconds, passing it the `I like JavaScript and Java!` string. The third timeout invokes `changeText()` after six seconds, passing it the `I like Java!` string. Finally, the fourth timeout invokes `accessApplet()` after eight seconds to cause the entire process to be repeated.

The `changeText()` function invokes the `setText()` method of the `FancyText` class defined in Listing 15.6. It uses `setText()` to change the text displayed by the applet.

To see the effect of using the JavaScript of Listing 15.7 with the Java of Listing 15.6, open `use-app1.htm` with your browser. Your browser will initially display the text shown in Figure 15.6. After two seconds, your browser will display the text shown in Figure 15.7. After two more seconds, your browser will display the text shown in Figure 15.8.

FIGURE 15.6:

Initial text display
(Listing 15.7)

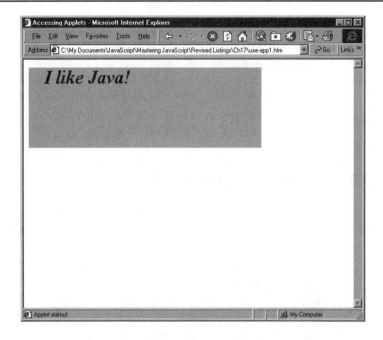

FIGURE 15.7:

The display after two
seconds (Listing 15.7)

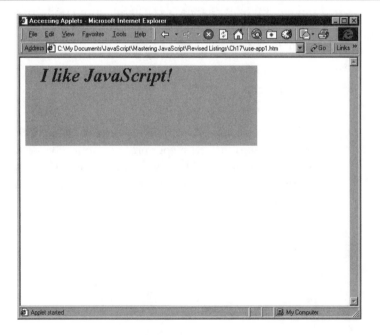

The display after four
seconds (Listing 15.7)

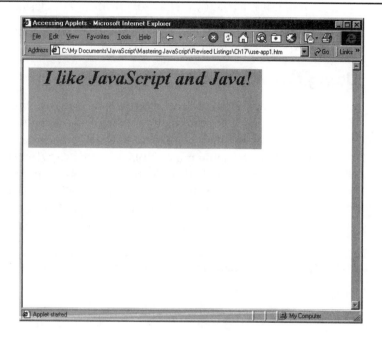

Using JavaScript in an Applet

So far you have learned how to access and control Java applets from within
JavaScript. But what if you want to do the converse, that is, access JavaScript
objects and functions from within an applet? Both LiveConnect and the Internet
Explorer Object Model provide an interface between Java and JavaScript that
allows you to do this. However, as with JavaScript-to-Java communication, there
are a few steps involved:

1. Use the MAYSCRIPT attribute of the <applet> tag to permit an applet to
    access a script.

2. Import the netscape.javascript package into your applet.

3. Create a handle to a JavaScript window using the JSObject class and the
    getWindow() method.

4. Use the getMember() method of the JSObject class to obtain access to
    JavaScript objects.

5. Use the eval() method of the JSObject class to invoke JavaScript methods.

These steps are covered in the following subsections.

Using the *MAYSCRIPT* Attribute

For an applet to be able to access a JavaScript object or function, the applet must be given explicit permission to do so. This prevents the applet from modifying other areas of a Web page without the Web page designer knowing about it. The MAYSCRIPT attribute must be placed in the `<applet>` tag to allow an applet to access JavaScript. If an applet tries to access JavaScript without the MAYSCRIPT attribute being specified, then the applet will generate an exception, display an error message, and stop running. In Listing 15.8, the ReadForm applet is loaded and given permission to access JavaScript objects and functions.

Listing 15.8   **Accessing JavaScript from an Applet (use-app2.htm)**

```
<HTML>
<HEAD>
<TITLE>Accessing JavaScript from an applet</TITLE>
</HEAD>
<BODY>
<FORM NAME="textForm">
<P>Enter some text and then click Display Text:
 <INPUT TYPE="text" NAME="textField" SIZE="20"></P>
</FORM>
<APPLET CODE="ReadForm.class" WIDTH=400 HEIGHT=100
 NAME="readApp" MAYSCRIPT>
[The ReadForm Applet]
</APPLET>
</BODY>
</HTML>
```

Importing *netscape.javascript*

In order for an applet to access JavaScript objects and functions, it must import the JSObject and JSException classes of the `netscape.javascript` package. The import statements shown in Listing 15.9 may be used to import these classes. You only need to import JSException if you plan to handle this exception within your applet. The use of JSObject in Java-to-JavaScript communication is covered in the following sections.

NOTE

The file `java40.jar` must be in your CLASSPATH in order to access the `netscape.javascript` package.

WARNING

In some cases, importing `netscape.javascript.*`; may lead to a compilation error. To avoid this problem, import `JSObject` and `JSException` via separate import statements as shown in Listing 15.9.

Listing 15.9   Reading a JavaScript Form (ReadForm.java)

```java
import java.applet.*;
import java.awt.*;
import java.awt.event.*;
import netscape.javascript.JSObject;
import netscape.javascript.JSException;
public class ReadForm extends Applet {
 String text="Enter some text for me to display!";
 Font font = new Font("TimesRoman",Font.BOLD+Font.ITALIC,24);
 JSObject win, doc, form, textField;
 public void init() {
  win = JSObject.getWindow(this);
  doc = (JSObject) win.getMember("document");
  form = (JSObject) doc.getMember("textForm");
  textField = (JSObject) form.getMember("textField");
  setLayout(new BorderLayout());
  Panel buttons = new Panel();
  Button displayTextButton = new Button("Display Text");
  displayTextButton.addActionListener(new ButtonEventHandler());
  buttons.add(displayTextButton);
  add("South",buttons);
 }
 public void paint(Graphics g) {
  g.setFont(font);
  g.drawString(text,30,30);
 }
 class ButtonEventHandler implements ActionListener {
  public void actionPerformed(ActionEvent e){
   String s = e.getActionCommand();
```

```
if("Display Text".equals(s)) {
 text= (String) textField.getMember("value");
 win.eval("alert(\"This alert comes from Java!\")");
 repaint();
}
}
}
}
```

Creating a Handle to a JavaScript Window

When accessing JavaScript methods and functions from within Java, one of the first things that you'll want to do is to gain access to the JavaScript window object associated with the window in which the applet is loaded. By doing so, you'll be able to access other objects (document, form, image) that are created in the Navigator instance hierarchy.

To access the JavaScript window object, declare a variable of type JSObject and use the getWindow() method of the JSObject class to assign the window object to the variable. For example, in Listing 15.9 the win variable is declared as class JSObject. The first statement in the init() method of the ReadForm class assigns the window object to the win variable. The this parameter that is passed to the getWindow() method causes getWindow() to return the window object associated with the window containing the applet.

Using *getMember()*

The getMember() method of the JSObject class is used to access objects and values that are properties of a JSObject object. This method takes a String argument that identifies the object or value to be accessed. For example, in the init() method of Listing 15.9, the following lines of code use getMember() to access objects that are properties of other JavaScript objects:

```
doc = (JSObject) win.getMember("document");
form = (JSObject) doc.getMember("textForm");
textField = (JSObject) form.getMember("textField");
```

The first statement invokes getMember() for the win variable used to reference the current document window. The "document" string is passed as an argument.

getMember() returns the JavaScript object corresponding to window.document and assigns it to the doc variable. The doc, form, and textField variables are all declared as class JSObject in the beginning of the definition of the ReadForm class.

In the second statement, getMember() is invoked for doc and returns the JavaScript object corresponding to window.document.textForm. This object is the form defined in Listing 15.4. It is assigned to the form variable.

The third statement invokes getMember() for the form variable. getMember() returns the JavaScript object window.document.textForm.textField. This object is assigned to the textField variable.

In the actionPerformed() method of Listing 15.9, the following statement is used to retrieve the value of an HTML text field and assign it to the Java text variable:

```
text= (String) textField.getMember("value");
```

Notice that in this statement, the value returned by getMember() is coerced into a value of the String class via the (String) type cast operator.

Using *eval()*

The eval() method of the JSObject class is used to invoke a method of a JavaScript object and make the value returned by the method available to a Java variable. It is used in the actionPerformed() method of Listing 15.9 to display the alert dialog box:

```
win.eval("alert(\"This alert comes from Java!\")");
```

Note that double quotes should be replaced by their escape character sequence \" when used as arguments to a method that is being evaluated.

Reading Values Entered in a Form

Now that you've covered the basics of Java-to-JavaScript communication, let's walk through the example provided by Listings 15.8 and 15.9.

Open use-app2.htm with your browser. It displays the Web page shown in Figure 15.9. Type *Hello JavaScript!* in the form's text field and click on the Display Text button. The Java applet generates the alert dialog box shown in Figure 15.10. After you've clicked OK, the applet uses JavaScript to read the text you typed into the HTML form and displays it in the applet area of the window, as shown in Figure 15.11. This small example shows how Java, JavaScript, and HTML can communicate to produce an interesting Web page effect.

FIGURE 15.9:

Accessing JavaScript from an applet (Listing 15.8)

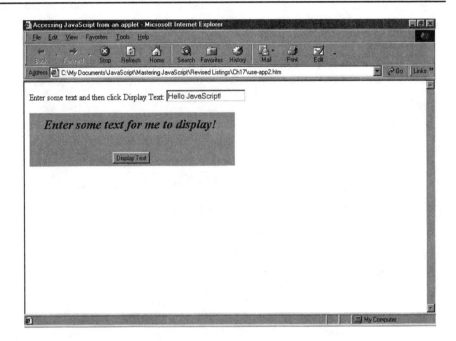

FIGURE 15.10:

Java generates a JavaScript alert dialog box (Listing 15.8).

The HTML file shown earlier in Listing 15.8 combines a simple form with the ReadForm applet. No JavaScript code is used in the file. The applet shown in Listing 15.9 accesses the HTML form via the JavaScript objects that are automatically created by your browser. Note that the win, doc, form, and textField variables are declared as class JSObject. These variables are used with the getWindow() and getMember() methods to provide access to the text field of the form. The actionPerformed() method handles the clicking of the Display Text button and uses the eval() method to display the JavaScript alert dialog box.

FIGURE 15.11:

Java uses JavaScript to read the HTML form and displays its value in the applet window area (Listing 15.8).

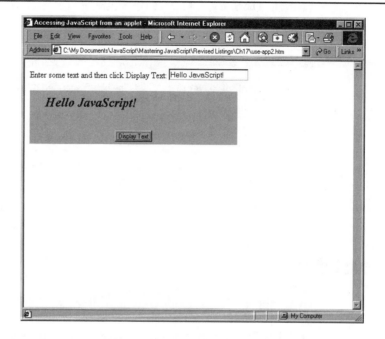

Other *JSObject* Methods

The JSObject class provides other methods besides getWindow(), getMember(), and eval(). Table 15.1 contains a complete list of the JSObject methods.

TABLE 15.1: Methods of the JSObject Class

Method	Description
call(String, Object[])	Invokes the JavaScript method specified by String and passes it the arguments specified in Object[]
eval(String)	Invokes the JavaScript method specified by String
finalize()	Decrements the reference count on a JavaScript object
getMember(String)	Returns the object or value specified by String
getSlot(int)	Returns the object array element specified by int
getWindow(Applet)	Returns the window containing the specified Applet

Continued on next page

TABLE 15.1 CONTINUED: Methods of the JSObjectt Class

Method	Description
removeMember(String)	Removes the object specified by `String`
setMember(String, Object)	Sets the object specified by `String` to the value specified by `Object`
setSlot(int,Object)	Sets the value of the object array element specified by `int` to the value specified by `Object`
toString()	Converts the JSObject to a `String` value

GraphIt!

JavaScript and Java provide complementary capabilities for Web page development:

- JavaScript provides a way to control the entire browser window.

- Java provides a capability to execute advanced programs within a limited area of the browser window.

- LiveConnect and the Internet Explorer Object Model provide the capability to link events that occur in the larger JavaScript-controlled window area to the Java methods that control the applet's operation.

The example presented in this section shows how JavaScript can easily interface with and make use of Java components. This example creates a Web application called *GraphIt!*, which allows a user to specify points to be plotted on a graph. The user types the coordinates of individual points he or she wishes to have included on the graph, and the applet draws line segments to connect the points. *GraphIt!* connects points according to their x coordinates, starting with the leftmost point and moving to the right. If two points have the same x coordinate, the applet connects to the lower point before drawing a line to the higher one. The user can also direct *GraphIt!* to remove a point from the graph, and the applet redraws to show the new result.

The *GraphIt!* example illustrates the symbiosis between JavaScript and Java. The applet designer, on the one hand, is free to design the applet without having to develop an explicit control interface; all he or she has to do is provide methods for adding and deleting points of the graph. The Web page designer, on the other hand, is able to use the applet without having to figure out the details of its operation; all she or he has to do is learn how to use the methods for adding and deleting points.

To see how the example works, open `graph.htm` (Listing 15.10) with your browser. The Web page displayed by your browser should look like Figure 15.12. The drawing area shows the intersection of x and y axes. Initially, the drawing area extends to +1 and -1 in each axis direction.

FIGURE 15.12:

The initial graph display (top) (Listing 15.10)

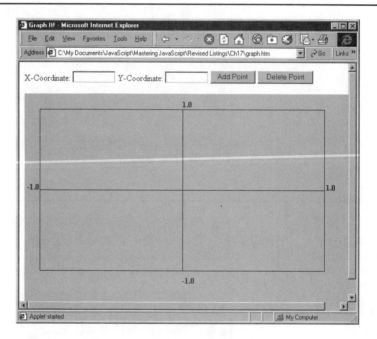

Perform the following steps to see *GraphIt!* in action:

1. For the first point on the graph, enter **2** in the X-Coordinate text field and **1** in the Y-coordinate text field to indicate the point (2,1). Then, click on the Add Point button. Because the graph contains only one point so far, no line is displayed, but the drawing area is automatically rescaled to accommodate this point. Refer to Figure 15.13.

2. Now add a second point (-2,-3) by entering **-2** and **-3** in the text fields. Then, click on Add Point. Notice how the drawing area is rescaled again to accommodate the greater value along the Y axis. Also, a line is drawn connecting the two points, as shown in Figure 15.14.

FIGURE 15.13:

When you add a first point (2,1), the drawing area automatically rescales to include the point (Listing 15.10).

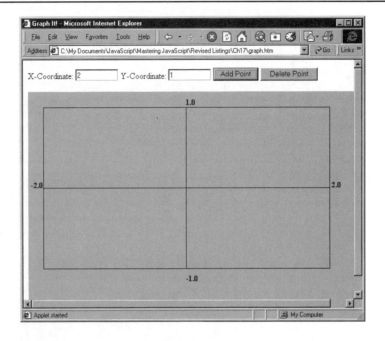

FIGURE 15.14:

The drawing area is rescaled again after adding (2,1) and (-2,-3). The graph begins to take shape, with a line drawn to connect the two points. (Listing 15.10)

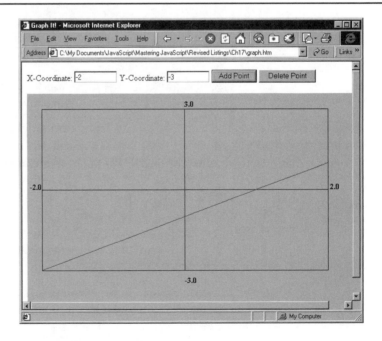

3. Add a third point (-1,1), as shown in Figure 15.15. Note how the graph is automatically updated to include this point. Because it connects the points in left-to-right, bottom-to-top order, it connects the point (-2,3) to (-1,1) and then connects (-1,1) to (2,1).

FIGURE 15.15:

The graph now connects all three points the user has entered: (2,1), (-2,-3), and (-1,1). (Listing 15.10)

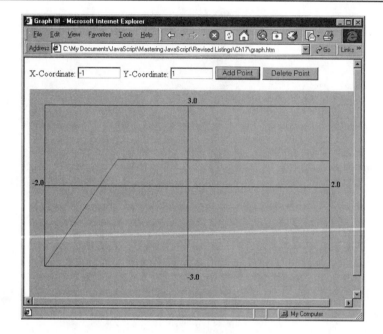

4. Now add the following points, one at a time: (3,-2), (4,2), (-4,1), (-6,-3), and (6,2). Your browser should look like that shown in Figure 15.16.

5. To see how the Delete Point feature works, delete the point (3,-2) by entering the coordinates in the text fields and clicking on the Delete Point button. The results are shown in Figure 15.17. Compare this to the graph shown in Figure 15.16; notice how the graph was redrawn to eliminate the deleted point.

FIGURE 15.16:

The graph connecting (2,1), (-2,-3), (-1,1), (3,-2), (4,2), (-4,1), (-6,-3), and (6,2) (Listing 15.10)

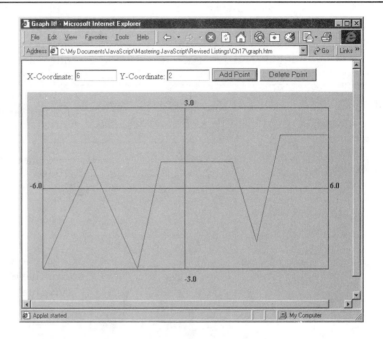

FIGURE 15.17:

The graph after deleting (3,-2) (Listing 15.10)

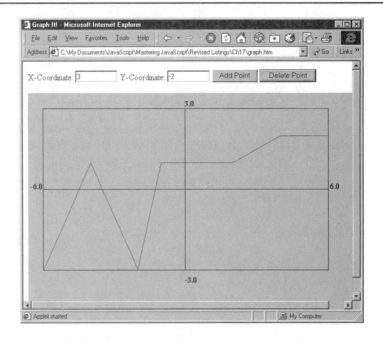

The graph.htm file is shown in Listing 15.10. It creates a simple form for specifying the points that are to be added and deleted from a graph. The addPoint() and deletePoint() functions handle the onClick events associated with the Add Point and Delete Point buttons. The addPoint() function reads the x and y coordinates entered by the user, converts them to floating point, and passes them to the addPoint() method of the GraphApp class. The deletePoint() function interfaces with the deletePoint() method of the GraphApp class in a similar manner.

Listing 15.10   A Graph Control Form (graph.htm)

```
<HTML>
<HEAD>
<TITLE>Graph It!</TITLE>
<SCRIPT LANGUAGE="JavaScript"><!-
function addPoint() {
 var x=parseFloat(window.document.xy.x.value)
 var y=parseFloat(window.document.xy.y.value)
 window.document.graph.addPoint(x,y)
}
function deletePoint() {
 var x=parseFloat(window.document.xy.x.value)
 var y=parseFloat(window.document.xy.y.value)
 window.document.graph.deletePoint(x,y)
}
// -></SCRIPT>
</HEAD>
<BODY>
<FORM NAME="xy">
X-Coordinate: <INPUT TYPE="text" NAME="x" SIZE="10">
Y-Coordinate: <INPUT TYPE="text" NAME="y" SIZE="10">
<INPUT TYPE="button" VALUE="Add Point"
 onClick="addPoint()">
<INPUT TYPE="button" VALUE="Delete Point"
 onClick="deletePoint()">
</FORM>
<APPLET CODE="GraphApp.class" NAME="graph" WIDTH=650 HEIGHT=400>
[Graph applet]
</APPLET>
</BODY>
</HTML>
```

The GraphApp.java file, shown in Listing 15.11, defines three classes: Float-Point, PointSet, and GraphApp. The first one, FloatPoint, is used for storing two-dimensional floating-point coordinates. The second class, PointSet, is used for manipulating and graphing sets of points. (I'll present this class's functions below.) The third class, GraphApp, implements the basic applet code. It creates an object of class PointSet and uses addPoint() and deletePoint() for adding and deleting points to the PointSet object. The paint() method invokes the displayGraph() method of the PointSet class to draw the graph.

The variables and functions of the PointSet class are as follows:

The *v* Variable

This variable is assigned a Vector object that is used to store the points added by the user.

The *xUL* and *yUL* Variables

These variables specify the location of the upper-left corner of the graph with respect to the upper-left corner of the applet window.

The *width* and *height* Variables

These variables identify the dimensions of the graph in pixels.

The *xOrig* and *yOrig* Variables

These variables identify the location of the point (0,0) on the graph.

The *numPoints* Variable

This variable identifies the number of points in the graph.

The *xMin*, *xMax*, *yMin*, and *yMax* Variables

These variables identify the minimum and maximum coordinates of the points to be included in the graph. These values are used to rescale the graph to automatically accommodate newly added points.

The *xDelta* and *yDelta* Variables

These variables identify the range of points that are to be included along each axis. (Note that x and y axes are not of the same scale.)

The *add()* Method

This method adds a point to v.

The *delete()* Method

This method deletes a point from v.

The *displayGraph()* Method

This method invokes the following five methods to display the graph:

> **updateGraphParameters()**   This method sets the values of xUL, yUL, width, height, xOrig, and yOrig. It then calculates the values of xMax, yMax, xMin, yMin, xDelta, and yDelta based upon the points entered by the user.
>
> **drawGraphBox()**   This method draws the drawing area—the rectangle surrounding the graph area.
>
> **drawAxes()**   This method draws x and y axes.
>
> **labelAxes()**   This method displays the values of the x and y axes at their intersections with the graph boundary.
>
> **drawPoints()**   This method invokes sortPoints() to sort v and then creates the vTrans vector to translate the absolute coordinates to points within the Graphics object on which the graph is to be displayed. It then draws a line between consecutive points of the vTrans vector.

The *sortPoints()* Method

This method sorts the points contained in the v Vector object from left to right and bottom to top.

Listing 15.11　　**The Graphing Applet (GraphApp.java)**

```java
import java.applet.*;
import java.awt.*;
import java.util.*;
class FloatPoint {
 public float x;
 public float y;
 public FloatPoint(float x,float y) {
  this.x=x;
  this.y=y;
 }
 public String xVal() {
  return String.valueOf(x);
 }
 public String yVal() {
  return String.valueOf(y);
 }
}
class PointSet {
 Vector v = new Vector();
 int xUL, yUL, width, height, xOrig, yOrig, numPoints;
 float xMin, xMax, yMin, yMax, xDelta, yDelta;
 public void add(FloatPoint p) {
  for(int i=0;i<v.size();++i) {
   FloatPoint q=(FloatPoint) v.elementAt(i);
   if(q.x==p.x && q.y==p.y) return;
  }
  v.addElement(p);
 }
 public void delete(FloatPoint p) {
  for(int i=0;i<v.size();++i) {
   FloatPoint q=(FloatPoint) v.elementAt(i);
   if(q.x==p.x && q.y==p.y){
    v.removeElementAt(i);
     break;
   }
  }
 }
 public void displayGraph(Graphics g) {
  updateGraphParameters();
```

```
 drawGraphBox(g);
 drawAxes(g);
 labelAxes(g);
 drawPoints(g);
}
public void updateGraphParameters() {
 xUL=30;
 yUL=30;
 width=550;
 height=300;
 xOrig=xUL+(width/2);
 yOrig=yUL+(height/2);
 numPoints=v.size();
 if(numPoints==0){
  xMax=1;
  yMax=1;
 }else if(numPoints==1){
  FloatPoint p=(FloatPoint) v.firstElement();
  xMax=Math.abs(p.x);
  yMax=Math.abs(p.y);
 }else{
  FloatPoint p=(FloatPoint) v.firstElement();
  xMax=Math.abs(p.x);
  yMax=Math.abs(p.y);
  for(int i=0;i<numPoints;++i) {
    p=(FloatPoint) v.elementAt(i);
    if(Math.abs(p.x)>xMax) xMax=Math.abs(p.x);
    if(Math.abs(p.y)>yMax) yMax=Math.abs(p.y);
  }
 }
 xDelta=xMax*2;
 yDelta=yMax*2;
 xMin=-xMax;
 yMin=-yMax;
}
public void drawGraphBox(Graphics g) {
 g.drawRect(xUL-1,yUL-1,width+2,height+2);
}
public void drawAxes(Graphics g) {
 g.drawLine(xUL,yOrig,xUL+width,yOrig);
 g.drawLine(xOrig,yUL,xOrig,yUL+height);
}
```

```java
public void labelAxes(Graphics g) {
 g.setFont(new Font("TimesRoman",Font.BOLD,14));
 int offset1=5;
 int offset2=25;
 g.drawString(String.valueOf(xMin),xUL-offset2,yOrig);
 g.drawString(String.valueOf(xMax),xUL+width+offset1,yOrig);
 g.drawString(String.valueOf(yMax),xOrig,yUL-offset1);
 g.drawString(String.valueOf(yMin),xOrig,yUL+height+offset2);
}
public void drawPoints(Graphics g) {
 sortPoints();
 Vector vTrans = new Vector();
 for(int i=0;i<numPoints;++i) {
  FloatPoint p = (FloatPoint) v.elementAt(i);
  int xTrans=xOrig;
  int yTrans=yOrig;
  xTrans+=Math.round(((float)width/2.0)*(p.x/xMax));
  yTrans-=Math.round(((float)height/2.0)*(p.y/yMax));
  vTrans.addElement(new Point(xTrans,yTrans));
 }
 Color currentColor = g.getColor();
 for(int i=0;i<numPoints-1;++i) {
  Point p1=(Point) vTrans.elementAt(i);
  Point p2=(Point) vTrans.elementAt(i+1);
  g.setColor(Color.red);
  g.drawLine(p1.x,p1.y,p2.x,p2.y);
 }
 g.setColor(currentColor);
}
public void sortPoints() {
 boolean again=true;
 while (again) {
  again=false;
  for(int i=0;i<numPoints-1;++i) {
    FloatPoint p1=(FloatPoint) v.elementAt(i);
    FloatPoint p2=(FloatPoint) v.elementAt(i+1);
    if(p2.x<p1.x || (p2.x==p1.x && p2.y<p1.y)){
     v.setElementAt(p2,i);
     v.setElementAt(p1,i+1);
     again=true;
    }
  }
```

```
    }
   }
  }
 public class GraphApp extends Applet {
  PointSet ps=new PointSet();
  public void paint(Graphics g) {
   ps.displayGraph(g);
  }
  public void addPoint(float x,float y) {
   FloatPoint p=new FloatPoint(x,y);
   ps.add(p);
   repaint();
  }
  public void deletePoint(float x,float y) {
   FloatPoint p=new FloatPoint(x,y);
   ps.delete(p);
   repaint();
  }
 }
```

Summary

In this chapter, you were introduced to Java and learned about its capabilities. You covered the similarities and differences between Java and JavaScript, and learned how to develop simple Java programs and applets. You also learned how to use JavaScript to communicate with Java applets and how to invoke JavaScript functions from within an applet. In the next chapter, you'll learn about ActiveX and how Internet Explorer supports communication between JavaScript, Java applets, and ActiveX components.

Scripting ActiveX Components

- What Is ActiveX?

- Using ActiveX Components

- Accessing ActiveX Components from within JScript

- Using the ActiveX Control Pad

ActiveX is an approach to developing and using software components that Microsoft created. ActiveX is an extension of the Object Linking and Embedding (OLE) and the Component Object Model (COM) technologies that were developed for Windows 3.1. ActiveX allows these technologies to be used with Web applications. In this chapter, you'll learn the basics of ActiveX, how to use ActiveX components in your Web applications, and how to script ActiveX components, using JScript. When you finish this chapter, you'll be able to integrate ActiveX components with your scripts.

What Is ActiveX?

As I mentioned above, ActiveX is an extension of the OLE and COM technologies that were developed for Windows 3.1. To understand ActiveX, you must understand how it evolved from these earlier technologies. Microsoft developed OLE to simplify the process by which Windows programs could exchange information. OLE was developed to allow objects that were developed in one program to be displayed and edited in other. For example, it allowed an Excel spreadsheet to be pasted into a Word document, and then displayed and edited from within the Word document.

This document-centric approach to object sharing is organized according to the program in which an object is embedded, referred to as the OLE container, and the program that creates the embedded object, referred to as the OLE server. In the example of the embedded Excel spreadsheet, Excel would be the OLE server, and Word would be the OLE container.

After having developed and deployed OLE in Windows 3.1, Microsoft realized that the capability to embed objects within documents was only one aspect of the more general problem of how software components should interact in a client-server framework. Based on this realization, Microsoft developed COM. COM provides a general approach for software components to communicate and exchange services.

Because of COM's power and flexibility, it quickly emerged as the basis for the development of Windows software components. ActiveX was introduced in 1996 as an attempt to transition COM-based software components to the Internet. The intent of ActiveX was to allow COM components to be used with Web browsers, Web servers, and other Internet-based software applications.

Microsoft portrayed ActiveX as a new technology, but it is essentially COM for the Internet. Since its introduction, ActiveX has been expanded to include a variety of related technologies. Some of these technologies are as follows:

ActiveX Components   COM components that can be used in Internet applications. ActiveX components that are GUI controls are referred to as ActiveX controls.

ActiveX Scripting   The use of JScript, VBScript, and other scripting languages to integrate ActiveX controls in Web applications.

Active Server Pages (ASP)   The extension of ActiveX components to Web servers.

ActiveX Data Objects   Provide the capability to access databases through the use of COM and OLE.

Active Documents   An extension of OLE to allow documents to be more accessible within an ActiveX container, such as Internet Explorer.

ActiveX Conferencing   ActiveX technologies, such as NetMeeting, that support conferencing over the Internet.

In this chapter, I'll concentrate on the first two. You'll learn how to use ActiveX controls in your Web pages and how to script them using JScript. In Chapter 22, "Scripting Microsoft Servers," you'll learn about Active Server Pages and ActiveX data objects.

NOTE   The term "ActiveX" is becoming more generic and is often used to refer to COM technologies in general, whether or not they are used in Internet applications.

Using ActiveX Components

Once you get the hang of it, ActiveX components are easy to insert and use in your Web pages. There is, however, somewhat of a learning curve, due to the arcane information required to include ActiveX components in your scripts. I'll start by showing you some scripted ActiveX components in action. After that, I'll show you the syntax required to include the components in a Web page and access them from JScript. Don't be daunted when you see the information required to use ActiveX. I'll show you a tool, referred to as the ActiveX control pad, that will greatly simplify the process of working with ActiveX components.

> **NOTE**   To run the examples in this chapter, you'll need Internet Explorer 5 (Beta 2) or later.

Download `axdemo.htm` (Listing 16.1) from this book's page on the Sybex Web site. When you open it, it will display the Web page shown in Figure 16.1. Note the two custom components displayed on the page. The top component is a progress bar. Its initial value is zero, so there is no progress. The bottom component is a slider. Its initial value is also set to zero. Both the slider and the progress bar are ActiveX components. Their interaction is scripted using JScript.

FIGURE 16.1:

Using some basic ActiveX controls (Listing 16.1).

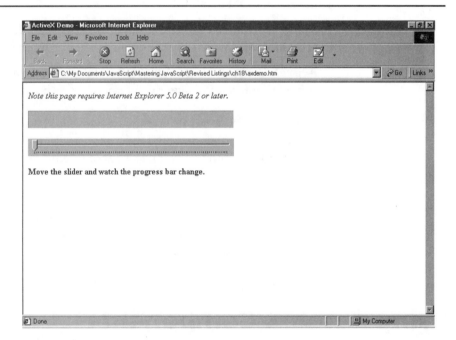

Move the slider to the right, you'll notice that the value of the progress bar changes to match the value of the slider. Refer to Figure 16.2. Once you understand how the interaction between the slider and progress bar is implemented in JScript, and how these components are inserted into a Web page, you'll be well on the way to scripting ActiveX components.

FIGURE 16.2:

Moving the slider causes
the progress bar to change
(Listing 16.1).

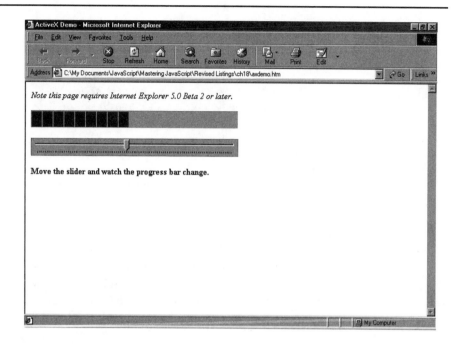

Listing 16.1   Using ActiveX Components with JScript (axdemo.htm)

```
<HTML>
<HEAD>
<TITLE>ActiveX Demo</TITLE>
</HEAD>
<BODY>
<P><I>Note this page requires Internet Explorer 5.0 Beta 2
or later.</I></P>
    <OBJECT ID="ProgressBar1" WIDTH=400 HEIGHT=33
     CLASSID="CLSID:0713E8D2-850A-101B-AFC0-4210102A8DA7">
        <PARAM NAME="_ExtentX" VALUE="10583">
        <PARAM NAME="_ExtentY" VALUE="873">
        <PARAM NAME="_Version" VALUE="327682">
        <PARAM NAME="Appearance" VALUE="1">
    </OBJECT>
<P>
    <SCRIPT LANGUAGE="JavaScript" FOR="Slider1" EVENT="Change()">
<!-
ProgressBar1.value = Slider1.value
->
```

```
</SCRIPT>
<OBJECT ID="Slider1" WIDTH=400 HEIGHT=33
  CLASSID="CLSID:373FF7F0-EB8B-11CD-8820-08002B2F4F5A">
      <PARAM NAME="_ExtentX" VALUE="10583">
      <PARAM NAME="_ExtentY" VALUE="873">
      <PARAM NAME="_Version" VALUE="327682">
      <PARAM NAME="Max" VALUE="100">
</OBJECT>
<P><B>Move the slider and watch the progress bar change.</B></P>
</BODY>
</HTML>
```

The first thing that you should notice about Listing 16.1 is the use of the
<OBJECT> tags. The two <OBJECT> tags are used to include the progress bar and
slider. This is the typical way that ActiveX controls are included in a Web page.
You should also notice a script nestled between the two <OBJECT> tags. This
script is used to enable interaction between the two ActiveX controls. We'll look
at the <OBJECT> tags first and then come back to the controls.

The first <OBJECT> tag consists of the following:

```
<OBJECT ID="ProgressBar1" WIDTH=400 HEIGHT=33
      CLASSID="CLSID:0713E8D2-850A-101B-AFC0-4210102A8DA7">
          <PARAM NAME="_ExtentX" VALUE="10583">
          <PARAM NAME="_ExtentY" VALUE="873">
          <PARAM NAME="_Version" VALUE="327682">
          <PARAM NAME="Appearance" VALUE="1">
      </OBJECT>
```

The ID attribute provides an identifier for the control. You can use this identifier
to access the control from your scripts. The WIDTH and HEIGHT attributes specify
the control's dimensions in pixels. You can resize the progress bar by altering these
values. The CLASSID attribute contains an alphanumeric value like none other. The
monstrous value of this attribute is used to uniquely identify the ActiveX object.
Every COM object (and therefore every ActiveX component) is an instance of a
class. The class identifier (specified by the CLASSID attribute) uniquely identifies
the class to which a COM object belongs. This identifier is used to tell the COM
library (a creator of COM objects) which class to use to create an object. Don't
worry about having to create these identifiers; they are automatically created for
you when you use the ActiveX control pad.

The <PARAM> tags are similar to the <PARAM> tags used with Java applets. They specify the names of ActiveX component parameters and the values of these parameters. The <PARAM> tags are also filled in by the ActiveX control pad.

The script that occurs between the two <OBJECT> tags consists of one line. It sets the value of the ProgressBar1 object to the value of the Slider1 object. The <SCRIPT> tag's FOR and EVENT attributes are used to connect events to scripts. The FOR attribute identifies the object for which the event occurs, and the EVENT attribute identifies the event. These attributes are used to identify the script as an event handler for the Change event of the Slider1 object.

Accessing ActiveX Components from within JScript

Now that you know the basics of using ActiveX components, let's take it one step further. Listing 16.2 shows an adaptation of Listing 16.1 that uses JScript to control both the slider and the progress bar. These controls are randomly updated as the result of the script's operation. Figure 16.3 provides a snapshot of the output it generates.

FIGURE 16.3:

The script causes the slider and progress bar to be randomly updated (Listing 16.2).

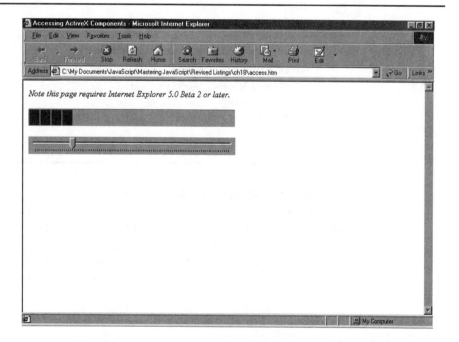

Listing 16.2   **Accessing ActiveX Controls (access.htm)**

```
<HTML>
<HEAD>
<TITLE>Accessing ActiveX Components</TITLE>
<SCRIPT LANGUAGE="JavaScript">
function accessActiveX() {
 var newValue = (1000*Math.random()) % 101
 ProgressBar1.Value = newValue
 Slider1.Value = newValue
}
</SCRIPT>
</HEAD>
<BODY onLoad='setInterval("accessActiveX()",2000)'>
<P><I>Note this page requires Internet Explorer 5.0 Beta 2 or
later.</I></P>
    <OBJECT ID="ProgressBar1" WIDTH=400 HEIGHT=33
     CLASSID="CLSID:0713E8D2-850A-101B-AFC0-4210102A8DA7">
        <PARAM NAME="_ExtentX" VALUE="10583">
        <PARAM NAME="_ExtentY" VALUE="873">
        <PARAM NAME="_Version" VALUE="327682">
        <PARAM NAME="Appearance" VALUE="1">
    </OBJECT>
<P>
    <OBJECT ID="Slider1" WIDTH=400 HEIGHT=33
     CLASSID="CLSID:373FF7F0-EB8B-11CD-8820-08002B2F4F5A">
        <PARAM NAME="_ExtentX" VALUE="10583">
        <PARAM NAME="_ExtentY" VALUE="873">
        <PARAM NAME="_Version" VALUE="327682">
        <PARAM NAME="Max" VALUE="100">
    </OBJECT>
</BODY>
</HTML>
```

You should notice that the <OBJECT> tags are the same as in Listing 16.1. The only difference between access.htm and axdemo.htm is the script it contains in its head. The onLoad event handler of the <BODY> tag causes the accessActiveX() function to be invoked every two seconds. This function generates a random value between 0 and 100 and sets the value of the progress bar and slider to these values. As you can see from this example, ActiveX controls are easy to manipulate with scripts.

Using the ActiveX Control Pad

Now that you have a feel for how ActiveX controls are implemented, I'll show you how to use the ActiveX control pad to insert them in your Web pages. The ActiveX Control Pad is available from Microsoft's Web site at `http://microsoft.com/workshop/misc/cpad/default.asp`. Go ahead and download and install ActiveX control pad before continuing.

When the Control Pad is launched, it displays the window shown in Figure 16.4.

FIGURE 16.4:

The ActiveX Control Pad
opening window
(Listing 16.3)

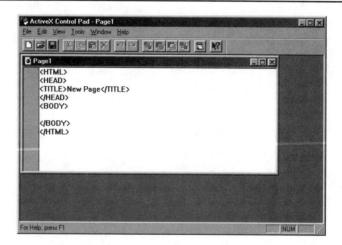

At first glance, the Control Pad looks like a basic HTML editor, but it is much more than that. You can use it to do the following:

- Insert ActiveX controls

- Attach scripts to the controls

- Create HTML layouts

- Work with both JScript and VBScript

I'll show you how to do the first two using JScript. You can learn more about the Control Pad through its extensive help information.

Let's work through an example to show how the Control Pad works. We'll use it to produce the Web page shown in Listing 16.3. Please follow these steps:

1. If you haven't done so already, launch the Control Pad.

2. Change the document title to *Picture Viewer*.

3. Select Edit ➢ Insert ActiveX Control. The dialog box shown in Figure 16.5 is displayed.

FIGURE 16.5:

Use the Insert ActiveX Control dialog box to insert controls into the control pad (Listing 16.3).

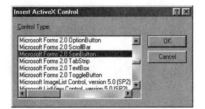

4. Select Microsoft Forms 2.0 SpinButton and click OK. The Properties dialog box shown in Figure 16.6 is displayed.

FIGURE 16.6:

The Properties sheet makes it easy to change an object's properties (Listing 16.3).

5. Change the spin button's orientation to horizontal. Then set its width to 71 and its height to 32.

6. Close the Edit ActiveX Control window.

7. Select Edit ➢ Insert ActiveX Control and insert a Microsoft ActiveX Image Control 1.0 object into your page (underneath the spin button).

8. Set the AutoSize property to *true*, the height to 320, and the width to 427.

9. Close the Edit ActiveX Control window.

10. Select Edit ➤ Insert ActiveX Control and insert a Microsoft Forms 2.0 Label object into your page (underneath the image).

11. Set the foreground color to blue, background color to white, font to 14pt Arial, height to 50, and width to 150.

12. Close the Edit ActiveX Control window.

You've inserted all the ActiveX components you need for the example. We'll now use the control pad to script these components.

1. Select Tools ➤ Options ➤ Script. Refer to Figure 16.7. Click the Code View and JavaScript radio buttons and then click OK.

FIGURE 16.7:

Use the script options to select a scripting language and view of your code (Listing 16.3).

2. Now select Tools ➤ Script Wizard. The window shown in Figure 16.8 is displayed.

FIGURE 16.8:

The Script Wizard makes scripting ActiveX components a snap (Listing 16.3).

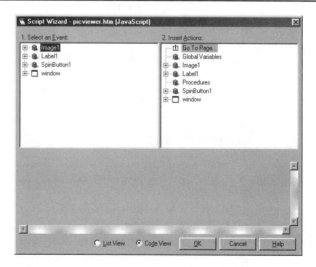

3. In the Select an Event pane, click on the `window` object and the `onLoad` event. Then type the following code in the lower half of the window (refer to Figure 16.9):

```
currentImage = 0
Image1.PicturePath = "image0.jpg"
Label1.Caption = "image0.jpg"
```

FIGURE 16.9:

Type your code into the script text area (Listing 16.3).

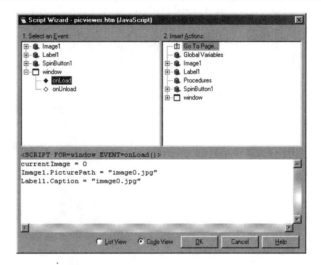

4. Now select the `SpinDown` event for `SpinButton1` (in the upper-left pane) and type the following code in the script text area:

```
currentImage += 7
currentImage %= 8
Label1.Caption = "image"+currentImage+".jpg"
Image1.PicturePath = Label1.Caption
```

5. Select the `SpinUp` event for `SpinButton1` and enter the following code:

```
currentImage += 1
currentImage %= 8
```

```
Label1.Caption = "image"+currentImage+".jpg"
Image1.PicturePath = Label1.Caption
```

6. You're almost done. Close the Script Wizard by clicking the OK button. The control pad window has the code for your application. Enter ** ** between each pair of <OBJECT> tags, as shown in Figure 16.10.

FIGURE 16.10:

Insert a nonbreaking space between the objects (Listing 16.3).

7. Save your file as picviewer.htm.

To use the picviewer application, you need some image files. I've included eight files with this chapter's code. You can use these files or substitute files of your own. Figure 16.11 shows the window displayed by the picviewer application. Use the spin buttons to move through the list of images that it displays.

FIGURE 16.11:

The window displayed by the picviewer application (Listing 16.3).

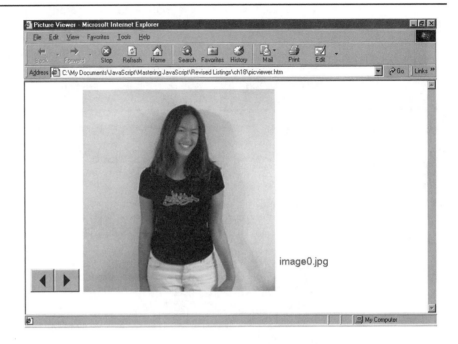

Listing 16.3 **The File That Is Generated by the ActiveX Control Pad (picviewer.htm)**

```
<HTML>
<HEAD>
    <SCRIPT LANGUAGE="JavaScript" FOR="window" EVENT="onLoad()">
<!-
currentImage = 0
Image1.PicturePath = "image0.jpg"
Label1.Caption = "image0.jpg"
->
    </SCRIPT>
<TITLE>Picture Viewer</TITLE>
</HEAD>
<BODY>
    <SCRIPT LANGUAGE="JavaScript" FOR="SpinButton1" EVENT="SpinDown()">
<!-
currentImage += 7
currentImage %= 8
Label1.Caption = "image"+currentImage+".jpg"
Image1.PicturePath = Label1.Caption
```

```
    ->
      </SCRIPT>
      <OBJECT ID="SpinButton1" WIDTH=95 HEIGHT=43
       CLASSID="CLSID:79176FB0-B7F2-11CE-97EF-00AA006D2776">
          <PARAM NAME="Size" VALUE="2505;1129">
          <PARAM NAME="Orientation" VALUE="1">
      </OBJECT>
       
      <OBJECT ID="Image1" WIDTH=569 HEIGHT=427
       CLASSID="CLSID:D4A97620-8E8F-11CF-93CD-00AA00C08FDF">
          <PARAM NAME="AutoSize" VALUE="-1">
          <PARAM NAME="BorderStyle" VALUE="0">
          <PARAM NAME="SizeMode" VALUE="3">
          <PARAM NAME="Size" VALUE="15064;11289">
          <PARAM NAME="PictureAlignment" VALUE="0">
          <PARAM NAME="VariousPropertyBits" VALUE="19">
      </OBJECT>
       
      <OBJECT ID="Label1" WIDTH=200 HEIGHT=67
       CLASSID="CLSID:978C9E23-D4B0-11CE-BF2D-00AA003F40D0">
          <PARAM NAME="ForeColor" VALUE="16744448">
          <PARAM NAME="BackColor" VALUE="16777215">
          <PARAM NAME="Size" VALUE="5292;1764">
          <PARAM NAME="FontName" VALUE="Arial">
          <PARAM NAME="FontHeight" VALUE="280">
          <PARAM NAME="FontCharSet" VALUE="0">
          <PARAM NAME="FontPitchAndFamily" VALUE="2">
          <PARAM NAME="FontWeight" VALUE="0">
      </OBJECT>
  </BODY>
  </HTML>
```

Summary

In this chapter, you were introduced to ActiveX and learned how to include
ActiveX controls in your Web pages. You also learned how to use JScript to access
the properties, methods, and events of ActiveX controls. Finally, you learned how
the ActiveX control pad can simplify the process of working with ActiveX controls. In the next chapter, you'll switch back to Navigator and learn how to access
plug-ins from your scripts.

CHAPTER

SEVENTEEN

17

How Plug-Ins Work

- ■ Popular Plug-Ins

- ■ Working with MIME Types

- ■ Determining Installed Plug-Ins

- ■ Accessing Plug-Ins from within JavaScript

- ■ Listing Plug-In Methods

- ■ Synchronizing Multiple Plug-Ins

- ■ Assisting Users in Installing Plug-Ins

Plug-ins provide the capability to extend your browser in a variety of ways. You can use a plug-in to listen to a radio broadcast, watch a video, or control another computer remotely. The potential applications for plug-ins are limitless. In this chapter, you'll learn all about plug-ins—how they work, how they are used, and how they interface with Navigator. You'll also access plug-ins from JavaScript. When you finish this chapter, you'll have a good understanding of how plug-ins work and how to use them in your Web applications.

NOTE   Although Netscape plug-ins are supported by Internet Explorer, Internet Explorer plug-ins are typically implemented as ActiveX components (see Chapter 16, "Scripting ActiveX Components"). This chapter shows how to use Navigator plug-ins from JavaScript with Netscape's LiveConnect. If you want to learn how to access an Internet Explorer plug-in from JScript, refer to Chapter 16.

Popular Plug-Ins

Since Netscape first introduced them, a large variety of attractive and useful plug-ins has been developed. They range from inline viewers like the Adobe Acrobat viewer, for example, to complete browser-embedded applications, such as SCIENCE.ORG's transferRNA. The Netscape Plug-In page provides links to many exciting and useful plug-ins. It is located at the URL `http://home .netscape.com/plugins/`.

The following are a few of the most popular browser plug-ins:

LiveAudio   Netscape's LiveAudio plug-in comes standard with Netscape. It plays audio files in WAV, AU, AIFF, and MIDI formats. LiveAudio is LiveConnect-capable and may be accessed from JavaScript.

LiveVideo   The Netscape LiveVideo plug-in is LiveConnect-capable and can be accessed from JavaScript. It is used to display videos that are in the Windows AVI format.

Cosmo Player   Cosmo Player is a LiveConnect-capable Virtual Reality Modeling Language (VRML) plug-in that works with both Navigator and Internet Explorer. It is an excellent viewer for displaying the three-dimensional worlds of VRML. You can download it from `http://vrml .sgi.com/cosmoplayer`.

QuickTime   The QuickTime plug-in displays QuickTime video files in an area of a browser window. The QuickTime plug-in was developed by Apple and is available at `http://www.apple.com/quicktime/download/index.html`.

Adobe Acrobat   Adobe's Acrobat plug-in allows you to display documents that are in Adobe's portable document format (PDF). PDF files have become a standard for distributing documents in electronic form. Acrobat is available from Adobe's home page at `http://www.adobe.com`.

Pointcast   The Pointcast Network plug-in allows up-to-the-minute news, weather, sports, and other information to be broadcast to your browser. It is available from the Pointcast home page at `http://www.pointcast.com`.

Macromedia Shockwave   The Macromedia Shockwave plug-in displays animations, movies, and other multimedia presentations that are produced by the Macromedia Director. It is available from the Macromedia home page at `http://www.macromedia.com`.

NCompass ScriptActive   The NCompass ScriptActive plug-in allows ActiveX-based applications to be displayed via Netscape Navigator. It is available from the NCompass Labs home page at `http://www.ncompasslabs.com`.

The plug-ins listed above are some of the most useful and popular ones that are available. However, they are only a small sample of what's available in plug-in technology. To find more information about what plug-ins are available for different applications, consult the BrowserWatch—Plug-In Plaza! Web page at `http://browserwatch.iworld.com/plug-in.html`.

Plug-Ins in Action

Plug-ins are independently developed software components that execute in the context of a browser window. They are compiled in the native executable code format of the operating system and computer in which they are run. Plug-ins are installed for use with Navigator by placing them in Navigator's `Plugins` directory and registering them for use with documents of a particular MIME type.

Plug-ins provide the capability to view documents of different MIME types. The documents can be viewed in *embedded mode* or in *full-page mode*. When a plug-in operates in embedded mode, it is assigned a dedicated part of a loaded HTML document in which to display information to the user and to respond to user-generated events, such as mouse and keyboard actions. When a plug-in operates in full-page mode, it is not displayed as part of a larger HTML document. Instead, it is given an entire browser window in which to operate.

Whether a plug-in document is viewed in embedded mode or full-page mode depends on how it is included in a document. If a plug-in document is inserted in an HTML document using the <embed> tag then it is viewed in embedded mode. If a plug-in document is referenced as part of a URL, then it is displayed in full-page mode.

The following sections describe the uses of embedded and full-page mode.

WARNING   Plug-ins, unlike HTML, JavaScript, and Java, are platform dependent. This means that some plug-ins do not exist for users of certain operating systems. Most plug-ins, however, support Windows and Macintosh platforms.

Embedded Plug-In Documents

Plug-in documents are inserted in a Web page using the <embed> tag. The syntax of the <embed> tag is as follows:

```
<embed attributes>
```

An <embed> tag must contain either a SRC or a TYPE attribute. The SRC attribute, which identifies the document to be viewed by the plug-in, is used more often than the TYPE attribute. The TYPE attribute is used by plug-ins that aren't principally used as viewers, but rather are used to create browser-based applications that are not necessarily document-specific. This is discussed in the section, "Plug-Ins as Embedded Applications," later in this chapter.

There are numerous other embed attributes that can be included in addition to the SRC and TYPE attributes. For example, other important and frequently used attributes are the NAME attribute and the HEIGHT and WIDTH attributes. The NAME attribute is used in JavaScript to access the plug-in object by name. The HEIGHT and WIDTH attributes are used to specify the location of the window area that is assigned to the plug-in. These dimensions are important to the plug-in's appearance. The attributes of the <embed> tag are summarized in Table 17.1.

TABLE 17.1: The Attributes of the <embed> Tag

Attribute	Description
HEIGHT	Specifies the vertical dimension of the plug-in area.
HIDDEN	Specifies whether the plug-in is to be hidden or visible.
NAME	Associates a name with the plug-in instance.
PALETTE	Specifies the mode of the plug-in's color palette.
PLUGINSPAGE	Specifies a URL containing instructions for installing the plug-in. This helps you to assist the user in installing a plug-in needed for a particular MIME type.
SRC	Specifies the document to be displayed by the plug-in.
TYPE	Specifies the MIME type associated with the plug-in.
WIDTH	Specifies the horizontal dimension of the plug-in area.
UNITS	Specifies the units of measurement associated with the HEIGHT and WIDTH attributes. The default is pixels.

Plug-ins are free to define additional attributes beside those listed in Table 17.1. These are usually defined on the plug-in developer's Web site. The values of these plug-in-specific attributes are automatically passed to the plug-in by Navigator.

How the *SRC* Attribute Is Processed

When an <embed> tag contains a SRC attribute, the value of the attribute is a URL that identifies the location of a document to be viewed by a plug-in. For example, consider the following <embed> tag:

```
<embed SRC="movie.avi">
```

When your browser loads an HTML file containing the above tag, it asks the Web server at the document's location what the document's MIME type is. When your browser receives the MIME type information from the Web server, it checks in its MIME type table to see if there is a plug-in associated with that MIME type. If a registered plug-in is found, then the plug-in is loaded into memory and a specific instance of the plug-in is created.

After a plug-in instance is created, the document identified by the SRC attribute is retrieved from its Web server by your browser. The contents of this document are then passed to the plug-in as a data stream. The plug-in reads the data stream and processes and displays the data in accordance with its MIME type. The plug-in is free to interact with the user via its allocated window area (if it requires one). It may access other network resources by instructing the browser to get information at a specific URL or to post information to a URL.

When the page containing a plug-in document is no longer displayed in a browser window, the plug-in instance associated with the document is deleted. When all instances of a plug-in have been deleted, the plug-in is removed from memory.

Plug-In Documents Referenced as URLs

When a plug-in document is to be displayed in full-page mode, it is not referenced using an `<embed>` tag. Instead, it is referenced directly via a URL. For example, consider the following link:

```
<A HREF="manual.pdf">Link to a plug-in document.</A>
```

When you click on the above link, your browser attempts to load the `manual .pdf` document. First, it queries the Web server at the document's location to determine the document's MIME type. It then processes the MIME type information in the same way that it would for embedded plug-in documents. It looks in its table of registered MIME types to determine what plug-in (if any) is registered for that MIME type. If a registered plug-in is found, then the plug-in is loaded into memory and an instance of that plug-in is created.

The plug-in instance is given an entire Navigator window in which to interact with the user. This is the only difference between the ways that full-page and embedded plug-ins are handled. The plug-in instance is deleted either as the result of its window being closed or as the result of a different document being loaded into its window. The plug-in is removed from memory when all of its instances are deleted.

Plug-Ins as Embedded Applications

Back in the early days of the Web, separate helper programs, referred to as *external viewers*, were launched by a browser to display documents of those MIME types that could not be handled by the browser. These ancestors of modern plug-ins were cumbersome to install and work with.

Plug-ins were originally developed as *inline viewers*. This means they were used to integrate external viewers into the browser application. Most plug-ins still serve this purpose—they display plug-in documents in embedded or full-page mode. However, a new breed of plug-in is becoming popular: embedded *applications* that execute in the context of a browser window. These embedded applications might or might not display documents—their main purpose is to perform a service that is independent of a particular document. For example, SCIENCE.ORG's transfer-RNA plug-in is used to transfer files from one user to another. You can download this plug-in at `http://computers.science.org/transferRNA/nptrna.zip`.

You may wonder how these plug-ins work if they aren't associated with a document of a specific MIME type. The answer is that they *are* associated with a MIME type, but not with a specific document of that MIME type.

Embedded application plug-ins are identified using the TYPE attribute of an `<embed>` tag as opposed to the SRC attribute. Consider the following example:

```
<embed TYPE="application/x-transferRNA" HEIGHT="390" WIDTH="600"
ShowRecvPage="0">
```

The above `<embed>` tag may be used to include the transferRNA plug-in within your Web page. When your browser encounters the above `<embed>` tag in a document, it uses the TYPE attribute to determine what MIME type is associated with the plug-in, and then looks in its MIME type table to see what plug-in (if any) is registered for that MIME type. (In this case, the plug-in is the transferRNA plug-in. Note that in this case the MIME type was named after the plug-in.) Your browser then loads the transferRNA plug-in.

Working with MIME Types

MIME types are fundamental to the operation of the Web. Browsers use MIME types to determine how to display files that are retrieved from Web servers. Similarly, in order to use a plug-in, it must be associated with a MIME type. The `mimeTypes` array, a property of the `navigator` object, describes all of the MIME types that are known to the browser.

The elements of the `mimeTypes` array are `mimeTypes` objects. Table 17.2 summarizes the properties of the `mimeTypes` object. These properties describe the MIME type and identify the plug-in that is installed and enabled to handle the MIME type. The `mimeTypes` object has no methods and is not associated with any events.

TABLE 17.2: Properties of the mimeTypes Object

Property	Description
type	The name of the MIME type.
description	A description of the MIME type.
enabledPlugin	The plugins object that is enabled to handle the MIME type. If no enabled plug-in is associated with the MIME type, then this value is null.
suffixes	A comma-separated list of the file extensions associated with the MIME type.

NOTE The plugins object is covered in the next section.

Listing 17.1 shows how the mimeTypes array is used. Download mime.htm from this book's Web page at http://www.sybex.com. When you open it, it will display a list of the MIME types that your browser is familiar with. Figure 17.1 shows the MIME types that my browser displayed. Your browser may display a different list depending on the plug-ins you've installed.

Listing 17.1 **Using the *mimeTypes* Object (mime.htm)**

```
<HTML>
<HEAD>
<TITLE>Determining how MIME types are handled</TITLE>
</HEAD>
<BODY>
<SCRIPT LANGUAGE="JavaScript"><!-
m=navigator.mimeTypes
for(var i=0;i<m.length;++i){
 with(document){
  writeln('<P><B>MIME type: </B>'+m[i].type+'</P>')
  writeln('<P><B>Description: </B>'+m[i].description+'</P>')
  writeln('<P><B>Suffixes: </B>'+m[i].suffixes+'</P>')
  writeln('<HR>')
 }
}
// -></SCRIPT>
</BODY>
</HTML>
```

FIGURE 17.1:

Displaying the MIME types that are familiar to your browser (Listing 17.1)

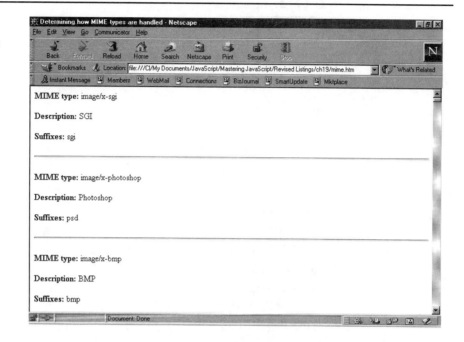

The script shown in Listing 17.1 iterates through the mimeTypes array and displays each mimeTypes object's type, description, and suffixes properties.

Determining Installed Plug-Ins

One of the first things that you'll want to do in order to use plug-ins is to determine which plug-ins are installed for a browser. JavaScript provides the plugins array for that purpose.

The plugins array is a property of the navigator object. It contains an entry for each plug-in that is installed for a browser. Each element of the array is a plugins object.

The plugins object has the five properties described in Table 17.3. It does not have any methods, and is not associated with any events. It does provide the capability to completely describe all plug-ins installed for a particular browser.

TABLE 17.3: Properties of the plugins Object

Property	Description
name	The name of the plug-in, as specified in the <embed> tag.
filename	The name of the file from which the plug-in is loaded.
description	The description of the plug-in provided by the plug-in's developer.
length	The number of MIME types supported by the plug-in.
[]	An array of the MIME types supported by the plug-in. Each element is a mimeTypes object.

Each plugins object is also an array of mimeTypes objects. This is confusing, so I'll summarize here how the plugins array and plugins object fit into the navigator object hierarchy:

- The plugins array is a property of the navigator object.
- Each element of the plugins array is a plugins object.
- The plugins object has five properties.
- One of those properties is an array of mimeTypes objects.
- The elements of this array are accessed by indexing the plugins object.

To clarify how the plugins array and the plugins object are used in a script, open plugins.htm (Listing 17.2) with your browser. Your browser will display a Web page similar to the one shown in Figure 17.2. As you can see, the information provided by the plugins object is very comprehensive.

Listing 17.2   Displaying Plug-In Information (plugins.htm)

```
<HTML>
<HEAD>
<TITLE>Determining Installed Plug-ins</TITLE>
</HEAD>
<BODY>
<SCRIPT LANGUAGE="JavaScript"><!-
p=navigator.plugins
for(var i=0;i<p.length;++i){
 with(document){
```

```
    writeln('<P><B>Plugin: </B>'+p[i].name+'</P>')
    writeln('<P><B>File name: </B>'+p[i].filename+'</P>')
    writeln('<P><B>Description: </B>'+p[i].description+'</P>')
    writeln('<P><B>MIME Types: </B>')
    for(var j=0;j<p[i].length;++j)
     writeln(p[i][j].type+'</BR>')
    writeln('</P><HR>')
   }
 }
// -></SCRIPT>
</BODY>
</HTML>
```

FIGURE 17.2:

My browser's plug-in information (Listing 17.2)

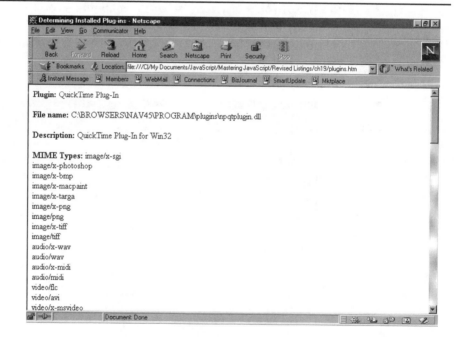

Listing 17.2 shows the contents of plugins.htm. A single script is included in the document's body. This script uses the p variable to refer to the plugins array. It then loops through each element of the plugins array and displays the name, filename, and description properties of the plugins objects. The length property is used to determine how many MIME types are supported by the plugins object. The type property of each of the mimeTypes objects referenced by each plugins object is printed.

NOTE
The way that Netscape designed the `plugins` object is very messy. Instead of defining each `plugins` object as an array of `mimeTypes` objects, it would have been much cleaner to have given the `plugins` object a `mimeTypes` property that would consist of an array of `mimeTypes` objects.

How About Plug-Ins Works

When you select Help ➣ About Plug-Ins in Navigator, your browser displays a description of all plug-ins supported by your browser, in the format shown in Figure 17.3. If you select View ➣ Document Source, you'll see the HTML file shown in Listing 17.3. This file provides a good example of how the `plugins` and `mimeTypes` objects can be used together to list and describe all of the `plugins` known to a browser.

FIGURE 17.3:

The About Plug-Ins display (Listing 17.3)

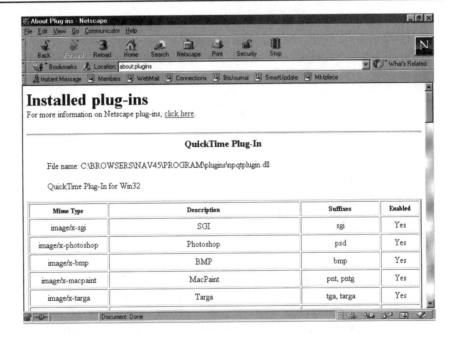

Listing 17.3   The About Plug-Ins Script (about.htm)

```
<HTML>
<HEAD>
<TITLE>About Plug-ins</TITLE>
</HEAD>
<BODY>
<SCRIPT language="javascript">
<!- JavaScript to enumerate and display all installed
 plug-ins ->
numPlugins = navigator.plugins.length;
if (numPlugins > 0)
  document.writeln("<b><font size=+3>Installed plug-ins
    </font></b><br>");
else
 document.writeln("<b><font size=+2>No plug-ins are
   installed.</font></b><br>");
 document.writeln("For more information on Netscape
  plug-ins, <A HREF=http://home.netscape.com/comprod/
  products/navigator/version_2.0/plugins/index.html>
  click here</A>.<p><hr>");
for (i = 0; i < numPlugins; i++)
{
 plugin = navigator.plugins[i];
 document.write("<center><font size=+1><b>");
 document.write(plugin.name);
 document.writeln("</b></font></center><br>");
 document.writeln("<dl>");
 document.writeln("<dd>File name:");
 document.write(plugin.filename);
 document.write("<dd><br>");
 document.write(plugin.description);
 document.writeln("</dl>");
 document.writeln("<p>");
 document.writeln("<table width=100% border=2 cellpadding=5>");
 document.writeln("<tr>");
 document.writeln("<th width=20%><font size=-1>Mime Type</font>
   </th>");
 document.writeln("<th width=50%><font size=-1>Description
   </font></th>");
 document.writeln("<th width=20%><font size=-1>Suffixes</font>
```

```
 </th>");
document.writeln("<th><font size=-1>Enabled</th>");
document.writeln("</tr>");
numTypes = plugin.length;
for (j = 0; j < numTypes; j++)
{
 mimetype = plugin[j];

 if (mimetype)
 {
  enabled = "No";
  enabledPlugin = mimetype.enabledPlugin;
  if (enabledPlugin && (enabledPlugin.name == plugin.name))
   enabled = "Yes";
  document.writeln("<tr align=center>");
  document.writeln("<td>");
  document.write(mimetype.type);
  document.writeln("</td>");
  document.writeln("<td>");
  document.write(mimetype.description);
  document.writeln("</td>");
  document.writeln("<td>");
  document.write(mimetype.suffixes);
  document.writeln("</td>");
  document.writeln("<td>");
  document.writeln(enabled);
  document.writeln("</td>");
  document.writeln("</tr>");
 }
}

 document.write("</table>");
 document.write("<p><hr><p>");
}
</SCRIPT>
</BODY>
</HTML>
```

The about.htm file contains a single script in the document body. The numPlugins variable is set to the number of plugins objects contained in the plugins array. After displaying header information, the script loops through the plugins array and displays the name, filename, and description properties of each plugins object. The script then constructs a table to describe the mimeTypes objects associated with each plugins object. The table lists the type, description, and suffixes properties, and contains a fourth column that identifies whether an enabled plug-in exists for the MIME type.

The numTypes property is set to the length property of each plugins object. The script then loops through the array of mimeTypes objects of each plugins object and displays the table data. The enabledPlugin variable is set to the value of the mimeTypes object's enabledPlugin property.

The if statement that follows this assignment checks if enabledPlugin is *true* (that is, not null) and that the name property of enabledPlugin is the same as that of the plugins object with which the mimeTypes object is associated. The reason for this check is that enabledPlugin could be null, indicating that no plug-in is enabled for the MIME type, or enabledPlugin could have its name property set to a different plugins object, indicating that the another plug-in is enabled for the MIME type.

Detecting Plug-Ins

The plugins array may be indexed by the name of a plug-in, and the mimeTypes array may be indexed by the name of a MIME type. This feature provides a handy capability for determining whether a browser is capable of supporting a particular plug-in or MIME type. When the plugins or mimeTypes arrays are accessed with unsupported values, a null value results.

Listing 17.4 (detect.htm) provides an example of using the above features to determine whether or not a video should be displayed. Open detect.htm with your browser. If the LiveVideo plug-in is installed for your browser then your browser will display the video as shown in Figure 17.4. If the LiveVideo plug-in is not installed for your browser then a message will be displayed in lieu of the video.

NOTE The AUTOSTART attribute can be set to *true* or *false* to specify whether or not LiveVideo is to automatically start playing the video without the user clicking the Play button. Later in this chapter, in the sections, "Plugging into LiveVideo" and "Listening to LiveAudio," I'll cover the Netscape documentation for LiveVideo and LiveAudio.

FIGURE 17.4:

The video is displayed
(Listing 17.4).

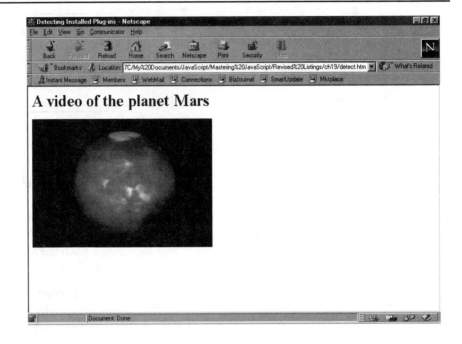

Listing 17.4   **Determining Whether the LiveVideo Plug-In Is Installed (detect.htm)**

```
<HTML>
<HEAD>
<TITLE>Detecting Installed Plug-ins</TITLE>
</HEAD>
<BODY>
<H1>A video of the planet Mars</H1>
<SCRIPT LANGUAGE="JavaScript"><!-
plugins=navigator.plugins
if(plugins["NPAVI32 Dynamic Link Library"]){
 document.write('<EMBED SRC="mars.avi" AUTOSTART="TRUE"')
 document.writeln('WIDTH="350" HEIGHT="270">')
}else{
 document.write('Sorry. Your browser does not have ')
 document.writeln('LiveVideo installed.')
}
// -></SCRIPT>
</BODY>
</HTML>
```

NOTE   If your browser does not support LiveVideo, you should upgrade to a version that does. If you are using a non-Windows OS then you'll have to follow along with the book. The reason I use LiveVideo and AVI files in this chapter is that LiveVideo provides full support of LiveConnect and therefore allows plug-in methods to be accessed from JavaScript.

Accessing Plug-Ins from within JavaScript

With LiveConnect, accessing plug-ins is easy—you use the embeds array. The embeds array is a property of the document object. The embeds array contains an entry for each of the document's <embed> tags. Each element of the embeds array is a plugin object.

The plugin object is different from the plugins object. The plugins objects, on the one hand, are elements of the plugins array, which is a property of the navigator object. The plugin objects, on the other hand, are elements of the embeds array, which is a property of the document object. Further, whereas the plugins object describes a plug-in, the plugin object provides access to the properties and methods of a plug-in.

Each plugin object is also a property of the document object. If an <embed> tag contains a name attribute, then the plugin object can be accessed by its name.

Listing 17.5 (access.htm) provides an example of how the plugin object may be used to access and control a plug-in. Open access.htm with your browser. After a few seconds, your browser loads and plays a Mars video, as shown in Figure 17.5. This is the same video as shown in Figure 17.4 except for one difference: this time you are controlling it from within JavaScript. Click the Start button and the video is rewound to the beginning, as shown in Figure 17.6. Click the Play button and the video begins playing again. Click the Stop button to freeze the video on a particular frame. Use the Frame Forward and Frame Backward buttons to advance or rewind the video one frame at a time. Click the End button to go to the last frame of the video, as shown in Figure 17.7.

FIGURE 17.5:

The video automatically
plays when the page loads
(Listing 17.5).

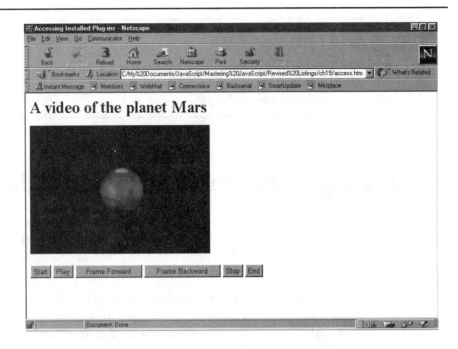

FIGURE 17.6:

Clicking the Start button
rewinds the video to the
beginning (Listing 17.5).

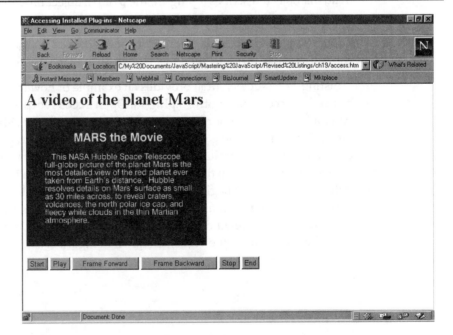

FIGURE 17.7:

Clicking the End button forwards the video to the end (Listing 17.5).

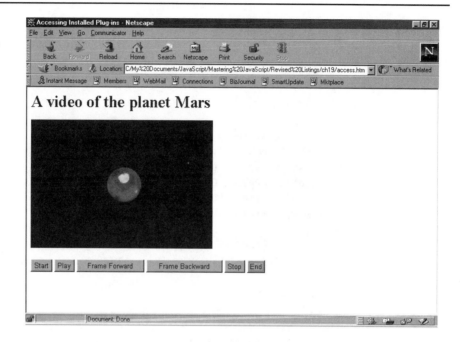

Listing 17.5   Accessing a Plug-In (access.htm)

```
<HTML>
<HEAD>
<TITLE>Accessing Installed Plug-ins</TITLE>
<SCRIPT LANGUAGE="JavaScript"><!-
function playVideo() {
 window.document.mars.play()
}
function stopVideo() {
 window.document.mars.stop()
}
function rewindVideo() {
 window.document.mars.rewind()
}
function forwardVideo() {
 window.document.mars.forward()
}
function forward() {
```

```
    window.document.mars.frameBack()
    }
    function back() {
    window.document.mars.frameForward()
    }
    // -></SCRIPT>
    </HEAD>
    <BODY>
    <H1>A video of the planet Mars</H1>
    <SCRIPT LANGUAGE="JavaScript"><!-
    plugins=navigator.plugins
    if(plugins["NPAVI32 Dynamic Link Library"]){
    document.write('<EMBED SRC="mars.avi" NAME="mars" ')
    document.writeln('AUTOSTART="TRUE" WIDTH="350" HEIGHT="240">')
    }else{
    document.write('Sorry. Your browser does not have ')
    document.writeln('LiveVideo installed.')
    }
    // -></SCRIPT>
    <FORM>
    <INPUT TYPE="BUTTON" VALUE="Start" onClick="rewindVideo()">
    <INPUT TYPE="BUTTON" VALUE="Play" onClick="playVideo()">
    <INPUT TYPE="BUTTON" VALUE="Frame Forward" onClick="forward()">
    <INPUT TYPE="BUTTON" VALUE="Frame Backward" onClick="back()">
    <INPUT TYPE="BUTTON" VALUE="Stop" onClick="stopVideo()">
    <INPUT TYPE="BUTTON" VALUE="End" onClick="forwardVideo()">
    </FORM>
    </BODY>
    </HTML>
```

Listing 17.5 shows how easy it is to access and control a plug-in from JavaScript. The onClick event handlers of the form's buttons are JavaScript functions that invoke the methods of the LiveVideo plug-in.

NOTE   Note that the frameBack() and frameForward() methods of the LiveVideo plug-in work in an opposite manner than you might expect—frameBack() causes the video to move forward, and frameForward() causes the video to move back.

The script in the document body is similar to the one used in Listing 17.4. The only difference is that the <embed> tag is given a name attribute.

Netscape's Plug-In Documentation

When you worked the LiveVideo example, you were probably wondering how I was able to determine what methods were supported by the LiveVideo plug-in. Part of the answer is that Netscape provides plug-in documentation at its Web site. This documentation includes the description of the `netscape.plugin` `.Plugin` Java class, which defines the minimal set of functions to be implemented by any LiveConnect-capable plug-in (and therefore the LiveVideo plug-in).

The other part of the answer is that LiveConnect lists all of the properties and methods of a plug-in as properties of whichever `plugin` object is associated with the plug-in. This lets you use the `for in` statement to list all of the plug-in's properties and methods.

The following subsections summarize the plug-in documentation provided by Netscape for LiveVideo and LiveAudio. Subsequent subsections describe the `netscape.plugin.Plugin` class and show how to use the `for in` statement to list all of a plug-in's properties and methods.

Plugging into LiveVideo

You've already used LiveVideo and are familiar with most of its methods. Live-Video plays video files that are in the AVI format. Although it is LiveConnect-capable, it is currently supported only on the Windows 95, 98, and NT operating system platforms.

In this section, I'll summarize the LiveVideo documentation provided by Java-Script. In the later section, "Listing Plug-In Methods," you'll learn how to list all of the properties of a plug-in.

The LiveVideo plug-in supports three application-specific attributes: AUTOSTART, LOOP, and ALIGN. The AUTOSTART and LOOP attributes take on the values of *true* or *false*. Their default values are *FALSE*. The AUTOSTART attribute determines whether the plug-in should automatically play the movie when the page is loaded. The LOOP attribute determines whether the video should be played in a continuous loop. The ALIGN attribute controls text alignment around the video display area. It is used in the same way as the `<img>` tag.

The LiveVideo documentation identifies four methods that may be used with the LiveVideo plug-in. These methods are described in Table 17.4. You'll learn additional methods in the section, "Listing Plug-In Methods," later in this chapter.

TABLE 17.4: Documented LiveVideo Plug-In Methods

Method	Description
play()	Plays the video starting at the current frame
stop()	Stops playing the video at the current frame
rewind()	Sets the current frame to the first frame of the video
seek(n)	Sets the current frame to the frame specified by **n**

Listening to LiveAudio

LiveAudio is a very powerful LiveConnect-capable audio player that is capable of playing audio files that are in the WAV, AIFF, AU, and MIDI formats. You've used the Netscape LiveAudio plug-in in examples in previous chapters. You probably thought that it was awkward to work with. It *is* awkward to work with, at least in its default configuration. However, LiveAudio provides a number of configuration options that can be used to tailor the way it appears and behaves.

Table 17.5 describes attributes that can be used with the LiveAudio plug-in. They can be used to hide or change the appearances of the audio player or to customize the way that an audio file is played.

TABLE 17.5: Attributes of the LiveAudio Plug-In

Attribute	Description
ALIGN	Controls the way text is displayed around the audio player's controls. It is used in the same manner as the <img> tag.
AUTOSTART	When set to *true*, the audio player begins playing the audio file when the Web page is loaded. It is set to *false* by default.
CONTROLS	May be set to CONSOLE, SMALLCONSOLE, PLAYBUTTON, PAUSEBUTTON, STOPBUTTON, or VOLUMELEVER to identify what type of audio control is to be displayed.
ENDTIME	Takes a *minutes:seconds* value that identifies where in the audio file the playback is to end.

Continued on next page

TABLE 17.5 CONTINUED: Attributes of the LiveAudio Plug-In

Attribute	Description
HIDDEN	When set to *true*, this attribute causes the audio controls to be hidden.
LOOP	Takes the values *true*, *false*, or an integer. If set to *true*, it causes the audio file to be played in a continuous, looping fashion. If set to *false*, it turns off looping. If an integer value is supplied, then the audio file is repeatedly played the specified number of times.
MASTERSOUND	This attribute is used with the name attribute to identify which file contains the actual file to be played.
NAME	Rather than naming the plug-in so that it can be accessed from JavaScript, this attribute is used to name a group of controls that apply to a single sound.
STARTTIME	Takes a *minutes:seconds* value that identifies where in the audio file playback is to start
VOLUME	Uses the values 0 to 100 to specify the percentage of the volume setting at which the audio file is to be played.

Table 17.6 identifies LiveAudio methods provided for use by JavaScript. These methods provide all of the capabilities needed to implement custom audio controls.

TABLE 17.6: Methods of the LiveAudio Plug-In

Method	Description
end_time(n)	Sets the end time n in seconds
fade_from_to(v1,v2)	Fades the volume level from v1 to v2
fade_to(v)	Fades the volume level to v
GetVolume()	Gets the current volume level
IsPaused()	Returns *true* if the audio player is currently paused
IsPlaying()	Returns *true* if the audio player is currently playing
IsReady()	Returns *true* if the audio player has been loaded
pause()	Causes the audio player to pause
play()	Causes the audio player to start playing

Continued on next page

TABLE 17.6 CONTINUED: Methods of the LiveAudio Plug-In

Method	Description
play(n,url)	Causes the audio player to start playing the first n seconds of the file located at the specified URL
setvol(v)	Sets the volume to the specified level
start_at_beginning()	Sets the start time to the beginning of the file
start_time(n)	Sets the start time to the specified number of seconds
stop()	Stops the playing of the audio file
stop_at_end()	Sets the end time to the end of the file

NOTE   Volume levels in LiveAudio methods are expressed as an integer in the range of 0 to 100.

The *netscape.plugin.Plugin* Class

The interface to LiveConnect-capable plug-ins is specified by the netscape.plugin .Plugin class. LiveConnect-capable plug-ins are subclasses of this class and add methods to it to enable the plug-ins to be accessed from Java and JavaScript. The netscape.plugin.Plugin class is of primary interest to plug-in developers, but as you'll see in the next section, it is good for you to know which methods it defines. This knowledge will help you to identify which methods are inherited from the Plugin class and which are specific to a particular plug-in. The methods of the netscape.plugin.Plugin class are described in Table 17.7.

TABLE 17.7: Methods of the netscape.plugin.Plugin Class

Method	Description
Plugin()	The class constructor
destroy()	Automatically invoked when the plug-in is destroyed
getPeer()	Returns the native object corresponding to the plug-in instance

Continued on next page

TABLE 17.7 CONTINUED: Methods of the `netscape.plugin.Plugin` Class

Method	Description
getWindow()	Returns the JavaScript window in which the plug-in displays its results
init()	Automatically invoked to initialize a plug-in
isActive()	Determines whether the plug-in is active

Listing Plug-In Methods

The publicly accessible properties and methods of LiveConnect-capable plug-ins are accessible as the properties of `plugin` objects. This lets you use the `for in` statement to find all of the undocumented features of a plug-in. Listing 17.6 (`listprop.htm`) illustrates this technique. When you open `listprop.htm` with your browser, it displays a Web page like that shown in Figure 17.8. Because I did not use the `WIDTH` and `HEIGHT` attributes in the `<embed>` tag, the video player display (the dark box at the top of the Web page) is minimized. This is fine because we are more interested in LiveVideo's properties and methods than in watching the video.

FIGURE 17.8:

The properties of the LiveVideo plugin object (Listing 17.6)

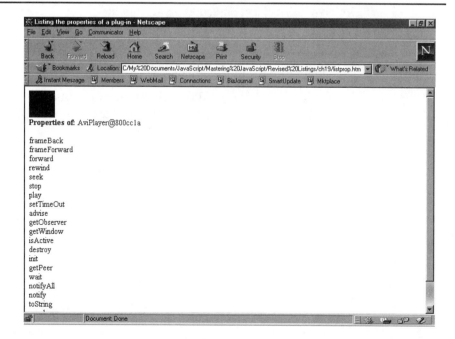

Listing 17.6   **Listing Plug-In Properties (listprop.htm)**

```
<HTML>
<HEAD>
<TITLE>Listing the properties of a plug-in</TITLE>
<SCRIPT LANGUAGE="JavaScript"><!-
function listProperties(obj) {
 document.writeln("<B>Properties of: </B>"+obj+"<BR>")
 for(var p in obj)
   document.writeln(p+"<BR>")
}
// -></SCRIPT>
</HEAD>
<BODY>
<EMBED SRC="Mars.avi"><BR>
<SCRIPT LANGUAGE="JavaScript"><!-
listProperties(document.embeds[0])
// -></SCRIPT>
</BODY>
</HTML>
```

---

listprop.htm uses an <embed> tag to display the Mars.avi file. The script in the document's body invokes the listProperties() function with the Live-Video plugin object passed as an argument.

listProperties() uses the for in statement to loop through and display the properties of the obj parameter.

listprop.htm may be easily adapted to display the properties of other plug-ins. Listing 17.7 shows the listaud.htm file that lists the properties of the LiveAudio plug-in. Figure 17.9 shows the Web page it displays.

FIGURE 17.9:

The properties of the
LiveAudio plug-in object
(Listing 17.7)

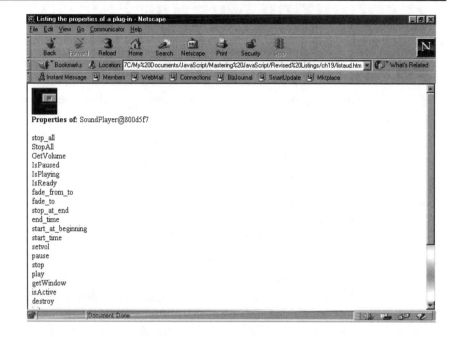

Listing 17.7   **Tailoring *listprop.htm* (listaud.htm)**

```
<HTML>
<HEAD>
<TITLE>Listing the properties of a plug-in</TITLE>
<SCRIPT LANGUAGE="JavaScript"><!-
function listProperties(obj) {
 document.writeln("<B>Properties of: </B>"+obj+"<BR>")
 for(var p in obj)
   document.writeln(p+"<BR>")
}
// -></SCRIPT>
</HEAD>
<BODY>
<EMBED SRC="test.wav"><BR>
<SCRIPT LANGUAGE="JavaScript"><!-
listProperties(document.embeds[0])
// -></SCRIPT>
</BODY>
</HTML>
```

Synchronizing Multiple Plug-Ins

In some multimedia applications you may wish to use two or more plug-ins. For example, the `Mars.avi` video that you used in this chapter was converted from a NASA MPEG video, and it does not contain any sound. If you're creating a multimedia application that uses the `Mars.avi` video, you may want to add an audio file to provide a narration for the video.

When using two or more plug-ins on the same Web page you may need to synchronize the plug-ins so that they start and stop together and display the correct information at the right time.

In general, most plug-ins do not provide synchronization primitives. To ensure that your plug-ins operate in tandem you can provide synchronization at the user interface level. Listing 17.8 (`synchro.htm`) provides a simple example of this type of synchronization.

Open `synchro.htm` with your browser. It displays the Web page shown in Figure 17.10. Click the Play button, and the video and audio files are played simultaneously. Click the Stop button, and the video and audio players stop at the same time. Click Play again, and they both play where they left off. The Start button "rewinds" the video and audio files, and the End button displays the last frame of the video file and stops the audio file.

FIGURE 17.10:

The initial script display (Listing 17.8)

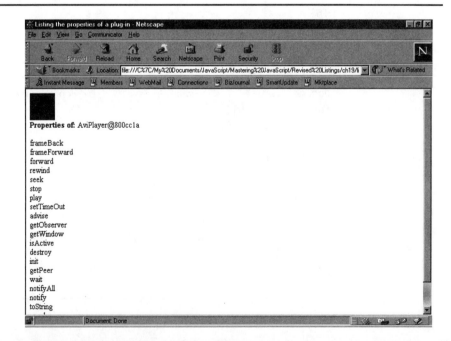

Listing 17.8   Synchronizing Two Plug-Ins (synchro.htm)

```html
<HTML>
<HEAD>
<TITLE>Synchronizing Plug-ins</TITLE>
<SCRIPT LANGUAGE="JavaScript"><!-
function play() {
 window.document.embeds[0].play()
 window.document.embeds[1].play()
}
function stop() {
 window.document.embeds[0].stop()
 window.document.embeds[1].pause()
}
function start() {
 window.document.embeds[0].rewind()
 window.document.embeds[1].stop()
}
function end() {
 window.document.embeds[0].forward()
 window.document.embeds[1].stop()
}
// -></SCRIPT>
</HEAD>
<BODY onLoad="start()">
<H1>The Planet Mars</H1>
<EMBED SRC="mars.avi" NAME="video" AUTOSTART="TRUE"
 WIDTH="350" HEIGHT="240">
<EMBED SRC="mars.wav" HIDDEN="TRUE">
<FORM>
<INPUT TYPE="BUTTON" VALUE="Start" onClick="start()">
<INPUT TYPE="BUTTON" VALUE="Play" onClick="play()">
<INPUT TYPE="BUTTON" VALUE="Pause" onClick="stop()">
<INPUT TYPE="BUTTON" VALUE=" End " onClick="end()">
</FORM>
</BODY>
</HTML>
```

Listing 17.8 shows how the two plug-ins are synchronized. The document body loads the LiveVideo plug-in to display the mars.avi file. It then loads the LiveAudio plug-in to play the mars.wav file. The <body> tag's onClick event handler invokes the start() function to ensure that both files are rewound upon document loading. The four functions in the document header are used as follows.

The *play()* Function

This function invokes the play() method of both plug-ins to cause the plug-ins to begin playing at the same time. It handles the clicking of the Play button.

The *stop()* Function

This function invokes the stop() method of the LiveVideo plug-in and the pause() method of the LiveAudio plug-in to cause both plug-ins to stop playing at the current position within their respective files. It handles the clicking of the Stop button.

The *start()* Function

This function invokes the rewind() method of the LiveVideo plug-in and the stop() method of the LiveAudio plug-in to cause both plug-ins to rewind their respective files to their initial position. It handles the clicking of the Start button.

The *end()* Function

This function invokes the forward() method of the LiveVideo plug-in and the stop() method of the LiveAudio plug-in. This causes the LiveVideo plug-in to display its last frame and the LiveAudio plug-in to restart. The end() function handles the clicking of the End button.

Assisting Users with Installing Plug-Ins

Navigator provides a special feature to assist the user with installing plug-ins that may be required by a script. When a user displays a page that requires a new plug-in to be installed, it displays a plug-in icon in place of the plug-in and launches a dialog box that provides the user with two buttons: Get the Plugin and Cancel.

If the user clicks Get the Plugin, then Navigator opens the URL specified by the PLUGINSPAGE attribute of the plug-in's <embed> tag. The designated URL should contain instructions on how to download and install the plug-in. (If the PLUGINS-PAGE attribute is not supplied, then the Netscape plug-ins page—maintained by Netscape—is loaded.) If the user clicks the Cancel button instead of the Get the Plugin button, then the assisted plug-in installation process is aborted. If the user changes their mind then they can click the plug-in icon again and the dialog box will be redisplayed.

Listing 17.9 (assist.htm) shows how assisted plug-in installation is implemented. It contains an <embed> tag with the SRC attribute set to test.ijk and the PLUGINSPAGE attribute set to the following URL:

http://www.jaworski.com/javascript/install.htm

I've configured my Web server to return a MIME type of application/x-ijk for files with the .ijk suffix.

Listing 17.9   Assisted Plug-In Installation (assist.htm)

```
<HTML>
<HEAD>
<TITLE>Assisted Plug-In Installation</TITLE>
</HEAD>
<BODY>
<H1>This page uses the ijk plugin</H1>
<EMBED SRC="test.ijk"
  PLUGINSPAGE="http://www.jaworski.com/javascript/install.htm">
</BODY>
</HTML>
```

In order to see how it works, you'll have to load it from my Web server. (If you load it from your local file system the correct MIME type will not be returned.) Open http://www.jaworski.com/javascript/assist.htm with your browser. It will display the Web file shown in Figure 17.11. Note how the plug-in object is displayed in the upper-left corner of the window.

FIGURE 17.11:

The plug-in object
(Listing 17.9)

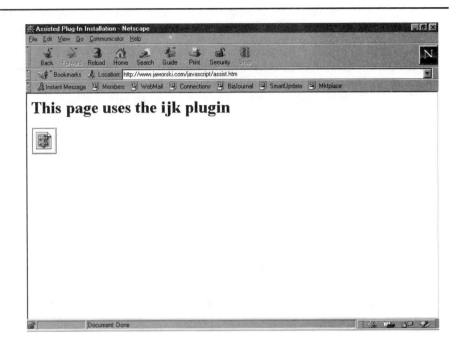

Immediately after the Web page shown in Figure 17.11 is loaded, the dialog box shown in Figure 17.12 is displayed. This dialog box gives you the option of obtaining and installing the plug-in. Click Get the Plugin and the Web page shown in Figure 17.13 (Listing 17.10) is loaded and displayed. This Web page would be used to provide instructions on downloading and installing the plug-in.

FIGURE 17.12:

The plug-in dialog box
(Listing 17.9)

FIGURE 17.13:

The installation instructions (Listing 17.10)

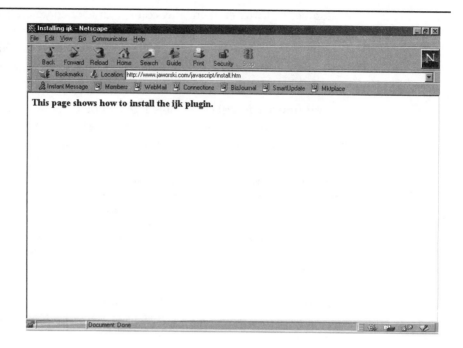

| Listing 17.10 | The Installation Instructions (install.htm) |

```
<HTML>
<HEAD>
<TITLE>Installing ijk</TITLE>
</HEAD>
<BODY>
<H3>This page shows how to install the ijk plugin.</H3>
</BODY>
</HTML>
```

Developing Your Own Plug-Ins

There are over 100 Navigator plug-ins currently available. In almost all cases, therefore, you'll be able to use an available plug-in for your Web application development. However, there may come a time when you'll need to develop your own plug-ins. Fortunately, all the information you'll need for this task is available online in the documentation section of the Netscape library. You can access the library at the URL `http://developer.netscape.com/library/documentation/index.html`.

The documents described in Table 17.8 will help you get started in developing your plug-in. Links to these documents may be found on the author's *Mastering JavaScript and JScript* home page at `http://www.jaworski.com/javascript/`.

TABLE 17.8: Documentation Available for Developing Your Own Plug-Ins

Document	Description
LiveConnect/Plug-In Developer's Guide	The complete guide to writing Navigator plug-ins. It describes the user's and programmer's view of plug-ins, documents the Plug-In API, and identifies the steps involved in creating a plug-in.
LiveConnecting Plug-Ins with Java	This document shows how to interface plug-ins with Java. It covers calling Java methods from plug-ins and calling plug-in methods from Java.
The Java Runtime Interface (JRI)	The JRI provides a standard interface to Java services. This document describes the JRI and shows how to use it to develop applets and plug-ins independent of the particular Java version used by Navigator.
LiveConnect Communication	This is a section of the *JavaScript Guide* that shows how to use LiveConnect to interface JavaScript with Java and plug-ins.
Using LiveConnect	This is a summary description of LiveConnect.

If you are going to be developing your own plug-in, you'll also need a version of the LiveConnect/Plug-In software development kit (SDK) for the particular OS platform on which your plug-in will run. Versions of the SDK are available for several operating system platforms. The SDK provides the header files, common source code and binary files, and tools that you'll need to develop a plug-in. It also provides a lot of useful examples. Links to the SDK can be found in the *LiveConnect/Plug-In Developer's Guide*.

NOTE Links to the documents identified in this section are provided in online Appendix B, "Accessing Online Resources."

Summary

In this chapter, you learned how to use JavaScript to work with plug-ins. You learned how to use the `plugins` and `mimetypes` objects to detect available plug-ins and determine the MIME types associated with these plug-ins. You learned how to use LiveConnect to communicate with plug-ins and control their behavior. You learned how to work with multiple plug-ins and various approaches to synchronizing plug-ins. You also learned how to assist users in installing plug-ins. In the next chapter, you'll learn how to work with Netscape and Microsoft's versions of DHTML.

PART V

Programming Servers

■ CHAPTER 18: Using Style Sheets and DHTML

■ CHAPTER 19: Creating Multimedia Applications

CHAPTER
EIGHTEEN

18

Using Style Sheets and DHTML

- What Are Style Sheets?

- JavaScript Style Sheets vs. Cascading Style Sheets

- Defining Style Sheets

- Using the <LINK> Tag to Include Styles

- Using Multiple Style Sheets

- Using Internet Explorer's DHTML Capabilities

One of the most exciting capabilities provided with HTML 3.2 is the capability to specify the style in which different HTML elements are formatted and displayed. Before the advent of style sheets, Web page authors were confined to using the standard formatting provided by individual HTML elements. Headings, paragraphs, lists, and other text elements provided little variety or flexibility in the way that they were presented. Style sheets changed all that—now Web authors can control the color, font, margins, and many other aspects of individual HTML elements. This powerful new capability results in Web pages that are livelier, more colorful, and more closely tailored to their target audience. This means that you can create, on the one hand, more stirring pages for those who want to be moved, and, on the other hand, more tightly organized pages for those who admire standardization.

In this chapter, you'll be introduced to style sheets. You'll learn the differences between JavaScript style sheets and the *Cascading Style Sheets (CSS)* that have been developed by the World Wide Web Consortium. You'll cover the tags, properties, and attributes used with JavaScript style sheets and learn how to work with both internally and externally defined styles. You'll also learn how styles can be dynamically updated using Internet Explorer's DHTML capabilities. When you finish this chapter, you'll be able to take advantage of JavaScript style sheets, CSS style sheets, and DHTML to add both flair and consistency to your Web applications. Throughout this chapter, I'll refer to CSS style sheets. Keep in mind that JavaScript's support corresponds to CSS1 and not CSS2.

What Are Style Sheets?

Style sheets provide the capability to control the way in which HTML elements, such as headings, paragraphs, and lists, are laid out and displayed. They enable Web page designers to use standard HTML elements in a limitless variety of new ways. For example, before style sheets were developed, Web authors had six heading levels to work with. These headings could be right-justified, left-justified, or centered. They could be made to use a different size font or display style, but not much more. Style sheets let you specify the display of different level headings with various colors, font styles, font sizes, and more. You can also specify the way that headings are laid out—the spacing before and after the heading and the margins used with the heading. You can collect styles for certain types of projects and save them in style sheets. Style sheets give you complete flexibility and control in the way that the pages of your Web applications are presented.

You may wonder what possible uses you can make of all this flexibility. Well, if you develop Web pages for a number of different audiences, then style sheets are an absolute must. You can create a standard company style sheet to lay out the pages that you develop at work, a style sheet to lay out documents that are unique to your department at school, a style sheet to create your own casual-looking personal Web pages, and a style sheet of really outrageous styles for the Web pages that you develop for your friends, kids, or hobbies.

Within an organization, different styles can be used for different departments (engineering vs. marketing), different types of documents (product descriptions vs. design specifications), or different types of information (company sensitive vs. material that can be distributed freely).

JavaScript Style Sheets vs. Cascading Style Sheets

Much of the underlying technology of the Web, including HTML, Web browsers, and Web servers, was developed at the CERN physics laboratory in Geneva, Switzerland. For a bunch of scientists, they sure turned out some amazing internetworking technologies. Style sheets are another development of CERN. In 1994, work on HTML style sheets was initiated, and, in December 1996, a specification called Cascading Style Sheets was proposed. The style sheets are referred to as *cascading* because the specification allows for multiple levels of styles to be applied to a single document where the output of some styles are the input of others.

The Cascading Style Sheets, referred to by their acronym CSS1, are a natural outgrowth of CERN's involvement in the development of HTML 3.2. HTML 3.2 and CSS1 are implemented by several browsers, including Netscape Navigator 4 and 4.5, Internet Explorer 3 and 4, and HotJava 1. In addition to supporting CSS1, Netscape Navigator 4 also supports a JavaScript-based approach to style sheets, referred to as JavaScript style sheets, or JSS for short. JavaScript style sheets support the styles provided by CSS1 and have the advantage of making these styles available as JavaScript properties. This advantage enables style properties to be created, read, and updated via JavaScript scripts. You can think of JavaScript style sheets as CSS1 style properties that have become JavaScript enabled.

Being a JavaScript programmer, you will find JSS more intuitive and easier to use than CSS. You will also appreciate the capability to work with style properties within scripts. However, the advantages are offset by the fact that only Navigator 4 supports JSS. This means that only users with Navigator 4 (and beyond) will be able to view the fancy styles that you specify with JSS. All other users will view your Web pages using the default HTML style. This trade-off is not all that bad, really—with JSS you can still appeal to the majority of Web users, because its fallback mode for those users who do not take advantage of Navigator 4's browsing capabilities is still as appealing as it has always been.

NOTE　The remainder of this chapter focuses on JavaScript style sheets with CSS examples. For a complete treatment of Cascading Style Sheets, refer to the W3C CSS1 proposal. It is available at the URL `http://www.w3.org/pub/WWW/TR/REC-CSS1`.

An Introductory Example

To give you a better feel for how style sheets work, we'll start off with a simple example. Listing 18.1 contains a document that displays a few headings and paragraphs in different colors using JSS. Figure 18.1 provides a black-and-white representation of the Web page that is displayed by Navigator 4. Listing 18.2 provides an equivalent CSS example.

FIGURE 18.1:

A simple introduction to
JavaScript style sheets

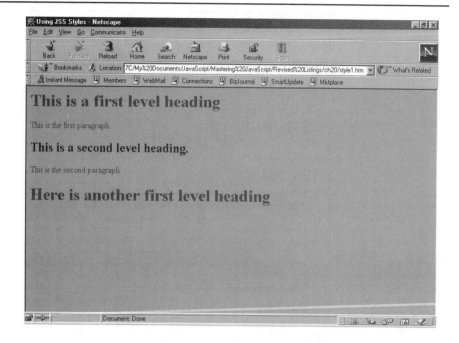

Listing 18.1   An Introductory Style Sheet Example (style1.htm)

```
<HTML>
<HEAD>
<TITLE>Using JSS Styles</TITLE>
<STYLE TYPE="text/javascript">
document.tags.BODY.backgroundColor = "cyan";
document.tags.H1.color="red";
document.tags.H2.color="blue";
document.tags.P.color="green";
</STYLE>
</HEAD>
<BODY>
<H1>This is a first level heading</H1>
<P>This is the first paragraph.</P>
<H2>This is a second level heading.</H2>
<P>This is the second paragraph.</P>
<H1>Here is another first level heading</H1>
</BODY>
</HTML>
```

Listing 18.2   **A CSS-Equivalent to Listing 18.1 (css-style1.htm)**

```
<HTML>
<HEAD>
<TITLE>Using CSS Styles</TITLE>
<STYLE TYPE="text/css">
body {
 background-color: "cyan";
}
h1 {
 color: "red";
}
h2 {
 color: "blue";
}
p {
 color: "green";
}
</STYLE>
</HEAD>
<BODY>
<H1>This is a first level heading</H1>
<P>This is the first paragraph.</P>
<H2>This is a second level heading.</H2>
<P>This is the second paragraph.</P>
<H1>Here is another first level heading</H1>
</BODY>
</HTML>
```

Open `style1.htm` with your browser (Navigator 4 or better) to see how the document is displayed. You'll probably be aghast at the awful color scheme that I've chosen—style sheets make it as easy to convey a poor sense of style as a well-developed sense of style. But please bear with me. Your document background color should be set to cyan. The first and last headings in the document are level-1 headings that are displayed in red. In the middle of the document is a level-2 heading that is displayed in blue. The document contains two one-line paragraphs that are displayed in green.

If you look at Listing 18.1, you'll see that except for the <STYLE> element in the document head, the rest of the document appears to be just regular HTML. That's the power of style sheets—you can change the formatting and display of an entire document by just changing the style of the document. In the case of style1.htm, all you had to do was add the <STYLE> element to change a very normal-looking HTML document into a very unusual-looking one.

The <STYLE> tags shown in Listing 18.1 are surrounding tags. They surround four JavaScript statements that assign color values to different subproperties of the document.tags property. The <STYLE> tag uses the TYPE attribute to determine what type of style sheet is in effect. The text/javascript value is used to identify a JavaScript style sheet. The text/css value would be used to identify a Cascading Style Sheet as shown in Listing 18.2.

> **NOTE**   The tags property always applies to the current document. You do not need to explicitly reference the document object.

Defining Style Sheets

As you saw in the previous example, using JavaScript style sheets is easy. You write your HTML documents using traditional HTML tags and then define a style sheet to specify the style changes to be used with selected HTML elements. This is the preferred way to use style sheets, although a number of usage options are provided.

JavaScript style sheets, like Cascading Style Sheets, may be defined in any of the following ways:

- The <STYLE> tag may be used to define styles in the document head.

- The <LINK> tag may be used to refer to a style sheet that is in a separate, external document.

- The <SPAN> tag may be used to surround text to which a particular style is to be applied.

The following sections show how to use each of the above mechanisms to define and use JavaScript styles within your documents.

The *<STYLE>* Tag

You've already learned to use the <STYLE> tag in the first example of this chapter:

- You put <STYLE> and </STYLE> tags in a document's header.

- You set the TYPE attribute to `text/javascript`.

- You placed JavaScript statements that defined styles between the <STYLE> tags.

The <STYLE> tag is very easy to use. The hard part is figuring out what kind of styles you want to define.

The styles used in Listing 18.1 showed how the styles associated with individual HTML elements can be defined. Basically, you redefined all level-1 and level-2 headings and paragraphs to use certain colors. The statements that are included between the <STYLE> tags may be used to provide much more power and flexibility in the way that styles are defined. For example, you can use JavaScript statements to

- Specify the style and size of fonts to be used with specific HTML elements

- Specify the way that text is to be aligned (vertically and horizontally), indented, capitalized, and decorated (underline, overline, blink, and strikethrough)

- Specify foreground and background colors and the use of background images

- Identify the margins, borders, padding, and alignment to be used to lay out block-formatted HTML elements

- Define classes of styles and specify which HTML elements belong to each class

- Define exceptions to a style or class of styles

- Insert comments that document your style definitions

While the above list may seem daunting, don't worry, we're going to cover each of the above capabilities, one at a time, in the following sections.

NOTE   If your machine doesn't have a font that JavaScript needs, your browser will try to find a font with the closest fit to the one it requires.

Inserting Comments

JavaScript comments /* */ and // can be used to document your style sheets.

The *tags* Property

The tags property is a property of the document object that allows you to define the style for individual HTML tags. You used the tags property in Listing 18.1 to redefine the styles of level-1 and level-2 headings and paragraphs. The tags property is typically set in an assignment statement as follows:

```
tags.tagID.property = value;
```

where tagID is the HTML tag that you want to define (for example, BODY, H1, P, and so on, without the angle brackets), property is the style property that you want to change (such as color, fontStyle, and so on), and value is the value that you want to change the property to (for instance, red, italic, small-caps, and so on). In subsequent sections of this chapter, you'll learn more about the properties and values that can be specified.

The *ids* Property and *ID* Attribute

While the tags property is used to redefine all instances of a particular HTML tag, the ids property is used to create specific exceptions to a style definition. For example, you can create an ID to specify that a particular HTML element is to be displayed in red. The ids property is typically set in an assignment statement as follows:

```
ids.ID.property = value;
```

where ID is the name of the ID that you want to define. The ID is then used as an attribute value, as shown in Listing 18.3. Listing 18.4 shows a CSS equivalent to Listing 18.3.

Listing 18.3   **Using the *ids* Property and *ID* Attribute (ids.htm)**

```
<HTML>
<HEAD>
<TITLE>Using the JSS ids property and ID attribute</TITLE>
<STYLE TYPE="text/javascript">
tags.BODY.backgroundColor="white";
tags.P.color="blue";
ids.WARNING.color="red";
</STYLE>
</HEAD>
<BODY>
<P>This is the first paragraph.
It uses the redefined paragraph style.</P>
<P ID="WARNING">This is the second paragraph.
It has its ID attribute set to WARNING.</P>
<P>This is the third paragraph.
It uses the redefined paragraph style.</P>
<H1>This is a normal H1 heading.</H1>
<H1 ID="WARNING">This H1 heading uses the WARNING ID.</H1>
</BODY>
</HTML>
```

Listing 18.4   **A CSS Equivalent to Listing 18.3 (css-ids.htm)**

```
<HTML>
<HEAD>
<TITLE>Using the CSS ID attribute</TITLE>
<STYLE TYPE="text/css">
BODY {background-color: "white";}
P {color: "blue";}
#WARNING {color: "red";}
</STYLE>
</HEAD>
<BODY>
<P>This is the first paragraph.
It uses the redefined paragraph style.</P>
<P ID="WARNING">This is the second paragraph.
It has its ID attribute set to WARNING.</P>
<P>This is the third paragraph.
```

```
It uses the redefined paragraph style.</P>
<H1>This is a normal H1 heading.</H1>
<H1 ID="WARNING">This H1 heading uses the WARNING ID.</H1>
</BODY>
</HTML>
```

The `tags` property is used to define styles for the `<BODY>` and `<P>` tags. The `ids` property is used to define an ID, named `WARNING`, that is used in the second paragraph and the last heading. This causes the second paragraph and last heading shown in Figure 18.2 to be displayed in red.

FIGURE 18.2:

How the `ids` property and ID attribute are used

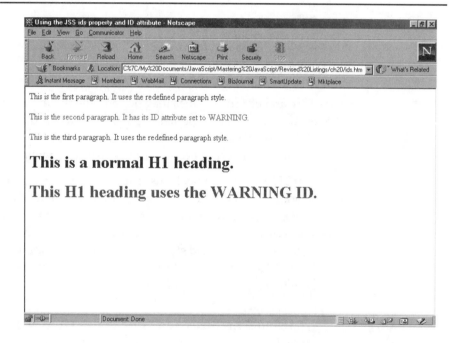

In general, you use the `ids` property to define an ID. Then set the `ID` attribute of an HTML tag to the ID that you've defined. By using IDs, you can create specific exceptions to the styles that you define using the `tags` and `classes` properties (covered later in this chapter in the section "Using Classes").

Setting Font Properties

The `fontStyle` and `fontSize` properties of an HTML element may be specified as part of the element's style definition. For example,

```
<STYLE TYPE="text/javascript">
tags.H1.fontStyle="italic";
tags.H1.fontSize="smaller";
</STYLE>
```

The `fontStyle` property may be assigned the following values:

- `normal`
- `italic`
- `oblique`
- `small-caps`

The `italic` and `oblique` values may be combined with `small-caps`. Use of the `oblique` style causes text to be slanted to the left; this is different from an italic font, which is explicitly designed to look slanted to the right. Use of `small-caps` causes text to appear in uppercase, but with a much smaller font.

The `fontSize` property may be used to change the size of the font in which text is displayed. Displayed font sizes depend upon the table of font sizes that your browser uses. Your browser may not have the exact font size that you specify; if this is the case, it will try to find the one closest to it in the table. Listing 18.5 shows how the font sizes and styles of the first four heading levels may be redefined. Figure 18.3 shows how a browser displays the new headings. Listing 18.6 shows how font styles are supported by CSS.

| Listing 18.5 | Using Font Sizes and Font Styles (fonstyle.htm) |

```
<HTML>
<HEAD>
<TITLE>Using JSS Font Sizes</TITLE>
<STYLE TYPE="text/javascript">
tags.BODY.backgroundColor="white";
tags.H1.fontSize="10pt";
tags.H2.fontSize="20pt";
tags.H2.fontStyle="italic";
tags.H3.fontSize="30pt";
tags.H4.fontSize="40pt";
tags.H4.fontStyle="italic";
```

```
</STYLE>
</HEAD>
<BODY>
<H1>A level 1 heading</H1>
<H2>A level 2 heading</H2>
<H3>A level 3 heading</H3>
<H4>A level 4 heading</H4>
</BODY>
</HTML>
```

Listing 18.6   CSS Font Styles (css-fonstyle.htm)

```
<HTML>
<HEAD>
<TITLE>Using CSS Font Sizes</TITLE>
<STYLE TYPE="text/css">
body {
 background-color: "white";
}
h1 {
 font-size="10pt";
}
h2 {
 font-size="20pt";
 font-style="italic";
}
h3 {
 font-size="30pt";
}
h4 {
 font-size="40pt";
 font-style="italic";
}
</STYLE>
</HEAD>
<BODY>
<H1>A level 1 heading</H1>
<H2>A level 2 heading</H2>
<H3>A level 3 heading</H3>
<H4>A level 4 heading</H4>
</BODY>
</HTML>
```

FIGURE 18.3:

Redefining the first four heading levels using font sizes and font styles

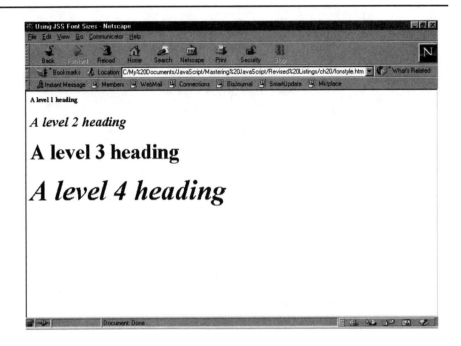

Setting Text Properties

You can define a number of properties that govern the display of text within an HTML element:

- `lineHeight` controls the spacing between lines of text.

- `textAlign` specifies the horizontal alignment of text within an HTML element.

- `verticalAlign` specifies the vertical alignment of text within an HTML element.

- `textTransform` specifies the case to be used for text within an HTML element.

- `textDecoration` specifies how text is to be adorned using underline, overline, blink, and strikethrough.

The lineHeight property is set to a number— such as 1.5 for space-and-a-half, 2 for double spacing, 3 for triple spacing, and so on—that identifies the line spacing to be used between adjacent lines of text.

The textAlign property can be set to left, right, center, or justify to alter the way that text is aligned with respect to an HTML element.

The verticalAlign property may be set to the values baseline, sub, super, top, text-top, middle, bottom, and text-bottom. The sub and super values are used to create subscripts and superscripts. The other values are similar to the HTML attribute values used to align images.

The textTransform property may be set to uppercase, lowercase, capitalize, or none. The none value turns off capitalization.

The textDecoration property may be set to the values none, underline, overline, line-through, or blink. The none value turns off any previously assigned decorations. The overline value is not currently supported.

Listing 18.7 provides an example of using text properties. Figure 18.4 shows how these properties are reflected in a browser's display. Listing 18.8 provides a CSS equivalent of Listing 18.7.

Listing 18.7   **Using Text Properties (textyle.htm)**

```
<HTML>
<HEAD>
<TITLE>Using JSS Text Properties</TITLE>
<STYLE TYPE="text/javascript">
tags.BODY.backgroundColor="white";
ids.HALF.lineHeight=.5;
ids.ONEPT5.lineHeight=1.5;
ids.ONEPT5.textAlign="center";
ids.ONEPT5.textTransform="uppercase";
ids.ONEPT5.textDecoration="blink";
ids.DOUBLE.lineHeight=2;
ids.DOUBLE.textTransform="lowercase";
ids.DOUBLE.textDecoration="underline";
ids.TRIPLE.lineHeight=3;
ids.TRIPLE.textTransform="capitalize";
ids.TRIPLE.textDecoration="line-through";
</STYLE>
</HEAD>
```

```
<BODY>
<P>This is paragraph 1.</P>
<P ID="HALF">This is paragraph 2.</P>
<P ID="ONEPT5">This is paragraph 3.</P>
<P ID="DOUBLE">This is paragraph 4.</P>
<P ID="TRIPLE">This is paragraph 5.</P>
</BODY>
</HTML>
```

Listing 18.8   **A CSS Equivalent to Listing 18.7 (css-textyle.htm)**

```
<HTML>
<HEAD>
<TITLE>Using CSS Text Properties</TITLE>
<STYLE TYPE="text/css">
BODY {background-color: "white";}
#HALF {line-height: .5;}
#ONEPT5 {lineHeight: 1.5;
 text-align: "center";
 text-transform: "uppercase";
 text-decoration: "blink";}
#DOUBLE {line-height: 2;
 text-transform: "lowercase";
 text-decoration: "underline";}
#TRIPLE {line-height: 3;
 text-transform: "capitalize";
 text-decoration: "line-through";}
</STYLE>
</HEAD>
<BODY>
<P>This is paragraph 1.</P>
<P ID="HALF">This is paragraph 2.</P>
<P ID="ONEPT5">This is paragraph 3.</P>
<P ID="DOUBLE">This is paragraph 4.</P>
<P ID="TRIPLE">This is paragraph 5.</P>
</BODY>
</HTML>
```

FIGURE 18.4:

Changing paragraph formats using text styles

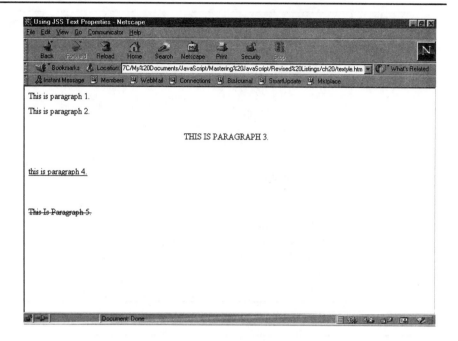

Using Colors and Background Images

You are already familiar with using the color and backgroundColor properties from previous examples in this chapter. The color property is used to set the text foreground color and the backgroundColor property is used to set the color of the background occupied by an HTML element. The RGB values of custom colors may be specified using the rgb() function. Consult online Appendix B, "Accessing Online References," for a link to an RGB color chart. For example, a color with a 50 red value, 100 green value, and 150 blue value may be specified using rgb(50,100,150). Listing 18.9 shows how background and foreground colors can be specified using the backgroundColor and color properties. Figure 18.5 shows a black-and-white version of the Web page displayed by Listing 18.9. If it were in color, it would show a white document background, a level-1 heading with red foreground and yellow background colors, and a paragraph with white foreground and blue background colors. Note that the heading is displayed using a paragraph-like font style. Listing 18.10 provides a CSS equivalent to Listing 18.9.

Listing 18.9   Using Backgrounds and Foregrounds (colors.htm)

```
<HTML>
<HEAD>
<TITLE>Using JSS Colors</TITLE>
<STYLE TYPE="text/javascript">
tags.BODY.backgroundColor="white";
tags.H1.backgroundColor="yellow";
tags.H1.color="red";
tags.P.backgroundColor="blue";
tags.P.color="white";
</STYLE>
</HEAD>
<BODY>
<H1>This is a level 1 heading.</H1>
<P>This is a paragraph.</P>
</BODY>
</HTML>
```

Listing 18.10   A CSS Equivalent to Listing 18.9 (css-colors.htm)

```
<HTML>
<HEAD>
<TITLE>Using CSS Colors</TITLE>
<STYLE TYPE="text/css">
BODY {background-color: "white";}
H1 {background-color: "yellow";
 color: "red";}
P {background-color: "blue";
 color: "white";}
</STYLE>
</HEAD>
<BODY>
<H1>This is a level 1 heading.</H1>
<P>This is a paragraph.</P>
</BODY>
</HTML>
```

FIGURE 18.5:

Background and foreground colors may be set using color properties.

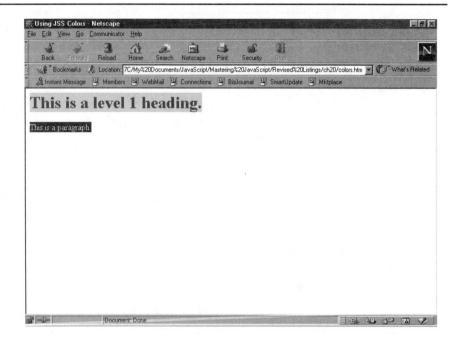

The backgroundImage property may be used to identify a background image to be used with an HTML element. The property takes a URL as its value. Background images are typically used with the document as a whole, by assigning an image to the <BODY> tag. However, JavaScript style sheets allow background images to be assigned to block-formatted elements. Block-formatted elements are covered next.

Laying Out Block-Formatted Elements

Block-formatted elements are HTML elements that begin on a new line. Examples are headings, paragraphs, and lists. The margins, border, and padding of block-formatted elements can be defined by JavaScript style sheets.

Margins are defined using the marginsRight, marginsLeft, marginsTop, and marginsBottom properties. The margins() method sets all four margins at the same time. It takes four arguments that can be used to set the top, right, bottom, and left margins as follows:

```
margins(top,right,bottom,left)
```

The width of the border around a block element is set using the `borderLeft-Width`, `borderRightWidth`, `borderTopWidth`, and `borderBottomWidth` properties. The `borderWidths()` method can be used in the same manner as the `margins()` method to set the width of all four borders at once. The `borderStyle` property sets the style of the border to `solid`, `3D`, or `none`.

The padding between a block element and its border is set using the `padding-Right`, `paddingLeft`, `paddingTop`, and `paddingBottom` properties. The `paddings()` method sets all four padding values.

The `width` and `height` properties specify the dimensions to be used in laying out block elements. If the `width` and `height` properties are set to `auto`, then any replacement for the block element, such as a loaded image, will cause the block to be automatically resized. If the properties are not set to `auto`, then the replacement will be resized to fit the block. The `align` property may be set to `left`, `right`, or `none`. It is used in the same manner as the `ALIGN` attribute of the `image` tag. The `clear` property may be set to `left`, `right`, `none`, or `both`. It may be set in the same manner as the `CLEAR` attribute of the `break` tag.

Listing 18.11 provides an example of block formatting. Figure 18.6 shows how the block formatting attributes affect the margins, border, and padding of paragraphs. Listing 18.12 shows how to accomplish the same effect using CSS.

Listing 18.11   Using Block-Formatting Properties (blocks.htm)

```
<HTML>
<HEAD>
<TITLE>Formatting JSS Block Properties</TITLE>
<STYLE TYPE="text/javascript">
tags.BODY.backgroundColor="white";
tags.P.marginLeft=10;
tags.P.borderLeftWidth=1;
tags.P.borderStyle="solid";
tags.P.backgroundColor="cyan";
ids.para2.marginLeft=50;
ids.para2.paddingLeft=10;
ids.para2.paddingTop=15;
```

```
ids.para2.paddingBottom=0;
</STYLE>
</HEAD>
<BODY>
<P>This is a paragraph.</P>
<P ID="para2">This is another paragraph.</P>
</BODY>
</HTML>
```

Listing 18.12   **Formatting Blocks with CSS (css-blocks.htm)**

```
<HTML>
<HEAD>
<TITLE>Formatting CSS Block Properties</TITLE>
<STYLE TYPE="text/css">
BODY {background-color: "white";}
P {margin-left: 10;
 border-left-width: 1;
 border-style: "solid";
 background-color: "cyan";}
#para2 {margin-left: 50;
 padding-left: 10;
 padding-top: 15;
 padding-bottom: 0;}
</STYLE>
</HEAD>
<BODY>
<P>This is a paragraph.</P>
<P ID="para2">This is another paragraph.</P>
</BODY>
</HTML>
```

FIGURE 18.6:

Block-formatting properties can be used to change the margins, border, and padding of block elements.

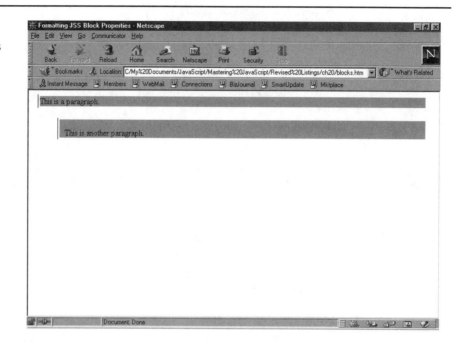

Using Measurement Units

JavaScript style sheets support the measurement units defined in Section 6.1 of the Cascading Style Sheets proposal (http://www.w3.org/pub/WWW/TR/REC-CSS1). These measurement units are used to specify font sizes, margins, and other element properties. They are organized into three categories:

Absolute units   These units specify the actual magnitude of a property. For example, 14pt may be used to identify a 14-point font.

Relative units   These units specify the magnitude of a property relative to the element being defined. For example, 5em may be used to identify a 5-em margin. (An *em* is a real unit of measure: It's defined as the width of the capital letter *M*. Obviously, this unit changes from one font to another.)

Proportional units   These units specify the size of a property in proportion to the element being defined. For example, 50% may be used to reduce the font size of a heading by half.

Listing 18.13 shows how absolute, relative, and proportional units may be used in JavaScript style sheets. Listing 18.14 provides a CSS equivalent document. Figure 18.7 shows how the document of Listing 18.13 is displayed.

Listing 18.13   Using Measurement Units (units.htm)

```
<HTML>
<HEAD>
<TITLE>JSS Measurement Units</TITLE>
<STYLE TYPE="text/javascript">
tags.BODY.backgroundColor="white";
tags.H1.fontSize="75%";
tags.P.marginLeft="5em";
ids.para2.fontSize="36pt";
</STYLE>
</HEAD>
<BODY>
<H1>This level 1 heading is reduced 75%.</H1>
<P>This is a normal paragraph with a 5 em margin.</P>
<P ID="para2">This paragraph uses a 36 point font and
has a 5 em margin.</P>
</BODY>
</HTML>
```

Listing 18.14   Using Measurement Units with CSS (css-units.htm)

```
<HTML>
<HEAD>
<TITLE>CSS Measurement Units</TITLE>
<STYLE TYPE="text/css">
BODY {background-color: "white";}
H1 {font-size: "75%";}
P {margin-left: "5em";}
#para2 {font-size: "36pt";}
</STYLE>
</HEAD>
<BODY>
<H1>This level 1 heading is reduced 75%.</H1>
<P>This is a normal paragraph with a 5 em margin.</P>
<P ID="para2">This paragraph uses a 36 point font and
```

```
has a 5 em margin.</P>
</BODY>
</HTML>
```

CSS measurement units may be used in JavaScript style sheets.

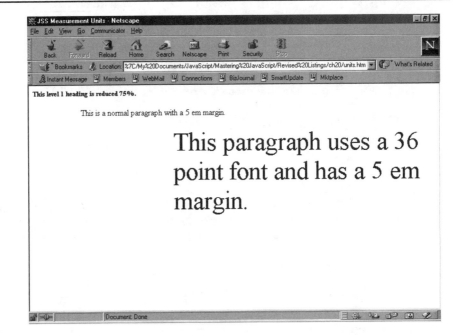

Using Classes

JavaScript style sheets can be used to define classes of styles that can be applied to different parts of a document. For example, you can define a class for marking company-sensitive data within a document, for highlighting important text, or for inserting revisions into a document. Classes are defined using the classes property. They are typically defined in assignment statements using the following syntax:

```
classes.className.tag.property = value;
```

where className and tag are the name of the class and tag being defined. The all keyword may be used to apply the property to all HTML tags.

Classes are applied to HTML elements by setting their CLASS attribute. Listing 18.15 shows how this is done. Figure 18.8 shows how the document described by Listing 18.15 is displayed. Listing 18.16 shows how classes are implemented using CSS.

Listing 18.15   Using Classes to Define Important Text (classes.htm)

```
<HTML>
<HEAD>
<TITLE>Using JSS Classes</TITLE>
<STYLE TYPE="text/javascript">
tags.BODY.backgroundColor="white";
classes.important.H1.fontSize="36pt";
classes.important.P.fontSize="18pt";
classes.important.UL.fontSize="12pt";
classes.important.all.textDecoration="underline";
classes.important.all.fontStyle="italic";
classes.important.all.textDecoration="underline";
classes.important.all.color="red";
classes.important.all.backgroundColor="yellow";
</STYLE>
</HEAD>
<BODY>
<H1>This is a normal heading.</H1>
<P>This is a normal paragraph.</P>
<H1 CLASS="important">This is an important heading.</H1>
<P CLASS="important">This paragraph contains some important informa-
tion.</P>
<P>This is a normal paragraph, but an important list follows.</P>
<UL CLASS="important">
<LI>item 1
<LI>item 2
<LI>item 3
</UL>
</BODY>
</HTML>
```

Listing 18.16   **How Classes Are Implemented Using CSS (css-classes.htm)**

```
<HTML>
<HEAD>
<TITLE>Using CSS Classes</TITLE>
<STYLE TYPE="text/css">
BODY {background-color: "white";}
.important {text-decoration: "underline";
 fontStyle: "italic";
 text-decoration: "underline";
 color: "red";
 background-color: "yellow";}
H1.important {font-size: "36pt";}
P.important {font-size: "18pt";}
UL.important {font-size: "12pt";}
</STYLE>
</HEAD>
<BODY>
<H1>This is a normal heading.</H1>
<P>This is a normal paragraph.</P>
<H1 CLASS="important">This is an important heading.</H1>
<P CLASS="important">This paragraph contains some important informa-
tion.</P>
<P>This is a normal paragraph, but an important list follows.</P>
<UL CLASS="important">
<LI>item 1
<LI>item 2
<LI>item 3
</UL>
</BODY>
</HTML>
```

FIGURE 18.8:

Classes add power and
flexibility to JavaScript style
sheets.

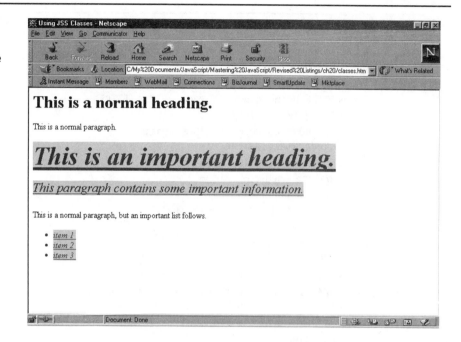

The *<SPAN>* Tag

What happens if you want to change the style of a selected portion of text and
do not want to redefine other logical and physical formatting tags? For example,
suppose that you want to develop a style, called highlight, that merely changes
the color of the selected text to magenta so that it will stand out. You could redefine the <EM> tag, but you still want to be able to emphasize text that is highlighted. The <SPAN> tag provides the solution you need.

The <SPAN> tag is used to apply styles to selected text. Use the <SPAN> and
</SPAN> tags to surround the text to which the style is to be applied. You can
then use the CLASS and ID attributes to apply a style to the text.

For example, consider Listing 18.17. It defines a highlight style that changes the
text foreground color to magenta. Highlighted text is selected by the <SPAN> tags, and
the ID attribute of the <SPAN> tag is set to highlight. Use of the <SPAN> tags does not
conflict with the <EM> tag. Figure 18.9 shows how the document of Listing 18.17 is
displayed. Listing 18.18 provides a CSS equivalent to Listing 18.17.

Listing 18.17   Using the <SPAN> Tag to Change the Style of Selected Text (span.htm)

```
<HTML>
<HEAD>
<TITLE>Using the SPAN tag in JSS</TITLE>
<STYLE TYPE="text/javascript">
tags.BODY.backgroundColor="white";
tags.P.fontSize="36pt";
tags.P.marginLeft="5em";
tags.P.marginRight="5em";
tags.P.marginTop="1em";
ids.highlight.color="magenta";
</STYLE>
</HEAD>
<BODY>
<P>This paragraph contains some
<SPAN ID="highlight">highlighted</SPAN> text.</P>
<P>This paragraph contains some
<SPAN ID="highlight">highlighted and <EM>emphasized</EM></SPAN>
text.</P>
</BODY>
</HTML>
```

Listing 18.18   Using the <SPAN> Tag with CSS (css-span.htm)

```
<HTML>
<HEAD>
<TITLE>Using the SPAN tag with CSS</TITLE>
<STYLE TYPE="text/css">
BODY {background-color: "white";}
P {font-size: "36pt";
 margin-left: "5em";
 margin-right: "5em";
 margin-top: "1em";}
.highlight {color: "magenta";}
</STYLE>
</HEAD>
<BODY>
<P>This paragraph contains some
```

```
<SPAN CLASS="highlight">highlighted</SPAN> text.</P>
<P>This paragraph contains some
<SPAN CLASS="highlight">highlighted and <EM>emphasized</EM></SPAN>
text.</P>
</BODY>
</HTML>
```

FIGURE 18.9:

The <SPAN> tag allows styles to be applied to selected text.

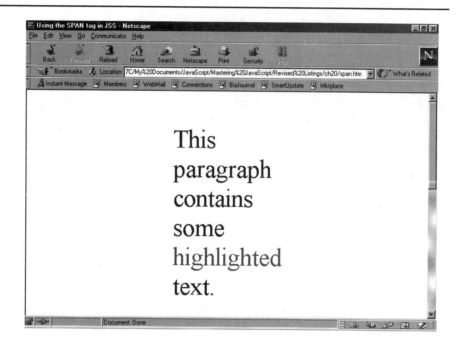

Using the *<LINK>* Tag to Include Styles

Now that you are familiar with JavaScript styles, you're probably wondering whether you have to reenter your favorite style definitions in the documents that use those styles. The answer is no—you can use the <LINK> tag to use styles that are defined in external files. This means that you can define your styles once and then reuse them over and over again. It also means that you can update the styles used for multiple documents by changing a single file.

The external style files define styles using the tags, classes, and ids properties. JavaScript style assignments are inserted into the file without the surrounding <STYLE> tags. For example, Listing 18.19 contains style definitions for the document body and paragraph tags. Listing 18.20 shows how these style definitions are made using CSS.

Listing 18.19   **External Style Definitions (favstyle)**

```
tags.BODY.backgroundColor="blue";
tags.P.fontSize="24pt";
tags.P.fontStyle="italic";
tags.P.color="white";
tags.P.marginLeft="5em";
tags.P.marginRight="5em";
tags.P.marginTop="5em";
```

Listing 18.20   **SS Style Definitions (css-favstyle)**

```
BODY {background-color: "blue";}
P {font-size: "24pt";
 font-style: "italic";
 color: "white";
 margin-left: "5em";
 margin-right: "5em";
 margin-top: "5em";}
```

The style definitions of Listing 18.19 can be included using the following <LINK> tag:

```
<LINK REL=STYLESHEET TYPE="text/JavaScript" HREF="favstyle">
```

The <LINK> tag corresponding to Listing 18.20 would be

```
<LINK REL=STYLESHEET TYPE="text/css" HREF="css-favstyle">
```

The <LINK> tag is defined in the HTML 3.2 specification (http://www.w3
.org/pub/WWW/TR/REC-html32.html). The REL attribute identifies the relationship with the linked document. It should always be set to STYLESHEET. The TYPE

attribute identifies the MIME type of the linked file. It should always be set to text/JavaScript. The HREF attribute identifies the URL of the external file containing the style definitions.

Listings 18.21 and 18.22 show how the <LINK> tag can be used to include externally defined styles. Figure 18.10 shows how this document is displayed.

Listing 18.21   Using the <LINK> Tag (usestyle.htm)

```
<HTML>
<HEAD>
<TITLE>Using the LINK tag</TITLE>
<LINK REL=STYLESHEET TYPE="text/JavaScript" HREF="favstyle">
</HEAD>
<BODY>
<P>This paragraph uses the style sheet that is contained in
the favstyle file. You can modify favstyle to update the styles
used for all of your favorite documents.</P>
</BODY>
</HTML>
```

Listing 18.22   Using the <LINK> Tag with CSS (css-usestyle.htm)

```
<HTML>
<HEAD>
<TITLE>Using the LINK tag</TITLE>
<LINK REL=STYLESHEET TYPE="text/css" HREF="css-favstyle">
</HEAD>
<BODY>
<P>This paragraph uses the style sheet that is contained in
the css-favstyle file. You can modify css-favstyle to update the styles
used for all of your favorite documents.</P>
</BODY>
</HTML>
```

FIGURE 18.10:

The <LINK> tag allows externally defined styles to be included in a document.

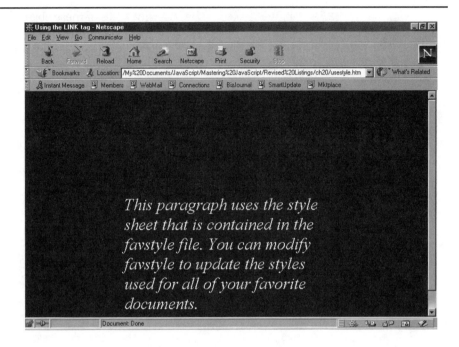

Using Multiple Style Sheets

Multiple JavaScript style sheets can be used in a single document. Externally defined style sheets can also be combined with internally defined style sheets. The internally defined styles take precedence over the externally defined styles. Later referenced external styles take precedence over earlier referenced external styles.

Using Internet Explorer's DHTML Capabilities

Internet Explorer's scripting support for styles goes way beyond that of Navigator. In Internet Explorer 4 and later, all HTML elements in a document are accessible as JScript objects. What's more, the CSS styles of these objects are also accessible through JScript. Internet Explorer goes one step further and allows these styles to be dynamically updated and redisplayed during a script's execution. I'll cover each of these features in the following subsections.

Accessing HTML Elements as Objects

In JScript, the `document` object has the `all` property, which is a collection of all the HTML element objects in a document. These objects can be accessed by supplying an index to the `all` collection. For example, `document.all(4)` returns the object corresponding to the fifth HTML element in a document because counting starts at 0. Note that all required HTML elements, such as the document `HTML`, `HEAD`, `TITLE`, and `BODY` tags, have a corresponding JScript object and are included (even if they are not explicitly identified within a document). The objects of the `all` collection are organized according to the order that they appear in the document. For example, the following code identifies all the objects of the `all` collection (that is, all the HTML elements in a document):

```
for(var i=0; i<document.all.length; ++i) {
    document.writeln(document.all(i).tagName+"<BR>")
}
```

The `tagName` property of an HTML element object identifies the name of the element's tag.

The `all` collection has the `length` property, which identifies the length of the collection, and two methods, `item()` and `tags()`.

The `item()` method returns a subcollection of the elements contained in the `all` collection, a single element, or the `null` value. It may take a string argument, numeric argument, or both. If a string argument is provided, then it is used to select all elements with matching `NAME` or `ID` attributes. For example, `document.all.item("myClass")` returns a collection of objects corresponding to all HTML elements with `NAME` or `ID` attribute set to `"myClass"`. If the collection consists of a single object with the specified attribute, then a single object (not a collection) is returned. If the collection is empty, then `null` is returned.

If the argument to the `item()` method is an integer, then it returns the element of a collection at the specified index. For example, `document.all.item(5)` returns the sixth element of the `all` collection. If the arguments to the `item()` method are a string followed by an integer, then the subcollection specified by the string argument is determined and the object at the specified index is returned. For instance, `document.all.item("myClass",3)` returns the object corresponding to the fourth element of a document with its NAME or ID attribute set to `"myClass"`.

The `tags()` method returns a collection of HTML element objects with a specified tag name or `null` if the collection is empty. For example, `document.all.tags("P")` returns the collection of all objects corresponding to a document's P tags and `document.all.tags("H1")` returns the collection of all objects corresponding to a document's H1 headings.

Listing 18.23 illustrates the use of the `all` collection and `tags()` methods. It displays the following output:

```
All Tags
HTML
HEAD
TITLE
SCRIPT
BODY
H1
P
H1
P
H1
P
All H1 Headings
H1
H1
H1
```

Listing 18.23   Using the all Collection (all.htm)

```
<HTML>
<HEAD>
<TITLE>Using the all Collection</TITLE>
<SCRIPT LANGUAGE="JavaScript"><!-
function display(s,c) {
 win.document.writeln("<H1>"+s+"</H1>")
 if(c==null) return
 if(c.length==null) return
 if(c.length==0) return
```

```
  for(var i=0;i<c.length;++i)
    win.document.writeln(c.item(i).tagName+"<BR>")
  }
  function displayAll() {
   var allTags = document.all
   var allH1 = document.all.tags("H1")
   win = window.open("","output")
   display("All Tags",allTags)
   display("All H1 Headings",allH1)
  }
  //–></SCRIPT></HEAD>
  <BODY onLoad="displayAll()">
  <H1>Heading 1</H1>
  <P>Paragraph 1</P>
  <H1>Heading 2</H1>
  <P>Paragraph 2</P>
  <H1>Heading 3</H1>
  <P>Paragraph 3</P>
  </BODY>
  </HTML>
```

The Style Property

Each HTML object has a `style` property that can be used to access the CSS styles of the corresponding HTML element. This `style` property is an object itself, referred to as the `style` object, and has properties that correspond to the CSS style properties. Table 18.1 lists these properties. The `style` object also has three methods, `getAttribute()`, `setAttribute()`, and `removeAttribute()`. These methods are used to access the style attributes of an HTML element object.

TABLE 18.1: Properties of the `style` Object

Properties	Description
Background backgroundAttachment backgroundColor backgroundImage backgroundPosition backgroundPositionX backgroundPositionY backgroundRepeat	The CSS **background** attributes

Continued on next page

TABLE 18.1 CONTINUED: Properties of the `style` Object

Properties	Description
Border borderBottom borderBottomColor borderBottomStyle borderBottomWidth borderColor borderLeft borderLeftColor borderLeftStyle borderLeftWidth borderRight borderRightColor borderRightStyle borderRightWidth borderStyle borderTop borderTopColor borderTopStyle borderTopWidth borderWidth	The CSS `border` attributes
clear	The CSS `clear` attribute
clip	The CSS `clip` attribute
color	The CSS `color` attribute
cssText	Identifies the CSS style rule
cursor	Identifies the type of cursor to display when the cursor is over the element
display	The CSS `display` attribute
filter	The CSS `filter` attribute
Font fontFamily fontSize fontStyle fontVariant fontWeight	The CSS `font` attributes

Continued on next page

TABLE 18.1 CONTINUED: Properties of the `style` Object

Properties	Description
height	The CSS height attribute
left	The CSS left attribute
letterSpacing	The CSS letter-spacing attribute
lineHeight	The CSS line-height attribute
ListStyle listStyleImage listStylePosition listStyleType	The CSS list attributes
Margin marginBottom marginLeft marginRight marginTop	The CSS margin attributes
overflow	The CSS overflow attribute
PaddingBottom paddingLeft paddingRight paddingTop	The CSS padding attributes
PageBreakAfter pageBreakBefore	The CSS page-break attributes
PixelHeight pixelLeft pixelTop pixelWidth	The dimensions and position of the element in pixels
position	The CSS position attribute
PosHeight posLeft posTop posWidth	The dimensions and position of the element in units specified by the CSS height, left, top, and width attributes

Continued on next page

TABLE 18.1 CONTINUED: Properties of the `style` Object

Properties	Description
styleFloat	The CSS `float` attribute
TextAlign textDecoration textDecorationBlink textDecorationLineThrough textDecorationNone textDecorationOverline textDecorationUnderline textIndent textTransform	The CSS `text` attributes
top	The CSS `top` attribute
verticalAlign	The CSS `vertical-align` attribute
visibility	The CSS `visibility` attribute
width	The CSS `width` attribute
zIndex	The CSS `z-index` attribute

The important point about the `style` object is that you can dynamically change the CSS style of an HTML object by setting the properties of its `style` object. You'll see an extended example of this in the next section.

A Style Sampler

To appreciate the power of Internet Explorer's dynamic style scripting capabilities, you need to see them in action. I'll give you a short tour and then explain how the scripts work. Open `ie-dhtml.htm` (Listing 18.24) with Internet Explorer 4 or later. It displays the screen shown in Figure 18.11. Click the Apply DHTML Style button, and the characteristics of the displayed text are updated, as shown in Figure 18.12. Click the button again, and the text colors change, as shown in Figure 18.13. Click one more time, and the text layout is altered, as shown in Figure 18.14.

FIGURE 18.11:

Displaying simple text

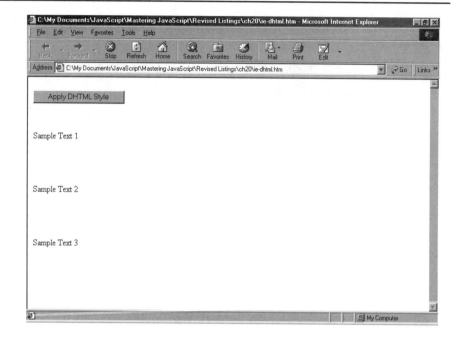

FIGURE 18.12:

Changing the text's font characteristics

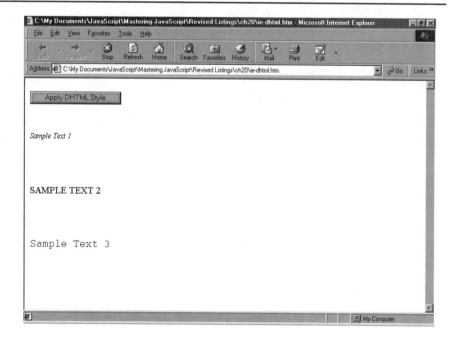

FIGURE 18.13:

Changing text colors

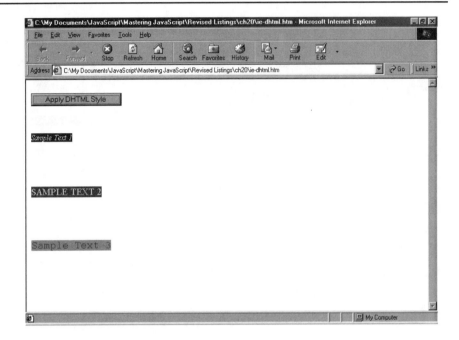

FIGURE 18.14:

Changing the text's position

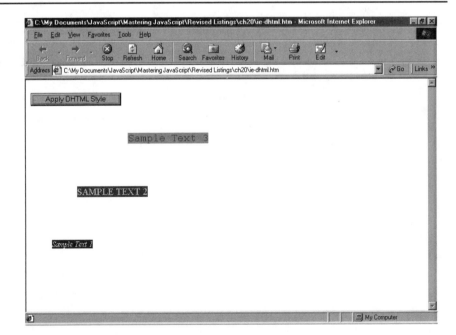

If you think that what you have seen so far is impressive, hang in there because it gets better. Click the Apply DHTML Style button again, and the text is animated, as shown in Figure 18.15. Click the button again, and the animation stops with the text aligned as in Figure 18.16. Click one more time, and the area occupied by each text segment is enlarged, as shown in Figure 18.17.

FIGURE 18.15:

Animating the text

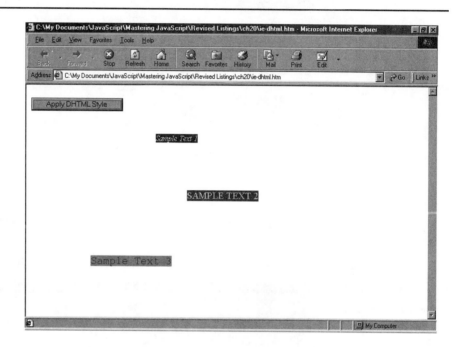

You're almost at the end of the style sampler. Click the Apply DHTML Style button three more times, and the text regions move and overlap, as shown in Figure 18.18. Click one last time, and the content, location, and font characteristics of the text is dynamically updated in an animation effect, as shown in Figure 18.19.

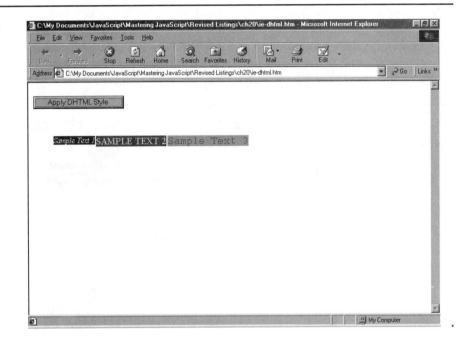

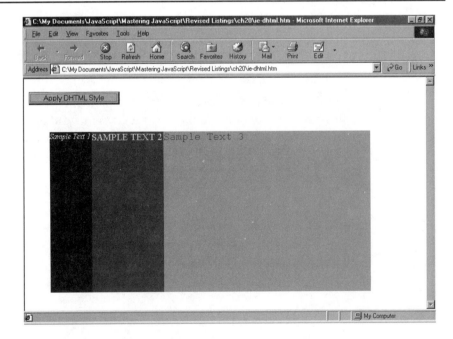

FIGURE 18.18:

Overlapping text regions

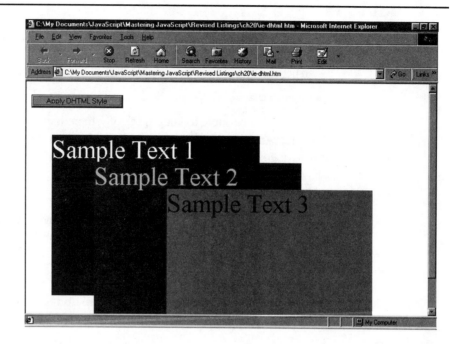

FIGURE 18.19:

More text animation

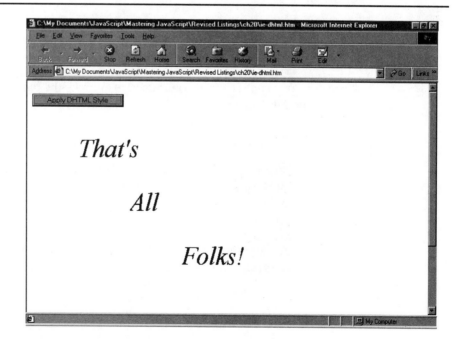

How the Style Sampler Works

The scripting behind the style sampler script is actually fairly simple. The `apply-DHTML()` function is invoked to handle the button's `onClick` event. This function creates an array of paragraph objects via the `all` collection and `tags` method:

```
paragraph=document.all.tags("P")
```

It uses the `state` variable to keep track of which display state it is in and updates the `style` object of each paragraph object in a long case statement. Each case is described in the following paragraphs:

case 0:

The `fontSize`, `fontStyle`, `fontVariant`, and `fontFamily` properties of the paragraphs' `style` objects are updated to change the text styles.

case 1:

The `backgroundColor` and `color` properties are updated to change the text background and foreground colors.

case 2:

The position of each paragraph is updated via the `posLeft` and `posTop` properties.

case 3:

The `moveParagraphs()` function is used to animate the paragraphs by moving them around the document window.

case 4:

The animation is stopped via the `clearInterval()` method and the paragraphs are lined up at 100 pixels from the top of the page.

cases 5–7:

The stacking order (`zIndex`) of each paragraph is updated to place it above the others and its `height` and `width` dimensions are enlarged.

case 8:

The paragraphs are converted to a 48pt Times font and repositioned.

case 9:

The paragraphs are converted to black-and-white, hidden, and repositioned to the left of the document window. The text of each paragraph is then changed. The slideText() function is invoked to animate each paragraph so that the paragraph moves from left to right while its font size increases. The italicize() method is then invoked to change each paragraph's text to italics.

Listing 18.24   **Dynamically Updating Styles Using Internet Explorer (ie-dhtml.htm)**

```
<HTML>
<HEAD>
<TITLE></TITLE>
<SCRIPT LANGUAGE="JScript"><!-
state = 0
function moveParagraphs() {
 paragraph[0].style.posLeft = Math.random()*400
 paragraph[0].style.posTop = Math.random()*400
 paragraph[1].style.posLeft = Math.random()*400
 paragraph[1].style.posTop = Math.random()*400
 paragraph[2].style.posLeft = Math.random()*400
 paragraph[2].style.posTop = Math.random()*400
}
function slideText(n) {
 paragraph[n].style.visibility = "visible"
 for(var i=0;i<(n+1)*100;++i) {
  setTimeout("paragraph["+n+"].style.posLeft++",500)
 }
}
function italicize() {
 paragraph[0].style.fontStyle = "italic"
 paragraph[1].style.fontStyle = "italic"
 paragraph[2].style.fontStyle = "italic"
}
function applyDHTML() {
 paragraph=document.all.tags("P")
 switch(state) {
```

```
case 0:
 paragraph[0].style.fontSize = 14
 paragraph[0].style.fontStyle = "italic"
 paragraph[1].style.fontSize = 18
 paragraph[1].style.fontVariant = "small-caps"
 paragraph[2].style.fontSize = 24
 paragraph[2].style.fontFamily = "Courier"
 break;
case 1:
 paragraph[0].style.backgroundColor = "blue"
 paragraph[0].style.color = "white"
 paragraph[1].style.backgroundColor = "green"
 paragraph[1].style.color = "yellow"
 paragraph[2].style.backgroundColor = "orange"
 paragraph[2].style.color = "red"
 break;
case 2:
 paragraph[0].style.posLeft = 50
 paragraph[0].style.posTop = 300
 paragraph[1].style.posLeft = 100
 paragraph[1].style.posTop = 200
 paragraph[2].style.posLeft = 200
 paragraph[2].style.posTop = 100
 break;
case 3:
 interval = setInterval("moveParagraphs()",750)
 break;
case 4:
 clearInterval(interval)
 paragraph[0].style.posLeft = 50
 paragraph[0].style.posTop = 100
 paragraph[1].style.posLeft = 132
 paragraph[1].style.posTop = 100
 paragraph[2].style.posLeft = 272
 paragraph[2].style.posTop = 100
 break;
case 5:
 paragraph[0].style.zIndex = 100
 paragraph[0].style.width = 400
 paragraph[0].style.height = 300
 break;
case 6:
```

```
      paragraph[0].style.zIndex = 0
      paragraph[1].style.zIndex = 100
      paragraph[1].style.width = 400
      paragraph[1].style.height = 300
      break;
    case 7:
      paragraph[1].style.zIndex = 1
      paragraph[2].style.zIndex = 100
      paragraph[2].style.width = 400
      paragraph[2].style.height = 300
      break;
    case 8:
      for(var i=0;i<3;++i) {
       paragraph[i].style.fontFamily = "Times"
       paragraph[i].style.fontSize = 48
       paragraph[i].style.fontStyle = "normal"
       paragraph[i].style.fontVariant = "normal"
      }
      paragraph[1].style.posTop += 50
      paragraph[2].style.posTop += 100
      break;
    case 9:
      for(var i=0;i<3;++i) {
       paragraph[i].style.color = "black"
       paragraph[i].style.backgroundColor = "white"
       paragraph[i].style.visibility = "hidden"
       paragraph[i].style.posLeft = 0
       paragraph[i].style.posTop = (i+1)*100
      }
      paragraph[0].innerText="That's"
      paragraph[1].innerText="All"
      paragraph[2].innerText="Folks!"
      setTimeout("slideText(0)",500)
      setTimeout("slideText(1)",1500)
      setTimeout("slideText(2)",2500)
      setTimeout("italicize()",5000)
      break;
    }
   state = state + 1 % 10
}
//--></SCRIPT>
</HEAD>
```

```
<BODY>
<P STYLE="position:absolute; top:100">Sample Text 1</P>
<P STYLE="position:absolute; top:200">Sample Text 2</P>
<P STYLE="position:absolute; top:300">Sample Text 3</P>
<FORM STYLE="position:absolute; top:25">
<INPUT TYPE="BUTTON" VALUE="Apply DHTML Style"
 onClick="applyDHTML()">
</FORM>
</BODY>
</HTML>
```

Summary

In this chapter, you were introduced to style sheets and covered several examples of their application. You learned about the differences between Netscape's JavaScript style sheets and the Cascading Style Sheets developed by the World Wide Web Consortium. You covered the tags, properties, and attributes used with JavaScript style sheets and learned how to work with both internally- and externally-defined styles. Finally, you looked at Internet Explorer's support for style sheets and DHTML. You learned how to use Internet Explorer to dynamically script styles and interesting effects to your Web pages.

In the next chapter, you'll learn to use another important capability provided by JavaScript 1.2—layers. You'll learn how to use layers to create multiple levels of multimedia overlays that will add a new dimension to your application's appearance and appeal. You'll also learn how Internet Explorer supports the same capabilities as layers through the division tag and div object.

Creating Multimedia Applications

- Using Layers and Divisions

- Working with Audio

- Performing Animation

- Using Video

Multimedia features, such as audio, video, and animation, can add to the effectiveness and appeal of your Web pages. You learned how to work with multimedia features in Part IV, "Communicating with Java, ActiveX, and Plug-Ins," when you studied plug-ins. The introduction of *layers* with Navigator 4 added to the multimedia capabilities provided by plug-ins. Layers can be used to move and control the display of different objects within a Web page. JavaScript 1.2 provides access to layers and allows you to manipulate the positioning and display of layers during a script's execution. While Netscape invented layers, Microsoft followed a more standard approach and provided full scripting support for the HTML <DIV> tag and Cascading Style Sheets in Internet Explorer 4. These features, referred to as Dynamic HTML (DHTML), provide the same capabilities as Netscape's layers and more.

In this chapter, you'll learn how to use the <LAYER> and <DIV> tags to integrate multimedia capabilities in your Web applications. You'll cover the JavaScript layer and div objects and learn how to use their properties and methods to enhance animations, create slide shows, and increase the effectiveness of videos. When you finish this chapter, you'll be able to use layers and divisions to augment the multimedia features of your Web applications.

Using Layers

Layers are one of the most attractive capabilities introduced with Navigator 4. They allow you to organize your documents into multiple levels of opaque or transparent sections that can be overlaid, moved, or selectively displayed. Each layer is able to contain HTML content; thus each layer can include other layers, Java applets, forms, and plug-ins. Layers can be combined to produce the effect of multiple documents being dynamically integrated within a single window. When used to create multimedia effects, layers can be used to create PowerPoint-like slide shows, perform advanced animation, or add new dimensions to the ways that plug-ins are displayed.

The Layer Tags

The <LAYER> and <ILAYER> tags are used to define layers. The <LAYER> tag is used to define a fixed position layer, while the <ILAYER> tag is used to define a layer that is formatted as part of the document's natural flow that is relative to other document elements. Both tags are surrounding tags and are used as follows:

```
<LAYER attributes>
HTML tags included within layer
</LAYER>
```

or

```
<ILAYER attributes>
HTML tags included within layer
</ILAYER>
```

The <LAYER> and <ILAYER> tags use the same attributes, as described in Table 19.1. All of these attributes are optional.

TABLE 19.1: Attributes of the <LAYER> and <ILAYER> Tags

Attribute	Description
ABOVE	Identifies the layer that is positioned immediately above the layer being defined.
BACKGROUND	Specifies the background image to be used with the layer.
BELOW	Identifies the layer that is positioned immediately below the layer being defined.
BGCOLOR	Specifies the background color to be used with the layer.
CLIP	Identifies the clipping rectangle of the layer. This attribute takes four comma-separated arguments of the form CLIP = *left*, *top*, *right*, *bottom*. These arguments identify the number of pixels from each side that should be clipped when the layer is displayed. The clipping rectangle can also be specified as two numbers CLIP = *right*, *bottom*. In this option, the left and top values are assumed to be 0.
LEFT	Identifies the horizontal distance from the left side of the window (<LAYER> tag) or from its normal positioning (<ILAYER> tag) where the layer is to be displayed.
HEIGHT	Determines the height of the layer's display.
ID	Uniquely identifies the layer.
NAME	Identifies the window's name.
PAGEX and PAGEY	Specifies the position of the layer with respect to the enclosing document.
SRC	Specifies a URL from which the contents of the layer should be loaded.

Continued on next page

TABLE 19.1 CONTINUED: Attributes of the <LAYER> and <ILAYER> Tags

Attribute	Description
TOP	Identifies the vertical distance from the top of the window (<LAYER> tag) or from its normal positioning (<ILAYER> tag) where the layer is to be displayed.
VISIBILITY	Identifies whether the layer is to be displayed.
WIDTH	Determines the width of the layer's display.
Z-INDEX	Specifies a positive integer that is used to determine how the layer is positioned with respect to other layers.

Layers are ordered according to a *stacking* order. This means that layers are stacked over each other like a deck of cards. This order is called a *z-order*. The Z-INDEX, ABOVE, and BELOW attributes are used to create this ordering. Only one of these three attributes can be used for a given layer definition. The Z-INDEX attribute is used to identify a layer's position within the ordering: layers with higher Z-INDEX attribute values are stacked above those with lower values. The ABOVE attribute identifies the layer (by name) that is immediately above the layer being defined. The BELOW attribute identifies the layer (by name) that is immediately below the layer being defined.

A layer is either transparent or opaque. A layer is opaque if its BACKGROUND or BGCOLOR attributes are specified; otherwise it is transparent. The VISIBILITY attribute is set to hide, show, or inherited. The show value causes a layer to be displayed. The hide value causes a layer to be hidden. The inherited value causes the visibility of a layer to be that of its parent (that is, an outer layer in which it is enclosed). If a layer has no parent, then setting its visibility to inherited is the same as setting it to show.

The SRC attribute loads the content of a layer from the document specified by a URL. The HTML elements contained in the file should be those that can appear within a document's body.

Windowed Elements

Forms, plug-ins, and applets are referred to as *windowed* elements. Windowed elements are always displayed, regardless of whether they are in a non-visible layer. In addition, windowed elements disappear if any part of the element is moved outside the visible area of a window. In comparison, *windowless* plug-ins are specially designed so that they can be hidden in non-visible layers.

The *layers* Array and *layer* Object

JavaScript provides access to layers via the `layers` array and the `layer` object. The `layers` array is a property of the `document` object that contains an entry for every layer defined within the document. The `layers` array does *not* contain entries for layers that are defined *within* layers; these layers can be accessed via a second-level or third-level `layers` array. For example, the second sublayer of the fourth layer of a document can be referenced as `document.layers[3].layer[1]`. The name of a layer can also be used as its index into the `layers` array.

The `layer` object is a property of the `document` object that is used to provide access to the attributes of an individual layer. Layers can be accessed by name or via the `layers` array. The properties of the `layer` object mimic the attributes of the <LAYER> tag. These properties include `above`, `background`, `below`, `bgColor`, `clip`, `left`, `name`, `src`, `top`, `visibility`, `width`, and `zIndex`. The `clip` property has `top`, `left`, `right`, `bottom`, `width`, and `height` properties.

In addition, the layer object also has the `height`, `layers`, `parentLayer`, `siblingAbove`, and `siblingBelow` properties. The `parentLayer` property is used to identify the layer in which a layer is nested. The `siblingAbove` and `siblingBelow` properties identify layers above or below a layer that share the same parent.

The methods of the `layer` object are described in Table 19.2.

TABLE 19.2: Methods of the `layer` Object

Method	Description
`captureEvents(eventType)`	Allows the layer to capture all events of the specified type
`handleEvent(event)`	Invokes the event handler for the specified event
`load(source, width)`	Loads the file specified by source and wraps data at the specified width
`moveAbove(layer)`	Moves the layer above the identified layer
`moveBelow(layer)`	Moves the layer below the identified layer

Continued on next page

TABLE 19.2 CONTINUED: Methods of the `layer` Object

Method	Description
moveBy(*x*, *y*)	Moves the layer by the specified x and y pixel increments
moveTo(*x*,*y*)	Moves the layer to the specified position within its container (layer or document)
moveToAbsolute(*x*,*y*)	Moves the layer to the specified position within the overall document
releaseEvents(*eventType*)	Ends the capturing of the specified event type
routeEvent(*event*)	Causes a captured event to be processed in a normal fashion
resizeBy(*width*, *height*)	Resizes the layer by the specified dimensions
resizeTo(*width*, *height*)	Resizes the window to the specified dimensions

A Slide Show Example

We've talked about layers long enough—it's time to get busy using them in an example. Listing 19.1 shows how layers can be used to create a slide show–like presentation. While this script won't knock PowerPoint off of the software charts, it does illustrate how JavaScript and layers can be combined to produce some interesting effects.

Download `slideshow.htm` from this book's page on the Sybex Web site. Open it using your browser. It displays the browser window shown in Figure 19.1. This window shows the first slide of a five-slide presentation about layers. The slide show is controlled by four buttons—First Slide, Previous Slide, Next Slide, and Last Slide. Click the Next Slide button and your browser displays the slide shown in Figure 19.2. You can quickly move to the last slide of the briefing by clicking the Last Slide button, or the previous slide by clicking the Previous Slide button. Play around with the script until you become familiar with its operation.

FIGURE 19.1:

The slide show opening display

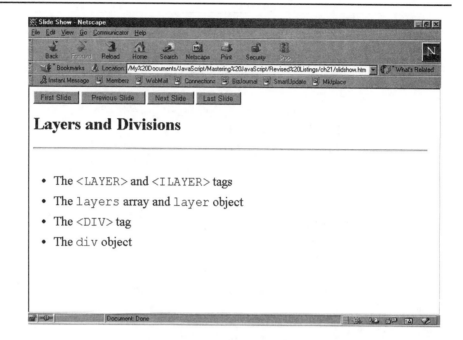

FIGURE 19.2:

Clicking the Next Slide button causes the next slide in the briefing to be displayed.

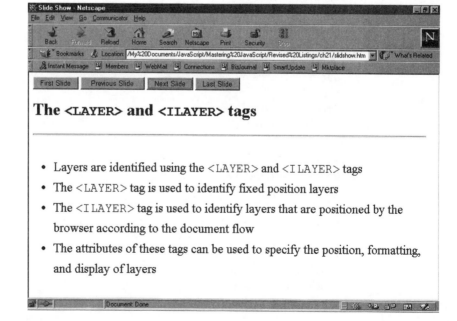

Listing 19.1   A Layer-Based Slide Show (slideshow.htm)

```
<HTML>
<HEAD>
<TITLE>Slide Show</TITLE>
</HEAD>
<SCRIPT LANGUAGE="JavaScript"><!-
function hideAll(){
 for(var i=0;i<document.layers.length;++i)
  document.layers[i].visibility="hide"
}
function getCurrent(){
 for(var i=0;i<document.layers.length;++i)
  if(document.layers[i].visibility!="hide") return i
 return 0
}
function makeVisible(i){
 document.layers[i].visibility="inherit"
}
function lastSlide(){
 return document.layers.length-1
}
function first(){
 hideAll()
 makeVisible(0)
}
function prev(){
 var i=getCurrent()
 hideAll()
 if(i>0) makeVisible(i-1)
 else makeVisible(i)
}
function next(){
 var i=getCurrent()
 hideAll()
 if(i<lastSlide()) makeVisible(i+1)
 else makeVisible(i)
}
function last(){
 hideAll()
 makeVisible(lastSlide())
```

```
}
// -></SCRIPT>
<STYLE TYPE="text/javascript">
 tags.UL.fontSize="18pt"
 tags.UL.lineHeight=2
</STYLE>
<BODY BGCOLOR="white">
<FORM>
<INPUT TYPE="BUTTON" VALUE="First Slide" ONCLICK="first()">
<INPUT TYPE="BUTTON" VALUE="Previous Slide" ONCLICK="prev()">
<INPUT TYPE="BUTTON" VALUE="Next Slide" ONCLICK="next()">
<INPUT TYPE="BUTTON" VALUE="Last Slide" ONCLICK="last()">
</FORM>
<LAYER NAME="slide0" BGCOLOR="white" VISIBILITY="SHOW">
<H1>Layers and Divisions</H1>
<HR>
<UL>
<LI>The <CODE>&lt;LAYER&gt;</CODE> and
<CODE>&lt;ILAYER&gt;</CODE> tags
<LI>The <CODE>layers</CODE> array and <CODE>layer</CODE> object
<LI>The <CODE>&lt;DIV&gt;</CODE> tag
<LI>The <CODE>div</CODE> object
</UL>
</LAYER>
<LAYER NAME="slide1" BGCOLOR="white" VISIBILITY="HIDE">
<H1>The <CODE>&lt;LAYER&gt;</CODE> and
<CODE>&lt;ILAYER&gt;</CODE> tags</H1>
<HR>
<UL>
<LI>Layers are identified using the
<CODE>&lt;LAYER&gt;</CODE> and
<CODE>&lt;ILAYER&gt;</CODE> tags
<LI>The <CODE>&lt;LAYER&gt;</CODE> tag is used to identify
fixed position layers
<LI>The <CODE>&lt;ILAYER&gt;</CODE> tag is used to identify
layers that are positioned by the browser according to
the document flow
<LI>The attributes of these tags can be used to specify
the position, formatting, and display of layers
</UL>
</LAYER>
<LAYER NAME="slide2" BGCOLOR="white" VISIBILITY="HIDE">
```

```
<H1>The <CODE>layers</CODE> array and <CODE>layer</CODE>
object</H1>
<HR>
<UL>
<LI>Access to layers from JavaScript is provided by the
<CODE>layers</CODE> array and <CODE>layer</CODE> object
<LI>The <CODE>layers</CODE> array identifies all layers
in a document
<LI>The <CODE>layer</CODE> object provides access to the
attributes of an individual object
</UL>
</LAYER>
<LAYER NAME="slide3" BGCOLOR="white" VISIBILITY="HIDE">
<H1>The <CODE>&lt;DIV&gt;</CODE> tag</H1>
<HR>
<UL>
<LI>The <CODE>&lt;DIV&gt;</CODE> tag is used with cascading
style sheets
<LI>It allows styles to be applied to all HTML elements contained
within the tags
<LI>This includes font, color, display, and other attributes
<LI>It provides a capability similar to that provided by the
<CODE>&lt;LAYER&gt;</CODE> tag
</UL>
</LAYER>
<LAYER NAME="slide4" BGCOLOR="white" VISIBILITY="HIDE">
<H1>The <CODE>DIV</CODE> object</H1>
<HR>
<UL>
<LI>The <CODE>div</CODE> object is supported by Internet
Explorer
<LI>It allows styles to be dynamically applied during
a script's execution
<LI>It can be used to alternately hide and display
different sets of HTML elements
</UL>
</LAYER>
</BODY>
</HTML>
```

The slide show script makes extensive use of layers. Five layers, named slide0 through slide4, are defined in the document body. The layers all have a white background color, but only the first slide is initially visible. Each layer contains an HTML description of its associated slide's contents. A simple four-button form is included at the top of the document body. These buttons invoke the first(), prev(), next(), and last() methods to move between slides.

The <STYLE> tags in the document head are used to change the list items of each slide to a larger font (18pt) and to display them using double-spacing.

The script in the document head defines eight functions, whose descriptions follow.

The *hideAll()* Function

The hideAll() function loops through all layers defined in the current document, and sets their visibility property to hide.

The *getCurrent()* Function

The getCurrent() function loops through all layers defined in the current document and returns the index of the layer whose visibility is not set to hide.

The *makeVisible()* Function

The makeVisible() function sets the visibility of a specified layer to inherit. This causes the layer to inherit the visibility of the overall document and therefore be displayed.

The *lastSlide()* Function

The lastSlide() function returns the index of the last layer in the layers array.

The *first()* Function

The first() function hides all layers using the hideAll() function, and then invokes the makeVisible() function to display the first slide in the slide show.

The *prev()* Function

The prev() function invokes getCurrent() to get the index of the currently visible layer and then hides all layers using the hideAll() function. If the current slide is not the first slide then the makeVisible() function is invoked to display the previous slide in the slide show.

The *next()* Function

The next() function invokes getCurrent() to get the index of the currently visible layer, and then hides all layers using the hideAll() function. If the current slide is not the last slide, then the makeVisible() function is invoked to display the next slide in the slide show.

The *last()* Function

The last() function hides all layers using the hideAll() function, and then invokes the lastSlide() and makeVisible() functions to display the last slide in the slide show.

Using Divisions

The division tag (<DIV>) is a generic block formatting tag that supports the creation of HTML sections that can be nested. It is not a new HTML tag; it has been around since HTML 3.2 and is supported by Navigator and Internet Explorer. What's new and interesting about the division tag is the DHTML support provided by Internet Explorer 4 and later.

As you learned in Chapter 18, "Using Style Sheets and DHTML," Internet Explorer provides access to all HTML elements contained within a Web page and allows those elements to be individually (and dynamically) scripted. What's more, Internet Explorer allows the CSS styles of these elements to be dynamically updated during a script's execution.

Getting back to divisions, Internet Explorer provides a unique div object for every division that occurs within an HTML document. You can script this object using its properties and methods. The most useful property of the div object is its style property. You can use the div object and its style property to do everything you can with Netscape layers and more.

Listing 19.2 (ie-slide.htm) shows how to use the division tag, div object, and its style property to duplicate the layers example of Listing 19.1. When you open ie-slide.htm in Internet Explorer 4 or later, it behaves exactly like its layers counterpart.

Listing 19.2   A Division-Based Slide Show (ie-slide.htm)

```
<HTML>
<HEAD>
<TITLE>Slide Show</TITLE>
</HEAD>
<SCRIPT LANGUAGE="JScript"><!-
function hideAll(){
 var divisions = document.all.tags("div")
 for(var i=0;i<divisions.length;++i)
  divisions[i].style.display = "none"
}
function getCurrent(){
 var divisions = document.all.tags("div")
 for(var i=0;i<divisions.length;++i)
  if(divisions[i].style.display == "block") return i
 return 0
}
function makeVisible(i){
 var divisions = document.all.tags("div")
 divisions[i].style.display = "block"
}
function lastSlide(){
 var divisions = document.all.tags("div")
 return divisions.length-1
}
function first(){
 hideAll()
 makeVisible(0)
}
function prev(){
 var i=getCurrent()
 hideAll()
 if(i>0) makeVisible(i-1)
 else makeVisible(i)
}
```

```
function next(){
 var i=getCurrent()
 hideAll()
 if(i<lastSlide()) makeVisible(i+1)
 else makeVisible(i)
}
function last(){
 hideAll()
 makeVisible(lastSlide())
}
// -></SCRIPT>
<STYLE TYPE="text/css">
 ul  {
  font-size: 20pt;
 }
 div {
  background-color: white;
  color: black;
  display: none;
 }
</STYLE>
<BODY BGCOLOR="white">
<FORM>
<INPUT TYPE="BUTTON" VALUE="First Slide" ONCLICK="first()">
<INPUT TYPE="BUTTON" VALUE="Previous Slide" ONCLICK="prev()">
<INPUT TYPE="BUTTON" VALUE="Next Slide" ONCLICK="next()">
<INPUT TYPE="BUTTON" VALUE="Last Slide" ONCLICK="last()">
</FORM>
<DIV NAME="slide0">
<H1>Layers and Divisions</H1>
<HR>
<UL>
<LI>The <CODE>&lt;LAYER&gt;</CODE> and
<CODE>&lt;ILAYER&gt;</CODE> tags
<LI>The <CODE>layers</CODE> array and <CODE>layer</CODE> object
<LI>The <CODE>&lt;DIV&gt;</CODE> tag
<LI>The <CODE>div</CODE> object
</UL>
</DIV>
<DIV NAME="slide1">
<H1>The <CODE>&lt;LAYER&gt;</CODE> and
<CODE>&lt;ILAYER&gt;</CODE> tags</H1>
```

```
<HR>
<UL>
<LI>Layers are identified using the
<CODE>&lt;LAYER&gt;</CODE> and
<CODE>&lt;ILAYER&gt;</CODE> tags
<LI>The <CODE>&lt;LAYER&gt;</CODE> tag is used to identify
fixed position layers
<LI>The <CODE>&lt;ILAYER&gt;</CODE> tag is used to identify
layers that are positioned by the browser according to
the document flow
<LI>The attributes of these tags can be used to specify
the position, formatting, and display of layers
</UL>
</DIV>
<DIV NAME="slide2">
<H1>The <CODE>layers</CODE> array and <CODE>layer</CODE>
object</H1>
<HR>
<UL>
<LI>Access to layers from JavaScript is provided by the
<CODE>layers</CODE> array and <CODE>layer</CODE> object
<LI>The <CODE>layers</CODE> array identifies all layers
in a document
<LI>The <CODE>layer</CODE> object provides access to the
attributes of an individual object
</UL>
</DIV>
<DIV NAME="slide3">
<H1>The <CODE>&lt;DIV&gt;</CODE> tag</H1>
<HR>
<UL>
<LI>The <CODE>&lt;DIV&gt;</CODE> tag is used with cascading
style sheets
<LI>It allows styles to be applied to all HTML elements contained
within the tags
<LI>This includes font, color, display, and other attributes
<LI>It provides a capability similar to that provided by the
<CODE>&lt;LAYER&gt;</CODE> tag
</UL>
</DIV>
<DIV NAME="slide4">
<H1>The <CODE>DIV</CODE> object</H1>
```

```
<HR>
<UL>
<LI>The <CODE>div</CODE> object is supported by Internet
Explorer
<LI>It allows styles to be dynamically applied during
a script's execution
<LI>It can be used to alternately hide and display
different sets of HTML elements
</UL>
</DIV>
<SCRIPT LANGUAGE="JScript"><!-
makeVisible(0)
//-></SCRIPT>
</BODY>
</HTML>
```

As you can see from Listing 19.2, ie-slide.htm closely resembles the layers-based slideshow.htm. Instead of five layers, ie-slide.htm contains five divisions. Each division corresponds to a slide in the slide show. A CSS style sheet is substituted for the JavaScript style sheet. The makeVisible(0) function call in the document body is used to make the first division visible and all others invisible.

The eight functions in the document head correspond one-for-one to the eight functions used by slideshow.htm. The first(), prev(), next(), and last() functions are identical. The four remaining functions each begin by setting the divisions variable to an array of all div objects contained in the document. The hideAll() function sets the display property of each div object's style property to "none" to cause the division to be hidden. The getCurrent() method returns the index of the first division that has style.display set to "block". (The "block" value is used to make a division visible.) The makeVisible() function makes a specified division visible. The lastSlide() function returns the last index in the divisions array.

Working with Audio

The topic of this chapter is multimedia, so let's look at how we can integrate multimedia features with layers and divisions. The slide show example of the previous section is a good place to start. Listing 19.3 shows how we can add an audio narrative to each slide. This example works with Netscape layers. I'll provide an Internet Explorer–compatible division-based example next. Open `audiosho.htm` with Navigator, and you'll hear me providing a slide-by-slide commentary.

Listing 19.3   **An Audio-Enhanced Slide Show (audiosho.htm)**

```
<HTML>
<HEAD>
<TITLE>Slide Show with Audio</TITLE>
</HEAD>
<SCRIPT LANGUAGE="JavaScript"><!-
function hideAll(){
 for(var i=0;i<document.layers.length;++i){
  document.layers[i].visibility="hide"
  document.embeds[i].stop()
 }
}
function getCurrent(){
 for(var i=0;i<document.layers.length;++i)
  if(document.layers[i].visibility!="hide") return i
 return 0
}
function makeVisible(i){
 document.layers[i].visibility="inherit"
 document.embeds[i].play()
}
function lastSlide(){
 return document.layers.length-1
}
function first(){
 hideAll()
 makeVisible(0)
}
function prev(){
 var i=getCurrent()
 hideAll()
 if(i>0) makeVisible(i-1)
 else makeVisible(i)
}
function next(){
 var i=getCurrent()
```

```
 hideAll()
 if(i<lastSlide()) makeVisible(i+1)
 else makeVisible(i)
}
function last(){
 hideAll()
 makeVisible(lastSlide())
}
// -></SCRIPT>
<STYLE TYPE="text/javascript">
 tags.UL.fontSize="24pt"
 tags.UL.lineHeight=2
</STYLE>
<BODY BGCOLOR="white">
<FORM>
<INPUT TYPE="BUTTON" VALUE="First Slide" ONCLICK="first()">
<INPUT TYPE="BUTTON" VALUE="Previous Slide" ONCLICK="prev()">
<INPUT TYPE="BUTTON" VALUE="Next Slide" ONCLICK="next()">
<INPUT TYPE="BUTTON" VALUE="Last Slide" ONCLICK="last()">
</FORM>
<LAYER NAME="slide0" BGCOLOR="white" VISIBILITY="SHOW">
<H1>Using Layers</H1>
<HR>
<UL>
<LI>The <CODE>&ltLAYER&gt</CODE> and
<CODE>&ltILAYER&gt</CODE> tags
<LI>The <CODE>layers</CODE> array and <CODE>layer</CODE> object
<LI>Properties of the <CODE>layer</CODE> object
<LI>Methods of the <CODE>layer</CODE> object
</UL>
</LAYER>
<LAYER NAME="slide1" BGCOLOR="white" VISIBILITY="HIDE">
<H1>The <CODE>&ltLAYER&gt</CODE> and
<CODE>&ltILAYER&gt</CODE> tags</H1>
<HR>
<UL>
<LI>Layers are identified using the
<CODE>&ltLAYER&gt</CODE> and
<CODE>&ltILAYER&gt</CODE> tags
<LI>The <CODE>&ltLAYER&gt</CODE> tag is used to identify
fixed position layers
<LI>The <CODE>&ltILAYER&gt</CODE> tag is used to identify
```

```
layers that are positioned by the browser according to
the document flow
<LI>The attributes of these tags can be used to specify
the position, formatting, and display of layers
</UL>
</LAYER>
<LAYER NAME="slide2" BGCOLOR="white" VISIBILITY="HIDE">
<H1>The <CODE>layers</CODE> array and <CODE>layer</CODE>
object</H1>
<HR>
<UL>
<LI>Access to layers from JavaScript is provided by the
<CODE>layers</CODE> array and <CODE>layer</CODE> object
<LI>The <CODE>layers</CODE> array identifies all layers
in a document
<LI>The <CODE>layer</CODE> object provides access to the
attributes of an individual object
</UL>
</LAYER>
<LAYER NAME="slide3" BGCOLOR="white" VISIBILITY="HIDE">
<H1>Properties of the <CODE>layer</CODE> object</H1>
<HR>
<UL>
<LI>The properties of the <CODE>layer</CODE> object
correspond to the attributes of the
<CODE>&ltLAYER&gt</CODE> and <CODE>&ltILAYER&gt</CODE>
tags
<LI>These properties may be used to change the location
and visibility of a layer
</UL>
</LAYER>
<LAYER NAME="slide4" BGCOLOR="white" VISIBILITY="HIDE">
<H1>Methods of the <CODE>layer</CODE> object</H1>
<HR>
<UL>
<LI><CODE>offset(x, y)</CODE>
<LI><CODE>moveTo(x, y)</CODE>
<LI><CODE>resize(width, height)</CODE>
<LI><CODE>moveAbove(layer)</CODE>
<LI><CODE>moveBelow(layer)</CODE>
</UL>
</LAYER>
```

```
<EMBED SRC="slide0.wav" HIDDEN="true" AUTOSTART="true">
<EMBED SRC="slide1.wav" HIDDEN="true" AUTOSTART="false">
<EMBED SRC="slide2.wav" HIDDEN="true" AUTOSTART="false">
<EMBED SRC="slide3.wav" HIDDEN="true" AUTOSTART="false">
<EMBED SRC="slide4.wav" HIDDEN="true" AUTOSTART="false">
</BODY>
</HTML>
```

The inclusion of audio narration can make a presentation more interesting and effective. You can record .wav files using a microphone with your computer's sound board. I recorded the files slide0.wav through slide4.wav using the built-in microphone that came with my computer. These files are included at the bottom of the document's body using <EMBED> tags. Their HIDDEN attributes are set to *true* in order to hide the plug-in's toolbar. The AUTOSTART attribute of the first sound file is set to *true* so that it starts playing when the document is loaded. The AUTOSTART attributes of the other files are set to *false* so that they remain silent until they are explicitly played.

The only other changes (from Listing 19.1) required to implement the audio narration are in the hideAll() and makeVisible() methods. The hideAll() method is modified to stop the playing of all plug-ins by invoking the stop() method for each element of the embeds array. The makeVisible() method is updated to invoke the play() method for the plug-in corresponding to the layer being displayed.

Doing It with Divisions and ActiveX

The ie-slide.htm example of Listing 19.2 can also be updated to use audio. Listing 19.4 (ieaudiosho.htm) shows how. Because this example is geared toward Internet Explorer, I used the ActiveMovie ActiveX control (refer to Chapter 16, "Scripting ActiveX Components") to play the audio files. The only scripting change occurred in the makeVisible() function. This function was updated to stop the currently playing audio file, and then select and play a new audio file.

Listing 19.4   An ActiveX-Based Audio Slide Show (ieaudiosho.htm)

```
<HTML>
<HEAD>
<TITLE>Slide Show</TITLE>
</HEAD>
<SCRIPT LANGUAGE="JScript"><!-
function hideAll(){
 var divisions = document.all.tags("div")
 for(var i=0;i<divisions.length;++i)
  divisions[i].style.display = "none"
}
function getCurrent(){
 var divisions = document.all.tags("div")
 for(var i=0;i<divisions.length;++i)
  if(divisions[i].style.display == "block") return i
 return 0
}
function makeVisible(i){
 var divisions = document.all.tags("div")
 divisions[i].style.display = "block"
 ActiveMovie1.Stop()
 ActiveMovie1.FileName = "slide"+i+".wav"
 ActiveMovie1.Play()
}
function lastSlide(){
 var divisions = document.all.tags("div")
 return divisions.length-1
}
function first(){
 hideAll()
 makeVisible(0)
}
function prev(){
 var i=getCurrent()
 hideAll()
 if(i>0) makeVisible(i-1)
 else makeVisible(i)
}
function next(){
 var i=getCurrent()
```

```
 hideAll()
 if(i<lastSlide()) makeVisible(i+1)
 else makeVisible(i)
}
function last(){
 hideAll()
 makeVisible(lastSlide())
}
// -></SCRIPT>
<STYLE TYPE="text/css">
 ul  {
  font-size: 20pt;
 }
 div {
  background-color: white;
  color: black;
  display: none;
 }
</STYLE>
<BODY BGCOLOR="white">
<FORM>
<INPUT TYPE="BUTTON" VALUE="First Slide" ONCLICK="first()">
<INPUT TYPE="BUTTON" VALUE="Previous Slide" ONCLICK="prev()">
<INPUT TYPE="BUTTON" VALUE="Next Slide" ONCLICK="next()">
<INPUT TYPE="BUTTON" VALUE="Last Slide" ONCLICK="last()">
</FORM>
<DIV NAME="slide0">
<H1>Layers and Divisions</H1>
<HR>
<UL>
<LI>The <CODE>&lt;LAYER&gt;</CODE> and
<CODE>&lt;ILAYER&gt;</CODE> tags
<LI>The <CODE>layers</CODE> array and <CODE>layer</CODE> object
<LI>The <CODE>&lt;DIV&gt;</CODE> tag
<LI>The <CODE>div</CODE> object
</UL>
</DIV>
<DIV NAME="slide1">
<H1>The <CODE>&lt;LAYER&gt;</CODE> and
<CODE>&lt;ILAYER&gt;</CODE> tags</H1>
<HR>
```

```
<UL>
<LI>Layers are identified using the
<CODE>&lt;LAYER&gt;</CODE> and
<CODE>&lt;ILAYER&gt;</CODE> tags
<LI>The <CODE>&lt;LAYER&gt;</CODE> tag is used to identify
fixed position layers
<LI>The <CODE>&lt;ILAYER&gt;</CODE> tag is used to identify
layers that are positioned by the browser according to
the document flow
<LI>The attributes of these tags can be used to specify
the position, formatting, and display of layers
</UL>
</DIV>
<DIV NAME="slide2">
<H1>The <CODE>layers</CODE> array and <CODE>layer</CODE>
object</H1>
<HR>
<UL>
<LI>Access to layers from JavaScript is provided by the
<CODE>layers</CODE> array and <CODE>layer</CODE> object
<LI>The <CODE>layers</CODE> array identifies all layers
in a document
<LI>The <CODE>layer</CODE> object provides access to the
attributes of an individual object
</UL>
</DIV>
<DIV NAME="slide3">
<H1>The <CODE>&lt;DIV&gt;</CODE> tag</H1>
<HR>
<UL>
<LI>The <CODE>&lt;DIV&gt;</CODE> tag is used with cascading
style sheets
<LI>It allows styles to be applied to all HTML elements contained
within the tags
<LI>This includes font, color, display, and other attributes
<LI>It provides a capability similar to that provided by the
<CODE>&lt;LAYER&gt;</CODE> tag
</UL>
</DIV>
<DIV NAME="slide4">
<H1>The <CODE>DIV</CODE> object</H1>
<HR>
```

```
<UL>
<LI>The <CODE>div</CODE> object is supported by Internet
Explorer
<LI>It allows styles to be dynamically applied during
a script's execution
<LI>It can be used to alternately hide and display
different sets of HTML elements
</UL>
</DIV>
<OBJECT ID="ActiveMovie1" WIDTH=0 HEIGHT=0
 CLASSID="CLSID:22D6F312-B0F6-11D0-94AB-0080C74C7E95">
    <PARAM NAME="Appearance" VALUE="0">
    <PARAM NAME="AutoStart" VALUE="0">
    <PARAM NAME="AllowChangeDisplayMode" VALUE="-1">
    <PARAM NAME="AllowHideDisplay" VALUE="0">
    <PARAM NAME="AllowHideControls" VALUE="-1">
    <PARAM NAME="AutoRewind" VALUE="0">
    <PARAM NAME="Balance" VALUE="0">
    <PARAM NAME="CurrentPosition" VALUE="0">
    <PARAM NAME="DisplayBackColor" VALUE="0">
    <PARAM NAME="DisplayForeColor" VALUE="16777215">
    <PARAM NAME="DisplayMode" VALUE="0">
    <PARAM NAME="Enabled" VALUE="-1">
    <PARAM NAME="EnableContextMenu" VALUE="-1">
    <PARAM NAME="EnablePositionControls" VALUE="-1">
    <PARAM NAME="EnableSelectionControls" VALUE="0">
    <PARAM NAME="EnableTracker" VALUE="-1">
    <PARAM NAME="Filename" VALUE="">
    <PARAM NAME="FullScreenMode" VALUE="0">
    <PARAM NAME="MovieWindowSize" VALUE="0">
    <PARAM NAME="PlayCount" VALUE="1">
    <PARAM NAME="Rate" VALUE="1">
    <PARAM NAME="SelectionStart" VALUE="-1">
    <PARAM NAME="SelectionEnd" VALUE="-1">
    <PARAM NAME="ShowControls" VALUE="0">
    <PARAM NAME="ShowDisplay" VALUE="0">
    <PARAM NAME="ShowPositionControls" VALUE="0">
    <PARAM NAME="ShowTracker" VALUE="0">
    <PARAM NAME="Volume" VALUE="-290">
```

```
</OBJECT>
<SCRIPT LANGUAGE="JScript"><!-
makeVisible(0)
//-></SCRIPT>
</BODY>
</HTML>
```

Performing Animation

As you have probably surmised, layers and divisions can be used to extend JavaScript's animation capabilities. Two different types of animation can be supported by using layers and divisions:

- You can create a stack of layers or divisions that contain the slides of an image's animation, and then flip through the slides to cause the animation effect.

- You can place an animated image in a layer or division and then move the layer or division around the screen to further increase the image's animation effect.

Listing 19.5 shows how layers can be used to implement the second kind of animation. Open anilayer.htm with Navigator and you'll see an animated image of an airplane fly from the bottom of your screen to the top of your screen. The page includes sound effects of the plane's engine. The plane flies between a set of clouds as shown in Figure 19.3. Some of the clouds are displayed in front of the plane and others are displayed in back of the plane. The plane then flies behind the heading as shown in Figure 19.4. You can let the animation run to observe its behavior. It loops to repeat itself over time.

FIGURE 19.3:

The plane is able to fly between the clouds.

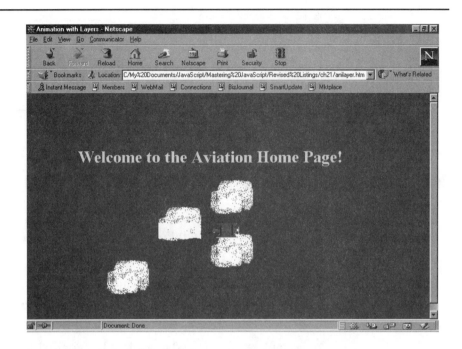

FIGURE 19.4:

The plane flies behind the heading.

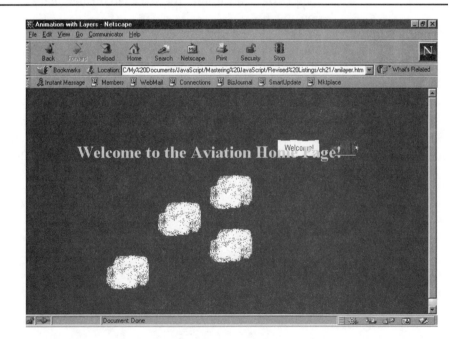

Listing 19.5   Using Layers to Support Animation (anilayer.htm)

```
<HTML>
<HEAD>
<TITLE>Animation with Layers</TITLE>
</HEAD>
<SCRIPT LANGUAGE="JavaScript"><!-
function fly() {
 var plane=window.document.layers["plane"]
 if(plane.top<10) plane.moveTo(0,400)
 else plane.offset(8,-5)
 setTimeout("fly()", 10);
}
// -></SCRIPT>
<STYLE TYPE="text/javascript">
tags.H1.color="yellow"
</STYLE>
<BODY BGCOLOR="blue" ONLOAD="fly()">
<LAYER NAME="heading" VISIBILITY="SHOW" LEFT=100 TOP=100>
<H1>Welcome to the Aviation Home Page!</H1>
</LAYER>
<LAYER NAME="plane" VISIBILITY="SHOW" ABOVE="heading"
 LEFT=0 TOP=400>
<IMG SRC="plane.gif">
</LAYER>
<LAYER NAME="cloud1" VISIBILITY="SHOW" BELOW="plane"
 LEFT=150 TOP=300>
<IMG SRC="cloud.gif">
</LAYER>
<LAYER NAME="cloud2" VISIBILITY="SHOW" BELOW="cloud1"
 LEFT=250 TOP=200>
<IMG SRC="cloud.gif">
</LAYER>
<LAYER NAME="cloud3" VISIBILITY="SHOW" ABOVE="plane"
 LEFT=350 TOP=150>
<IMG SRC="cloud.gif">
</LAYER>
<LAYER NAME="cloud4" VISIBILITY="SHOW" ABOVE="cloud3"
 LEFT=350 TOP=250>
<IMG SRC="cloud.gif">
</LAYER>
```

```
<EMBED SRC="plane.wav" HIDDEN="true" AUTOSTART="true"
 LOOP="true">
</BODY>
</HTML>
```

NOTE   All coordinate references are in pixels with (0,0) located in the upper-left corner of the browser window.

The anilayer.htm file defines six layers in the document body—heading, plane, and cloud1 through cloud4. The heading layer displays the welcome message heading. It is positioned at (100,100). The plane layer displays the airplane, initially at (0,400). The heading layer is identified as being above the plane layer. The cloud1 layer displays a cloud at (150,300) and specifies the plane layer as being below it. The cloud2 layer displays a cloud at (250,200) above the cloud1 layer. The cloud3 layer displays a cloud below the plane layer and the cloud4 layer displays a cloud below the cloud3 layer. All four clouds display the same image. The ordering of the layers is what causes the plane to fly in front of some objects and behind others.

The flying of the airplane is initiated when the document is loaded. The onLoad event is handled by invoking the fly() method. This method checks to see if the plane is within 10 pixels of the top of the window, and if so, moves the plane back to its original position. Otherwise, the position of the plane is moved 8 pixels to the right and 5 pixels up the page. The setTimeout() method is used to invoke the fly() method after 10 milliseconds have transpired. This repeated calling of fly() causes the plane to move across the page.

Flying Divisions

Listing 19.6 (ie-anim.htm) shows how the animation can be accomplished using divisions. Each of the six layers of Listing 19.5 are replaced by equivalent divisions of the same name. The CSS position, left, top, and z-index attributes are used to position the divisions in the same manner as the original layers. An ActiveMovie control is used to make the airplane sound.

The fly() method uses the style property of the plane division to move the plane. The posLeft and posTop properties of the style are used to reposition the plane during the animation. These properties identify the plane division's horizontal and vertical coordinates.

Listing 19.6   **Flying the Plane Using Divisions (ie-anim.htm)**

```
<HTML>
<HEAD>
<TITLE>Animation with Divisions</TITLE>
</HEAD>
<SCRIPT LANGUAGE="JScript"><!-
function fly() {
 var planeStyle=window.document.all.plane.style
 window.defaultStatus = planeStyle.posTop
 if(planeStyle.posTop < 10) {
  planeStyle.posLeft = 0
  planeStyle.posTop = 400
 }else{
  planeStyle.posLeft += 8
  planeStyle.posTop -= 5
 }
 setTimeout("fly()", 10);
}
// -></SCRIPT>
<STYLE TYPE="text/css">
 h1 {
  color: "yellow";
 }
</STYLE>
<BODY BGCOLOR="blue" ONLOAD="fly()">
<DIV NAME="heading" STYLE="position:absolute;left:100;top:100;z-
index:3">
<H1>Welcome to the Aviation Home Page!</H1>
</DIV>
<DIV ID="plane" STYLE="position:absolute;left:0;top:400;z-index:2">
<IMG SRC="plane.gif">
</DIV>
<DIV ID="cloud1" STYLE="position:absolute;left:150;top:300;z-index:3">
<IMG SRC="cloud.gif">
</DIV>
<DIV ID="cloud2" STYLE="position:absolute;left:250;top:200;z-index:3">
<IMG SRC="cloud.gif">
</DIV>
<DIV ID="cloud3" STYLE="position:absolute;left:350;top:150;z-index:1">
<IMG SRC="cloud.gif">
</DIV>
<DIV ID="cloud4" STYLE="position:absolute;left:350;top:250;z-index:1">
```

```
<IMG SRC="cloud.gif">
</DIV>
<OBJECT ID="ActiveMovie1" WIDTH=0 HEIGHT=0
 CLASSID="CLSID:22D6F312-B0F6-11D0-94AB-0080C74C7E95">
    <PARAM NAME="AudioStream" VALUE="-1">
    <PARAM NAME="AutoSize" VALUE="0">
    <PARAM NAME="AutoStart" VALUE="-1">
    <PARAM NAME="AnimationAtStart" VALUE="-1">
    <PARAM NAME="AllowScan" VALUE="-1">
    <PARAM NAME="AllowChangeDisplaySize" VALUE="-1">
    <PARAM NAME="AutoRewind" VALUE="0">
    <PARAM NAME="Balance" VALUE="0">
    <PARAM NAME="BaseURL" VALUE="">
    <PARAM NAME="BufferingTime" VALUE="5">
    <PARAM NAME="CaptioningID" VALUE="">
    <PARAM NAME="ClickToPlay" VALUE="-1">
    <PARAM NAME="CursorType" VALUE="0">
    <PARAM NAME="CurrentPosition" VALUE="0">
    <PARAM NAME="CurrentMarker" VALUE="0">
    <PARAM NAME="DefaultFrame" VALUE="">
    <PARAM NAME="DisplayBackColor" VALUE="0">
    <PARAM NAME="DisplayForeColor" VALUE="16777215">
    <PARAM NAME="DisplayMode" VALUE="0">
    <PARAM NAME="DisplaySize" VALUE="4">
    <PARAM NAME="Enabled" VALUE="-1">
    <PARAM NAME="EnableContextMenu" VALUE="-1">
    <PARAM NAME="EnablePositionControls" VALUE="-1">
    <PARAM NAME="EnableFullScreenControls" VALUE="0">
    <PARAM NAME="EnableTracker" VALUE="-1">
    <PARAM NAME="Filename" VALUE="plane.wav">
    <PARAM NAME="InvokeURLs" VALUE="-1">
    <PARAM NAME="Language" VALUE="-1">
    <PARAM NAME="Mute" VALUE="0">
    <PARAM NAME="PlayCount" VALUE="0">
    <PARAM NAME="PreviewMode" VALUE="0">
    <PARAM NAME="Rate" VALUE="1">
    <PARAM NAME="SAMILang" VALUE="">
    <PARAM NAME="SAMIStyle" VALUE="">
    <PARAM NAME="SAMIFileName" VALUE="">
    <PARAM NAME="SelectionStart" VALUE="-1">
    <PARAM NAME="SelectionEnd" VALUE="-1">
    <PARAM NAME="SendOpenStateChangeEvents" VALUE="-1">
    <PARAM NAME="SendWarningEvents" VALUE="-1">
    <PARAM NAME="SendErrorEvents" VALUE="-1">
```

```
        <PARAM NAME="SendKeyboardEvents" VALUE="0">
        <PARAM NAME="SendMouseClickEvents" VALUE="0">
        <PARAM NAME="SendMouseMoveEvents" VALUE="0">
        <PARAM NAME="SendPlayStateChangeEvents" VALUE="-1">
        <PARAM NAME="ShowCaptioning" VALUE="0">
        <PARAM NAME="ShowControls" VALUE="0">
        <PARAM NAME="ShowAudioControls" VALUE="-1">
        <PARAM NAME="ShowDisplay" VALUE="0">
        <PARAM NAME="ShowGotoBar" VALUE="0">
        <PARAM NAME="ShowPositionControls" VALUE="0">
        <PARAM NAME="ShowStatusBar" VALUE="0">
        <PARAM NAME="ShowTracker" VALUE="0">
        <PARAM NAME="TransparentAtStart" VALUE="0">
        <PARAM NAME="VideoBorderWidth" VALUE="0">
        <PARAM NAME="VideoBorderColor" VALUE="0">
        <PARAM NAME="VideoBorder3D" VALUE="0">
        <PARAM NAME="Volume" VALUE="-290">
        <PARAM NAME="WindowlessVideo" VALUE="0">
    </OBJECT>
    </BODY>
    </HTML>
```

Using Video

When we think of multimedia, we generally think of audio, video, and animation combined. As you have seen from previous examples in this chapter, audio and animation capabilities can easily be added to your documents through the use of layers. Video is also easy to work with, but has some drawbacks that must be considered. Video files of any meaningful length are huge by Web standards—on the order of megabytes. This means that users will have to wait to download any video files that you insert in your Web documents. Audio and image files are usually far less than a megabyte in size.

Furthermore, because of their large size, video dimensions are usually kept small—not much larger than a postage stamp. Videos are usually very short, too. Finding a video lasting longer than a minute or two is unusual on the Web. The small dimensions of videos and their short length tend to limit the effectiveness of videos in enhancing the information presented on your Web pages.

Despite the limitations identified above, videos can be used to contribute to your Web pages' appeal and effectiveness. Listings 19.7 and 19.8 provide an example that shows how videos can be easily used with both Navigator and Internet Explorer.

Open MoviePlayer.htm with your browser. A selection list is displayed along with the Play Movie button. The selection list contains the names of five airplane types. Select an airplane type from the list and a video of the plane in action is displayed in the middle of the page. Refer to Figure 19.5.

FIGURE 19.5:

Displaying a video of a real plane

Listing 19.7   **The MoviePlayer Frame Set (MoviePlayer.htm)**

```
<HTML>
<HEAD>
<TITLE>Movie Player</TITLE>
</HEAD>
<FRAMESET ROWS="150,*" BORDER="0">
<FRAME SRC="player.htm">
<FRAME SRC="blank.htm">
</FRAMESET>
</HTML>
```

Listing 19.8   The Form for Selecting and Playing a Video (player.htm)

```
<HTML>
<HEAD>
<TITLE>Movie Player</TITLE>
<SCRIPT LANGUAGE="JavaScript"><!-
function showMovie() {
 var movie = new Array("SR-71","X-1","X-15","X-31","XB-70")
 var selectedMovie=  document.forms[0].elements["movies"].selectedIndex
 alert("Please wait while movie loads.")
 parent.frames[1].location.href = movie[selectedMovie]+".mov"
}
//-></SCRIPT>
</HEAD>
<BODY>
<P ALIGN="CENTER">
<FORM>
<SELECT NAME="movies" SIZE="1">
<OPTION SELECTED VALUE="SR-71">SR-71
<OPTION VALUE="X-1">X-1
<OPTION VALUE="X-15">X-15
<OPTION VALUE="X-31">X-31
<OPTION VALUE="XB-70">XB-70
</SELECT>
 
<INPUT TYPE="BUTTON" NAME="play" VALUE="Play Movie"
 onClick="showMovie()">
</FORM>
</P>
</BODY>
</HTML>
```

Summary

In this chapter, you learned how to use layers to integrate multimedia capabilities in your Web applications. You covered the JavaScript layer object and learned how to use its properties and methods to create animations, develop slide shows, and increase the effectiveness of videos. This chapter concludes Part V, "Developing Advanced Applications." In Part VI, "Programming Servers," you'll learn all about server-side Web programming using JavaScript.

PART VI

Programming Servers

■ CHAPTER 20: Interfacing JavaScript with CGI Programs

■ CHAPTER 21: Scripting Netscape Servers

■ CHAPTER 22: Scripting Microsoft Servers

■ CHAPTER 23: Securing Your Scripts

CHAPTER
TWENTY

20

Interfacing JavaScript with CGI Programs

- When to Use CGI Programs

- How CGI Programs Work

- Getting Data from the Web Server

- Sending Data Back to the Web Server

- A Shell Script Example

- Interfacing JavaScript Scripts with CGI Scripts

- Returning JavaScript from CGI Programs

The Common Gateway Interface (CGI) is the standard for communication between Web servers and server-side Web programs. Netscape, Microsoft, and most other Web servers support the Common Gateway Interface. Thus, for the most part, Web application designers can develop server-side programs that will work regardless of the particular type of Web server used at a Web site. If you want to write a server-side program that will have the greatest portability, then develop it as a CGI program or a Java servlet.

In this chapter, you'll learn how CGI programs work. We'll cover the types of Web applications in which CGI programs are used. On the one hand, you'll learn how to interface JavaScript scripts with CGI scripts, and on the other hand, you'll learn how to use CGI programs to generate JavaScript code. When you finish this chapter, you'll know how to combine JavaScript scripts with CGI programs in your Web applications.

When to Use CGI Programs

Previous chapters stressed the need to perform as much processing as possible on the browser, rather than on the server, to conserve precious communication bandwidth and server-processing resources. Any processing that is performed locally reduces the load on your Web server.

However, for some Web applications, server-side processing is absolutely essential. These applications include any that collect and store data about multiple users (for example, online registration forms and customer surveys). Applications that require significant database support (for example, large catalogs and search engines) also fall into this category.

CGI programs provide the interface between Web browsers and online databases. They also provide gateways to other online services, such as Gopher and WAIS (though, admittedly, the popularity of these services has declined with the rise of the World Wide Web). Any Web application that requires server-side storage or access to non-Web resources is a potential candidate for the use of a CGI program.

How CGI Programs Work

CGI programs (also referred to as CGI scripts) are the external programs I was talking about when I said that the CGI is a standard interface for communication between Web servers and external programs. The CGI specification identifies how data is to be passed from a Web server to a CGI program, and back from the CGI program to the Web server.

> **NOTE**
>
> Refer to Chapter 1, "Learning the Fundamentals," for a general overview of CGI programs. Refer to Chapter 7, "Processing Forms," for a discussion and examples of using CGI programs with forms.

The following points summarize how the CGI works:

- A browser requests a CGI program by specifying the CGI program's URL. The request arises as the result of the user submitting a form or clicking a link. (The browser may insert into the URL a query string or extra path information.)

- When a Web server receives a URL request, it determines whether the URL refers to a CGI program. Most Web servers identify CGI programs by the path in which they are located or by their filename extension. For example, all files in the path /cgi-bin/ or with the extensions .CGI or .PL could be considered CGI programs.

- When a Web server identifies a request for a CGI program, it executes the CGI program as a separate process and passes any data included in the URL to the program.

- The CGI program performs its processing and then returns its output to the Web server. The conventions defined by the CGI specification determine how CGI programs receive data from and return data to Web servers. These conventions are described in the following sections.

The overall process is depicted in Figure 20.1.

FIGURE 20.1:

Web servers communicate with external programs using the conventions of CGI (will be 2/3 as deep as a regular screen image).

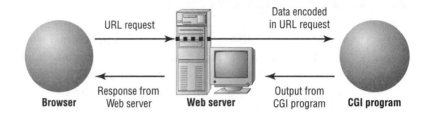

Getting Data from the Web Server

When a CGI program is executed, one of its first tasks is to determine what data was passed to it by the Web server. This data may be passed in the following ways:

- Command-line arguments
- Environment variables
- The program's standard input stream

Command-line arguments and the standard input stream are supported by almost all programming languages. Environment variables are less commonly used outside of Web applications. The following subsections describe when and how CGI programs receive data via each of these mechanisms.

Command-Line Arguments

Command-line arguments are parameters that are passed to programs via the command line that is used to execute the program. For example, the following command line executes the `search` program and passes it the string `news` as an argument:

```
search news
```

HTTP `ISINDEX` queries are the means of passing data to CGI programs as command-line arguments. CGI programs read the command-line arguments via the mechanisms provided by the programming language in which they are written. For example, the C programming language provides the `argc` and `argv` variables for accessing command-line arguments. The Perl programming language provides the `@ARGV` array for the same purpose.

Environment Variables

Environment variables are the primary mechanism by which Web servers communicate with CGI programs. All CGI programs can receive data from Web servers via environment variables.

Environment variables are variables that are external to a program's execution. They are used to define the environment in which a program executes. Table 20.1 identifies the environment variables defined by CGI version 1.1. The most important of these variables are CONTENT_LENGTH, which identifies the number of bytes that are passed via standard input, and PATH_INFO and QUERY_STRING, which identify data that is passed via extra path information or a query string.

TABLE 20.1: Environment Variables Used by CGI

Environment Variable	Description
AUTH_TYPE	The authentication scheme used to validate the user requesting access to a Web page.
CONTENT_LENGTH	The number of characters that have been passed via standard input.
CONTENT_TYPE	The MIME type associated with the data available via standard input.
GATEWAY_INTERFACE	The version of the CGI specification supported by the server.
HTTP_*	The contents of the various HTTP headers received by the Web server. "HTTP_" is prepended to the name of the header. For example, the ACCEPT header is represented by the HTTP_ACCEPT environment variable, and the USER_AGENT header is represented by the HTTP_USER_AGENT variable.
PATH_INFO	The extra path information added to the URL of the CGI program.
PATH_TRANSLATED	The full path name that was translated from the URL by the Web server.
QUERY_STRING	The query string portion of the URL.
REMOTE_ADDR	The IP address of the host associated with the requesting browser.
REMOTE_HOST	The name of the host associated with the requesting browser.
REMOTE_IDENT	The verified name of the host associated with the requesting browser.
REMOTE_USER	The name of the user associated with the requesting browser.
REQUEST_METHOD	The method associated with the browser request: GET, POST, HEAD, and so on.

Continued on next page

TABLE 20.1 CONTINUED: Environment Variables Used by CGI

Environment Variable	Description
SCRIPT_NAME	The path and name of the CGI program.
SERVER_NAME	The name of the Web server host.
SERVER_PORT	The HTTP port number (usually 80) used by the Web server.
SERVER_PROTOCOL	The name and version of the protocol used by the requesting browser to submit the request.
SERVER_SOFTWARE	The name and version number of the Web server software.

The environment variables shown in Table 20.1 are available to all CGI programs regardless of whether the CGI program was executed as the result of an ISINDEX query, a form submission, or the clicking of a hyperlink.

Many programming languages provide special mechanisms for accessing environment variables. For example, Perl provides the $ENV array, and C provides the getenv() library function. Because the capability to read environment variables is important for any nontrivial CGI programs, it should be a primary consideration when selecting a CGI programming language.

TIP

Some Web servers, such as Netscape servers, define server-specific environment variables in addition to those defined by the CGI. If you want your CGI programs to be portable between Web servers, you should not use these server-specific environment variables.

Reading Query String Data   When data is passed to a CGI program via the QUERY_STRING environment variable, the data is encoded using the following conventions. These coding conventions are referred to as *URL coding*:

- Spaces are replaced by plus (+) signs.

- Other characters may be replaced by character codes of the form %xx (with the xx being replaced by two hexadecimal digits). For example, %2a is used to encode a plus sign.

CGI programs must decode the data passed via the QUERY_STRING variable. This is accomplished by replacing plus signs with spaces, and sequences of the form %xx with their character equivalent. This decoding is known as *URL decoding*.

Form Data Coding　In addition to query string encoding, other application-specific codings may be used. For example, form data is encoded as a sequence of name=value pairs, separated by ampersands (the & symbol), with name being replaced by the form field's name attribute and value being replaced by the field's value when submitted by the user. Any equals signs or ampersands appearing in the data are encoded using the %xx hexadecimal coding scheme covered in the previous section.

When the form uses the GET method, form data is passed to CGI programs via the QUERY_STRING environment variable. When the form uses the POST method, form data is passed to the CGI programs via standard input. The use of standard input is covered in a later section of this chapter.

CGI programs should decode form data by using the ampersands to separate the query string into name=value pairs, using the equals signs to separate the name and value portions, and then decoding the name and value portions using the URL decoding conventions.

Reading Extra Path Data　Extra path information is data that is added to a URL as additional path information following the path to the CGI program. The extra path information is passed to a CGI program using the PATH_INFO environment variable. For example, in the following URL, `http://www.jaworski.com/cgi-bin/echo-query/extra/path/info`, the path `/extra/path/info` that follows `echo-query` would be passed to the echo-query program via PATH_INFO as "/extra/path/info". Extra path information is an easy way to send fixed information to CGI programs. It is usually used with non-form URLs.

TIP

If you intend to use extra path information to send data to CGI programs, you should use URL-coding to ensure that the data is correctly processed by Web browsers and servers.

The Standard Input and Output Streams

Standard input refers to the keyboard input received by character-mode programs, such as non-graphical DOS programs and UNIX and Windows NT command-line programs. Relatedly, *standard output* refers to the visible output produced by these programs: characters that are displayed on the console monitor (in this context, this would normally be the *server's* console window, not the user's).

NOTE

The physical console of olden days has been replaced by a command-line console window on modern windowing systems.

In addition to treating users' input and output in standard ways, most operating systems have the capability of allowing command-line programs to run in an environment where the user's keyboard and display monitor can be *simulated*. This means that input other than the user's keyboard input (for instance, a query string or extra path information in a URL, or data from a browser form) can be *redirected* to a program *as* standard input. The program can process the data regardless of the fact that the data came from some source other than the standard source (keyboard input). Similarly, a program's output can be redirected by a server to the user's browser as though it were standard output to the server's own console display. Web servers make use of this redirection capability to process posted form data, as shown in Figure 20.2.

FIGURE 20.2:

Web servers redirect the standard input and output streams of CGI programs to support browser/CGI program communication (will be 2/3 as deep as a regular screen image).

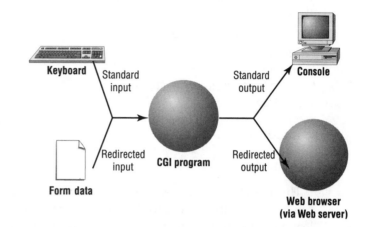

When the POST method is used to submit a form, the form's data is sent by the Web server to a CGI program as standard input to the CGI program. When a Web server creates a process to execute a CGI program, it redirects the form's data to the standard input stream of the CGI program. This data appears to a CGI program as if it were typed by a user at a keyboard. (*Note:* The amount of data that can be redirected in this manner is subject to limitation. You can use the CONTENT_LENGTH environment variable to identify the number of bytes to be made available via standard input.)

The output of the CGI program is returned to the Web server so that it can be redirected to the user's browser. By redirecting standard input and output, the Web server allows CGI programs to be designed using the simple character-stream approach common to DOS and UNIX programs. Almost all programming languages provide capabilities to read data from the standard input stream and write data to the standard output stream.

Sending Data Back to the Web Server

A CGI program returns data to the requesting browser via the Web server. In all cases, it returns the data by writing it to the standard output stream. The output of the CGI program must begin with a header line, followed by a blank line, and then by the data to be displayed by the browser. The header line usually consists of a Content-type header that specifies the MIME type of the data returned by the CGI program. In most cases, the MIME type will be text/html, as shown in the following example:

```
Content type: text/html
<HTML>
<HEAD>
<TITLE>CGI Results</TITLE>
</HEAD>
<BODY>
<H1>It worked!</H1>
</BODY>
</HTML>
```

The header line does not have to be a Content-type header; a CGI program can instead return a Location header that specifies the name of a URL to be loaded. For example, consider the following program output. The Location header specifies that the results.htm file that is located at the partial URL /javascript/results.htm is to be returned as the result of the CGI program's execution.

```
Location: /javascript/results.htm
blank line
```

TIP   When using a Location header, be sure to follow it by a single blank line, even if the header is the entirety of your script.

Using Nonparsed Header Programs

As mentioned in the previous section, CGI programs normally return data to the requesting browser via the Web server, which takes care of providing all of the required HTTP headers. It is possible, however, for CGI programs to bypass the Web server and return data directly to the requesting browser. Of course, when you do this, your CGI program is then responsible for providing all of the required headers.

CGI programs that bypass the Web server and return data directly to Web browsers are referred to as *nonparsed header programs*. Most Web servers require nonparsed header CGI programs to begin with the characters nph- (nph followed by a hyphen) to help servers differentiate between regular CGI programs and nonparsed header programs.

When should you use nonparsed header programs? The answer is almost never. By going through the Web server, your CGI programs can be designed much more simply and easily. The only time it makes sense to bypass the Web server is when your CGI program returns a large amount of data and you don't want the server to delay transmission of the data to the browser.

The General Design of a CGI Program

Now that you've learned how CGI programs receive data from and return data to Web servers, we'll cover the general design of typical CGI programs.

Most CGI programs are *transaction oriented*. They receive input data from a browser, perform processing based on the data received from the browser, and return the results of the processing to the browser. The way that a CGI program reads and processes its data depends on the way that is requested by a browser.

ISINDEX Queries

The CGI program looks for input data by checking its command-line arguments. If it does not have any data, then it returns a Web page containing an ISINDEX tag to the requesting browser. This allows the user to submit data to the CGI program. If the CGI program does contain data in its command-line arguments, then it decodes the data using URL decoding, processes the ISINDEX query, and sends the results of the query to the requesting browser.

Form Processing

CGI programs that process form data access the form data in different ways depending on whether the form is submitted using the GET or POST method. If the form is submitted via the GET method, then the form data is read from the QUERY_STRING variable. If the form is submitted via the POST method, then the form data is read from the standard input stream.

When the form data has been read, it is decoded and processed. The data returned by the CGI program can consist of other forms, other Web pages, or files of other MIME types.

Server-Side Image-Map Queries

CGI programs that process image-map queries read the coordinates of the user's click from the QUERY_STRING environment variable. These programs perform their processing based on the coordinates of the click and a map file. The map file associates image regions with URLs.

The particular map file to be used can be specified as extra path information. The image-map program returns the URL associated with the coordinates of the user's click.

Using Custom Hyperlinks to Invoke CGI Programs

Some CGI programs may be invoked as the result of the user clicking a hyperlink. Data may be passed to the CGI program via a query string or extra path information contained in the URL. The CGI program uses command-line arguments and environment variables to access this data. It performs its processing and then returns its output to the browser.

A Shell Script Example

By now, you are probably anxious to see an example of a CGI program. Listing 20.1 provides a CGI script written in the Linux shell programming language. Don't worry if you don't understand Linux shell programming; the script only uses the echo and cat commands. The first line of the script identifies the file as a shell script. The second line writes the Content-type header to standard output. The third line writes the required blank line to standard output. Subsequent lines write an HTML document to standard output.

The first part of the document identifies the command-line arguments that are passed to the CGI program. The $# variable identifies the number of command-line arguments and the $* variable identifies the values of these arguments.

Listing 20.1   **The *echo-query* Script (echo-query)**

```
#!/bin/sh
echo Content-type: text/html
echo
echo "<HTML>"
```

```
echo "<HEAD>"
echo "<TITLE>Echo CGI Request</TITLE>"
echo "</HEAD>"
echo "<BODY>"
echo "<H1>CGI Request</H1>"
echo "<H2>Command Line Arguments</H2>"
echo "<P>Number of command line arguments: $#</P>"
echo "<P>Command line arguments: "$*"</P>"
echo "<H2>Environment Variables</H2>"
echo "<PRE>"
echo AUTH_TYPE = $AUTH_TYPE
echo CONTENT_LENGTH = $CONTENT_LENGTH
echo CONTENT_TYPE = $CONTENT_TYPE
echo GATEWAY_INTERFACE = $GATEWAY_INTERFACE
echo HTTP_ACCEPT = "$HTTP_ACCEPT"
echo HTTP_USER_AGENT = "$HTTP_USER_AGENT"
echo PATH_INFO = "$PATH_INFO"
echo PATH_TRANSLATED = "$PATH_TRANSLATED"
echo QUERY_STRING = "$QUERY_STRING"
echo REMOTE_ADDR = $REMOTE_ADDR
echo REMOTE_HOST = $REMOTE_HOST
echo REMOTE_IDENT = $REMOTE_IDENT
echo REMOTE_USER = $REMOTE_USER
echo REQUEST_METHOD = $REQUEST_METHOD
echo SCRIPT_NAME = "$SCRIPT_NAME"
echo SERVER_NAME = $SERVER_NAME
echo SERVER_PORT = $SERVER_PORT
echo SERVER_PROTOCOL = $SERVER_PROTOCOL
echo SERVER_SOFTWARE = $SERVER_SOFTWARE
echo "</PRE>"
echo "<H2>Standard Input</H2>"
cat
echo "</BODY>"
echo "</HTML>"
```

The second part of the returned document identifies the environment variables that are passed to the CGI program. These variables are referenced by prepending a $ to the name of the environment variable.

The last part of the returned document identifies the data that is sent to the CGI program via the standard input stream. The `cat` command is used to read CONTENT_ LENGTH characters from standard input and write them to standard output.

NOTE
The `echo-query` program shown in Listing 20.1 is accessible via the URL `http://www.jaworski.com/cgi-bin/echo-query.cgi`.

In order to use the `echo-query` script, you need to create an HTML document to access the script's URL. Listing 20.2 provides such a document. It contains a link to `echo-query` with both extra path information and a query string appended.

Open `cgi-test.htm` with your browser. Figure 20.3 shows the Web page that is displayed. Click the link to the CGI program. Figure 20.4 shows the Web page that is returned. Note the value of the QUERY_STRING and PATH_INFO variables.

TIP
The `echo-query` script is a useful tool for testing your links in order to see how the data they encode is passed to a CGI program.

Listing 20.2   **Accessing the *echo-query* Script (cgi-test.htm)**

```
<HTML>
<HEAD>
<TITLE>CGI Test</TITLE>
</HEAD>
<BODY>
<A HREF="http://www.jaworski.com/cgi-bin/echo-
query.cgi/extra/path/info?f1=v1&f2=v2">
Click here to access echo-query</A>
</BODY>
</HTML>
```

FIGURE 20.3:

The Web page generated by cgi-test.htm (Listing 20.2)

FIGURE 20.4:

The results returned by echo-query (Listing 20.2)

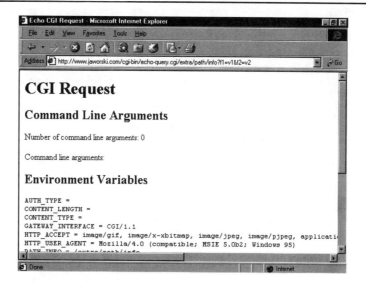

Interfacing JavaScript Scripts with CGI Scripts

JavaScript scripts can make use of CGI programs to access online databases, Internet services, or perform other types of server-side processing. The interface between a JavaScript script and a CGI program is through the CGI program's URL. Scripts can use the URL to invoke a CGI program and pass data to it as a query string or extra path information. If a CGI program is accessed via an HTML form, then the form's data can be used to control the CGI program's behavior.

The js2cgi.htm file, shown in Listing 20.3, demonstrates how CGI programs can be accessed via JavaScript. Open js2cgi.htm with your browser. It generates the HTML form shown in Figure 20.5. Fill out the form and click the Submit button. Your form data is sent to the add2db.cgi CGI program at the URL http://www.jaworski.com/cgi-bin/add2dbcgi and the Web page shown in Figure 20.6 is displayed.

FIGURE 20.5:

Using JavaScript to process a form's data and send it to a CGI program (Listing 20.3)

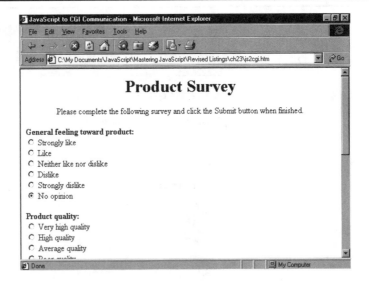

FIGURE 20.6:

The survey results are displayed using JavaScript generated by a CGI program (Listing 20.5)

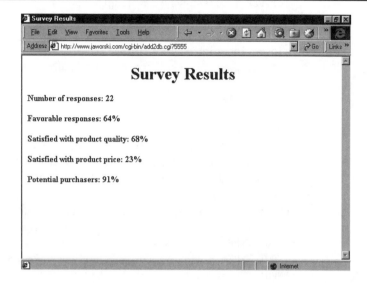

The js2cgi.htm file consists of an HTML form with four sets of radio buttons. The user clicks the radio buttons to fill out the product survey. The sendToCGI() function handles the onClick event of the Submit button by determining which buttons were selected and creating a four-character text string (stored in the results variable) that summarizes the form's data. For example, suppose a user selected the third value of the first set of radio buttons, the fourth value of the second set, the first value of the third set, and the last value of the last set. The value of the results variable would be *2305*.

The value of the results variable is appended to the URL of the CGI program as a query string, and the href property of the current window's location object is set to the URL. This causes the URL of the CGI program to be requested.

Listing 20.3   **Interfacing JavaScript with a CGI Program (js2cgi.htm)**

```
<HTML>
<HEAD>
<TITLE>JavaScript to CGI Communication</TITLE>
<SCRIPT LANGUAGE="JavaScript"><!-
function sendToCGI() {
 results=""
 surveyForm=window.document.survey
```

```
  for(var i=0;i<surveyForm.length-1;++i)
   if(surveyForm.elements[i].checked)
    results+=i%6
  window.location.href=
   "http://www.jaworski.com/cgi-bin/add2db.cgi?"+results
 }
 // -></SCRIPT>
 </HEAD>
 <BODY BGCOLOR="white"">
 <H1 ALIGN="CENTER">Product Survey</H1>
 <P ALIGN="CENTER">Please complete the following survey and
 click the Submit button when finished.</P>
 <FORM NAME="survey">
 <P><B>General feeling toward product:</B><BR>
 <INPUT TYPE="radio" NAME="g1"> Strongly like<BR>
 <INPUT TYPE="radio" NAME="g1"> Like<BR>
 <INPUT TYPE="radio" NAME="g1"> Neither like nor dislike<BR>
 <INPUT TYPE="radio" NAME="g1"> Dislike<BR>
 <INPUT TYPE="radio" NAME="g1"> Strongly dislike<BR>
 <INPUT TYPE="radio" NAME="g1" CHECKED> No opinion<BR>
 </P>
 <P><B>Product quality:</B><BR>
 <INPUT TYPE="radio" NAME="g2"> Very high quality<BR>
 <INPUT TYPE="radio" NAME="g2"> High quality<BR>
 <INPUT TYPE="radio" NAME="g2"> Average quality<BR>
 <INPUT TYPE="radio" NAME="g2"> Poor quality<BR>
 <INPUT TYPE="radio" NAME="g2"> Very poor quality<BR>
 <INPUT TYPE="radio" NAME="g2" CHECKED> No opinion<BR>
 </P>
 <P><B>Product pricing:</B><BR>
 <INPUT TYPE="radio" NAME="g3"> Price is very high<BR>
 <INPUT TYPE="radio" NAME="g3"> Price is high<BR>
 <INPUT TYPE="radio" NAME="g3"> Price is about right<BR>
 <INPUT TYPE="radio" NAME="g3"> Price is low<BR>
 <INPUT TYPE="radio" NAME="g3"> Price is very low<BR>
 <INPUT TYPE="radio" NAME="g3" CHECKED> No opinion<BR>
 </P>
 <P><B>Purchase plans:</B><BR>
 <INPUT TYPE="radio" NAME="g4"> Plan to purchase<BR>
 <INPUT TYPE="radio" NAME="g4"> May purchase<BR>
 <INPUT TYPE="radio" NAME="g4"> May purchase if price is
  lowered<BR>
```

```
<INPUT TYPE="radio" NAME="g4"> May purchase if quality is
 improved<BR>
<INPUT TYPE="radio" NAME="g4"> Do not plan to purchase<BR>
<INPUT TYPE="radio" NAME="g4" CHECKED> No opinion<BR>
</P>
</TABLE>
<INPUT TYPE="BUTTON" VALUE="Submit"
 onClick="sendToCGI()">
</FORM>
</BODY>
</HTML>
```

When my Web server receives the URL request for add2db.cgi, it executes the Perl script shown in Listing 20.4. Because the query string passed by js2cgi.htm is a single value and not a name=value pair, my Web server assumes that the request is an ISINDEX query and passes the data contained in the URL's query string as a command-line argument.

The add2db.cgi script works as follows. The first line identifies the location of the Perl interpreter. The second line opens the file db.txt with append access. This means that anything written to db.txt will be appended to the end of the file. The third line writes the value of the command-line argument to the db.txt file. This value is the four-character form processing result that was appended to the URL of add2db.cgi. The fourth line writes a new line character to db.txt. The fifth line closes the db.txt file, and the last line returns the file located at http://www .jaworski.com/javascript/results.htm as the result of the CGI program's processing. Figure 20.6 shows how results.htm is displayed.

Listing 20.4   A Perl Program That Stores the Form Data on the Server (add2db.cgi)

```
#!/usr/bin/perl
open (OUTPUT, ">>db.txt");
print OUTPUT @ARGV;
print OUTPUT "\n";
close (OUTPUT);
print "Location: /javascript/results.htm\n\n";
```

Returning JavaScript from CGI Programs

One of the more powerful techniques of integrating client-side JavaScript scripts with CGI programs is to use CGI programs to return JavaScript code. In doing so, your Web applications become more dynamic and efficient by allowing browsers to perform some of the CGI program's processing. Instead of responding with a static Web page, your CGI programs are able to perform the minimum amount of server-side processing and return a JavaScript script that completes the application processing on the browser.

The following example shows how CGI programs can be used to return JavaScript code. This example builds on the add2db.cgi example of the previous section.

In the last line of Listing 20.4 the results.htm file is returned to complete the processing of add2db.cgi. Listing 20.5 shows the contents of results.htm. It contains two scripts in the document head. The first script includes JavaScript code from the URL http://www.jaworski.com/cgi-bin/getdb.cgi. But this is the URL of a CGI program. Listing 20.6 shows the source code of getdb.cgi.

Because the output of getdb.cgi is crucial to the operation of results.htm, we'll examine the operation of getdb.cgi before continuing with the discussion of results.htm. The file getdb.cgi is a Perl script that summarizes the data contained in db.txt and returns its results as a JavaScript array. Recall that each line of db.txt is a four-digit value that describes the data entered into the form shown in Listing 20.3. The getdb.cgi script reads through db.txt and counts how many times radio buttons 1 through 6 are selected for survey topics 1 through 4. This results in a 24-value array. A 25th value is added that identifies the number of lines in db.txt.

getdb.cgi performs its processing as follows:

Line 1 Identifies the location of the Perl interpreter. Note that the .cgi extension was not used with getdb.cgi—it was left off in order to prevent the browser from expecting a file of a different MIME type.

Line 2 Identifies the MIME type of the data returned by getdb.cgi as application/x-javascript. Note that a blank line follows the Content header.

Line 3 Returns the beginning of a JavaScript array definition that is assigned to variable r.

Lines 4-6 Open db.txt for input, initialize the @totals array to 0, and set $num to 0.

Lines 7-15 Loop through db.txt and read each line. $num counts the number of lines read. $totals[6*$i+$n] counts the number of times radio button $n is selected for topic $i.

Lines 16-19 Print the values of $totals to the JavaScript output.

Lines 20-21 Add the number of lines in db.txt as the 25th value of the r array.

Getting back to results.htm, the second script contains two functions, display-Results() and writeResult(). The first of these, displayResults(), performs further processing on the r array to summarize and display the results of the survey. It sets n to r[24] which is the number of lines in db.txt. It then calculates the percentage of favorable responses, the percentage of responses in which the product quality and price were acceptable, and the percentage of respondents who are potential purchasers. These results are then displayed using the writeResult() function.

Listing 20.5   **Displaying the Results of the Product Survey (results.htm)**

```
<HTML>
<HEAD>
<TITLE>Survey Results</TITLE>
<SCRIPT LANGUAGE="JavaScript"
 SRC="http://www.jaworski.com/cgi-bin/getdb.cgi"><!-
// -></SCRIPT>
<SCRIPT LANGUAGE="JavaScript"><!-
function displayResults() {
 var n=r[24]
 var favorable=(r[0]+r[1])/n
 favorable=Math.round(favorable*100)
 var quality=(r[6]+r[7]+r[8])/n
 quality=Math.round(quality*100)
 var price=(r[14]+r[15]+r[16])/n
 price=Math.round(price*100)
 var purchase=(n-r[22])/n
 purchase=Math.round(purchase*100)
 document.write("<P><B>Number of responses: "+n+"</B></P>")
 writeResult("Favorable responses: ",favorable)
```

```
   writeResult("Satisfied with product quality: ",quality)
   writeResult("Satisfied with product price: ",price)
   writeResult("Potential purchasers: ",purchase)
  }
  function writeResult(s,n) {
   document.write("<P><B>"+s+n+"%</B></P>")
  }
  // -></SCRIPT>
  </HEAD>
  <BODY>
  <H1 ALIGN="CENTER">Survey Results</H1>
  <SCRIPT LANGUAGE="JavaScript"><!-
  displayResults()
  // -></SCRIPT>
  </BODY>
  </HTML>
```

Listing 20.6 **A CGI Script That Returns Its Results as JavaScript (getdb.cgi)**

```perl
#!/usr/bin/perl
print "Content-type: application/x-javascript\n\n";
print "r= new Array(";
open (INPUT,"db.txt");
@totals=(0,0,0,0,0,0,0,0,0,0,0,0,0,0,0,0,0,0,0,0,0,0,0,0);
$num=0;
while(<INPUT>) {
 $num++;
 chop;
 $line=$_;
 for($i=0;$i<4;$i++){
  $n=substr($line,$i,1);
  $totals[6*$i+$n]++;
 }
}
for($i=0;$i<24;$i++){
 print $totals[$i];
 print ",";
}
print $num;
print ")\n";
```

Summary

In this chapter, you learned how CGI programs work and saw the types of Web applications in which CGI programs are used. You learned how to interface JavaScript scripts with CGI scripts and how to use CGI programs to generate JavaScript code. In the next chapter, you'll learn how to use LiveWire with JavaScript to develop integrated server-side Web applications with Netscape Web servers.

CHAPTER
TWENTY-ONE

21

Scripting Netscape Servers

- ■ LiveWire

- ■ Application Manager

- ■ Server-Side JavaScript Programming

- ■ Server-Side Objects

- ■ LiveWire Database Services

- ■ The database Object

- ■ Structured Query Language (SQL)

In the previous chapter, you learned how to develop server-side Web programs using the CGI and how to use client-side JavaScript scripts with CGI programs. In this chapter, you'll learn how to use LiveWire to create Web applications that eliminate the need for CGI programs. You'll learn how to use JavaScript's server programming capabilities to process data received from browsers and to dynamically return new Web pages to browsers. You'll also learn how to use LiveWire Database Services to access online databases. You'll learn how to use the `database` object to open database connections, add data to databases, and perform database queries. You'll be introduced to the Structured Query Language (SQL) and learn how to execute SQL statements using the methods of the `database` object. When you finish this chapter, you'll be able to use the server-side programming and database capabilities of LiveWire in your own Web applications.

Server-Side Scripting with LiveWire

In the previous chapter, you learned how to write server-side programs that communicate with Web servers using the CGI. You might have been thinking, "Oh great! Now I have to learn Perl or some other server-side scripting language." You may have been a little perturbed at the thought of having to develop your server-side programs independent of your HTML and JavaScript files. If you were, then you would have had a legitimate gripe—there ought to be a way to develop all parts of a Web application in an integrated fashion. LiveWire is an answer to that need.

LiveWire is a Web application development environment that works with Netscape FastTrack and Enterprise servers. It provides the solution to the problem of developing both browser and server-side parts of Web applications using a common language and an integrated development environment. It allows JavaScript to be used to write server-side scripts that eliminate the need for CGI programs. These scripts are developed, integrated, and maintained with the HTML and client-side JavaScript displayed by the browser.

Browser and server elements of Web applications are compiled into `.web` files that are used by Netscape servers to handle browser requests. The compilation process integrates HTML and client- and server-side JavaScript into a single application file and eliminates the need to separately develop and manage browser and server elements of the same Web application.

To run LiveWire, you'll need access to a FastTrack or Enterprise server. Like most Netscape products, LiveWire runs on a variety of OS platforms, including Windows NT. Trial versions of Netscape servers may be downloaded from Netscape's Web site at `http://home.netscape.com`. These products are easy to install and come with excellent documentation. The examples in this chapter were created using FastTrack version 3.01 running under Windows NT 4 (with Service Pack 4). To run the database examples, you'll also need Microsoft Access.

A *Simple* LiveWire Example

In order to quickly get you up to speed using LiveWire, we'll start with a simple example. In this example, you'll be exposed to server-side JavaScript and learn how to use the LiveWire tools to compile a Web application and install it on your Web server. The example will provide you with an overview of how LiveWire is used. Later sections of this chapter will fill in the details.

The example application presents you with the Web page shown in Figure 21.1. It displays a *Hello From LiveWire!* message followed by information about your browser and Web server. This is a very simple application, but it illustrates concepts and approaches common to all LiveWire applications.

FIGURE 21.1:

A simple application that shows how to use LiveWire (Listing 21.1)

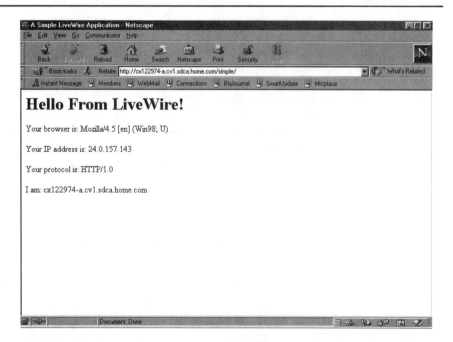

Building the Example Application

Building the example *Simple* application involves the following steps:

1. Enter the source code found in the file `simple.htm`.

2. Compile `simple.htm` using the LiveWire compiler.

3. Move the compiled application file to your Netscape Web server.

4. Install the application using Application Manager.

Listing 21.1 contains the source HTML and JavaScript code for the *simple* application.

NOTE   LiveWire no longer supports the Site Manager tool or the `lwcomp` compiler. You must compile your Web applications using the `jsac` compiler.

You probably have a few questions on how `simple.htm` works. Hang in there. The `<server>` tag and the enclosed JavaScript is covered in the section "How the *Simple* Application Works," later in this chapter.

Listing 21.1   **Your First LiveWire Application (simple.htm)**

```
<HTML>
<HEAD>
<TITLE>A Simple LiveWire Application</TITLE>
</HEAD>
<BODY>
<H1>Hello From LiveWire!</H1>
<SERVER>
write("Your browser is: "+request.agent+"<P>")
write("Your IP address is: "+request.ip+"<P>")
write("Your protocol is: "+request.protocol+"<P>")
write("I am: "+server.hostname)
</SERVER>
</BODY>
</HTML>
```

After creating the `simple.htm` file, you need to compile it. You use the Live-Wire compiler (`jsac.exe`) directly via the command line. To use the LiveWire compiler, first put it in your program PATH. Then enter the following at the command-line prompt while in the directory in which `simple.htm` is located:

```
jsac -v -o simple.web simple.htm
```

The –v switch tells the compiler to generate verbose output and the –o switch tells the computer to generate a `.web` file. The above command produces the following output:

```
C:\WINNT\Profiles\Administrator\Desktop\ch24>jsac -v -o simple
  .web simple.htm
JavaScript Application Compiler Version 21.10
Copyright (C) Netscape Communications Corporation 1996 1997
All rights reserved
Reading file simple.htm
Compiling file simple.htm
Writing .web file
C:\WINNT\Profiles\Administrator\Desktop\ch24>
```

Having compiled the *Simple* application, it is now necessary to move the `simple.web` file to your Web server. If your Web server is on the same machine, you can copy the file to a directory under your server's root directory. If your server is on a different machine, you can use FTP to move the file.

Once you've moved the `simple.web` file to your Web server, you must install the *simple* application using Application Manager. Open Application Manager (`http://your.server.com/appmgr/`) and click on the Add link. Figure 21.2 shows the Application Manager Add Application form. Set the fields of this form as shown in Table 21.1 and click on the OK button. Application Manager displays the output shown in Figure 21.3.

TABLE 21.1: Filling Out the Add Application Form

Field	Value
Name	**simple**
Web File Path	*(Type the full path to the* `simple.web` *file's location on your Web server)*
Default Page	**simple.htm**
Initial Page	*(Leave blank)*

Continued on next page

TABLE 21.1 CONTINUED: Filling Out the Add Application Form

Field	Value
Maximum Database Connections	**0**
External Libraries	*(Leave blank)*
Client Object Maintenance	**client-cookie**

FIGURE 21.2:

The Application Manager Add Application form

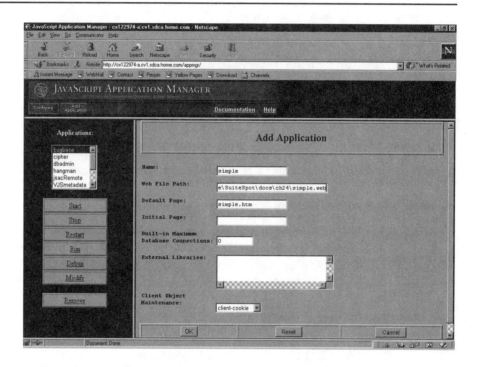

One more step to go. In the left frame of the Application Manager window, click on the Start link. This starts the *Simple* application. It is now ready to run.

FIGURE 21.3:

The output produced by Application Manager after adding the *Simple* application.

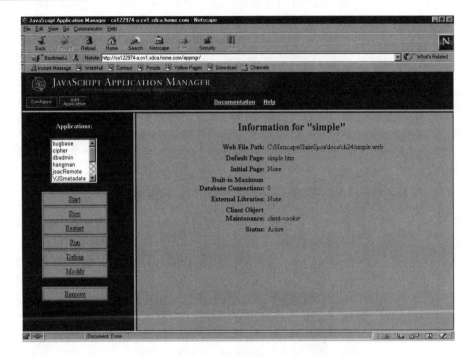

Running the Application

You can run the *Simple* application in two ways:

- In the left frame of the Application Manager window, click on the Run link. This launches Navigator and opens the link at `http://your.server.com/simple/` where your Web server's host name is substituted for `your.server.com`.

- Use your browser to open the URL `http://your.server.com/simple/` as described in step 1 in the previous section.

When you access the application's URL, your Web server first checks with LiveWire to determine whether the URL refers to a LiveWire application. If it does, then the LiveWire application is executed. Otherwise, your Web server looks for the path specified in the URL in the server's document directory.

TIP

Make sure that you don't name your application with the same name as a path in your server's document directory. If you do, the documents in your server's document directory will become inaccessible.

How the *Simple* Application Works

Now that you have the *Simple* application up and running, let's take a look at how it works.

The first thing that you probably noticed is the use of the `<server>` tags. As you might have guessed, the `<server>` tags enclose server-side JavaScript statements. These statements generate HTML and client-side JavaScript that is sent to and displayed by browsers. The `write()` function operates in the same way as it does in client-side JavaScript. However, instead of generating HTML to be displayed to a document window, it generates HTML that is returned from the LiveWire application to the browser. The properties of the `request` and `server` objects are written to the document displayed by the browser. These objects are described later in this chapter in the sections "The `request` Object" and "The `server` Object."

Figure 21.4 shows the source document displayed by my browser when it accesses the *Simple* application. Note the HTML that was generated by the server-side JavaScript.

FIGURE 21.4:

The source document displayed by your browser is generated by the *Simple* application.

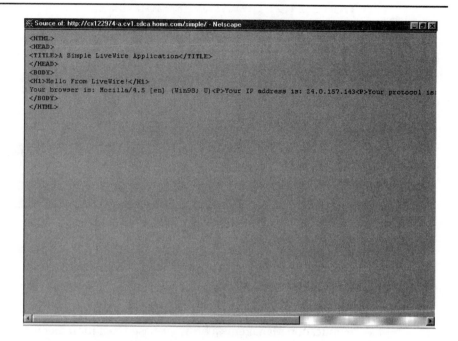

The LiveWire Compiler

The LiveWire compiler translates files containing HTML, client-side JavaScript, and server-side JavaScript into bytecode-executable files with the .web extension. These files are installed as part of the LiveWire server extension by Application Manager. The .web files are in a format that can be executed by the LiveWire server extension.

The compiler command-line syntax is as follows:

```
jsac [options] HTML_files [JavaScript_files]
```

The HTML and JavaScript files are the source files used in the application. The compiler options are described in Table 21.2. Spaces should be used to separate options and files. The -o option should be the last option that is specified.

T A B L E   2 1 . 2 : LiveWire Compiler Command-Line Options

Option	Description
-c	Checks syntax without generating a .**web** file
-d	Displays the JavaScript statements that are generated
-o *outfile*	Identifies the .**web** file to which the output should be written. (*NOTE:* If you're using more than one option from this table, be sure to put this option last.)
-v	Requests verbose output that results in more detailed error messages from the compiler.
-?	Causes compiler help information to be displayed

Application Manager

Application Manager is a browser-based tool for managing LiveWire applications. (In fact, Application Manager is itself a LiveWire application.) It provides a set of links and forms that allow you to

- Add new LiveWire applications to the LiveWire server extension.
- Modify existing applications.
- Start, stop, and restart applications.
- Run and debug applications.
- Also, you can use it to manage Netscape Web servers remotely from anywhere on the Web.

To start Application Manager, open your browser to the URL `http://your` `.server.com/appmgr/` (but replace the host name *your.server.com* with the host name of your Web server).

WARNING   Make sure that you use your server's access-control features to prevent the world at large from running Application Manager on your server.

To use Application Manager, just click on the appropriate link in the left frame of the Application Manager window. Application Manager provides online help via the Help link.

When adding or modifying a LiveWire application, Application Manager prompts you for some basic information about your application. Table 21.3 explains how to fill out each of the fields in the Add Application form.

TABLE 21.3: Filling Out the Add Application Form

Field	How to fill out
Name	Identify the name of your application. If your application's name is *appname* and your Web server's address is *your.server.com* then the URL of your application is `http://your.server.com/appname`.
Web File Path	Enter the full path to the `.web` file to be used in the application. Use the path-naming conventions of your local operating system.
Default Page	Identify the Web page to be loaded for an application if no other page has been specified. The first time a user runs the application, the Initial Page (identified in the next field) is served before the Default Page.
Initial Page	Identify the Web page that LiveWire serves when a user first runs an application. This page is used to perform any required initialization. The Default Page (identified in the previous field) is served after the Initial Page has been processed.
Maximum Database Connections	Enter the maximum number of database connections allowed by your database server license. You can enter 0 if you are not accessing a database. Enter at least 1 for any database-related application. For test purposes, I generally use a value of 10 or higher.
External Libraries	If your application needs to access any external functions written in C, C++, or other programming language, then enter the location of the external libraries here. The development of external libraries is platform-specific. Windows platforms use dynamic link libraries. Unix platforms use shared objects. Consult your LiveWire documentation for more information.
Client Object Maintenance	Select client-cookie, client-URL, server-IP, server-cookie, or server-URL. See the section "State Maintenance," later in this chapter, for more information on the meaning of each of these options.

NOTE The Default Page, Initial Page, and External Libraries fields are optional.

TIP

Remember to use Application Manager's Restart link to restart any applications that have been modified or recompiled. You must restart an application for any changes to take effect.

NOTE

On UNIX systems, you may need to stop and restart your Web server when new applications are added.

Server-Side JavaScript Programming

Server-side JavaScript programs are developed as LiveWire applications. The same steps used to develop the *Simple* application earlier in this chapter are used in all LiveWire applications. The only differences between the *Simple* application and other LiveWire applications are the contents of their source files and their Application Manager installation parameters. With this in mind, learning server-side JavaScript programming consists of the following:

1. Learning to create source files using HTML, client-side JavaScript, and server-side JavaScript. (You already know how to use HTML and client-side JavaScript. The rest of this chapter shows you how to use server-side JavaScript.)

2. Learning to use the LiveWire compiler to compile source files into `.web` files. (You already know how to do this, and you'll get more experience in subsequent examples.)

3. Learning to use Application Manager to install compiled applications. (You already know how to use Application Manager. The section entitled "State Maintenance," later in this chapter, explains how to use the client-object state-maintenance feature of LiveWire.)

Server-side JavaScript is included in LiveWire source files in three different ways:

- By enclosing the JavaScript statements within `<server>` tags
- By surrounding the JavaScript statements with back quotes (`) or (\Q)
- By putting the JavaScript statements in a `.js` file

You already learned how to use the `<server>` tags with the *Simple* application earlier in this chapter. The `<server>` tags are the most common way of using server-side JavaScript. Use the `write()` function within the `<server>` tags to generate HTML that will be sent to the browser.

Back quotes (`` ` ``) are used within an HTML tag to specify attributes or attribute values based on the value of JavaScript expressions. For example, suppose the value of the imageName variable is *image10.gif*. The following image tags are equivalent:

> <img src="image10.gif">
>
> <img src=\QimageName\Q>
>
> <img src=`imageName`>

NOTE   LiveWire automatically surrounds back-quoted (`` ` ``) expressions with double quotes
(") when generating HTML.

JavaScript (`.js`) source files are used in the same way for server-side JavaScript as for client-side JavaScript. However, server-side `.js` files do not need to be referenced via an SRC attribute to be included in an application. Simply reference the `.js` file in the LiveWire compiler command line, or include the file in the site being compiled by Site Manager.

Within the `<server>` tags, back quotes, and `.js` files, server-side JavaScript scripts are written in the same way as client-side JavaScript scripts. The language syntax remains the same. The only difference is in the objects, methods, properties, and functions available on the server. The following sections introduce these new language elements, beginning with server-side objects.

Server-Side Objects

LiveWire provides four objects that are at the heart of any server-side JavaScript application: `request`, `client`, `project`, and `server`. These objects are referred to as the *LiveWire object framework* and are used to simplify the process of application development. After having experimented with writing CGI programs in the previous chapter, you'll appreciate the features provided by these objects. Figure 21.5 summarizes how the LiveWire object framework is used to develop server-based applications.

FIGURE 21.5:

The LiveWire object framework simplifies the development of server-based applications.

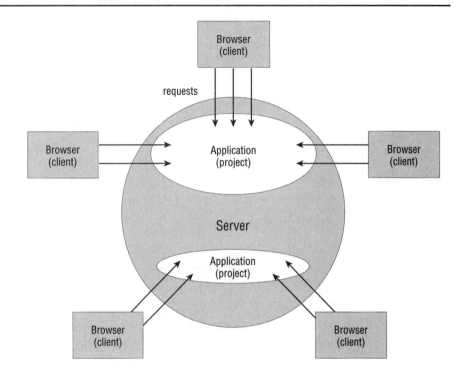

The properties of the request object provide basic information about the browser requesting the URL of a LiveWire application. Its properties also provide easy access to the information contained in a URL request, such as form data, image map coordinates, and data that is included in a query string. You can also define additional request properties for use in your application. A request object only exists until the application finishes responding to the request.

The client object maintains information about an individual browser across browser requests. The properties of the client object are application specific and are maintained using the client object maintenance mechanism specified when an application is installed via Application Manager. LiveWire maintains client information in a near-transparent manner—you don't have to worry (very much) about programming cookies or encoding data in URLs to maintain client properties. A client object exists for a predefined duration; the default is 10 minutes.

The project object maintains information that is common to all clients that access an application. This information is stored using application-specific properties of the project object. The project object exists until the application is stopped or restarted.

The `server` object maintains information that is common to all projects that are running on a server. The `server` object exists until the server is stopped or restarted.

The following subsections explain how to use each of the objects of the LiveWire object framework.

The *request* Object

The `request` object encapsulates a browser's request of an application URL. Unique `request` objects are created for each instance of a URL request. All `request` objects have the four predefined properties described in Table 21.4. A `request` object also contains properties that provide access to data sent by the browser to the application. These properties contain the values of form fields, image map clicks, and query string data encoded in URLs. Table 21.5 summarizes the `request` properties that are created for URL requests. These properties greatly simplify the processing of browser data. All the overhead of parsing query strings, common to CGI programs, is automatically handled by LiveWire.

TABLE 21.4: Predefined `request` Properties

Property	Description
agent	The name and version of the browser making the URL request
ip	The IP address of the host from which the request is made
method	The HTTP method used with the request
protocol	The version of the HTTP protocol used by the requesting browser

TABLE 21.5: Properties That Are Created for URL Requests

Request Type	Properties That Are Created
Form submission (GET or POST)	The form elements are given properties of the form `request.name` where **name** is the name of the form element. For example, if a form has text fields named **address** and **city** then the properties `request.address` and `request.city` are created to provide access to the data submitted in these fields.

TABLE 21.5 CONTINUED: Properties That Are Created for URL Requests

Request Type	Properties That Are Created
Server-side image map click	The properties `request.imageX` and `request.imageY` are created to provide access to the coordinates of the mouse click.
Link with appended query string	If the query string contains *name=value* pairs of the form `?name1=value1& ... namen=valuen` then the `request` properties `request.name1` through `request.namen` are created with values *value1* through *valuen*.

> **NOTE**   The *file upload* form element cannot be used in LiveWire applications.

The *Simple* application presented earlier in this chapter showed how to use the predefined `request` properties. The following sections provide examples of server-side scripts that show how to access data that is sent by browsers in URL requests.

A Form Example

Listing 21.2 shows the contents of the `form.htm` file. This file contains a simple HTML form with the `newuser.htm` file specified as the `ACTION` attribute of the form. The form is used to get the first name, last name, and e-mail address of a user in order to register the user at the Web site.

Listing 21.3 shows the contents of `newuser.htm`. This file contains server-side JavaScript that displays the values of the `firstName, lastName`, and `email` fields that are received when the form of Listing 21.2 is submitted.

To see how `form.htm` and `newuser.htm` work together as part of a LiveWire application, use the following statement to compile the files into an application file named `register.web`:

```
jsac -v -o register.web form.htm newuser.htm
```

Now move `register.web` to a directory on your Web server. Use Application Manager to add the application to LiveWire. Then set the application name to `register` and the default page to `form.htm`. Now start the application by clicking on the Start LiveWire link. Finally, click Run to run the `register` application.

It will generate a Web page, as shown in Figure 21.6. Fill out the registration form and click on Submit Registration. This will result in a Web page similar to the one shown in Figure 21.7. (Note how the values you entered in the form are displayed by the server script contained in newuser.htm.)

Listing 21.2   A Registration Form (form.htm)

```
<HTML>
<HEAD>
<TITLE>Registration Form</TITLE>
</HEAD>
<BODY>
<H1>Please Register</H1>
<FORM NAME="registration" ACTION="newuser.htm">
Firt Name: <INPUT TYPE="text" NAME="firstName">
Last Name: <INPUT TYPE="text" NAME="lastName"><P>
E-Mail Address: <INPUT TYPE="text" NAME="email" SIZE="50"><P>
<INPUT TYPE="SUBMIT" VALUE="Submit Registration">
</FORM>
</BODY>
</HTML>
```

Listing 21.3   Displaying Submitted Form Data (newuser.htm)

```
<HTML>
<HEAD>
<TITLE>Thank You</TITLE>
</HEAD>
<BODY>
<H1>Thanks for registering</H1>
<P>Your registration information is as follows:</P>
<P><SERVER>
write(request.firstName+" "+request.lastName+"<BR>")
write(request.email)
</SERVER></P>
</BODY>
</HTML>
```

FIGURE 21.6:

A registration form that is used to send sample form data to a server-side script (Listing 21.2)

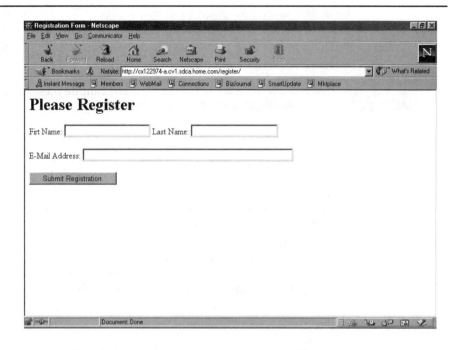

FIGURE 21.7:

A server-side script that displays the form data it receives from the browser (Listing 21.3)

An Image Map Example

Listing 21.4 shows the contents of the map.htm file. This file displays a simple server-side image map. The coordinates of the user's clicks are sent to the file disp-xy.htm, shown in Listing 21.5. The files, map.htm and disp-xy.htm, work together as part of a LiveWire application. Compile these files using

```
jsac -v -o imagemap.web map.htm disp-xy.htm
```

Move imagemap.web and shapes.gif to a directory on your Web server. Use Application Manager to add the application to LiveWire. Then set the application name to imagemap and the default page to map.htm. Now start and run the imagemap application. It will generate a Web page, as shown in Figure 21.8. Click on the image. This will result in a Web page similar to the one shown in Figure 21.9. (Note how the values of your click are displayed by the server script contained in disp-xy.htm.)

Listing 21.4   A Simple Image Map (map.htm)

```
<HTML>
<HEAD>
<TITLE>Using Image Maps</TITLE>
</HEAD>
<BODY>
<H1>Using Image Maps</H1>
<A HREF="disp-xy.htm">
<IMG SRC="shapes.gif" ISMAP="ISMAP">
</A>
</BODY>
</HTML>
```

Listing 21.5   Displaying Image Map Coordinates (disp-xy.htm)

```
<HTML>
<HEAD>
<TITLE>Image Map Processing</TITLE>
</HEAD>
<BODY>
<H1>You clicked at
<SERVER>
write("("+request.imageX+","+request.imageY+")")
</SERVER>
.<H1>
</BODY>
</HTML>
```

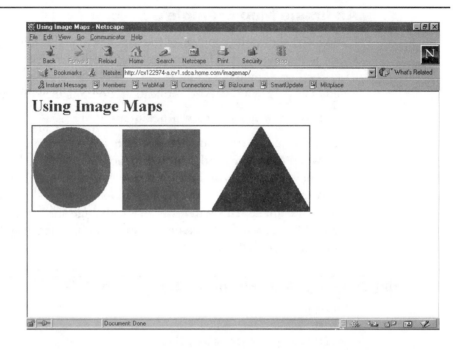

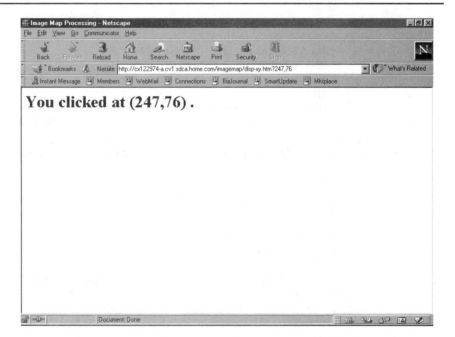

A Custom URL Example

Listing 21.6 shows the contents of the qstring.htm file. This file displays a link with an attached query string. When the user clicks on this link the query string is forwarded to the file disp-qs.htm, shown in Listing 21.7. The files qstring.htm and disp-qs.htm work together as part of a LiveWire application. Compile these files using

```
jsac -v -o querystring.web qstring.htm disp-qs.htm
```

Move querystring.web to a directory on your Web server. Use Application Manager to add the application to LiveWire. Then set the application name to querystring and the default page to qstring.htm. Now start and run the querystring application. It will generate a Web page, as shown in Figure 21.10. Click on the link. This will result in a Web page similar to the one shown in Figure 21.11. (Note how the query string values are displayed by the server script contained in disp-qs.htm.)

Listing 21.6   A Link with a Query String (qstring.htm)

```
<HTML>
<HEAD>
<TITLE>Query String Test</TITLE>
</HEAD>
<BODY>
<A HREF="disp-qs.htm?var1=LiveWire&var2=is&var3=great">
disp-qs.htm?var1=LiveWire&var2=is&var3=great
</A>
</BODY>
</HTML>
```

Listing 21.7   Displaying Query String Values (disp-qs.htm)

```
<HTML>
<HEAD>
<TITLE>Query String Results</TITLE>
</HEAD>
<BODY>
<P>The method associated with the URL is:
<B><SERVER>write(request.method)</SERVER></B></P>
<P>The value of var1 is:
<B><SERVER>write(request.var1)</SERVER></B></P>
<P>The value of var2 is:
<B><SERVER>write(request.var2)</SERVER></B></P>
<P>The value of var3 is:
<B><SERVER>write(request.var3)</SERVER></B></P>
</BODY>
</HTML>
```

FIGURE 21.10:

The link is used to send a query string to a server-side script (Listing 21.6).

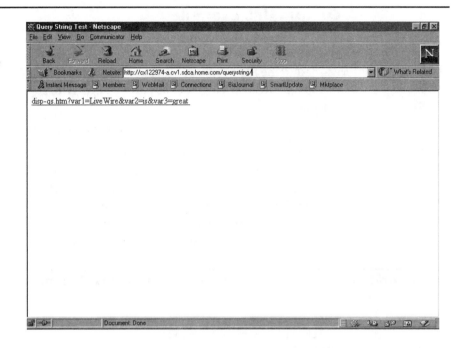

FIGURE 21.11:

The server-side script displays the query string values (Listing 21.7).

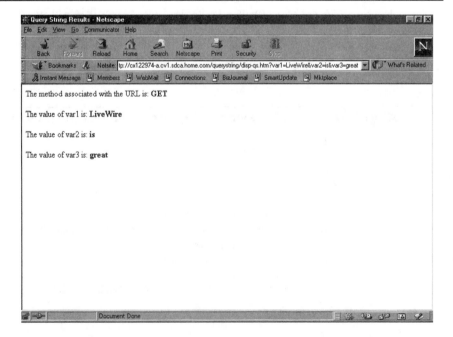

The *client* Object

The client object provides the capability to maintain client-specific information across multiple browser requests. This allows you to keep track of the application state of individual clients. For example, the client.id property could be defined to assign a unique ID to the client for the duration of a browser session. As another example, consider an online sales application. The client.selections array could be used to keep track of the products a user selected for purchase.

The client object does not have any predefined properties. Client properties are created by the application by assigning a value to the property. For example, the following statement creates the client.id property and assigns it the value of the nextID() function.

```
client.id = nextID()
```

By default, client objects expire and cease to exist after 10 minutes. This default expiration time can be changed using the expiration() method. This method takes as a parameter the number of seconds that a client is allowed to exist before it expires. For example, the following statement extends the lifetime of a client object to an hour:

```
client.expiration(3600)
```

The destroy() method can be used to destroy a client object immediately. Use this method to destroy a client object's property values. Use expiration(0) to remove all client property information stored on a user's browser.

> **NOTE** Client expiration does not apply if the client-url approach is used to maintain client data. See the section "State Maintenance," later in this chapter, for more information.

The *project* Object

The project object allows properties to be specified that apply to an entire application. These properties are accessible to all clients that use the application. For example, a project.counter can be defined to count the number of times an application has been accessed. As another example, consider a project.nextID property that is used to assign user IDs to individual clients.

The `project` object does not have any predefined properties. Application-specific properties are created in the same way that they are with the `client` object. The `project` object exists until the application is stopped or restarted.

Because the `project` object is shared among multiple clients, a special mechanism, referred to as *locking*, is implemented to prevent one client from interfering with the processing of another.

The `lock()` method is used to lock the `project` object. When the `project` object is locked, only the script instance that invoked the `lock()` method is able to modify any properties of the `project` object. (A *script instance* is a script that is executing in response to a browser request.) All other script instances attempting to modify `project` properties must wait until the lock is released. The `unlock()` method is used to release a lock on the `project` object. Because other script instances may be waiting for a project to be unlocked, it is important to minimize the code that is executed between invoking `lock()` and `unlock()`.

> **NOTE**   LiveWire automatically prevents a project property from being modified (by another script) when a script reads or writes a project property. Locking is used to prevent any modifications between reads and writes.

The *server* Object

The `server` object is used to store information that is common to all applications supported by a server. The `server` object has the predefined properties shown in Table 21.6. In addition to these properties, application-specific properties may be defined in the same way as with the `client` and `project` objects. For example, the `server.nextUserID` property may be used to assign a user ID for each user who accesses applications on a server.

TABLE 21.6: The Predefined Properties of the `server` Object

Property	Description
hostname	The name of the host and protocol port used by the server
host	The name of the host on which the server runs
protocol	The protocol used by the server *(http:)*
port	The protocol port used by the server

The server lock() and unlock() methods support server object locking in the same manner as for the project object. The server object exists until the server is stopped or restarted.

File Input and Output

Because all objects of the LiveWire object framework expire at some point in time, it is important to maintain permanent copies of critical application information. The LiveWire File object provides the capability to access files in the server's file system. You can use File to store critical data so that it can be used by LiveWire-external applications and to back up project and server properties.

File objects are created using the new operator as follows:

```
var=new File(path)
```

var is the variable to which the file object is assigned, and path is the path to the file, written in the local operating system format. For example, the statement

```
f1=new File("db.txt")
```

creates a new File object that can be used to access the db.txt file.

TIP

If f is a variable that is assigned a File object, then write(f) produces the name of the file to which f refers.

Opening Files

Once a File object is created, it must be opened before it can read or written. The open() method of the File object opens the File object and returns a Boolean value indicating whether or not the open was successful. The open() method takes a string parameter that specifies the mode in which the file is to be opened. These mode strings are defined in Table 21.7.

TABLE 21.7: Mode Strings for the open() Method of the File Object

String	Description
a	The file is opened in write-only text mode. All data that is written to the file is appended at the end of the file. If the file does not exist, then it is created.
a+	The file is opened in text mode for both reading and writing. All read-and-write operations occur at the end of the file. If the file does not exist, then it is created.
r	If the file exists, then it is opened in read-only text mode. Reading starts at the beginning of the file. If the file does not exist, then false is returned.
r+	If the file exists, then it is opened in read-and-write text mode. Reading and writing starts at the beginning of the file. If the file does not exist, then false is returned.
w	The file is opened as an empty file in write-only text mode. Writing starts at the beginning of the file. If the file does not exist, then it is created.
w+	The file is opened as an empty file in read-and-write text mode. Reading and writing start at the beginning of the file. If the file does not exist, then it is created.

On Windows platforms, the argument **b** may be appended to any of these mode strings to open the file in binary mode instead of text mode.

Suppose the f variable is assigned the File object created from db.txt. If db.txt exists, the following statement opens the file for reading and writing:

```
status=f.open("r+")
```

The open() method returns true if db.txt exists and false otherwise.

Closing Files

The close() method is used to close a file after access to the file is no longer needed. It returns a Boolean value indicating the success (*true*) or failure (*false*) of the close operation.

Accessing Files

The File object provides several methods for reading and writing files. These methods are summarized in Table 21.8. The byteToString() and stringTo-Byte() methods are static. This means that they apply to the File object type and not to specific File objects. Thus, you must precede static methods by the name of the object type instead of the name of an object instance. For example, the following statement converts the number 49 to its corresponding ASCII string and assigns it to the `str` variable.

```
str=File.byteToString(49)
```

TABLE 21.8: Methods of the `File` Object

Method	Description
byteToString(*n*)	A static method that returns the ASCII string corresponding to the byte value *n*
clearError()	Resets any errors or end-of-file conditions associated with a file
close()	Closes a file that was previously opened
eof()	Returns **true** if the file pointer is passed the end of the file and **false** otherwise
error()	Returns operating system–specific error status codes
exists()	Returns **true** if a file exists and **false** otherwise
flush()	Writes any buffered output to a file
getLength()	Returns the length of a file
getPosition()	Returns the current position of the file pointer
open(*modeString*)	Opens a file for reading or writing (see Table 21.7)
read(*n*)	Reads *n* number of bytes from the file starting at the pointer position. The data is returned as a string. The pointer is moved by the number of characters read.
readByte()	Reads the next byte in a file that is opened in binary mode. The byte is returned as an integer and the file pointer is incremented by one byte.
readln()	Reads a line of characters from a file and returns it as a string. Moves the file pointer to the beginning of the next line.
setPosition(*position* [,*reference*])	Sets the file pointer to *position*. The optional *reference* parameter specifies the relative location of *position*. If *reference* is 0 then *position* is relative to the beginning of the file. If *reference* is 1 then *position* is relative to the current position. If *reference* is 2 then *position* is relative to the end of the file.
stringToByte(*string*)	A static method that converts the first character of a string to its ASCII byte value

TABLE 21.8 CONTINUED: Methods of the File Object

Method	Description
write(*expression*)	Writes the string value of *expression* to a file and advances the file pointer by the number of bytes written
writeByte(*n*)	Writes the byte specified by integer *n* to a file that is opened in binary mode. The file pointer is advanced by one byte.
writeln(*expression*)	Writes *expression* as a line of text. The file pointer is advanced by the number of bytes written.

Many of the File methods make use of a mechanism known as the file *pointer*. The file pointer is the position within a file at which the next read or operation is to take place. When the file pointer is positioned past the last character of a file, it is said to be at the end of the file.

Locking File Access

Because application files may be shared by several concurrently executing script instances, it is important to implement precautions designed to prevent file access conflicts. The project- and server-locking mechanisms can be used to prevent these conflicts.

When you invoke project.lock(), all other application script instances are prevented from accessing files. These scripts must wait until project.unlock() is invoked before resuming execution.

If a file is shared by two or more applications, use server.lock() and server.unlock() to prevent scripts from one application from conflicting with the file accesses being made by scripts of another application.

A Fuller Example—*Diskette*

In this section, you'll develop an application that uses all of the objects of the LiveWire object framework, uses the File object to store application data, and integrates client- and server-side JavaScript. This application, which I call

Diskette, is an online storefront that specializes in the sale of high-density, double-sided, 3-½ inch diskettes. This application takes user orders and stores them in a disk file. Although the application is quite simple—it was designed that way—it illustrates many important aspects of LiveWire application development. A real online ordering application would dress up the site with fancy graphics and provide a mechanism for online payment.

The next section introduces the files that make up the *Diskette* application. The section after that shows how to build, install, and run the application.

Up until now, I've asked you to run an application before I explained how it works. In the *Diskette* application, I'm going to reverse this process. When you study the *Diskette* application files, see if you can visualize how they work in advance of compiling and running the application. This will give you a more thorough understanding of how each of the individual application files work together.

The Files of the *Diskette* Application

The *Diskette* application is made up of the following four files:

start.htm   This file is the default page for the *Diskette* application. It presents a price list and order form to the user. When the order form is submitted, the form data is sent to `process.htm`.

process.htm   This file processes the data entered by the user in the order form of `start.htm`. It combines client- and server-side JavaScript to display the user's order. It then prompts the user to enter name and address information. This information is combined with the locally calculated price of the user's order and submitted to `display.htm`.

display.htm   This file takes the form data submitted by `process.htm` and stores it in `client` properties. It then displays the data collected by `start.htm` and `process.htm` so that the user may check their order.

finish.htm   This file writes the user's order to the `orders.txt` file and thanks the user for their order.

These files are analyzed in the following subsections.

The *start.htm* File

The start.htm file is shown in Listing 21.8. It is a simple HTML file that displays a tabular price list and an order form. The only distinguishing feature of this file is that the ACTION attribute of the form points to an HTML file (process.htm) instead of to a CGI program. This is possible because process.htm is part of the *Diskette* application and it uses server-side JavaScript to access the data submitted in the order form.

Listing 21.8   **The Opening Page of the Diskette Application (start.htm)**

```
<HTML>
<HEAD>
<TITLE>Diskette Center</TITLE>
</HEAD>
<BODY BGCOLOR="white">
<H1 ALIGN="CENTER">Welcome to Diskette Center</H1>
<P ALIGN="CENTER"><I>The cheapest diskettes on the Web.</I>
</P>
<P>All orders are sent COD.</P>
<H2>Price List (High Density Double-Sided Dikettes)</H2>
<TABLE>
<TR><TH>Quantity</TH><TH>Price per diskette</TH></TR>
<TR><TD>1-20</TD><TD>25 cents</TD></TR>
<TR><TD>21-100</TD><TD>20 cents</TD></TR>
<TR><TD>101-500</TD><TD>15 cents</TD></TR>
<TR><TD>500-1000</TD><TD>10 cents</TD></TR>
<TR><TD>over 1000</TD><TD>7.5 cents</TD></TR>
</TABLE>
<H2>Place your order and click Continue.</H2>
<FORM ACTION="process.htm">
Number of diskettes:
<INPUT TYPE="TEXT" SIZE="10" NAME="number">
<INPUT TYPE="Submit" VALUE="Continue">
</FORM>
</BODY>
</HTML>
```

The *process.htm* File

The process.htm file is shown in Listing 21.9. It is an example of how application processing can be divided between client and server scripts.

In the head of process.htm is a client-side script that contains the display-Order() function. This function displays a breakout of the cost of the user's order. It calculates the total cost of the order and assigns it to the total variable. The function has a single argument that identifies how many diskettes the user ordered.

The body of process.htm begins with server-side JavaScript that uses the write() function to generate client-side JavaScript. The generated JavaScript is a call to the displayOrder() function, with the number of diskettes ordered by the user passed as a parameter. This number is passed to process.htm as request.number where number is the name of the field in the order menu of start.htm. The request.number property is assigned to client.number. This enables the value to survive the life span of the request object and be available in subsequent application Web pages.

The body of process.htm displays a form which requests name and address information from the user. The form is submitted to the display.htm file. Note that the form contains a hidden field named total. The value of this field is set in the client script that immediately follows the form, using the total value calculated by the displayOrder() function as the result of earlier processing. This is a good example of how a client-side script is able to send a locally calculated result to a server-side script.

Listing 21.9　　**Combining Client- and Server-Side JavaScript (process.htm)**

```
<HTML>
<HEAD>
<TITLE>Diskette Center</TITLE>
<SCRIPT language="JavaScript">
function displayOrder(n) {
 with(document){
  if(n<21) rate=.25
  else if(n<101) rate=.2
  else if(n<501) rate=.15
  else if(n<1001) rate=.10
  else rate=.075
  subtotal=n*rate
```

```
      subtotal=Math.round(subtotal*100)/100
      total=subtotal+10
      write("<H2>You ordered:</H2>")
      write(n+" disks at $"+rate+" per disk: "+subtotal+"<BR>")
      write("Tax: included"+"<BR>")
      write("Shipping: $10"+"<BR>")
      write("Total: "+total+"<BR>")
    }
  }
</SCRIPT>
</HEAD>
<BODY>
<SERVER>
client.number=request.number
write("<SCRIPT language='JavaScript'>")
write("displayOrder("+client.number+")")
write("</SCRIPT>")
</SERVER>
<H2>Please fill out the following information.</H2>
<FORM ACTION="display.htm">
First Name: <INPUT TYPE="TEXT" NAME="firstName"><BR>
Last Name: <INPUT TYPE="TEXT" NAME="lastName"><P>
Address:<BR>
<INPUT TYPE="TEXT" NAME="addr1" SIZE="40"><BR>
<INPUT TYPE="TEXT" NAME="addr2" SIZE="40"><BR>
City: <INPUT TYPE="TEXT" NAME="city">
State: <INPUT TYPE="TEXT" NAME="state" SIZE="5">
Postal Code: <INPUT TYPE="TEXT" NAME="zip" SIZE="10"><BR>
Country: <INPUT TYPE="TEXT" NAME="country"><P>
Phone: <INPUT TYPE="TEXT" NAME="phone"><P>
E-mail address:     <INPUT TYPE="TEXT" NAME="email" SIZE="40">
<INPUT TYPE="HIDDEN" NAME="total"><P>
<INPUT TYPE="SUBMIT" VALUE="Continue">
</FORM>
<SCRIPT language="JavaScript">
document.forms[0].total.value=total
</SCRIPT>
</BODY>
</HTML>
```

The *display.htm* File

The display.htm file (Listing 21.10) contains a server-side script that assigns the form data of process.htm to client object properties. Note that the hidden total field of process.htm is also stored as a client property. This value was calculated locally by the displayOrder() function of process.htm.

The second half of the server script displays the client properties to the user so that they can review their order. The server script is followed by a form that contains a Continue button. This form is submitted to finish.htm.

Listing 21.10   Using the Client Object to Store Data between Web Pages (display.htm)

```
<HTML>
<HEAD>
<TITLE>Diskette Center</TITLE>
</HEAD>
<BODY>
<H1>Please check your order:</H1>
<SERVER>
client.firstName=request.firstName
client.lastName=request.lastName
client.addr1=request.addr1
client.addr2=request.addr2
client.city=request.city
client.state=request.state
client.country=request.country
client.zip=request.zip
client.phone=request.phone
client.email=request.email
client.total=request.total
write(client.firstName+" "+client.lastName+"<BR>")
write(client.addr1+"<BR>")
write(client.addr2+"<BR>")
write(client.city+", "+client.state+" "+client.zip+"<BR>")
write(client.country+"<BR>")
write(client.phone+"<BR>")
write(client.email+"<P>")
write(client.number+" diskettes<BR>")
write("$"+client.total+" US dollars<BR>")
</SERVER>
```

```
<FORM action="finish.htm">
<INPUT TYPE="SUBMIT" VALUE="Continue">
</FORM>
</BODY>
</HTML>
```

The *finish.htm* File

This file (see Listing 21.11) saves the user's order in the `orders.txt` file on the server. It begins by locking the `project` object to prevent any conflicts with other concurrently executing scripts. The `project.nextOrder` property is used to assign a number to each customer order. It is a `project` property because it is shared among all clients.

The `if` statement checks `project.nextOrder` to see if it is null. This is the case when the application is started or restarted. In this case, it is initialized to 1000. The `client.order` property is set after incrementing `project.nextOrder`.

NOTE   The properties of the `request`, `client`, `project`, and `server` objects are stored as strings. Use the `parseInt()` and `parseFloat()` functions to convert from string to integer and floating-point values.

A `File` object is created for the file `orders.txt` and assigned to the `f` variable. The file is opened in append mode. The `writeln()` method is used to write the user's order to the file. The file is closed and the `project` object is unlocked.

The file ends with the user being thanked and informed of the order number.

Listing 21.11   **Saving Customer Orders in a File (finish.htm)**

```
<HTML>
<HEAD>
<TITLE>Diskette Center</TITLE>
</HEAD>
<BODY>
<SERVER>
project.lock()
if(project.nextOrder==null) project.nextOrder=1000
```

```
project.nextOrder=parseInt(project.nextOrder)+1
client.order=project.nextOrder
f=new File("orders.txt")
f.open("a")
f.writeln(client.order+" "+client.number+" "+client.total)
f.writeln(client.firstName+" "+client.lastName)
f.writeln(client.addr1)
f.writeln(client.addr2)
f.writeln(client.city+" "+client.state+" "+client.zip)
f.writeln(client.country)
f.writeln(client.phone)
f.writeln(client.email)
f.close()
project.unlock()
</SERVER>
<H1>Thank you for your order!</H1>
<H2>Your order number is <SERVER>
write(client.order)
</SERVER>.</H2>
</BODY>
</HTML>
```

Building and Running the *Diskette* Application

Use the following command to compile the *Diskette* application:

```
jsac -v -o diskette.web start.htm process.htm display.htm finish.htm
```

Next, move diskette.web to your server. Use Application Manager to install it, and set the default page to start.htm.

Run the *Diskette* application by clicking on the Application Manager Run link. It displays the Web page shown in Figure 21.12. Enter the number of diskettes you want to order and click on the Continue button.

The number of diskettes ordered is passed to process.htm and the Web page shown in Figure 21.13 is displayed. Note how the server-side JavaScript displays the user's order information. This is an example of how client-side JavaScript can be used to take some of the processing load off the server. Fill out the name and address information and click on the Continue button.

FIGURE 21.12:

The order form prompts you to enter the number of disks you are ordering (Listing 21.8).

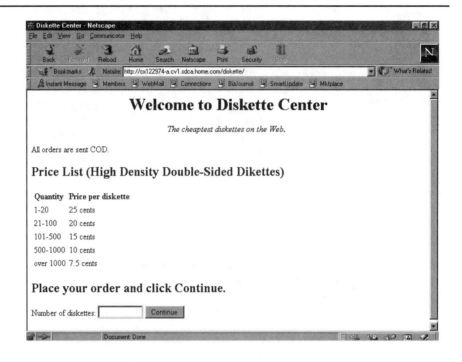

FIGURE 21.13:

This form collects name and address information from the user (Listing 21.9).

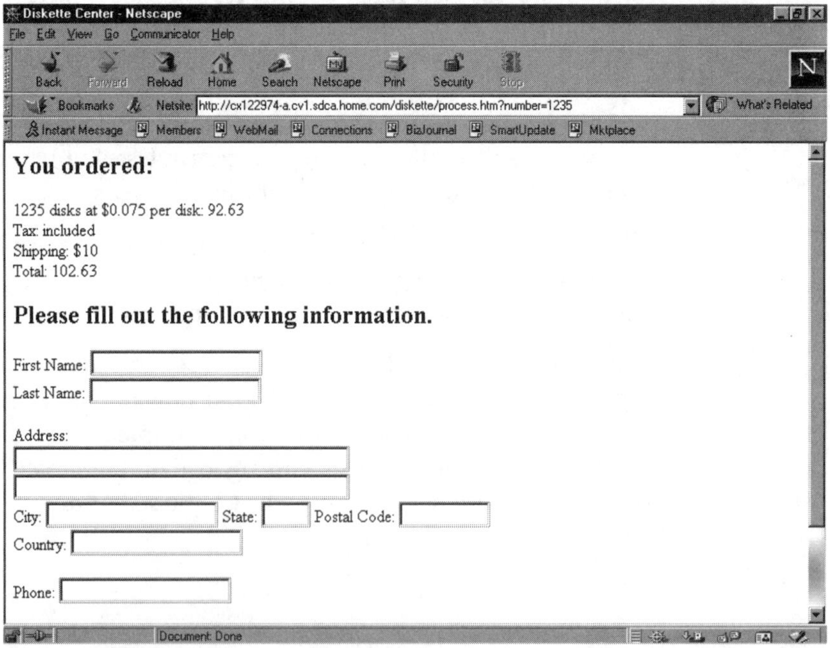

The information provided in the name and address form is forwarded to display.htm along with the calculated total price and the number of diskettes from the first form. This information is displayed, as shown in Figure 21.14. Go ahead and click on the Continue button.

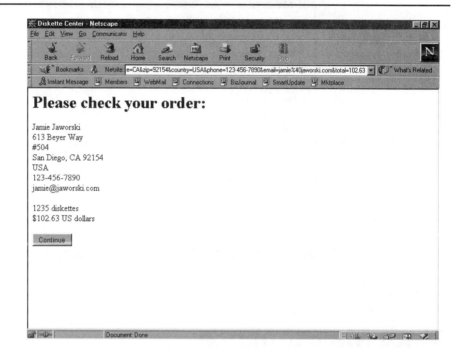

The data collected in previous forms is forwarded to finish.htm. The Java-Script code in finish.htm writes the order data to the orders.txt file. A Web page like the one shown in Figure 21.15 is displayed.

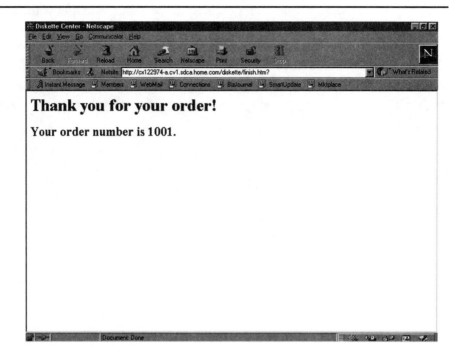

FIGURE 21.15:

The user is thanked and informed of the order number (Listing 21.11).

State Maintenance

A popular application that serves many browser clients simultaneously may need a great deal of memory to store client information. The Client Object Maintenance field of Application Manager's Add Application form allows LiveWire applications to choose between five different approaches to storing client information:

- Client-cookie
- Client-URL
- Server-IP
- Server-cookie
- Server-URL

LiveWire provides these five alternatives so that you can choose the particular approach that is best suited for your application. The following subsections describe these approaches and summarize the advantages and disadvantages of each approach.

The Client-Cookie Approach

In Chapter 8, "Using Hidden Fields and Cookies," you learned how to use cookies to maintain state information across multiple Web pages. The client-cookie approach uses cookies to store `client` object information in the `cookies.txt` file of each of the browsers accessing the application. The *advantage* of client-cookie is that it is client-based and does not require server memory resources. The *disadvantages* are as follows:

- It only works with browsers that support cookies.

- It is limited to 20 properties with a maximum of 4K bytes each.

- The `client` object properties must be set before the application generates 64K bytes of output. Any new or modified client properties after the application has generated 64K bytes of output will be lost.

- It increases network traffic.

The Client-URL Approach

In the client-URL approach, LiveWire encodes the `client` object properties as *name=value* pairs that are appended to the URLs used to link to other application pages. When these URLs are requested by a browser, the encoded information is sent back to the browser. The *advantages* of this approach are as follows:

- It is client based and does not require server storage.

- It works with all browsers.

- The `client` object information does not expire.

The *disadvantages* of this approach are as follows:

- The `client` object properties are transmitted multiple times if the generated Web page contains multiple URLs. This may significantly increase network traffic for some applications.

- The size of a URL is limited to 4K bytes. The actual number of bytes available for client object storage is slightly less than 4K bytes.

- It does not work correctly with forms.

- The `client` object properties must be set before the application generates 64K bytes of output. Any new or modified client properties after the application has generated 64K bytes of output will be lost.

- Dynamically generated links must add the client properties to the URL via the `addClient()` function.

The Server-IP Approach

In this approach, the client's IP address is used to index `client` object information on the server. The *advantage* of this approach is that it does not place any limit on the number or size of cookie properties. It has the following *disadvantages*:

- The `client` object information is lost when the server is restarted.

- It consumes server memory resources.

- It may malfunction with applications that use frames.

- It does not work correctly with browsers that are proxied by a firewall.

- It may malfunction for browsers on hosts that do not have fixed IP addresses.

- It may malfunction on hosts that support multiple concurrent browser sessions.

WARNING In most cases, server-IP is the least reliable way to maintain `client` object information.

The Server-Cookie Approach

In the server-cookie approach, a single cookie value is generated and sent to the browser. This value is used as an index to `client` object information that is stored on the server. The *advantage* of this approach is that it does not place any limit on the number or size of cookie properties. The *disadvantages* of this approach are that

- The `client` object information is lost when the server is restarted.

- It consumes server memory resources.

- It may malfunction with applications that use frames.

- It only works with browsers that support cookies.

The Server-URL Approach

The server-URL approach stores an index on the browser. This index is used to access `client` object information that is stored on the server. The index is stored by encoding application URLs in the same way as the client-URL approach. The *advantages* of this approach are that

- It does not place any limits on the number or size of client properties.

- It works with all browsers.

The *disadvantages* of this approach are that

- The `client` object information is lost when the server is restarted.

- It consumes server memory resources.

- It may malfunction with applications that use frames.

- It does not work correctly with forms.

- Dynamically generated links must add the index to the URL via the `add-Client()` function.

Which Approach Should You Use?

With five different approaches to maintaining `client` object properties, each with their own advantages and disadvantages, you may wonder which approach to use for your application. Your decision process is driven by the following questions:

- Do you need to take advantage of client storage capabilities?

- Can you limit your application to browsers that support cookies?

If you need to take advantage of client storage, then your options are client-cookie and client-URL. If the application can be limited to cookie-capable browsers, then choose client-cookie because it eliminates all of the overhead associated with URL encoding.

If you don't need to take advantage of client storage, then your choices are server-IP, server-cookie, and server-URL. The required assumptions for using server-IP are so limiting that it should never be considered as a viable option unless you have complete control over all clients who could access an application. This leaves server-cookie and server-URL. If the application can be limited to cookie-capable browsers, then choose server-cookie because it eliminates problems associated with URL encoding.

Server Functions

LiveWire provides several functions that can be used in server-side scripts. These functions are in addition to the functions provided by client-side JavaScript.

The *addClient(URL)* Function

When the client-URL or server-URL approach is used to maintain client object properties, these properties must be encoded as *name=value* pairs in application URLs. If you dynamically generate a URL and are using client-URL or server-URL, then you must use addClient() to add the client properties to the URL. The addClient() function returns a string that contains the URL with the client properties appended as a query string.

The *debug(expression)* Function

This function is used in conjunction with the Application Manager's Debug command. It writes the value of the expression to the Application Manager's Debug window.

The *flush()* Function

When the write() function is used to generate HTML, its output is buffered in 64K chunks before being sent to the browser. The flush() function causes buffered output to be immediately sent to the browser. All client object properties should be set before invoking flush().

The *getOptionValue(name,n)* Function

The getOptionValue() function returns the text of the *n*th option of the HTML selection list of the specified name.

The *getOptionValueCount(name)* Function

The getOptionValueCount() function returns the number of options selected in the select list of the specified name.

The *redirect(URL)* Function

The redirect() function redirects the browser to immediately load the specified URL. All subsequent JavaScript statements are ignored.

The *write(expression)* Function

The write() function generates the HTML specified by the expression.

NOTE   LiveWire provides additional functions for accessing external functions written in other languages, such as C and C++. Consult Netscape's LiveWire documentation for more information on accessing external functions.

File-Oriented Systems vs. Database Management Systems

Many small computer applications are centered on the creation, development, management, and display of documents that are organized into files. Your word processor is used to create and manage word processing documents. Your HTML editor is used to develop Web pages. Your spreadsheet program is used to work with spreadsheets. And so on.

Most personal computer programs are perfectly suited to file-oriented applications because the focus of the application is the application *document* (.doc, .html, or .xls), which is comprised of one or more application files. However, for medium- to large-scale applications that focus on the collection, analysis, and reporting of information, a simple file-based approach is quite limiting.

As an example, consider the *Diskette* application. It just takes customer orders and appends them to the end of the file `orders.txt`. This simple application works well for recording orders, but it wouldn't fit all of the needs of the "Diskette Center" business. For example, those employees who are responsible for filling orders would need a capability to view the `orders.txt` file. (Of course, they could always write an application to display the contents of `orders.txt` in some formatted fashion.) Other employees would be required to maintain the status of the individual orders. (These employees could write an application to update `orders.txt` with status information.) And of course, management would need to get involved in determining how well (or poorly) the whole process works. A script that could provide the capability to analyze `orders.txt` would also be helpful.

File-Oriented Systems

Are you starting to get the picture? Most file-oriented systems break down when a few different groups need to maintain the file information for different purposes. The main deficiencies of file-oriented systems are that they are structurally rigid, difficult to maintain, less reliable and secure, and do not support custom information sharing. The following is a summary list of these issues:

- File-oriented systems are *structurally rigid and difficult to maintain*, because once a file format has been developed, its very difficult to change the format without having to change everybody's file access scripts.

- They are *less reliable and less secure*, because anyone with access to the file has access to the entire contents of the file. All it takes is one individual with an update script that malfunctions to ruin the file data used by everyone else.

- File-oriented systems *do not support custom information sharing*, because with file-oriented systems you have two query options: Use an existing query script or write your own. For those who do not have the resources to write their own scripts, the available options become rather limited.

Database Management Systems

Database management systems remove many of the limitations of file-oriented systems. A database management system, abbreviated as *DBMS*, is a system of software tools for storing, updating, retrieving, analyzing, reporting, and managing information. A good DBMS would provide all of the employees at the imaginary "Diskette Center" with the capabilities they need to efficiently carry out their work. For example, compare these characteristics of a DBMS with the drawbacks mentioned above for file-oriented systems:

- A typical DBMS is much more flexible when it comes to structural changes. You can change the structure and organization of your database without losing any of your data. For this reason, a database is usually much easier to maintain.

- A good DBMS promotes reliability by validating data before adding it to the database. Many DBMSs usually have security features for limiting user access to certain types of database information.

- Probably the most compelling reasons for using a DBMS are the capabilities that it provides for querying and reporting information. Many database management systems provide a query language, such as the Structured Query Language or SQL, for asking a database about the information it contains. The query language is often integrated with a set of report-generation tools, which take the results of database queries and format them into custom reports.

Figure 21.16 contrasts DBMS-oriented systems with file-oriented systems.

FIGURE 21.16:

DBMS-oriented systems have many advantages over file-oriented systems.

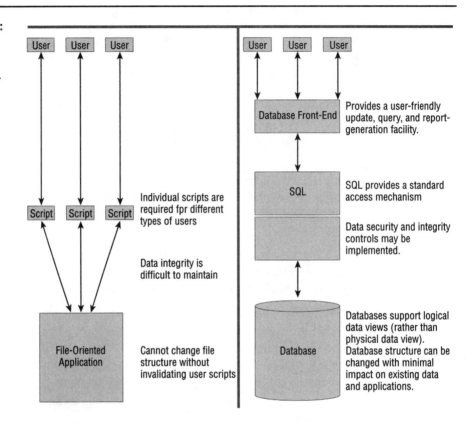

Individual scripts are required fpr different types of users

Data integrity is difficult to maintain

Cannot change file structure without invalidating user scripts

Provides a user-friendly update, query, and report-generation facility.

SQL provides a standard access mechanism

Data security and integrity controls may be implemented.

Databases support logical data views (rather than physical data view). Database structure can be changed with minimal impact on existing data and applications.

Among the various types of database management systems, the *relational* database management system, or RDBMS, has become the most successful and popular. The success of such systems lies in the use of a relational model for organizing the information contained in the database. In the relational model, a database is organized into one or more *tables*, which contain data that is arranged according to the table's *columns*. Each *row* of the table represents an individual table *record*. For example, a database of taxpayers' names and addresses may have the following table columns: taxID, address, city, state, zip code, and country. A record about me in that table would consist of the following *row:*

taxID	address	city	state	zip code	country
123-45-6789	613 Beyer Way #504	San Diego	CA	92154	USA

One or more of the columns of a table are used as *keys* for the table. A key is a group of columns that uniquely identify each row of the table. Take note of that qualifying word "uniquely": In the above taxpayer table, the `taxID` column could be a key, but the `city` column cannot, because a `city` value of San Diego could easily identify hundreds, if not thousands, of table entries. Figure 21.17 summarizes the organization of a relational database.

FIGURE 21.17:

Relational database systems are organized into a series of tables.

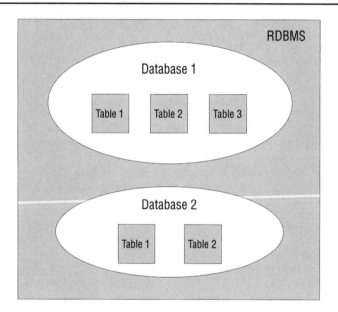

NOTE   An RDBMS can manage more than one database at a time.

The reason for the popularity and success of relational database management systems is that their tabular approach allows databases to be defined in ways which promote consistency by eliminating redundant information. RDBMs are also storage-efficient and are easily updated and queried.

LiveWire Database Services to the Rescue

With all the benefits of using an RDBMS, you're probably wondering why the capability to work with databases was left out of LiveWire. The answer is that it wasn't; in fact, LiveWire provides a `database` object that can be used to access online databases. What LiveWire is lacking is the server. *A database server* is the portion of a distributed database system that manages the database and provides service by responding to database update and query requests. *A database client* is used to send queries and updates to the database and to provide access to the responses of the queries and updates. LiveWire Database Services acts as a database client.

These concepts are illustrated in Figure 21.18.

FIGURE 21.18:

Distributed database systems use a client-server approach.

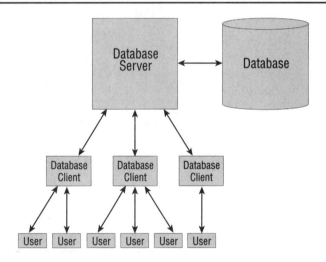

> **NOTE**   LiveWire Database Services works with many database servers, such as those provided by Informix, Oracle, Sybase, and Microsoft.

Setting Up a Microsoft Access Database for Use with LiveWire

I've included a Microsoft Access 97 database named orders.mdb in this chapter's files. Copy this database to your Netscape Web server. You'll need to install Microsoft Access 97 to use this database. In addition, once you've installed Access, you'll need to set up the orders database as an Open Database Connectivity (ODBC) data set. This will allow the database to be accessed from LiveWire.

To set up the data set, open the 32-bit ODBC applet found in the system Control Panel. Refer to Figure 21.19. Click on the System DSN tab and then the Add button. Select the Microsoft Access database driver, and then click the Finish button. The dialog box shown in Figure 21.20 is displayed. Set the Data Source Name to orders, and click the Select button. Find the orders.db file in the Select Database dialog box and click OK.

FIGURE 21.19:

The ODBC setup applet

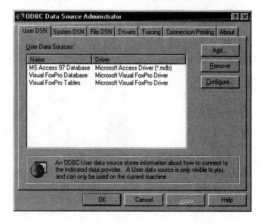

FIGURE 21.20:

The setup dialog box

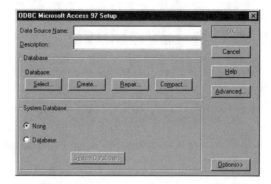

You'll return to the setup dialog shown in Figure 21.21. Click the Advanced button, and fill in the user name and password fields. I use the values `user` and `password` in the examples in this chapter. You can use these values for working with this chapter's examples. When you develop your own applications, make sure that you use a more secure password and a more appropriate user name. Click OK until you are out of the ODBC setup applet.

FIGURE 21.21:

Filling in the setup dialog

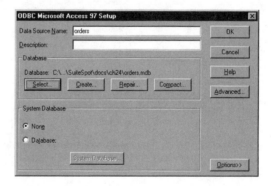

Now that you've set up your database, you can use LiveWire's *dbadmin* application to set up and test the connection between LiveWire and your database. To use *dbadmin*, open the URL http://your.server.com/dbadmin. You'll see the page shown in Figure 21.22. Click the Connect to Database link, and the database connection test page shown in Figure 21.23 is displayed. Fill in the form as shown in Figure 21.23, substituting the user and password values you selected in the ODBC setup.

FIGURE 21.22:

The *dbadmin* opening display

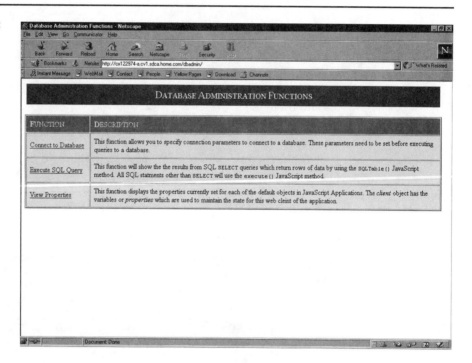

Click the Connect button to connect to your ODBC data set. You'll see (if successful) the Execute Query form shown in Figure 21.24. Change the SQL statement to SELECT * FROM custorder, and click the Execute button. You should see the Web page shown in Figure 21.25. Congratulations! Your database is set up and ready to go!

FIGURE 21.23:

The connection test page

FIGURE 21.23:

The connection test page

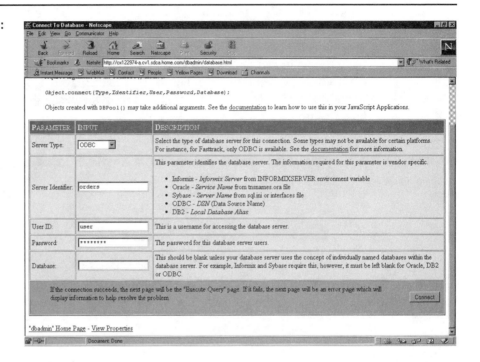

FIGURE 21.24:

The Execute Query
test page

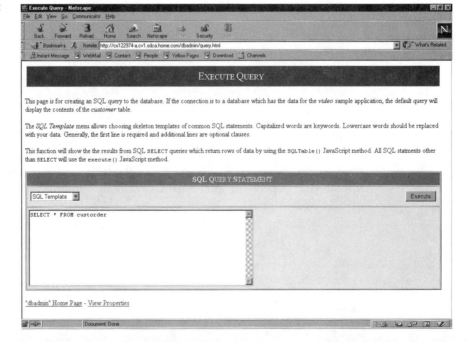

FIGURE 21.25:

The results of the test query

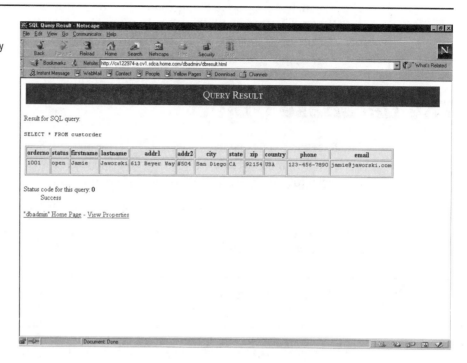

Using LiveWire Database Services

Now that you've installed the test database, you're probably wondering how you go about using LiveWire Database Services. This involves the following steps:

1. Create a database on the database server. (You've done that.)

2. Create one or more database tables to store information. (A table is already in the orders database.)

3. Use the `database` object within a JavaScript script to connect to the database.

4. Use the methods of the `database` object to add data to the database, view data stored in the database, or modify or delete database information.

The first two steps involve the use of your database server (in this case, Microsoft Access). The third and fourth steps involve the use of the `database` object, which is covered in the next section. The fourth step also involves the use of SQL statements. A quick-and-dirty introduction to SQL is provided in the section "Structured Query Language," later in this chapter.

The *database* Object

The `database` object is a server-side JavaScript object. There is only one `database` object; it is named `database`. To use it, you must invoke its `connect()` method to connect it to a database. This is accomplished as follows:

```
database.connect("ODBC","orders","user","password","")
```

In the above statement, `user` is the user name you supplied in the ODBC setup and *password* is the password. The `orders` parameter is the name of the data set.

NOTE   If you use a database other than Access, you'll need to supply other parameters for the connect method. Consult the Netscape documentation for these parameters.

The invocation of the `connect()` method marks the beginning of all database activity. After connecting, you'll use the methods of the `database` object to interact with the database and then disconnect from the database when finished. Table 21.9 summarizes the methods of the `database` object. The following subsections show how to use these methods.

TABLE 21.9: The Methods of the database Object

Method	Description
beginTransaction()	Starts a new database transaction
commitTransaction()	Commits all actions since the last `beginTransaction()` method was invoked
connect(*dbType*, *databaseServer, user, password, database*)	Connects to a database
connected()	Determines whether you are currently connected to a database
cursor(*sqlSelect* [,*updateable*])	Creates a `cursor` object that contains the result of the *sqlSelect* statement. The *updateable* parameter specifies whether the cursor is updateable.

Continued on next page

TABLE 21.9 CONTINUED: The Methods of the database Object

Method	Description
disconnect()	Disconnects from the database
execute(*sql*)	Executes the *sql* statement and returns an error status code
majorErrorCode()	Returns the major error code that is provided by the database server in response to a failed method invocation
majorErrorMessage()	Returns the major error message that is provided by the database server in response to a failed method invocation
minorErrorCode()	Returns the minor error code that is provided by the database server in response to a failed method invocation
minorErrorMessage()	Returns the minor error message that is provided by the database server in response to a failed method invocation
rollbackTransaction()	Undoes all database modifications since the last **beginTransaction()** method was invoked
SQLTable(*sqlSelect*)	Displays the results of the *sqlSelect* statement as an HTML table

NOTE You can only access one database at a time in JavaScript. For most applications, however, a single database is sufficient. If you need to access multiple databases, you can do so sequentially by disconnecting from one and then connecting to another.

Locks and Connections

Two types of database connections may be used to access a database from JavaScript—*standard* or *serial*. A standard connection occurs when the `project` object is not locked. A serial connection occurs when the `project` object is locked.

Under the standard approach, only one connection is required per application—all script instances of the same application share the single connection. This approach lets LiveWire and the database server handle any issues that may be related to concurrent access to the database; it also greatly simplifies database access. However, it has the disadvantage that you may too easily reach the maximum number of database connections allowed by your database license. In addition, all database connections share the same user name and password, and therefore all have equivalent database access.

Under the serial approach, only one script instance is allowed to access the database at a time. The script instance acquires the project lock and retains access to the database until the project is unlocked. Each script instance connects individually and therefore can be assigned different user names and passwords. The drawback to this approach is the overhead required for the project locking and for establishing the database connections.

NOTE   The examples in this chapter use the standard approach but add additional checks to ensure that a database connection is established before performing any database operations.

Executing SQL

Once a connection to a database has been established, the `execute()`, `SQLTable()`, and `cursor()` methods can be used to execute SQL statements that update or query the database.

NOTE   If you are not familiar with SQL, the section "The Structured Query Language," later in this chapter, provides a quick introduction.

The `execute()` method takes a string containing a SQL statement as a parameter, executes the statement, and returns an error status code. The SQL statement may be any SQL statement that does not return an answer set. These statements are database updates rather than queries. The "Error Handling" section, later in this chapter, shows how to handle the error status codes returned by methods that execute SQL statements. An example of the `execute()` method follows:

```
database.execute("DELETE FROM custorder WHERE orderno < 2000")
```

The above statement tells the database server to delete all rows in the custorder table where the value of the orderno column in less than 200.

The `SQLTable()` method is an invaluable tool for querying a database. It takes a SQL SELECT statement as a parameter, executes the statement, and displays the result of the query as an HTML table. For example, the following statement queries the database for all rows of the custorder table sorted by the orderno column:

```
database.SQLTable("SELECT * FROM custorder ORDER BY orderno)
```

The cursor() method can be used to query or update a database. It takes a SQL SELECT statement as a parameter and an optional Boolean value, indicating whether or not the cursor is updateable. It executes the SQL statement and stores the resulting answer set as a cursor object. The cursor object can be used to perform subsequent database operations, as described in the next section. An updateable cursor object is one that can be used to update the database. A cursor object that is not updateable (the default case) can only be used to query the database. The following statement creates a cursor object that contains all rows of the custorder table for which the status column is open:

```
database.cursor("SELECT * FROM custorder WHERE status = 'open'",true)
```

This cursor can be updated.

Using the Cursor

A cursor object is created as the result of invoking the cursor() method of the database object. The cursor object contains the answer set that results from a SQL SELECT statement. The properties and methods of the cursor object can then be used to perform operations on the answer set. The methods of the cursor object are summarized in Table 21.10.

T A B L E 2 1 . 1 0 : Methods of the cursor Object

Method	Description
close()	Closes the cursor object and releases memory resources that it used
columnName(n)	Returns the name of the *n*th column of the cursor object (starts at 0)
columns()	Returns the number of columns in a cursor object
deleteRow(table)	Deletes the row in *table* corresponding to the current row of the cursor. Returns an error status code. The cursor must be updateable.
insertRow(table)	Inserts the row in *table* corresponding to the current row of the cursor. Returns an error status code. The cursor must be capable of being updated.
next()	Moves to the next row of the answer set associated with the cursor. Returns **false** if the current row is the last row of the cursor (before movement) and **true** otherwise.
updateRow()	Updates the row in *table* corresponding to the current row of the cursor. Returns an error status code. The cursor must be capable of being updated.

The `cursor` object is associated with a pointer, which indicates the rows in the `cursor` object's answer set. This pointer is initially placed before the first row. The `next()` method is used to move the pointer to the first row and then to subsequent rows. The current row is the row at which the pointer is currently located.

NOTE   LiveWire Database Services automatically closes all `cursor` objects at the end of a client request.

The columns of a `cursor` object are properties of the `cursor` object. They can be referred to by name or by indexing the `cursor` object. For example, suppose the `rows` variable is assigned a `cursor` object as the result of the following statement:

```
rows=database.cursor("SELECT orderno, status, lastname FROM custorder")
```

The answer set has the three columns orderno, status, and lastname. You can refer to the column values of the current row using `rows.orderno`, `rows.status`, and `rows.lastname`. You can also refer to these values using `rows[0]`, `rows[1]`, and `rows[2]`.

Each of the columns of the current row is itself a `cursorColumn` object with two methods—`blobImage()` and `blobLink()`, as described below. (The acronym *BLOb* stands for *Binary Large Object*; it refers to large objects, such as images and multimedia objects, that are stored in the database.)

The *blobImage()* Method

The `blobImage()` method causes the value of the `cursorColumn` object to be displayed using an `<img>` tag. Its syntax is as follows:

```
cursor.column.blobImage(format [, alt] [, align] [,width] [,height]
[,border] [,ismap])
```

The *format* parameter may be GIF, JPEG, or any other MIME image format. The *alt, align, width, height,* and *border* attributes specify the corresponding attributes of the image tag. The *ismap* parameter is `boolean`; if it's `true`, then an ISMAP attribute is added to the `image` tag.

To see how `blobImage()` works, consider the following code:

```
rows=database.cursor("SELECT imageID, title, image FROM imageTable")
rows.next()
write(rows.image.blobImage("GIF"))
```

The above code generates an image tag containing the name of a temporary .gif image generated by the database from the BLOb contained in the image column of the first row of the cursor object assigned to the rows variable.

The *blobLink()* Method

The blobLink() method is used to create a hyperlink to a BLOb. Its syntax is as follows:

```
cursor.column,blobLink(mimeType, text)
```

where *mimeType* is the MIME type of the BLOb, and *text* is the text to be used in the link. For example, the following code:

```
rows=database.cursor("SELECT imageID, title, image FROM imageTable")
rows.next()
```

```
write(rows.image.blobLink("image/gif","Click here to see an image."))
```

creates a hyperlink to the .gif image contained in the BLOb with the text, "Click here to see an image."

Transaction Processing

Most databases allow database updates to be performed as *transactions*. A transaction consists of one or more database operations that are grouped together. Transaction processing causes the transaction to be performed as a single unit. A lock is acquired during the processing of the transaction and prevents other script instances from creating conflicts with the transaction that is in progress. Transactions are also used to perform database operations that can be undone if an error occurs before all steps of the transaction are completed. The database object supports transaction processing.

Invoke the beginTransaction() method to start a transaction and the commitTransaction() method to end the transaction. If you want to undo a transaction before it is committed, invoke the rollbackTransaction() method.

If transaction processing is not specified, it is implicitly performed on a statement-by-statement basis, as each SQL statement is executed.

NOTE   A transaction is automatically committed when the HTML page containing the script of the transaction processing is no longer being processed.

Error Handling

Error status codes are returned for the following methods of the `database` object:

- `beginTransaction()`
- `commitTransaction()`
- `execute()`
- `rollbackTransaction()`

Error status codes are also returned for the following methods of the `cursor` object:

- `deleteRow()`
- `insertRow()`
- `updateRow()`

An error status code of 0 indicates a successful database operation. When the error status code is 5 (server error) or 7 (vendor library error), you can use the following methods of the `database` object to find out more information about the error:

- `majorErrorCode()`
- `majorErrorMessage()`
- `minorErrorCode()`
- `minorErrorMessage()`

The major and minor error codes are the primary and secondary codes returned by the server. The major and minor messages are the messages associated with these error codes.

Structured Query Language

So far you've learned how the methods of the database and cursor objects can be used to update and query an online database by executing SQL statements. You've seen some examples of SQL statements in the descriptions of these methods. But what exactly is SQL?

SQL is a language for accessing RDBMSs that was developed by IBM during the early days of RDBMS research. It was standardized during the later 1980s and has become the de facto standard query language for RDBMSs. The following URL is the SQL Standards Home Page and contains links to all types of information about SQL: `http://www.jcc.com/sql_stnd.html`.

The next URL contains a great tutorial on learning SQL. If you are new to SQL, I highly recommend taking this tutorial: `http://w3.one.net/~jhoffman/sqltut.htm`.

> **NOTE**   The SQL acronym is pronounced "sequel."

While an introduction to SQL is a book in itself, in this section I'll try to give you enough of a background to get you going. For a more thorough introduction, I recommend taking the aforementioned tutorial and browsing the SQL Standards Home Page.

In any database application there are a number of core operations that you'll want to perform:

- Create and modify a database
- Create and modify a database table
- Add rows to the table
- Delete rows from the table
- Update rows in the table
- Query tables

There are SQL statements that allow you to do each of the above. Once you learn how to use these statements, you will have a basic knowledge of database programming.

> **NOTE**   In the following paragraphs I'll present the basic information you'll need for performing these core operations. For the first two operations, however—creating or modifying a database or a database table—refer to the documentation provided by your database management system.

Adding, Deleting, and Updating Rows

You add rows to a table using the INSERT statement, delete rows from a table using the DELETE statement, and update a table row using the UPDATE statement. Pretty simple.

For the purposes of this section and the next, let's suppose our database consists of a single `custorder` table with the following columns: orderno, status, firstName, lastName, addr1, addr2, city, state, zip, phone, and email. Let these columns correspond to the `client` properties of the `diskette` application.

The *INSERT* Statement

There are two forms for the INSERT statement. The syntax of the first form is

```
INSERT INTO table VALUES (value1, value2, …, valuen)
```
where *table* is the name of the table into which the row is to be inserted and *value1* through *valuen* are the values of the row. For example, the following statement inserts a row into the `custorder` table.

```
INSERT INTO custorder VALUES ('1001','open','Don','Woodbridge','714 Elm
Street', 'Apartment B', 'Scranton', 'PA', '18504', 'USA', '717-555-
5555', 'woody@work.com')
```

Note that a value for each column is specified. To enter a row without specifying all of the columns, use the second form of the INSERT statement, the syntax of which follows:

```
INSERT INTO table (columnA, columnB, …, columnJ) VALUES (valueA,
valueB, …, valueJ)
```

The values for *columnA* through *columnJ* are the names of the columns into which data is inserted, and *valueA* through *valueJ* are the values to be placed in these columns. All other columns in the row are assigned a null value. For example, the following statement inserts a row into `custorder` with the `orderno` column set to 1111, the firstName column set to `Fred`, and the lastName column set to `Masters`.

```
INSERT INTO custorder (orderno, firstName, lastName) VALUES ('1111',
'Fred', 'Masters')
```

The *DELETE* Statement

The syntax of the DELETE statement is as follows:

```
DELETE FROM table [WHERE condition]
```

The *condition* specifies a condition that must be met for a row to be deleted. The following are examples of using the DELETE statement.

```
DELETE FROM custorder WHERE orderno < 1001
DELETE FROM custorder WHERE lastName = 'Jones'
DELETE FROM custorder WHERE orderno > 5000 AND status = 'open'
```

> **WARNING** If the WHERE clause of the DELETE statement is omitted, then all rows of the table are deleted.

The *UPDATE* Statement

The syntax of the UPDATE statement is as follows:

```
UPDATE table SET [columnA = valueA, …, columnJ = valueJ] [WHERE
condition]
```

The *columnI = valueI* expressions specify how selected columns of a row are to be updated. The *condition* selects the rows that are to be updated. If the WHERE clause is omitted, all rows of the table are updated. An example of the UPDATE statement is as follows:

```
UPDATE custorder SET status = 'West Coast' WHERE zip >= 9000
```

It sets the status column of all rows where the zip code is 9000 or higher to West Coast.

Querying Tables

SQL provides in the SELECT statement all of the capabilities that you'll likely need for querying data from a database. The SELECT statement returns rows consisting of selected columns from one or more tables that meet certain conditions. The rows returned from a SELECT statement are referred to as an *answer set*. In JavaScript, the answer set is either displayed by the SQLTable() method or returned as a cursor object.

While a complete treatment of the SELECT statement is beyond the scope of this section, I'll present a limited description of the SELECT syntax that will get you started. For a more detailed treatment of the SELECT statement, check out the Web tutorial at http://w3.one.net/~jhoffman/sqltut.htm.

The following is a limited description of the SELECT statement syntax that is used in typical database queries:

```
SELECT columnList FROM tableList [WHERE condition] [ORDER BY column]
```

In the above description, *columnList* is a comma-separated list of columns and *tableList* is a comma-separated list of tables. The answer set generated by the SELECT statement contains exactly those columns specified. These columns may come from one or more tables. The rows in the answer set must meet the *condition* of the WHERE clause and are sorted by the *column* specified in the ORDER BY clause.

The following is an example of the SELECT statement that returns an answer set consisting of the order, status, lastName, and phone columns from the custorder table:

```
SELECT orderno, status, lastName, phone FROM custorder WHERE status =
'open' ORDER BY orderno
```

These rows must have open as the value of the status column and are sorted by the orderno field.

Updating the *Diskette* Application

Now that we've covered all of the required background information, let's update the *Diskette* application to take advantage of LiveWire Database Services. We'll use the orders database (and its custorder table) that you set up earlier in the chapter. We'll then update diskette to add customer orders to the database.

After porting *Diskette* over to LiveWire Database Services, we'll create two new applications—orders and updateDB—that will let employees of the imaginary "Diskette Center" view the contents of their database and update the database using SQL. You can use these two new applications to experiment with and learn SQL on your own.

Adding Database Support to *Diskette*

In this section, we'll update *Diskette* to work with the orders database instead of with a text file. The start.htm, process.htm, and display.htm files will not need to be modified. Only finish.htm will need to be changed. Go ahead and update it as shown in Listing 21.12. Also create the thanks.htm and error.htm files shown in Listings 21.13 and 24.14.

What Are the Changes to *finish.htm*?

The `connected()` method is used to determine whether the database is currently connected. If it is not, then the `connect()` method is used to connect to the `orders` database.

The second invocation of `connected()` determines whether the `connect()` method succeeded. If it did not, then the `error.htm` file is loaded to display an error message. Otherwise, the `insertSQL` variable is used to build a SQL INSERT statement from the properties of the `client` object. The `execute()` method is invoked to execute the SQL statement. The resulting error status is used to determine whether the `thanks.htm` file is loaded to thank the user or the `error.htm` file is loaded to display an error message.

Listing 21.12   **Updating finish.htm to Use the Orders Database (finish.htm)**

```
<HTML>
<HEAD>
<TITLE>Diskette Center</TITLE>
</HEAD>
<BODY>
<SERVER>
project.lock()
if(project.nextOrder==null) project.nextOrder=1000
project.nextOrder=parseInt(project.nextOrder)+1
client.orderno=project.nextOrder
project.unlock()
client.status="open"
if(!database.connected())
 database.connect("ODBC","orders","user","password","")
if(database.connected()){
 insertSQL="INSERT INTO custorder VALUES ("
 insertSQL+="'"+client.orderno+"',"
 insertSQL+="'"+client.status+"',"
 insertSQL+="'"+client.firstName+"',"
 insertSQL+="'"+client.lastName+"',"
 insertSQL+="'"+client.addr1+"',"
 insertSQL+="'"+client.addr2+"',"
 insertSQL+="'"+client.city+"',"
 insertSQL+="'"+client.state+"',"
```

```
insertSQL+="'"+client.zip+"',"
insertSQL+="'"+client.country+"',"
insertSQL+="'"+client.phone+"',"
insertSQL+="'"+client.email+"')"
errorStatus=database.execute(insertSQL)
client.errorStatus="Execute error: "+errorStatus
if(errorStatus!=0) redirect("error.htm")
redirect("thanks.htm")
}else{
client.errorStatus="Can not open database."
redirect("error.htm")
}
</SERVER>
</BODY>
</HTML>
```

Listing 21.13   Thanking the User for the Order (thanks.htm)

```
<HTML>
<HEAD>
<TITLE>Diskette Center</TITLE>
</HEAD>
<BODY>
<H1>Thank you for your order!</H1>
<H2>Your order number is <SERVER>
write(client.orderno)</SERVER>.</H2>
</BODY>
</HTML>
```

Listing 21.14   Displaying an Error Message to the User (error.htm)

```
<HTML>
<HEAD>
<TITLE>Diskette Center</TITLE>
</HEAD>
<BODY>
<H1>Sorry! Your order could not be processed.</H1>
<H2><SERVER>write(client.errorStatus)</SERVER></H2>
</BODY>
</HTML>
```

Compiling and Running *Diskette*

Use the following command to compile the application:

```
jsac -v -o diskette.web start.htm process.htm display.htm finish.htm
thanks.htm error.htm
```

After moving it to your Web server, launch Application Manager, and then modify the *Diskette* application to give it at least one database connection. When you're finished, restart *Diskette*, and then run it by clicking on the Run link of Application Manager. Use *Diskette to* add a few orders to the database. (I know this is boring, but do it anyway—you'll need some data to work with in the next section). When you add each order, you should receive a customer order number, as shown in Figure 21.26.

FIGURE 21.26:

Each order added to the database results in a new order number being generated (Listing 21.13).

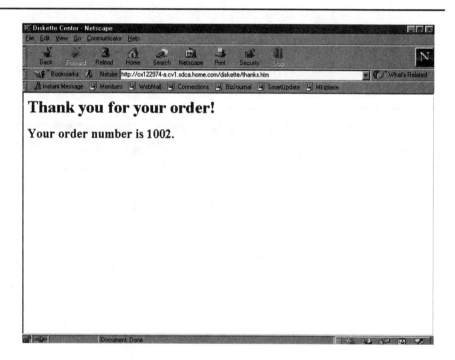

Viewing the Database

So far all we've done is update *Diskette* to use the `orders` database instead of the `orders.txt` file. We need to provide a way for the employees of the Diskette Center to view the contents of the database so that they can see what orders need to be filled. That's what we'll do in this section. We'll do it by creating a new project, called `orders`, that will let users view all or part of the `custorder` table of the `orders` database.

This project illustrates the power and simplicity of using a SQL-capable database with server-side JavaScript. It consists of the single file, `viewdb.htm`, shown in Listing 21.15. Compile the file using the following command:

```
jsac -v -o orders.web viewdb.htm
```

and move the `orders.web` file to your Web server. Start Application Manager, and add the `orders` application. Be sure to give it at least one database connection. When you run `orders`, it displays the contents of your database, as shown in Figure 21.27. Experiment with the SQL SELECT statement to view different subsets of the database.

FIGURE 21.27:

The SQL SELECT statement provides a powerful tool for querying a relational database (Listing 21.15).

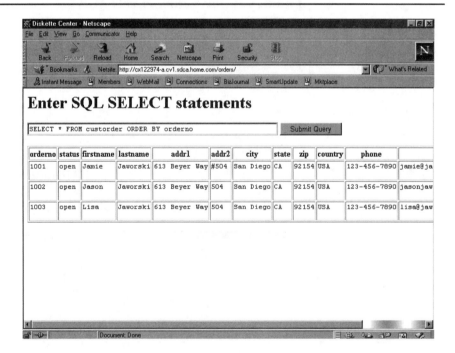

Listing 21.15	Using the SQL SELECT Statement in Your Database Applications (viewdb.htm)

```
<HTML>
<HEAD>
<TITLE>Diskette Center</TITLE>
</HEAD>
<BODY>
<H1>Enter SQL SELECT statements</H1>
<FORM ACTION="viewdb.htm">
<INPUT TYPE="TEXT" SIZE="60" NAME="sql"
 VALUE="SELECT * FROM custorder ORDER BY orderno">
<INPUT TYPE="SUBMIT">
</FORM>
<SERVER>
if(!database.connected())
 database.connect("ODBC","orders","user","password","")
if(database.connected())
 if(request.sql==null)
  database.SQLTable("SELECT * FROM custorder ORDER BY orderno")
 else
  database.SQLTable(request.sql)
else write("<H1>Could not connect to database.</H1>")
</SERVER>
</BODY>
</HTML>
```

How *viewdb.htm* Works

The body of viewdb.htm consists of a simple HTML form that contains a text field for entering SQL SELECT statements. The default value of the field is a SQL statement that selects all rows and columns of the custorder table. The form is submitted to itself for processing.

The server script within viewdb.htm begins by connecting to the orders database. It checks to see if the value of the sql text field submitted is null, which is the case the first time viewdb.htm is loaded. In this case, it selects all columns and rows of custorder.

If the value of the sql field is not null, then the submitted SQL statement is executed.

Providing SQL Access to *orders*

We now can add data to `orders`, using the *Diskette* application, and view its contents, using the *Orders* application, but there's still something missing. We need to add the capability to update specific rows of the database and to directly insert and delete table rows. To do this, we'll build an `updateDB` application that will consist of three files—`getsql.htm`, `dosql.htm`, and `error.htm`. The `getsql.htm` file is shown in Listing 21.16, and `dosql.htm` is shown in Listing 21.17. The `error.htm` file is the same as that shown earlier, in Listing 21.14. The `getsql.htm` file is the default page for the `updateDB` application.

Compile the three files to create `updateDB.web` using the following compiler command:

```
jsac -v -o updateDB.web getsql.htm dosql.htm error.htm
```

Move `updateDB.web` to your Web server, and create the `updateDB` application using Application Manager. When you run `updateDB`, it displays the Web page shown in Figure 21.28. Enter a couple of SQL UPDATE and DELETE statements to update your database. You can use this application to practice your SQL.

FIGURE 21.28:

SQL statements can also be used to update a relational database (Listing 21.16).

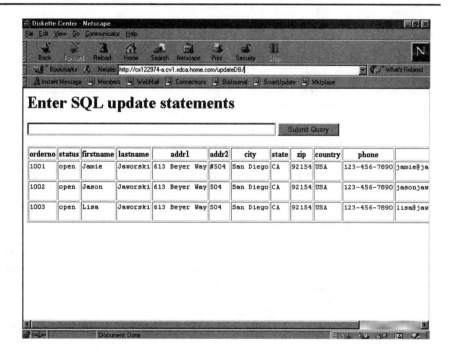

**Listing 21.16   Getting a Database Update Command from the User
(getsql.htm)**

```
<HTML>
<HEAD>
<TITLE>Diskette Center</TITLE>
</HEAD>
<BODY>
<H1>Enter SQL update statements</H1>
<FORM ACTION="dosql.htm">
<INPUT TYPE="TEXT" SIZE="60" NAME="sql">
<INPUT TYPE="SUBMIT">
</FORM>
<SERVER>
if(!database.connected())
 database.connect("ODBC","orders","user","password","")
if(database.connected())
 database.SQLTable("SELECT * FROM custorder ORDER BY orderno")
else write("<H1>Could not connect to database.</H1>")
</SERVER>
</BODY>
</HTML>
```

Listing 21.17   Processing the Database Update Command (dosql.htm)

```
<HTML>
<HEAD>
<TITLE>Diskette Center</TITLE>
</HEAD>
<BODY>
<SERVER>
if(!database.connected())
 database.connect("ODBC","orders","user","password","")
if(database.connected()){
 errorStatus=database.execute(request.sql)
 if(errorStatus!=0){
  client.errorStatus="Error: "+errorStatus
  redirect("error.htm")
 }else redirect("getsql.htm")
}else{
```

```
 client.errorStatus="<H1>Could not connect to database.</H1>"
 redirect("error.htm")
}
</SERVER>
</BODY>
</HTML>
```

How *updateDB* Works

The getsql.htm file is similar to viewdb.htm in that it consists of a SQL entry form, followed by a server script. In the case of getsql.htm, the SQL entry form is used to enter SQL UPDATE, DELETE, and INSERT statements. The form is submitted to dosql.htm for processing. The server script that follows the form uses the SQLTable() method to display the entire contents of the custorder table. This allows you to view the effects of any database updates.

The dossql.htm file processes the getsql.htm form data by executing the SQL statement entered into the sql field using the execute() method. Errors are processed by loading error.htm. If no errors occur, the getsql.htm file is reloaded.

Summary

In this chapter, you learned how to use LiveWire to create Web applications that eliminate the need for CGI programs. You learned how to use JavaScript 's server programming capabilities to process data received from browsers and to dynamically return new Web pages to browsers. You also learned how to use LiveWire Database Services to access online databases. You learned how to use the database object to open database connections, add data to databases, and perform database queries. You were introduced to the Structured Query Language (SQL) and learned how to execute SQL statements using the methods of the database object. In the next chapter, you'll learn how to use JScript to program Microsoft servers.

CHAPTER
TWENTY-TWO

22

Scripting Microsoft Servers

- Active Server Pages

- ASP Scripting

- Server-Side Objects

- Connecting to Databases

- Windows Scripting Host

- Remote Scripting

In the previous chapter, you learned how to develop server-side scripts with Netscape servers. Chapter 21 covered the basics of server-side scripting, database access, and SQL. This chapter shows how to apply the same techniques that you learned in Chapter 21 to Microsoft servers. It begins with Active Server Pages (ASP) and ASP scripting and shows how the Web applications you developed in Chapter 21 can be translated into Active Server Pages. It describes approaches to database communication with ASP and covers Windows Scripting Host (WSH) and remote scripting technologies. When you finish this chapter, you'll be familiar with the basics of Microsoft's server-side scripting technologies.

Active Server Pages

Active Server Pages (ASP) is Microsoft's name for its server-side scripting environment. ASP is analogous to Netscape's LiveWire. ASP supports the development of Web applications that integrate HTML, server-side JScript, and server-side ActiveX components. In this chapter, I'll concentrate on the server-side JScript aspect of ASP.

NOTE   The ASP examples in this chapter were developed on Windows 98 using Personal Web Server. Personal Web Server is provided on the Windows 98 installation CD. Personal Web Server also runs on Windows NT Workstation 4 and Windows 95. It can be downloaded from Microsoft's Web site. The ASP examples in this chapter also work with Microsoft's Internet Information Server (IIS) 4.

Active Server Pages are implemented in terms of an ASP processor that is integrated with Microsoft Web servers. When an `.asp` file is requested from the Web server, the server passes the requested file to the ASP processor. The ASP processor reads through the file and executes any scripts that are embedded in the file. The ASP processor formats the Web page with the results of the script execution and sends them to the requesting browser. Figure 22.1 provides an overview of this process.

FIGURE 22.1:

How ASP works.

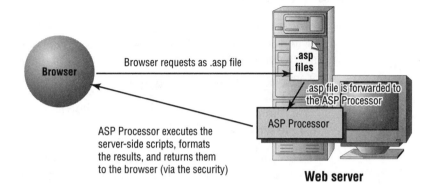

The ASP processor transforms the results of server-side scripts to standard HTML (even though the file might have an .asp extension) before forwarding the scripts to Web browsers. This allows any Web browser to interact with ASP. The ASP processor can also be instructed (through server-side scripts) to interact with databases and server-side ActiveX components. This capability allows server-side scripts to integrate corporate databases and business applications into the ASP environment.

NOTE   ASP supports other scripting languages, such as VBScript and Perl.

ASP Scripting

ASP makes use of Web pages with the `.asp` extension. You can create `.asp` files immediately by just changing the extensions of your `.htm` and `.html` files to `.asp`. That's all it takes to create `.asp` pages. However, to include server-side scripts in `.asp` pages, you'll need to learn the about the server-side objects supported by ASP and the syntax for including scripts in `.asp` pages. I'll start with the basic syntax in this section and cover the server-side object in the next section.

ASP Directives

Because ASP supports a variety of server-side scripting languages, you should always indicate to ASP what scripting language you use in a particular `.asp` file. This is accomplished by placing the following line at the beginning of an `.asp` file:

```
<%@ LANGUAGE=ScriptingLanguage %>
```

In the case of JScript, the above line is as follows:

```
<%@ LANGUAGE=JScript %>
```

If you only include HTML in an `.asp` file, you do not need to add the above line. Your Web server may allow you to configure the default scripting language to use with ASP. In this case, you do not need to include a directive in every `.asp` file. However, it is good practice to do so and will avoid any problems if you move your `.asp` files to a new Web server.

TIP   ASP supports other directives besides the language directive. Consult the ASP manual that comes with your Web server for more information on these directives.

Script Delimiters and the = Operator

Server-side scripts are identified within an `.asp` file by the <% and %> delimiters. Listing 22.1 provides an example of an `.asp` page that embeds a script using these delimiters. This file is a conversion of the *Simple* application of Chapter 21, "Scripting Netscape Servers," from LiveWire to ASP.

NOTE   To install `simple.asp` or any of the `.asp` files in this chapter, just put the file in a directory that is accessible from your Microsoft Web server. To run the file, simply open the file's URL in your Web browser.

In LiveWire (refer to Chapter 21), the `write()` method is used to inject the results of server-side scripts into the Web pages it produces. ASP uses the = operator instead of the `write()` method. The = operator writes the string value of an expression to the Web page produced by the ASP processor. Figure 22.2 shows the result of executing simple.asp (see Listing 22.1). It informs the user of her or his browser type, IP address, HTTP version, and the host name of the Web server.

FIGURE 22.2:

The results of executing
simple.asp (Listing 22.1).

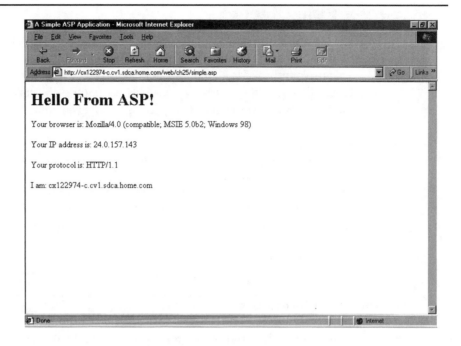

Listing 22.1	The Simple Application of Chapter 21 Converted to ASP (simple.asp)

```
<%@ LANGUAGE=JScript %>
<HTML>
<HEAD>
<TITLE>A Simple ASP Application</TITLE>
</HEAD>
<BODY>
<H1>Hello From ASP!</H1>
Your browser is: <% =Request.ServerVariables("HTTP_USER_AGENT") %><P>
Your IP address is: <% =Request.ServerVariables("REMOTE_ADDR") %><P>
Your protocol is: <% =Request.ServerVariables("SERVER_PROTOCOL") %><P>
I am: <% =Request.ServerVariables("SERVER_NAME") %>
</BODY>
</HTML>
```

Server-Side Objects

The scripts of Listing 22.1 make extensive use of the **Request** object. This object is analogous to the **request** object of LiveWire. In addition, to the **Request** object, ASP also supports the **Response**, **Session**, **Application**, and **Server** objects. Table 22.1 shows the correspondence between these objects and the LiveWire objects you studied in Chapter 21, "Scripting Netscape Servers."

TABLE 22.1: ASP Objects vs. LiveWire Objects

ASP Object	LiveWire Object
Request	request
Session	client
Application	project
Server	server

I'll cover each of these objects and the **Response** object in the following sections.

The *Request* Object

The Request object of ASP is logically equivalent to (but syntactically different from) the request object of LiveWire. It encapsulates the browser's request of the server. You can use its properties to access the information that is passed in an HTTP request. These properties are as follows:

ClientCertificate   The values of fields sent in any client certificate

Cookies   A collection of cookie values sent by the browser in the HTTP request

Form   A collection of posted form values

QueryString   A collection of values associated with a **request** query string

ServerVariables   A collection of environment variables related to the HTTP request

TotalBytes   The total number of bytes sent in the body of a request

The Request object supports the BinaryRead() method, which is used to access binary data that is supplied as the result of an HTTP POST.

Listing 22.1 shows how the ServerVariables collection is used to access the HTTP_USER_AGENT, REMOTE_ADDR, SERVER_PROTOCOL, and SERVER_NAME environment variables of the HTTP request. Listings 22.2 and 22.3 show how the Form collection is used to gain access to submitted form values. The form.asp and newuser.asp files are analogous to the form.htm and newuser.htm LiveWire files of Chapter 21, "Scripting Netscape Servers." By comparing these files, you can see just how similar the ASP Request object is to the LiveWire request object. Figures 22.3 and 22.4 show the browser output generated by form.asp and newuser.asp.

FIGURE 22.3:

An HTML registration form (Listing 22.2)

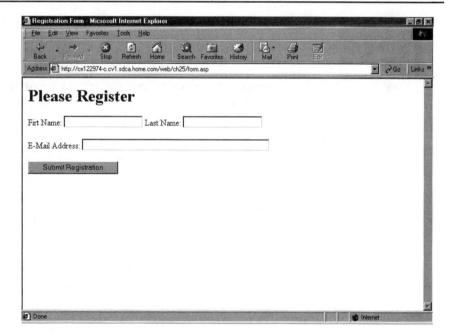

FIGURE 22.4:

Displaying the
information received
by ASP (Listing 22.3)

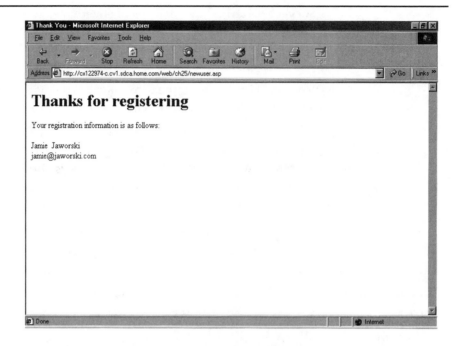

Listing 22.2   **A Registration Form That Sends Its Results to an ASP File
(form.asp)**

```
<HTML>
<HEAD>
<TITLE>Registration Form</TITLE>
</HEAD>
<BODY>
<H1>Please Register</H1>
<FORM NAME="registration" ACTION="newuser.asp"
 METHOD="POST">
```

```
Firt Name: <INPUT TYPE="text" NAME="firstName">
Last Name: <INPUT TYPE="text" NAME="lastName"><P>
E-Mail Address: <INPUT TYPE="text" NAME="email" SIZE="50"><P>
<INPUT TYPE="SUBMIT" VALUE="Submit Registration">
</FORM>
</BODY>
</HTML>
```

Listing 22.3   An ASP File That Reads and Displays the Form Results (newuser.asp)

```
<%@ LANGUAGE=JSCRIPT %>
<HTML>
<HEAD>
<TITLE>Thank You</TITLE>
</HEAD>
<BODY>
<H1>Thanks for registering</H1>
<P>Your registration information is as follows:</P>
<P>
<% =Request.Form("firstName") %>
 <% =Request.Form("lastName") %>
<BR>
<% =Request.Form("email") %>
</P>
</BODY>
</HTML>
```

Listings 22.4 and 22.5 show how the QueryString collection is used in ASP. The map.asp and disp-xy.asp files are analogous to the map.htm and disp-xy.htm files of Chapter 21, "Scripting Netscape Servers." Figures 22.5 and 22.6 show the output produced by the ASP files.

FIGURE 22.5:

A client-side image map
(Listing 22.4)

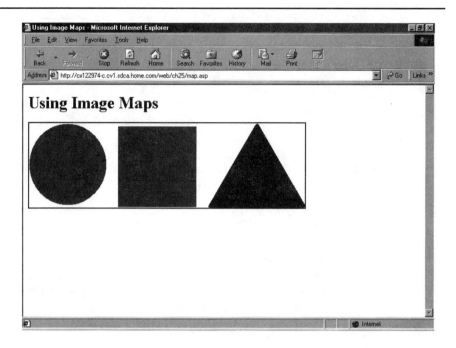

FIGURE 22.6:

Displaying the image map
information received by
ASP (Listing 22.5)

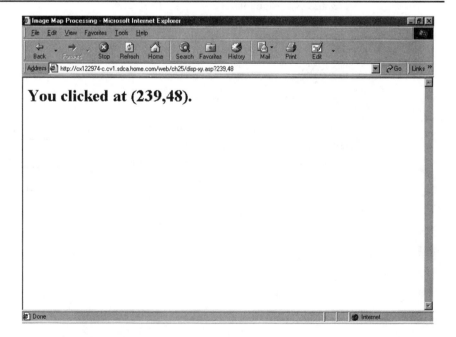

Listing 22.4   An Image Map That Sends Its Results to an ASP File (map.asp)

```
<HTML>
<HEAD>
<TITLE>Using Image Maps</TITLE>
</HEAD>
<BODY>
<H1>Using Image Maps</H1>
<A HREF="disp-xy.asp">
<IMG SRC="shapes.gif" ISMAP="ISMAP">
</A>
</BODY>
</HTML>
```

Listing 22.5   An ASP File That Reads and Displays the Results of the User's Click (disp-xy.asp)

```
<%@ LANGUAGE=JSCRIPT %>
<HTML>
<HEAD>
<TITLE>Image Map Processing</TITLE>
</HEAD>
<BODY>
<H1>You clicked at
(<% =Request.QueryString %>).
</H1>
</BODY>
</HTML>
```

Listings 22.6 and 22.7 are ASP conversions of the `qstring.htm` and `disp-qs.htm` files of Chapter 21, "Scripting Netscape Servers." The output of these files is provided in Figures 22.7 and 22.8.

FIGURE 22.7:

A link with a custom query string (Listing 22.6)

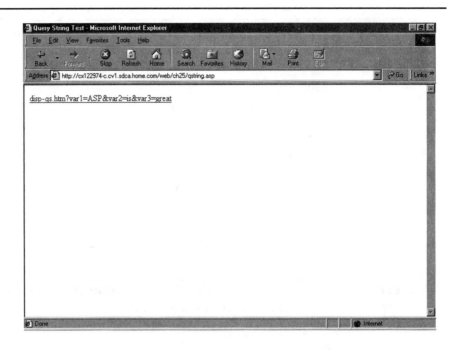

FIGURE 22.8:

Displaying the query string information received by ASP (Listing 22.7)

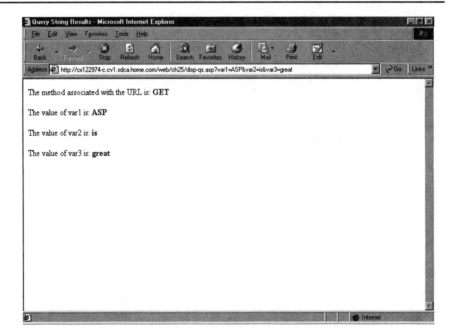

Listing 22.6   **A Custom Link That Sends Its Results to an ASP File (qstring.asp)**

```
<HTML>
<HEAD>
<TITLE>Query String Test</TITLE>
</HEAD>
<BODY>
<A HREF="disp-qs.asp?var1=ASP&var2=is&var3=great">
disp-qs.htm?var1=ASP&var2=is&var3=great
</A>
</BODY>
</HTML>
```

Listing 22.7   **An ASP File That Reads and Displays the Results of the Query String (disp-qs.asp)**

```
<%@ LANGUAGE=JSCRIPT %>
<HTML>
<HEAD>
<TITLE>Query String Results</TITLE>
</HEAD>
<BODY>
<P>The method associated with the URL is:
<B><% =Request.ServerVariables("REQUEST_METHOD") %></B></P>
<P>The value of var1 is:
<B><% =Request.QueryString("var1") %></B></P>
<P>The value of var2 is:
<B><% =Request.QueryString("var2") %></B></P>
<P>The value of var3 is:
<B><% =Request.QueryString("var3") %></B></P>
</BODY>
</HTML>
```

The *Response* Object

The Response object is used to formulate an HTTP response that is sent back to the user's browser. It does not have a LiveWire analogy. Its properties and methods are used to provide low-level control of server-to-browser communication. In most cases, you won't need this fine level of control and can use the simple = operator, as shown in the examples in the previous section. One Response method of note is the Redirect() method, which you can use to redirect the user's browser to a new URL other than the one it originally requested. The ASP documentation contains much more information on the Response object and the Redirect() method than I have covered here.

The *Session* Object

The Session object is analogous to the LiveWire client object. It is used to span multiple requests from the same browser. A Session object exists for the duration of a browser's interaction with a set of Web pages from a particular server directory path. A Session object also expires after a predefined timeout period. The default value for this timeout is 20 minutes. The properties of the Session object are as follows:

CodePage Provides access to the language encoding used for ASP output

Contents Identifies the script-defined session variables

LCID Identifies the Web server's locale (country/language)

SessionID Provides access to the session identifier used by ASP

StaticObjects Provides access to any server-side objects (server-side ActiveX controls) that are created with the <OBJECT> tag

Timeout The session's timeout period in minutes

The Session object supports the Abandon() method, which is used to destroy a Session object and release its associated resources.

You'll learn how to use the Session object later in this chapter in the section, "The *Diskette* Application."

The *Application* Object

The Application object is analogous to LiveWire's project object. It maintains information about multiple sessions that interact with a particular Web application. It is used to share common objects across user sessions. It supports the

`Contents` and `StaticObjects` properties and the `Lock()` and `Unlock()` methods. The `Contents` property is a collection that identifies the application variables created by user scripts. The `StaticObjects` property is a collection that provides access to server-side objects identified by the `<OBJECT>` tag. The `Lock()` and `Unlock()` methods are analogous to the `lock()` and `unlock()` methods of LiveWire's `project` object. They are used to synchronize access to shared variables across multiple user sessions. The section, "The *Diskette* Application," provides an example of using the `Application` object.

The *Server* Object

The `Server` object provides access to server-wide resources. It is typically used to create instances of server-side ActiveX objects. The `ScriptTimeout` property specifies the amount of time that a script may execute before it times out. The default value is 90 seconds. The `Server` object supports the following methods:

CreateObject()   Used to create an instance of a server-side COM (ActiveX) object

HTMLEncode()   Used to encode a string with HTML encoding

MapPath()   Used to map a virtual server path to a physical directory path

URLEncode()   Used to encode a string with URL encoding

The above methods are available to all applications, sessions, and request-processing scripts.

File Input and Output

Like LiveWire, ASP provides objects for accessing the server's native file system. These objects are as follows:

FileSystemObject   Provides a gateway to the server's file system

Folder   Provides access to a file system directory

File   Provides access to a specific file within the file system

TextStream   Provides sequential read/write access to a text file

We'll use the `FileSystemObject` and `TextStream` object in the *Diskette* application of the following section.

The *Diskette* Application

Listings 22.8 through 22.11 illustrate the use of the Request, Session, Application, FileSystemObject, and TextStream objects. These listings are the ASP equivalent of the diskette application of Chapter 21, "Scripting Netscape Servers." Place these in a directory that is accessible from your Web server, and then open the URL of the start.asp file. The Web page shown in Figure 22.9 is displayed. Enter a value for the number of diskettes, and click the Continue button. The form shown in Figure 22.10 is displayed. Fill out the form, click Continue, and the results of your order are displayed, as shown in Figure 22.11. Click Continue again, and your order number is displayed. Figure 22.12 shows how the transaction is completed. If all this seems familiar, it should be; you've just executed the ASP equivalent of the LiveWire *Diskette* application introduced in Chapter 21.

FIGURE 22.9:

Starting the *Diskette* application(Listing 22.9)

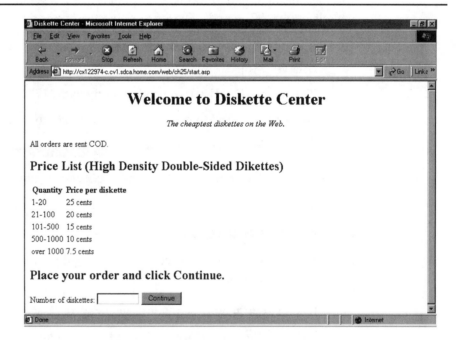

FIGURE 22.10:

Processing the user's order
(Listing 22.10)

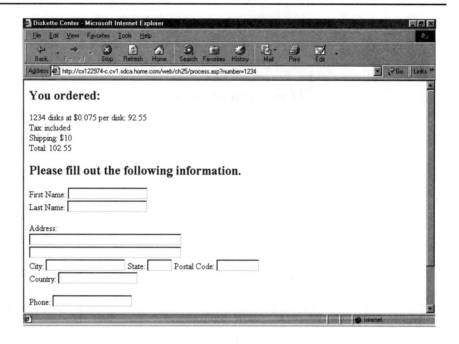

FIGURE 22.11:

Displaying the user's order
(Listing 22.11)

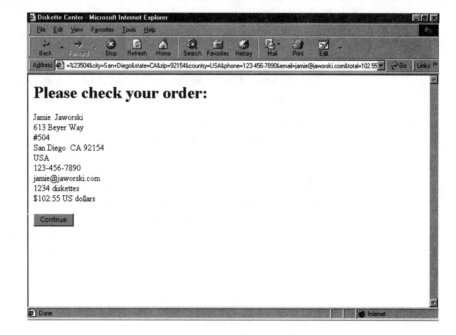

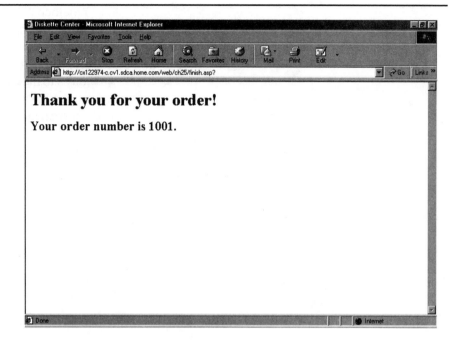

After having covered the *Diskette* application in Chapter 21, "Scripting Netscape Servers," you should be familiar with its structure and operation. The only new material is the use of ASP objects in place of LiveWire objects. These differences are as follows:

start.asp   The reference to proces.htm was changed to a reference to process.asp.

process.asp   The Session object is used to record the number of diskettes ordered by the user. This number is passed as an argument to display-Order(). The reference to display.htm was changed to display.asp.

display.asp   The values of the QueryString properties of the Request object are assigned to properties of the same name in the Session object. Note that the Form properties could have been substituted for the Query-String properties. The Session properties are displayed to the user. The reference to finish.htm is changed to finish.asp.

finish.asp The Lock() and Unlock() methods of the Application object are used to synchronize access to the application's nextOrder variable and the orders.text file. The nextOrder variable is incremented and assigned to the session's order variable. A FileSystemObject object is created (as an ActiveX object) to obtain access to the server's file system. A TextStream object is created on the orders.txt file from the FileSystem-Object via the OpenTextFile() method. The parameter 8 indicates that the file should be opened for append access. The true parameter indicates that the file should be created if it currently does not exist. The WriteLine() method of the TextStream object is used to write the Session property values to the orders.txt file. This file is then closed via the Close() method.

As you can see from the above summary, the changes needed to convert from LiveWire to ASP were minimal.

Listing 22.8   **Starting the Diskette Application (start.asp)**

```
<HTML>
<HEAD>
<TITLE>Diskette Center</TITLE>
</HEAD>
<BODY BGCOLOR="white">
<H1 ALIGN="CENTER">Welcome to Diskette Center</H1>
<P ALIGN="CENTER"><I>The cheapest diskettes on the Web.</I>
</P>
<P>All orders are sent COD.</P>
<H2>Price List (High Density Double-Sided Dikettes)</H2>
<TABLE>
<TR><TH>Quantity</TH><TH>Price per diskette</TH></TR>
<TR><TD>1-20</TD><TD>25 cents</TD></TR>
<TR><TD>21-100</TD><TD>20 cents</TD></TR>
<TR><TD>101-500</TD><TD>15 cents</TD></TR>
<TR><TD>500-1000</TD><TD>10 cents</TD></TR>
<TR><TD>over 1000</TD><TD>7.5 cents</TD></TR>
</TABLE>
<H2>Place your order and click Continue.</H2>
<FORM ACTION="process.asp">
Number of diskettes:
<INPUT TYPE="TEXT" SIZE="10" NAME="number">
<INPUT TYPE="Submit" VALUE="Continue">
```

```
</FORM>
</BODY>
</HTML>
```

Listing 22.9   Processing the User's Order (process.asp)

```
<%@ LANGUAGE=JSCRIPT %>
<HTML>
<HEAD>
<TITLE>Diskette Center</TITLE>
<SCRIPT language="JavaScript">
function displayOrder(n) {
 with(document){
  if(n<21) rate=.25
  else if(n<101) rate=.2
  else if(n<501) rate=.15
  else if(n<1001) rate=.10
  else rate=.075
  subtotal=n*rate
  subtotal=Math.round(subtotal*100)/100
  total=subtotal+10
  write("<H2>You ordered:</H2>")
  write(n+" disks at $"+rate+" per disk: "+subtotal+"<BR>")
  write("Tax: included"+"<BR>")
  write("Shipping: $10"+"<BR>")
  write("Total: "+total+"<BR>")
 }
}
</SCRIPT>
</HEAD>
<BODY>
<% Session("number") = Request.QueryString("number") + "" %>
<SCRIPT language="JavaScript">
displayOrder("<% =Session("number") %>")
</SCRIPT>
<H2>Please fill out the following information.</H2>
<FORM ACTION="display.asp">
First Name: <INPUT TYPE="TEXT" NAME="firstName"><BR>
Last Name: <INPUT TYPE="TEXT" NAME="lastName"><P>
Address:<BR>
<INPUT TYPE="TEXT" NAME="addr1" SIZE="40"><BR>
<INPUT TYPE="TEXT" NAME="addr2" SIZE="40"><BR>
City: <INPUT TYPE="TEXT" NAME="city">
```

```
State: <INPUT TYPE="TEXT" NAME="state" SIZE="5">
Postal Code: <INPUT TYPE="TEXT" NAME="zip" SIZE="10"><BR>
Country: <INPUT TYPE="TEXT" NAME="country"><P>
Phone: <INPUT TYPE="TEXT" NAME="phone"><P>
E-mail address:    <INPUT TYPE="TEXT" NAME="email" SIZE="40">
<INPUT TYPE="HIDDEN" NAME="total"><P>
<INPUT TYPE="SUBMIT" VALUE="Continue">
</FORM>
<SCRIPT language="JavaScript">
document.forms[0].total.value=total
</SCRIPT>
</BODY>
</HTML>
```

Listing 22.10   Displaying the User's Order (display.asp)

```
<%@ LANGUAGE=JSCRIPT %>
<HTML>
<HEAD>
<TITLE>Diskette Center</TITLE>
</HEAD>
<BODY>
<H1>Please check your order:</H1>
<%
Session("firstName")=Request.QueryString("firstName")+""
Session("lastName")=Request.QueryString("lastName")+""
Session("addr1")=Request.QueryString("addr1")+""
Session("addr2")=Request.QueryString("addr2")+""
Session("city")=Request.QueryString("city")+""
Session("state")=Request.QueryString("state")+""
Session("country")=Request.QueryString("country")+""
Session("zip")=Request.QueryString("zip")+""
Session("phone")=Request.QueryString("phone")+""
Session("email")=Request.QueryString("email")+""
Session("total")=Request.QueryString("total")+"" %>
<% =Session("firstName") %> 
<% =Session("lastName") %><BR>
<% =Session("addr1") %><BR>
<% =Session("addr2") %><BR>
<% =Session("city") %> 
<% =Session("state") %> <% =Session("zip") %><BR>
<% =Session("country") %><BR>
<% =Session("phone") %><BR>
```

```
<% =Session("email") %><BR>
<% =Session("number") %> diskettes<BR>
$<% =Session("total") %> US dollars<BR>
<FORM action="finish.asp">
<INPUT TYPE="SUBMIT" VALUE="Continue">
</FORM>
</BODY>
</HTML>
```

Listing 22.11   Finishing the Transaction (finish.asp)

```
<%@ LANGUAGE=JSCRIPT %>
<HTML>
<HEAD>
<TITLE>Diskette Center</TITLE>
</HEAD>
<BODY>
<%
Application.Lock()
var nextOrder = parseInt(Application("nextOrder"))
if(isNaN(nextOrder)) Application("nextOrder")=1000
Application("nextOrder")=parseInt(Application("nextOrder"))+1
Session("order")=parseInt(Application("nextOrder"))
var fs = new ActiveXObject("Scripting.FileSystemObject")
var f = fs.OpenTextFile("orders.txt",8,true)
f.WriteLine(Session("order")+" "+Session("number")+"
"+Session("total"))
f.WriteLine(Session("firstName")+" "+Session("lastName"))
f.WriteLine(Session("addr1"))
f.WriteLine(Session("addr2"))
f.WriteLine(Session("city")+" "+Session("state")+" "+Session("zip"))
f.WriteLine(Session("country"))
f.WriteLine(Session("phone"))
f.WriteLine(Session("email"))
f.Close()
Application.Unlock()
%>
<H1>Thank you for your order!</H1>
<H2>Your order number is <% =Session("order") %>.</H2>
</BODY>
</HTML>
```

Connecting to Databases

In Chapter 21, "Scripting Netscape Servers," we upgraded the *Diskette* application to replace the `orders.txt` file with a Microsoft Access database. ASP provides a similar database capability through its Microsoft Data Access Components technology. You can use it to integrate your server-side scripts with databases in the same manner as LiveWire Database Services. The operations required to do this are essentially the same as the LiveWire database application of Chapter 21. Only the object names, methods, and syntax are changed. Both Microsoft Data Access Components and LiveWire Database Services support the industry-standard Structured Query Language (SQL) that was covered in Chapter 21. Your Personal Web Server or Internet Information Server contains documentation on using Microsoft Data Access Components.

Windows Scripting Host

Recognizing the value of JScript in both client and server Web applications, Microsoft extended the use of JScript and other scripting languages to general desktop applications. This scripting technology is referred to as Windows Scripting Host (WSH). WSH is documented at Microsoft's scripting Web site located at `http://msdn.microsoft.com/scripting/`.

WSH supports JScript, VBScript, Perl, and other scripting languages through the use of a language-independent scripting framework. WSH allows scripts to execute using windows or command-line text input and output. It provides a basic set of objects from which simple desktop applications may be constructed. These objects are as follows:

Wscript   The basic object of a WSH application; provides access to other WSH objects

WshArguments   Provides access to the arguments of a WSH application

WshCollection   Used to provide a collection of network drives and available printers

WshEnvironment   Provides access to environment variables

WshNetwork   Provides access to network resources

WshShell Provides access to popup windows, the system registry, executable programs, and special system folders

WshShortcut Encapsulates a shortcut to Windows's objects

WshSpecialFolders Provides access to special windows directories, such as the desktop and Start menu

WshURLShortcut Encapsulates a shortcut to objects that are accessed via a URL

Listing 22.12 provides an example of a WSH script. This script creates a Wsh-Shell object and assigns it to the shell variable. It then invokes the display-Environment() function to display selected environment variables and the runProgram() function to run explorer.exe.

The displayEnvironment() function creates a WshEnvironment object and assigns it to the environ variable. It then uses the object to access the PATH, PROMPT, WINDIR, TEbMP, and TMP environment variables. The values of these variables are put into a string that is displayed in a pop-up window. The Popup() method of the WshShell object displays the string with a timeout of 0 seconds and a title of "Environment Settings."

The runProgram() function simply invokes the Run() method of the WshShell object.

To run Listing 22.12, you'll need to have WSH installed on your system. You can check for wscript.exe in your \Windows directory. If it does not exist, download WSH from Microsoft's scripting Web site at http://msdn.microsoft.com/scripting/. After installing WSH, simply double-click on the icon for wsh-environ.js to run the script. Figure 22.13 shows the pop-up window displayed when I run wsh-environ.js on my system.

FIGURE 22.13:

A simple WSH program that displays environment variables and launches Explorer (Listing 22.12)

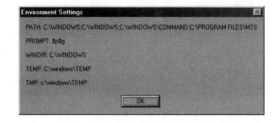

Listing 22.12   A WSH Script That Displays Environment Variables and Launches Explorer (wsh-environ.js)

```javascript
function displayEnvironment() {
 var environ = shell.Environment("Process")
 var edata = "PATH: "+environ("PATH")+"\n\n"
 edata += "PROMPT: "+environ("PROMPT")+"\n\n"
 edata += "WINDIR: "+environ("WINDIR")+"\n\n"
 edata += "TEMP: "+environ("TEMP")+"\n\n"
 edata += "TMP: "+environ("TMP")+"\n"
 shell.Popup(edata,0,"Environment Settings")
}
function runProgram(p) {
 shell.Run(p)
}
shell = WScript.CreateObject("WScript.Shell")
displayEnvironment()
runProgram("explorer.exe")
```

Remote Scripting

Microsoft's latest advance in scripting technology is referred to as "remote scripting." Remote scripting provides for closer integration between client-side and server-side scripts. In the current scripting paradigm, server-side scripts execute on Web servers and produce Web pages containing client-side scripts that are executed on Web browsers. In order for a client-side script to communicate with a server-side script, it must request the Web page containing the server-side script. The client and server scripts must also use a protocol, such as the cookie protocol, for maintaining the state of Web applications.

Remote scripting was developed to simplify the communication between client and server scripts. It allows scripts executing on Internet Explorer to invoke functions or object methods contained in an ASP page. This invocation occurs without the need for the browser to request the ASP page from the Web server. It greatly improves the efficiency with which clients and servers communicate, but it suffers from the fact that it is a Microsoft-only technology. You must have a Microsoft Web browser and Microsoft Web server for it to work.

Remote scripting is implemented using a client proxy process. When a browser executes a remote function, it invokes the function on the client proxy. The client proxy (a Java applet) requests the ASP page containing the remote function. The server loads the page, executes the function, and returns the result to the client proxy. The client proxy then returns the result to the client script that initiated the process.

Remote methods can be implemented in either a synchronous or asynchronous fashion. When a remote script is implemented in a synchronous fashion, the calling script must wait until the Web server returns the result of the method execution (via the client proxy) before continuing. When a remote script is implemented in an asynchronous fashion, the calling script can continue to execute while the Web server processes the method execution. More information on remote scripting can be obtained from Microsoft's scripting Web site at `http://msdn.microsoft.com/scripting/`.

Summary

In this chapter, you learned how to use the server-side scripting capabilities of Microsoft servers. You covered ASP scripting, database connectivity, WSH, and remote scripting. In the next and final chapter, you'll learn about the security threats faced by Web developers and users and how to minimize the security risks associated with these threats.

CHAPTER

TWENTY-THREE

Securing Your Scripts

- Internet Security Threats

- Web Security Issues

- Spying Scripts and JavaScript Security Policy

Congratulations, you've made it to the last chapter of this book! If you've worked your way through the previous chapters, then by now you are adept at client- and server-side JavaScript and have been exposed to CGI and database programming. With these new skills, you are probably eager to go out and develop your own Web applications. The purpose of this chapter is to temper your enthusiasm with some practical cautions related to Web security vulnerabilities.

This chapter covers Web security from two perspectives—the Webmaster's and the user's:

- The Webmaster-oriented discussion describes issues related to Web site security and emphasizes server-side application development.

- The user-oriented discussion describes the security risks associated with using the Web and identifies ways to protect your personal computer from Web-based attacks.

In addition to the above discussions, this chapter points out security issues that are specific to JavaScript and identifies the ways in which Navigator and Internet Explorer address these issues.

When you finish this chapter, you'll be able to develop your Web applications with a better understanding of the security issues involved.

Internet Security Threats

The following sections cover Internet security threats from the perspective of the Web site manager and the Web user.

Threats to the Web Site Manager

As a Web content developer and as a user, the Internet security threats that you face depend on who you are and what you have to protect. For example, if you are the Webmaster for a high-profile organization, such as the CIA or the U.S. Department of Justice, then you'll be the target of all those hackers merely for the challenge you present; many hackers want the fame associated with penetrating one of the big guys. Even if your Web site is not in the hacker "Top 40," if it is not well protected, it may be penetrated just because it is an easy target.

If your Web site is involved with any type of financial transactions or controls any valuable assets, directly or even indirectly, then it could be the target of a more professional type of criminal than the recreational hacker. These cyber thieves may try to penetrate your Web site in order to get access to such things as credit card numbers, software, sensitive information, or physical assets, such as products that may be purchased through your Web site.

An attack on your Web site may be the first stage of a concerted attack on your organization as a whole. If your Web server is inside your organization's firewall, then a penetration of your Web server could lead to a serious security breach of site-internal networks. If your Web server is outside your organization's firewall, then an attacker may attempt to install clandestine software to monitor network traffic at the firewall's external interface.

Due to the growing importance of the Web to commerce, a company's ability to conduct business can be affected by attacks on its Web site. While most businesses don't prey on each other through the Internet, a third party could manipulate a company's Web presence to reap financial gain.

Threats to the Web User

The security threats faced by the individual user are somewhat different than those of the Webmaster. First of all there isn't much prestige in breaking into someone's PC. This rules out some, but not all, recreational hackers. If someone wants to get access to your PC, then it is probably someone who is intent on collecting information about you or sabotaging the data on your PC. This special someone could be an acquaintance, a competitor, or anyone else who has an interest in knowing or stopping what you're doing. Due to the rise of electronic commerce on the Web, some electronic pickpockets have surfaced. These small-time cyberthieves snoop on users' PCs in order to collect credit card numbers, passwords, and information that can be used to forge digital certificates.

Most indiscriminate attacks on individuals come in the form of malicious software, such as viruses—yes, they are still out there. Future attacks will probably include executable Web content (JavaScript, Java, ActiveX) and executable e-mail, such as that provided by Netscape Messenger, Outlook, and other mail programs.

Web Security Issues

To some, the Internet itself is just one big security vulnerability. However, for most of us, it is a vulnerability that we have to live with. While a complete treatment of Internet security vulnerabilities is beyond the scope of this book, the following subsections describe Web-specific security issues from the point of view of the Webmaster and the user.

The Webmaster's Perspective

Running a secure Web server is not an easy task. Security vulnerabilities can, potentially, exist anywhere—in CGI programs, in the server setup, or in the Web server itself. These vulnerabilities could lead to embarrassing modifications to Web content, the theft of sensitive information, or the complete shutdown of your Web site.

To run a secure Web site, the Webmaster must keep abreast of the latest Web vulnerabilities and implement security countermeasures as needed. The World Wide Web Security FAQ, located at `http://www.genome.wi.mit.edu/WWW/faqs/www-security-faq.html` can help you get started. It discusses many of the known Web vulnerabilities and offers good advice on how you can protect your Web site.

Server Software

Web site security begins with the Web server. Unfortunately, not all Web servers are secure. Security holes have been identified in both commercial and public domain servers. Although these holes have been patched in later versions of the server software, the potential for the introduction of new vulnerabilities cannot be dismissed.

Publicly available Web servers, such as the Apache server, offer a high level of security and reliability. However, if security is of paramount concern, then you may want to consider a commercial server by a major vendor, such as Netscape. While commercial servers are not immune to security flaws, reputable vendors tend to respond quickly to security holes once they are identified, in order to stay in business. Publicly developed Web servers, such as Apache, also have quick turnarounds for bug fixes—in some cases, even faster than commercial developers. However, there is no one to blame if and when a problem does occur.

Server Capabilities

New server products continue to add features, such as server-side JavaScript, server plug-ins, and database connectivity that increase the overall complexity of the server software. While the Webmaster looks at the capabilities of a Web server and visualizes all of the ways in which these capabilities could be used to build a better Web site, the penetrator examines each capability in terms of how it could be used to circumvent, defeat, and disable the security of the server as a whole.

Server-side *includes* are examples of server features that are also a bonus to the penetrator. A server-side include is a sequence of commands that is embedded in an HTML document. When a Web server requests the document, the server scans the document for the embedded commands and executes them. The results of the command execution are used to update the HTML document before it is sent to the browser. One of the commands, `exec`, allows arbitrary operating system commands to be executed. This capability is very powerful—both for you and the penetrator. When server-side includes are enabled, a person with minimal Web-publishing capabilities gains the extra privilege of being able to execute operating system commands.

The best way to avoid security vulnerabilities with new server features is to assess the capabilities provided by each feature and determine which ones pose unacceptable security risks. Minimally, you must consider the following to be risks:

- The feature can be used to execute external programs or operating system commands

- The feature can be used to read or write arbitrary files located on the server

- The feature maintains client information on the browser using cookies or URL encoding

The above risks only determine whether the feature has the capability to cause security problems—it doesn't mean that the feature is necessarily insecure. For example, CGI programs, ASP, and LiveWire applications are risky according to all three risk indicators. Once you identify a feature as risky, you have to determine whether secure applications can be built using the feature despite its inherent risks and whether the benefits provided by the feature are worth taking a chance. In the case of CGI programs, ASP, and LiveWire applications, the answer is usually yes.

CGI Programs

There is nothing inherently insecure about CGI itself. However, CGI programs are a prime source of server-side vulnerabilities. By deploying a CGI program, you are allowing others to execute programs on your Web server. From the penetrator's perspective, every CGI program is a potential tool with which to attack your system. Any security flaws in your CGI programs are directly and continually accessible, and penetrators are free to repeatedly probe and cajole these flaws until they succeed in accomplishing their clandestine objectives.

Do flaws exist in CGI programs? You bet. Some flaws let attackers read data that should otherwise be concealed. Other flaws let hackers trash data that is collected from Web users. The most devastating flaws let penetrators remotely execute operating system commands and programs of their choosing.

How do flaws in CGI programs occur? How are they exploited? In many cases, these flaws occur because of poor parameter checking and faulty assumptions on the part of the programmer. For example, consider the case where a CGI program invokes a search program and passes it the value of a decoded query string. The programmer assumes that the search program will simply search for whatever value is passed. But when the query string is passed, the following is executed:

```
search string; cat /etc/passwd
```

In this case, the CGI program returns much more than the search results—it appends the contents of your password file to the search results. The penetrator can then use a password-cracking program to find a password that will let him or her log into your system.

You may wonder why anyone would develop CGI programs that would allow such serious breaches of security. Some programmers don't know any better—they are oblivious to the fact that their programs may be misused. Some are so focused on developing their Web applications that security is put on the back burner—permanently. However, the biggest problem, by far, is that in most CGI programs, security flaws are difficult to spot. In the cases where they are found, they are often dismissed. "But no one would ever do that" is a common justification for failing to remove an exploitable flaw.

Another problem facing CGI programmers is the fact that the odds are heavily stacked against them. The programmers must eliminate all possible security flaws in order to make their CGI programs secure. The penetrator need only find a single exploitable flaw in order to break into the Web server.

ASP and LiveWire Applications

Although ASP and LiveWire applications provide the same capabilities as CGI programs, they are far less prone to security vulnerabilities. There are a number of reasons why these applications are inherently more secure:

- They automatically parse data that is passed to applications and make it available in an easy-to-use manner. This reduces the likelihood of a flaw occurring in the input parsing functions.

- Their applications have predefined objects at their disposal, which reduce the complexities of maintaining client information, sharing data between clients, and sharing data between applications. By making it easier to perform common server-side functions, ASP and LiveWire help you to develop more reliable and error-free code, thereby lowering the likelihood of an exploitable security flaw.

- LiveWire and ASP applications are written in JavaScript and JScript. This eliminates the potential problems associated with using a second, less familiar, language for writing CGI programs. The less experience a programmer has with a language, the more likely she or he is to make mistakes—potentially exploitable ones.

The above features significantly reduce the likelihood of security vulnerabilities in LiveWire and ASP applications. However, the potential for some vulnerability still exists. For example, suppose an application is designed in such a way that a LiveWire `redirect()` method takes a client property as a parameter. A penetrator could modify client properties (client cookies or URLs) to cause the `redirect()` function to return a file of the penetrator's choosing.

Server-Side Plug-Ins

Netscape and Microsoft Web servers provide other server-side programming features, such as Java and server-side plug-ins. In general, any server-side programming mechanism has the potential to be exploited.

Server-side plug-ins are compiled and integrated with the Web server software. They allow server-side applications to be developed that perform better than server-side JavaScript applications and CGI programs. This is because they are called directly by the server instead of being run as a separate process.

The performance gain of server-side plug-ins is offset by the difficulty of developing them. Because server-side plug-ins are closely integrated with the server, any errors in the plug-in could easily result in the complete failure of the server.

Web Application Access Controls

Most Web servers provide the capability to control access to certain Web pages and their associated Web applications. These controls may be based on host name, IP address, user name and password, or other identification and authentication mechanisms. Failure to implement restrictions on some applications, such as your server's management software, could lead to serious security holes.

File Permissions

Operating-system file permissions are closely related to Web-application access controls. These permissions determine which files users and applications are able to read, write, and execute. These controls are important to protecting your Web site. In particular, write permission to the directories containing CGI programs and server-configuration files should be limited to the most trusted users. Failure to do so weakens the security of your Web server, opening it up to a broader spectrum of attacks.

If your server stores financial information, such as credit card data, the permissions of these files should be set to prevent them from being read by other applications. If at all possible, these files should be made write-only.

In the event that your server is penetrated, the privileges of your server become those of the penetrator. Therefore, the login privileges of the Web server itself should be limited to the minimum needed to perform its function.

Other Server-Side Security Considerations

In addition to the vulnerability mentioned in the previous sections, Web servers are vulnerable to a wide range of attacks aimed at their application services and communication protocols. If a Web server supports other Internet services, such as telnet or FTP, then the server inherits all of the vulnerabilities of these services. The good news is that you can eliminate these vulnerabilities by turning off the additional services.

If a Web server is on the Internet, then it, by definition, must support the Transmission Control Protocol/Internet Protocol (TCP/IP). TCP/IP is notorious for its security vulnerabilities. These vulnerabilities include susceptibility to spoofing, session hijacking, and session monitoring. While these vulnerabilities are common to all systems that are on the Internet, they need to be considered when assessing the risk of setting up a Web server. If the perceived risk is too high, then you may want to implement a firewall or another network security countermeasure.

As a final consideration, the operating system platform on which the Web server runs is also a potential source of security vulnerabilities. In general, multi-user operating systems, such as UNIX, pose a higher risk than single-user systems, such as the Macintosh and Windows 98. The security of most multiuser systems depends on the reliability and trustworthiness of all system users. If a single user is careless or untrustworthy, then the security of the entire system could be jeopardized. Most multiuser operating systems provide security controls, such as file permissions, that prevent a user from viewing or modifying the files of others. However, to be effective, these controls must be correctly applied.

Although Web servers exist for the Macintosh, Windows 98, and Windows 95 platforms, most midlevel-to-high-end servers run on Windows NT and UNIX platforms. This is because Windows NT and Unix provide a fuller set of operating system services for implementing more complex and capable server software.

Both Windows NT and Unix have advantages and disadvantages as far as security goes. The main advantage of Windows NT is that it does not support (without additional software purchases) many of the services, such as Telnet, Internet mail, and the X Windows System, that are provided out of the box with UNIX systems. These services may be used by a penetrator to gain remote access to a UNIX system.

The primary advantage of UNIX is its maturity. It has been subjected to hacking for many years, including years before Windows NT was conceived. As a result, most of the UNIX security bugs have been identified and countermeasures have been implemented. Under a security-conscious system administrator, a UNIX Web site can be made as secure as it would be using other operating-system platforms.

NOTE   While this section has covered the merits of one operating system over another, it is important to keep in mind that many break-ins occur as the result of social engineering—duping people into divulging their passwords or other bad security practices.

The Web User's Perspective

Although the risk of using the Web is small, it still merits some consideration. The basic question that you need to ask is, "What do I have to lose?" If you use your PC purely for recreation and don't perform any financial transactions over the Web, then the answer is, "Not much." However, if you use your PC to store your diary and sensitive company documents and use the Web to make online purchases, then you may want to examine your risk more closely.

For users, Web security begins with the browser and, for most of us, that means a Netscape or Microsoft browser. Netscape Navigator and Microsoft Internet Explorer provide a number of features that go beyond simple Web-page display. Both browsers support executable content—Java and, of course, JavaScript. In addition to executable content, both browsers support plug-ins (Internet Explorer supports Navigator plug-ins and ActiveX controls, in addition to its own), cookies, Secure Sockets Layer (SSL) communication, and digital certificates. Each of these features has implications for user security, as described in the following subsections.

Dealing with Executable Content

When most people think of browser vulnerabilities they think of Java, JavaScript, and ActiveX. For most of us, the thought of opening a Web page and automatically having a program load and execute on their computer is a bit frightening. There is a good reason for this fear—it is very difficult to allow executable content without leaving yourself wide open to a Trojan horse attack.

A Trojan horse is a program that appears to provide a useful function while, in reality, it is attacking your system. The name comes from the legend of the huge wooden horse that was left as a gift at the gates of Troy. When the Trojans opened the gates of their city to bring in the horse, Greek soldiers who had been hiding inside the horse poured out and attacked the Trojans.

Each of the three major browser-programming technologies uses a different approach to protecting against Trojan horses:

- Java code executes in the Java Virtual Machine (JVM), which is part of the Java runtime system. The runtime system is designed to prevent operations that would violate the browser's security policy.

- JavaScript eliminates Trojan-horse code by not providing objects or methods that could be used to cause damage or violate the user's privacy.

- ActiveX components do not provide any inherent protection against damage. Instead, these components are digitally signed. The signature provides a high degree of assurance that the component originated from the organization that it claims.

Navigator and Internet Explorer 4 also support signed Java applets. The signature can be used to determine whether the applet should be given extra privileges beyond those allowed by the default Navigator security policy.

Of the three approaches, JavaScript's is the most secure. By not providing a mechanism for creating damage, it is able to prevent the damage from occurring. But how do we know that no object or method can be used to cause damage? The answer is extensive analysis and testing. Could something have been overlooked? Try writing a JavaScript script that could damage your system.

Java's approach is next best when it comes to security. The Java runtime system is capable of supporting multiple security policies. For example, Java programs that are loaded from your hard disk are allowed more privileges than applets that are loaded over the network. Signed applets are given more privileges than unsigned applets. Java's approach, in allowing multiple security policies to be enforced, is daring. Except for a few early flaws, the Java runtime system has held up to its claims of security.

ActiveX uses the least secure of the three approaches. The signature attached to an ActiveX component does not provide any assurance that the component won't destroy your system; it just tells you who to go after in case it does.

Both Navigator and Internet Explorer provide the capability to selectively turn off these browser programming capabilities. If you simply can't take the chance of Trojan-horse software being loaded into your computer, then you should take advantage of this option.

Plug-In and ActiveX Vulnerability

Nearly 200 plug-ins are available for Navigator and Internet Explorer. In addition, Internet Explorer supports numerous ActiveX controls, which expose the same vulnerabilities as plug-ins. These plug-ins execute as native code extensions to the browser. As such, plug-ins can do anything that your browser can. From a penetrator's perspective, this means that a plug-in can cause any sort of damage.

With nearly 200 available plug-ins to choose from, what do you think the chances are that one of them contains an exploitable security vulnerability? The same holds true for ActiveX controls. Just because a control is signed, it doesn't mean that it is error free. Due to the capability to invoke plug-in functions and ActiveX control methods from Java and JavaScript, what do you think is the likelihood of a plug-in or ActiveX vulnerability being exploited?

As an example of this type of risk, consider the programs that are available for viewing Microsoft Word documents. With the capability to embed macros in a Word document, what do you think is the likelihood that a macro virus could be injected into your system via a Word document? If your experience with Word is like mine, you've probably had your share of macro virus attacks.

Plug-ins and ActiveX controls pose a potential risk to browser security. The more of them you use, the greater the risk. Fortunately, there is an easy way to lower this risk—only install the ones that you absolutely need.

Protecting Financial Information

If you plan on purchasing any merchandise or performing other types of financial transactions over the Web, you should be aware of the security mechanisms being used by your browser. The lower-left corner of the Navigator window displays an indicator that shows the level of security that is currently in force. A broken key indicates that no encryption is being used. A solid key with a single tooth indicates that international security (40-bit) encryption is in use. A solid key with two teeth indicates that domestic security (128-bit) encryption is in use.

Both international and domestic security use the Secure Sockets Layer (SSL) for encryption. SSL uses public key cryptography to exchange keys that are used for private key encryption. Digital certificates are used to verify the identity of the organization with which you are communicating.

How strong is the security provided? If no encryption is used, then you should assume that whatever information you send can be intercepted.

If international (40-bit) encryption is used, then your encrypted communication is probably secure from a hacker without many computational resources, but not from anyone else. This encryption scheme has already been broken several times.

If domestic (128-bit) encryption is used, then you are probably secure from most eavesdroppers. However, absolute security cannot be guaranteed. SSL only protects information while it is in transit. Whatever information you send is unprotected before it is transmitted by your browser and after it is received by the server.

Maintaining Privacy

How private is your interaction with the Web? Not very private. Whenever you request a document from a Web server, your request is usually logged by that server. The log record doesn't identify you by name, but it does include your IP address. If you use a static IP address, then you are positively identified. If you use a dynamic IP address, then the log information could apply to other users of your Internet service provider.

Both Navigator and Internet Explorer support cookies. When cookies were first introduced, they were the subject of some concern. Because they can be used to maintain information about a user on the user's browser, cookies were looked at as the instrument of Big Brother. As it turns out, cookies can be used to maintain information about users—that was their original intent. Is this a problem? It depends. If you look at cookies as a way to improve Web services, then you'll want to keep them. If you look at cookies as a means to spy on you, then your best bet is to periodically delete your cookie files. This will let you use cookies when you need to and will make it difficult for anyone to maintain consistent information about you. You can also make your cookie files read-only.

Spying Scripts and JavaScript Security Policy

In addition to the security issues addressed in the previous sections, there are some security issues that are specific to JavaScript. These issues involve user privacy and the protection of sensitive user information. These issues center around the way in which JavaScript prevents scripts from one Internet host from accessing the data of scripts that are from other Internet hosts.

A script that executes in one browser window or frame has the capability to access data entered by a user in another window or frame. You've seen several examples of how this can be done in Part II, "Using Predefined Objects and Methods." In most cases, this is a desirable feature. However, under some scenarios it can pose a security risk. For example, consider the case where a user is browsing a hacker Web site in one browser window and performing an online purchase in another. What prevents an untrusted script from the hacker's Web site from reading the credit card information that you enter into the shopping form of the other window? This is what *spying scripts* do.

The answer to this potential security problem has been addressed since JavaScript 1. However, the specific manner in which it has been resolved has changed with JavaScript 1.1 and 1.2. In JavaScript 1, a script that executes in the context of a document loaded from one Internet host is prevented from accessing the properties and methods of documents that are loaded from other Internet hosts. This provided a simple solution to the spying script problem. This solution is referred to as the *Same Origin Security Policy*.

However, in JavaScript 1.1, Netscape lost its flair for simplicity and came up with an approach for allowing scripts from one host to *securely* access the properties of documents that are loaded from other hosts. This approach was called *data tainting*. It was implemented in Navigator 3, ignored by Internet Explorer 4, and replaced in Navigator 4 and later.

When data tainting is turned on (as the result of a complex user configuration process), scripts from one host are allowed to access the properties of documents from other hosts. However, the capability to identify security-sensitive properties as private (referred to as *tainting*) is provided. Tainted values cannot be disclosed without the user's permission. When data tainting is turned off (the default), the JavaScript 1 Same Origin Security Policy is in effect.

The good point about data tainting is that it allows some flexibility in security. However, this benefit was outweighed by the cumbersome process by which it was implemented; the requirement to taint properties to keep them secure; and the fact that the whole process confused the user. More information on data tainting is provided in online Appendix A, "Comparing JavaScript and JScript." Data tainting is essentially a dead approach and should be avoided.

In JavaScript 1.2, data tainting was replaced by signed scripts and the *Object Signing Security Policy*. This approach involves the following:

Principal   The principal is a person or organization that signs a script.

Target   The target is the script or portion of a script that is signed.

Signature   The principal creates the signature by applying a private encryption key to the contents of the target (script). The signature indicates that the signer has (or should have) verified that the script is trustworthy. The signature also acts as a seal in that it can be used to verify that the script has not been altered after it has been signed. The signature can be verified as being from the principal using cryptographic methods involving the principal's public key.

Privilege   When a signed script executes, it requests privileges from the browser and user. The browser presents information about the script's signature to the user so that the user can make informed decisions about whether he or she should grant the privileges requested by the script. A privilege generally involves permission to perform a security-sensitive operation, such as collecting information from other windows or generating e-mail on behalf of the user.

Certificate   A certificate is an electronic document that attests to the fact that a principal can be recognized by a particular public key. Anyone can sign a script. However, to have your signature recognized, the public key associated with your signature must itself be signed by a recognized certificate authority (such as Verisign). This boils down to the fact that you must pay the certificate authority to give you a certificate. The certificate authority generally performs some investigation to see if you are indeed who you say you are.

The details of object signing delve into cryptographic methods. Links to these details are provided in online Appendix B, "Accessing Online References."

Internet Explorer maintains the simple same-origin security policy in all of its browser versions. To get around this policy, you'll need to develop a custom ActiveX control and sign the control using Microsoft's code-signing tools. Consult Microsoft's Site Builder Workshop at `http://www.microsoft.com/workshop/` `c-frame.htm#/workshop/components/default.asp` for more information on how to do this.

Having covered the evolution of Netscape security policy related to spying scripts, you may wonder how this affects your script development. In general, if your scripts do not have any compelling need to access the properties of documents that are loaded from other Web sites in other frames and windows, you have nothing to worry about. Both Navigator and Internet Explorer default to the same origin security policy. If, for some reason, your scripts need to access the properties of these other documents or to send information, such as e-mail, on behalf of the user, you'll have a security problem. To solve this problem, you'll need to implement a Navigator-specific solution and an Internet Explorer–specific solution. You'll need to use signed scripts with Navigator and signed ActiveX controls with Internet Explorer. In both cases, you'll need to get a code-signing certificate from a certificate authority and sign your scripts using appropriate code-signing tools. Online Appendix B, "Accessing Online References," contains links to certificate authorities as well as Netscape and Microsoft security tools.

Summary

In this chapter, you learned about Web security from the perspective of the Web-master and the user. You learned about the security issues related to Web site development and how to protect your personal computer from Web-based attacks. You also covered JavaScript-specific security issues. You should now be able to develop your Web applications with a better understanding of the security issues involved.

This is the final chapter of the book. Thanks for staying the course. I hope that it helped you to learn JavaScript well enough that you'll be able to use it effectively and creatively in your Web applications. Be sure to check out the book's Web page at `http://www.Sybex.com`. If you have any questions, you can e-mail me at `jamie@jaworski.com`.

INDEX

Note to the Reader: Throughout this index **boldfaced** page numbers indicate primary discussions of a topic. *Italicized* page numbers indicate illustrations.

SYMBOLS

& (ampersands)
  in assignment operators, 85
  in bit operators, 84
  for entities, 43
  in form data coding, 721
  in logical operators, 82
  precedence of, 93
<> (angle brackets) in HTML, 8
* (asterisks)
  in assignment operators, 85
  for comments, 44, 637
  for multiplication, 82
  precedence of, 93
` (backquotes) for LiveWire, 751
\ (backslashes) in string values, 58–59
{} (braces)
  for entities, 43
  for functions, 111
  for if statements, 98–99
  for with statements, 119
^ (carets)
  in assignment operators, 85
  as bit operator, 84
  precedence of, 93
: (colons)
  in conditional expressions, 85–86
  precedence of, 93
  in URLs, 357
, (comma) operator, 86

, (commas) for parameters, 204
$ (dollar signs) in names, 50–51
" (double quotes)
  for attributes, 138
  for string values, 58
= (equal signs)
  in Active Server Pages, 816
  in assignment operators, 85
  in comparison operators, 83
  in form data coding, 721
  precedence of, 93
! (exclamation points)
  for comments, 38
  for comparison operators, 83
  for logical operators, 82
  precedence of, 93
/ (forward slashes)
  in assignment operators, 85
  for comments, 38, 44, 637
  for division, 82
  in HTML, 8
  precedence of, 93
  in URLs, 14–15, 357
> (greater than signs)
  in assignment operators, 85
  as bit operator, 84
  in comparison operators, 83
  precedence of, 93
< (less than signs)
  in Active Server Pages, 816
  in assignment operators, 85
  as bit operator, 84

in comparison operators, 83
precedence of, 93
- (minus signs)
in assignment operators, 85
in decrement operators, 82
precedence of, 93
for subtraction, 82
() (parentheses)
for conditions, 98–99
for methods, 204
for operator precedence, 93–94
% (percent signs)
in Active Server Pages, 816
in assignment operators, 85
for modulus operator, 82
precedence of, 93
in query strings, 721
+ (plus signs)
for addition, 82
in assignment operators, 85
in increment operators, 82
with mixed types, 62–67, 67
precedence of, 93
in query strings, 357, 507, 720
for string concatenation, 84
(pound signs) in URLs, 357–358
? (question marks)
in conditional expressions, 85–86
precedence of, 93
in query strings, 357, 507
; (semicolons)
for attributes, 138
for statements, 97
' (single quotes)
for attributes, 138
for string values, 58
[] (square brackets) for arrays, 70
~ (tildes), precedence of, 93
_ (underscore characters) in names, 50
| (vertical bars)
in assignment operators, 85
as bit operator, 84
in logical operators, 82
precedence of, 93

A

a mode string, 764
<A> tag, 132, 596
Abandon() method, 826
abort events, 132
about.htm file, **602–605**, *602*
about protocol, **361**, *362–363*
ABOVE attribute, 681–682
abs() function, 225, 416
absolute measurement units, 650
access
controls for, **848**
to documents, **276–277**, *278*
to form elements, **292–299**, *299*
in Java
to applets, **550–553**, *554–555*
to methods, **548–549**, *549–550*
to LiveWire files, **764–766**
to plug-ins, **607–610**, *608–609*
access.htm file, **581–582**, *581*, **607–610**, *608–609*
Access program for LiveWire, **787–789**, *787–791*
accessActiveX() function, 582
accessApplet() method, 552
accessories
assembling, **456–458**, *457*
calculator, **443–448**, *444*
calendar, **434–443**, *437*, *439–440*
to-do list, **448–454**, *449–450*
world clock, **454–456**, *455*
acos() function, 225, 417
Acrobat plug-in, 593
ACTION attribute, 313, 327
action property, 291
actionPerformed() method, 560
Active Server Pages (ASP), **22–23**, **814–815**, *815*
Application object in, **826–827**
connecting to databases, **835**
directives in, **816**
for Diskette application, **828–834**, *828–830*
file system in, **827**
Request object in, **818–825**, *819–820*, *822–824*
Response object in, **825–826**
scope delimiters in, **816**

scripting in, **815–817**, *817*
Server object in, **827**
Session object in, **826**
ActiveX technology, **18–19**, **576–577**
    ActiveX components, **577–582**, *578–579*, *581*
    ActiveX Control Pad, **583–589**, *583–588*
    in multimedia, **698–703**
    scripts for, 20
    security in, 851
Add Application form, 743–744, *744–745*, 749–750
add-in modules, **12**
add() method, 569–570
add2db.cgi file, 733
add2db.pl file, 730
addClient() function, 780
addDecimalPoint() function
    in calc, 445
    in math, 421, 427
addDigit() function
    in calc, 444–445
    in math, 421, 426
adding
    methods to object types, **237–240**, *240*
    rows in SQL, **800**
addition, 82
addPoint() function
    in graph, 567
    in GraphApp, 573
Adobe Acrobat plug-in, 593
advertiseLink() function, 143–145
agent property, 753
airplane in animation, **703–709**, *704*
alert() method, 137, 163, 250, 255
algebraic functions, 225, 416
ALIGN attribute
    in LiveAudio, 612
    in LiveVideo, 611
align property, 648
alinkColor property, 273, 279
all collection, 661–662
all.htm file, 662–663
altKey property, 175
altView() function
    in catform2, 478, 483
    in catform3, 490

ampersands (&)
    in assignment operators, 85
    in bit operators, 84
    for entities, 43
    in form data coding, 721
    in logical operators, 82
    precedence of, 93
anchor() method, 384
Anchor object, 206, **384–385**
anchor property, 273
anchors array, 206, 208, 384
anchors property, 273
and operators
    bit, 84
    logical, 82
Andreessen, Marc, 5
angle brackets (<>) in HTML, 8
anilayer.htm file, **703–706**, *704*
animate() function, 401, 403
animate.htm file, **400–403**
animation
    images with, **399–403**, *400*
    layers in, **703–709**, *704*
API (Application Programming Interface) for Java,
    533–534, **540**
appCodeName property, 281
appendDigit() function
    in calc, 445
    in math, 421, 427
Applet class, 547
Applet object and applets, **18**, 206, 209, **552–553**
    accessing, **550–553**, *554–555*
    in HTML, 18, 547
    in Java, 532, 534, **540–541**, **545–548**, *547*
    JavaScript in, **555–562**
    limitations of, 538
    loading, **551–552**
    signed, 851
applet property, 273
<APPLET> tag, 18, 547
applets array, 206, 208–209
applets property, 273
Application Manager, 743–744, *744–745*, **748–750**
Application object, **826–827**
application/octet-stream MIME type, 13

Application Programming Interface (API) for Java, 533–534, **540**
application/x-javascript MIME type, 13
applications
    distributed, **25**
    embedded plug-in, **596–597**
    helper, **11–14**
apply() method, 222
applyDHTML() function, 672–674
applyFunction() function, 423, 428
AppMinorVersion property, 281
appName property, 281
appointments, calendar for, **434–443**, *437*, *439–440*
appVersion property, 281
Area object and areas, 206
    events for, 132
    and image maps, **403–404**
area property, 208, 273
<AREA> tag, 132, 157, 403
arguments
    for CGI programs, 718
    for functions, **110–113**
    for methods, 204
arguments array, 113–114
arguments property, 221
arithmetic operators, **81–82**
arity property, 221
Array object and arrays, **70–72**, *71*, **215–217**, *217*
    of arrays, **74–75**, *76*
    declaring, **72–74**, *74*, 98
    dense, **74**, 98
    elements of, **74–75**, *76*
    for layers, **683–684**
    object type for, **215–217**, *217*
ASCII files
    for HTML, 8
    MIME type for, 13
asin() function, 225, 417
askAboutProducts() function, 331–332
askNextQuestion() function, 345, 347–348
ASP. *See* Active Server Pages (ASP)
.asp files, 815
assigning properties, **232–233**
assignment operators, **84–85**
assignment statements, 97

assist.htm file, **620–621**, *622*
asterisks (*)
    in assignment operators, 85
    for comments, 44, 637
    for multiplication, 82
    precedence of, 93
atan() function, 225, 417
atan2() function, 225, 417
attributes and attribute values in HTML, 9
audio
    MIME type for, 13
    for online catalogs, **485–495**, *486*
    in slide shows, **694–698**
audio/x-wav MIME type, 13
audiosho.htm file, **694–698**
AUTH_TYPE environment variable, 719
authoring tools, 5
AUTOSTART attribute
    in LiveAudio, 612
    in LiveVideo, 605, 611
axdemo.htm file, **578–581**, *578–579*

B

\b character, 59
back() function
    in access, 610
    in history, 386
background
    in document, 279
    properties for, **203**, *204*
    style sheets for, **645–647**, *647*
BACKGROUND attribute
    with <ILAYER> tag, 681–682
    with <LAYER> tag, 681–682
background properties, **663**, 672, 683
backgroundColor property, 645
backgroundImage property, 647
backquotes (`) for LiveWire, 751
backslashes (\) in string values, 58–59
backspace character, 59
badGuess() function, 306, 309
bars (|)

in assignment operators, 85
as bit operator, 84
in logical operators, 82
precedence of, 93
beginning tags in HTML, 8
beginTransaction() method, 792, 797–798
BELOW attribute, 681–682
below property, 683
Berners-Lee, Tim, 5, 10
BGCOLOR attribute
with <ILAYER> tag, 681–682
with <LAYER> tag, 681–682
bgColor property
in document, 273, 279
in layer, 683
binary operators, 81
BinaryRead() method, 819
bit manipulation operators, **84**
blank.htm file, **266**, 367
blobImage() function, **796–797**
blobLink() function, **797**
block-formatted elements, **647–649**, *650*
blocks.htm file, 648–649, *650*
blur events, 133–135
blur() method
for form elements, 296–297
in window, 250
board.htm file, **264–265**
body code for quiz, **347**
<BODY> tag, 9, 133, 262
Boole, George, 57
Boolean object, **218**
Boolean values, **56–57**, *57*
BORDER attribute
for forms, 326
with <TABLE> tag, 67
border properties in style, **664**
border property, 391–392
borderBottomWidth property, 648
borderLeftWidth property, 648
borderRightWidth property, 648
borderStyle property, 648
borderTopWidth property, 648
borderWidths() method, 648
bottom property, 683
braces ({})

for entities, 43
for functions, 111
for if statements, 98–99
for with statements, 119
brackets ([]) for arrays, 70
brackets (<>) in HTML, 8
break statements, **104–106**, *105*, 108
browser.htm file, **282–284**, *284–285*
browserLanguage property, 281
browsers and browser objects, 5–6
hierarchy of, **208–209**
identifiers for, **209–214**, *214–215*
ignoring JavaScript code in, **37–38**, *37–39*
in Java vs. JavaScript, **538**
and JavaScript, **28–33**, *29–33*
navigator object for, **280–284**, *284–285*
scripts for, 20
security in, 850
bubbling, event, **182–185**, *183–184*
buildHitList() function, 519–520
Button object and buttons, 207, 209, 293
events for, 134
methods of, 294
properties of, 294
button property
for event object, 175
for form object, 291
buttonClickHandler() function, 183, 185
byte code
in Java, 536
in LiveWire, 747
byteToString() method, 764–765

(

-c compiler option, 748
C++ language, 533–534
cache status, 361, *362*
cal.htm file, 439, *440*
cal-clock.htm file, 457–458
calc() function
in calc, 445–446
in math, 422, 428

calc.htm file, **443–448**, *444*
calculateOperation() function
    in calc, 446
    in math, 422, 428
calculator
    desktop, **443–448**, *444*
    scientific, **418–428**, *418–420*
calendar, **434–443**, *437, 439–440*
Calendar() function, 435, 437
calendar.htm file, **442–443**
calendar.js file, **435–438**
call() method
    in Function, 222
    in JSObject, 561
caller property, 221
cancelBubble property, 175
captureEvents() method
    in layer, 683
    operation of, 178–179
capturing events, **178–181**, *180, 182*
carets (^)
    in assignment operators, 85
    as bit operator, 84
    precedence of, 93
carriage returns, 59
Cascading Style Sheets (CSS), **11**, **631–632**
case keyword, 108
case-sensitivity
    of attributes, 138
    of variable names, 50–51
catalog.htm file, 463, *464*
catalog2.htm file, *476*, 477
catalog3.htm file, 485–486
catalogs, online
    without CGI programs, **462–475**, *464*
    multimedia features for, **485–495**, *486*
    user preferences with, **475–485**, *476*
catch statement, 96, **121–126**
categoryName() function
    in product3, 492
    in products, 474
catform.htm file, **465–469**
catform2.htm file, **475–485**
catform3.htm file, **485–492**
ceil() function, 225, 416

CERN, 5–6, 10
certificates, 855
CGI (Common Gateway Interface) programs,
    16–17, 30–31, **716**
    command-line arguments for, **718**
    for cookies, **335–337**
    design of, **725**
    environment variables for, 313, **719–722**
    example, **726–728**, *729*
    forms with, **312–317**, *316*, **725**
    hyperlinks for, **726**
    image map queries for, **726**
    input and output streams for, **722–723**, *723*
    JavaScript code from, **734–736**
    JavaScript interfacing with, **730–733**, *730–731*
    non-parsed headers in, **724–725**
    operation of, **717**, *718*
    for search forms, **507**
    security with, **846**
    Web server data for, **718–723**, *723*
    Web server data from, **723–725**
cgi-test.htm file, 727–728, *729*
ch03-01.htm file, 87–92
ch03-02.htm file, 100–101
ch03-03.htm file, 103
ch03-04.htm file, 104–106
ch03-05.htm file, 107
ch03-06.htm file, 109–110
ch03-07.htm file, 112
ch03-08.htm file, 116
ch03-09.htm file, 123
ch03-10.htm file, 125–126
ch04-01.htm file, 136–137
ch04-02.htm file, 140
ch04-03.htm file, 141
ch04-04.htm file, 143–145
ch04-05.htm file, 145–146
ch04-06.htm file, 146–147
ch04-07.htm file, 148–149
ch04-08.htm file, 150
ch04-11.htm file, 153
ch04-12.htm file, **157–159**
ch04-13.htm file, **161–162**, *163–164*
ch04-14.htm file, **163–166**, *166*
ch04-15.htm file, **166–167**, *168*

ch04-16.htm file, **170**
ch04-17.htm file, **171–173**, *172*
ch04-18.htm file, 176–177, *177*
ch04-19.htm file, 179–181, *180*
ch04-20.htm file, 181, *182*
ch04-21.htm file, 183–184, *183*
ch04-22.htm file, 186–187, *187*
ch04-23.htm file, 188–190, *189*
ch05-01.htm file, 203
ch05-02.htm file, **210–214**, *214–215*
ch05-03.htm file, 216–217, *217*
ch05-04.htm file, **220**
ch05-05.htm file, 222, *223*
ch05-06.htm file, **226**
ch05-07.htm file, **229–230**, *230*
ch05-09.htm file, **236**, *237*
ch05-10.htm file, **239–240**, *240*
ch06-01.htm file, **252–253**, *254*
ch06-02.htm file, 253
ch06-03.htm file, 256, *257*
ch06-04.htm file, **259**, *260*
ch06-15.htm file, **276–277**, *278*
ch06-16.htm file, **279–280**, *279*
change events, 134–135
changeColor() function, 261
changeSign() function
    in calc, 445
    in math, 421, 427
changeText() method, 552–553
charAt() method, 228
charCodeAt() method, 228
checkAnswers() function, 345–346, 348–349
Checkbox object, 207, 209, 293
    events for, 135
    methods of, 294
    properties of, 294
checkbox property, 291
checked property, 294
checks, form handling of, 301
child types, inheritance from, 198
<CITE> tag, 49
classes, 196
    COM, 19
    and inheritance, **199–200**

    in Java, 541–542, 551
    style sheets for, **652–654**, *655*
classes.htm file, 652–653
classes property, 652
CLASSID attribute, 580
clear property
    for block-formatted elements, **648**
    in style, 664
clearDisplay() function
    in calc, 445
    in math, 421, 427
clearError() method, 765
clearInterval() method
    purpose of, 260
    in text animation, 672
    in window, 250
clearTimeout() method, 250, 258
clearTimer() function, 259
click events, 132–135, 301
click() method, 296–297
click1.htm file, **369–377**
click2.htm file, **377–380**
clickHandler() function, 176, 178
client-cookie approach in LiveWire, **777**
client object in LiveWire, **761**
Client Object Maintenance field, 744, 749, **776–780**
client-side processing
    Form object and forms, **312**
    image maps, **155–156**, *156*
client-URL approach in LiveWire, **777–778**
ClientCertificate property, 818
clients, database, 786, *786*
clientX property, 174
clientY property, 174
CLIP attribute, 681–682
clip property
    in layer, 683
    in style, 664
clock, world, **454–456**, *455*
clock.htm file, **454–456**, *455*
close() method
    in cursor, 795
    in document, 274–276
    in File, 764–765
    in window, 250–252

closed property, 249
closing
    files in LiveWire, 764
    windows, **252–255**, *255*
closing tags in HTML, 8
CodePage property, 826
coding and decoding URLs, 720–721
colons (:)
    in conditional expressions, 85–86
    precedence of, 93
    in URLs, 357
color
    constants for, **231**
    with documents, **279–280**, *279*
    style sheets for, **645–647**, *647*
Color class, 544
color property
    purpose of, 645
    in style, 664
colorDepth property, 285
colors.htm file, 645–646, *647*
colorWrite() function, 238–240
COLS attribute, 263
columnName() method, 795
columns in databases, 784
columns() method, 795
COM (Component Object Model), 18–19, **576–577**
comma (,) operator, 86
command-line arguments for CGI programs, **718**
commas (,) for parameters, 204
comments
    in HTML, **44–45**, *45*
    for non-JavaScript browsers, **37–38**, *39*
    in style sheets, 637
commitTransaction() method, 792, 797–798
Common Gateway Interface. *See* CGI (Common
        Gateway Interface) programs
communication, window object for, **255–256**, *257*
company.htm file, 408, *410*
comparisons
    functions for, 225, 416
    operators for, **83**
compilers
    in Java, **535–536**
    for LiveWire, **747–748**

compiling
    diskette example
        in LiveWire, **773**
        in LiveWire Database Services, **805**
    Java programs, 543
    LiveWire files, 743, *745*
complete property, 391, 393
Component Object Model (COM), 18–19, **576–577**
composition, object, **197**
computerMoves() function, 269–271
computers.science.org site, 597
concatenation of strings, 84
conditional expressions, **85–86**
confirm() method, 250, 255–256
confirmLink() function
    in ch04–03, 141–142
    in ch04–05, 145–146
connect() method, 792, 803
connected() method, 792, 803
connections in LiveWire, **793–794**
connectionSpeed property, 281
console.htm file, **548–549**, *549–550*
console programs, **540–542**
ConsolePrg.java file, 541–542
constants
    for color, **231**
    for Math, **414–415**
constructors, **205**
    for Date, 219–220
    for image, 391–393
    for table, 232–233
    in WindowsPrg, 544
containers, OLE, 576
CONTENT_LENGTH environment variable, 719,
        723, 728
CONTENT_TYPE environment variable, 719
Content-type headers, 723–724
Contents property
    in Application, 827
    in Session, 826
continue statements, **106–107**, *107*
control.htm file
    for calendar, **440–442**
    for forms, 326–327
    for Tic Tac Toe game, **266–267**

Control Pad, **583–589**, *583–588*
controlForm variable, 327
CONTROLS attribute, 612
conversions
    with comparison operators, 83
    functions for, **68–69**, *69*
    between types, **62–69**, *63, 67, 69*
convertToQueryString() function
    in engines2, 510–511
    in engines3, 519–520
cookie.js file, 452–453, 465, **470**
cookie property, 273
cookieEnabled property, 281
cookies, **334–335**
    vs. hidden fields, **352–353**
    for history quiz, **342–352**, *342–343*
    information in, **335–337**
    for LiveWire, 777
    as privacy concern, 853
    using, **338–340**, *340–341*
Cookies property, 818
cookies.txt file, 334, 777
cooktest.htm file, **339–340**, *340–341*
correct() function, 346, 349
correctAnswers variable, 348
cos() function, 225, 417
Cosmo Player plug-in, 592
cpuClass property, 281
createFrames() function, 510–511
CreateObject() method, 827
createSummary() function, 276–277
css-blocks.htm file, 649
css-classes.htm file, 654
css-colors.htm file, 646
css-favstyle.htm file, 658
css-fonstyle.htm file, 641
css-ids.htm file, 637–638
css-span.htm file, 656
css-style1.htm file, 634
css-textyle.htm file, 644
css-units.htm file, 651
css-usestyle.htm file, 659
cssText property, 664
ctrlKey property, 175
curly braces ({})
    for entities, 43

    for functions, 111
    for if statements, 98–99
    for with statements, 119
current property, 385
currentMonth() function, 441–442
currentQuestion variable, 347
cursor() method, 792, 794–795
cursor object, **795–797**
cursor property, 664
custom URL example, **759**, *760*

D

-d compiler option, 748
data declarations, **97–98**
data for CGI programs, **312–313**
data property, 174
data tainting, 282, 854
data types. *See* types
database connectivity, 33, *33*
database management systems (DBMSs), 783
database object and databases, **791–793**
    vs. files, **781–785**, *784–785*
    in LiveWire. *See* LiveWire Database Services
Date object and dates
    with javascript protocol, 358, *359*
    object type for, **218–220**, *221*
dateTime() function, 455–456
db array, 522–523
db.js file, **522–527**
dbadmin application, 789, *789*
DBMSs (database management systems), 783
debug() function, 780
decimal integers, 53
decimal points, 55
declaring
    arrays, **72–74**, *74*, 98
    data, **97–98**
    Java elements, 543, 551
    local variables, **114–116**, *115, 117*
decode() function, 451, 453–454
decoding URLs, 720
decrement operator, 82
Default Page field, 743, 749

default statements with switch, 108
defaultChecked property, 294
defaultStatus property, 249, 257
defaultValue property, 294–296
defining
    functions, **111–114**, *113*
    methods, **233–234**
    object types, **231–240**
    style sheets, **635–657**
    table object, **234–236**
    variables, **45–47**, *46–47*
delay variable, 402
delete() method, 569–570
delete operator, 86, **240–241**
DELETE statement in SQL, **800–801**
deletePoint() function, 567, 573
deleteRow() method, 795, 798
deleting
    properties and methods, **240–241**
    rows in SQL, **800–801**
delta variable, 402
dense arrays, **74**, 98
deptURLs array, 522
describeBrowser() function, 210–212, 214
describeDocument() function, 211, 213
describeForm() function, 211, 213
describeForms() function, 211, 213
describeLinks() function, 211, 213
describeWindow() function, 211–213
description property
    in error object, 188
    in mimeTypes, 598–599, 605
    in plug-ins, 600–601, 605
descriptions for plug-ins, **602–605**, *602*
desktop accessories
    assembling, **456–458**, *457*
    calculator, **443–448**, *444*
    calendar, **434–443**, *437*, *439–440*
    to-do list, **448–454**, *449–450*
    world clock, **454–456**, *455*
desktop.htm file, 456–457, *457*
destroy() method
    in client, 761
    in Plugin, 614
detect.htm file, **605–607**, *606*

detecting plug-ins, **605–607**, *606*
developing plug-ins, **623–624**
DHTML, **660–661**
    accessing HTML elements in, **661–663**
    divisions in, 690
    style property in, **663–666**
    style sampler in, **666–676**, *667–671*
dialog boxes, window object for, **255–256**, *257*
dictionary array, 522
digital certificates and signatures, 851, 854
dimensions of applets, 547
directions() function, 252–253
directives in Active Server Pages, **816**
directories option with open() method, 251
disabling JavaScript, **39–40**, *40–41*
disconnect() method, 793
diskette example
    Active Server Pages for, **828–834**, *828–830*
    in LiveWire, **767–768**
        building and running, **773**, *774–775*
        display.htm file in, **771–772**
        finish.htm file in, **772–775**
        process.htm file in, **769–770**
        start.htm file in, **768**
    in LiveWire Database Services, **802**
        compiling and running, **805**
        database for, **802–810**
        SQL access in, **808–810**, *808*
        viewing database in, **806–807**, *806*
disp-qs.asp file, 823–825, *824*
disp-qs.htm file, 759, *760*
disp-xy.asp file, 821–823, *822*
disp-xy.htm file, **757**, *758*
display.asp file, *829*, 830, **833–834**
display() function
    in all, 662–663
    in calc, 445
    in math, 421, 427
display.htm file, **771–773**
display monitor, 722, *723*
display properties
    for images, **392**
    in style, 664
displayAll() function, 663

displayAltView() function
 in catform2, 478, 481
 in catform3, 488
displayAnswers() function, 345, 348
displayBrowserProperties() function, 283–284
displayByCat() function
 in catform2, 477, 480
 in catform3, 487
displayByProduct() function
 in catform2, 478, 480
 in catform3, 487
displayByRoom() function
 in catform2, 477, 480
 in catform3, 487
displayCalendar() function, 435–437
displayCalendarHeader() function, 435, 437
displayCatalogForm() function
 in catform, 465
 in catform3, 487
displayCategories() function
 in catform, 466, 468
 in catform2, 478, 481–482
 in catform3, 488–489
displayCategoryForm() function, 477, 480
displayCatList() function
 in catform2, 478, 482–483
 in catform3, 489–490
displayCell() function
 in click1, 372, **374**
 in click2, 378
 in match, 379
displayDates() function, 436, 438
displayed array, 376
displayedImages cookie, 373–374
displayEnvironment() function, 836–837
displayExplorerProperties() function, 283–284
displayFormData() function, 298–299
displayGraph() method, 569–571
displayGuessed() function, 306, 309
displayHangman() function, 306, 309
displayLine() function, 229–230
displayMatchStatus() function, 380–381
displayNavigvatorProperties() function, 282–284
displayOrder() function, 769

 in process.asp, 832
 in process.htm, 769
displayProducts() function
 in catform, 466, 468
 in catform2, 478, 482
 in catform3, 489
displayProductsList() function
 in catform2, 478, 483
 in catform3, 490
displayResults() function, 735–736
displayRooms() function
 in catform, 465, 467–468
 in catform2, 478, 481
 in catform3, 488
displayScreenProperties() function, 286
displaySquared() function, 116
displayTable() function
 in click1, 373
 in pairs.htm, 395, 398
 in pairs.js, 376–377
displayTaggedText() function, 112
displayToGuess() function, 306, 309
displayTopics() function, 502–504
distributed applications, **25**
<DIV> tag, **690–694**
division, 82
divisions
 in animation, **706–709**
 in slide show, **690–694**
divURLs array, 522
do while statements, **101–102**
doc1.htm file, 150
doc2.htm file, 151
document body, events for, 133
document object and documents, 206, **273–275**, 661
 accessing contents of, **276–277**, *278*
 color with, **279–280**, *279*
 embedded plug-in, **594–595**
 generating contents of, **275–276**
Document Object Model (DOM), 21
document property, 208, 249
documentation
 for developing plug-ins, **623–624**

for LiveAudio, **612–614**, **616–617**
for LiveVideo, **611–612**
documentClickHandler() function, 183
dollar signs ($) in names, 50–51
DOM (Document Object Model), 21
domain field, **337**
domain property, 273
DosLynx, 37, *38*
dosql.htm file, 808–810
double.htm file, 515
double quotes (")
for attributes, 138
for string values, 58
drawAxes() method, 569, 571
drawGraphBox() method, 569, 571
drawPoints() method, 569, 572
drawString() method, 544
dynamic image display, **393–398**, *397*
dynamic links, 356

E

E constant, 224, 415
E in floating-point numbers, 55
echo-query script, **726–728**, *729*
ECMAScript language, 21
Edit ➤ Insert ActiveX Control command, 584–585
elements
of arrays, **74–75**, *76*
in Form, accessing, **292–299**
elements array, 209, 293, 299
elements object, 207
elements property, 291
em units, 650
embed object, 207
<EMBED> tag, **594–597**, 621
embedded applets, 538
embedded plug-in documents, **594–597**
embedding JavaScript in HTML, **34–43**, *35*
embeds array, 607
embeds property, 273
enabledPlugin property, 598, 605
encapsulation, **197–198**

encode() function, 451, 453–454
encoding property, 291, 313
encryption, 852, 854
ENCTYPE attribute, 313
end() method, 619–620
end_time() method, 613
ending tags in HTML, 8
endQuiz() function, 346
ENDTIME attribute, 612
engines1.htm file, **505–506**
engines2.htm file, **509–515**
engines3.htm file, **519–522**
entities, **43**
environment variables, 313, **719–722**
eof() method, 765
equal signs (=)
in Active Server Pages, 816
in assignment operators, 85
in comparison operators, 83
in form data coding, 721
precedence of, 93
error events, 132–133
error.htm file, 804
error() method, 765
error object, 121–122, **187–190**, *188–189*
errorHandler() function, 186–187
errorMessage parameter, 186
errors and error handling
events for, **185–190**, *187–189*
exception-handling statements for, **121–126**, *121*
in LiveWire, **798**
objects for, **241**
escape characters, 58
escape() method
for encoding and decoding, 721
in Global, 224
eval() method
for conversions, **68**
in Global, 224
in JSObject, **559–561**
evaluation of expressions, 81
event handlers, 20
event object, 173, **241**
for capturing events, **178–181**, *180*

properties for, **173–175**
using, **176–178**, *178*
events and event handling, 29–31, **130–139**, *130,*
137, 142
   bubbling, **182–185**, *183–184*
   capturing, **178–181**, *180, 182*
   for error handling, **185–190**, *187–189*
   event object for, **173–178**
   form, **159–167**, *163–164, 166, 168*, **301–311**,
303–305
   image, **152–154**, *154–155*
   image map, **155–159**, *155–156, 159*
   within JavaScript, **168–170**, *171*
   link, **142–146**, *144, 146*
   simulation methods for, **171–173**, *172*
   window, **146–152**, *147, 149, 151–152*
exception-handling statements, **121–126**, *121*
exclamation points (!)
   for comments, 38
   for comparison operators, 82
   for logical operators, 82
   precedence of, 93
exclusive or operator, 84
executable content and security, **850–851**
execute() method, 793–794, 798
exists() method, 765
exit() method, 544
exp() function, 225, 417
expiration() method, 761
expiration time for client, 761
expires field for cookies, **336**
exponential functions, 225, 416–417
exponents in floating-point numbers, 55
export statement, 96
expressions, **80–81**
   conditional, **85–86**
   for entities, **43**
extensions
   to HTML, 11–12
   with MIME, 13
external files for style sheets, **657–659**, *660*
External Libraries field, 744, 749
external viewers, **12**, 596–597
extranets, **25**

F

\f character, 59
fade_from_to() method, 613
fade_to() method, 613
false/true values, **56–57**
FancyText.class file, **553**, *554–555*
FancyText.java file, 551
favstyle.htm file, 658, *660*
fgColor property, 273, 279
field.htm file, 408, *410*
fields
   hidden, **322–333**, *323–325*, **352–353**
   in Java, 541
File object, **763–766**, 827
file offsets in URLs, 358
file protocols in URLs, **14–15**
filename property, 600–601, 605
files
   in Active Server Pages, **827**
   vs. databases, **781–785**, *784–785*
   in LiveWire
     accessing, **764–766**
     closing, 764
     locking, **766**
     opening, **763–764**
   permissions for, **848**
FileSystemObject object, 827
FileUpload object, 207, 209, 293
   methods for, 296
   properties for, 294
FileUpload property, 291
filter property, 664
finalize() method, 561
financial information, security for, **852**
finish.asp file, *830*, **831**, **834**
finish.htm file, **772–775**, **802–804**
finishWindow() function, 211, 213–214
first() function
   in audiosho, 695
   in ie-slide.htm, 691, 694
   in ieaudiosho, 699
   in slideshow, 686, 689

floating-point types
   in graphing, 568
   literals, **55–56**, *56*
FloatPoint class, 568
floor() function, 225, 416
flow control statements
   if, **98–99**
   loop, **100–107**, *101*
flush() method, 765, 780
fly() function
   in anilayer, 705–706
   in ie-anim, 706–707
flying animation, **703–709**, *704*
focus events, 133–135, 302
focus() method
   for form elements, 296–297
   in window, 250
Folder object, 827
fonstyle.htm file, 640–641, *642*
font properties in style, 664, 672
fonts, style sheets for, **640–641**, *642*
fontSize property, 640–641, *642*
fontStyle property, 640–641, *642*
FOR attribute, 581
for statements, **102–103**
for in statements, **120**
form-acc.htm file, **298–299**, *299*
form.asp file, 819–821, *819*
form data for CGI programs, **721**
form feeds, 59
form.htm file, **754–755**, *756*
Form object and forms, 206, 209, **290–292**
   accessing elements in, **292–299**, *299*
   with CGI, **312–317**, *316*, **725**
   client-side processing of, **312**
   events for, 133, **159–167**, *163–164, 166, 168,*
      301–311, *303–305*
   hidden fields in, **322–333**, *323–325*, **352–353**
   for LiveWire, **754–755**, *756*
   reading values from, **559–560**, *560–561*
   search, **498–505**, *499–500*, **507**, *508–509*
form property
   in document, 273
   in Request, 818
<FORM> tag, 133
form1.htm file, **327–329**

form2.htm file, **329–330**
form3.htm file, **330–333**
formClickHandler() function, 183
forms array, 206, 208–209
forms property, 273, 292
forward() function
   in access, 609–610
   in history, 386
forward slashes (/)
   in assignment operators, 85
   for comments, 38, 44, 637
   for division, 82
   in HTML, 8
   precedence of, 93
   in URLs, 14–15, 357
forwardVideo() function, 609
fractions in floating-point numbers, 55
Frame class, 544
frame object and frames, 206, **262–263**
   events for, 133
   loading, **148–152**
   for Tic Tac Toe game, **263–272**
frame sets, 133, 262
<FRAME> tag, 133, 262
frameBack() method, 610
frameForward() method, 610
frames array, 206, 208
frames property, 249
frames2.htm file, 514
frames3.htm file, 514
frames4.htm file, 514
frames5.htm file, 515
frames6.htm file, 515
<FRAMESET> tag, 133, 262–263
fromElement property, 175
ftp protocol identifier, 14
full-page plug-in mode, 594
Function object and functions, **110–111**, **221–222**,
   223. See also methods
   for conversions, **68–69**, *69*
   defining, **111–114**, *113*
   for event handlers, 141–142
   for Math, **415–418**
   parameters for, **110–113**
   return statements in, **117–118**
   variables in, **114–116**, *115, 117*

G

gallows array, **308–309**
game programming
    Hangman, **302–311**, *303–305*
    pair-matching, **369–381**, *370–371*, **394–398**, *397*
    Tic Tac Toe, **263–272**, *264*, *270*
GATEWAY_INTERFACE environment variable, 719
generateError() function, 188, 190
GET method
    in CGI programs, 312–313, 721, 725
    in HTTP, **16**
getAttribute() method, 663
getCookieValue() function
    in cookie, 453, 470
    in notes, 452
    in pairs, 375–376
getCurrent() function
    in audiosho, 695
    in ie-slide.htm, 691, 694
    in slideshow, 686, 689
getDate() method, 218, 220
getDay() method, 218, 438
getdb file, 734–735
getFullYear() method, 219
getHours() method, 218, 220
getLength() method, 765
getMember() method, **558–561**
getMilliseconds() method, 218
getMinutes() method, 218, 220
getMonth() method, 219–220
getNumberValue() function, 344, 348
getOptionValue() function, 781
getOptionValueCount() function, 781
getPeer() method, 614
getPosition() method, 765
getSeconds() method, 219–220
getSlot() method, 561
getsql.htm file, 808–809
getTime() method, 219
getTimeZoneOffset() method, 219
getUTCDate() method, 218
getUTCDay() method, 218
getUTCFullYear() method, 219
getUTCHours() method, 218

getUTCMilliseconds() method, 218
getUTCMinutes() method, 218
getUTCMonth() method, 219
getUTCSeconds() method, 219
getValue() function, 235
GetVolume() method, 613
getWindow() method
    in JSObject, 558, 560–561
    in Plugin, 615
getYear() method, 219–220
GIF files
    helper applications for, 11
    MIME type for, 13
Global object, **223–224**
global variables, 97, 114–116, *117*
go() method, 386
goFaster() function, 401, 403
goSearch() function
    in engines1, 505–507
    in engines2, 509–511
    in engines3, 519–520
goSlower() function, 401, 403
gotFocus() function, 151
graph.htm file, **562–567**, *563–566*
GraphApp class, 568, 573
GraphApp.java file, **568–573**
graphics, helper applications for, 11
Graphics class, 544
GraphIt application, **562–573**, *563–566*
greater than signs (>)
    in assignment operators, 85
    as bit operator, 83
    in comparison operators, 83
    precedence of, 93
guess() function, 307, **311**
guessChoices array, 310
guessed field, 310–311
guesses variable, 309

H

<H1> tag, 10
handleEvent() method, 179
    in layer, 683

in link, 369
in ReadForm, 557–558
handler1() function, 169–170
handler2() function, 169–170
handles to windows, **558–559**
Hangman game, **302–311**, *303–305*
hangman.htm file, **302–311**
hash elements in URLs, 357–358
hash property
    in area, 404
    in link, 368
    in location, 363
head code for quiz, **348–349**
HEAD method, **16**
<HEAD> tag, 9
header programs, non-parsed, **724–725**
headings, 10, 34, **45–47**, *46–47*
HEIGHT attribute
    with <APPLET> tag, 547
    with <EMBED> tag, 594–595
    with <ILAYER> tag, 681
    with <LAYER> tag, 681
    with <OBJECT>, 580
height option with open() method, 252
height property
    in event, 174
    in HTML, 648
    in image, 391–392
    in layer, 683
    in screen, 285
    in style, 665
height variable, 568
Hello World! program, 34–35, *35*
Help ➤ About Plug-Ins command, **602–605**, *602*
helper applications, **11–12**
    external viewers and plug-ins, **12**
    and MIME types, **12–14**
hexadecimal integers, 53–54, *54*
HIDDEN attribute
    with <EMBED> tag, 595
    in LiveAudio, 613
hidden fields, **322–333**, *323–325*, **352–353**
Hidden object, 207, 209, 293
    methods of, 296
    properties of, 294

hidden property, 291
hideAll() function
    in audiosho, 695
    in ie-slide.htm, 691
    in ieaudiosho, 699
    in slideshow, 686, 689
hiding information, **198**
hierarchy of browser objects, **208–209**
history.js file, 343, **349–351**
history object, 206, 208, **385–386**
history of JavaScript, **19–21**
history property, 208, 249
history quiz, **342–352**, *342–343*
hitList array, 520
horizontal rules in HTML, 8–10
horizontal tab character, 59
host property
    in area, 404
    in link, 368
    in location, 363
    in server, 762
hostname element in URLs, 357
hostname property
    in area, 404
    in link, 368
    in location, 363
    in server, 762
<HR> tag, 8–10
HREF attribute
    with <A> tag, 384
    with <AREA> tag, 157, 403
href property
    in area, 404
    in link, 368
    in location, 363–364
hspace property, 391–392
.htm extension, 13
HTML (HyperText Markup Language), **8–10**, *10*
    comments in, **44–45**, *45*
    development of, **10–11**
    DHTML. *See* DHTML
    embedding JavaScript in, **34–43**, *35*
    entities in, **43**
    generating, **48–50**, *49*
    heads in, 10, 34, **45–47**, *46–47*

horizontal rules in, 8–10
for ignoring JavaScript code, **37–38**, *37–39*
<NOSCRIPT> tag in, **39–40**, *40–41*
parsing in, 28, *30*, 62, *63*
<SCRIPT> tag in, **41–42**, *42*
HTML 3.2, 10
HTML 4, 11
.html extension, 13
<HTML> tag, 9
HTMLEncode() method, 827
HTTP_ environment variables, 719
HTTP (HyperText Transfer Protocol), 6, 7, **15–16**
HTTP-NG, 16
http protocol identifier, 14
hyperlinks for CGI programs, **726**
HyperText Markup Language. *See* HTML (Hyper-
    Text Markup Language)
HyperText Transfer Protocol (HTTP), 6, 7, **15–16**

I

ID attribute
    in <OBJECT>, 580
    in <STYLE>, **637–638**, *639*
id property, 761
identifiers for browser objects, **209–214**, *214–215*
identifying properties, **232–233**
ids.htm file, **637–638**, *639*
ids property, **637–638**, *639*
ie-anim.htm file, **706–709**
ie-dhtml.htm file, **666–676**, *667–671*
ie-slide.htm file, **691–694**
ieaudiosho.htm file, **698–703**
if statements, **98–99**
ignoring JavaScript code, **37–38**, *37–39*
IIS (Internet Information Server), 20
<ILAYER> tag, **680–682**
image/gif MIME type, 13, 276
image/jpeg MIME type, 13
image maps
    and area object, **403–404**
    with CGI programs, **726**

event handling in, **155–159**, *155–156*, *159*
for LiveWire, **757**, *758*
working with, **404–408**, *406*, *409–410*
image object and images, 206, 208, **390**
    with animation, **399–403**, *400*
    dynamic display, **393–398**, *397*
    events for, 132, **152–154**, *154–155*
    properties for, **390–393**
image property, 273
<IMAGE> tag, 18
imageAborted() function, 153–154
imageError() function, 154
imageLoaded() function, 153
images array, 206, 208, 376
images property, 273
imageSequence array, 398
imageSequence cookie, 373–374
imageSource array, 398
imap.htm file, 404–405, *406*
<IMG> tag, 132, 390–391
import statement, 96, 542
importing packages in Java, 541, **556–557**
incorrect() function, 346, 349
increment operator, 82
index.htm file, 14
indexes for arrays, 70, 75
indexOf() method, 228, 309–310
Infinity property, 224
information hiding, **198**
inheritance, **198–200**
init() method
    in Plugin, 615
    in ReadForm, 557–558
Initial Page field, 743, 749
initialize() function
    in animate, 400–402
    in pairs, 394–395, **398**
initializeDisplayedArray() function, 375, 377
initializeImageArray() function, 375, 377
initializing arrays, 73
inline viewers, 597
input streams for CGI programs, **722–723**, *723*
<INPUT> tag, 134–135
Insert ActiveX Control dialog box, 584, *584*

INSERT statement in SQL, **800**
inserting source files for scripts, **41–42**
insertRow() method, 795, 798
install.htm file, 622–623, *623*
installed plug-ins, determining, **599–602**, *601*
installing plug-ins, **620–623**, *622–623*
instances
   declaring, 98
   hierarchies of, 208–209
   of objects, **196**, 201–202, **205**
instantiable object types, 237
integers, **53–54**, *54*
interfaces, COM, 19
interfacing JavaScripts with CGI programs,
   730–733, *730–731*
internal Internets, **24–25**
Internet Explorer
   scripts in, 37, *37*
   security in, 850
Internet Explorer 2, 37, *37*
Internet Explorer 3, 20
Internet Information Server (IIS), 20
Internet Protocol (IP), 6
interpreters, **536**
intervals, **260–261**, *262*
intranets, **24–25**
invoking Java methods, **548–549**
IP (Internet Protocol), 6
ip property, 753
isActive() method, 615
isBlank() function
   in ch04–13, 161–162
   in ttt, 268, 270–271
isFinite() method, 224
isHeader() function, 235–236
ISINDEX queries, **718**, 720, **725**
isNan() method, 224
IsPaused() method, 613
IsPlaying() method, 613
IsReady() method, 613
isTicTacToe() function, 268, 271
italicize() function, 673
item() method, 661–662

J

Java
   API for, **540**
   applets in, **18**, 532, 534, **540–541**, **545–548**, *547*,
      550–553, *554–555*
   browser interaction in, **538**
   compilation in, **536**
   for console program, **541–542**
   features of, **534**
   Java Development Kit in, **539**, *539*
   vs. JavaScript, **535–538**
   learning, **540**
   method access in, **548–549**, *549–550*
   as object-oriented language, **533–534**, **536–537**
   platform independence of, **532–533**
   programs in, **540–541**
   security in, **535**, **850–851**
   simplicity and reliability of, **534**
   strong typing in, **537–538**
   for window program, **543–545**
java.applet package, 547
java.awt package, 543
Java Development Kit (JDK), 532, **539**, *539*
java.lang package, 543
Java Runtime Environment (JRE), 533
Java Runtime Interface (JRI) guide, 624
Java Virtual Machine (JVM), 533, 850
javac compiler, 543
javaEnabled() method, 282
javascript protocol for URLs, **358–360**, *359–360*
JavaScript Style Sheets (JSS), 11, **631–632**
JavaScript1.1 LANGUAGE attribute, 35
JavaScript1.2 LANGUAGE attribute, 35
JavaScript1.3 LANGUAGE attribute, 36
JavaSoft company, 532
JDK (Java Development Kit), 532, **539**, *539*
join() method, 216
joining strings, 84
.jpe extension, 13
.jpeg extension, 13
JPEG files
   helper applications for, 11
   MIME type for, 13

.jpg extension, 13
JRE (Java Runtime Environment), 533
JRI interface, 624
.js extension, 41, 751
js2cgi.htm file, **730–733**, *730–731*
JScript language, 20
    accessing ActiveX components from, **581–582**, *581*
    accessing HTML elements from, **661**
JScript LANGUAGE attribute, 36
JSException class, 556–557
JSObject class
    in Java, 556–559
    methods in, 561–562
JVM (Java Virtual Machine), 533, 850

K

keyboard, 722, *723*
keycode property, 175
keys in databases, 785
keywords
    in Java, 541
    in search scripts, **516–517**, *517–518*

L

labelAxes() method, 569, 572
labels, **104**
    for break statements, 104
    for continue statements, 106
LANGUAGE attribute, **34–37**, 83
LANGUAGE directive, 816
Language property, 281
last() function
    in audiosho, 695
    in ie-slide.htm, 692, 694
    in ieaudiosho, 700
    in slideshow, 686–687, 689–690, 696
lastIndexOf() method, 228

lastModified property, 274
lastSlide() function
    in audiosho, 695
    in ie-slide.htm, 691, 694
    in ieaudiosho, 699
    in slideshow, 686, 689
layer object and layers, **683–684**
    in animation, **703–709**, *704*
    in HTML, **680–682**
    in slide show, **684–690**, *685*
<LAYER> tag, **680–682**
layers array, 683–684
layerX property, 174
layerY property, 174
layout documents, load events for, **147–148**
LCID property, 826
learning Java, **540**
LEFT attribute, 681–682
left property
    in layer, 683
    in style, 665
left shift operator, 84
len variable, 309
length of arrays, 72–73, *74*
length property
    in Array, 215
    in document, 661
    in Form, 291
    for form elements, 295, 299
    in Function, 221
    in history, 385
    of objects, 76
    in plugins, 600–601, 605
    in string, 228
    in window, 249
less than signs (<)
    in Active Server Pages, 816
    in assignment operators, 85
    as bit operator, 84
    in comparison operators, 83
    precedence of, 93
letterSpacing property, 665
libraries, COM, 19
line parameter in onError, 186

lineHeight property, 642–643, 665
link() method, **382–384**, *383*
Link object and links, 206, 356, **368–369**
  to blobs, 797
  color of, 279
  events for, 132, **142–146**, *144*, *146*
  URLs for. *See* URLs (Uniform Resource Locators)
  using, **369–381**, *370–371*
link property, 274
<LINK> tag, **657–659**, *660*
linkColor property, 274, 279
links array, 206, 208, 368, 384–385
links property, 274
linkx.htm file, 382–383, *383*
list selection, form handling of, 302
listaud.htm file, **616–617**, *617*
listprop.htm file, **615–616**, *615*
listProperties() function
  in listaud, 617
  in listprop, 616
listStyle property, 665
listStyleImage property, 665
listStylePosition property, 665
listStyleType property, 665
listURLs() function, 520–521
literals, **51–52**
  Boolean, **56–57**, *57*
  null, **61**
  numbers, **53–56**, *54*, *56*
  strings, **58–60**, *59*, *61*
LiveAudio plug-in, 592, **612–614**, **616–617**
LiveConnect
  for graphing, **562**
  in Internet Explorer Object Model, 548
LiveConnect Communication guide, 624
LiveConnect/Plug-In Developer's Guide, 624
LiveConnecting Plug-Ins with Java guide, 624
LiveScript, 19–20
LiveVideo plug-in, 592
  detecting, **605–607**, *606*
  documentation for, **611–612**
LiveWire, **22**, **740–741**, *741*
  accessing files in, **764–766**

Application Manager for, 743, *744–745*, **748–750**
building applications for, **742–744**, *744–745*
client object in, **761**
closing files in, 764
compiler for, **747–748**
custom URL example, **759**, *760*
diskette example, **767–768**
  building and running, **773**, *774–775*
  display.htm file in, **771–772**
  finish.htm file in, **772–775**
  process.htm file in, **769–770**
  start.htm file in, **768**
forms for, **754–755**, *756*
image maps for, **757**, *758*
locking files in, **766**
opening files in, **763–764**
project object in, **761–762**
request object for, **753–759**
running applications in, **745–746**
security with, **847**
server functions for, **780–781**
server object in, **762–763**
server-side objects for, **751–763**, *752*, *756*, *760*
server-side programming for, **750–751**
for state maintenance, **776–780**
LiveWire Database Services, **22**, **786**, *786*
  Access setup for, **787–789**, *787–791*
  cursor object in, **795–797**
  database object in, **791–793**
  diskette example in, **802**
    compiling and running, **805**
    database for, **802–810**
    SQL access in, **808–810**, *808*
    viewing database in, **806–807**, *806*
  error handling in, **798**
  locks and connections in, **793–794**
  with SQL, **794–795**, **798–802**
  transaction processing in, **797**
  using, **791–792**
LN2 constant, 224, 415
LN10 constant, 224, 415
load events, 132–133, **146–150**, *147*, *149*
load() method, 683
load-url.htm file, 365–367, *366*

loadFrames() function
  in engines2, 510, 512
  in url-form, 367–368
loading
  applets, **551–552**
  frames, **148–152**
  images, **152–154**, *154*
loadNextFrame() function, 510, 512–513
loadNotes() function, 450, 453
local search engines, **515–527**
local variables, **114–116**, *115*, *117*
Location headers in CGI programs, 724
location object, 206, **363–368**, *366*
location option with open() method, 251
location property, 208, 249
lock() method
  in Application, 827
  in project, 762, 766
  in server, 763, 766
locks
  in LiveWire, **766**
  in LiveWire Database Services, **793–794**
log() function, 225, 416
LOG2E constant, 224, 415
LOG10E constant, 225, 415
logarithmic functions, 225, 416
logical operators, **82**
logical values, **56–57**, *57*, 98–99
LOOP attribute
  in LiveAudio, 613
  in LiveVideo, 611
loop statements
  break, **104–106**, *105*
  continue, **106–107**, *107*
  do while, **101–102**
  for, **102–103**
  for in, **120**
  while, **100–101**, *101*
loosely coupled objects, 198
loosely typed languages, **537–538**
lostFocus() function, 151
lowsrc property, 391–392
Lynx browsers, 39

M

Macromedia Shockwave plug-in, 593
main() method
  in ConsolePrg, 542
  in Java, 541
  in WindowsPrg, 543
maintenance
  in DBMSs, 783
  state, **776–780**
majorErrorCode() method, 793, 798
majorErrorMessage() method, 793, 798
makeHeader() function, 235–236
makeHeaderColumn() function, 235–236
makeHeaderRow() function, 235–236
makeNormal() function, 235–236
makeVisible() function
  in audiosho, 695
  in ie-slide.htm, 691, 694
  in ieaudiosho, 699
  in slideshow, 686, 689
map.asp file, 821–823, *822*
map.htm file, 405–406, **757**, *758*
<MAP> tag, 404
MapPath() method, 827
Margin property, 665
marginBottom property, 665
marginLeft property, 665
marginRight property, 665
margins
  for images, 392
  in style sheets, 647, 665
margins() method, 647
marginsBottom property, 647
marginsLeft property, 647
marginsRight property, 647
marginsTop property, 647
marginTop property, 665
markup in HTML, 8
Mars.avi file, 618, *618*
MASTERSOUND attribute, 613
match.htm file, **379–381**
math.htm file, **418–428**, *418–420*

Math object, **224–226**, *226*
 for calculator, **418–428**, *418–420*
 constants for, **414–415**
 functions for, **415–418**
max() function, 225, 416
MAX_VALUE property, 227
max variable, 309
Maximum Database Connections field, 744, 749
MAYSCRIPT attribute, **556**
measurement units, **650–652**, *652*
menubar option with open() method, 252
method property
 in Form, 291
 in request, 753
methods, 76, **118–119**, 194–195. *See also* Function
  object and functions
 COM, 19
 for cursor, 795–796
 for database, 792–793
 for Date, 218–219
 defining, **233–234**
 deleting, **240–241**
 for document, 274
 for File, 765
 for Form, 291
 for form elements, 296–297
 for frame, 263
 in Java, 541
  accessing, **548–549**, *549–550*
  declaring, 551
 in JSObject, 561–562
 for layer, 683–684
 for LiveAudio, 613–614
 for location, 364–365
 for Math, 225
 for objects, **204–205**, **237–240**, *240*
 for plug-ins, **615–617**, *615, 617*
 for string, 228–229
 for window, 250
MIME (Multipurpose Internet Mail Extension)
  types
 in CGI programs, 723–724
 descriptions for, 605
 with document, 275–276

and helper applications, **12–14**
 for plug-ins, **593–594**, **596–599**, *599*
mime.htm file, 598, *599*
mimeType object, 207
mimeTypes array, 209, **597–599**
mimeTypes property, 281
min() function, 225, 416
MIN_VALUE property, 227
minorErrorCode() method, 793, 798
minorErrorMessage() method, 793, 798
minus signs (-)
 in assignment operators, 85
 in decrement operators, 82
 precedence of, 93
 for subtraction, 82
modifiers property, 175
modularity, **198**
modulus operator, 82
monitors, 722, *723*
Mosaic browser, 5
mouseDownHandler() function, 179, 181
mouseMoveHandler() function, 181
mouseOut events, 132
mouseOver events, 132, 136–139, *137*
moveAbove() method, 683
moveBelow() method, 683
moveBy() method, 684
moveParagraphs() function, 672–673
moveTo() method, 684
moveToAbsolute() method, 684
MoviePlayer.htm file, **709–710**, *710*
msdn.microsoft.com site, 23–24, 838
multimedia
 ActiveX-based, **698–703**
 animation, **703–709**, *704*
 audio, **694–698**
 divisions in, **690–694**
 in online catalogs, **485–495**, *486*
 slide show, **684–690**, *685*
 video, **709–711**, *710*
multiple inheritance, **199–200**
multiple style sheets, 660
multiplication, 82

Multipurpose Internet Mail Extension (MIME)
    types
  in CGI programs, 723–724
  descriptions for, 605
  with document, 275–276
  and helper applications, **12–14**
  for plug-ins, **593–594**, **596–599**, *599*
multiuser operating systems, security in, 849
myEventHandler() function, 176
myEye() function, 157, 159
myMouth() function, 158–159
myNose() function, 157, 159

N

\n character, 59
NAME attribute
  with <EMBED> tag, 594–595
  for forms, 327
  with <ILAYER> tag, 681–682
  with <LAYER> tag, 681–682
  in LiveAudio, 613
Name field
  in Add Application form, 743, 749
  for cookies, 336
name property
  in Form, 291–293
  for form elements, 294–296
  in image, 391, 393
  in layer, 683
  in plugins, 600–601, 605
  in window, 249
nameDefined() function
  in cookie, 452, 470
  in notes, 452
  in pairs, 374, 376
names
  for browser objects, **209–214**, *214–215*
  for variables, 50
nameSelect() function, 161–162
name=value pairs in form data coding, 721
NaN (not a number) value, 61

NaN property
  in Global, 224
  in Number, 227
National Center for Supercomputing Applications
    (NCSA), 5–6
Navigator objects, **206–208**, **280–284**, *284–285*
NCompass ScriptActive plug-in, 593
NCSA (National Center for Supercomputing
    Applications), 5–6
negation, 82
NEGATIVE_INFINITY property, 227
nesting exception-handling statements, **124–126**,
    125, *127*
netscape.javascript package, **556–557**
Netscape Navigator, security in, 850
netscape.plugin package, **614–615**
network programming, Java for, 534
new line character, 59
new operator, 86, 98, 230
newFrames array, 148
newuser.asp file, 819, *820*, 821
newuser.htm file, **754–755**, *756*
next() function
  in audiosho, 695–696
  in cursor, 796
  in ie-slide.htm, 692, 694
  in ieaudiosho, 699–700
  in slideshow, 686, 689–690
next property, 385
nextImage variable, 402
nextMonth() function, 441–442
NOHREF attribute, 157
non-parsed header programs, **724–725**
<NOSCRIPT> tag, **39–40**, *40–41*
not a number (NaN) value, 61
not logical operator, 82
notes, to-do lists for, **448–454**, *449–450*
notes-calc.htm file, 457–458
notes.htm file, **449–452**, *449–450*
null values, 52, **61**, 67
Number object, **227**
number property, 188
number types, **52–56**, *54*, *56*
numberOfDays() function, 436, 438

numberOfQuestions variable, 348
numberOfSearchSites() function, 510–511
numPlugins variable, 605
numPoints variable, 568
numTypes property, 605

0

-o compiler option, 747–748
o.htm file, 272
object-access statements, **118–119**
object-based languages, 194–195, **200–202**
object framework in LiveWire, 751
Object Linking and Embedding (OLE), 576
Object object, **227–228**
object-oriented programming, **196**
 in Java, **533–534**
 in JavaScript, **536–537**
Object Signing Security Policy, **854–855**
<OBJECT> tag, 580–581
objects, 76, **194–195**
 Array, **215–217**, *217*
 Boolean, **218**
 COM, 19
 composition of, **197**
 Date, **218–220**, *221*
 error-handling, **241**
 Function, **221–222**, *223*
 Global, **223–224**
 HTML elements as, **661–663**
 inheritance in, **198–200**
 instances of, **196**, 201–202, **205**
 JavaScript features for, **200–202**
 for layers, **683–684**
 Math, **224–226**, *226*
 methods for, **204–205**, **237–240**, *240*
 Navigator, **206–214**, *214–215*, **280–284**, *284–285*
 Number, **227**
 Object, **227–228**
 properties for, **202–203**, *204*
 RegExp, **231**
 screen, **285–286**, *287*
 string, **228–231**, *230*
 types for. *See* types

octal integers, 53–54, *54*
ODBC applet, 787, *787*
offscreenBuffering property, 249
offsets in URLs, 358
offsetX property, 174
offsetY property, 174
OLE (Object Linking and Embedding), 576
onAbort attribute, 138, 153, *154*
onBlur attribute, 138
 for forms, 160
 for window events, **149–151**
onChange attribute, 138, **166–167**, *168*
onClick attribute, 137–138
 for forms, **163–166**, *166*, 169–170
 for link events, **145–146**
onDblClick attribute, 138, 157
onDragDrop attribute, 138
onError attribute, 138
 for error handling, **185–187**, *187*
 for images, 152–154, *154*
onFocus attribute, 138
 for forms, 160
 for window events, **149–151**
onHead() attribute, 157, 159
onKeyDown attribute, 138
onKeyPress attribute, 138
onKeyUp attribute, 138
online catalogs
 without CGI programs, **462–475**, *464*
 multimedia features for, **485–495**, *486*
 user preferences with, **475–485**, *476*
onLine property, 281
online tutorial for Java, 540
onLoad attribute, 138
 for images, 152–153, *154*
 for window events, **146–150**, *147, 149*
onMouseDown attribute, 138
onMouseMove attribute, 138, **181**, *182*
onMouseOut attribute, 138–139
 for area, 404
 for image maps, 157
 for link events, **143–145**, *144*
onMouseOver attribute, 136–138
 for area, 404

for image maps, 157, 159, *159*
for link events, 142
onMouseUp attribute, 139
onReset attribute, 138, 160
onResize attribute, 138
onSelect attribute, 138, 160
onSubmit attribute, 138, **160–162**, 298
onUnload attribute, 138, **147–150**, *147*, *149*
open() method
in document, 274–276
in File, 763–765
in window, 210, **250–253**
opener property, 250, 258
opening
files in LiveWire, **763–764**
windows, **251–253**, *254*
opening tags in HTML, 8
Opera browsers, 21, 36
operands, 80
operators, **80–81**
arithmetic, **81–82**
assignment, **84–85**
bit manipulation, **84**
comparison, **83**
logical, **82**
precedence of, **93–94**
special, **86–87**
string, 84
summary table for, **87–92**, *92*
option object, 207
options for window, 251–252
options property, 295
or operators
bit, 84
logical, 82
order of operations, 81
orderfrm.htm file, **314–317**, *316*
orders application, **806–810**, *806*, *808*
orders.mbd file, 787
orders.txt file, 773, *774*, *782*
output streams for CGI programs, **722–723**, *723*
overflow property, 665
owns() function, 268, 270–271

P

<P> tag, 10, 49
pack() method, 544
packages in Java, 541
padding() method, 648
paddingBottom property, 648, 665
paddingLeft property, 648, 665
paddingRight property, 648, 665
paddingTop property, 648, 665
pageBreakAfter property, 665
pageBreakBefore property, 665
pageHeading variable, 347
pages, objects for, **206–208**
PAGEX attribute
with event object, 174
with <ILAYER> tag, 681
with <LAYER> tag, 681
PAGEY attribute
with event object, 174
with <ILAYER> tag, 681
with <LAYER> tag, 681
paint() method
in FancyText, 551
in GraphApp, 573
in ReadForm, 557
in WebApp, 547
in WindowsPrg, 544–545
pair-matching game
with dynamic images, **394–398**, *397*
for link demonstration, **369–381**, *370–371*
pairs.htm file, **394–398**, *397*
pairs.js file, **373–376**
PALETTE attribute, 595
paragraphs in HTML, 10, 49
<PARAM> tag, 581
parameters
for CGI programs, 718
for functions, **110–113**
for methods, 204
parent property, 250
parent types, inheritance from, 198
parentheses ()
for conditions, 98–99

for methods, 204
for operator precedence, 93–94
parentLayer property, 250
parseFloat() function, **68**, 224
parseInt() function, **68**, 224
parsing, 28, *30*, 62, *63*, 81
Password object, 207, 209, 293
    methods of, 297
    properties of, 294
password property, 291
PATH_INFO environment variable, 719, 722
PATH_TRANSLATED environment variable, 719
pathname property
    in area, 404
    in link, 368
    in location, 364
paths
    for CGI programs, **721–722**
    for cookies, 337
    in URLs, 14, 357
pause() method, 613
percent signs (%)
    in Active Server Pages, 816
    in assignment operators, 85
    for modulus operator, 82
    precedence of, 93
    in query strings, 721
performOp() function
    in calc, 446
    in math, 422–423, 428
performSearch() function, 519–520
permissions for security, **848**
permuteString() function, 375, 377
PI constant, 225, 415
picviewer.htm file, **587–589**, *588*
pixelHeight property, 665
pixelLeft property, 665
pixelTop property, 665
pixelWidth property, 665
planning, calendar for, **434–443**, *437*, *439–440*
platform dependence of plug-ins, 594
platform independence of Java, **532–533**
platform property, 281
play() function
    in LiveAudio, 613–614

in LiveVideo, 612
in synchro, 619–620
player.htm file, 711
playerMoves() function, 269, 271
playSound() function, 485, 491
playVideo() function, 609
plug-ins, **12**, **592**
    accessing, **607–610**, *608–609*
    class for, **614–615**
    detecting, **605–607**, *606*
    developing, **623–624**
    documentation for, **611–615**
    embedded, **594–597**
    features of, **593–594**
    information about, **602–605**, *602*
    installed, determining, **599–602**, *601*
    installing, assistance for, **620–623**, *622–623*
    LiveAudio, **612–614**
    LiveVideo, **611–612**
    methods for, **615–617**, *615*, *617*
    and MIME types, 593–594, **596–599**, *599*
    popular, **592–593**
    security with, **847–848**, **851–852**
    status of, 361, *363*
    synchronizing, **618–620**, *618*
Plugin class, 611, **614–615**
plugin object, 207
plugin property, 274
plugins array, 209, **599–602**
plugins.htm file, **600–602**
plugins property, 281
PLUGINSPAGE attribute, 595, 621
plus signs (+)
    for addition, 82
    in assignment operators, 85
    in increment operators, 82
    with mixed types, 62–67, *67*
    precedence of, 93
    in query strings, 357, 507, 720
    for string concatenation, 84
Pointcast plug-in, 593
PointSet class, **568–573**
polymorphism, **200**
Popup() method, 836

port property
in area, 404
in link, 368
in location, 364
in server, 762
ports
for TCP, 15
in URLs, 357
posHeight property, 665
position property, 665
POSITIVE_INFINITY property, 227
posLeft property, 665, 672
POST method
in CGI programs, 312–313, 721, 725
in HTTP, **16**
posTop property, 665, 672
posWidth property, 665
pound signs (#) in URLs, 357–358
pow() function, 225, 416
precedence of operators, **93–94**
preference() method, 282
preformatted text, HTML tags for, 60
prev() function
in audiosho, 695
in ie-slide.htm, 691, 694
in ieaudiosho, 699
in slideshow, 686, 689–690
previous property, 385
previousMonth() function, 441–442
primeTest() function, 122–123
primitive data types, 51–52
principals in Object Signing Security Policy, 854
println() method, 542
privacy, security for, **853**
privileges in Object Signing Security Policy, 855
process.asp file, *829*, 830, **832–833**
process.htm file, **769–770**, 773
processArea() function, 502–503
processForm1() function, 327–328
processForm2() function, 329–330
processForm3() function, 333
processOrder() function, 314–315, 317
prod array, 475
Product() function
in product3, 493
in products, 474

product3.js file, **492–495**
productCategories array, 474
products.htm file, 404, 407–408, *409*, 463–465
products.js file, 465
programs
CGI. *See* CGI (Common Gateway Interface)
programs
in Java, **540–541**
in JavaScript, 5–6
project object, **761–762**
prompt() method, 250, 256
properties, 76, **118**, 169, 194–195
for area, **403–404**
deleting, **240–241**
for document, 273–274
for event, **173–175**
for Form, 291–292
for form elements, 293–296
for frame, 263
identifying and assigning, **232–233**
for image, **390–393**
for link, 368
for location, 363–364
for Math, 224–225
for mimeTypes, 598–599
for navigator, 281
for objects, **202–203**, *204*, **237–240**, *240*
for plugins, 599–600, 605
for request, 753, 818–819
for server, 762
for Session, 826
for style, **663–666**
styles as, 631
for window, 249–250
Properties dialog box, 584, *584*
proportional measurement units, 650
protocol property
in area, 404
in link, 368
in location, 364
in request, 753
in server, 762
protocols
communication, 6
for URLs, 14–15, **356–362**, *359–361*

prototype property, 237–238
   in Array, 215–216
   in Boolean, 218
   in Function, 221
   in image, 391, 393
   in Number, 227
public key encryption, 852, 854
public modifier in Java, 542, 551

Q

qstring.asp file, 823–825, *824*
qstring.htm file, 759, *760*
QUERY_STRING environment variable, 719–721, 725–726
query strings
   with LiveWire, **759**, *760*
   in URLs, 357, 507, 720
querying tables in SQL, **801–802**
QueryString property, 818
querystring.web file, 759
Question() function, 344, 348
question marks (?)
   in conditional expressions, 85–86
   precedence of, 93
   in query strings, 357, 507
QuickTime plug-in, 593
quiz.htm file, **342–349**, *342–343*

R

r array, 426
\r character, 59
r mode string, 764
radio buttons, 135
Radio object, 207, 209, 293
   methods of, 297
   properties of, 294–295
radio property, 291
random() function
   in ch04–07, 148
   in Math, 225, 272, 417

random numbers, 225, 272, 417
RDBMSs (relational database management systems), 784
re-use of objects, 197
read() method, 765
readByte() method, 765
readCookie() function
   in catform, 465, 467
   in catform2, 477, 480
   in catform3, 487
   in click1, **372–373**
   in click2, 377–378
   in match, 379
   in quiz, 344, 348
ReadForm.java file, **557–558**
reading
   query string data, **720–721**
   values from forms, **559–560**, *560–561*
readln() method, 765
reason property, 175
records in databases, 784
redirect() function
   in LiveWire, 781, 847
   in Response, 826
redirecting input and output, 722, 723
referrer property, 274
RegExp object, **231**
register.web file, 754
regular expressions, **231**
relational database management systems (RDBMSs), 783
relational operators, **83**
relative measurement units, 650
releaseEvent() method, 179
releaseEvents() method, 684
reliability
   in DBMSs, 783
   of Java, 534
   strong typing for, 537
reload() method, 364
remainder operator, 82
REMOTE_ADDR environment variable, 719
REMOTE_HOST environment variable, 719
REMOTE_IDENT environment variable, 719
remote scripting, 21, **23–24**, **837–838**
REMOTE_USER environment variable, 719

removeAttribute() method, 663
removeBlanks() function
    in cookie, 452–453, 470
    in notes, 452
    in pairs, 374–376
    in quiz, 344–345, 348
removeMember() method, 562
replace() method, 364–365
Request for Comments (RFC) documents, 313
REQUEST_METHOD environment variable, 719
request object
    in Active Server Pages, **818–825**, *819–820,
        822–824*
    in LiveWire, **753–759**
reset events, 133
reset() method, 291
Reset object, 207, 209, 293
    methods of, 297
    properties of, 295
reset property, 291
resetImages() function, 396, 398
resetting forms, 302
resizable option with open() method, 252
resize() method, 684
Response object, **825–826**
restart() function, 266–267
restartQuiz() function, 346, 349
results.htm file, **734–736**
return statements, **117–118**
returnValue property, 175
reverse() method, 216
rewind() method, 612
rewindVideo() function, 609
RFC (Request for Comments) documents, 313
rgb() function, 645
right property, 683
right shift operator, 84
rollbackTransaction() method, 793, 797–798
roomCategories array, 475
roomName() function
    in product3, 492
    in products, 470–471, 474
roomProductCategory() function
    in product3, 493
    in products, 475

rooms array, 474
round() function
    in ch04–07, 148
    in Math, 225, 272, 416
rounding functions, 416
routeEvent() method, 179, 684
ROWS attribute with <FRAMESET> tag, 263
rows in databases, 784, **800–801**
running
    diskette example
        in LiveWire, **773**
        in LiveWire Database services, **805**
    LiveWire applications, **745–746**
runProgram() function, 836–837

S

Same Origin Security Policy, 854
saveNotes() function, 451, 453
schedules, calendar for, **434–443**, *437, 439–440*
schemes in URLs, 14
scientific calculator, **418–428**, *418–420*
scope delimiters, **816**
scope variable, 519
score variable, 348
screen object, **285–286**, *287*
screenX property, 174
screenY property, 174
scrElement property, 174
scrFilter property, 175
SCRIPT_NAME environment variable, 720
Script Options dialog box, 585, *585*
<SCRIPT> tag, 20, 34, 37, **41–42**, *42,* 83
Script Wizard, 585, *585*
ScriptActive plug-in, 593
scripts
    browser, 20
    instances of, 762
ScriptTimeout property, 827
scroll() method, 250
scrollbars option with open() method, 252
SDK (Software Development Kit) for LiveConnect,
        624

search elements in URLs, 357
search engines, **505–506, 509–515**
    connecting search forms to, **507**, *508–509*
    local, **515–527**
search forms, **498–505**, *499–500*, **507**, *508–509*
search.htm file, **498–501**
search property
    in area, 404
    in link, 368
    in location, 364
searchString variable, 511
second-level frames, **267–272**
sectURLs array, 522
secure field for cookies, 337
Secure Sockets Layer (SSL), 852
security
    access controls for, **848**
    and browser restrictions, 538
    with CGI programs, **846**
    in DBMSs, 783
    and executable content, **850–851**
    file permissions for, **848**
    for financial information, **852**
    in Java, **535, 850–851**
    with LiveWire applications, **847**
    with plug-ins, **847–848, 851–852**
    for privacy, **853**
    and server capabilities, **845**
    for server software, **844**
    and spying scripts, **853–856**
    strong typing for, 537
    threats to, **842–843**
    from user perspective, **850–853**
    from Webmaster perspective, **844–849**
seek() method, 612
Select Database dialog box, 787
select() method, 296–297
Select object, 207, 209, 293
    methods of, 297
    properties of, 295
select property, 291
SELECT statement in SQL, 795, **801–802, 806–807**,
    806
selected() function, 124–126
selected text with style sheets, **655–657**, *657*

selectedIndex property, 295
selectFrames() function, 148–149
selectFromBigList() function
    in catform2, 479, 484
    in catform3, 484, 491
selections, events for, 134–135
selectProduct() function
    in catform, 466, 469
    in catform2, 479, 484
    in catform3, 484, 491
selectProductCat() function
    in catform2, 479, 484
    in catform3, 491
selectProductType() function
    in catform, 466, 469
    in catform2, 479, 483
    in catform3, 491
selectRoom() function
    in catform, 466, 468–469
    in catform2, 479, 483–484
    in catform3, 490–491
self property, 250, 258
semicolons (;)
    for attributes, 138
    for statements, 97
sendToCGI() function, 731–733
separating tags in HTML, 8–9
serial connections in LiveWire, 793–794
server-cookie approach in LiveWire, **778–779**
server functions for LiveWire, **780–781**
server-IP approach in LiveWire, **778**
SERVER_NAME environment variable, 720
server object
    in Active Server Pages, **827**
    in LiveWire, **762–763**
SERVER_PORT environment variable, 720
SERVER_PROTOCOL environment variable, 720
server-side image maps
    for CGI programs, **726**
    handling, **155–156**, *156*
server-side includes, **845**
server-side objects
    in Active Server Pages, **818–834**, *819–820*,
        822–824
    in LiveWire, **751–763**, *752, 756, 760*

server-side processing. *See* CGI (Common Gateway Interface) programs
server-side scripting, 20–22, 31–32, *32*
   in Active Server Pages, **22–23**
   in LiveWire, **740–741**, **750–751**
SERVER_SOFTWARE environment variable, 720
<SERVER> tag, 746, 751
server-URL approach in LiveWire, **779**
servers, 6
   ASP for. *See* Active Server Pages (ASP)
   CGI data for, **723–725**, *723*
   CGI data from, **718–723**
   COM, 19
   database, 786, *786*
   and JavaScript, **28–33**, *29–33*
   OLE, 576
   security issues in, **844–845**, **847–848**
ServerVariables collection, 819, *819*
ServerVariables property, 819
Session object, **826**
SessionID property, 826
Set-Cookie header, 335–336
set() function, 235
setAttribute() method, 663
setColor() method, 544
setCookie() function
   in catform, 466, 469
   in catform2, 479, 484–485
   in catform3, 491–492
setDate() method, 218
setFont() method, 544
setFrames() function, 148
setFullYear() method, 219
setHours() method, 218
setInterval() method
   purpose of, **260–261**, *262*
   in window, 250
setMember() method, 562
setMilliseconds() method, 218
setMinutes() method, 218
setMonth() method, 219
setOwner() function, 268, 270–271
setPosition() method, 765
setSearch() function, 502
setSeconds() method, 219

setSize() method, 544
setSlot() method, 562
setStart() method, 400
setStartState() function
   in calc, 444
   in math, 420, **426**
setText() method, 551, 553
setTime() method, 219
setTimeout() method, 250, 258, 399
setTimer() function, 259
setTo() function, 421, 427
setupWindow() function, 210, 212
setUTCDate() method, 218
setUTCFullYear() method, 219
setUTCHours() method, 218
setUTCMilliseconds() method, 218
setUTCMinutes() method, 218
setUTCMonth() method, 219
setUTCSeconds() method, 219
setValue() function, 233
setvol() method, 614
setYear() method, 219
sform.htm file, 501
shift operators, 84
shiftKey property, 175
Shockwave plug-in, 593
show() method, 544
showcal.htm file, **438–439**, *439–440*
showMovie() function, 711
showResults() function, 164, 166
siblingAbove property, 683
siblingBelow property, 683
signatures, 851, 854
simple.asp file, 816, *817*
simple.htm file, 741, *741*
   building, **742–744**
   operation of, 746, *747*
   running, **745–746**
simulation methods for events, **171–173**, *172*
sin() function, 225, 417
single inheritance, **199**
single quotes (')
   for attributes, 138
   for string values, 58
SIZE attribute with <HR> tag, 9–10

size of applets, 547
slashes (/)
    in assignment operators, 85
    for comments, 38, 44, 637
    for division, 82
    in HTML, 8
    precedence of, 93
    in URLs, 14–15, 357
slide shows, **684–690**, *685*
    ActiveX-based, **698–703**
    audio in, **694–698**
slider ActiveX component, **578–581**, *578–579*
slideshow.htm file, **684–690**, *685*
slideText() function, 673
software, security issues in, **844**
Software Development Kit (SDK) for LiveConnect,
    624
sort() method, 216
sortPoints() method, 569, 572
sound
    MIME type for, 13
    for online catalogs, **485–495**, *486*
    in slide shows, **694–698**
source files for scripts, **41–42**
spaces in query strings, 357, 507, 720
spacing for images, 392
span.htm file, **655–657**, *657*
<SPAN> tag, **655–657**, *657*
special operators, **86–87**
split() method, 228
spying scripts, **853–856**
SQL (Structured Query Language), **798–799**
    adding rows in, **800**
    deleting rows in, **800–801**
    in diskette, **808–810**, *808*
    executing, **794–795**
    querying tables in, **801–802**
    updating rows in, **801**
SQLTable() method, 793–794, 801
sqrt() function, 225
SQRT1_2 constant, 225, 415
SQRT2 constant, 225, 415
square brackets ([]) for arrays, 70
square4.htm file, **267–268**
SRC attribute
    with <EMBED> tag, **594–596**

with <ILAYER> tag, 681–682
with <LAYER> tag, 681–682
with <SCRIPT> tag, **41–42**, *42*
src property
    in image, 391–393
    in layer, 683
SSL (Secure Sockets Layer), 852
stacking order for layers, 682
standard connections in LiveWire, 793–794
standard input and output streams for CGI pro-
    grams, **722–723**, *723*
start.asp file, *828*, **830–832**
start_at_beginning() method, 614
start.htm file, **768**
start() method, 619–620
start_time() method, 614
startAgain() function, 306, **309**, 311
startAnimation() function, 401–402
startColorChange() function, 261
STARTTIME attribute, 613
state information
    cookies for, **334–353**, *340–341*
    hidden fields for, **322–333**
    maintaining, **321**
state maintenance, LiveWire for, **776–780**
state variable, **426**
stateless design for Web, 320
statements, **94–97**
    assignment, 97
    data declaration, **97–98**
    exception-handling, **121–126**, *121*
    if, **98–99**
    for in, **120**
    loop, **100–107**, *101*, *107*
    object-access, **118–119**
    return, **117–118**
    switch, **108–110**
    with, **119–120**
static links, 356
static modifier in Java, 542
StaticObjects property
    in Application, 827
    in Session, 826
status bar, properties for, 250, 257
status field, 309–311
status information, **257**

status option with open() method, 252
status property, 250, 257
stayAway() function, 306, 311
stop_at_end() method, 614
stop() function
  in LiveAudio, 614
  in LiveVideo, 612
  in synchro, 619–620
stopVideo() function, 609
strict equality, 83
String object and strings, **228–231**, *230*
  concatenation of, 84
  query, 357, 507, 720, **759**, *760*
  support for, **58–60**, *59, 61*
stringToByte() method, 764–765
strongly typed languages, **537–538**
Structured Query Language (SQL), **798–799**
  adding rows in, **800**
  deleting rows in, **800–801**
  in diskette, **808–810**, *808*
  executing, **794–795**
  querying tables in, **801–802**
  updating rows in, **801**
style property, **663–666**
style sampler in DHTML, **666–676**, *667–671*
style sheets, **11**, **630–631**
  for block-formatted elements, **647–649**, *650*
  for classes, **652–654**, *655*
  for color and background images, **645–647**, *647*
  comments in, 637
  defining, **635–657**
  and DHTML. *See* DHTML
  example, **632–635**, *633*
  for font properties, **640–641**, *642*
  ids property and ID attribute for, **637–638**
  JavaScript vs. cascading, **631–632**
  <LINK> tag for, **657–659**, *660*
  for measurement units, **650–652**, *652*
  multiple, 660
  <SPAN> tag for, **655–657**, *657*
  <STYLE> tag for, **635–654**, *639, 642, 647, 650, 652, 655*
  tags property for, **637**
  for text properties, **642–644**, *645*
<STYLE> tag, **635–654**, *639, 642, 647, 650, 652, 655*

style1.htm file, **632–635**
styleFloat property, 666
submit events, 30, 133, 302
submit() method, 291, 313–314, 317
Submit object, 207, 209, 293
  methods of, 297
  properties of, 295
submit property, 292
subscripts
  for arrays, 70, 75
  precedence of, 93
substring() method, 229
subtraction, 82
suffixes property, 598–599, 605
summary forms, **314–317**, *316*
super() method, 544
surrounding tags in HTML, 8–9
survey.htm file, **323–327**, *323–325*
switch statements, **108–110**
synchro.htm, **618–620**, *618*
synchronizing plug-ins, **618–620**, *618*
synonyms for window, 249, 258
System class, 542
System DSN tab, 787
System.out variable, 542
systemLanguage property, 281

T

\t character, 59
table_colorWrite() function, 238–240
table() constructor, 235
table_getValue() function, 234
table_isHeader() function, 234–235
table.js file, **234–236**
table_makeHeader() function, 234–235
table_makeHeaderColumn() function, 234–235
table_makeHeaderRow() function, 234–235
table_makeNormal() function, 234–235
table object and tables, 67–68, *67*
  in databases, 784
  defining, **234–236**
  methods for, **233–234**

properties for, **232–233**
querying, **801–802**
using, **236**, *237*
table_set() function, 234–235
table_setValue() function, 233–234
<TABLE> tag, 67
table_write() function, 234–235
tabs, 59
tagName property, 661
tags in HTML, 8–9. *See also* HTML (HyperText
    Markup Language)
tags() method, 661–662
tags property, 635, **637**
taintEnabled() method, 282
tainting, 282, 854
tan() function, 225, 417
TARGET attribute
    with <AREA> tag, 403
    for forms, 327
target property
    in area, 404
    in event, 174
    in Form, 292
    in link, 368
targets in Object Signing Security Policy, 854
TCP (Transmission Control Protocol), 6, 15
TCP/IP, security with, 848–849
<TD> tag, 67
templates, object types as, 196
ternary operator, 85–86
text files for HTML, 8
text/html MIME type, 13, 275, 724
Text object and text, 207, 209, 293
    color of, 279
    events for, 134, 301
    in HTML. *See* HTML (HyperText Markup
        Language)
    methods of, 297
    properties of, 295
    style sheets for, **642–644**, *645*
text/plain MIME type, 13
text property, 292
textAlign property, 642–643, 666
Textarea object and text areas, 134, 207, 209, 293
    methods of, 297
    properties of, 295

textarea property, 292
<TEXTAREA> tag, 134
textDecoration properties, 642–643, 666
textIndent property, 666
TextStream object, 827
textTransform property, 642–643, 666
textyle.htm file, 643–644, *645*
<TH> tag, 67
thanks.htm file, 804
throw statements, 96, **121–126**
Tic Tac Toe game, **263**, *264*
    blank.htm for, **266**
    board.htm for, **264–265**
    control.htm for, **266–267**
    implementation of, **268–269**, *270*
    second-level frame for, **267–272**
    square4.htm for, **267–268**
    top-level frame for, **264–267**
    ttt.js for, **268–272**, *270*
    values.htm for, **265–266**
tick() function, 455–456
ticTacToe() function, 268, 271
tildes (~t), precedence of, 93
time zones in clock, 454
Timeout property in Session, 826
timeoutProcessing() method, 258–259
timeouts, **258–259**, *260*
times
    object type for, **218–220**
    world clock for, **454–456**, *455*
title property, 274
<TITLE> tag, 9
to-do lists, **448–454**, *449–450*
toElement property, 175
toGMTString() method, 219
toGuess field, 309–311
toLocaleString() method, 219
toLowerCase() method, 229
toolbar option with open() method, 251
Tools ➤ Options ➤ Script command, 585
Tools ➤ Script Wizard command, 585
TOP attribute, 682
top-level frames, **264–267**
top property
    in layer, 683

in style, 666
in window, 250, 258
Topic() constructor, 501–503
topic.htm file, **501–505**
topics arrays, 502
toString() method
    in Array, 216
    in Boolean, 218
    in Date, 219
    in Function, 222
    in JSObject, 562
    in Number, 227
    in Object, 227
    in String, 229
TotalBytes property, 819
toUpperCase() method, 229
toUTCString() method, 219
<TR> tag, 67
transaction processing, **797**
Transmission Control Protocol (TCP), 6, 15
trigonometric functions, 225, 417
Trojan horses, **850–851**
true/false values, **56–57**
try statement, 96, **121–126**
ttt.htm file, 263, *264*
tutorials, 540
TYPE attribute
    with <EMBED> tag, 594–595, 597
    with <STYLE> tag, 635
type property
    for event object, 174
    for form elements, 294–296
    in mimeTypes, 598–599, 605
type/subtype MIME naming scheme, 13
typeof operator, 86
types, **51–52**, **196**
    arrays, **70–77**, *71*
    Boolean, **56–57**, *57*
    conversions between, **62–69**, *63*, *67*, *69*
    creating, **197–200**
    defining, **231–240**
    in Java, **537–538**
    null, **61**
    numbers, **52–56**, *54*, *56*
    properties and methods for, **237–240**, *240*

strings, **58–60**, *59*, *61*
strongly typed vs. loosely typed languages,
    537–538
and variables, **51**

U

unary operators, 81
undefined values, **61**
underscore characters (_) in names, 50
unescape() method
    for encoding and decoding, 721
    in Global, 224
UNITS attribute, 595
units.htm file, 650–651, *652*
Unix, security in, 849
unload events, 133
unlock() method
    in Application, 827
    in project, 762, 766
    in server, 763, 766
UPDATE statement in SQL, **801**
updateCalendar() function, 441–442
updateCookie() function
    in cooktest, 339
    in quiz, 346, 349
updateDB.htm, **808–810**
updateGraphParameters() method, 569, 571
updateOrder() function, 166
updateRow() method, 795, 798
updateSearch() function, 519, 521
updating rows in SQL, **801**
upperCaseResults() function, 165–166
url-form.htm file, 367–368
url parameter, 186
URL property, 274
urlDescs array, 522
URLEncode() method, 827
URLs (Uniform Resource Locators), **14–15**, 356–358
    anchor object for, **384–385**
    with CGI programs, 717
    coding and decoding, 720–721

custom, **759**, *760*
history object for, **385–386**
link() method for, **382–384**, *383*
link object for, **368–381**, *370–371*
location object for, **363–368**, *366*
for plug-in documents, **596**
protocols for, 14–15, **356–362**, *359–361*
urlSet variable, 520
use-app1.htm file, **552**
use-app2.htm file, **556**, **559–560**, *560–561*
USEMAP attribute, 157
user actions with forms, **301–311**, *303–305*
user interaction in Java vs. JavaScript, **538**
user preferences, catalogs based on, **475–485**, *476*
userAgent property, 281
userClick() function
    in click1, 372, **374**
    in click2, 378–379
    in pairs, 395–396, 398
userLanguage property, 281
userProfile property, 281
users, security threats to, **843**, **850–853**
usesProducts() function, 330–333
usestyle.htm file, 659
Using LiveConnect guide, 624

V

-v compiler option, 748
v variable in PointSet, 568
validate() function, 161, 163
validateEmail() function, 161, 163
validateEssay() function, 161
validateForm() function, 161, 163
value property, 294–296
valueOf() method
    in Boolean, 218
    in Date, 219
    in Function, 222
    in Number, 227
    in Object, 227
    in String, 229

values.htm file, **265–266**
variables
    defining, **45–47**, *46–47*
    global, 97, 114–116, *117*
    in Java, 541, 551
    local, **114–116**, *115*, *117*
    and types, **50–61**
vertical bars (|)
    in assignment operators, 85
    as bit operator, 84
    in logical operators, 82
    precedence of, 93
verticalAlign property, 642–643, 666
video
    with layers, **709–711**, *710*
    MIME type for, 13
video/mpeg MIME type, 13
video/quicktime MIME type, 13
View ➢ Document Source command, 602
viewdb.htm file, **806–807**
viewers, **12**
viewing databases, **806–807**, *806*
VISIBILITY attribute, 682
visibility property, 666, 683
vlinkColor property, 274, 279
void keyword in Java, 542
void operator, 87, 360
VOLUME attribute, 613
vrml.sgi.com site, 592
vspace property, 391–392

W

w mode string, 764
w3.one.net site, 799, 801
Web and Web sites, **4–6**, *7*
    browsers for. *See* browsers and browser objects
    objects for, **206–208**
    threats to, **842–849**
Web Diner page, **166–167**, *168*
Web File Path field, 743, 749
.web files, 740, 747

web.htm file, **546–557**
Web servers, 6
   CGI data for, **723–725**, *723*
   CGI data from, **718–723**
WebApp.java file, **545–548**
well-known ports, 357
whatsnew.htm file, 407, *409*
which property, 174
while statements, **100–101**, *101*
WIDTH attribute
   with <APPLET> tag, 547
   with <EMBED> tag, 594–595
   with <ILAYER> tag, 681–682
   with <LAYER> tag, 681–682
   with <OBJECT>, 580
width option with open() method, 252
width property
   in event, 174
   in HTML, 648
   in image, 391–392
   in layer, 683
   in screen, 285
   in style, 666
width variable, 568
window object and windows, 206, **248–250**
   closing, **252–255**, *255*
   for dialog boxes, **255–256**, *257*
   events for, **146–152**, *147*, *149*, *151–152*
   handles to, **558–559**
   hierarchy of, **208–209**
   opening, **251–253**, *254*
   for status information, 258
   synonyms for, 258
window programs, 534, 540, **543–545**
window property, 250, 258
windowClosing method, 544–545
windowed elements, 682–683
WindowEventHandler class, 544
windowless plug-ins, 683
Windows NT, security in, 849
Windows Scripting Host (WSH), **23**, **835–837**, *836*
WindowsPrg class, **543–545**
WindowsPrg() constructor, 544

winner() function
   in hangman, 306–307, 310–311
   in match, 380–381
with statements, **119–120**, 225, 417
Word documents, security threats from, 852
world clock, **454–456**, *455*
write() function
   in document, 274–275
   in File, 766
   in LiveWire, 781
   in table, 234–236
   in window, 249
writeByte() method, 766
writeDate() function, 436, 438
writeDocument() function
   in catform, 466, 469
   in catform2, 479, 484
   in catform3, 491
writeln() method
   in document, 274–275
   in File, 766
writeResult() function, 735–736
Wscript object, 835
WSH (Windows Scripting Host), **23**, **835–837**, *836*
wsh-environ.js, 837
WshArguments object, 835
WshCollection object, 835
WshEnvironment object, 835
WshNetwork object, 835
WshShell object, 836
WshShortcut object, 836
WshSpecialFolders object, 836
WshURLShortcut object, 836
www.adobe.com site, 593
www.apple.com site, 593
www.genome.wi.mit.edu site, 844
www.javasoft.com site, 532, 535
www.jaworksi.com site, 313, 730
www.jcc.com site, 799
www.macromedia.com site, 593
www.ncompasslbas.com site, 593
www.netscape.com site, 337
www.operasoftware.com site, 21

www.pointcast.com site, 593
www.sybex.com site, 598
www.w3.org site, 632, 650

X

x.htm file, 272
x property, 174
xDelta variable, 569
xMax variable, 568
xMin variable, 568
XOrig variable, 568
xUL variable, 568
xVal() method, 570

Y

y property, 174
yDelta variable, 569
yMax variable, 568
yMin variable, 568
YOrig variable, 568
yUL variable, 568
yVal() method, 570

Z

Z-INDEX attribute, 682
z-order for layers, 682
zIndex property, 666, 683

SYBEX BOOKS ON THE WEB

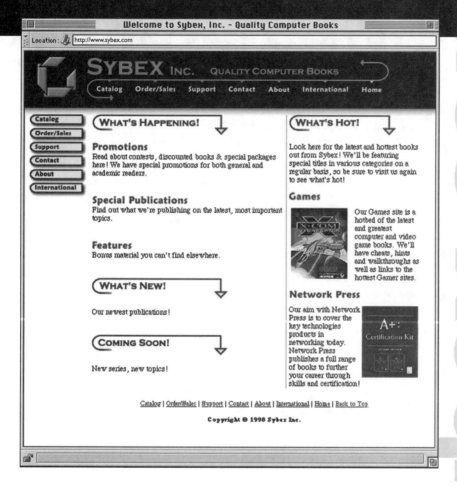

At the dynamic and informative Sybex Web site, you can:

- view our complete online catalog
- preview a book you're interested in
- access special book content

- order books online at special discount prices
- learn about Sybex

www.sybex.com